RAPE IN
MARRIAGE

S0-AHY-717

JAN 23 2004

RAPE IN MARRIAGE

Expanded and Revised Edition
with a New Introduction

DIANA E. H. RUSSELL

INDIANA UNIVERSITY PRESS

Bloomington and Indianapolis

The author gratefully acknowledges permission to reprint excerpts from:
"A Man's Madness: Could 2 Lives Have Been Saved?" by Narda Zacchino. Copyright, 1977, Los Angeles Times. Reprinted by permission.
"Wife's Grisly Story" by George Williamson. © San Francisco Chronicle, 1979. Reprinted by permission.
"Man's Wives Have a Tragic History." © San Francisco Chronicle, 1980. Reprinted by permission.
"'Battered Wife' Cleared in Shooting Husband," by William Carlsen. © San Francisco Chronicle, 1981. Reprinted by permission.
"Spousal Rape: A Story of Human Suffering," by Pat Lakey in *Record Searchlight*. Reprinted courtesy of Record Searchlight, Redding, California.
"Marital Rape: What Happens When Women Fight Back?" by Teresa Priem. Reprinted courtesy of Teresa Priem and the National Clearinghouse on Marital Rape. (Reprint available from the marital rape collection, Women's Studies Library, University of Illinois, Urbana, Il. 61807.)
Battered Wife, Murderer, and Feminist Hero," by Bill Shaw. Reprinted courtesy of Bill Shaw.
"Sex Torture Charges Unveiled in Burnham Trial," by Sylvia Wharton. Reprinted courtesy of the *Sun-Star*, Merced, California.
"Marine to Be Tried for Wife's Rape," by Santa Ana Associated Press. Reprinted by permission of the Associated Press.
"I Kept Thinking Maybe I Could Help Him," by Michelle Celarier. Reprinted courtesy of *In These Times*.
The Battered Woman by Lenore E. Walker. Copyright © 1979 by Lenore E. Walker. Reprinted by permission of Harper & Row, Publishers, Inc.
"In 44 States, It's Legal to Rape Your Wife" by Moira K. Griffin. Reprinted from *Student Lawyer*, © 1980, American Bar Association.

© 1982, 1990 by Diana E. H. Russell
All rights reserved
Originally published 1982 by Macmillan Publishing Company

No part of this book may be reproduced or utilized in any form or by any means, electronic or mechanical, including photocopying and recording, or by any information storage and retrieval system, without permission in writing from the publisher. The Association of American University Presses' Resolution on Permissions constitutes the only exception to this prohibition.

The paper used in this publication meets the minimum requirements of American National Standard for Information Sciences—Permanence of Paper for Printed Library Materials, ANSI Z39.48-1984. ∞

Manufactured in the United States of America

Library of Congress Cataloging-in-Publication Data

Russell, Diana E. H.
Rape in marriage / Diana E.H. Russell.
p.   cm.
"Reissue with new introduction."
Includes bibliographical references.
ISBN 0-253-35055-7. — ISBN 0-253-20563-8 (pbk.)
1. Rape in marriage—United States.   I. Title.
HV6561.R89 1990
362.82'92'0973—dc20   89-24650
                                                              CIP

1 2 3 4 5   94 93 92 91 90

To the women who had
the courage to tell the truth
about their husbands

CONTENTS

INTRODUCTION TO NEW EDITION

Wife Rape: From the 1980s to the 1990s

"I don't think this should be a crime, because after all, this is
what men get married for."
— Mother of convicted wife rapist, 1984[1]

"Cathy and I were having problems in our marriage for the
last two years. She could have claimed 'rape' any time during that time. Half of the married men in the country are
guilty of the same thing, if that's rape. . . . This [spousal
rape] law is wrong. I don't doubt that for a minute."
— Hughlen Watkins, first husband in the U.S. convicted of marital rape committed while still living
with his wife, 1980[2]

"It would be only a slight exaggeration to say that a man has a better
chance of surviving a nuclear holocaust than winning a legal contest
with a woman," lamented divorce lawyer Sidney Siller in a *Penthouse* article titled "'Wife Rape'—Who Really Gets Screwed."[3]

"Your wife can accuse you of rape at any time during your marriage,"
he complained. "That charge can lead to your arrest, prosecution, and
incarceration in many of the fifty states. Your protection against this conjugal lie is absolutely nil."[4] Like many others in this country, Siller does
not believe that a wife has the right to decline her husband's sexual advances, so he does not think it should be considered rape when a husband forces sexual intercourse on his wife. And, despite the fact that he
is a lawyer, he talks as if a woman's mere accusation of wife rape will
result in her husband's incarceration. I would have anticipated that a
lawyer would be the first to understand that there is a system of criminal
justice whose task it is to evaluate the truth of criminal charges, including those of wife rape.*

After the publication of *Rape in Marriage* in 1982, I had the misfortune
to be on Phil Donahue's show with this spokesperson for the rights of

---

*Siller subsequently became one of the founders of the National Organization for Men.
He believes that the women's movement will achieve its goals to win more power for
women "unless men organize in self-defense."

men to rape their wives. Not that Siller himself would use the word *rape* in this context. He denied that a husband *could* rape his wife. Placing legal sanctions on what he views as the conjugal rights of the husband would violate the sanctity and privacy of the marital bed, he maintained. Since feminists started taking action on this issue, "the specter of the women's liberation movement is now in your bedroom," Siller warned.[5]

Donahue had set up his show on wife rape as a debate, with me and Laura X—an expert on wife rape and the director of the National Clearinghouse on Marital and Date Rape—pitted against Sidney Siller. I doubt that Donahue would have felt equally comfortable about inviting someone on his show in 1982 who believes that rape by a stranger is impossible, but he apparently considered it fine to give TV time to someone with Siller's point of view on wife rape. For one thing, it permitted Donahue to play the role of the good guy to Siller's bad guy, while Laura and I could barely get a word in edgewise. "These women have come here to tell the world . . .," Donahue proclaimed on at least three occasions, making it impossible for us to speak for ourselves.

Laura X has observed from years of campaigning to reform the laws relating to wife rape in 45 states that a commonly held right-wing position on wife rape is that to criminalize such behavior is a violation of family privacy, while many political liberals have protested that it is an unacceptable intrusion into the privacy of the bedroom.[6] I would add that when it comes to crime, the political left has traditionally been preoccupied with the rights of offenders, ignoring the rights of victims as well as their suffering. As far as women are concerned, this mostly boils down to siding with male offenders (since most offenders are male), including men who rape their wives.

So, nine years after *Rape in Marriage* was first published, I find that many people—like the two cited in the epigraphs that open this introduction—still believe that "when a woman says 'I do,' she gives up her right to say 'I won't.'"[7] One woman put it this way: "If you're married you belong to the man. . . . My husband says it's my duty. And he says he has a right to force me if I don't want to."[8] In chapter 6 of this book there are many other examples of women who feel they have no right to decline their husbands' sexual advances. This might be one way to avoid being raped by one's husband (although it is not effective with battering husbands, many of whom force sex on their terrified wives after a beating). However, the impact of unwanted sex, of feeling that they do not own their own bodies, of permanent submission to another human being, must surely take its toll.

Just fifty years ago the scene of wife rape in *Gone with the Wind* was considered the height of conjugal passion.[9] Has that perception really changed? Who, watching Rhett Butler and Scarlett O'Hara even today, thinks of rape when Rhett swoops Scarlett up in his arms, carries her screaming and fighting up the stairs to "have his way" with her? Do people think it wasn't rape because she was married to him? Or because she succumbed to his passion, surrendering to the "wild thrill" of it? ("He had humbled her, hurt her, used her brutally through a wild mad night, and she had gloried in it. . . .")[10]

Whatever the reason, journalist Mike Capuzzo observes that: "the 'love scene' in *Gone with the Wind* endures as the most famous moment in a classic that defined romance in America. . . . In the olden days, men and women called this courtship, romance. Today it's in the courts, and they call it something different: rape."[11] Can we be surprised that many men are still resisting this change? That few women believe anything has really happened, even those who live in states where laws have been passed criminalizing wife rape? That many people subscribe to the common male fantasy in which women, like Scarlett O'Hara, actually enjoy forced sex? And that many people also believe that women say "no" when they truly mean "yes"?

In the light of all this skepticism, it is tempting for advocates of wife rape victims to focus on the more extreme examples of wife rape in an effort to force people to recognize the absurdity of the notion that women would want or enjoy such violation and pain. Similarly many advocates for battered women and incest survivors have focused on the more extreme cases. An unfortunate consequence of our doing this is that the women with less extreme experiences often do not identify themselves as victims of wife rape, battery, or incest. Equally important, they are not seen as victims by others, which reinforces abused women's own denial.

While I am very careful in *Rape in Marriage* to include the whole range of wife rape experiences, from cases where there was no additional physical violation to the more violent and sometimes grotesquely sadistic cases,[12] I will be focusing in this introduction on one of the more extreme and deviant cases (the Burnhams') as well as on one that is less so (the Evans'). I decided to go into the Burnham story in particular detail for several reasons: 1) it is described at some length in this book (pp. 279–80); 2) it reemerged as a case once more, in 1989; and 3) there are a number of important points that it brings out, despite its unusualness. I hope my citing this case will not obscure the point that rape in marriage does not have to be complicated and bizarre in order to justify being considered as such.

My appearance on the Donahue show was at the beginning of my publicity tour for *Rape in Marriage*. By the end of it, I had become more accustomed to—if not more accepting of—a media approach to wife rape. But I was totally unprepared for an experience I had after returning home to the California Bay Area. I was invited to give a three-hour seminar on wife rape to the San Francisco-based Institute for the Advanced Study in Sexuality. Perhaps I should have been better prepared for what happened there. After all, this institute is headed by Kinsey researcher Wardell Pomeroy, who has been known to defend incestuous relationships.* I ended my lecture by reading a few illustrative accounts of wife rape, concluding with a particularly shocking case perpetrated by Victor Burnham, a thirty-five-year-old construction worker who lived (and still lives) in Merced, California. Before California's spousal rape legislation made rape in marriage illegal in 1980, Victor Burnham could not have been prosecuted for raping his third wife, Rebecca. So although he had also raped his two ex-wives, both of whom testified against him at his trial in 1981, these rapes were not prosecutable. Even after 1980, because California's spousal rape law set a thirty-day time limit on reporting, most of the rapes that had occurred during Rebecca's two-and-a-half-year marriage were dismissed.

In an article entitled "Sex Torture Charges Unveiled in Burnham Trial," the Merced prosecutor was reported to have described Rebecca Burnham's marriage as "a bondage similar to that of a prisoner of war." [13] I was particularly impressed by this description, since some time before this I had been struck by the similarity between the effects—as well as the kinds—of torture inflicted by men on their wives and the torture that is experienced by some hostages, political prisoners, and prisoners of war.**

Reporter Sylvia Wharton wrote that Burnham's two former wives testified to episodes of torture with a battery-charged cattle prod and an egg beater and to forced intercourse with her husband's male acquaintances. The first Mrs. Burnham also reported that her husband had purchased a large dog and trained it to have sex with her. Watching this occur enabled him to become sufficiently aroused to have intercourse with her. All three women told the court that "they were unwilling participants in the events recounted," but that they did not feel able to escape them because they "feared for their lives." [14] In addition, "all three have said they have been choked, beaten, struck with gun butts, held at gunpoint, and continually threatened." [15]

---

*For example: "When we examine a cross-section of the population, as we did in the Kinsey Report, . . . we find many beautiful and mutually satisfying relationships between fathers and daughters. These may be transient or ongoing, but they have no harmful effects." Wardell Pomeroy, "A New Look at Incest," *Forum* (November 1976), p. 101.

**See chapter 20 on the torture of wives.

The testimony of these women was supported by a man who said that he went for sex-and-photo sessions with two of Burnham's wives. Another male testified that he believed Rebecca Burnham would be hurt if he did not do as his friend, Victor Burnham, suggested. Additional compelling evidence in Rebecca Burnham's case was available in the form of two photograph albums which contained "a pictorial record of Burnham's wife's forced sexual activities." Members of the jury are reported to have been "horrified."[16]

The outcome of this trial was that Victor Burnham was found guilty of spousal rape, bestiality, and intent to commit great bodily harm. For these crimes he was sentenced to thirteen years in state prison.

I concluded my lecture at the institute by reading a longer version than this of the Burnham case (see chapter 20) to my audience of approximately fifty male and female students. I had done this elsewhere on several other occasions. Instead of the shared sense of outrage and horror that I was accustomed to, a man at the back of the room who identified himself as a therapist asked me why I assumed that Rebecca Burnham had not consented to her husband's sexual practices. Though stunned by his skepticism, I referred to the photographic evidence, the corroboratory evidence by his two ex-wives, both of whom had left Victor, and the statements of two of the men who had participated in sexually abusing Rebecca Burnham, one of whom had expressed his fears for her safety.

My male questioner remained skeptical, claiming to know something about the case, and making it clear that he believed that Rebecca Burnham was into sadomasochism, and that the charge of rape was therefore inappropriate. Up jumped an angry young woman in the audience to argue with him. I breathed a sigh of relief to find someone else willing to take on this man. "I strongly resent what you said," she shot at him. "I'm a sadomasochist, and I'll have you know that this doesn't mean I cannot be raped!" Naturally, I agreed. Nevertheless, I found myself thinking that the fashionability of sadomasochistic depictions in pornography and its practice in people's lives[17] has likely contributed to the reemergence of what I hoped had become a passé question: how do you know she didn't want to be tied up? forced? raped? So I didn't relish finding myself on the same side of this argument as a sadomasochist.

I tried again. "Do you really think Rebecca Burnham wanted to have sex with the family dog?" I asked. "Dogs don't fuck you," someone offered with great conviction, "unless you want it!" "Is this the sort of thing they have courses on here?" I wondered, my head reeling. "But . . .," I struggled on, drawing on my very limited knowledge of these matters, "in her book, *Ordeal*, Linda Marchiano describes how she was subjected to sex with a dog although she detested both the idea and the experience."[18] "Her whole *book* is a crock of shit," someone else volunteered. "I guess I'd flunk out of this program," I thought, now at my wits' end. Pomeroy seems to have attracted a bunch of like-minded students, I noted to myself, as I hastened to get away, back to a more familiar and sane world.*

As it turned out, the man who questioned me about the Burnham case was not as out of touch with the thinking in the world as I was. After Victor Burnham served three years in prison, his 1981 conviction was overturned by the Fifth District Court of Appeals in Fresno, California, because the judge had failed to instruct the jury that Rebecca Burnham could have consented to the rapes and torture about which she had testified. The State Supreme Court upheld this decision by refusing to hear the case, thereby allowing Victor Burnham to go free.

Eight years later in July 1989, forty-three-year-old Victor Burnham faces four counts of rape, one count of attempted rape, two counts of forcible oral copulation, and one count of false imprisonment of his live-in lover. Diane Booth, staff writer for the Merced *Sun-Star* (July 4, 1989), described Burnham's latest crime spree as follows:

According to court records, Burnham is charged with forcing his 30-year-old live-in girlfriend to engage in sex acts with several men while he watched.

The woman, who is pregnant, told investigators she complied with Burnham's demands since December [1988] because of threats against her life, as well as that of her unborn child, daughter, and other family members. . . .

Court records state Burnham also forced his girlfriend to call friends to ask them if they were "open-minded" enough to participate in three-way sex.

One man invited to have sex as a threesome with Burnham said he changed his mind when the woman became upset and appeared to have second thoughts about the encounter.

Another man said the woman called him asking if he wanted a three-way sex experience, but he declined. The woman later called him back to apologize, explaining she was forced by Burnham to make the phone call.

On June 20, [1989] the woman contacted police because Burnham threatened to kill her and her family.

She told police Burnham beat her two weeks earlier, refused to let her use the phone and wouldn't let her out of his sight, even accompanying her to the bathroom.

How, I wonder, will this story end? Will the testimony of four women be enough finally to keep this man where he belongs, in prison for life? Or do the lives of four women not yet equal the worth of one man? Are

---

*In the interests of fairness, I should add that there were divergent opinions among the students on other matters, and probably on this one too, and that it was evident that some people at the institute *did* recognize sexual abuse of women as a problem.

the men who run the judicial system, like Sidney Siller, so terrified of the thought that their wives could accuse *them* or their buddies of rape that they will allow Victor Burnham to go free once more, giving him the opportunity to replay his predictable scenario with yet another woman? [19]

Victor Burnham is an unemployed construction worker with a prison record. As well as the rape charges made by three of his ex-wives and one live-in lover, he was also on trial back in 1981 for child molesting. How many more women and girls would have had to accuse him of rape before he would have been convicted—and *stayed* convicted—had he been a doctor, lawyer, or teacher? Despite the formidable skepticism encountered by those women who do accuse men of sexual assault, many people continue to express bewilderment over the fact that so few women turn to the judicial system for help. Women's reluctance to do so even makes them suspect in many people's eyes, including law enforcement personnel. "Why didn't you report this sooner?" they frequently ask. The implication of such a question is that the length of the delay in reporting correlates with the fraudulence of the report or with the lack of trauma of the sexual assault.

The Burnham case demonstrates several important points about wife rape. First, that it is easier to make rape in marriage illegal than it is to exorcise the appallingly woman-hating attitudes toward the victims of wife rape revealed by the Burnham case. Having access to the Berkeley-based National Clearinghouse's extensive collection of newspaper clippings, I could have chosen many other cases besides the Burnhams to demonstrate the continuing prevalence of reactionary attitudes to wife rape. For example, in July 1989, San Diego Superior Court Judge Bernard Revak sentenced Navy Commander Larry Evans to 11 years in prison for pistol-whipping and raping his wife. Although the Probation Department recommended a 14-year sentence, the length of the sentence is less revealing than Judge Revak's "20-minute soliloquy on how sorry he was to so strictly sentence a man with such professional potential and such an honorable background." [20]

Judge Revak stated that "this was probably the most difficult sentence in which he had been involved in more than twenty-four years as a prosecutor and a judge, . . . not only because of the individuals involved but because state law required him to sentence Evans to prison." [21] He went on to assure Evans that, "If I had the discretion, I would grant you probation." Judge Revak said he also would have chosen to sentence Larry Evans to the arduous task of performing community service for battered women and poor people. [22]

Despite the fact that Larry Evans was convicted of the following assaults on his wife, Mary Evans: "rape, rape with a foreign object, forced oral copulation, assault with force likely to create great bodily harm, and assault with a deadly weapon," causing black eyes, a broken ear drum, a chipped tooth, an injury to her nose, as well as emotional trauma, Judge Revak concluded that, "I think both of you have to share a lot of responsibility for what went on."[23] One of the reasons for this judgment was that Mrs. Evans had engaged in sexual relations with her husband after having obtained a restraining order against him. "I think it created a false sense of security or home for Mr. Evans," said the judge, totally empathizing with the perpetrator and failing to investigate whether— given her fear of her violent husband—rape rather than "sexual relations" might have been a more accurate description of what had occurred.

Joyce Faidley, author of the *Los Angeles Times'* account of the Evans trial I am citing here, observed that wife rape and beating are often condoned when the perpetrator is very successful, is very intelligent, and has an accomplished educational background. "Would we examine the bank robber's educational background and potential for career advancement," Faidley asks, "and would we ask the bank teller he held up why she let the crime happen?"[24]

All during Evans' trial, the courtroom was packed with advocates for battered women. How much more sympathy Judge Revak might have expressed for Mr. Evans had these women not been present, we can only guess. Perhaps his prison sentence would also have been considerably lighter, or waived completely as Revak so keenly wanted. Craig Weinerman, the attorney for Larry Evans, wrote a long letter of rebuttal to the *Los Angeles Times* in response to Joyce Faidley's article, congratulating Revak "for resisting this lynch-mob mentality."[25]

Weinerman also asked a couple of revealing questions: "Will Cmdr. Evans' serving 11 years in prison solve the complex problem of spousal rape? Are the three children better off with their father in prison and unable to support them? . . . Perhaps Mary Evans will realize one day that Revak understands the tragedy of family violence far better than Faidley and her battered-women groups do."[26]

A logical interpretation of Weinerman's argument is that no employed man should ever go to prison for beating or raping his wife. Indeed, not if he tortured her for years or even killed her. The notion that the male breadwinner should be the beneficiary of some special immunity because of his family's economic dependence on him is not new. It is frequently advanced in cases of father-daughter incest. On the basis of such an argument, it follows that it would be a violation of the principle of equity to incarcerate men who beat and/or rape women who are *not* their wives. Specifically, it would not be fair to the wives and children of

employed stranger rapists, acquaintance rapists, date rapists, lover rapists, authority figure rapists, or rapists who rape their friends. Why
should these families have to endure the loss of their breadwinners if the
families of husband rapists are spared this hardship?

While some rape apologists argue that men who rape their wives
should be freed to feed and house their families, others maintain that
women are responsible for their own rape. When I was on the Geraldo
show recently on the topic of "Why Men Rape," the only male guest argued fervently that rape happens because women have all the sexual
power. "Women are always the ones in a position to say 'no' to having
sex with men," he pointed out, resentfully. "So," I said, "Your solution
to the rape problem would appear to be that women should stop saying
no."[27] I might have added that then, instead of being called rape, all sexual acts would be considered consensual and the law would not have to
be involved in people's sex lives anymore. Then the courts' backlog of
cases would be eased, and they could get on with trying some of the
really serious offenders.

Not only does the Burnham case illustrate the entrenchment of misogyny in our judicial system, it also reveals a dramatic shift in the public's interest away from wife rape. Consider, for example, the interest
generated by the Greta and John Rideout case in December 1978. In contrast, there seems to be little public interest in wife rape today. The National Clearinghouse on Marital and Date Rape, in Berkeley, California,
a speaking and consulting firm, pays Allen's newspaper clipping service
to send them all the articles on wife rape (as well as other forms of rape)
published throughout the United States. Allen's sent nothing on the
Burnham case from any paper outside of Merced. It appears that a gory
and scandalous story of rape and torture in a sleepy little California
town cannot generate enough interest in 1989 to get outside the town
limits. Assuming that Allen's clipping service does a reasonably competent job, one is compelled to ask why this is so.

Feminists fought a long and hard battle to outlaw the previously
mandatory instruction by judges to juries in rape trials that "rape is a
charge easily made and difficult to defend against." But the Court of Appeals that opened the prison door for Victor Burnham appears unable to
see any contradiction between the outlawing of this instruction and
their requiring another that presumes that women are as likely as not to
consent to the following acts, repeated over a period of years: beatings,
being struck by gun butts, being held at gunpoint, being threatened
with death, being tied up and raped, being forced to solicit strange men
for sexual three-somes, being photographed in pornographic poses,

being shocked with an electric cattle prod, and being forced to have sex with the family dog.

It is very difficult to believe that the judge in a trial of the captors of American hostages would be required to instruct the jury to consider whether the hostages might have consented to their own torture. And I sincerely hope the same instruction was never required in cases of unsuccessful lynchings or savage beatings of slaves by their masters. Yet it is seen as reasonable in both our culture and our judicial system to believe that women want to be mistreated, brutalized, raped, and tortured. Despite all the work feminists have done over the years to try to dispel the myth that females are inherently masochistic, the Burnham case shows that this goal has yet to be attained.

It is clear that renewed efforts by feminists and our allies are needed to protest the sexist application of the marital rape laws. And further reforms in these laws themselves are also needed in many states. For example, Burnham was originally charged with about seventy counts of wife rape by Rebecca Burnham, but most of these were dismissed because California's law set a thirty-day limit on reporting wife rape to the police. Although this time limit has since been extended to ninety days, no time limit is required in California for the reporting of any other crime, including rape by other kinds of perpetrators.

We know that wife rape, like wife beating and battery, frequently occurs over a period of many years. Secondly, we know that there are all sorts of obstacles discouraging women from reporting these experiences, not the least of which is the treatment they can anticipate from the criminal justice system. These are but two reasons among many why I consider a limitation on the reporting time to be insensitive to the realities of women's experiences of wife rape.

While much work remains to be done on the issue of wife rape—an issue that affects all married women, since they are all potential victims—it is important to be aware of the enormous strides that have been made during the past decade in the formulation and implementation of new laws on rape in marriage. In July 1980, only eight states had passed laws criminalizing rape in marriage. Just nine years later, forty-two states have instituted such laws.* The women's movement can take great pride in the considerable gains that have been made in a fairly short period of time.

Lobbying for marital rape legislation has often been difficult. According to Marjory Fields, problems arise when victims attempt to relate to

---

*These 42 states are listed in chapter 2.

male legislators "the physical and emotional horrors that have been committed by husbands." [28] For example, a male judge cut off a woman when she tried to relate her personal experience of a brutal rape by her husband, saying: "I don't want to hear about these things. You're a married woman." [29]

A form that was drawn up by a Montana legislator as a joke and circulated to other senators during a campaign to criminalize wife rape, also reveals why women lobbyists often encounter resistance.

Form Drawn Up by Montana Legislator*

Due to a situation in Oregon in which a man is on trial for raping his wife, the following "Consent Form" is being furnished as a public service for Montana's males.

It's recommended that no sexual contact be made by Montana's males with their wives until this form has been filled out and signed.

Remember, tonight she may be willing but tomorrow YOU MAY BE CHARGED WITH RAPE.

Agreement

I, _____

do hereby on this _____ day of _____,

(Check one) _____ Beg
             _____ Request
             _____ Agree
             _____ Grudgingly agree (please pull down
                     my nightgown when you're through)

to have sexual relations with my husband between the hours

of _____ and _____.

_____
(Signed)

Public Service Form No. 61600

Legally, this form is but a one-time agreement, of course. Any sexual contact other than on the above date and at the above time shall require a new agreement.

Additional copies of this form can be obtained from State Senator Pat Regan.

It is satisfying to discover that the sexist buffoonery of these legislators amounted to the kick of a dying horse. Montana subsequently criminalized rape in marriage, as did Colorado more recently. In Colo-

*This form was given to me by women working in the women's center at the University of Montana.

rado, legislator Anne Tebedo expressed a similarly sexist attitude. She was one of two House members to vote against a 1988 bill to make rape in marriage illegal in her state.

"'Prove rape by my husband, for gosh sakes,' Tebedo said. 'This kind of thing just takes another chink out of the sanctity of marriage. . . . There are some areas the state just doesn't belong in. . . . These are personal things. . . .

"'I think if a woman is having problems, she might abuse it,' she added. 'All of a sudden she gets tired of him and she yells "Rape!"'"[30]

Given the prevailing denial of the seriousness and significance of the problem of wife rape, it is rather hard to explain why there has been such remarkable progress in criminalizing rape in forty-two states. Perhaps just as racist legislators are often unwilling to articulate their racist views in public, so many sexist legislators may have become less willing to publicly vote for a husband's right to rape his wife. This in turn may reflect a growing awareness of this issue among their constituents.

One thing is clear. Again and again, when legislators debate the pros and cons of passing a law to make marital rape a crime, they take great comfort in testimony that reassures them that they need not be afraid that every second woman will flock to the police station to report having been raped by her husband. In the preface, I describe the occurrence of this phenomenon in California in 1979, and it is still happening a decade later. More recently in 1988, Anne Byrne of Denver's Rape Assistance and Awareness Program was brought in to calm down the nervous Colorado legislators, telling them "not to expect an immediate flurry of cases if the measure passed. . . . When the victim is married to the perpetrator," Byrne reassured them, "chances of reporting are very small."[31] Byrne was right. Only three cases of wife rape were reported in Colorado one year after rape in marriage had been criminalized. Byrne no doubt knew that most wives are reluctant to report because of the humiliating aspects of the trial and the lack of public sympathy for their plight. The firing of Martha Warren from her job after her husband was tried and convicted for wife rape in Georgia in 1985 constitutes a particularly shocking example of punitiveness toward the victim.[32]

Colorado Senator Al Meikeljohn's response to this minute report rate was that, "the limited number of cases 'do not raise my apprehensions.'"[33] Of course, if he and other legislators had had the interests of women in mind, they would have been deeply concerned by the prediction that very few married women would likely make use of the law. In the case of the Colorado legislators, they did not even have the excuse of ignorance, since they had been educated during the legislative hearings in 1988 that there had been at least 400 sexual assaults on wives in the Denver area in 1987.[34] In addition, they learned that 40 percent of 1,200 battered women staying in shelters in Denver reported having been sexually assaulted by a husband or boyfriend, and that one third of the 40 percent had been sexually assaulted at least once a month.[35]

The relief of most legislators on learning that few women will actually benefit from the marital rape statutes the lawmakers pass demonstrates the intensity with which they protect male interests. Even assuring these distinguished gentlemen of the improbability of successfully prosecuting a false report fails to completely settle their misgivings. Judging from their debates, the hazard of a single bogus accusation disturbs them far more than all the pain endured by countless numbers of women who, for whatever reason, cannot seek justice.

A final point about the Burnham case: the silence of feminists in the aftermath of the scandalous decision to free Victor Burnham from prison eight years before his sentence would have expired, and his subsequent arrest for repeating his pattern of multiple torture/rape and death threats, is very troubling. Having fought so hard and so successfully to reform the marital rape laws in most states throughout the country, "the battle is winding down," observed criminal justice professor and shelter board member Martin Schwartz, in a 1989 speech.[36]

"There is only one problem," Schwartz continued. "Nothing has changed, except possibly the state legislators are no longer being pestered on this issue by reformers." Why? Because "we all went home," Schwartz concluded. "We . . . essentially dropped the issue as completed once we obtained the change in the state laws. We have not created the political climate to allow the police to arrest and the prosecutors to prosecute."[37]

Although Schwartz granted that many of the men who administer the law enforcement and judicial systems still subscribe to the myths that kept the marital rape exemption in place, and that these attitudes contribute to the lack of prosecutions for cases of wife rape, he still maintained that "the major problem . . . is with us [social reformers]. Marital rape," he argued, "has never occupied a central theoretical role in the discussions of marriage or the victimization of women in American society. One reason the police do not worry about marital rape is that few people care enough to discuss the issue in public."[38]

Unfortunately, the fault for the lack of contemporary concern about wife rape does not only lie with social reformers in general, but also with many feminists. Even many of the women who work in the anti-rape and anti-wife abuse movements* appear to share with other feminists, as well as with the public at large, an attitude of indifference to wife rape. Could it be that feminists failed to protest the decision to release Victor Burnham from prison after he had served only three years of his thirteen-year sentence because he was tried for spousal rape rather than for stranger rape or domestic violence?

Neither the National Coalition Against Sexual Assault (NCASA) nor the National Coalition Against Domestic Violence (NCADV) has ever had a keynote speech on the topic of wife rape. Generally, they have but one workshop on the subject. There was nothing whatsoever on wife rape at the most recent annual NCASA conferences in 1989. Laura X describes her many years of experiences offering workshops for both these organizations as extremely frustrating. Although her workshops— when permitted—are well attended, and many individual shelter and rape crisis workers show great interest in learning more about wife rape, Laura feels that many of the conference organizers have denied the importance of the topic. Likewise, several NCADV and NCASA spokeswomen have told her that "women who are *just raped* don't need to be in shelters." [39]

"I have struggled year after year," Laura X told me, "but often in vain. NCASA and NCADV have rarely wanted to deal with the issue of marital rape, especially legislatively. Nor are the organizers very interested in the experiences of marital rape survivors, even though Carol Coady [an outspoken survivor of wife rape who led the Pennsylvania campaign for legal reform] and I (as another kind of survivor and resource person) were both founders of the former victim/survivor caucus in NCASA, and Carol initiated a survivor workshop at NCADV as well." [40]

Unfortunately, NCADV and NCASA's seeming indifference to wife rape is far from unique. Laura X reported similar experiences at the annual National Women and Law Conferences. Indeed, ignoring the reality and significance of wife rape seems to be the norm among feminists as well as in the society at large. In my federally funded study of the prevalence of different types of sexual assault, 44 percent of my probability sample of 930 women in San Francisco reported an experience of rape or attempted rape at some time in their lives, 38 percent reported an experience of child sexual abuse, 16 percent disclosed an experience of incestuous abuse, and 14 percent of the women who had married once or more reported having been raped by their husbands.

Despite the fact that these prevalence rates are all substantially and

---

*I feel uncomfortable using the phrase *domestic violence* (although it is the label chosen by many involved in the movement), since it conceals the fact that the vast majority of cases of intra-couple violence involve a male perpetrator and a female victim.

significantly higher than those reported in prior studies,[41] little contro-versy seems to have been generated by these figures among activists in the field of violence against women. For example, while I am frequently approached about my prevalence statistics and other research findings on child sexual abuse, including having been asked to give scores of key-note speeches to feminist gatherings on the subject, I have received very few requests to talk about my research on wife rape.

But why are my data on child sexual abuse considered so important, while my shocking findings of a 44 percent prevalence rate for rape and attempted rape by all types of perpetrators, and a 14 percent prevalence rate for wife rape from the same study, are virtually ignored? This, de-spite the fact that my figure on rape by all kinds of perpetrators com-bined is significantly higher than the statistic usually reported by rape crisis centers.[42] There appears to be no rational basis for such a different receptivity to the information on these forms of sexual assault. But this does not mean there is no explanation for it.

Despite the fact that wife rape is the most prevalent form of rape (see chapter 5), and that it was found in my study to be just as traumatic as rape by a stranger,* it could be that people—including many femi-nists—still hold victim-blaming attitudes toward women who are raped by their husbands. They may find it easier to empathize with young, in-nocent children who have been sexually abused, and to recognize that they are not responsible for their victimization.

The rape of adolescent and adult women was of interest to the public for a short period in the early 1970s when it was still a novelty to hear women talking about it, but that time has passed. Although it makes a great deal of difference to the lives of women whether the percentage of females who are raped is 10, 30, 50, or 60, women in the 1980s do not seem willing to think about which of these figures might be accurate, and most men could care less. More importantly, if so many of the women who work with rape survivors are not interested in obtaining the most accurate statistics available, why should one expect the public to care?

Another reason for the neglect of wife rape by rape crisis centers is that they are ill-equipped to deal with wife rape. It does not fit neatly into the definitions established for the clientele they are trying to help. The circumstances of women who are married to their rapists are ex-ceedingly different from those of survivors of rape by non-intimates, in particular, strangers and acquaintances. Above all, many victims of wife

---

*Stranger rape is often regarded as the most traumatic type of rape. See chapter 14 for a detailed analysis of the trauma of wife rape as compared with rape by other perpetrators.

rape need a place to stay in order to get away from their abusive husbands. Rape crisis centers do not have such facilities. Many rape crisis workers therefore feel that battered women shelters are better suited to helping victims of wife rape on the physical safety issue. I think they are right, but this is not a satisfactory reason for failure to include wife rape as a major topic in their crisis training and public educational efforts, nor their failure to participate in court and legislative advocacy for the victims of wife rape.

I sometimes wonder if rape crisis workers, regardless of what their efforts may have accomplished in the past, have any significant impact on current attitudes toward rape. Aside from the worthy task of assisting rape victims in all possible ways, many rape crisis centers have become preoccupied with keeping funding sources happy. But how is their work contributing to the eradication of rape? These centers provide a much needed band-aid on the rape problem, like all good social work, but why aren't the rape crisis workers taking to the streets to make a hue and cry about cases like Victor Burnham?

In addition, while rape crisis workers are often oppressively busy helping survivors, the multi-billion dollar pornography industry continues to encourage increasing numbers of men to act out their rape desires.[43] What are the rape crisis centers doing or saying about this? It seems to me that rape crisis work is in serious danger of becoming deradicalized, institutionalized, and pacified.

Nor do the workers in battered women shelters appear to recognize the role of pornography in the abuse of wives, particularly sexual abuse. The shelter workers are in an ideal position to find out about battered women's experiences of pornography and to publicize the destructive role pornography plays in many of these women's lives, but most of these workers appear to shut their eyes to this problem. What do they even *know* about pornography? How often does NCADV or NCASA include a workshop on this subject at their conferences or in their training? The answer—according to Laura X—is very, very rarely.

As previously mentioned, I think battered women's shelters are better equipped to help victims of wife rape than rape crisis centers, and some of them do so. But many shelter workers do not want to deal with wife rape victims who are not also being beaten, because wife rape in and of itself is often not considered life-threatening. Hence, because of the lack of appropriate facilities on the part of rape crisis centers and the limited understanding and interest on the part of many battered women's shelters, help for victims of wife rape is frequently unavailable or highly inadequate.

This was as true when *Rape in Marriage* was first published in 1982 as it is today. I anticipated that an increase in awareness and concern about wife rape would result from the many campaigns in different states to reform the laws relating to wife rape, as well as from the availability of my book and other research (see the selected bibliography on wife rape). I expected that better services to victims of wife rape would follow. Not only does this not seem to be the case, but it appears also that the magnitude of the problem of sexual abuse by husbands and the trauma that usually results from it are not sufficiently understood or addressed by the workers in most battered women's shelters and many rape crisis centers.

The above analysis and critique is confirmed by a national survey of services for wife rape victims undertaken by the Executive Director of the Austin Rape Crisis Center—Lynn Thompson-Haas—the first person in the country to facilitate a support group for victims of wife rape.[44] She mailed 1,864 self-administered questionnaires to all rape crisis centers and battered women's shelters in the United States to find out how these organizations were meeting the needs of wife rape victims. Spokespersons for just under half of these organizations returned her questionnaire (a 46 percent return rate). Thompson-Haas suggests that the survey results likely over-report the level of wife rape services available because those who answered the questionnaire were probably more responsive to this form of rape than those who did not.[45]

Thompson-Haas affirmed the point already made that "many sexual assault programs see marital rape as a 'family violence problem,' and many programs for battered women see it as a 'sexual assault issue.'"[46] Some of the reasons given by the respondents for the failure to serve the victims of wife rape were:

"Our services are for sexual assault [as if wife rape is not sexual assault]. Tennessee law does not recognize marital rape."

"We are a shelter. Our group is not *involved* with rape."

"We are a family violence program. Domestic violence survivors are given priority at our center."

"We think it is important. We just don't know how to deal with it."

"We rarely see marital rape as traumatic in women. . . . It isn't the main problem" [by a shelter worker].[47]

Thompson-Haas also told me that one of the survivors of wife beating and rape in a therapy group she facilitated reported that shelter workers had requested that she not talk about her experiences of sexual abuse by her husband in her group therapy sessions.[48]

Many of Thompson-Haas' respondents in her national survey did not answer the question about what types of intervention they had found to be the most successful in helping wife rape victims to recover from the trauma, "because they feel they are not adequately addressing the problem and thus are not qualified to respond."[49]

Although it has been found that at least 40 percent of the women in battered women's shelters have also been raped by their husbands,[50] Thompson-Haas found that the majority of shelter workers did not encourage their clients to talk about their experiences of sexual assault. Only 34 percent of the programs that combined their rape crisis and shelter work routinely ask their clients if they have been sexually assaulted in a marital or cohabiting relationship. However, even fewer of the rape crisis centers ask this question (19 percent).

Despite the importance of asking the victims of wife rape about their experiences in order to encourage disclosure, some of the survey respondents reported "that they do not deal with marital rape because survivors do not want to discuss it."[51] First of all, this is a myth. Secondly, I presume that shelter workers would ask about battery even if the survivors did not want to talk about it. As Thompson-Haas points out, "Survivors are usually silent because: (1) the counselor is not ready to deal with the issue and or (2) the woman does not know that others view her experience as rape, and that services are available."[52]

For example, Thompson-Haas found that if outreach is done to battered women on this issue, they are eager to discuss their pain about being raped or sexually abused in other ways by their husbands. Thompson-Haas told me that when she offered women at a battered women's shelter the opportunity to attend a weekly support group to discuss their experiences of sexual abuse in marriage, "virtually every woman at the shelter attended."

Thompson-Haas also found that "marital rape is a part of staff training in only 40 percent of the battered women's programs; 72 percent of the sexual assault programs; and 77 percent of the combination programs."[53] Furthermore, although volunteers usually play a very significant role in these service organizations, Thompson-Haas reports that even fewer of them receive training about wife rape, and for those who do, the training is often minimal. Although California has passed a law that requires all state-funded shelters to include wife rape in their training and public education materials, Thompson-Haas found that many programs in California are not fulfilling either of these requirements.

Thompson-Haas points out that it is important that workers in both rape crisis centers and shelters "should be aware of the prevalence of marital rape, the impact, the laws, and ways to facilitate disclosure and resolution of the trauma."[54] In addition, she stresses the important point that it is not only imperative that victims of wife rape receive appropriate counseling, but that the many wives who have been sexually abused— but not raped—also have access to such help.

When comparing the shelters and the rape crisis centers in their handling of wife rape, Thompson-Haas reported that the shelters had a significantly poorer record on a number of items. For example, they were much less likely to include a discussion of wife rape at the crisis intervention stage (69 percent versus 97 percent), in their follow-up counseling (46 percent versus 86 percent), in advocating for the victims during their interviews with hospitals and law enforcement personnel (32 percent versus 84 percent), and in offering support groups for the victims of wife rape (17 percent versus 54 percent).[55] On the other hand, no significant differences were evident on these factors when rape crisis centers that were combined with shelters were compared with rape crisis centers that were not.

Only 40 percent of the shelter staff received training about wife rape, compared to 72 percent of the rape crisis center staff. Similarly, only 39 percent of the shelters included knowledge about the emotional reactions to wife rape in their staff trainings, compared to 72 percent of the rape crisis centers.[56]

In summary, we see that the problem of wife rape is being seriously overlooked, particularly by many of the battered women's shelters—the facilities best suited to deal with it.

As the cases cited in *Rape in Marriage* will show, some women are raped by their husbands but not beaten by them or threatened with weapons. Unfortunately, much of the limited research that has been done on wife rape has overlooked this group of abused wives and has focused instead on battered women who are also raped by their husbands. Many people would like to see wife rape as one more traumatic assault experienced by the already battered woman. Perceived in this way, wife rape does not appear to be relevant to all the women who are not beaten by their husbands. But as I suggest in the following pages, rape in marriage should rather be seen as being at one end of a marital sex continuum, with voluntary, mutually desired and satisfying sex at the other end. Rape-like behavior such as coercive sex (without physical force or threat of physical force), unwanted sex, sex in which the wife is totally passive, servicing her husband, would be somewhere in the middle of such a continuum. Taking wife rape out of a violent, battering context, as I do in this book, highlights the connections between wife rape and other prevalent negative marital sexual experiences reported by women.*

Some research findings published since *Rape in Marriage* first appeared in 1982 offer additional reasons why shelter workers need to take

---

*This idea of a continuum is further developed in chapter 6.

the issue of wife rape much more seriously than many of them have heretofore.

• Jacquelyn Campbell points out that in several studies the percentages of physically abused women who were also raped by their husbands ranged from a low of 33 to a high of 59 percent.[57] (The comparable figure was 51.5 percent in Campbell's study.)[58] Hence, wife rape is an experience that affects many of the battered women that shelter workers serve.

• When comparing battered women who had been raped with those who had not been so victimized, Campbell found significantly more serious physical violence in the sexually abusive relationships in terms of the severity and frequency of the aggression as well as the severity of the resulting injuries.[59] Similarly, Irene Frieze, Nancy Shields, and Christine Hanneke found that wife rape was associated with more severe battering than was observed for battered wives who were not raped.[60]

• Because of the finding reported above, Shields and Hanneke controlled for the severity of the physical abuse. Having done this, they found that battered women who were also raped had significantly lower self-esteem than women who had only been battered.[61] Campbell also reports that women in her study who were raped and battered by their male partners had significantly lower self-esteem than those who had not been raped, "even if it happened only once or early in the relationship."[62] Hence, shelter workers need to make a special effort to help the victims of wife rape to improve their self-esteem. Such efforts are likely to be ineffective if they fail to deal with its cause.

• According to Campbell's Danger Assessment measure, victims of wife rape are at greater risk of being murdered by their husbands, or of murdering them, than battered women who are not also sexually violated.[63] This is extremely important information for shelter workers. Battering husbands are particularly liable to become murderous toward their wives when their wives succeed in leaving them. It could be lifesaving for shelter workers to know which husbands are likely to be particularly dangerous. This knowledge could help them to gauge when to assist a woman to escape from the shelter in the event that her husband finds out where it is located. It could also help in deciding when it might be necessary to explain to battered women who are at particularly high risk of killing or being killed, why they cannot see their husbands as long as they live in the shelter, and the extreme risk they would be taking should they be tempted to return to their abusers.

It is also in the self-interest of shelter workers to know which battered women in their facility are most at risk of homicide, since they themselves are at some risk of being targeted by these dangerous men.

Hence, knowledge that can assist shelter workers in predicting which husbands are particularly dangerous could save their lives.

• Campbell also found that battered women who were raped by their male partners were significantly more likely to have been beaten during pregnancy than those who had not been raped.[64] Awareness of this finding could help to alert shelter workers to probe even more carefully for experiences of wife rape when women report such an experience.

• Shields and Hanneke reported that the women who were victims of wife rape and battering scored significantly higher on anxiety, paranoid ideation, and psychoticism, and were less likely to be able to enjoy sex than battered women who had not been raped and women who had been raped by strangers.[65] Again, these findings indicate the greater trauma suffered by battered women who are also raped by their husbands. If battered women reveal any of these traits, shelter workers should be alerted to the probability that they have been sexually assaulted by their mates.

• Campbell found that female victims of male partner rape and battery suffered significantly more from a damaged body image than the women who were battered but not raped by their partners, even if the rape happened only once or early on in the relationship. In addition, she and Peggy Alford report that battered women who had been raped by their partners were significantly more likely to suffer from certain health problems than were battered women who had not been so raped. "Sequelae of marital rape can include sexually transmitted diseases, urinary tract infections, decreased sexual desire and pleasure, hemorrhoids, and other genitourinary tract problems," Campbell noted.[66]

"It is clear," concluded Campbell, "that battered women will need to be specifically asked about sexual abuse in whatever shelter or health setting they are seen."[67] Experiences of wife rape are unlikely to be revealed voluntarily. If a woman is asked about rape in marriage in an insensitive or judgmental way, she will be even less inclined to discuss her experience. The questioner must proceed cautiously, without blaming or appearing to blame the victim for her ordeal. Ideally, the interviewer will be a woman who does not flinch at the details of sexual coercion and sexual brutality. Careful selection and thorough training of shelter workers about wife rape will enable them to support and encourage the victims of wife rape to talk about their painful experiences.

The finding of Jacquelyn Campbell (who has conducted other important research on the much-neglected topic of misogynist murder of women)[68] that battered women who are also raped are significantly more at risk of being murdered by their husbands than battered women who are not so abused, provides an extremely important reason for battered women advocates to become as knowledgeable as possible about wife rape as well as wife murder.[69]

My decision to be critical of those branches of the women's movement that are most relevant to wife rape was a difficult one. But I have come to realize that my previously non-critical stance has been singularly ineffective in getting the movement to take more responsibility for the victims of wife rape, and in getting all women to realize that this is *their* issue, because any married or cohabiting woman can become a victim of wife or partner rape. My hope is that a fact-based critical approach might be more effective.

Since the sections of this book on the current status of the laws on wife rape and the bibliography are the only out-of-date parts of the first edition of *Rape in Marriage,* these are the only sections that have been revised for this new edition; that is, the second half of chapter 2 on wife rape and the law, and Appendix II on the legal statutes on marital rape in each state. In addition, the selected bibliography on wife rape has been greatly expanded.

This revised edition of *Rape in Marriage* is dedicated to the very radical idea of ending wife rape, the most neglected but the most prevalent form of rape in the United States, and probably throughout the world. As Susan Brownmiller so eloquently stated: "If women are to be what we believe we are—equal partners—then intercourse [I'd say sexual relations] must be construed as an act of mutual desire and not as wifely 'duty,' enforced by the permissible threat of bodily harm or of economic sanctions."[70]

PREFACE

I began my research on rape in the fall of 1971 in response to a rape trial that occurred in San Francisco earlier that year. As usual, it was the victim who appeared to be on trial, and the man she accused of raping her was acquitted. I was a sufficiently conscious feminist at that time to be aware of the double standard that was applied. The victim was assumed to be unrapeable because she had an active sex life, whereas the man she accused of raping her was seen as an unlikely rapist because of his far more active sex life.

I realized then how little I knew about the experience of rape from the victim's perspective. Several trips to the library revealed that I was not alone in my ignorance. I decided a study was needed, and applied to the National Science Foundation for funding. In the letter I received in response I was told: "You have not made it clear that rape is an important problem or whether it is just the concern of a bunch of looney women." Shocked by this hostile reaction, but not discouraged, I embarked on my interviews with rape victims without benefit of funding.

I wanted the broadest possible range of victim experiences to be represented in this study, and because no women who had been raped by a husband, a father, or other family member were volunteering, I put up signs and placed ads encouraging women with these experiences to volunteer. Only one of the ninety women I eventually interviewed came to talk specifically about an experience of rape by a husband. Another woman described how she was raped at the age of four years by two foster brothers, molested by her stepfather, and raped by her husband because she couldn't have "vaginal" orgasms. This woman had not originally intended to talk about the experience of wife rape; it came out unexpectedly while I was trying to assess the impact of the earlier experiences on her life. A third woman's experience of wife rape also came out only incidentally: her husband forced intercourse on her after she was still recovering from a traumatic and physically injurious rape by a stranger. I recorded these three cases of wife rape in my book *The Politics of Rape*, published in 1975. They are, to my knowledge, the first cases of rape in marriage to appear in the social scientific literature on rape.

In 1977 I received funding from the National Institute of Mental Health to do a large-scale survey of women residents in San Francisco, to try to ascertain the prevalence of marital and extramarital rape and other sexual assault. While I was still analyzing the data resulting from the survey, legislation making "spousal rape" a crime in California was passed by the State Assembly in June 1979. The bill was sponsored by Assemblyman Floyd Mori who had been working against strong opposition to obtain this legal reform since 1976. One of the opponents to this bill, Walter Ingalls, argued that "it would subject husbands to the 'traumatic social stigma' of being faced with 'the horrible charge of rape.' For God's sake, don't make us look as ridiculous as Oregon," he exhorted.[1] Nevertheless, the measure was sent to the Senate Judiciary Committee on a vote of 50 to 18.

Given the paucity of information on wife rape, particularly information obtained from a scientifically sound survey, I was asked to be an expert witness in support of this legislation when it was to come before the all-male Senate Judiciary Committee. I agreed to do this. With the opportunity to use my data on wife rape to help change the law, I stopped everything else I was doing to focus on analyzing the material on rape in marriage. But as it turned out, I never got to give my testimony. Nor did seventeen others—almost all women—who had gone to Sacramento for that purpose, for a last minute decision was made to allow only four men and one woman to testify. It seemed clear to me, based on the questions posed to those selected and on their responses, that their major function was to assure the legislators that even if the law were passed, probably very few wives would ever try to prosecute their husbands. District Attorney Peter Sandrock from Oregon, one of those who testified, reassured these worried male senators that "the Oregon law has not unleashed a flood of rape accusations by unhappy wives. 'The often-repeated fear that vindictive women will falsely charge their husbands has not, most emphatically has not, been the experience in Oregon,' Sandrock said."[2] I began to think it was fortunate that I was not permitted to testify that in our survey, 14 percent of the women who had ever been married had been raped by a husband.

To relieve the anxieties of the senators, Mori agreed to several last minute compromises; for example, that rape by a husband must be reported to the police within thirty days (to prevent opportunistic wives from using "the threat of a rape charge to try to win custody disputes and property settlements at the time of divorce").[3]

Other such compromises followed, the vote was taken, and the bill was approved unanimously (9 to 0). After approval by the Senate, it was signed into law by Governor Jerry Brown a month later, becoming effective on January 1, 1980. Although only one woman was allowed to offer expert testimony in support of the measure that day, the presence of all the women who could not testify must have made it clear that many women in California had strong feelings about the issue. Mori himself cited "overwhelming grassroots support for the final breakthrough. The bill was backed," his press release stated, "by women's groups and rape crisis centers statewide, as well as district attorneys, the A.C.L.U. and countless individuals who maintained their efforts despite repeated setbacks."[4]

While my role in contributing to a change in the California law ended up being a token one, I had become aware of the need for wide availability of substantive information about wife rape, not only as a tool for those seeking to change the law in other states, but also to bring public attention to what is happening in the American family today in the hope that this will provide an incentive for people to seek and find non-legal solutions to this problem. And so the idea of writing this book was born.

ACKNOWLEDGMENTS

The study on which this book is based began in April 1977. Four and a half years later, literally hundreds of people have been involved in widely varying capacities. Even the list of project personnel at the end of these acknowledgments does not fully represent all those who contributed. Though it is impossible to name all who helped, I want to express my gratitude to all who did so. And to those individuals who were of outstanding help, I would like to express my special appreciation.

Peter Melvin from the Institute for Scientific Analysis was responsible for informing me about the availability of funding for research on rape from the then newly formed National Center for the Prevention and Control of Rape at the National Institute of Mental Health. Kristin Luker gave generously of her time in the development of the research proposal; her considerable skill in offering constructive criticism greatly strengthened the proposal, and likely played a significant role in its being funded. Kristin was also extremely helpful in other phases of the research; consequently, I see her as one of the mid-wives of this entire project. I am also grateful to "The Rape Center" at NIMH for their funding of the early stages of this research (Grant # RO1MH 28960).

Laura Tow worked with me from the beginning of the project through all the early phases, developing the interview schedule, hiring staff, coordinating the fieldwork, and suggesting avenues for future analysis. Aside from being the person who more than anyone else shared the headaches and responsibilities as well as the joys and excitement evoked by our ambitious project, her knowledge of survey research methodology, her considerable organizing skills, and her generally optimistic and positive approach to problems, were quite indispensable to me.

Sandy Hunter did a very fine job of organizing and overseeing the preliminary trial run of the survey, and Mei Sun Li and Carol McElheney were excellent interviewer supervisors during the main study itself. Interviewing 930 women about their experiences of rape and other sexual abuse evoked a great deal of feeling, as did the budget problems that developed, but Mei Sun and Carol were able to maintain an admirably high professional standard and sense of responsibility to the research goals throughout. Mei Sun did an equally impressive job hiring and supervising coders and overseeing parts of the analysis. For this I am extremely grateful. She has played an indispensable role in this research, not only by virtue of her considerable talents but also because of her extraordinary faithfulness and commitment to the project.

Joie Hubbert was friendly and supportive to work with, and through her, the excellent services of Field Research Associates were employed to draw our sample. The support and the methodological expertise and advice of Pat Miller, Michelene Skronski and Barbara Heyns in the early phases of the project were very valuable and much appreciated, as was that of Arlene Daniels, to whom I have turned for all manner of assistance throughout all phases of the research and writing.

Sandra Butler was enormously helpful in numerous ways both during and after the field work period, as was Connie Janssens, who also deserves mention as a most outstanding interviewer. Her skill at gaining the trust of a wide diversity of women and her ability at obtaining rich and detailed information was very impressive.

Karen Trocki has been responsible for the quantitative analysis of the data, and I am very grateful to her for her skillful handling of a very complex task, as well as her patience in working with me on these matters. I am also grateful to David Jenkins and Bill Wells, both computer programmers, for their help with the data analysis.

My research assistants and typists; Jone Lemos, Judy Okawa, Susan Broadhead, Jan Dennie, Julie Mahoney, and Chantal Rohlfing, as well as two of the coders, Joan Monheit and Kathy Bowden, deserve special mention for their excellent help and contributions to this research. In particular I want to thank Jone Lemos for her superb and intelligent secretarial help, and for donating many hours of work to the project when funds had run out.

Most of the typing of the qualitative interview materials was done by Jan Dennie, who also, together with me, coded this material on marital rape, keyed the entire manuscript into the computer, and patiently endured all the redrafts. In many ways she—more than anyone else—has shared the responsibility with me of completing this book, making my deadlines her own, and frequently doing what seemed undoable, with a patience and generosity of spirit for which I feel both enormously fortunate and enormously grateful.

Laura X and her National Clearinghouse on Marital Rape (P.O. Box 9245, Berkeley, CA 94709) have both been invaluable resources on the subject of wife rape. Laura has often been the first to inform me about a relevant article, newspaper story, or panel on wife rape, and her files of clippings on the subject have been extremely useful. Many cases cited in this book would not otherwise have come to my attention. I feel very lucky to be living in the same city where the Clearinghouse is located, and so to have had such ready accessibility to it and to Laura. I also want to express my appreciation to the librarians at Mills College, particularly Eda Regan, for providing me with statistics, addresses, and references as needed, thereby saving me hours of work.

I am very grateful to Joanne Schulman for her willingness to take time she did not have to prepare the state-by-state analysis of laws relating to wife rape that appears in this book, as well as for her comments on Chapter 2 on the Law. I also appreciate very much David Finkelhor's willingness to share his ideas and information about wife rape with me, as well as the stimulating colleagial relationship we have developed over the past two years.

Clare Fischer, Margrit Brückner, Lene Sjørup, Karen Trocki, Arlene Daniels, Jill Hall, and Jack Fremont gave thoughtful and useful feedback and criticism of various chapters when still in their first draft. Rachel Kahn-Hutt read the entire manuscript in its first draft, and gave me extremely helpful suggestions and criticism. Laura Tow applied her excellent editing skills to a few of the chapters. Cheryl Colopy read all the subsequent drafts of each chapter and her recommendations, both substantive and editorial, have, I believe, greatly improved this book. I am also extremely grateful to Pat Loomes for her very valuable comments and suggestions on several different drafts of the manuscript. In addition, I wish to express my enormous appreciation for her sympathetic and supportive ear throughout the four and a half years that it has taken to complete my study and to produce this book, as well as for her sound advice on the great variety of questions and concerns involved in this research and the writing of this book.

I am also extremely grateful to Nancy Howell for her careful reading of the entire manuscript at the galley stage, as well as her general feedback and suggestions.

Others who have given me much needed moral support and encouragement at various times during this project are Marie Hart, Donnis Thompson, Mildred Pagelow, Doree Allen, and Jane Loebel.

I want to express my appreciation to Jonathan Dolger, my agent, for his encouragement, his patience, his availability, and his faith in me and this book. I am also very grateful to my editor, Wendy Goldwyn, for the considerable and excellent job she has done in making this a more readable and a more powerful book, as well as her enthusiasm and conviction regarding its importance. She is also the first editor I have worked with who has encouraged me to feel that this was my book rather than the publisher's, and hence, who allowed me the final say.

Finally, I want to thank all the women, in this country and abroad, who had the courage to talk honestly about their experiences with their husbands. It is only through the openness of women like them that rape in marriage can become at last the focus of public attention and efforts at solution.

LIST OF PROJECT PERSONNEL

Data Analysts
Eleanor Engram

Karen Trocki

Programmers
Michael Jang
Deborah Brecher

David Jenkins
William Wells

Project Coordinator
Laura Tow

Supervisors and Consultants
Martha Burt
Winnie Chu
Charlotte Coleman
Lorraine Copeland
Jan Faulkner
Shirley Feldman-Summers
Meg E. Goldfeather
Diane Horowitz
Joan Huber
Alice Henry
Barbara Heyns
Joie Hubbert
Alexandra (Sandy) Hunter
Connie Janssens
Kimmy Johnson
Ellen Katzman
Camille LeGrand
Mei Sun Li

Robin Linden
Amarylis Lipscomb
Kristin Luker
Carol McElheney
Aviva Menkes
Patricia Miller
Judith Musick
Thom Rhue
Sandra Salazar
Sandye Sanders-West
Judith Schlecter
Judy Stacey
Joan Straub
Lorna Wallace
Carol Walton
Sandra Wara
Rhea Wilson
Penelope Wong

Research Assistants
Jan Dennie
Julie Mahoney

Judy Okawa
Chantal Rohlfing

Interviewers

Catherine Allan
Robbie Brandwynne
Katherine Brown-Keister
Sandra Butler
Patricia Butorac
Tisa Casas
Joyce Chong
Linda Cole
Linda Collins
Peggy Collins
Barbara Crockenberg
Clara Davis
Aledjimanduna Estrada
Cuchiya Font
Aixa Gannon
Luz Guerra
Susan Kitazawa
Sarah Lawrence
Patricia Lehrman
Cynthia Leung

Stephanie Liu
Willie McGowen
Christina Medina
Wilma Montanez
Cherríe Moraga
Aurora Morales
Nancy Peterson
Vincenza Petrilli
Manuela Ramirez
Joan Schretlen
Susan Sher
Louise Swig
Kitty Tsui
Yeh Tung
Katherine Wilson
Cathleen Wolf
Judith Woolridge
Maxine Yee
Felice Yeskel

Coders

Rick Barth
Kathy Bowden
Alexandra Brady
Phillip Chin
Betty Chow
Julie Keyes

Vann McGee
Joan Monheit
Linda Pacheco
Gil Schaeffer
Michelle Smith

Interview Editors and Office Workers

Susan Broadhead
Midge Edwards
Mary Griffin
Kris Hartman
Mary Kae Josh
Maureen Judge
Chris Kobayashi

Jone Lemos
Jeanne Marguerite
Barbara Noda
Grace Shimizu
Alice Sokolow
Sandra Wallenstein

RAPE IN
MARRIAGE

1

Introduction:
The Crime in the
Closet

"I would never think of taking it by force—except from my wife. I don't think I could get it up in a rape situation. It so appalls me that I couldn't do it."

"I don't think I have ever wanted to rape a woman except maybe my wife and I am not sure why I would want to rape her at this point. . . . I don't even believe in rape in marriage."

—Male respondents, *The Hite Report on Male Sexuality,* Shere Hite, 1981

In recent years, growing attention has been paid to various types of violence in the family. Nonsexual child abuse, particularly the physical beating of children as well as their gross emotional neglect or maltreatment, was the first type of violence in the family to be generally acknowledged. This was followed by attention to nonsexual wife abuse—"wife-battering," as it has been termed—and more recently, to child *sexual* abuse, particularly incest. The increased attention has produced a number of books on all three issues, and in turn these books have helped foster concern about these problems.

This is the first book to be published in the English language on the violent sexual abuse of women by their husbands.[1] However, the recent recognition in some states that rape in marriage is legally possible, combined with the publicity surrounding a few controversial trials of husbands accused of raping their wives, indicates that the problem of rape in marriage is finally being recognized. It is the goal of this book to increase this recognition; to provide an understanding of why the problem of wife rape exists; to show how it is connected with other problems such as unwanted sex in marriage, wife beating, and even the torture and killing of wives; and to suggest solutions to these problems.

The study I undertook and will report on here, and which informs this book, is the only study of wife rape in the United States to be based on interviews with a random sample of women. *Fourteen percent (14%) of the 930 women interviewed who had ever been married had been raped by a husband or ex-husband.* To the extent that this finding may be generalized to the population at large,[2] it suggests that at least one woman out of every seven who has ever been married has been raped by a husband at least once, and sometimes many times over many years. In other words, we all know women who have been raped by husbands. (Chapter 5 considers the likelihood that this is in fact a considerable underestimate of the prevalence of rape by husbands, as well as how it compares with the prevalence of rape by strangers, acquaintances, friends, dates, lovers, authority figures, and relatives besides husbands.)

The fact that these women were located by a random sample is important, because the results of studies based on volunteers from nonrepresentative populations may not be generalized, since volunteers are likely to be different from non-volunteers. For a start, those willing to seek out a stranger to talk to about being raped are more likely to have an experience that fits the stereotyped notion of what rape is. In particular, they are more likely to have been raped by a stranger. That is why it would be totally invalid to generalize about rape victims from the sample of volunteers whose experiences are described in *The Politics of Rape.* The most uniquely valuable aspect of the data to be presented here is that they show neither a selection of the most extreme cases, nor of the least extreme cases, but reveal the full gamut of such experiences.

Wife rape has presumably been with us as long as the institution of marriage—at least in western culture.* Though no one has yet written a history of wife rape, Susan Brownmiller does address the issue in her brilliant and comprehensive history of rape in general, *Against Our Will.* According to Brownmiller: "The exemption from rape prosecutions granted to husbands who force their wives into acts of sexual union by physical means is as ancient as the original definition of criminal rape, which was synonymous with that quaint phrase of Biblical origin, 'unlawful carnal knowledge.' To our Biblical forefathers," she continues, "any carnal knowledge outside the marriage contract was 'unlawful.' And any carnal knowledge within the marriage contract was, by definition, 'lawful.' Thus, as the law evolved, the idea that a husband could be prosecuted for

---

*Margaret Mead has claimed that a society called the Arapesh in New Guinea knew nothing of rape except that it was the unpleasant custom of another nearby society. Certainly, given Mead's description of the loving, gentle, nurturant relationships between Arapesh men and women, as well as between the parents and their children, it would be surprising to learn that rape in marriage occurred there. Presumably a few other societies once existed like the Arapesh. *Sex and Temperament in Three Primitive Societies* (New York: Dell, 1935), p. 110.

raping his wife was unthinkable, for the law was conceived to protect *his* interests, not those of his wife."[3]

As Brownmiller and other feminist writers (such as Florence Rush in *The Best Kept Secret: Sexual Abuse of Children* and Lorenne Clarke and Debra Lewis in *Rape: The Price of Coercive Sexuality*) have shown, the idea that females are the property of males is the key to understanding the history of extramarital rape and the laws pertaining to it. This has been so well presented, I take it as a premise without going through the argument. Many cases cited in this book will show that the notion of wives as property is equally fundamental to an understanding of wife rape. Not only are wives commonly viewed as the property of their husbands, but more specifically, they are seen as the *sexual* property of their husbands. As John Stuart Mill pointed out in *The Subjection of Women* published in 1869:

[A] female slave has (in Christian countries) an admitted right, and is considered under a moral obligation, to refuse to her master the last familiarity. Not so the wife: however brutal a tyrant she may unfortunately be chained to—though she may know that he hates her, though it may be his daily pleasure to torture her, and though she may feel it impossible not to loathe him—he can claim from her and enforce the lowest degradation of a human being, that of being made the instrument of an animal function contrary to her inclinations.*

But the viewing of wives as their husbands' property is not inevitable; it is part of our patriarchal heritage. The phenomenon of wife rape must be seen in the context of the patriarchal family.

Patriarchy refers to "a form of social organization in which the father is recognized as the head of the family." Outside of the family it also refers to "government by men."[4] The key elements of the contemporary patriarchal family involve the husband-father as the primary breadwinner, and the wife-mother as having the primary responsibility for child-rearing and housework. Whether or not the wife also has paid employment outside the home is significant, and often has some impact on the balance of power within the family, but it certainly does not equalize the power between husband and wife as long as the basic division of labor and responsibility within the family is unchanged. This conclusion is supported by the fact that in the Soviet Union and other socialist countries, where a much higher percentage of married women work outside the home than in western nations, and where women have more access to high status jobs, wives still have the primary responsibility for housework and child care.[5] The concept of "the double day" for

---

*The so-called right of the female slave mentioned by Mill hardly served as an effective protection. The right of women to reject the sexual advances of men other than their husbands was and is also constantly violated.

working women, and the quip that in socialist countries women are free to do two jobs, one paid and one unpaid, reflect this situation. The same "double day" applies to working women in western nations.

The point is not that any differentiated division of labor results in inequality (though it often does), but rather that the particular division of labor characteristic of the patriarchal family leads to inequality. This division of labor has been more or less culturally universal, with a few exceptions;[6] the oppression of women as a class by men as a class has been equally universal. The typical division of labor in patriarchal societies places the husband in the position of economic power, and the wife in the position of economic as well as status dependency. Given that women only earn fifty-nine cents to every dollar earned by a man, this economic dependence is diminished when wives have jobs outside the home, but the economic power imbalance is still present in most two-parent American families. If there are children, this economic dependency becomes economic vulnerability for the woman; if either the husband or the wife decides to end the marriage, the wife-mother can find herself in a critical economic situation, particularly if the children are young, and particularly in countries like the United States that have very few and very poor childcare facilities. Many wives in this situation can be coerced by their vulnerability into living with objectionable or abusive husbands. And if their husbands become disaffected with the marriage, wives may be forced to placate and accommodate them in an attempt to prevent being abandoned.

Having the primary responsibility for the care of children who are dependent and vulnerable and who demand much time and emotion, leaves mothers unable to pursue their own interests, unless they are willing to reject the notion that children are their responsibility. Rejecting this role sometimes requires a willingness to abandon the children. Most mothers cannot do this. Most mothers feel this responsibility far more strongly than most fathers feel their responsibility to support the family, as evidenced by the fact that very few husbands continue to pay child support when a marriage breaks up, while the vast majority of wives continue to take care of the children (unless their economic situation makes this quite impossible).

The primary problem, however, is not that husbands or ex-husbands are being irresponsible. The problem is that the division of labor in the patriarchal family both reflects and perpetuates the husband's power over the wife. This is the context within which wife rape and wife beating occur, and often continue. Wife rape and wife beating are two very serious and cruel forms of husbands' abuse of their power over their wives. They are both extreme acts of domination. Other forms of domination that are effected without violence can be as devastating—for example, extreme verbal cruelty, or inordinate possessiveness. The fundamental problem is not that husbands abuse their power, but that they have so much of it in the first place. Not everyone who has power in an unbalanced power situation abuses it, but in general, where there is power imbalance, there is abuse.

WIFE RAPE AND SOCIAL SCIENCE RESEARCH

Wife rape was rarely mentioned in social science literature until very recently. Even feminist analyses of rape have given little attention to wife rape. One exception: feminist sociologist Pauline Bart reported in 1975 that in her analysis of 1,070 questionnaires completed by rape victims who responded to a request published in *Viva* magazine, only four of the women had been raped by their husbands (i.e., 0.4 percent). Bart attributed this low figure to the fact that wife rape is legal in most states in the United States, so victims of wife rape were as unlikely as the law to recognize themselves as rape victims.[7] This is no doubt true, but another factor is the tendency already referred to for women with rape experiences that seem to be atypical to be less inclined to volunteer. This includes completing a questionnaire.

The first article to appear in a scholarly journal on the subject of wife rape was Richard Gelles' "Power, Sex, and Violence: The Case of Marital Rape," published in 1977.[8] Although Gelles deserves credit for being one of the first to introduce the problem to the scholarly community, he makes some very questionable statements.* For example, he writes that "labeling sexual intercourse forced on a wife by a husband 'marital rape' implies a major value judgment by the labeler concerning appropriate interpersonal relations between family members."[9] Clearly, however, *not* labeling such an act marital rape implies a major value judgment, too. Gelles next raises the question: "If the victim herself is unlikely to view the behavior as 'rape,' how can we discuss the phenomenon 'marital rape'?" But sociologists have never limited themselves to studying only phenomena where the participants or victims subscribe to the same phenomenological viewpoint as themselves. Incest victims, for example, may never have heard the word incest, but that does not mean sociologists cannot study incest. It may simply mean they should not use the word incest when talking to the victims.

In this article Gelles offers as "one reason why so little attention has

*In his first book *The Violent Home,* Gelles even maintained that "sex-related violence is one of the types of violence where husbands and wives are equally aggressive." (Beverly Hills, Calif.: Sage Publications), p. 84.

been directed toward forced sexual intercourse in marriage" the notion that "this is not viewed as a problem by most wives."[10] My own view is that it has been the researchers rather than the wives who did not see forced sex in marriage as a problem.*

For all the shortcomings of this article, Gelles did emphasize that "the topic of marital rape is an important area of investigation for social scientists," and that "the head-in-the-sand approach to marital rape is no longer acceptable."[11]

In 1978, Edward Sagarin, a well-known sociologist and past president of the American Society of Criminology, wrote in answer to the question "Is it legally possible to 'rape' one's own wife?":

The rationale for not including an assault on the wife as rape was that marriage gave the husband the right to sexual intercourse with his spouse; that it did not give the woman the same right may be regarded by many as grossly unfair, but there are many obvious biological and physiological impediments to forcible sexual relations demanded by a willing woman of an unwilling man.[12]

Sagarin implies here that the essential problem is the inequity of married women not being able to rape their husbands; this indicates a serious misunderstanding of the issue.†

In 1979, Nicholas Groth included some discussion of wife rape in his book *Men Who Rape,* which he expanded on in an article published in 1981.[13] Based on extensive research with incarcerated sexual offenders, Groth observed that: "Some offenders assault only their own wives, others rape only strangers, and some sexually assault both. However, based on our clinical experience with identified offenders, *it makes little difference whether the victim is wife or stranger, the dynamics of the offender are the same*"[14] (emphasis mine). Unfortunately, Groth's data base does not make such a generalization permissible: his data are particularly poor as a basis for discussing and analyzing husbands who rape their wives, since they were collected on over five hundred offenders, all of whom had been convicted of raping someone *other than* their wives—usually strangers. This is an exceedingly select group. Groth shows extraordinary naïveté when he optimistically states: "There is no way of determining whether the subjects we have worked with and studied constitute a random sample of all men

---

*A similar phenomenon occurred in the area of child abuse. Researchers failed for years to ask women and children whether or not they had been sexually abused in their early years.

†Sagarin goes on to caution his readers as follows: "Some people are agitating for a change in legal definitions of rape so that a husband can be held accountable as a rapist. Although it would meet the cannons of fairness, such a law would be virtually unenforceable and it is unlikely that a successful prosecution could be made." (Ibid.) Fortunately, Sagarin has already been proved wrong, as will be evident from the many cases of wife rape that have already been prosecuted, some of which are cited in Appendix I.

who rape. They are representative, however, of those offenders who directly or indirectly come to the attention of criminal justice and mental health agencies and with whom law enforcement officials and providers of social services are expected to deal in some effective manner."[15]

First, we can be sure that it is not a random sample, because Groth did not apply random sampling techniques. Second, identified sexual aggressors—as he sometimes refers to them—are a unique group who in no way represent the population of rapists at large. The psychological and social characteristics (e.g., race, social class) of rapists who are not apprehended are likely to be very different from their less fortunate brothers. Brownmiller is among those suggesting that it is only the most disturbed rapists who are convicted, though studies on this issue are inconsistent.[16] Third, reported cases are not representative of unreported cases: only a fraction of the reported cases of rape ever result in offenders who "come to the attention of criminal justice and mental health agencies." Hence, if reported rape is the tip of the iceberg, the rapist who becomes an offender known to the criminal justice system is the speck of dust on the tip of the iceberg.

I think Groth's study is very valuable. I object only because he generalizes from this highly select and unrepresentative group to men who rape in general. For example, Groth states: "Although there is a wide variety of individual differences among men who rape, there are certain general characteristics that men who are prone to rape appear to have in common."[17] He goes on at length to enumerate these supposedly common characteristics, for example:

His overall mood state, then, is dysphoric, characterized by dull depression, underlying feelings of fear and uncertainty and an overwhelming sense of purposelessness.

At the root of all this are deep-seated doubts about his adequacy and competency as a person. He lacks a sense of confidence in himself as a man in both sexual and nonsexual areas—a feeling that is often unacknowledged since he exhibits little capacity for self-awareness.[18]

Groth proceeds to describe 10 percent of these men as being in a psychotic state at the time of the offense, and maintains that 56 percent "were diagnosed as belonging to various types of personality disorders (inadequate, antisocial, passive-aggressive, borderline, and the like)."[19] This picture may well be appropriate for incarcerated rapists; however, it is hopelessly limited and inadequate for the many different types of men who rape women in a culture that has itself been described as a "rape culture."[20] An account of the results of psychological research that has been conducted in the last few years should bring this point home.

Sociologist Martha Burt has reported that over half of a representative sample of 598 residents of Minnesota believed in the following kinds of rape myths: "Any healthy woman can resist a rapist"; "In the majority of rapes, the victim was promiscuous or had a bad reputation"; "If a girl engages in necking or petting and she lets things get out of hand, it is her fault if her partner forces sex on her"; "One reason that women falsely report a rape is that they frequently have a need to call attention to themselves."[21]

Burt found that rapists also believe such myths and that they "use them to excuse or deny their behavior after the fact."[22] She concluded that these attitudes effectively support rape, and hence that it is appropriate to talk about this being a rape supportive culture. Burt's findings have been supported by other researchers who have used college students as their subjects.[23]

In the first of a series of experiments, psychologist Neil Malamuth and his colleagues Scott Haber and Seymore Feshbach asked a sample of fifty-three male students to read a five-hundred-word "rape story," an excerpt of which follows:

Bill soon caught up with Susan and offered to escort her to her car. Susan politely refused him. Bill was enraged by the rejection. "Who the hell does this bitch think she is, turning me down," Bill thought to himself as he reached into his pocket and took out a Swiss army knife. With his left hand he placed the knife at her throat. "If you try to get away, I'll cut you," said Bill. Susan nodded her head, her eyes wild with terror.

"The story then depicted the rape. There was a description of sexual acts with the victim continuously portrayed as clearly opposing the assault."[24] As is customary in much psychological research, the students were not drawn by any random sampling process; they volunteered to participate in the research as part of a requirement of introductory psychology courses. After they had read the rape story they were asked whether they personally would be likely to act as the rapist did in the same circumstances. The same question was then repeated, this time with an assurance that they would not be punished. The results: "On a response scale ranging from 1 to 5 (with 1 denoting 'none at all' and 5 'very likely'), 17 percent of the men specified 2 or above when asked if they would emulate such behavior 'under the same circumstances.'[25] But a total of 51 percent responded that they might do it if they were assured that they would not be caught."[26]

This study has since been replicated, mostly with college students in various areas of North America including Los Angeles and Palo Alto in California, and Winnipeg in Canada. Malamuth writes that across these varied studies, an average of about 35 percent of the males surveyed indicated at least some likelihood of raping if they could get away with it, and an average of about 20 percent reported a higher likelihood of raping, also if they could be assured of no punishment.[27] In a study by John Briere and his colleagues which focused on male students' willingness to force sex on a woman as well as to rape, 60 percent of their sample indicated some likelihood of rape or force or both given the right circumstances.[28] They concluded that their findings "reinforce the contention of feminist writers that there exists within the general population many males with a propensity toward sexual violence."[29]

Although male college students are clearly not representative of the male population at large, many researchers in this field would argue that college students are less inclined to rape than non-college students.[30] In a study of high school students, Roseann Giarusso and her colleagues report that more than 50 percent of the high school males they interviewed believed it was acceptable ". . . for a guy to hold a girl down and force her to have sexual intercourse in instances such as when 'she gets him sexually excited' or 'she says she's going to have sex with him and then changes her mind.' "[31]

Groth's psychological portrait (an extract of which was cited above) is supposed to apply to "men who are prone to rape." But the accumulating research that reveals how widespread the proclivity to rape is in the male population argues strongly against Groth's notion that 66 percent of all rape-prone men have psychotic episodes or suffer from clinically diagnosable personality disorders.

TERMINOLOGY

The term "wife rape" is preferred over "marital rape" or "spousal rape" because it is not gender neutral. The term "spousal rape" in particular seems to convey the notion that rape is something that wives do to husbands, if not as readily as husbands do it to wives, at least sufficiently often that a gender neutral term should be used. When the spousal rape legislation was being discussed in the Senate Committee in California, use of this phrase seemed to help foster the illusion that the protection of husbands was being sought, not just the protection of wives. It was repeatedly emphasized that this legislation would also allow a husband to charge his wife with rape. The legislators, it seems, were believed to be more likely to support legislation that on the surface at least, was not totally inimical to their interests as males. But since all other researchers appear to prefer the term marital rape, it will necessarily be used here from time to time, particularly when discussing their work. The term husband-rapist will sometimes be used for husbands who rape their wives.

The two terms most widely used to describe violence in marriage aside

from rape are "wife beating" and "wife battering." Both are highly problematic. The term "battering," for example, conveys the notion of extreme violence, and is appropriate only when the violence *is* extreme. It is
not a suitable phrase to describe a marriage in which a woman is slapped
from time to time. It is equally inappropriate to use the word rape to apply to all degrees of sexual abuse and assault. One of the consequences of
using words like battery or rape to apply to all degrees of violence or sexual abuse is that less drastic but nevertheless serious experiences can easily be neglected. Hence in this book, the term "battered" will be reserved
for severe violence such as repeated beating, slugging, kicking, choking,
use of weapons, and the like.

"Wife beating" is a term with less extreme connotations. However,
not all violence in marriage can accurately be described as beating. For example, the use of weapons to coerce, hurt, or even kill, is not always accompanied by beating. Throwing an object at another person is usually
violent and may be highly dangerous, but it is not a beating. Violent acts
such as shoving someone against a wall, throwing her to the floor, twisting an arm behind her back, are not accurately described by the term
beating. Even slapping or being struck once, as opposed to repeatedly,
seems to be too "minor" to warrant the term.

However, introducing a new phrase such as "husband violence" results in other problems. It is often necessary to differentiate between rape
and other violent behavior, but to use the term "husband violence" for
everything aside from rape implies that rape itself is not violent. Hence,
the reader should be aware that when the term "wife beating" is used, it
may refer to a wide range of violent acts toward wives, not beating alone.

CASE MATERIAL

As Jessie Bernard pointed out in *The Future of Marriage,* in every marriage there are two marriages—his and hers.[32] This is true of sexual assault as well. Since it is a patriarchal culture, we have mostly heard and
seen things from "his" point of view. This study, in contrast, will be totally focused on "her" perspective of sexual abuse in marriage. Eighty-
seven women who were victims of wife rape will describe their
eighty-nine experiences (two of the women were raped by two husbands)
in their own words.

In presenting case material I had to choose between selecting appropriate passages to quote as illustrative material for different topics, or
keeping the entire experience intact. I chose the latter course since (1) it
better allows the reader to get an overall sense of the woman's whole experience; and (2) it offers the reader important "raw data" on wife rape,

data nowhere else available at this time except in the form of single cases. Quoting a woman's experience in full also allows the reader to draw her or his own conclusions, apart from those I offer.

What I have done, then, is to study each of these eighty-nine experiences of wife rape with great care to decide which topics I thought each case best illustrated. Sometimes particular cases illustrated several topics very well; other cases contained less powerful illustrative material. Except for one case, which simply was too brief and unrevealing, I allocated all cases to one chapter or another. In contrast, since there is now considerable case material on wife beating in the published literature, I have been more selective about the material on this form of abuse, using only a small part of the case material available. No case is ever cited in full more than once. However, short excerpts from the complete accounts are sometimes quoted in more than one chapter.

When a woman has been both raped and beaten by a husband, the latter experience will be quoted with the former. When a woman says she submitted to her husband's demands out of fear of his using physical force, it is helpful to know about any other physical abuse that she had experienced from him. When there is no additional information on wife beating in the cases to be quoted, it means that the woman was not subjected to non-rape related violence from that husband.

A choice also had to be made regarding the format of the interview material presented. Several people suggested that the interviewer's questions should be "edited out" because they were distracting and intrusive; others suggested that the interviewer's questions should be fully written out and that each question should appear on a separate line like the dialogue in a play. I chose a middle course between these two options. It seemed to me a great distortion of the data to follow the first suggestion by editing out the interviewer's questions. Indeed, I don't see how it could be done without putting words into the respondent's mouth. For example, if the interviewer asks: "Did he force intercourse on you?" and the respondent replies: "Yes, he did so often," how does one "edit out" the interviewer? The interview was an interactive process. Few women simply held forth with a lengthy monologue. The interviewer's questions clearly greatly affected what the women said. Hence, the questions are included but in a paraphrased form to render them less distracting and obtrusive.

Some people believe that it is only necessary to quote one example to illustrate a point. This seems often to be a wise policy. However, when a problem has been denied for as long as wife rape has been denied, and when many people would prefer to believe that the victims of wife rape are exceptional and that the problem of wife rape has no bearing on the lives of most women and men, then I believe there is considerable value in citing many illustrative examples. The great volume of examples cited here along with the supporting statistics will, I hope, inspire the already concerned and convince the skeptical that the problem of wife rape is a serious one, deserving of our attention and urgent efforts at solution.

Race and Ethnicity

Statistical data on the race and ethnicity of the women in the study and the husbands who raped them are presented in Chapters 10 and 13. However, it seemed preferable not to describe the race or ethnicity of the respondent and her husband when presenting the case material, unless it seemed relevant. For example, in a few instances the responses of family members to women who were abused in inter-racial marriages were particularly cruel, and the women attributed these reactions to the fact that their marriage was inter-racial. In such cases, the racial identification of the couple will be mentioned. For the most part, however, given the great sensitivity of this issue, mentioning the respondents' race in a routine fashion would seem to distract attention from what the respondent has said.

Anonymity

Anonymity is of course a crucial issue in a study of this kind. All respondents' names have been changed. Pseudonyms were obtained by random selection from the San Francisco telephone directory. However, since certain racial or ethnic groups have distinctive names, it would be very confusing for the reader to try to remember that Mrs. Chan, say, might be an Anglo woman, and Mrs. Fernandez might be Chinese. Hence, names that are exclusively associated with a particular ethnic group were omitted.

Each respondent is referred to by the same name throughout this book. To further ensure anonymity in some cases, other changes were made that would not affect the substance of what was said in any important way.

Finally, a word about what to expect in the ensuing pages may be helpful. I have written this book with two major purposes in mind: first, that it provide heretofore unavailable information about wife rape, and place it in an appropriate context that will enlighten the general public, and provide both ammunition and inspiration to those who seek to change the conditions that have caused the problem, as well as to those who seek to help the victims of wife rape. The second major purpose is to have an impact on the scholars working in the areas of violence against women, marriage, heterosexual sexuality, rape, and the oppression of women in general. In order to increase the chances that the latter purpose will be achieved, a few chapters may seem frustratingly academic to many readers, particularly Chapters 3, 5, 7, 8, and 9. I want to urge readers who find one or more of these chapters a little difficult, dry, or uninteresting, to realize that they are there for an important purpose, and to read them selectively. Non-fiction books are usually written for either an academic market (so-called textbooks) or the non-academic market (so-called trade books). This book is written for both. Though I have attempted to use nontechnical language as much as possible, a few chapters will be of primary interest to scholars; by far the majority of chapters will hopefully be of interest to scholars and non-scholars.

Because this is the first book on rape in marriage, I felt it was important to include materials from all sources, published and unpublished, scholarly and journalistic, that I could find on this subject. This book does not attempt to provide a well-rounded picture of marriage today, or in the past, but instead, focuses on an ugly form of violation that occurs in many more marriages than most people would like to believe. My hope is that this book will make it impossible for the crime of wife rape to remain in the closet any longer.

PART ONE

THE LAW

2

Wife Rape and
the Law

I can not say that I think you very generous to the Ladies, for whilst you are proclaiming peace and good will to men, Emancipating all Nations, you insist upon retaining an absolute power over Wives. But you must remember that Arbitrary power is like most other things which are very hard, very liable to be broken. . . .

   —Abigail Adams to John Adams, 1776, *Familiar Letters of John Adams and His Wife, Abigail Adams, During the Revolution*, ed. Charles Francis Adams, 1876

The marriage license [is] a raping license.

   —David Finkelhor and Kersti Yllo, "Forced Sex in Marriage," 1980

The laws relating to rape in most states of this nation, and in most countries of the world, include what is commonly referred to as "the marital rape exemption." These laws usually define rape as *the forcible penetration of the body of a woman, not the wife of the perpetrator,* and so according to them, rape in marriage is a legal impossibility.

The origin of this exemption is invariably traced to a pronouncement by Matthew Hale, Chief Justice in England in the 17th century. As published in *History of the Pleas of the Crown* in 1736, it reads as follows:

But the husband cannot be guilty of a rape committed by himself upon his lawful wife, for by their mutual matrimonial consent and contract the wife hath given up herself in this kind unto the husband which she cannot retract.

The rationale behind the rule seems to have been the idea that "marriage, with the promise to obey, implied the right to sexual intercourse with the wife upon all occasions."[1] This idea, in turn, rested upon the notion that women were the property of their husbands, and procreation was the sole purpose of marriage.[2] Though Hale offered no legal authority in support of his opinion, case law in the United States "indicates an unquestioning acceptance of the Hale *dictum,* almost as if the courts were incapable of conceiving other resolutions of the issue."[3] Even the knowledge that Hale "made a name for himself by presiding over 'witch' trials and leading juries to convictions over enormous odds" does not seem to have made any dent in the credibility of this 17th century misogynist.[4]

The women's movement was very successful in drawing public attention to the issue of rape in the early 1970's, and equally successful in pressuring for changes in the laws pertaining to extramarital rape. For example, almost every state had passed some form of rape reform legislation by 1980.[5] Common reforms include limiting the cross-examination of the victim about her sexual history, disallowing what used to be a routine cautionary instruction given by the judge to the jury that rape is an easy charge to make but a difficult one to defend against, redefining rape to acknowledge that males as well as females can be victimized, and including forced oral or anal penetration in the definition of rape. However, these reforms did not sail through the state legislative bodies; rather they came after a considerable grass-roots lobbying effort by a coalition of feminists and law and order groups.[6] The slow progress in the passage of rape reform legislation has been compared by Hubert Feild and Leigh Bienen with the rapid and enthusiastic enactment of legislation against the exploitation of children in the pornography industry in 1978.[7]

There seems to have been an even greater reluctance to change laws condoning wife rape. One explanation for this is that "the matter may be too close for personal comfort for the well-placed, married males who make up the vast majority of the membership of American state legislatures. It may take only a little imagination for them to create a scenario in which, in their worst forebodings, they are cast as the protagonist in a Kafka-like performance."[8] Some of the arguments that have greeted legislative efforts to outlaw rape in marriage give strong support to this thesis. The following are examples of such arguments described as "typical" by the National Center on Women and Family Law:

"The State of Florida has absolutely no business intervening into the sexual relationship between a husband and a wife. . . . We don't need Florida invading the sanctity and the intimacy of a relationship." (Rep. Tom Bush, May 29, 1980)

"[T]he Bible doesn't give the state permission anywhere in that Book for the state to be in your bedroom, and that is just exactly what this bill has gone to. It's meddling in your bedroom; the State of Florida, as an entity, deciding what you can do and what you can't do." (Rep. John Mica, May 29, 1980)

"But if you can't rape your wife, who can you rape?" (California State Senator Bob Wilson, addressing a group of women lobbyists, spring 1979).[9]

THE RIDEOUT CASE IN OREGON

The spousal immunity clause was deleted from Oregon's rape statute in 1977. A year later in that state, John Rideout was indicted for raping his wife, Greta, and he thus became the first husband charged with marital rape while still living with his wife to be criminally prosecuted. Although there have been several other cases of husbands charged with rape in various states since then, the Rideout case is best known, or more accurately, most notorious. Despite the fact that the publicity about this case was often critical of Greta Rideout and the fact that a husband could be accused of raping his wife, it has done more than any other to raise consciousness about the issue of wife rape. The case was described in the media of the time:[10]

A twenty-three-year-old woman who'd been physically and psychologically abused by her husband for over two years, [Greta Rideout] found that as soon as she quit submitting to his desires, her husband's sexual aggression became so violent she could label it nothing less than rape. . . .

She had met John Rideout four years ago (in 1974) in Portland. . . . Before they were married (shortly after their two-and-a-half-year-old daughter, Jenny, was born), Greta said he'd slapped her face and "demolished" the house they were living in. She left him then—the first of three times.

"Two months after we were married, he began the mental abuse—calling me a dumb bitch, accusing me of being with someone else," she said, "but I was trying to deal with it. I wanted the marriage to work out, for better or worse. And believe me, most of it was worse."

Slowly she began to see a change taking place. The first time he gave her a black eye was a year and a half ago (in 1976). Aggressive sex, too, began to be a part of the pattern, according to Greta. "He was highly obsessed with sex; he wanted it two or three times a day. No matter what I gave him, he was never totally satisfied."

What seemed to give him the most pleasure, she reflected, was the violent sex which became a once-a-week occurrence. "And the more riled I got, the more he seemed to enjoy it."

Like most battered women, Greta Rideout had been afraid to fight back. The relationship became one of "love-hate, love-hate." John even threatened to sexually manipulate their daughter and told his wife he would show Jenny "what sex is all about" when she became an adolescent. . . .

She left him for the third time in July but returned for the same reason she had done so before. She couldn't support her daughter on the part-time minimum wages of her cashier's job or on welfare. She said she considered leaving Jenny with friends while she got on her feet financially, but thought John would accuse her of abandoning the child and try to take Jenny from her. Many of their arguments had been over money; John's work as a gas station attendant plus her meager wages "barely covered essentials," she said.

When she returned for the last time, her plan was to save up enough money to be able to leave for good.

"Before this point I had submitted. Now I was swimming to the surface to get out of the gutter, and he knew it. He saw the strength rising in me. . . ." It was around this time that his violence toward her seemed to intensify. "At times I'd be laying watching TV, and he'd walk up and kick me. I started feeling, God, he's weird." But he told her, "You're my wife; I can do what I want."

"He was in love with me when I was weak, but when I showed any strength, he hated my guts," she recalled. At the same time, she now realizes, he both loathed and was excited by strong women.

"He would see pretty women, strong career women, on TV or in magazines, and they seemed 'prudish' to him. He'd get worked up and say, 'Jeez, I'd like to rape that bitch's ass.' "

On October 10 (1978), John and Greta had an argument over money. He'd quit his job to return to school on the GI Bill and she thought he was squandering money at bars, playing pool—and not attending classes. She ran away from him, but he chased her, locked her in the apartment and started demanding sex. When she refused, he beat her until finally, she testified in court, she submitted for fear he would break her jaw.

John Rideout and his attorney never denied that he beat her that day, or that they had sexual intercourse. Their marriage had a pattern of fight, make up, and make love, the men said. (By the time their fights were over, said Greta, she often just submitted to sex. On the day of the rape, she said she was "totally repulsed" by the idea of having sex with John.)

Greta's rape story was confirmed by the doctor who examined her afterward and the Crisis Center worker who'd answered her call. "She was so scared that I was shaking; she had me scared to death," remembered volunteer Wanda Monthey.[11]

On December 27, 1978, John Rideout was acquitted of the charge of first degree rape of his wife by a jury of eight women and four men.

On January 6, 1979, less than two weeks after John was found not guilty, the Rideouts announced their reconciliation. Their faces beamed out from the pages of newspapers across the nation. "The law is right," John Rideout was quoted as saying. "It's a hard thing for a person like me to come back and say he believes the law is right when the law was used on me."

In March 1979, the couple separated again. Greta was quoted as saying, "I was going to go mad if I stayed there any longer. He has some pretty wild ideas about marriage." She added, "He also said that the things he told me about women's rights after the trial were wrong." Jean Christensen, Greta's attorney, obtained a divorce for her. Greta resumed her maiden name.

A few months later, John Rideout was back in court. On September 4, 1979, he pled guilty to a charge of criminal trespass for breaking into his ex-wife's home on August 27. He was given a nine-month suspended jail sentence, put on two years' probation, and required to pay $15 for the door he damaged and to submit to psychiatric evaluation. In February of this year, John Rideout was sentenced once again to nine months in jail for harassing his ex-wife; probation would be considered if Rideout consented to mental counseling.

Rideout's continuing attacks upon his ex-wife [after the rape trial] did not receive the sensational headlines that had attended the trial and reconciliation, so people still remember the Rideouts when they announced they were back together. Reporter Rae Nadler, writing in the *Hartford Courant*, described them at the time: "They posed together, a handsome couple, while the headlines declared 'Rideouts Will Ride It Out.' The world grinned and shook its head."

The reconciliation of John and Greta Rideout, though brief, was seen as confirmation by those who opposed the striking out of the marital exemption in Oregon's rape laws, that the state had no business meddling in the private affairs of married couples. And it was received as a blow to those who favored the legal reform and/or who believed Greta's story of wife rape. It was seen to demonstrate that, though she had been raped, it could not have been that upsetting an experience or she would not have become reconciled with her husband. But such a conclusion shows little understanding of the dynamics of relationships, particularly those in which women are being battered; for Greta was not just a victim of wife rape, she was a battered wife as well.

The issues of battered women and rape victims emerged as public concerns at different times and have developed in this and other countries as if they were two totally different problems. Separate literatures have developed around each, different institutions have been developed for handling them, and different people have been attracted to working with either rape victims or battered women, each often remaining quite ignorant of the other problem.

The Rideout case is one of many in which it is impossible to separate these two forms of male violence. But although ongoing intimate heterosexual relationships that are violent often involve both rape and beating, it is also important to recognize that the issues of wife rape and wife beating can be quite separate in many marriages, and that wife rape is not merely one more abuse suffered by the already battered woman.

MARITAL RAPE LEGISLATION AND COURT DECISIONS: THE CONTEMPORARY SCENE IN THE UNITED STATES

In July 1980 only Oregon, Nebraska, and New Jersey had completely abolished the marital rape exemption, and California, Delaware, Hawaii, Minnesota, and Iowa had partially stricken it. Nine years later in July 1989, husbands can be prosecuted for raping their wives in forty-two states, the District of Columbia, and on all federal land. This represents an extraordinary achievement on the part of many feminists and their allies who have had to work very hard to break through the resistance on the part of mostly male legislators. These forty-two states are listed in the two left-hand columns of the chart below.

The sixteen states in the far left column of the chart are those that no longer permit a marital rape exemption. This is to say that wife rape is a crime in these states, regardless of whether the couple lives together or apart.

In the twenty-six states in the middle column of the chart, husbands can be prosecuted for raping their wives in some circumstances, but they are totally exempt from prosecution in others that are prosecutable for non-marital rape. For example, in some states, so-called lower degrees of rape are not considered crimes in cases of wife rape: for instance, rape imposed by force but without the wife's suffering additional degrees of violence such as kidnapping or being threatened with a weapon; and non-forceful rape that is imposed when the woman is unable to consent because she is unconscious, drugged, asleep, ill, or physically or mentally helpless in some other way.

In my new introduction I discuss the fact that California's spousal rape law still requires that the victim report the crime within ninety days of its occurrence. One reason for this provision is to protect men from the assumed-to-be-numerous vindictive and dishonest wives who are by this provision rendered less able to fabricate a charge of marital rape in divorce cases. For instance, this provision attempts to prevent a woman from being able to report during divorce proceedings or custody battles that her husband raped her throughout her marriage. Or, if she does make such a charge, these rapes are not prosecutable offenses. There are numerous other such exemptions built into the California spousal rape law,* as in many of the other 25 states in the middle column of the chart.

In the eight remaining states (those on the far right of the chart), wife rape is not a crime. If a husband rapes his wife when they are living apart or have obtained a legal separation, or when one of the parties has filed for a divorce or for an order of protection, the couple is defined as unmarried for the purposes of prosecution. As marital rape expert Laura X states: "The seventeenth century legal definition of 'married' (i.e., a wife gives up her right to consent) is thus reinforced in these states."[12]

*1. Other circumstances in which wife rape in California is not a crime are as follows:
   a) The wife is incapable of giving consent because of a mental disorder, developmental or physical disability about which her husband is or should be cognizant.
   b) The wife is prevented from resisting due to intoxicating, anesthetic or controlled substances (illegal drugs, mostly narcotics, and others such as barbiturates) administered by her husband or about which he is cognizant.
   c) The wife is unconscious of the nature of the act at the time it occurred.
   d) Intercourse is forced on the wife by threat of deportation or incarceration (for example) by a husband who is a public official such as a policeman or immigration official—or who poses as such—when the wife has reason to believe that her husband has such authority. (This circumstance is particularly endemic in Los Angeles and other areas where brides are imported as sex slaves either by United States GIs or by men of their own or other cultures. In these cases the woman is often kept at home, terrorized, and because she does not understand the language, she cannot learn the truth about her husband's occupation.)
2. The convicted husband/rapist does not have to report as a sex offender.
3. Husband/rapists are the only rapists who can be charged with a misdemeanor instead of a felony for the crime of rape.
Source: National Clearinghouse on Marital and Date Rape, document prepared by Laura X, 1989.

State Law Chart*

Husbands Can Be Prosecuted for Raping Their Wives		Husbands Cannot Be Prosecuted Unless Couple Living Apart or Legally Separated or Filed for Divorce or Order of Protection
No Exemptions	*Some Exemptions*	
N = 16	N = 26	N = 8
Alabama	Arizona	Kentucky
Alaska	California	Missouri
Arkansas	Connecticut	New Mexico
Colorado	Delaware	North Carolina
Florida	Hawaii	Oklahoma
Georgia	Idaho	South Carolina
Indiana	Illinois	South Dakota
Maine	Iowa	Utah
Massachusetts	Kansas	
Nebraska	Louisiana	
New Jersey	Maryland	
New York	Michigan	
North Dakota	Minnesota	
Oregon	Mississippi	
Vermont	Montana	
Wisconsin	Nevada	
(District of	New Hampshire	
Columbia, and	Ohio	
federal lands in	Pennsylvania	
any state)	Rhode Island	
	Tennessee	
	Texas	
	Virginia	
	Washington	
	West Virginia	
	Wyoming	

*This is an adaptation of an updated chart prepared by the National Clearinghouse on Marital and Date Rape, Berkeley, California, January 1990.

She goes on to point out that the husband in these eight states can continue to rape his wife until *she* takes action; the burden is on her to leave him or to file for divorce—sometimes life-threatening steps for her to initiate—instead of it being the state's responsibility to remove him from her, and from society, for raping her.[13]

The National Clearinghouse on Marital and Date Rape is the only source for national statistics on the outcome of wife rape cases that have been reported to the police. The Clearinghouse staff followed up information obtained from a newspaper clipping service and a vast network of contacts at rape crisis centers and battered women's shelters, with phone calls to the prosecutors, court officials, attorneys, and journalists—in short, anyone who could supply them with further information about the outcome of the cases they had learned about. Unfortunately, the Clearinghouse data cover only the period 1978 (after the acquittal of John Rideout) to 1985, when lack of funding prevented the continuation of this project. Although it can be assumed that their method of acquiring information did not enable the staff to draw up a complete compendium of all the wife rape cases reported in the United States between 1978 and 1985, it is nevertheless the most complete data available on the outcome of wife rape cases.

An adapted version of the National Clearinghouse's table on arrest, prosecution, and conviction statistics for marital rapists appears below.

TABLE 2–1   Outcome of Wife Rape Cases
Reported to the Police: 1978–1985

Outcome	Number of Cases
Husband Arrested	210
Charge Dropped	48
Case Still Pending (as of 1985)	44
Prosecution Ended with Acquittal	14
Prosecution Ended with Conviction	104
Total Prosecuted Cases	118
Convictions as a Percentage of Prosecuted Cases	88%

The 88 percent conviction rate for victims of wife rape whose reports to the police resulted in arrest is strikingly high. It is considerably higher than many people either anticipated or currently realize. It is also significantly higher than the conviction rate for *non*-marital rapes. This is surprising because it is generally true that the more intimate the relationship between the victim and the rapist, the less likely are reporting, arrest, and conviction.[14]

One reason for the high conviction rate for wife rape is probably that—contrary to the fears of many legislators—the wives who charge their husbands with rape have often been subjected to particularly brutal and/or deviant experiences (many examples of these cases are cited in Appendix I). The thousands of women who are raped by their husbands in more "ordinary" ways, without the employment of tire irons, dogs, strangulation, or death threats, are simply not reporting their experiences to the police. And it is doubtful that the vast majority ever will. Given the continuing misogyny of the legal and law enforcement systems, we should not delude ourselves that this is a problem that will be solved by having every victim of wife rape report her attack to the police.

I believe that the next steps in the campaign for the rights of wife rape victims (and all married women are potential wife rape victims) are for concerned women and men to mobilize for the pursuit of the following goals:

1. The criminalization of wife rape in the eight holdout states that have so far been unwilling to institute this reform.

2. The passing of laws in the twenty-six states which still treat some forms of rape by husbands as non-criminal, the implicit assumption being that wife rape is less serious than rape by other perpetrators.

Feminist legal theorists, such as Joanne Schulman (formerly the staff attorney of the National Center on Women and Family Law), Sarah Wunsch and Anne Simon (formerly at the Center for Constitutional Rights), have noted that proposed marital rape laws are often butchered by amendments before becoming law. This is what has happened in twenty-six states. In contrast, the highest courts in several states have simply struck down the marital rape exemption as an unconstitutional denial of equal protection for wives. Because the rape of unmarried women is considered a crime, some of them have argued that equity requires that it also be so for married women. The courts have not followed the practice of many legislatures in maintaining that wife rape is different from rape by other perpetrators.

These feminist attorneys therefore have proposed that the wives in the thirty-four states that either do not have a law against wife rape or that do not have a satisfactory law, should organize a class action suit in each of these states to have the exemptions struck down by the courts as unconstitutional.

3. Courts can also strike down the exemptions for husbands as unconstitutional if they agree, as in *Liberta* (New York),[15] with Friend of the Court briefs requesting such a decision.

4. Wives who reside in states where wife rape is still legal can sue their husbands for damages in civil court, as pioneering rape law analyst Camille Le Grand proposed in the seventies. However, she also pointed out that it would be easier to sue one's husband civilly in a state where wife rape was taken seriously enough to be considered criminal.

On the other hand, it is equally important for all of us to recognize that wife rape is not a problem that will ever be solved by turning to the law. As long as men are the ones to make and implement the laws, there will be no justice for women. I pointed out in my new introduction that the primary dedication of male legislators is to their own interests, not to women's. Taking their husbands to court is not an option that many wives will consider, for economic, social, and psychological reasons. In addition, many women realize that the system is unlikely to be fair to them. For some it would also be highly dangerous to report sexual assault by their husbands because of the vindictive and sometimes lethal violence to which they might then be subjected.

The solution to the problem of wife rape starts with breaking silence about it. Women must realize that rape in marriage is common, but illegal, and married women need to know that they have a *right* to decline their husbands' sexual advances whenever they want to. For these goals to be achieved, feminists—particularly those who work in battered women's shelters and rape crisis centers—must acknowledge the significance and seriousness of wife rape in the United States, and place it on their agenda of issues that must be confronted and remedied. Service workers must extend their services to the victims of wife rape, and include wife rape in their efforts to educate the community. These are some of the first steps toward creating new norms for men's behavior in marriage. New remedies will emerge once these norms have been established. This may involve publicly shaming men, as the Chinese battered wives did in their "speak bitterness" sessions after the Communist revolution. Whatever the method, one thing is clear. True gender equality in and outside of marriage is necessary before all wives will be free from the risk of rape by their husbands.

PART TWO
THE STUDY

3

The Rape Study

It is very little to me to have the right to vote, to own property, etc., if I may not keep my body, and its uses, in my absolute right. Not one wife in a thousand can do that now.

—Lucy Stone, in a letter to Antoinette Brown, 1855

THE SURVEY

Little research was done on rape, and particularly little on rape victims, prior to the early 1970's when the women's movement brought the
issue to the attention of the public. Since then almost all research undertaken has been based on nonrandom samples of one kind or another, such
as surveys of college students who attend certain courses accessible to
professors doing research, questionnaires returned by readers of particular
publications interested in surveying their readers, victims admitted to the
accident floor of a hospital, police records of reported rape, interviews
with victims who reported their victimization to the police, and victims
who seek counselling or therapy. The problem with using nonrandom
samples is that it is not possible to generalize any of the findings to a larger population. For example, if research is based on a nonrandom sample of
rape victims, it is not valid to draw conclusions about all rape victims. According to the rules of scientific sampling theory, it is only legitimate to
talk about the rape victims actually studied. This is because it has been
found that there are often large differences between those who volunteer
for a study and those who do not. For example, in my study of rape victims reported in *The Politics of Rape,* very few Black women volunteered for
the study. It would be quite wrong for me to draw the conclusion from
this fact that there are many more white victims in the population at large
than there are Black victims; all I can be sure of is that more white women
volunteered. In this case we know that my study was, in this respect, totally unrepresentative of reality since there is considerable data to show
that Black women are victimized by rape disproportionately more often
than white women. Nonrandom sampling procedures can be excellent for
raising hypotheses and doing exploratory research, but they are less helpful when one wishes to *test* hypotheses.

27

Prior to my current study, the most significant research on rape victimization based on random sampling techniques in this country was undertaken by the National Crime Panel Surveys, an ongoing study of many different kinds of criminal victimization sponsored by the Law Enforcement Assistance Administration of the United States Department of Justice.[1] Unfortunately, the manner in which information about rape victimization is obtained in these city-wide and national surveys is likely to result in a considerable underestimate of the prevalence of rape. Only one of the survey's questions comes close to asking about rape, and it is put so indirectly ("Did anyone TRY to attack you in some other way?") that many rape victims might not realize that their experience is being requested. Nor did interviewers receive any training to sensitize them to the issue of rape. Hence there is no reason to believe they would not subscribe to the rape myths still believed by most people.[2] Interviews by people who think rape victims are responsible for being raped or that being raped is evidence that a woman has a bad character—as most of the general population still believes—are unlikely to elicit much information about rape experiences.[3] The incidence of rape reported to these Census Bureau interviewers has, not surprisingly, usually been so low that in almost every city the small number of victims precluded more detailed statistical analysis. These studies therefore provide little information to enhance our understanding of rape.

The only other study of rape victimization based on a random sample was conducted by the National Opinion Research Center in 1967.[4] In this study any adult eighteen years and older available for an interview was asked if anyone in the household had been a victim of any crime within the previous year. But we know that many rape victims do not tell their families about their experiences.[5] In addition, one-third of the rapes reported were disqualified because they were deemed by the interviewers—who were also not sensitized to the issue—as improbable.

Thus, other research on rape victimization either was based on random sampling techniques but lacking in methodological soundness for others reasons, or, even when extremely sensitive and effective in suggesting hypotheses to be tested, has lacked the methodology that would allow for generalization to a larger population than the one studied. In designing my study, then, it was my intention to combine the most rigorous, scientifically sound methodology with a deep knowledge of, and sensitivity to, the issue of rape.

I began my study with the hypothesis that the percentage of women in the population at large who have been raped is much higher than the percentages obtained in previous studies for the reasons noted, and higher also than is commonly believed to be the case. Assuming that my research would confirm this hypothesis, my primary objective was to establish the magnitude of the problem, both in terms of the number of occurrences of rape as well as the effects, in order to stimulate concern and provide a basis for demanding that the problem receive greater attention and that more efforts to resolve it be made. I also wanted to find out the relative frequencies of rape by strangers, acquaintances, friends, lovers, husbands, other relatives, and authority figures (as well as answers to a host of other questions which I plan to report in subsequent books).

San Francisco was selected as the locale for this survey rather than Oakland or Berkeley or other communities near where I live, because it is by far the best known of these cities. We felt that the results were more likely to be taken as seriously as they deserve to be if the study were based in this large and prominent community. While San Francisco is known to have a large population of gay people, this fact, we thought, would likely have no impact on the prevalence of heterosexual rape. I assume in fact that the true prevalence of rape and other sexual assault is unlikely to be substantially different for San Francisco and other major cities. There are likely to be enormous inaccuracies in the *reported* rape rates for different cities because definitions of rape differ, and because of different reporting practices by the police. Nevertheless, it is of interest that the rape rate per 100,000 people in 1978 was very similar in the following cities: San Francisco, 86; Los Angeles, 83; Boston, 84; Cleveland, 88; Dallas, 91; and Tampa, 93.* Whether or not these figures have any relationship to the true incidence of rape, including unreported cases, it was my goal to gain some insight into prevalence rates, the relevance of which would not be limited to San Francisco.

Designing the Interviews

It was our objective to explore rape in marriage, as well as rape in all other kinds of relationships. But the problem arose: how could potential respondents, chosen on a random basis, be approached so that they would be willing to answer intimate questions about any experiences of sexual abuse they might have had, including experiences with their husbands, fathers, brothers, or other females? Experts were discouraging about the prospects, but we designed a preliminary interview schedule and worked for months on redrafts in response to sound objections and suggestions made by others. After going through ten drafts, we and others adminis-

---

*(Uniform Crime Reports, 1979) The rape rate per 100,000 people in San Francisco in 1978 was higher than some major cities, for example, New York, 55; Washington, D.C., 70; Chicago, 45; but it was lower than others, for example, Detroit, 107; Atlanta, 139; Memphis, 103. (Ibid.) These rates do not include marital rape.

tered the interview schedule to acquaintances and friends. This led to more revisions. Each revised draft was tested by administering it to volunteer respondents, then seeking their feedback. As we progressed, we administered later drafts to paid volunteers whom we did not know personally. This process of revision went on for eight months before we did our pre-test, much longer than we had anticipated. We knew, however, that without an excellent interview schedule, it would be impossible to obtain high quality interviews.

It is customary in survey research to do a pilot study to see whether the methods chosen (including sampling techniques, manner of locating respondents, interviewer training and instructions, as well as the usability of the interview schedule) are workable and sound. Eleven interviewers, after appropriate training, completed ninety-two interviews over a period of three weeks with women who had been randomly selected. The results were then analyzed and our methods evaluated. While further changes were made as a result of the pre-test, it served essentially to demonstrate that despite the warnings we had received about the extreme difficulty of conducting interviews on the subject of rape, we had succeeded in developing an excellent and workable methodology.

Since several Asian women consultants advised us that non-English speaking Asian women were likely to be extremely unwilling to talk honestly about their experiences of sexual assault, these women were not included in our study. Interviews were conducted in English or Spanish, according to the respondent's choice; hence, non-English and non-Spanish speaking women are not represented in this study.

The Sample

For the drawing of our sample, we sub-contracted with Field Research Corporation, a well-known and highly reputable marketing and public opinion research firm in San Francisco. They used their customary procedure of first selecting "key addresses" from the San Francisco telephone directory. Each address served as a starting point for obtaining a cluster of household listings. Enumerators used these key addresses as starting points for listing all the addresses on the entire side of that block.* We then applied another systematic randomizing procedure to select a number of addresses in each block proportional to the density of the block.

---

*Normally, Field Research instructs the enumerators to list a fixed number of addresses in the same block as each key address. We were advised, however, that this would likely result in a bias against higher density blocks, i.e., poor and minority neighborhoods. Since we wanted to interview at least the percentages of Black, Latina, Asian, and other Third World women residing in San Francisco, we felt it necessary to ask Field to make this small change in their methodology.

We had intended to obtain one thousand interviews with women eighteen years and older. Because of a high incidence of not-at-homes during the summer months when the interviews were conducted, and because of an unexpectedly large number of households in which no eligible woman resided, the original sample of two thousand households drawn by the methods described above proved insufficient for obtaining one thousand completed interviews. Part way through the field period, we therefore had to draw an additional sample of twelve hundred.

These changes, as well as many other factors, resulted in higher costs than anticipated, necessitating our completing only 930 interviews. Though we did not complete processing the second sample of twelve hundred, we did complete the first random sample of two thousand households. This enabled us to make a comparison between the first and second samples to determine whether the households in these samples are comparable to one another. Fortunately, it appears that there is no significant difference between the two samples, and therefore the quality of randomness is not jeopardized.

The Interviewers

After careful screening, thirty-three female interviewers were hired: seventeen white, six Asian, five Black, and five Latina. They were carefully selected not only for their interviewing skills, but also for their empathetic attitudes to rape victims. A serious attempt was made to hire interviewers from all class backgrounds, as well as all age groups. All were given approximately sixty-five hours of intensive, paid training, an amount extremely rare in survey research. Since a key hypothesis of our study was that with high quality interviewing by women who had been sensitized to the issue of sexual assault, we would find that rape and other kinds of sexual assault are quite prevalent, developing the best possible training therefore became a primary commitment. This training included at least ten hours of "consciousness raising" about rape and incestuous abuse, as well as a half day on defining and desensitizing sexual words so that interviewers would be as relaxed as possible with whatever vocabulary respondents might choose to use.

Interview Procedures

A "Dear Resident" letter in English, Spanish, and/or Cantonese (depending on the ethnic make-up of that particular block) was mailed to each address in the two samples. No mention was made of the fact that it was a survey about rape. The word "crime" was used instead, because we did not want husbands, fathers, and boyfriends objecting on behalf of a potential respondent.

An interviewer followed up the letter with a visit to the address. Her first task was to obtain a list of all members of the household, their ages, relationships with each other, and their marital and employment status. If there was more than one woman eighteen years or over in a given household, a random procedure was applied to select one of them. It was only upon speaking with the respondent herself that the interviewer divulged the subject matter of the interview. Respondents signed consent forms before the interview commenced. Anonymity and confidentiality were stressed. Interviews were held in private, and every effort was made to match the race and ethnicity of interviewer and respondent. Respondents were paid ten dollars for their participation. The length of the interviews varied from twenty minutes to just over eight hours. The average length of time was one hour and twenty minutes. Usually only one visit was necessary, once the interview had been arranged.

Twenty-two percent (22 percent) of the interviews were verified, which is an unusually high verification rate (about 10 percent is average). This means that the interviewer supervisors checked that the interviews had indeed happened in 22 percent of the 930 cases, and that they also checked the accuracy of two sample questions. All 22 percent of the respondents recalled the interview and said the interviewer had been polite. And there were very high correlations between the answers to both questions reported by the interviewer and then reported to the interviewer supervisors (these correlations were 0.91 and 0.99). All but twenty-two of these verifications were done by telephone, the remainder being done by postcard. At least half of the verified interviews were drawn at random.

According to the report of one of these supervisors, Mei Sun Li, near the end of the verification process:

Not one woman reached has expressed any negative response to the interview experience. In fact, the predominant reaction has been one of enthusiasm, great encouragement for the study, and highly complimentary regard for the interviewer. . . .

I am confident that our interviewers did a spectacularly fine and honest job in an area so sensitive that some people have questioned whether it could be done.

Although the thirty-three interviewers were selected with a great deal of care, and given a very thorough training, there is no doubt that some were more talented than others, particularly in evoking confidence and encouraging disclosure, but also in their skill at probing. Hence the richness of the data the interviewers gathered varied. Had all the interviewers been as skilled as the most highly talented of our interviewers, a higher figure for the prevalence of rape in marriage would no doubt have been obtained. I doubt very much that this variability in skill, or any other factor, resulted in the fabrication of experiences of wife rape either by respondents or by interviewers. Two factors were important in discouraging these possibilities: (1) Respondents were paid a flat fee of ten dollars whether or not they had any experiences to report, whether the interview took half an hour or five hours; (2) Interviewers were also paid by the hour, not by the number of completed interviews. It was believed that the latter policy might motivate some interviewers to keep interviews as short as possible by discouraging disclosure, or worse, to fabricate interviews entirely.

VALIDITY OF THE DATA

Refusal Rate

When random sampling is used, it is important that the percentage of selected respondents who complete interviews be as large as possible; or to put it another way, that the refusal rate be as low as possible. The higher the refusal rate, the more questionable is the validity of generalizing the findings beyond those interviewed.

There are several ways a refusal rate can be calculated. If one wants to know what proportion of respondents, knowing that the study was about rape, refused to participate, then our refusal rate was 19 percent. When including in the refusal rate those people (men as well as women) who declined even to give a listing of those in the household, the refusal rate increases to 36 percent. Finally, if one takes into account all households where no one was ever at home, or where the interviewer could not gain access to the house because of locked gates, fierce watchdogs, and the like, as well as those where the women randomly selected to be interviewed simply were never available because they were out of town, or because the husbands or some other persons would not give the interviewer access to the women, or for some other reason, then the refusal rate is 50 percent.

There are several significant factors which affected our refusal rate. First, the National Institute of Mental Health, which funded the research, because of its concern for protecting human subjects, forbade us to attempt to "change the minds" of those who refused by sending back to that household a second interviewer particularly adept at this task, or who was better matched for characteristics such as age and social class to the person who refused.

In addition, because the study was conducted in the summer, when most people take their vacations, there was no one home at an unusually large number of households in spite of repeated call-backs.

The larger the refusal rate, the more possible it is that the data might look significantly different if those refusing had instead given us completed interviews.*

One way of attempting to assess the bias introduced by refusals is to compare the characteristics of those who refuse with those who do not. Where this information was available such a comparison reveals that there is little or no difference in the race or ethnicity of these two groups, the number of persons living in each household, and the employment status (i.e., the percentage who were working full-time, part-time, laid off or looking for work, or retired). However, there is a significant difference in age and marital status. Women who refused to participate in the study were more likely to be older than those who agreed to be interviewed (an average age of 50 years versus 43 years) and married (60 percent versus 39 percent). To assess the effect of this potential bias on the sample, we used a weighting procedure in which married women and older women would count for more in the sample. Fortunately, application of this weighting procedure had only a small impact on the prevalence of wife rape (i.e., it lowered it by one percentage point).

Until the 1980 census data are available for factors besides race, it is impossible to assess how the refusals have skewed the sample of women who were interviewed. Comparison with the 1970 census data is not useful because there is reason to believe that factors such as age, marital status, number of single mothers, number of gays, have changed considerably in San Francisco in the last decade.† We know that the racial composition of San Francisco has changed dramatically since 1970. For example, the percentage of white people has dropped from 71 percent to 58 percent, and the percentage of Asian people has risen from 13 percent to 22 percent. (The percentage of Black people has remained the same—13 percent, but the category of "Other" has risen from 1 percent to 7 percent).[6]

Although overall our refusal rate is higher than we had hoped, we consider the data we have obtained no less remarkable and phenomenal, given the immense difficulties of tackling a random sample survey on this subject. It must be remembered that Kinsey and his colleagues, Masters and Johnson, and Shere Hite all based their studies on volunteers because

---

*By way of example, let's say 10 out of 100 selected respondents refuse and that the average age of the 90 who *are* interviewed is 30. Even if the average age of the 10 *not* interviewed is very different, e.g., 20, the overall average would change by only a year ([90 × 30] + [10 × 20] ÷ 100 = 29). However if 50 out of 100 refused, and the average age of those interviewed was 30, while the average age of those who refused was 20, the overall average would be quite altered ([50 × 30] + [50 × 20] ÷ 100 = 25).

†For example, marriage rates have dropped and divorce rates have increased; people are marrying later—thus there are larger numbers of never-married women, especially in their twenties; and there has been an increase in the number of gay men and women in San Francisco—a factor which would also affect marital status.

they considered a random sample unfeasible. A less than perfect random sample is still unprecedented for research in the area of sex or sexual abuse.

Alfred Kinsey and his collaborators (Wardell Pomeroy, Clyde Martin, and Paul Gebhard) in their classic studies of male and female sexual behavior, also used the interview method to obtain data about people's sexual feelings, preferences, and practices. Their questions also spanned people's entire lifetimes. Hence, there is considerable similarity between some of the problems we each faced. Some of the limitations of their methodology apply to our study as well.

Throughout research of the sort involved here, one needs to be continuously conscious . . . that it is impossible to get more than approximations of the fact on the incidences and frequencies of various types of human sexual behavior. Memory cannot be wholly accepted as a source of information on what has actually happened in an individual's history. There is both deliberate and unconscious cover-up, especially of the more taboo items; and in dealing with people of diverse mental levels and educational backgrounds, there are differences in their ability to comprehend and to answer questions with any precision in an interview.[7]

Several factors affected the validity of our data. First, how willing were respondents to tell us about unwanted sexual experiences with their husbands and how honest were they willing to be about all the details? Second, even when willing to disclose, what was their *capacity* to cooperate? For example, could they hear adequately? Could they understand the questions? Would they necessarily remember if they had had such experiences, and how accurate would their memories be? Third, how accurate and honest were the interviewers in recording the data?

Willingness to Disclose

Each interview concluded with a section on "Interviewer Observations." Two questions in this section concerned the interviewer's assessment of the respondent's willingness to disclose and her overall confidence in the validity of the data.

In answer to the question: *How willing do you think the respondent was to disclose experiences of sexual assault she might have had?* the interviewers answered as follows for the 87 victims of wife rape: 64 percent "very willing," 34 percent "willing," and 2 percent "unwilling." In answer to the even more important question: *In general, how confident are you about the validity of the data the respondents gave you?* 79 percent of the interviewers answered "completely confident," 16 percent "very confident," and 5 percent "somewhat confident" or "not very confident." It should be remembered, however, that these questions were not only addressed to the wife rape data, but to the entire interview.

Although interviewers were instructed to emphasize the importance of privacy during the interview, and even to insist on it, in a few cases respondents refused or were unable to control the situation. Of the eighty-seven victims of wife rape, in the interviewer's estimation, only three respondents were affected "some" by the presence of others, and for one, "much" effect was reported.

Respondents were also given a very brief self-administered questionnaire at the end of the interview. Two of the questions, along with the percentage breakdown of the answers given by the victims of wife rape follow. *How comfortable have you felt about answering the questions on unwanted sexual experiences?* Fifty-three percent (53 percent) of the victims of wife rape answered "very comfortable," 21 percent answered "somewhat comfortable," 17 percent answered "somewhat uncomfortable," and 8 percent answered "very uncomfortable." *How frank were you able to be during this interview about any unwanted sexual experiences you may have had?* Eighty-two percent (82 percent) circled the answer that read "I felt comfortable enough to answer *all* the questions as accurately as I could"; 15 percent admitted that they didn't feel comfortable enough to answer one or two of the questions accurately; and 2 percent admitted they had not answered "a few" or "some" questions accurately. (Again, these questions didn't necessarily relate to the wife rape experiences *per se,* since many respondents had other sexual assault experiences.)

Respondents were also asked to describe which questions they had felt unable to answer accurately. These answers provide unambiguous evidence that several women were unwilling to admit having forced sexual experiences with their husbands, and sometimes they were also unwilling to disclose their husband's other violence toward them. For instance, Mrs. Wolf was willing to talk about her husband's other violence, but while willing to admit she had experienced unwanted sex with him, she denied during the interview that it was ever physically forced. However, on the self-administered questionnaire she wrote that she had not felt able to be accurate about "my husband forcing unwanted sex."

Mrs. Johnson was also willing to admit unwanted sex with her husband ("I didn't feel like having sex but he was so eager that I gave in."), but during the interview she denied that he ever used force, or threat of force, or had sex when she was totally helpless. The interviewer was skeptical about this denial because Mrs. Johnson seemed very uncomfortable at the time, very defensive, and was unable to maintain eye contact. Though Mrs. Johnson was reluctant, she was willing to talk about her husband's other violence, though it seemed that there was underdisclosure about this, too. (For example, she said "if he was angry and drunk he would hit me. . . ." as if it were a general pattern, but then she said he had been violent only from 2–5 times over a period of one month.) On the self-administered questionnaire Mrs. Johnson first circled that she had not been able to answer one or two questions accurately. Then she erased this along with the beginning of an explanation, and circled that she had answered all questions accurately. The interviewer wrote that "Mrs. Johnson here proves that it's sometimes easier to lie than explain the nature of her difficulty."

Other women simply refused to answer the question on unwanted sexual experiences with their husbands. "That's a loaded question," said Mrs. Montgomery, and declined to say any more, though she answered questions about other violence very readily and in great detail. Mrs. Stevenson also refused to talk about "forced relations with my husband," but had no problem talking about other violence.

Still other women said enough to indicate that they had been raped by their husbands, but they would not answer additional questions about the experience. For example, Mrs. Underwood said: "I wanted him to love me, but he didn't. He forced me to have intercourse with him anyway; 'I'll do anything,' he said. He wanted me to suck his thing all the time and he wanted me to try to make him come." Mrs. Underwood refused to give any further information except to repeat that he made her do it several times against her will.

All Mrs. Spencer was willing to say about her experience of wife rape was: "Many nights, one in particular, I was exhausted but he wouldn't take no for an answer, and he forced me to have intercourse with him." When asked about her husband's other physical violence, she was only willing to say: "He beat me, he hit me with his fist in my upper chest and in the stomach. I was sick and had to be taken to the hospital." Mrs. Spencer also said that the violence had occurred from 6–10 times over a period of 4 years. On the self-administered questionnaire she wrote that she had not been able to be accurate on the following: "(1) In regards to an unwanted sexual experience with my husband. (2) In regards to being subjected to physical violence from my husband, the physical results of which are severe and painful. Many effects are also mental, but very many are physical."

A few other respondents admitted having been forced to have sex with their husbands but were nevertheless extremely evasive about the details. For example, after Mrs. Mayfield had said that she had many such experiences, she was asked to describe the most upsetting time.

It was all upsetting, but it happened so long ago—who can remember. *Does any incident stand out?* No, it was all the same. Always he wanted sex and I didn't. When you're married, or at least, when you're married to a jerk like that, it happens all the time. *Most upsetting time?* No, I told you they were all upsetting at the time but I can't remember them now. It's not worth it, who wants to dwell on that? He was a strange guy and it was a bad marriage. *What brought it to an end?* He stopped making sexual advances. He obtained a girl friend.

How upset were you by these experiences? Somewhat upset. *How much effect on your life?* A great effect. I'm suspicious, not of my present husband, but of people in general. I'm more wary and paranoid. *Why?* Because of my ex-husband. He had temper tantrums. He'd cry and over-dramatize. Sexually, it was terrible. He was maladjusted. For a couple of years, it made me bitter and closed-off to people. It taught me to look for ulterior motives in other people.

Most upsetting experience of other violence? It was all part of the experience of being married to this guy. He'd slap me around if he was frustrated. He always seemed frustrated. Then he'd go running off to his mother. *Can you be more specific?* No, I can't be specific. It was so long ago and I never wanted to dwell on it. I was just glad I got out. *One incident?* No, they were all the same.

Mrs. Mayfield said her ex-husband was violent from 11–20 times over a period of 10 years.

There were at least two women who denied any unwanted sexual experiences with their husbands, but who did not deny other marital violence. However, they refused to give any details. For example, Mrs Purcell:

Husband ever violent? Yes, he drank. He was mean to me. But I don't want to go into that. I don't want to think about it. I don't like to have to remember my husband that way.

The interviewer added: "Mrs. Purcell set her jaw and refused to answer any more questions."

Mrs. Evans at first maintained that her husband had just kicked her once and hit her a couple of times "not seriously." She added that "he'd be considered a gentleman, I think." Then later in another context Mrs. Evans told the interviewer that she'd lived a life of hell with her husband. "I've been called every name under the sun." Her only joy had been raising her son. She said she felt that "the good Lord" rewarded her with this son in return for her having to live with this man. Later she said: "I shouldn't have even mentioned it" (his violence).

Mrs. Peters had first intended not to disclose her husband's violence, but changed her mind because of the confidentiality oath required of the interviewers, and "in the interest of scientific study."

More women appear to have been willing to disclose violence in marriage than forced sex. Sexual abuse has been seen as even more taboo than other forms of abuse, including violence, for a long time. This is why the problem of child abuse and neglect has only recently come to include sexual abuse, and why research on wife abuse has almost always neglected the sexual aspects of this abuse. No examples of women willing to disclose forced sex in their marriage, but not other violence, were evident.

Indeed, judging from the answers to the self-administered questionnaire, it seems that honest disclosure of unwanted sexual experiences in marriage was more difficult for many women than disclosure of sexual abuse by all other categories of people, including victims of incestuous abuse.

Why are women so reluctant to talk about sexual abuse by husbands? Some women expressed a desire not to focus on the negative experiences in their marriages, or felt they were abusing the memory of a husband now dead and buried. Others saw it as a breach of confidence, or as reflecting badly on themselves, internalizing the notion that they are in some way responsible. And one woman was very clear about her reason: her husband is a voracious reader and she was afraid he might read the book and identify himself.

Capacity to Disclose

Willingness to disclose is one problem; capacity to disclose another. At the end of the interview the interviewer was asked whether the respondent had appeared to have any difficulty understanding the questions. Of the 87 victims of wife rape, 76 percent were judged to have no difficulty, 22 percent some difficulty, and 2 percent great difficulty. The difficulties referred to may in part be due to unfamiliarity with English. While all but three of these 87 interviews were conducted in English, 17 percent mentioned that a language other than English was spoken in their home at the time of the interview.

Six victims of wife rape were judged by the interviewer to have difficulty hearing the questions. Two had some difficulty reading (a few answers were broken down into categories, and handed to respondents on a card, so that they could simply give the number of the category that applied to them), and two others were judged as being unable to read.

Fortunately, the question on unwanted sex with a husband was not a particularly complex one. And if the respondent said she had had such an experience, the interviewer's task was to probe for whether it would meet our definition of rape or not. Difficulties in understanding and hearing are therefore likely to have been picked up by the interviewer in the course of obtaining a description of the attacks. However, if the woman simply answered no to the question on unwanted sex with a husband, then there would not have been an opportunity to rectify misunderstandings. Hence, if these methodological problems had any impact on the wife rape data, it was likely to be in the direction of respondents answering no to the question when they might have answered yes, rather than vice versa. Underestimation was thus far more likely to be a problem than overestimation.

As for memory, several respondents mentioned difficulty recalling not

simply details, but sometimes entire events. However, it seems most unlikely that they would be totally unable to recall an experience of wife
rape, had such an experience occurred to them. On the other hand, it is
quite likely that some women may not have recalled one or more incidents of *other* physical violence.

With regard to the accuracy of the data on the frequency and duration
of wife rape and other violence, we can learn from the Kinsey team's experience.

As usual, incidence figures [on whether or not a particular sexual behavior was
practiced] are more accurate than frequency data [how often the behavior oc-
curred]. Estimates of average frequencies are especially difficult for children, for
individuals of low mentality, and for most poorly educated individuals. Frequencies are more difficult to estimate when they concern remote periods.[8]

Much of the Kinsey team's discussion of the pros and cons of data based
on recall of recent events versus those in the distant past are also applicable to our research. First, they raise a question:

Since the subjects were of various ages when they contributed their histories, the
data shown for any particular age period have been obtained partly from the more
immediate recall of younger persons, and partly from the more remote—sometimes the quite remote—memory of older persons. Can data obtained by such different processes fairly be added together?"[9]

In answer, they offer some of the following points, presented here because of their relevance to our research.

More recent events seem, in general, to be recalled more easily, and more remote
events are recalled with greater difficulty. This seems reasonable enough, but it
proves nothing concerning the validity of the recall. It seems reasonable to believe
that more immediate and more easily recalled events would be reported with
greater accuracy, but there are at least certain circumstances where that is clearly
not so. . . .

The possibly greater accuracy of recent memory is at least partially offset by
the greater extent of coverup on recent events. . . . Consequently many subjects in
a case history study will admit participation in the more taboo sexual activities at
some time in the past, while insisting that such activities are no part of their current histories, or that the frequencies are now very much reduced. . . .

The generalization to be drawn from these several impressions is that the memory
of more recent events may be more accurate (except in the aged), but its accuracy
is more or less offset by a considerable amount of cover-up on more immediate
activities.[10]

These points suggest that the presumed advantages of incidence
(events occurring in the last twelve months) over prevalence data (events
occurring at some time in a person's life) do not necessarily hold, particularly when the subject being researched is very personal or painful.

In confirmation of Kinsey and his colleagues' observations, it has been my strong impression that women who are still married to a husband who is abusing them are less ready to divulge this, and if they do, they are more likely to downplay or discount the experience.

Only one of the thirty-eight questions in our survey actually used the word rape; rather than asking about wife rape directly, interviewers were instructed to ask the following question: *Because so few people think of husbands when they think of sexual assault, I want to ask you a question about that. Did you ever have any kind of unwanted sexual experience with your husband(s) or ex-husband(s)?* If the respondent answered in the affirmative she was asked: *Tell me briefly about that experience (each of those experiences).* It was the task of the interviewer then to probe for experiences that would meet our definition of rape or attempted rape.

For every case of rape and attempted rape (including the few cases of forced oral, anal, or digital sex), the interviewers administered a separate questionnaire which asked for a description of the assault, sufficiently detailed to ensure that one of the criteria for defining it as rape or attempted rape had been met. Women raped more than once by a husband were asked to describe the most upsetting time.

Lovers, including live-in lovers, were not included in the analysis of wife rape, but a few common-law marriages were included when the woman made it clear that she regarded the man as a husband.* One case of a live-in lover who was the biological and social father of the respondent's child was also included.

Our aim was to combine the most rigorous and scientifically sound methods of gathering and analyzing data on rape and other sexual assault, with a sophisticated and empathetic understanding of the experience of sexual victimization. I believe this combination made it possible to obtain the most valid and reliable material on wife rape and other forms of sexual assault, both quantitative and qualitative, heretofore available.

---

*For example, a few women described themselves as married and responded to the questions about husbands, but in answer to a later question, said that they were not technically married to these men, but that they regarded them as husbands. A few women also specifically described their spouses as common-law husbands.

4

What Is Wife
Rape?

There are some (wives) who still suffer strong pangs of guilt
over sex and only "allow" themselves to participate if it is
supposedly against their will.

If "everything is all right" once you get started, just remind yourself that you are committing rape-by-request and
contributing to your wife's over-all sexual satisfaction.

> —David Reuben's answer to a letter in his column
> "Reuben on Sex," *San Francisco Chronicle,* May 12,
> 1973

I thought of frigging, but an irrepressible desire for cunt,
cunt, and nothing but it, made me forget my fear, my dislike
of my wife, our quarrel, and everything else,—and jumping
out of bed I went into her room.

"I shan't let you,—what do you wake me for, and come to
me in such a hurry after you have not been near me for a
couple of months,—I shan't, you shan't,—I dare say you
know where to go."

But I jumped into bed, and forcing her on to her back,
drove my prick up her. It must have been stiff, and I violent,
for she cried out that I hurt her. "Don't do it so hard—what
are you about!" But I felt that I could murder her with my
prick, and drove and drove, and spent up her cursing. While I
fucked her I hated her—she was but my spunk-emptier.

> —Anonymous Victorian gentleman (sic), *My Secret
> Life,* c. 1890

DEFINING WIFE RAPE

The first question we must confront is: What exactly are we referring
to when we speak of wife rape? Do we include any kind of forced sex, or
do we have a narrower definition? And are there different types of wife
rape?

The legal definition of forcible rape in California at the time our research commenced, in 1977, was typical of that of most states. Forcible
rape (hereafter simply referred to as rape) included: (1) forced intercourse
(vaginal-penile penetration), or (2) intercourse obtained by threat of
force, or (3) intercourse when consent is impossible because the victim is

unconscious, severely drugged, asleep, or in some other way totally help-less.

Feminists have strongly opposed this traditional legal definition of rape, preferring a definition including "any sexual intimacy forced on one person by another,"[1] and feminist-initiated protests have resulted in changes in the rape laws of most states. A broader definition of rape has come to be favored by many people because they recognize that violation and trauma are not limited to acts of forced penile-vaginal intercourse. The focus on penetration of the vagina has often been seen as a vestige of an outdated patriarchal notion that female purity and virtue requires a vagina that has not been penetrated. According to this perspective a fe-male who has experienced all manner of "foreplay," including oral or anal sex, whether voluntary or involuntary, may still be regarded as a virgin.

Another rationale for focusing on forced sex instead of relying on a more traditional definition of wife rape is that few women define them-selves as having been raped by their husbands even when intercourse has been forced on them. Hence asking them whether their husbands ever raped them is an unpromising approach.[2]

We've arrived at a compromise between the traditional legal definition and the more modern, feminist-influenced definition, to include forced oral and anal sex as well as forced digital penetration.* We are, however, omitting consideration of a sizable number of other forced sex acts that are likely to occur even more frequently in and outside of marriage—for example: forced fondling of breasts or external female genitalia, forced fondling of the penis, and forced kissing. Such acts would nevertheless meet the definitions of wife rape used by some sociologists such as David Finkelhor, Kersti Yllo, and Irene Frieze. Frieze, for example, defines mari-tal rape as "forced sexual activity of a wife by her husband."[3] (Her defini-tion also makes it impossible for a husband to be raped by his wife.)

Following the traditional legal definition of rape, we have distin-guished between rape by force, rape by threat of force, and rape when the wife is in no position to consent because she is unconscious, drugged, asleep, or in some other way helpless. Examples may help delineate the differences between these three types of rape. The first experience to be described is an example of rape by force.

Force

Mrs. Morgan was a twenty-eight-year-old woman who was separated at the time of the interview from the husband who raped her. She was

---

*"Forced digital penetration" is the rather misleading phrase used to describe one case where a husband repeatedly forced his fist into his wife's vagina.

living with another man and one of her two children. She was working full-time as a clerk-typist.

Mrs. Morgan was twenty-four at the time her husband first raped her. She said the rapes occurred from 6–10 times over a period of 6 months, and his other physical violence occurred from 2–5 times.

He wanted me to have sex with him when I didn't want to. I had no desire. I didn't want him to touch me, so he forced me. He said I was his wife and I had to do it. I wanted to sleep on the couch but he forced me. *Forced intercourse?* Yes. *Verbal threats?* He said he was going to beat me. He called me names. He said I was his wife and he had a right to sleep with me when he wanted to. *Other times?* They were always much the same as I've said.

What brought it to an end? I left.

How upset? Somewhat upset. *How much effect on your life?* No effect.

Other physical violence? He'd start arguing and fighting with me. (*Mrs. Morgan took a long time to answer. She looked very upset and had tears in her eyes, so I did not probe further.*)

It seems that Mrs. Morgan's discounting of any long-term effects from the rapes may in part be explained by the fact that she is currently experiencing much worse abuse from the boyfriend with whom she is living. (This experience is described in Chapter 19.) Such down-playing may also be due to an acceptance that this treatment is normal in marriage.

Threat of Force

Mrs. Taylor was a seventy-year-old divorced woman who lived alone when she was interviewed. She had no children. Before her retirement, she had worked as the chief telephone operator in a legal office.

Always when he was drunk he wanted sex. I was afraid of him. He used to accuse me of looking at other men. *Did you have any unwanted sexual experiences with him?* Yes, I did—to keep myself from getting banged. It didn't happen too many times because when he was drunk he usually got it from other women. Later when I knew better, I'd hide in the bathroom until he passed out. *Did he do anything else to you?* He never forced me. He just did the normal things that a husband and wife do together. *What kinds of things?* Just normal things. There was nothing abnormal or unnatural about the sex we had. *Intercourse?* Yes. *Vaginal?* Yes. It was just that I didn't at all want to have it.

It is apparent that Mrs. Taylor herself makes a clear distinction between force and physical intimidation. She says she has had intercourse "to keep myself from getting banged," but answers decisively that "he never forced me." Yet Mrs. Taylor was afraid of her husband because he was a violent man. In answer to the question about her husband's violence, she described the most upsetting of more than twenty experiences that had occurred over a period of seven years as follows:

It was the time he kicked me in the leg in the street and I could hardly walk. He told me I was out with so and so, though I was never even in the bar. Fellows used to flirt with me and he got jealous. So he beat me up, slapped me in the face, and belted me in the jaw. Other times, he'd ask: "Where's my supper?" If it wasn't there, he'd hit me, even though I never knew when he'd be home because he was out with other women.

I never had to go to the hospital, but he knocked my tooth through my gums and once he gave me a black eye. Another time he came home with a gun. He said he was holding it for someone. I said I'd report him so he got rid of it the next day. *Used weapon against you?* No, he never actually used a weapon on me.

Once I had him put in jail overnight. The cop downstairs came up when I called. They took him down to headquarters for wife beating. He was released the next day when he was sober. *Other physical violence?* No, it was mainly kicking and slapping.

It seems from Mrs. Taylor's description that she was primarily a battered wife who was also intimidated into having sex from time to time. This situation is considered by many to be typical of wife rape cases, but the many experiences to be described throughout this volume will show that this is only one type of relationship within which wife rape occurs. Mrs. Taylor attempts to downplay her husband's force; she is typical of the many women who can discount experiences of rape by intimidation more easily than they can rape by force, perhaps because they are able to avoid the sense of their physical efforts and their will (as distinct from their wishes) being overcome.

Inability to Consent

Here are two examples of rape that occurred because the wives were unable to consent: one wife was asleep, and the other taken by surprise.

Mrs. Rice was thirty-nine years old at the time of the interview. She had two children, a six-year-old and a baby of one month, and she was in fact on maternity leave from her job as a clerical worker. She was still married to her husband, who worked as a parking attendant.

Mrs. Rice was raped in her sleep by her husband once five years prior to the interview.

One time my husband thought I was awake and started to approach me. He says that I answered him, but I was deeply asleep. We had just returned home from a week-long trip, so I was exhausted. I woke up about two hours later and I felt wet, and was without my panties. He said that I answered him but I never remembered anything. What a barbarity! I didn't know what happened. I didn't know if I enjoyed it or didn't enjoy it.

While some might question whether such an experience should be classified as rape, Mrs. Rice's sense of outrage (she calls it "a barbarity") is evident. But if a wife is *not* upset by her husband having intercourse with her in her sleep, or if she is not in any way traumatized by it, can it be regarded as rape?

In order to answer this question, we have to ask what it means for a wife or a husband to think it is acceptable for a husband to have sex with his wife if she neither consents nor participates. This acceptance often stems from the belief that wives are the sexual property of their husbands, and that it is natural male behavior to be able and willing to have sex with a woman who is passive or noncooperative. This acceptance also implies the belief that it is appropriate for wives to accommodate their husband's needs and desires as long as it doesn't hurt them. The notion that it is of little consequence for a husband to have intercourse with his wife when she cannot consent is another version of the view that wives have no right to refuse their husband's sexual advances. For if it doesn't matter whether a woman says "no," what does it mean for her to say "yes"?

Mrs. Haas was not so much forced as taken by surprise, and thus in no position to consent to several acts of anal rape. This happened from 2–5 times over a period of 3 months; it was not the result of a single misunderstanding between Mrs. Haas and her husband. (This was the only experience of rape by surprise that was disclosed, possibly because the interviewers were instructed to probe for force, threat of force, or total helplessness, not for being taken by surprise.)

Mrs. Haas was thirty-four years old at the time of the interview. She had remarried, and was living with her second husband and three-year-old child. She described herself as "keeping house," but had previously worked as a general office worker. Her first husband had worked as a bus driver.

He liked anal sex and I didn't. *Force?* He didn't really force it. I just didn't know what was happening. It happened so fast I didn't realize what he was doing. We were making love, he was on top and I was on my stomach. He just stuck his penis into my anus. I told him to stop. Finally I moved so I could get away because he wouldn't stop and it hurt like hell. He didn't care if I wanted it or not.

What finally brought it to an end? We separated.

How upset? Very upset. *How much effect on your life?* A little effect.

Other physical violence? The most upsetting time was when he pushed me out of the car when we were traveling about thirty miles per hour. Then he stopped the car abruptly and ran out and picked me up and threw me in the car. I had sidewalk burns and bruises on my arm.

Mrs. Haas reported that her husband's physical violence had occurred 11–20 times over a period of 2 years. There appears to be no connection between these violent incidents and the rape; we shall come to see that this is quite often the case.

Ambiguous Cases

While our categorization of rape works quite well for most rapes, the experiences described by some women are not always easily placed in one of them (force, threat, or nonconsent). For example, Mrs. Draper's experiences seem at first to be a clear-cut case of rape because of threat of force, but later it seems that she used sex to try to deflect her husband's anger and violence.

Mrs. Draper, who was twenty-eight years old at the time of the interview, was raising a two-year-old child. She was looking for work, her previous occupation having been as a counselor for a job placement program. Her husband worked as a mental health counselor.

We had a fight. He wanted sex and I didn't. I wouldn't say he physically forced me. It was more my fear of violence—of getting hit—that made me go along with him and have intercourse. I knew he'd hit his first wife, and I'd been pushed a couple of times by him. But I also used sex as a way of cooling down a fight. For example, a fight seemed to be getting out of hand. He threw something and it broke against a wall. I remember getting nervous. I can't really call it force—it was just the fear of it. I wasn't afraid of being hit, but of other kinds of violence. So we had intercourse.

Any other unwanted sex with him? It's hard to say when you're married. He has a really hot temper and it's hard to delineate what's wanted and what's not. You can't just call it quits and go home!

Verbal threats? Yes, as a way of venting his anger he'd say, "Would you like a fist in your face?" "Would you like your teeth broken?"

How upset? Extremely upset. *How much effect on your life?* A great effect. It clues me in to the fact that my marriage is in a lot of trouble and that my husband has emotional problems. *Other?* I'm afraid. I hope he gets counseling before things get worse. I go out of my way not to antagonize him. Also, I got an abortion because I felt our relationship wasn't such that I wanted to have another baby.

Other physical violence? He's not violent, but I'm afraid of his *becoming* violent. He's pushed me around; so I steer his violence toward sex rather than force. *Most upsetting time?* When he's pushed me or kicked me. Twice he kicked me and once he pushed me. What is upsetting is the tension in the air. It makes me afraid. *Most upsetting time?* He didn't want me to go out and he pushed me at the top of the stairs. He seemed out of control. Another time he kicked me in the middle of a fight and I left the house quickly. The third time, he kicked me when we were having an argument. It was not that heated a situation, but I was really scared and angry. I warned him I wouldn't take any more. It happened in front of his son, which particularly bothers me. Kids pick things like that up.

Mrs. Draper said that these three incidents occurred over a period of one and a half years.

Only the experience described by Mrs. Draper at the beginning of the section of her interview quoted above would qualify as rape (due to fear of force) by our definition. More frequently, it seemed Mrs. Draper had sex when she didn't want it, but she was the one initiating it in order to calm her husband down. It could be argued that she was in no position to consent because she lives in such fear of his becoming physically violent, but while there is merit to such an argument, it would be stretching our definition of total helplessness further than I am willing to do.

FORCE AND VIOLENCE

The women we interviewed defined force and violence very different-ly. For example, Mrs. Draper emphasized that she did not regard her husband's kicking and pushing her as violence, explaining that it was "never anything that really hurt." Mrs. Gordon said of her husband: "He started pushing me around, threw me on the bed and slapped me. He broke my beads and ripped my shirt. I don't think it was really violence." There were other cases in which the woman said she was forced to have sex with her husband, but in which it turned out that she *felt* forced by her own notion of her duty, or her husband's persistent nagging; she was not actually forced, nor in fear of physical force. Such cases were not counted as rape.

Though the women's own definitions of force and violence obviously influenced whether or not they told the interviewer about their experiences, as well as how they label their experiences, it is useful for our purposes here to devise a consistent definition of force, threat of force, and violence. For our study, we determined a minimal level of physical force, which included such acts as pushing, pinning, and being held down by a husband's weight so that the woman couldn't move.

Many, probably most, victims of wife rape do not perceive themselves as such. But in contrast, one of our respondents defined herself as having been raped by her husband, even though she insisted there had been no force or threat of force.

Mrs. Lawson related that:

He would rape me when I didn't want to be. *Forced?* No, it was not forced, I never refused him. I felt that it's the wife's duty to let her husband have intercourse with her even if she doesn't want to. *How do you mean rape?* Because he had intercourse with me when I didn't want to. *He never used physical force?* No.

This case was disqualified as a rape experience, and counted as an experience of unwanted sex. But although, as Mrs. Lawson's case illustrates, it was necessary to apply our own definition rather than simply accepting the women's definitions in our study, however specific any definition may be, there are always some borderline cases—for example, Mrs. Merrill and Mrs. Nash.

Mrs. Merrill was a thirty-three-year-old divorced woman at the time of the interview. She had borne one child who had died while still a baby. She worked full-time doing personnel work for a large corporation. When asked if she was married to the man who attacked her, Mrs. Merrill replied that she was not, but that she had lived with Mr. Merrill for twelve years "as if married." This met our criteria for a common-law marriage.

Mrs. Merrill was raped by her common-law husband once when she was twenty-five years old after eight years of living with him.

He came home one evening drunk and wanted to have intercourse immediately without the usual foreplay. He succeeded. *Against your wishes?* Yes. I was already in bed, and he got in bed and said, "I want to fuck." I said, "I don't." He said, "Too bad." I said it was okay after a few words; I'm not one to argue. His behavior was rather unusual. I was frightened of a big scene. *Did you resist at all?* No, but I didn't respond either. *Physical force?* He forced intercourse on me. It was physical in as much as he had intercourse with me when I didn't want him to. *Actual physical force used?* He pinned me down.

How upset? Very upset. *How much effect on your life?* Some effect. I saw a totally different side of him. It changed our relationship for a while. I felt he lacked respect for me, that he didn't regard my feelings. It kind of blew it for a while. We'd had a good relationship before that happened. *How much longer did you live with him after this?* Four years.

Had Mrs. Merrill not finally said "he pinned me down," her experience would not have qualified as rape by force. Nor would being "frightened of a big scene" qualify as *fear* of force. It is clear that there are many different methods of manipulation and coercion, but only physical coercion or fear of physical coercion constitutes rape, as defined here—and by law, at least in this country.

Mrs. Nash was a thirty-eight-year-old divorced woman at the time of the interview. She was working full-time as a secretary/receptionist. She was living with another woman and her two teenage children. Her husband had worked as a buyer for a large retail store.

Mrs. Nash was twenty-three years old when she was raped by her husband.

I wasn't interested in having sex and he wanted to. He said, "This is what we're going to do." I'd say there was some force. He'd had a few drinks or maybe we were fighting. *Forced?* Once I'd call it that. Another time it was kind of half and half. This second time we were arguing and it wasn't like the first time but still, I felt he forced himself on me. I guess the difference is sometimes a man wants to have sex and you don't, so he just imposes it on you. But there's not anger or violence or meanness; it's just having his way. In the first instance there *was* anger there, and a sense of violence and his wanting to degrade me. I felt like I'd really been raped. But that only happened once. *Would you be more specific?* My memory of it is that we were arguing about something—I don't know what. I was probably putting him down for something he did, and I probably refused to have sex. Then I remember he said, "Well, I'm gonna have sex, and you are too, whether you like it or not." I probably said "OK," I didn't fight him, but I felt like I'd been raped. It's like I couldn't get away—that he'd hit me if I tried to leave. I don't remember anymore, it only happened once.

Physical force? No, he never hit me. He wasn't a monster. He was just an angry, frustrated man. I don't want you to get the idea that my husband was an ogre. I'm sure it only happened once. He never used force except to hold me down. I don't want to talk about it any more.

Any other unwanted sex with him? My husband wanted to have anal intercourse, and we did it. I didn't like it. I felt like a dog! It was embarrassing. Not that it didn't feel good.

What brought it to an end? Divorce. That's not *why* we divorced, but there's no possibility it can happen now. All I'm saying by that is that there were times when I didn't want to have sex and he wanted to, so we had it.

How upset? Somewhat upset. *How much effect on your life?* Some effect. Maybe I should say a little effect. I want to change my answer. I can't think of any way it affected my life except that I'm determined I'm going to have my way in my life. I'm not interested in having a man support me, nor in my doing anything for a man or being obligated to one.

Other physical violence? The most upsetting time was when we were separated and he wanted me to sign a paper which I wouldn't sign. He pushed me down on the floor, then pulled me up, then pushed me down. He pushed me around till it got to the point where I told my daughter to call the police. I was definitely afraid something was going to happen. *Other violence?* He might have hit me or slapped me on the head and pressed me up against the wall.

Mrs. Nash said her husband's physical violence had occurred 2–5 times over a period of 7 years.

Mrs. Nash's account of what happened and how she felt about it reveals considerable confusion and many inconsistencies: on the one hand, she was so afraid when her husband was pushing her around and possibly slapping or hitting her that she had her daughter call the police; on the other hand, when discussing their sexual relationship, she says, "He never hit me. He wasn't a monster. He was just an angry frustrated man." Like many other women, she appears to separate the violence that was not related to sex, from the force that was. Mrs. Nash appears to need to downplay her experience of rape. After describing her husband as forcing sex on her at least one time, she later says, "He never used force *except to hold me down*" (my emphasis). This level of force meets our minimal criterion, hence qualifying as a case of rape by force. Mrs. Nash also claims that the experience had little effect on her life, but proceeds to describe considerable effects, including her wish never to be dependent on a man again.

Mrs. Nash's description of her experiences with her husband illustrates well how difficult it is to treat the subject of sexual assault in a categorical fashion. Mostly what she described was unwanted sex, but once it was forced, and another time it was "kind of half and half." She differentiated sex imposed on her accompanied by anger, violence, or meanness, from sex which was imposed but free of those sentiments. She regarded the latter as normal male behavior; the former as rape. Mrs. Nash is one of the minority of married women who specifically used the word rape to describe her experience, but she couldn't quite say that she had been raped by her husband; rather she said that she *felt* like she had been raped.

Almost all of the examples cited so far have involved penile-vaginal penetration, but oral and anal rape should also be considered. We encountered a number of cases: for example, those of Mrs. Davies and Mrs. Little.

Mrs. Davies was a fifty-year-old widow who lived alone at the time of the interview. She had raised six children and was working full-time as a pharmacy dispensing clerk. She said her husband had forced fellatio on her 2–5 times over a period of 7 months.

He was used to getting his way. He wanted me to go down on him, so he forced me. *How?* Held me and forced me. I'd gag and get sick to my stomach, but he didn't care. He just couldn't believe I didn't like it.
How upset? Somewhat upset. *How much effect on your life?* A little effect.

At the end of the interview the interviewer wrote, "The respondent has concluded that oral sex is for prostitutes and decent men would not ask her to do it." In the light of this, one would have thought she would have reported being more upset as a result of the forced fellatio in her marriage: gagging and getting sick are themselves unpleasant, aside from the other connotations that oral sex held for her.

Mrs. Little was twenty years old at the time of the interview. She was raising a nine-month-old child and working full-time as a computer operator. Her husband, who worked as a clerk, had forced anal intercourse on her starting when she was seventeen years of age.

He forced me to have anal intercourse. I don't like it, which he knows. I tried to get him off me. I said, "No, no." I was crying. But he forced me. He does it every two or three months.
Other physical violence? He kicked me in the behind when I was nine months pregnant. I tried to call the police, but my husband disconnected the phone.
How upset? Somewhat upset. *How much effect on your life?* Some effect. I don't trust men like before. I am afraid they are all going to do something to me.

In the brief self-administered questionnaire completed by each woman at the end of the interview, Mrs. Little admitted that she did not feel comfortable enough to answer accurately one or two questions about her experience with her husband.

Attempted Rape

The FBI and the on-going National Crime Panel Surveys always combine statistics for attempted rape and completed rape; we have chosen to do so as well. The following case is an example of attempted wife rape.

Mrs. Collins was a forty-one-year-old woman at the time of the interview. She had remarried and was living with her husband. She had no children, and was working full-time as an administrator in a large commercial loan company. She had been the primary supporter of her ex-husband, who also worked as manager of a small truck repairing business.

The attempted rape by her ex-husband occurred when she was twenty-five years old.

I consented to sex with him when I didn't want to in the period before we were divorced. It was out of duty, I guess you'd say. He somehow conveyed to me that he expected it of me because I was his wife. *Somehow?* Verbally. *Force?* On one occasion when I refused, he forced me. He did it with brute strength.

All I can remember is that we had an argument about something. Then he grabbed me and we struggled. *Succeeded in completing intercourse?* No. I can remember struggling for a long time, and that I did actually get away in the end. *How do you know he was attempting intercourse?* Well, he told me he was. He threw me down on the floor—that sort of thing.

Physical force? He used his arms. He grabbed me and held me down on the floor. *Else?* No. He was a very big person.

How upset? Extremely upset. *How much effect on your life?* Some effect. It influenced me to get a divorce. That's it. *Influenced?* It just added to the other reasons.

Other physical violence? Yes. *Which was the most upsetting time?* When he phoned my employer and told him I was quitting my job. Then he wouldn't let me go to work. Every time I would try to put my clothes on to get ready to go, he'd pull them away from me. He would shove me onto the bed and take my clothes away. He kept repeating that until I finally gave up. It seems to me he might have locked me in a room. I can't remember for sure.

Mrs. Collins reported that the physical violence occurred from 11–20 times over a period of a year.

Mrs. Collins' experience highlights a point crucial to an understanding of rape in marriage: many women may not be raped only because they do not say no to their husbands. During a particular period in her marriage, Mrs. Collins consented to sexual intercourse with her husband out of "duty." The one time she refused, he tried to force her. One wonders how many of the other women who submit to their husbands even though they do not want sex with them, or are repelled by it, would be raped if they did not submit.

WIVES' PERCEPTIONS OF RAPE IN MARRIAGE

Many victims of wife rape do not perceive themselves as such, a fact that has also been observed by other researchers.[4] Only 6 of the 87 victims of wife rape (7 percent) mentioned their experience with their husbands in answer to the one direct question on rape (*At any time in your life, have you ever been the victim of a rape, or attempted rape?*). Since this question was asked prior to the questions about experiences with their husbands, had they perceived themselves as victims of wife rape, this would have been the appropriate place to mention it. However, some of these women may have failed to mention a rape experience with their husbands at that point because of an unwillingness to disclose it rather than their not perceiving it as rape. Some women might also have assumed we were not seeking information on such experiences.

It may be considered strange that women who are victimized by rape could fail to see themselves as such. However, this probably says more about the myths surrounding the word rape (e.g., that it only happens between strangers), since it is clear that virtually all of these women did feel they had been sexually abused by their husbands. In addition, one might be equally struck by the fact that, though wife rape has been legally acceptable for so long, some women were able to see rape for what it is regardless of the law or the culture at large. In addition to the six victims of wife rape who mentioned the experience in answer to the one direct question on rape, eight of the eighty-seven women spontaneously described their husbands as raping them later in the interview. Five others made statements such as: "It was almost like rape"; or "He pinned me down like he was raping me"; or finally "It was just like a rape, except I was on the same bed." More often the word rape simply wasn't mentioned (our interviewers had been instructed not to use it unless the respondent did). However, since the women were not specifically asked whether they perceived their experiences with their husbands as rape, we cannot be sure that more than eight did not.

One aspect of being dominated is that the person who is in the subordinate position often perceives experiences from the perspective of the dominant person. In many marriages, this means women accept or are greatly influenced by their husbands' views of their relationships and the world around them. In her study of male sexuality, Shere Hite quotes several men who reveal that they do not perceive forcing their wives to have sex as "real" rape. For example, in answer to a question regarding whether they had ever raped a woman, one man answered: "No, unless you can call forcing myself on my wife after her continuous refusals over a long period of time."[5] And another man replied: "No, I've never raped a woman. Maybe sort of my wife once. I didn't want to hurt her. I guess I felt like she belonged to me."[6] No wonder, then, that women often concur. Had we followed the women's definitions, we would have obtained the erroneous information that rape in marriage is very rare, when unfortunately, this is not the case.

PART THREE

THEORY AND STATISTICS

5

The Prevalence of
Wife Rape

Woman was and is condemned to a system under which the
lawful rapes exceed the unlawful ones a million to one.

—Margaret Sanger, *Woman and the New Race,* 1920

The average woman's chances of actually being raped in her
lifetime are still minimal.

—Edward Shorter, "On Writing the History of
Rape," *Signs,* 1977*

Eighty-seven women in our sample of 930 women eighteen years and
older were the victims of at least one completed or attempted rape by
their husbands or ex-husbands. This constitutes 14 percent of the 644
women who had ever been married (286 of the 930 women had never
been married). This means that *approximately one in every seven women who has
ever been married in our San Francisco sample was willing to disclose an experience of
sexual assault by their husbands that met our quite conservative definition of rape.*

Seventy-four of these wives (85 percent) were subjected to completed
penile-vaginal rape by their husbands or ex-husbands; 9 (10 percent)
were victims of attempted penile-vaginal rape;† and 4 (5 percent) were
victims of forced oral sex, anal sex, or digital penetration, or attempts at
these acts.‡ Some of the victims of penile-vaginal rape were also subjected to additional experiences of forced oral or anal sex. But there were
only four women whose husbands did not rape them vaginally, but who
did force oral or anal sex, or digital penetration on them.

Three of the eighty-seven women were already divorced at the time of
the first "wife" rape. While rape by ex-husbands can be prosecuted as

---

*Vol. 3, No. 2.

†Cases in which husbands attempted to have intercourse with their wives while the latter were asleep, but who did not succeed because their wives woke up, were not counted as
attempted rape, because of our concern that this fairly common experience might be used to
discount the seriousness of the overall findings on marital rape.

‡The distinction between attempted and completed rape will no longer be maintained
except in the analysis of particular cases.

such in this country, rape by husbands separated from their wives cannot be prosecuted in most states.* Since separated husbands still have the right to rape their wives in most states, and since rape by separated husbands and ex-husbands seem both to result from some men's notion that even ex-wives are still their property, rape by the three ex-husbands is included in our 14 percent prevalence figure.

The significance of the fact that our prevalence figure of 14 percent was obtained from a random sample cannot be overemphasized, for it allows us to make valid generalizations from the findings of our study to the entire population of women eighteen years and older in San Francisco. And as I've noted earlier, while San Francisco is often seen as a uniquely progressive or radical city, and does indeed enjoy some unusual characteristics (for example, an extremely large and visible gay community, and the fact that one-quarter of the infants born in San Francisco are born outside of a marriage relationship) there is no reason to believe that San Francisco is significantly different from other large cities concerning the sexual assault of females.† The fact that the sample size is quite large (930 women) also adds to its significance. In fact, though, this 14 percent figure underestimates the true prevalence of wife rape. Several factors lead to this conclusion.

Our prevalence figure probably grossly underestimates the occurrence of forced oral, anal, or digital sex in marriage, since the interviewers were not seeking information about these acts; data were obtained only when the respondent interpreted "intercourse" to include them. Given the general social taboo on talking about these topics, it is likely that most women would only volunteer information about such experiences if specifically asked.

Although our study revealed 14 percent of the women as having been raped by a husband, many women not included in this group saw it as their "duty" to submit to sexual intercourse with their husbands, even when they had no desire for sex or were repulsed by the idea. In a sense, this attitude and behavior renders these wives "unrapeable" by their husbands. Another way to estimate the prevalence of rape in marriage would be to calculate the number of women raped by husbands as a percentage of wives who express their right to refuse sex with their husbands. By this method of calculation, the prevalence of wife rape would be considerably higher than 14 percent.

Several respondents made it clear that they were not willing to admit to experiences of forced sex by their husbands to the interviewers (this

*See Appendix II for information on which states still condone rape by husbands from whom wives are separated.

†See specific data on rape per 100,000 people in different cities in Chapter 3.

problem of underdisclosure was discussed at length in Chapter 3); and there were undoubtedly others who were not so frank about their unwillingness to disclose. It is of course impossible to know how many women withheld such information.

Sociologists such as David Finkelhor and Kersti Yllo have pointed out that violence occurs quite frequently in marriage as a means of "resolving" problems and that sexual conflict in marriage is also a common occurrence.[1] They make the convincing argument that given these two facts, one can anticipate that violence will quite often be used by husbands to get what they want sexually. (For more about this, see Chapter 11.) On the basis of this reasoning, one might again expect a prevalence rate of wife rape that would be much higher than 14 percent.

Our survey data included only household residents of San Francisco, not those of no fixed abode nor those residing in institutions such as mental hospitals, prisons, shelters, nursing homes, half-way houses, etc. It seems probable that women who have been subjected to very traumatic experiences including wife rape are over-represented in institutions, or among street people. Hence, our survey has excluded groups of women for whom the prevalence of wife rape is likely to be highest.

Two of the eighty-seven victims of wife rape we interviewed volunteered that they had been so upset by their husbands' abuse of them that they had attempted suicide. Several more women had been or still were afraid of being killed by their husbands. Obviously, it is not possible to interview those who did not survive the trauma of wife rape and other violence by their husbands. And we can be sure that some of the most traumatized women do not live to tell of their experiences, either because they do not wish to, or because they are murdered by their husbands. In 1978, the year of our survey, 1,095 wives were murdered by their husbands throughout the country.[2] Current research on some of the most badly battered women who seek the assistance of refuges reveals that at least one-third or more have also been raped by their husbands.[3] Hence, it is likely that a significant percentage of wives murdered by their husbands were also raped by them.

The bias toward underestimating the prevalence of wife rape indicated by the six points just noted is somewhat mitigated by the fact that our prevalence figure refers to the percentage of women who have ever been married who reported one or more experiences of wife rape; it does not refer to *marriages* in which wife rape has occurred or is occurring. Since many of these women were married more than once (and only two of them were raped by two husbands), the total number of marriages within which wife rape could potentially occur is considerably greater than the 930 women to whom it could potentially occur. A prevalence figure based on the percentage of marriages within which wife rape occurs, then, would be lower than one based on the percentage of women ever raped by a husband.

For the skeptic who believes that some wives might falsely report being raped by a husband, it might be helpful to point out that our methodology required that the wives describe their experience, and it was the task of the interviewer to continue questioning about the experience until she was satisfied either that our definition of rape had been met, or that it had not been. In short, we did not simply go along with the women's definitions of rape.

Taking all these factors into consideration, we can be certain that 14 percent is a very low estimate of the prevalence of wife rape in San Francisco, and by extension, in the U.S. in general.

Other Prevalence Estimates of Wife Rape

As recently as 1977 the sociologist Richard Gelles wrote about rape in marriage that "the research carried out to date allows no direct insights into the incidence or nature of the phenomenon."[4] In January 1979 one of the first articles on rape by husbands outside of the scholarly literature was written by Morton Hunt and published in *Family Circle.*[5] Since no statistics were available on the prevalence of wife rape at that time, the author attempted an estimate. First, he cited an estimate of two million battered wives in the United States which he attributed to Richard Gelles.[6] Then he suggested that "about one-fifth of all battered wives, to judge from several other studies, are forced by their husband to have sex as part of a beating or as a sequel to it."[7] Hunt, assuming that the problem of wife rape affects only battered women,* proceeded to estimate "that at least four hundred thousand wives are raped by their husbands each year."[8] However, he continued, "this figure is far too conservative, according to battered-wife expert Gelles, who says, 'I can't imagine a marriage where a husband beats his wife that doesn't also include forced sex at times. There may be four hundred thousand violent marital rapes per year, but if you include rape by intimidation—the threat of violence—it would be more like a couple of million.' "[9]

In the absence of any official statistics on the prevalence of wife rape, this ingenious estimate has come to be treated as if it were a known fact.[10] It is in fact just a speculation based on an estimate based on yet another estimate. Making estimates is all well and good as long as they are reported not as if they are facts, nor as if they have been based on appropriately sound research when this is not the case. Knowledge is not advanced in this fashion.

*The degree of overlap between wife rape and wife beating will be discussed at length in the next chapter.

A few researchers have investigated to what extent battered women are also victims of rape by husbands. Mildred Pagelow, for example, has reported that of the 325 women responding to a survey questionnaire item inquiring about sexual assault, over one-third (37 percent) said that their batterers had also sexually assaulted them.[11] Pagelow went on to say that "many of the women who had given a negative answer to this item explained that they submitted to sexual demands in order to prevent beatings, not because they wanted sex."[12] The latter experiences would also meet our definition of rape. Pagelow did not include in her 37 percent figure the women who were raped due to their fear of force, although she has said that at least 50 percent of her sample of battered women either defined themselves as having been raped by their husbands, *or* would be defined as such by our definitions.[13]

Irene Frieze reported that 34 percent of the 137 women in her self-selected sample of battered women had been raped at least once by their husbands.[14] (These women checked the statement "Husband has raped you" as applying to themselves.) Frieze's sample of women was "solicited from shelters for battered women, from lists of women who had filed a legal action against a physically abusive husband, and from posted notices asking for volunteers for a study of violence in marriage."[15] Frieze's data base is unique because she is able to compare this self-selected sample of abused women with a control group located in the following manner:

For each of the 137 battered women, a matched control woman was also interviewed using the same interview schedule. Matching was done by finding women in the same neighborhood as the battered women. . . . After the interviews were completed, we found that forty-eight of the control women had themselves been physically assaulted by their husbands. These women were considered as a separate "Battered–Control" group.[16]

Six percent (6 percent), then, of the 137 women in her Battered–Control group, and only 1 percent in the Non-Battered–Control group were raped at least once by their husbands.[17]

When a measure which did not include the word rape was used, higher percentages of wife rape were found in all groups. Forty-three percent (43 percent) of the Battered women group agreed with the item: "Sex is unpleasant because he forces you to have sex," as compared with 13 percent in the Battered–Control group, and 2 percent in the Non-Battered–Control group. When the latter two groups were combined, 6 percent of the women agreed with the item.[18] Following this analysis, Frieze concluded:

These data suggest that marital rape is relatively rare in the general population. Although not a statistical sampling of the country, or even of Pittsburgh, our

Control and Control Battered samples together should be a rough approximation of the general population in Southwestern Pennsylvania. Looking at the percentages of these combined control samples, only 3 percent of the women reported marital rape. . . . However, another way of looking at these data is to note that a serious problem experienced by 3 to 6 percent of all married women is indeed a serious one. These percentages are far higher than those for rape of women by those other than their husbands.[19]

It's obvious that this prevalence figure of from 3 to 6 percent is markedly lower than the 14 percent obtained in our survey. This is all the more surprising since Frieze's definition of rape is a broader one focusing on "forced sexual activity" and not limited to forced oral or anal sex, forced sexual intercourse, or forced digital penetration. However, by another criterion it is a narrower definition, insofar as Frieze excludes intercourse obtained by threat of force or when the wife was in no position to consent because she was unconscious, drugged, or in some other way totally helpless.

Frieze made a distinction in her study between wife rape and sexual pressure. Eleven percent (11 percent) of the women who had never been raped by their husbands, according to her report, were pressured into having sex by the violent threats of their husbands.[20] She concluded then that "the frequency of marital rape is probably higher than our earlier figures might indicate if we included situations which would be classified as rape if they did not occur in the marital situation.[21] Why, one wonders, is she so tentative about applying a definition that would be the same in or outside of marriage? Even the law recognizes intercourse by threat of force as rape.

In an effort to rectify Frieze's exclusion of rape by threat of force it is unfortunately not acceptable to add the 11 percent and 6 percent figures because Frieze did not indicate the number of Control group women who contributed to the 11 percent, and the number of women in the original Battered group. The latter is a highly unrepresentative group, and estimates of the prevalence of marital rape in the general population cannot be based on data on these women.*

A northern New Jersey newspaper with a circulation of approximately two hundred and fifty thousand middle and upper-middle class suburbanites carried in March 1979, a forty-four item questionnaire titled "You and Violence." All readers were asked to respond, whether or not they had ever experienced any sort of intimate violence, and 612 readers did so.[22] (As sociologist Julie Doron, the person who placed the questionnaire

---

*In a personal communication on this matter (June 10, 1981), Frieze said that most of the women who made up the 11 percent who had never been raped but who had been pressured into having sex by their husbands' violent threats, were in the original Battered group.

points out, this is a highly self-selected group, so it is therefore not possible to generalize the findings to the population of newspaper readers, let alone to the population at large.)

The readers were asked the following question: "Has your spouse or lover ever used violence or the threat of violence to force you to have sexual intercourse?" Forty (8 percent) out of the 505 women answered in the affirmative and 3 (3 percent) out of the 105 men answered likewise.[23] Unfortunately, Doron offered no explanation for the male victims, and in fact, she even failed to differentiate between the prevalence of male and female victimization (I calculated the percentages from the figures she provided). Also, since the question combined lovers with spouses, it is not possible to calculate the prevalence of wife and lover rape separately.

In a preliminary report of an exploratory study of wife rape reported by women who came to a family planning center in Portland, Maine, David Finkelhor and Kersti Yllo reported that 9 women (6 percent) out of the 133 who had been married to, or had cohabited with a partner, indicated that they had forced sex experiences with their husbands or live-in lovers.[24] However, "the rate among those who were married or who had once been married was 6 out of 68, or 9 percent." And "the rate among the divorced alone was 21 percent."[25]* Finkelhor and Yllo cautioned appropriately that "None of these rates is reliable because the sample was so small. For example, the actual rate (of 'marital' rape) for ever-married women in this clinic population could be anywhere from 2 percent to 16 percent using a 95 percent confidence interval."[26]

In her book *The Battered Woman*, Lenore Walker claims that "most of the women interviewed in this study felt they had been raped by their batterers."[27] Later "most" becomes "almost all."[28] But no precise number is ever offered. Walker's statements are most surprising since there is considerable evidence that many women who are raped by their husbands still cannot see themselves as having been raped by them.[29] Further confusion is added by the fact that in Walker's chapter on "Sexual Abuse," much of the sex described is not only not rape, it is not even abusive.†

---

*However, this 21 percent figure involves only 3 women.

†Walker herself even writes in this chapter that "There is real difficulty in distinguishing when such experiences were pleasurable and when they were coercive for the woman." Indeed, sometimes Walker appears to think that rape and battering are mutually exclusive phenomena, for example: "Despite the similarities between rape and battering, there are also significant differences that occur when sex between a couple is on a repetitive basis." (Ibid., p. 108.) And, later, Walker reveals a very stereotypic notion of rape as if it only applies to strangers: "Another major difference between sexual behavior in a battering relationship and rape is that the former begins with a touch of consensual illicitness, while rape never does." (Ibid., p. 112.)

Rape Prevalence Rates by Types of Assailant

Several of the people who have written about wife rape have speculated that rape by husbands occurs more frequently than rape by other kinds of assailants.[30] For example, Gelles wrote in 1977: "[W]e believe that a woman is most likely to be physically forced into having sexual intercourse by her husband."[31] Hunt was less tentative. "Incredible as it may seem, *more women are raped by their husbands each year than by strangers, acquaintances or other persons.*"[32]

The correctness of these speculations depends on the way the comparison is made. For example, according to the women who responded to our survey, if rapes by strangers, acquaintances, friends, dates, lovers and ex-lovers, authority figures, and relatives (aside from husbands) are combined into one category, this speculation would be wrong: many more women have been raped by men in these categories combined, than have been raped by husbands. Forty-four percent (44 percent) of the 930 women interviewed had been subjected to at least one rape or attempted rape in the course of their lives, but only 8 percent of the entire sample, which includes women who had never been married, had been raped by a husband.*

It makes more sense to break down extramarital rape into several categories than to combine all the various situations. I have for this reason broken out the rates for completed rape (excluding attempted rape) by ten different categories of rapists. As may be seen in Table 5–1, 8 percent of the women in the sample were raped by a husband or ex-husband—more than any of the other nine types of assailants. Five percent (5 percent) of the 930 women were raped by an acquaintance and 5 percent by a lover or ex-lover; 3 percent were raped by a stranger; 3 percent by a date; and 3 percent by a friend of the respondent. Two percent (2 percent) were raped by boyfriends and 2 percent by authority figures; 1 percent by a friend of the family; and 1 percent by relatives other than husbands.

However, when cases of completed and attempted rape are taken together as is generally the case with the official statistics, then the picture changes considerably. From Table 5–2 it is evident that the more intimate the relationship, the more likely the attempts at rape will succeed; thus the number of *attempted* rapes for husbands, lovers, and boyfriends are all very low in comparison to the number of attempted rapes by non-intimates. When rape and attempted rape are combined, acquaintances become the most prevalent type of rapists: 14 percent of the 930 women were victims of rape or attempted rape by acquaintances, 12 percent by

---

*The narrower, more traditional legal definition is here applied to wife rape, to make it comparable with rape by other kinds of assailants.

TABLE 5–1 Prevalence of Completed Rape by
Relationship between Victim and Assailant

RELATIONSHIP WITH VICTIM AT TIME OF FIRST RAPE	Number Women	Percent Women in Sample	Number Incidents with Different Assailants[1]	Percent Incidents[1]
Stranger	31	3	38	12
Acquaintance	47	5	55	17
Friend of family	8	1	8	2
Friend of respondent	25	3	26	8
Date	26	3	27	8
Boyfriend	15	2	15	5
Lover or ex-lover[2]	43	5	47	15
Authority figure[3]	20	2	21	7
Husband or ex-husband[4]	71	8	73	23
Other relative	13	1	13	4
TOTAL			323	101

[1]Many women were the victims of rape more than once by different assailants. A group or pair rape is counted as one incident. Multiple attacks by the same person are counted as one "incident."

[2]Lover was defined as a friend, date, or boyfriend with whom voluntary sexual intercourse had occurred prior to the first rape experience.

[3]Examples of authority figures are doctors, teachers, employers, ministers, therapists, policemen, and—for children—much older persons.

[4]Rape by husbands and ex-husbands is here presented as a percentage of the entire sample, not only women who have been married. Cases of forced oral, anal and digital sex by husbands are also excluded.

dates, 11 percent by strangers, 8 percent by husbands or ex-husbands, 6 percent by lovers or ex-lovers, 6 percent by authority figures, 6 percent by friends of the respondents, 3 percent by boyfriends, 3 percent by relatives other than husbands, 2 percent by friends of the family.

It could be argued that this is not an entirely reasonable comparison. It is possible for any woman to be raped by a stranger, an acquaintance, a friend, an authority figure, a relative other than a husband, and, assuming the woman had ever had a date, a boyfriend, and a lover; it is possible for her to have been raped by one or all of them, whereas only women who have ever been married can be raped by a husband. If rape and attempted rape by husbands and ex-husbands were calculated as a percentage of women who had ever been married rather than as a percentage of the whole sample, then the 12 percent figure would still place rape and attempted rape by husbands right after rape and attempted rape by acquaintances.

We can look at this issue another way. Since some women were raped by more than one stranger, or by more than one friend, some might argue for a comparison between the numbers of attackers in different categories of rapists. As indicated in Table 5–2 (column D), if multiple attacks by the same person are counted as one "incident," 23 percent of the 776 incidents were rapes or attempted rapes by acquaintances, 16 percent by dates, and 16 percent by strangers, as compared with only 10 percent by husbands or ex-husbands. This is because several women were raped by, say, more than one date, or by more than one acquaintance, whereas only two women were raped by more than one husband.

One of the problems with these comparisons is that multiple attacks by the same man are counted as if they were attacks that occurred only once. In order to correct this, we obtained data on the frequency of attacks for men who raped a woman on more than one occasion; that is, whether the attacks occurred from 2–5 times, from 6–10 times, from 11–20 times, and more than 20 times. These ranges were converted into their midpoints (3.5, 8.0, 15.5, and 30.0) so that if a woman had been raped by

TABLE 5–2 Prevalence of Rape and Attempted Rape (Combined) by Relationship between Victim and Assailant

RELATIONSHIP WITH VICTIM AT TIME OF FIRST RAPE	A Number Women	B Percent Women in Sample	C Number Incidents with Different Assailants[1]	D Percent Incidents[1]
Stranger	100	11	122	16
Acquaintance	134	14	178	23
Friend of family	15	2	17	2
Friend of respondent	54	6	64	7
Date	112	12	128	16
Boyfriend	27	3	29	4
Lover or ex-lover[2]	54	6	61	8
Authority figure[3]	57	6	65	8
Husband or ex-husband[4]	78	8	80	10
Other relative	29	3	32	4
TOTAL			776	98

[1]Many women were the victims of rape more than once by different assailants. A group or pair rape is counted as one incident. Multiple attacks by the same person are counted as one "incident."

[2]Lover was defined as a friend, date, or boyfriend with whom voluntary sexual intercourse had occurred prior to the first rape experience.

[3]Examples of authority figures are doctors, teachers, employers, ministers, therapists, policemen, and—for children—much older persons.

[4]Rape by husbands and ex-husbands is here presented as a percentage of the entire sample, not only women who have been married. Cases of forced oral, anal and digital sex by husbands are also excluded.

TABLE 5-3   The Prevalence of Rape and Attempted Rape by
Type of Assailant Adjusted for Multiple Attacks*

Type of Assailant	Total Number of Incidents	Percent	Number of Women for Whom Data on Frequency Available
Husband or ex-husband	979	38	74
Lover or ex-lover	344	13	61
Acquaintance	237	9	178
Other relative	209	8	32
Date	196	8	128
Authority figure	180	7	64
Boyfriend	165	6	29
Stranger	156	6	122
Friend of respondent	100	4	63
Friend of family	22	1	17
TOTAL	2,588	100	

*In order of highest prevalence to lowest

her lover, for example, from 6–10 times, it was counted as 8.0 incidents of rape rather than merely as one. As may be seen in Table 5–3, when rape and attempted rape are combined, this method of calculating the prevalence of rape by the type of assailant resulted in rape by husbands and ex-husbands being by far the most prevalent (979 incidents), followed by rape by lovers and ex-lovers (344 incidents), acquaintances (237 incidents), relatives other than husbands (209 incidents), dates (196 incidents), authority figures (180 incidents), boyfriends (165 incidents), strangers (156 incidents), friends of the respondent (100 incidents), and finally, friends of the family (22 incidents). But even by this method of calculation, rape by husbands can not be interpreted as occurring more frequently than *all* other types of assailants combined, as Hunt suggested.

It is clear that answers about prevalence depend greatly on how one chooses to approach the question. For example, in our study we chose to differentiate between lovers (defined as an unrelated person with whom the respondent has had intercourse at least once), boyfriends, and dates. The distinction between dates and boyfriends was left up to the respondent to make, but basically it seems that the term boyfriend was used for an on-going relationship in which there was some degree of commitment, whereas dates varied from blind dates or one-time social engagements to more regular ones. However, had we chosen to combine these categories (lovers, ex-lovers, boyfriends, or dates), our results would have been different.

Nevertheless, however one analyzes this question, wife rape is clearly one of the most prevalent types of rape, and by some measures, it is the most prevalent form.

WIFE RAPE IN OTHER COUNTRIES

West Germany

Though cross-national comparisons of statistics on reported rape are subject to even greater error than within-national comparisons, the statistics that are available indicate that extramarital rape occurs with much greater frequency in the United States than in any other western nation.[33] It would be interesting to know how the prevalence of wife rape in the rest of the world compares with our figure of 14 percent. This, however, is not possible as yet, for West Germany is the only country, to my knowledge, in which an attempt has been made to ascertain the prevalence of rape on the basis of a nation-wide representative quota sample.

The popular magazine *Stern* commissioned the Institut für Demoskopie Allensbach, a German institute that conducts representative opinion polls, to undertake a survey on wife rape in January 1976. Three hundred and thirty-two (332) married women aged from eighteen to seventy years were interviewed in person in their homes by seventy-two trained female interviewers.[34]

Interviewers were instructed as to the number of women to be interviewed, and for what characteristics they were to be selected. "On the basis of official statistics, the interview arrangements were distributed among the federal states and within the states, among the big cities, medium-sized cities, small towns and villages" and "among the various age groups, occupations and persons not actively employed."[35]

The women drawn in the sample were asked the following question:

In their research, scientists have found out that there are women who report that their husbands forced them to have marital intercourse against their will. When this was published many women reported that this had also happened to them. Has this also happened in your marriage?

Women who answered yes or said that it "used to happen" were asked how often it happened. They were then given a list and asked to "tell me which of these things apply to you?"

The list was as follows:

"When your husband forced you to have sexual intercourse, how did this occur?"

1) I told him that I didn't want to, but he didn't listen, just grabbed and attacked me.

2) He hit me.

3) I let it happen to me because otherwise I have to put up with his bad mood for days.

4) I am afraid and give in; I simply don't dare deny myself to him.

5) He held me against my will, so that I couldn't move.

Women who said they had not experienced forced marital intercourse were asked instead: "It's not so easy to say, but when you look at this list, is there anything that applies to you?" They were given the same list as those who admitted marital rape with the addition of a sixth item which read "Doesn't apply to me, my husband has never forced me to have sex."[36]

The results of this survey were as follows:

Eighteen percent (18 percent) of the married women—about one out of five—declare that they have been forced to participate in marital intercourse against their will.

Initially, only 10 percent of the married women responded positively to the key question "Has it ever occurred in your marriage that your husband forced you to have marital intercourse against your will?" However, an additional 5 percent declared that this had happened at an earlier time. Finally, we found 3 percent who first declared this had never occurred but who then described in the interview the particular circumstances that had led to this situation in their marriage.[37]

It should be emphasized that these women interviewed were all currently married. Since many women who are raped in their marriages leave their husbands, 18 percent undoubtedly understates the prevalence of wife rape in West Germany.

A table that is buried in the unpublished report by the Institut without comment in fact offers an alternative measure of wife rape in West Germany that is so high, it is difficult to know how to interpret it. The question asked was: "Married couples don't always have the same desires/interests. It sometimes happens that a husband forces himself on his wife when she's not in the mood. In your relationship, does this happen frequently or rarely?" Seven percent (7 percent) of the women answered "frequently," 57 percent "sometimes," 35 percent "never," and 1 percent did not answer. By this measure, 64 percent of the women reported being raped by a husband.[38] Most likely the question asked is being interpreted differently by German women than it would be by Americans. Certainly, the Institut stresses the 18 percent figure rather than 64 percent.

While the difference between 18 percent and 14 percent is not that great, several points of comparison between the German survey and our own deserve mention, factors that might help explain why the German figure is higher than ours.

The German definition of rape included one possibility not included in our definition: "I let it happen to me because otherwise I have to put up with his bad mood for days." This item does not relate to physical coercion. So in looking at the variance in our figures, the question is: What portion of the 18 percent of women who were considered raped by their husbands in Germany were included as such because they checked this particular option? Unfortunately, women were instructed that they could give multiple answers, and that is what they did. Fifty-two percent (52 percent)—the largest percentage by far—checked this particular item as an explanation for how it came about that their husbands "forced them to have marital intercourse against their will." Thirty-three percent (33 percent) checked number one ("I told him that I didn't want to, but he didn't listen, just grabbed me and attacked me"); 19 percent checked number 5 ("He held me against my will, so that I couldn't move"); 19 percent also checked number 4 ("I am afraid and give in; I simply don't dare deny myself to him"); and 3 percent checked number 2 ("He hit me").[39]

While we are not able to tell from these data what the prevalence of marital rape in West Germany would have been in 1976 if the definition had been limited to physical coercion, the fact that the item that included non-physical coercion was the most frequently chosen, suggests that the prevalence figure would likely drop were this item to have been eliminated.

The disclosure rate in the German survey was probably increased by the wording of the statement that preceded the question: "In their research, scientists have found out that there are women who report that their husbands forced them to have marital intercourse against their will. When this was published many women reported that this had also happened to them." This statement offered the victim of wife rape reassurance that she was not alone; scientists already knew about the problem and "many" other women were willing to speak up in confirmation of the scientists' findings. Some sociologists might criticize such a leading question as biasing the results. But in the area of wife rape, underdisclosure rather than fabrication is the problem. Hence making that statement was a sound strategy from a methodological point of view. The question we used did not inform the respondents that many other women had reported forced marital intercourse and that scientists were aware of this problem. Nor did those in our study who denied forced intercourse or intercourse because of threat of force or inability to consent receive a second chance to look at a list of five different kinds of forced sex and consider again if any applied to them.

There are, however, at least two reasons why one would expect the prevalence figure in our survey to be much higher than the one reported in the West German study. First, as already mentioned, the official statistics on rape indicate that there is a higher rape rate in this country than in most countries in the world for which statistics are available. Second, the West German study was limited to currently married couples. Our data indicate that divorced women report a much higher frequency of wife rape than women who are currently married.[40] Of the 87 victims of wife rape in our study, 51 percent were divorced or separated at the time of the interview, 9 percent were widowed and 40 percent were married—but not necessarily to the husband who raped them. Only 21 percent of the victims of wife rape were still married to the husband who had raped them. Hence, the fact that 18 percent of women in West Germany who were married at the time of the survey in 1976 reported forced intercourse with their husbands is strikingly high compared to our figure, but it is likely explained by the much broader definition of marital rape used by the Institut.

Australia

A questionnaire about child abuse, incest, and rape—including wife rape—was published in 1980 in *The Australian Women's Weekly*,[41] the most popular women's magazine in Australia, and considered "very influential with men as well as with women."[42] The opening question: "Have you ever been raped?" was followed by a question about who the attacker was, with "Husband" at the top of the list of possibilities.[43] Thirteen percent (13 percent) of the thirty thousand women who completed questionnaires and said they had been a victim of rape reported their husbands as their attacker.[44]

Because of the large number of replies, the survey was seen as "the most successful and widespread private survey ever conducted in Australia."[45] The claim was also made that the firm that conducted the survey "used widely accepted statistical methods to ensure that the results are accurate in every way and reflect the views of women in all parts of the country."[46] But of course, the readership of a magazine does not constitute a representative sample of the general population, and then again, not all women responded, so self-selection is involved here too. No matter how fine the statistical methods of the research firm, it is not legitimate to generalize from this sample to Australian women as a whole.

To understand what it means that 13 percent of women who completed questionnaires and who had been raped, said that it was their husband who raped them, we need to know how many women were raped in the first place. The answer is 8 percent. This means 2,400 out of the sample of 30,000. Thirteen percent (13 percent) of 2,400 represents 312 victims of wife rape. This in turn represents 1 percent of the sample of thirty thousand women.

Probably many factors combine to account for this very low prevalence figure for marital rape. Some important factors are certainly methodological. The question "Was your attacker—?" was asked as if victims of rape are only raped by one attacker. Had they been asked: "Were you ever raped by any of the following people?" the results would likely have been very different. Being asked in this indirect fashion to select only one category, respondents may have been more likely to think of the rape experience which was most frightening, or most recent, or which fit most closely with the public image of rapists, or to choose a rape experience that is less taboo than rape by a husband. In addition, we have seen that many women do not see rape in marriage as rape—just as the law has not seen it as such. Hence, the use of this word rather than a phrase like "forced intercourse" can also be expected to have had a considerable impact.

While I am attempting to explain why a prevalence rate for wife rape of 1 percent in Australia is so low, the government of New South Wales was shocked at how high it was. I was recently informed that "The N.S.W. government has just passed new legislation incorporating rape in marriage as an offence. . . . The fact that so many women reported being raped by their husbands was very significant and supported the findings of the Women's Advisory Council that there was strong community support for legislation enabling a wife to prosecute her husband."[47]

Hopefully, those remaining states in the U.S. which have not yet outlawed rape in marriage will be similarly shocked into doing it by the 14 percent rate found in the survey.

6

A Continuum of Sexual Relations

In lovemaking, the woman must be able to follow the man's lead and tune into his body rhythms and style. While occasionally nothing will delight him more than your taking the initiative, breaking rhythm and turning him into the follower, in the main he will not be happy unless he is controlling the lovemaking. He wants you to do everything imaginable to him, but he also wants to tell you when. Now, as never before, even the most fantastic lover needs to know that he is in full command of the scene sexually.

—"J," *The Sensuous Woman,* 1971

Rape is simply at the end of the continuum of male-aggressive, female-passive patterns, and an arbitrary line has been drawn to mark it off from the rest of such relationships.

—Andrea Medea and Kathleen Thompson, *Against Rape,* 1974

Woman's alienation from her own sexuality, man's resentment at having to purchase sexual fulfillment, the unequal bargaining that trades security for sex—all of these distortions of human sexuality make it inevitable that much sexual contact between men and women will necessarily be coercive in nature.

—Lorenne Clarke and Debra Lewis, *Rape: The Price of Coercive Sexuality,* 1977

Ever since Kate Millett's brilliant analysis of sexual politics was published in 1970, feminists have tended to emphasize the need to see rape in the context of other sexual abuse of women. For example, Germaine Greer pointed out connections between seduction and rape, Medea and Thompson wrote about a continuum that included the "little rapes" as well as rape as legally defined, Clarke and Lewis considered rape as at one end of a continuum of coercive sexuality, and I pointed out that the connection between sex and aggression does not necessarily express itself in rape; less extreme ways of expressing the connection are in fact more common. For example, some men prefer women to be passive, leaving all

73

the action to themselves. These men *do* things *to* women; the act is not a mutual one. Although this is not rape, if one sees sexual behavior as a continuum, with rape at one end, and sex liberated from sex roles at the other, this, a classic pattern, would be near the rape end.[1]

On a continuum of sexual behavior, much conventional sexual behavior is close to rape. As Germaine Greer so aptly put it: "A man is, after all, supposed to seduce, to cajole, persuade, pressurize, and even actually overcome."[2] Consider also "J's" advice to women in her best-selling book, *The Sensuous Woman:*

no woman of any sensitivity would refuse to make love to a man she cares for, just because she "doesn't really feel like it." You focus like mad on all the fantasies that stir your sexual juices, concentrate on making your body respond to the highest point possible and, if you really can't get to orgasm, to avoid disappointing him and spoiling his plateau of excitement and sexiness, you fake that orgasm.[3]

Since marriage is the only relationship in which a woman's duty to acquiesce to sexual demands is sanctioned by law, it should not surprise us that where rape in marriage does not occur, much rape-like behavior does.

Just over one-quarter (26 percent) of the 644 women of our sample who had ever been married replied affirmatively to the question: *Had they ever had any kind of unwanted sexual experience with their husband(s)?* It took further probing about whether the unwanted experiences had involved forced intercourse, or intercourse because of threat of force, or because they were unable to consent, to obtain the 14 percent prevalence figure for wife rape. Only 12 percent (80 of the 644 women who had ever been married) reported unwanted sexual experiences with their husbands that fell short of rape. (Twelve percent [12 percent] seems an extraordinarily low figure for unwanted sexual experiences in marriage, for after all, technically, an unwanted kiss would qualify as such. Almost three-quarters of these women [74 percent] are claiming that they have never once had an unwanted sexual experience with their husbands.)

Because marriage has customarily marked the end of a woman's sexual autonomy—as evidenced by the fact that rape in marriage has been legal for so long—the willingness of many women to acknowledge unwanted sexual experiences with their husbands, even to themselves, appears to be extremely low. Wives are expected to accommodate the sexual desires of their husbands, so many women simply do not ask themselves whether they want their husbands' sexual advances or not.

A question almost identical to the one pertaining to husbands was asked about females, i.e., *At any time in your life, have you ever had an unwanted sexual experience with a girl or a woman?* Only 8 percent of the sample answered in the affirmative, yet it was striking that many of the experiences mentioned were relatively trivial. Respondents said, for example: "She asked me for a date"; "It was the way she looked at me. I could tell she was having sexual thoughts about me"; "We were driving in the country and she leaned forward and touched my knee." For some heterosexual women, any suggestion of sex with another woman is taboo, and sometimes disgusting or frightening as well, while making sexual advances is seen as normal male behavior, and is likely to be tolerated to a great extent, even when the woman doesn't want them.

THE CONTINUUM OF SEXUAL BEHAVIOR

As we have already seen, categorization of an act as rape can be difficult. Some borderline cases presented to us in our study do not qualify as rape. They reflect the continuum of sexual behavior, not merely rape, or its absence.

Mrs. Raymond was a fifty-three-year-old divorced woman who was living alone at the time of the interview. She had raised two children and was working full-time as a writer and art teacher. The ex-husband with whom she had unwanted sexual experiences was a broker for an insurance company.

Mrs. Raymond was twenty-one years old when she first had an unwanted sexual experience with her then twenty-four-year-old husband. Her experiences do not qualify as rape because physical force was not used, nor threat of force, nor was she asleep when he had sex with her.

My first husband woke me up once when he wanted to have sex. I didn't want to, but he said he had to have sex because we were married. He kept telling me he wanted to have sex. He kept after me, until I did it. I didn't want to, I was tired and wanted to sleep. *Feel forced?* Yes. *Was he violent?* No. *How exactly did he force you?* He wouldn't take no for an answer. He said, "I'm married and I need it." After that experience I really felt that whenever he wanted it, I had to do it. I used to sleep soundly and it was difficult for me to wake up, but he wouldn't let me sleep. Finally when I was awake I did have sex with him. He kept talking to me until I was awake, then he'd start kissing me and getting me aroused. Usually I enjoyed it. *Did he use physical force?* Well, not in terms of violence, but he wouldn't take no for an answer. It was insistence more than physical force. Violence was not in his nature. But it came to the point that I had no say about what I wanted to do. The only way I could have changed that pattern would have been to leave him; in no way would he change his behavior. That's why I felt forced. It was an old pattern of sex as a woman's duty. That's what it came down to. *What brought it to an end?* I got pregnant. After the baby was born, we separated.

How upset? Somewhat upset. *How much effect on your life?* I really feel it affected my entire adult sexual life. I became so turned off to him that I never was really spontaneous sexually after that.

Mrs. Raymond was in fact raped by her second husband, who was also violent toward her twice. She reacted to her second husband's violence with enormous assertiveness, but was not assertive about unwanted sex with either of her husbands, even though this unwanted sex affected her deeply. Mrs. Raymond's husband used common tactics short of force to make his wife agree to sex, including persistence, seduction and attempts to make her feel guilty.

The wives who admitted to having unwanted sexual experiences with their husbands appeared to be talking mostly about vaginal intercourse. The focus of the questions about husbands was on whether wife rape had occurred, and not the type of unwanted sex these women might have experienced; few women spontaneously divulged information about unwanted oral or anal or other more unusual sexual practices. Nevertheless, unwanted oral sex was referred to by some women.

Mrs. Polk: It started with oral sex when I was first married and very young (nineteen years old). It was an alien idea to me. That includes having oral sex performed on me as well as being asked to perform it. It was a running argument for a year. It was not presented to me gradually, in a way that I could ever consent to. I was made to have oral intercourse. *Force?* No, it was more like coercion. He'd say: "If you love me of course you would do this. He was constantly trying to persuade me. *Physically threatened?* No. *Asleep?* No. *Other sex with force?* No. We had a very good sex life except for that one obsession of his. *After the first year?* I just stopped battling with him about it.

Mrs. Scott: He was more experienced than I. He wanted things I didn't want to do, like oral sex. I wasn't prepared to do that. *Force?* No, nor was I threatened, but he would be real insistent and get angry if I refused.

The brief accounts of Mrs. Scott and Mrs. Polk reveal three different tactics. Mrs. Scott's husband would get very angry if she refused; Mrs. Polk's husband used verbal persuasion and more specifically, an appeal to the notion of love—"if you love me of course you would do this."

Mrs. Thompson said her husband had tried to get her to be involved with other people. It was unclear whether she was referring to "group" sex, or whether he wanted her to have extramarital affairs.

There was a lot of unwanted intercourse, and he tried to force me to be involved with other people. He tried to set up intercourse with other people. *Ever use force on you?* It was more emotional than physical. *Physically threatened?* No. *Asleep, unconscious?* No.

Persuasion is a very common tactic, as we see in Mrs. Pierce's account:

I didn't want it but I decided for whatever reasons that it was okay. I was very passive—in the sense that I really didn't want it. There was a lot of persuasion. It wasn't forced. It was persuasion force. *Physical threat?* The threat was more emotional—that he would be upset if I didn't do it. *Asleep or helpless?* Yeah, there's been that kind of thing. But I wouldn't say it was forced. I could have gotten up and left or screamed and yelled. It was only psychological coercion.

Other men try to make their wives feel inadequate as a means of getting what they desire. For example, Mrs. Adams recounted that:

He wanted rectal intercourse. It pretty much never happened, but it came close. I didn't want it. I was quite aware I was being made to feel inadequate. *Physical force?* Not really. *Physical threat?* No. Just psychological, by making me feel inadequate.

Another means used is the threat of ostracism. At first it sounded as if Mrs. Bailey had been raped, but as so often, with a little additional probing, the picture changed.

I am sometimes asleep at night and I don't want to have sex and he does. He gets mad. He starts kissing me and pulls me over and forces me to have sex with him. Sometimes sex can be a bore. *Which was the most upsetting time?* He was working at night. He got home at 1:00 A.M. I was in bed sleeping. He came in kissing on me and trying to turn me over. That's what he does. I get mad and tell him to leave me alone, and try to go back to sleep. He'll leave me alone then; but he won't speak to me for a while.

Another common tactic mentioned was emotional withdrawal.

Mrs. Clarke: There were a reasonable number [of unwanted sexual experiences] a year before we split. I stopped wanting to make love, and it was constant pressure. *Physical force?* No, there was no physical coercion; it was just emotional withdrawal or no physical contact.

Some men, like Mrs. Carter's husband, tried to induce guilt.

Mrs. Carter: Sometimes when I didn't want to have intercourse and he did, he pushed it. He used verbal tactics. He laid guilt trips on me. Like when we would go for a long time without any sex he would demand it, and I would feel like I had to have sex though I didn't want it. I'd just be passive and let him have his way. I felt I had no way out.

WHY SEX UNWANTED

Respondents in our survey who admitted having unwanted sexual experiences with their husbands were not specifically asked why they did not want sex at those times.

However, in the survey conducted in West Germany described in Chapter 5, all the women who were considered wife rape victims by the researchers were asked the question: "What were your reasons for resisting your husband's advances until he overcame you with force?"[4] Their answers are listed in Table 6–1 in order from the most frequent to the

TABLE 6–1   Reasons Raped Wives in West Germany
Resisted Husbands' Sexual Advances

	Percent of Victims Answering Yes to Different Reasons
1. I wasn't in the mood	55
2. I didn't feel good	43
3. He was drunk/under the influence of alcohol	28
4. I don't care much for sex	17
5. I was afraid of getting pregnant	16
6. I had my period	14
7. He wants sex too often	14
8. I don't love him any more	12
9. It was at a time and place that didn't suit me	12
10. He wants me in positions that I don't like	5
11. I love my husband, but sex with him is unpleasant	2

least frequent reasons. These women were instructed to choose as many reasons as applied to them.

Though we have no comparable data from our survey, reasons why some wives did not want sex with their husbands did emerge.

Chronic Discrepancy in Sexual Desires or Needs

Mrs. Dennis: Our sex life was bad throughout the marriage. There were many times when I didn't want sex with him. The most upsetting time was when I was discharged from the hospital after my breakdown and I couldn't relate to him. He tried other techniques like oral sex and he was disgusted with me that they didn't work. It was upsetting to me that nothing turned me on to him.

Some people might be tempted to label Mrs. Dennis frigid, since she appeared to be "sexually cold."[5] But lack of interest can often be related to other aspects of the relationship, and we really don't know to what extent this was the case, and what could be attributed to a dislike of sex *per se.* Mrs. Norman, for example, hated sex with her first husband and believed herself frigid for eighteen years, but she then met another man with whom her experience was quite different. Had she not assumed the problem was hers, she might have spared herself some of the eighteen years of misery.

Mrs. Norman was fifteen years old the first time she had unwanted sex with her husband:

I couldn't respond to him. I couldn't stand him to touch me. I went to a doctor about it. I had two children, so there must have been sex. But every time he touched me I felt like a snake climbing up at me. Then we divorced and I met my darling and for the first time I knew what sex and love were all about.

I guess you could say I was frigid. I wanted him to hold me and caress me but when it came to sex, I didn't know anything about it, and I never wanted it.

Which time most upsetting? All the time was upsetting—eighteen years of it! *Why stayed that long?* For the sake of the kids. But that was wrong, very wrong. That was the only bad aspect of our married life. I was frigid and didn't know how to help myself. He tried to get me to enjoy sex and I couldn't. That's why I kept going back to the doctors. Every time we had sex it was unwanted, but I knew I had to do it because I was his wife.

I thought all men made me feel this way. *Why did you marry?* Because I thought I was in love with him. But when it came to sex, it made me sick and afraid, until I met Ted and everything changed.

Temporary Discrepancy in Sexual Desires or Needs

Being ill, in pain, or fatigued, are other common reasons for wives not to want sex.

Mrs. Beasley: Sometimes your husband wants to and you don't. Sometimes the man doesn't understand. *Force?* No, he just gets mad. Sometimes they accuse you of having someone, but a housewife is awfully tired and doesn't want to be bothered. My husband is not the kind that abuses. He always apologizes. I don't want you to misunderstand. There is no sexual problem, no cheating. We both come from good families. I have never had sex with any other man in my life. I was a virgin when I married him. We've been married forty-two years. It's been a good marriage. I have no regrets.

Although she acknowledges that she sometimes has sex with her husband when she doesn't want it, Mrs. Beasley refused to consider this a problem. "Problems" refer to things like infidelity.

Mrs. Charles: After giving birth to the first baby, I didn't want to have any sex because I thought it was too soon. *Intercourse?* Yes. I just didn't like it. *Physically threatened?* No. He'd be angry but I didn't think he'd hurt me.

Dislike of Being Woken for Sex

Being woken from sleep is one of the most common preludes to unwanted sex for wives in our sample.

Mrs. Parker: I was tired and didn't want to be bothered. Sometimes when I'm asleep, he just takes what he wants. Mostly it's when I'm tired. There is no struggle; I usually just give in. *Has it occurred while asleep?* No—I usually wake up and find him fumbling.

Mrs. Fowler: He'd wake me up when I was asleep and I'd get so mad at him. He'd go in and do his business. *Had intercourse?* Yes. *Use force?* Sometimes he did; sometimes he didn't. *What kinds of force?* He used to force me to wake up, but he was never a violent man.

Dislike of Husband's Behavior

Mrs. Gates: He was real big and he was going at me roughly and it really hurt.

Mrs. Harrington: When I was mad he'd play with me, soften me up, and afterward I'd be mad again because I didn't want it. *Did he force you?* No, he didn't force me, he just got at me.

Fighting as a Turn-Off

Many wives appear to be uninterested in sex during or after fighting, whereas many husbands appear to be interested in sex at those times.

Mrs. Greer: When we were fighting and I didn't want to, I just did it. You know how it is when you're married, you just do. It was never forced or anything like that.

Mrs. Kidd: After we have a fight, he wants to make love and I don't. He gets his way. I am sick of that situation. *Force?* Well, I guess not. Once I told him that I was not in the mood and that he was making love with a dead body. I did it because he was my husband.

Pre-Divorce Turn-Off

Once divorce has been decided upon, some wives become less interested in sex. However, this isn't always the case with their husbands.

Mrs. Jennings: I wanted a divorce. Sex was not wanted at that time, but no physical threat or force were used. It was an unpleasant time, but he never forced me or threatened me.

Obviously, there must be cases where the husband loses interest in sex prior to a divorce and his wife does not. Whether or not husbands acquiesce to their wives' desires as frequently as wives do to husbands in such cases, we do not know.

AQUIESCENCE TO UNWANTED SEX

Many people associate the idea of women having sex with their husbands out of a sense of duty with Victorian times, but this was by far the most frequent reason wives in our survey gave for submitting to their husbands when they did not want sex. Many wives appear to agree with their husbands' belief that they have a right to access to their wives' bodies whenever they wish. There is no way of knowing how many of the eighty wives who admitted to having an unwanted sexual experience with their husbands, but not to being forced, would have become rape victims had they refused.

In the national study of wife rape conducted in West Germany in 1976, married women were asked a question about so-called "marital duty": "Do you think that it's an appropriate part of marriage for a wife to perform sexually for her husband whenever he wants, or do you think that's not right?" Exactly two-thirds of the women (66 percent) answered that " 'marital duty' isn't right, in my opinion." Just over one-fifth (22 percent) said they upheld the idea, and 12 percent were not sure.[6]

A relationship was noted in the German study between the belief, on the part of women, in "marital duty," and age. "Only half as many wives under forty as those over fifty think 'that's part of being married.' Similar differences exist between urban and small-town women, and between women with different levels of education."[7] According to Imogen Seger-Coulborn, the author of the German study, this belief is gradually passing into oblivion. However, Seger-Coulborn also observed that the attitudes of the women with respect to the notion of marital duty seemed to have very little effect on their husbands' behavior.[8]

The statements of many of the respondents in our survey make it clear that the belief that wives have a duty to provide sex to their husbands on demand is far from having passed into oblivion in this country.

Wife Believes She Has No Right to Refuse Her Husband

Mrs. Keating: He'd want it, I'd be tired. This is a big complaint of wives. *Force?* No, only saying it. Many, many times I lay there. *No physical threat?* No, I'm a nice wife. I don't want, he want, okay, I lay there, just like a sick person. *Asleep, helpless?* When I'm sick, he won't do it. When I'm asleep, he wakes me up, tells me to take off my pants. He wants it, I do it.

Mrs. Korn: When things were not going well in my marriage, I felt obligated to sleep with my husband because I was his wife. I found it extremely unpleasant. It was out of a sense of duty. *Ever physical force?* I don't know. Several times it was unwanted, but I eventually went along with my husband anyway. He related to sex as if it were separate from love; as if sex was pornography.

Mrs. Randle: Many times I didn't feel like having sex but I did it. With a husband, you feel forced. I have an obligation to my husband which is very bad. It's always been a man's world.

Mrs. West: We were going through a divorce. I would acquiesce. I used to think that just because he rolled over in the middle of the night I had to acquiesce. *Physical force?* No, I always went along with it.

Mrs. Mathews: It wasn't forced, but I wasn't physically interested in him, and I only had sex with him because it was a wifely duty. It bothered me because it made me feel sexually abnormal. He was my first lover, and I felt there was something wrong with me not being physically turned on to him.

Sometimes the women we interviewed didn't actually say anything to suggest that they didn't feel they have a right to refuse their husband; this was implicit rather than explicit in what they said.

Mrs. Newman: It was not violent—just "grit your teeth and bear it honey." It's conditioning. It's not a case of the husband taking his marital rights, because someone's agreeing. But it comes down to being a victim of social conditioning.

Mrs. Oakes spoke about her first and second husbands at the same time: When they want it and I don't want it, it's against my will. *Did your husbands ever force you?* They don't force me but whenever they want to I always go along with them, even though I really don't want to.

Mrs. Paige: I have been married for four years and these kinds of things happen quite often. *Forced intercourse?* No. He would stop if I protested enough. I usually consent even though I'm not interested.

Mrs. Summers: Every married woman has those experiences. But it's not forced. I get disinterested and it becomes more of a chore than a pleasure. He gets the same way but it seems more necessary for the man. You'd rather turn over and go to sleep; it's just kind of a bother.

Mrs. Victor: When I'm sleeping I don't want to be bothered. He didn't force me but if I didn't want it, he'd do it anyhow. I didn't enjoy it. I'd just say "go ahead, but I'm not in the mood."

There are many other reasons why wives engage in unwanted sex. Some of the women we interviewed did so out of consideration or empathy, a desire to please their husbands, to stop an argument or avoid a fight, to try to prevent their husband's infidelity, or to avoid being overpowered.

Consideration and Empathy

Only one woman gave consideration and empathy as a reason for having sex with her husband when she didn't want it.

Mrs. Ward: If I'm not in the mood to make love, it's unwanted, but I want to be considerate of his needs. It's also out of empathy. If my own passion is not satisfied, it's painful. Rather than leave him frustrated, I try to satisfy him even if I'm not in the mood.

Taken at face value, Mrs. Ward's reasons for submitting seem quite healthy; the health of her marriage depends on whether this consideration and empathy are mutual.

Pleasing

The motive of pleasing seems to fall somewhere between consideration and empathy on the one hand, and a sense of duty on the other. Once again, one wonders if the husband does things just to please the wife as well; much research has shown that marriage is usually a pretty unequal collaboration, with the wife doing far more of the giving, giving up, and adaptation, than her husband.[9]

Mrs. Albert: Sometimes my husband wants to do things I don't want to do, or that are uncomfortable to me. Certain positions are uncomfortable or exhausting to me, like standing up. It's not forced like rape, but sometimes when I say no he doesn't ever force me, but I might do it to please him.

Stopping Arguments; Avoiding Fights

Mrs. Bishop: We were out for the evening and we had an argument, so I left and came home. When he came home I was asleep. He tried to make love to me which I didn't want; I just wanted to be left alone. He insisted, not violently, but saying, "Please, honey, let's forget about the argument," so I did. But I didn't want it; it was an unwilling thing.

This happened two or three times. I gave in to stop the arguing. But I didn't have the feeling that he would force me if I said no. *What brought it to an end?* I explained how I felt about it. It had to do with a family problem. He was drinking too much because of his mother's death. He stopped it then.

Mrs. Downing: I just didn't want to do it and he did, so we had sex anyway. I said I didn't want to and I didn't help it happen, but on the other hand, I wasn't forced. That probably happens a lot to married people. *Did you feel forced?* Yes, I felt forced to do it. Not physically. But you can't just start fighting with your husband. We weren't in good communication. It was our wedding night and I was really, really drunk. *Still conscious?* Just semi-conscious. I was feeling pretty sick.

Many other women made the distinction between *feeling* forced and *being* forced. This reflects the fact that factors other than physical force or threat can make one feel one has no real choice; the subjective feeling is not limited to physical coercion.

Preventing a Husband's Infidelity

Mrs. Fisher: It happens very often. If I refuse he will go to other women. Then it would be my fault and a sin. Whether I like it or not I have to give in.

Mrs. Gibbs: I was tired. I was working very hard. I wanted to sleep. Because he's my husband I couldn't say no. I never said "I have a headache" like American women, because then he would go someplace else. *Force, physical threat?* No. I didn't say no. I let him have it. It was no pleasure for me at all.

Mrs. Hicks: The way I grew up I was taught to please my husband. Now I'm more Americanized. In our culture we're taught to do what they want in order to keep them happy so they won't fool around.

Preventing Being Overpowered

Mrs. Ingalls: He didn't use physical force, but there was the feeling that "you might as well give in because he has the right to it." *Helpless?* I felt helpless in the sense that if we fought, he would have been stronger. But it didn't happen that way. I went along with him.

Many women may consciously or unconsciously assess their chances of avoiding being overpowered in this fashion. Women like this are borderline rape victims. While they do not submit out of fear of bodily harm or violence, they do submit out of fear of being forced.

UNWANTED MARITAL SEX AND PORNOGRAPHY

Since I was involved in the debate about whether or not pornography causes rape and other violence against women at the time our survey was being conducted, and since there was no information available on women's experience of victimization as a result of pornography, the women in our sample were asked, *Have you ever been upset by anyone trying to get you to do what they'd seen in pornographic pictures, movies or books?*

Twenty-one of the victims of wife rape (24 percent) answered yes, a considerably higher percentage than that reported by women drawn in the sample as a whole (10 percent). Those who answered yes were then asked to briefly describe the experience that upset them the most. Although women were not specifically asked what their relationship was to the person with whom they had this upsetting experience, in eight instances victims of wife rape volunteered that the person involved was a husband. This means that well over one-third (38 percent) of these unwanted experiences which the women believed were inspired by pornography, involved husbands. While nothing can be proven by this high percentage, particularly since only eight cases are involved, the fact that 9 percent of the victims of wife rape spontaneously mentioned that their husbands were influenced by pornography raises the question of whether there is a causative relationship between the husband's use of pornography and their sexual abuse of their wives.

Although some of the women were able to avoid doing what was asked or demanded of them, others were not so fortunate. And even in cases where the behavior was avoided, the woman often ended up feeling harassed or humiliated.

Mrs. Jones: Yes, my third husband. He tied me up against my will.

Mrs. Altman: It was S and M stuff—being asked if I would participate in being beaten up. It was a proposition. It never happened. I turned it off. I didn't like the idea of it.

Anything else? Anal intercourse. I have been asked to do that, but I don't enjoy it at all. I have had to do it very occasionally. [Elsewhere Mrs. Altman mentioned that the anal intercourse is no longer forced by her husband because she uses a drug to dull the pain.]

Mrs. King: My husband enjoys pornographic movies. He tries to get me to do things he finds exciting in these movies. They include twosomes and threesomes. I always refuse.

Also, I was always upset with his ideas about putting objects in my vagina, until I learned this is not as deviant as I used to think. He used to force or put whatever he enjoyed into me.

Mrs. Fulton: He forced me to go down on him. He said he'd been going to porno movies. He'd seen this and wanted me to do it. He also wanted to pour champagne in my vagina. I got beat up because I didn't want to do it. He pulled my hair and slapped me around. After that I went ahead and did it, but there was no feeling in it.

Mrs. Dean: He'd go to a porno movie, come home, and then want to try out what he'd seen. He'd put his penis in my rectum. I reminded him that my rectum was not for his penis. After I went to sleep on my stomach I felt a throbbing in my butt hole. He was trying to insert his penis. I tried to get up so that I could slap the shit out of him, but I couldn't move.

Mrs. Folger: My husband showed me a book of naked women. I don't like seeing it and I hate for him to show it to me. He tried to get me to stand and dance naked. I don't like for him to push me to do things like that. It's just not me.

Mrs. Goodner: It was oral sex. I didn't want to do it with him, but I was made to do it. I'd ask him "why are you making me do something I feel uncomfortable with?"

Mrs. Heller: He started bringing home shit. Dirty, kinky stories. He tells me to read them. I make a mockery of him. I tore them up. He's come up with a few dillies he'd like to do but he never forces me. It's more mental torment than physical torment.

While these statements by the eight wives don't justify the conclusion that pornography is *causing* the behavior described, I think one can conclude that at minimum, it *does* have some effect. Clearly, these women felt that they had been personally victimized by pornography. Regarding their husbands' behavior, it appears that some of them attempt to use pornography to get their wives to do what they want. It also seems likely that some pornography may have reinforced and legitimized these acts, including the assaultive behavior, in these men's minds. In some cases the actual *idea* of doing certain acts appears to have come from viewing pornography. Considerable experimental evidence is now available to substantiate these conjectures.[10]

This chapter has offered some anecdotal data on why some women have unwanted sexual experiences with their husbands, but further research is needed to obtain information on this subject in a more thorough and systematic fashion. In general, very little has been written in the social scientific literature about marital sexuality, particularly about unwanted experiences (as distinct from sexual problems such as impotence, premature ejaculation, frigidity). Kinsey and his associates have a long chapter on "marital coitus" which provides much information about women's orgasms and the frequency of intercourse, but nothing about the frequency of unwanted sex in marriage and why it occurs.[11] Shere Hite's two books on female and male sexuality include many relevant quotes, but never focus on marital sex *per se*.[12] Morton Hunt, who has been writing about sex, love, and marriage for over twenty years, is one of the few writers to give some attention to sex in marriage.[13] Hunt set out to evaluate the magnitude of changes in the sexual behavior of adults eighteen years and over in the United States since Kinsey *et al.*'s publications in 1948 and 1953. He directed a survey commissioned by the Playboy Foundation, in which questionnaires were completed by 982 males and

1044 females, 90 percent white and 10 percent Black.[14] (Like Kinsey's research it was not based on a random sample, so we can't generalize his findings to the population at large.)

Citing Masters and Johnson's guess that about 50 percent of all American marriages suffer from sexual dysfunction of one kind or another, Hunt offers a very different picture.[15] He concludes from his survey that "since Kinsey's time marital sex in America has become a good deal more egalitarian," and that "there is a considerable increase in the percentage of marital sexual experiences that yield genuine satisfaction to both persons."[16] Addressing the problem of nonpleasurable marital sex, Hunt reports a strong connection between the closeness of the marital relationship and sexual pleasure.[17] So, for example, 86 percent of the married women who defined their marital relationship as very close, reported that sex in the prior year had been very pleasurable or mostly pleasurable, whereas 62 percent of the married women who defined their relationship as "not too close, or very distant," reported that sex was "mostly or very nonpleasurable" or "neither pleasurable nor nonpleasurable."[18] Hunt concludes that "sexual pleasure and emotional intimacy are still strongly linked for most people."[19] He argues that the causal relationship goes both ways, that is, that pleasurable marital sex leads to closeness and closeness leads to pleasurable marital sex.[20]

One problem with this rosy picture is that it sidesteps the whole issue of abuse. One would never imagine on reading Hunt's chapter that 14 percent of wives who have ever been married have been raped by a husband, and that another 12 percent report other unwanted sexual experiences (which usually refers to unwanted intercourse, or oral or anal sex). But the so-called sexual revolution has not been as totally positive for women as Hunt (and many others) believes. Our survey data suggest not so much that Hunt asked the wrong questions as that additional questions on sexual abuse needed to be asked.

7

Wife Rape and
Wife Beating

[I]t is marriage and the taking on of the status of wife that
make a woman the "appropriate victim" of violence aimed at
"putting her in her place" and that differential marital responsibility and authority give the husband both the perceived right and the obligation to control his wife's behavior
and thus the means to justify beating her.

—R. Emerson Dobash and Russell Dobash, *Violence
Against Wives*, 1979

Whatever the motivation, male sexuality and violence in our
culture seem to be inseparable. James Bond alternately whips
out his revolver and his cock, and though there is no known
connection between the skills of gun-fighting and love-mak-
ing, pacifism seems suspiciously effeminate.

—Susan Griffin, "Rape: The All-American Crime,"
Ramparts, September 1971

OVERLAP BETWEEN WIFE RAPE AND WIFE BEATING

Eighty-seven (14 percent) of the women in our study who had ever
been married had been raped by a husband. Are these the same women
who are beaten by their husbands? Is wife rape a problem only for the
wife who is also subjected to other forms of violence? This is a very important question. To the extent that wife rape can be viewed as merely
one more abuse for the already most abused of women, then some of the
implications of wife rape for all women can more easily be ignored.

Until recently, as we have noted earlier, the issue of wife rape was totally ignored by sociologists, psychologists, and other non-legal researchers, except for a few feminists who gave wife rape passing attention. The
researchers who studied victims of violence by husbands largely ignored
rape as a form of violence, or sexual abuse in marriage as a form of abuse.
While a few of these researchers have finally given this issue some of
their attention, others appear to remain oblivious to the problem. For example, Murray Straus, Richard Gelles, and Suzanne Steinmetz in their recently published *Behind Closed Doors: Violence in the American Family*, have

not a word to say about wife rape. This no doubt made it easier for them to make their preposterous argument that "the larger problem we are facing is not one of a single class of people, sex, or age group in the family being the most victimized."[1]

Even thoughtful anti-sexist scholars like R. Emerson Dobash and Russell Dobash totally ignore the issue of rape in marriage in their recently published book *Violence Against Wives: A Case Against the Patriarchy;* the word rape does not even appear in the index, though it does appear in one table titled "Types of Physical Force Used During Violent Episodes." It is included in this table in a category labeled "Other" along with biting and being stood on.[2] Despite the fact that the Dobashs "recorded up to five different types of physical force in any single violent episode," they claim, with no comment about the low figures, that in only 1 percent of cases in their sample did rape, biting, or being stood on, occur in the first violent episode; in only 3 percent of the worst violent episodes; and in only 5 percent of the last episodes.[3] A more likely explanation for the very low prevalence is that the women were not asked about experiences of rape; it has become clear from research in this country that few women volunteer such taboo information until asked about it (though even then the word rape should not be used).

With the exception of Frieze, whose study design included a control group, researchers on battered women who are attending to the issue of wife rape are limited in what they can say about violence against wives in general or wife rape in particular, by the highly selected women they study. They can tell us what percentage of battered wives are also raped, but they are unable to tell us anything about the wives who are raped but not battered.[4] There is no problem with this limitation as long as the implications are not forgotten. But this is generally not the case, because over and over again, estimates of the prevalence of wife rape have been based on estimates of the percentage of battered wives who are probably raped, and the assumption implicit in this procedure has not been questioned. After a thorough review of what literature there is on wife rape, Irene Frieze concluded that: "All of this research would tend to suggest that marital rape is not really a very big problem and that the most likely situation for marital rape to occur in is in an otherwise violent relationship. However, none of the research found this to be a frequent component of battering relationships."[5] In other words, the research suggests that wife rape is but one more problem for the beaten wife, but not a very frequent one. Julie Doron, one of the few contemporary researchers on wife rape, is quoted as saying, "Marital rape doesn't occur without other forms of domestic violence."[6] The results of our survey clearly refute these findings and conclusions.

Discovering the relationship between wife beating and wife rape requires us to face a number of problems. For example, if a woman is beaten in the course of being raped, should she be seen as both a victim of wife rape *and* wife beating? If so, does any forceful rape automatically qualify as wife beating? Or should one differentiate rape-related violence from other violence, so that wife beating that occurs only in connection with rape would not be counted as wife beating but as rape? If so, is a beating before or after a rape automatically seen as rape-related? The answers to these questions obviously have a tremendous effect on what one then "finds." For example, the degree of overlap we find between wife rape and wife beating will be greatly influenced by how these questions are resolved. If one defines any force as violent and hence an instance of wife beating, then one would have to conclude that all wives who are raped are also beaten.

Fortunately, the answers of the women themselves provided guidance on how to deal with these questions. For example, women whose experience of wife rape was at the minimal level of force (being pushed, pinned, held down or struggled with but not hit, slapped, or beaten) rarely answered the question: *Was your husband (or ex-husband) ever physically violent with you?* in the affirmative, unless there had been additional violence unconnected with rape. There is a tendency, as this shows, to downplay the lower levels of violence when they are associated with sexual behavior. But when the husband's violence during a rape reached the level of slapping, hitting, or beating, women usually answered "Yes" to the question on whether or not their husbands had ever been physically violent, even when the violence was always rape related. For our purposes in the study, one such incident would thus be counted as an instance of both wife rape and of wife beating. However, wife rape and wife beating are often unconnected.

The question of overlap between wife rape and wife beating can be dealt with in different ways. With regard to our study, one can simply focus on the 644 women who had ever been married, and report the numbers and percentages of these women who experienced both wife rape *and* beating (63 women or 10 percent), as compared with those who experienced wife rape only (24 women or 4 percent), or wife beating only (75 women or 12 percent). (See Table 7–1.)

To look primarily at wife rape, categories 1 and 2 should be added (87 women), indicating a prevalence rate for wife rape of 14 percent; to focus on wife beating, categories 1 and 3 should be added (138 women), indicating a prevalence rate for wife beating of 21 percent.* To focus on the overlap between wife rape and wife beating, category 1 reveals that 10

*This percentage differs by one point from that which would be obtained by adding the percentages for the appropriate categories in Table 7–1 because of rounding to the nearest whole number.

TABLE 7–1   Number and Percentage of Women
Experiencing Wife Rape and Wife Beating*

	Number of Women	Percent of Ever-Married Women
1. Wife rape and beating	63	10
2. Wife rape only	24	4
3. Wife beating only	75	12
TOTAL	162	644

*A few of these women were beaten or raped in more than one marriage.

percent of the women reported both wife rape and wife beating, whereas the addition of categories 2 and 3 show that 15 percent * (99 women) reported one *or* the other (i.e., there was no overlap).

However, this approach ignores the fact that a woman may be a victim of wife rape and wife beating, but not necessarily by the same husband. If one examines instead *marriages* in which there was either wife rape or wife beating or a combination, the following breakdown emerges. (See Table 7–2.)

Prevalence rates cannot be ascertained from the data presented in Table 7–2 because the figures refer to marriages, not women, but the data give us a more meaningful assessment of the overlap between wife rape and beating. In almost half of these marriages (49 percent), wife beating occurred but no rape; in 37 percent of these marriages there was both wife rape and wife beating; and in only 14 percent was there wife rape with no wife beating.

In 21 percent of the marriages for which information on rape and beating was available, the rape and other violence occurred on the same occasion or occasions. In 56 percent of the marriages the rape and other violence occurred at a different time(s). In 25 percent of the marriages the rapes and beatings sometimes occurred at the same time and sometimes on different occasions.

*This percentage differs by one point from that which would be obtained by adding the percentages for the appropriate categories in Table 7–1 because of rounding to the nearest whole number.

TABLE 7–2   Number and Percentage of Marriages in Which
Wife Rape and Wife Beating Occurred

	Number of Marriages	Percentage
1. Wife rape and beating	64	37
2. Wife rape only	25	14
3. Wife beating only	86	49
TOTAL	175	100

TOWARD A TYPOLOGY OF WIFE ABUSE

Including women who are raped and beaten by their husbands in one category is imprecise, because such a group lumps together women who have been beaten every week for ten years and raped once, with those who were raped every week for ten years and slapped once. Hence, we have developed a typology that distinguishes five types of marriages within which violence toward wives occurs. As already mentioned, 25 (14 percent) of the marriages involved *wife rape only*, and 86 (49 percent) involved *wife beating only*. As may be seen in Table 7–3, in 16 (9 percent) of the marriages in which both rape and beating occurred, the woman's descriptions of her experiences suggested that she was a victim primarily of *wife rape* (i.e., that was the more significant problem), in 9 (5 percent) of the marriages she appeared to be a victim primarily of *wife beating,* and in 38 (22 percent) of the marriages the *rape and beating seemed to be of approximately equal significance.*

To further simplify these findings: in just over half (54 percent) of the marriages in which wives are abused, wife beating is the major or only problem. In close to one-quarter of the marriages (23 percent), wife rape is the major or only problem, and in just over one-fifth of the marriages (22 percent), wife rape and wife beating are problems of approximately equal significance. Illustrative examples of our typology will now be presented.

Wife Rape Only

Mrs. Bernard was a thirty-eight-year-old divorced woman at the time of the interview. She was rearing three teenage children and working full-time as an executive secretary. Her ex-husband had worked as a sales manager for an insurance company.

TABLE 7–3 Types of Wife Abuse

	Number of Marriages	*Percentage*	
1. Wife rape only	25	14 ⎤	
2. Primarily victim of wife rape	16	9 ⎦	23
3. Wife rape and wife beating of approximately equal significance	38	22	
4. Primarily victim of wife beating	9	5 ⎤	
5. Wife beating only	86	49 ⎦	54
TOTAL	174	99	

Missing data: 1

Mrs. Bernard's one experience of wife rape occurred four years prior to the interview.

One time he wanted to have relations and I didn't. You could say it was forceful. It was forceful enough that I did it. He had had a couple of drinks. He had me down on the bed and he was standing up. He didn't hurt me but it was a little scary. *How force?* He held my arms. That was it. *What next?* I went ahead with it. I was afraid of what might happen next, that he might become violent.

How upset? Extremely upset.

How much effect on your life? Some effect. It made me afraid of men, not all the time but occasionally. I'm afraid when I see certain similarities, like when a person has too much to drink and when he's always talking about who he can fight, then I become wary.

Mrs. Bernard was subjected to some force but for the most part she was raped by intimidation because of fear of force. There are other, more dramatic examples of non-violent rape than this one, but experiences like Mrs. Bernard's cannot be dismissed, for they are probably far more common than our data suggest. For reasons we've discussed, many wives would probably not have told us about experiences like Mrs. Bernard's.

Primarily a Victim of Wife Rape

Mrs. Arnold was a sixty-eight-year-old widow who was living alone at the time of the interview. She had raised one child and worked full-time as a sales clerk. The husband who raped her had worked as a police officer. He raped her more than twenty times over a period of fifteen years. Mrs. Arnold said that her husband's physical violence had occurred from 6–10 times over a period of 10 years. Mrs. Arnold was twenty-eight years old the first time her husband raped her.

He used to call me at work to come to him at once because he wanted sex. I used to work on Saturday and he didn't, so he wanted me home. *Force intercourse?* Of course he did. It was against my will. I didn't feel like having sex so often. He would get mad and insist.

We lived for about two years in a tent settlement in another country. He would push me into the tent and my son was in the next tent. He would put a pillow over my head when he wanted to have sex and I didn't. He didn't want others to hear me scream. Then he would have sex with me. *How force?* He put a pillow over my head and held my hands down. Sometimes I gave in but sometimes I fought. It was not right when he forced me. *Kind of sex?* Intercourse. He never cared if I didn't want it. He would make me. [Mrs. Arnold was getting upset at this point and starting to cry.]

How upset? Very upset.

How much effect on your life? I think it made for a very bad marriage. I guess I held it against him. He said before he died, "I know you never loved me." I said, "Yes, I did." But all the time he thought only of sex. If I didn't want it, he still made me.

Most upsetting physical violence? He always put a pillow on my head and held my hands down. *Ever hit?* Only once, in the face. We came home and had a quarrel after a party. He hit me with his fist on the side of my cheek. I don't remember what the fight was about. Probably it was about sex—that's what we always fought about. He slapped me sometimes, but mostly he used the pillow.

Violence was primarily connected with rape in this case. The degree of trauma experienced by Mrs. Arnold was evident when she started to cry when recounting the rape, even though the last episode had occurred twenty-five years previously. The interviewer wrote at the end of the interview that Mrs. Arnold "was most upset by questions regarding her husband. She stated that they had not had a happy marriage—mostly because of problems with sex. . . . Mrs. Arnold seems to have guilt that she did not treat him well when he was alive." That she feels guilt rather than anger could be seen as a tribute to her powerful socialization as a female.

Wife Rape and Beating of Equal Significance

Mrs. Joyce was a seventy-three-year-old divorced woman at the time of the interview. She had raised one child, but was living alone. She was physically disabled, but when she had worked, she had done office work and business administration. Her husband had worked as a foreman of a lumber yard.

Mrs. Joyce was twenty-one years old when her husband raped her for the first time. He raped her more than twenty times during the twenty years they lived together. Mrs. Joyce gave the same figures for her husband's other violence toward her.

I was built so small, and he was built so large. I was deformed. My pelvic area didn't grow after I was fourteen years old. I have never had a climax; and I have never had any sexual desire. It has to be my mother's training. *Your husband forced sexual intercourse?* Yes, every time he did, I bled. He was a brute. *Which husband?* My first husband. My second husband didn't force me.

What was the most upsetting time? I can't say. Like I said, most of the time I had no desire for sex because I was built so small. At the time I didn't realize that it was the way I was built that was the problem. *What usually happened?* I just laid there and took it. I didn't put on no acts. I couldn't bear him forcing me. He was strong; he just held my arms and put his weight on me. I didn't want to scream because I didn't want my mother, the blind man [a boarder at her mother's house], or my boy, to hear. I was embarrassed.

The doctors told me to get my boy and leave.

Verbal threats? "I'll kill you." He also threatened my mother and my boy.

Result of police report? He was arrested, and put in jail, but I was too scared to convict him. [Mrs. Joyce was scared it would be worse for her at home if she pressed charges.] *What brought it to an end?* Divorce—for mental and physical cruelty.

How upset? Extremely upset. *How much effect on your life?* A great effect. It hurt me. It made me bleed. *Else?* My nerves—I suffer from hypertension as a result. It made me a nervous wreck. I've had to fight my own battles: to nurse my mother and the blind man. I buried them all. It was a large responsibility. I've had little pleasure.

Other physical violence? Do you know what he beat me for? For putting baloney in his sandwich! I didn't know he didn't like baloney; he never told me. He would beat me and the boy. He'd take his fist and beat me black and blue, and he'd take a coat hanger to beat my boy. [Mrs. Joyce began to cry.] It brings back the past. I try never to look back; I try to throw it off. But he was vicious. I didn't know men were like that.

He ran with another woman, then married her youngest girl. [Mrs. Joyce's husband married his lover's youngest daughter after their marriage ended.] He's just trash. I think he and his family are mentally retarded.

The interviewer said that at the beginning of the interview Mrs. Joyce was "quite jovial, saying, 'No, nothing has happened to me' until we got to the questions about her husband. Then she became noticeably upset and cried, but was willing to go on."

Mrs. Joyce's explanation for why she didn't press charges against her husband after she had reported him, according to the interviewer's note, was that she was afraid she would have a worse time. Presumably this means she was afraid of more violence.

Primarily a Victim of Wife Beating

Mrs. Palmer was twenty-eight years old at the time of the interview. She had remarried and was living with her husband. She had one eight-year-old child who was not living with her at that time. She said she was receiving disability but that she had previously worked as a receptionist. The husband who raped and beat her had worked as the manager of a drive-in theater.

Mrs. Palmer said she had been forced to have intercourse once, and subsequently had been too afraid to refuse again. She said these experiences had happened from 11–20 times over a period of 10 years. Her husband had been violent toward her more than twenty times in the same period. Mrs. Palmer was nineteen years old the first time she was raped by her husband.

One time I had the flu and I didn't feel like having sex, but he forced me to anyway. *Force?* He used his arms and body to pin me down so I couldn't move. With all of the violence that had occurred before—him beating me all the time—I was afraid of him when he told me I better not move. *Intercourse?* Yes. He would be violent—and then he would want to have sex afterward. I didn't want to, but I was afraid not to. After the incident when I had the flu he only had to talk to me, to use verbal force, because I was afraid of him.

What brought it to an end? I left him.

Verbal threats? He said: "I'll kill you bitch."

How upset? Extremely upset.

How much effect on your life? Some effect. It made me very paranoid about other men. He had hidden his wild temper so I thought he was very gentle when we got married. Afterward he would have these outbursts. So I began to think all men were like that.

Most upsetting time he was physically violent? When he threw a lamp at me. It had a brass leaf at the top with a sharp point. He threw it at me but it struck the wall. It missed me by inches. After he threw the lamp, he hit me with his open hand. He only hit me one time with his fists. He said he was sorry for months after for hitting me like that.

His outbursts of violence would happen about every six months. His mother used to beat him when he was a child. He had marks on him from the beatings.

At the end of the interview, when Mrs. Palmer was asked if she had anything to add to what she'd already said, she responded: "My husband was so violent, I can't understand why I stayed with a man like that for ten years."

Mrs. Palmer's experiences, like Mrs. Arnold's, illustrate how difficult, or even impossible, it sometimes is to separate rapes and beatings. For Mrs. Arnold the violence always occurred in connection with sex, and for Mrs. Palmer the violence preceded the rape and intimidated her into submission.

The case of Mrs. Palmer also suggests how difficult it can be to try to determine the relative significance of wife rape versus wife beatings, particularly since respondents were not asked which bothered them the most. But when discussing the impact on her life, Mrs. Palmer focused on her husband's violence in general rather than the trauma of sexual violation *per se.* In addition the wife beating happened more often (over 20 times) than the rape (11–20 times).

Wife Beating Only

Mrs. Oliver was fifty years old at the time of the interview. She was separated and living with a male relative. Her three children were in their twenties and had left home. Mrs. Oliver was disabled, but had worked as a waitress.

Mrs. Oliver was married for fifteen years, and said that her husband had been violent toward her more than twenty times over a twelve year period.

My first husband was a gambler and didn't want to work. He'd gamble the rent money and my mother would have to give me money. He also believed in fighting. One day after gambling he came in and nearly blinded me with a hairbrush. *Most upsetting time?* I was pregnant and he kicked me and I almost lost my baby.

How many different times was he violent? It was *all* the time. I'm Catholic and didn't want to divorce him on account of the kids.

Mrs. Norris was also fifty years old at the time of the interview and had raised one child. She was divorced and living alone. She was not employed at the time (she described herself as in transition, having just moved), but she had previously worked as a nurse.

Mrs. Norris said her ex-husband had been violent toward her more than twenty times over a period of twelve years.

The worst time was when his aunt and uncle were visiting and he started slapping me around in front of them. He was pounding on me. They got scared and left for bed.

He turned the shower on and pushed me into the shower. He turned the water on and pushed me around. I awakened his relatives and he grabbed my son and was taking the baby to work with him in a jeep. His relatives said he'd kill me, and that I should divorce him. I ran out of the house, heard his jeep coming back, so I hid. Then I called the police. They told him to leave the baby at home.

I had this lovely child and beautiful home and I didn't want to divorce. *Other violence?* He threatened me a lot verbally. He pushed me around. He had terrible tantrums, but his verbal beatings were worse than his physical beatings.

One of the functions of a typology such as this one is that it helps to convey that there is more than one kind of marriage relationship within which sexual and/or other violent abuse occurs. With book titles such as *The Battered Woman* (as if there is just one type) and the notion of "the battered woman syndrome," there is a danger that new stereotypes are developing about abused wives. However, there is nothing sacrosanct about any one particular typology either: the typology one develops depends on what one wants to illuminate. For example, rather than focusing on the frequency and seriousness of different forms of abuse, someone might find it more helpful to differentiate between sex-related marital violence versus violence that is not sex-related, or violence-related sex versus pressured sex.

THE PREVALENCE OF WIFE BEATING

Earlier in this chapter I mentioned that in our survey, *21 percent of the 644 women who had ever married reported being subjected to physical violence by a husband at some time in their lives.* This figure may be lower than the true incidence of violence in marriage for a number of reasons. First, it was left to respondents to define what they thought constituted physical violence. They were simply asked the question: *Was your husband (or ex-husband) ever physically violent with you?* If they said no, there was no further probing. This is not the most reliable technique. In contrast, sociologists Murray Straus, Richard Gelles, and Suzanne Steinmetz asked their respondents whether or not they had engaged in a number of different types of violent behavior; in this way, their definition of violence was applied, not the definition of their respondents.[7] A battery of specific questions also often helps to jog people's memories. As we have seen, only 22 percent of the respondents in our survey answered yes to the direct question on rape. After many other questions were asked to help respondents focus on different times of their lives and different types of people who might have raped them, it turned out that twice the original number—44 percent—of respondents had been victims of rape or attempted rape. A similar methodology would likely have considerably increased the 21 percent prevalence of wife beating reported in our survey.

Second, while our survey left it up to the respondents to define physical violence, it seems clear from their accounts of their experiences, that most of them did not include behavior that other surveys often take into account. For example, almost all of them seemed to distinguish between violence and force: the latter referring to acts on the level of pushing, grabbing, shoving, pinning, and holding down; whereas hitting, kicking, and beating were seen as violent. In addition, few mentioned instances of having something thrown at them. Again in contrast, Straus *et al.* included "threw something at spouse" and "pushed, grabbed, shoved spouse," as well as other more extreme behaviors.[8]

Third, it seems that a few women in our survey who felt they could hold their own with their husbands in terms of physical force, might have answered in the negative. For example, Mrs. Emery first answered "Yes" to the question, then added: "But I was also physically violent with him. I wasn't a little flower myself. We were like two overgrown kids. So I'd say no."

Fourth, the focus of most of our interview was, of course, on experiences of sexual victimization. Throwing in one question about another form of abuse that may or may not be related, without building up to it, is likely to discourage disclosure. Too, there were probably other women besides Mrs. Emery who assumed we would only be interested in victimization experiences, or those in which they were unable to "give as good as they got."

Other Estimates of the Prevalence of Wife Beating

In her book *The Battered Woman,* Lenore Walker maintains that 50 percent of women were/would be battered in marriage. However, her sample of battered women clients in no way constitutes an appropriate group on whom to base such a generalization. It turns out that all but two of the other estimates of prevalence of wife beating were similarly based on very special samples of women. One exception is reported in *Behind Closed Doors* by Murray Straus, Richard Gelles, and Suzanne Steinmetz.[9]

The estimate of Straus, Gelles, and Steinmetz should be the most accurate if we look at resources available to them and ambitiousness of goals. Based on 2,143 interviews, theirs is the only national study of violence in American homes. As they point out: "There has never been a systematic study of violence based on a representative sample of even a single state or city, much less one that is representative of the whole country."[10] Straus *et al.* used two different measures of violence. The first one was very broad and included throwing something at a spouse, pushing, grabbing, shoving, or slapping a spouse, as well as more severe forms of violence. But Straus *et al.* do not report what percentage of wives subjected to violence at the more broadly defined level. This oversi̗ ... presumably reflects their strong commitment to the notion that violer is a spousal and/or family problem; hence, when considering the issue ᴜᵢ violence as most broadly defined, they only report on the prevalence of violence *between couples.*

They report that there is at least one violent act by a husband or a wife in 28 percent of American couples.[11] However, they argue that "it seems likely that *the true rate is closer to 50 or 60 percent of all couples than it is to the 28 percent who were willing to describe violent acts to our interviewers.*"[12] Their reasons are as follows:

(1) There is one group of people who are likely to "under-report" the amount of violence. For this group a slap, push, or shove (and sometimes even more severe violence) is so much a normal part of the family that it is simply not a noteworthy or dramatic enough event always to be remembered. Such omissions are especially likely when we asked about things which had happened during the entire length of the marriage.

(2) At the opposite end of the violence continuum, there is another group who fail to admit or report such acts because of the shame involved if one is the victim, or the guilt if one is the attacker. Such violent attacks as being hit with objects, bitten, beaten up, or attacked with a knife or gun go beyond the "normal violence" of family life and are often unreported.

(3) A final reason for thinking these figures are drastic underestimates lies in the nature of the sample. We included only couples currently living together. Divorced people were asked only about their present marriage. Since "excessive" violence is often a cause of divorce, the sample probably omits many of the high violence cases.[13]

Of the 28 percent of couples who reported at least one incident of violence at some time during their marriage, 49 percent were marriages in which both husband and wife had used violence,[14] 27 percent were marriages in which only the husband was violent, and 24 percent were marriages in which only the wife was violent.[15] (Note, since these are all percentages of 28 percent, a less misleading way to report these findings would be as follows: in 14 percent of the marriages in which some violence occurred, both the husband and the wife had used violence; in 8 percent, only the husband had used violence; and in 7 percent, only the wife had used violence.*)

These figures obscure the fact that a blow or beating by a man and a blow or beating by a woman frequently have very different physiological consequences. This and the failure to differentiate between defensive and offensive violence are tremendously significant oversights on the part of Straus *et al.* There is considerable evidence from other studies that when wives are violent, they are usually being defensive.[16] In our study, admittedly not designed to evaluate this issue, it was only in one out of one hundred and fifty marriages in which the wife was subjected to some degree of violence from her husband that she reported having initiated the violence.

For their second measure of violence, Straus *et al.* were willing to get away from looking at the couple as a unit. They developed a Wife-beating and a Husband-beating Index that focused on more severe levels of violence. "The Wife-beating Index consists of the extent to which the husband went beyond throwing things, pushing or grabbing, and slapping and attacked his wife by kicking, biting, or punching; hitting with some object; beating her up; threatening her with a gun or knife; or using a knife or gun."[17] The Husband-beating Index was identical. Straus *et al.* report a rate of 3.8 percent of wife beating and 4.6 percent of husband beating.[18] Since they found a higher percentage of husband beating than wife beating they concluded that "some revision of the traditional view about violence seems to be needed."[19]

This conclusion seems erroneous because the data on which it is based fail to distinguish between defensive and offensive violence, and because the statistics ignore the differences in strength and fighting skills between women and men. Most husbands are stronger than their wives; when they get into a mutual fight, the woman is more likely to get hurt. Though Straus *et al.* acknowledge these points, they do so in the form of an aside, which does not affect the thrust of their conclusions.[20]

In order to consider these factors seriously, those interviewed should have been asked about whether the violence was offensive or defensive; about the degree of hurt and injury resulting from the violence done by men and women, and the major problem should not be obscured by the use of the term "family violence." The percentage of women subjected to violence—as more broadly defined—should also have been identified.

On the basis of her research, Irene Frieze reported that most of the battered women in her sample fought back. However, Frieze maintained

*These figures add up to 29 percent rather than 28 percent because of rounding to the nearest whole number.

that only a few of the wives were as violent as their husbands, and there were no cases where the husbands of very violent women were not also violent. She concluded that her study therefore offered no support for the idea that there are many "battered husbands."[21]

Frieze reported a prevalence rate for wife beating of 34 percent in her sample. First, a reminder about her methodology might be helpful. One hundred and thirty-seven (137) women and 137 control women were interviewed in Frieze's study. The battered women were a self-selected group who had publicly identified themselves as such. "Control women were randomly selected as matches to battered women. For every battered woman, a control letter was sent to a woman from her same neighborhood to ask her to participate in a study of 'marriage dynamics.' Other control women were located through public notices which again asked for volunteers for a study of marriage dynamics."[22]

Using what she called a measure of "violent hurt,"* Frieze reported that 34 percent of her geographically selected control group reported experiencing some marital violence.[23] She concluded that: "This is probably our best estimate of the underlying frequency of marital violence in the city of Pittsburgh and in the surrounding suburban and rural communities. However," she cautioned, "this was not a random sample of the area."[24] Nevertheless, Frieze's study offers us the best estimate of the prevalence of wife beating currently available. The discrepancy between her figure and our 21 percent figure can partially be explained by her much broader definition of violence: she includes any force, even that resulting in no hurt. And in her violent action measure she included mild to moderate threats. In our survey no woman who only experienced a verbal threat reported that she had been a victim of husband violence.

It is clear from our survey that there is a large and significant group of women who experience both wife rape and wife beating, but that there is also a large and significant group of women who experience wife beating

---

*Frieze developed both a "violent hurt" and a "violent action" measure. These measures were highly correlated, particularly for the husbands' violence. Hence Frieze decided to use the hurt codes for the husband's worst violence as the measure for the level of wife battering, since she believed this to be most comparable to the definitions of earlier researchers. The violent hurt measure included: "1. Force used but no hurt; 2. No physical injury but some pain or damage (tearing clothing, break eyeglasses); 3. Simple, superficial injuries (splinters, bruises, cuts, mild burn, black eye, lose hair, etc.); 4. Severe, superficial injuries (severe bruises, severe cuts or burns, mild concussion, black eyes needing medical attention); 5. Severe physical or emotional trauma (traumatized joint, spinal injury, pelvic injury, broken bones, severe head injury, internal injuries requiring surgery, miscarriage, psychotic episode requiring hospitalization); 6. Extreme and permanent injuries (required hysterectomy, colostomy, bowel resection, permanent joint damage, permanent head injuries)" ("Causes and Consequences of Marital Rape," pp. 8–10).

but no rape, and a smaller but significant group of women who experience only wife rape. Recognizing wife rape requires recognition of a new group of abused wives, as well as of another form of abuse suffered by wives whose other abuse already has gained some recognition. Hence wife rape cannot and must not be subsumed under the battered woman rubric.

The tendency to see wife rape as the exclusive problem of battered women has led to an important segment of wife rape victims being overlooked—those who are never beaten, or those for whom wife beating is a much less significant problem than sexual abuse.

8

omit

Husband Battering,
Wife Battering,
and Murder

Witness the records of the courts with the wife-beaters and
slayers, the rapists, the seducers, the husbands who have deserted their families, the schemers who have defrauded wid-
ows and orphans—witness all these and then say if all men
are the natural protectors of women.

> —S. B. Anthony, I. H. Harper, eds., *History of Woman
> Suffrage*, IV, 1902

The real surprise lies in the statistics on husband-beating.
These rates are slightly higher than those for wife-beating!
Although such cases rarely come to the attention of the po-
lice or the press, they exist at all social levels.

> —Murray Straus *et al.*, *Behind Closed Doors*, 1980

When I started to do research on rape in 1971 I was astounded to find
how often men in particular would respond by asking me why I wasn't
doing research on the rape of men. I replied that rape of women was by
far the more pervasive problem, and that as a woman, I was more concerned about the danger of rape to women at the hands of men than I was
about the dangers of rape to men, also at the hands of men. Though most
experimental psychological research is done using men as subjects without so much as an explanation or an apology, it is amazing how often
when women are given the primary attention in research it is seen as narrow or sexist. One is put on the defensive about it—even with a subject
like rape.

Forewarned as I probably should have been by the experience, I was
nevertheless taken aback to find reputable scientists starting a few years
ago to proclaim that the problem of the battered husband is widespread
and comparable in many ways to that of the battered wife, and that
therefore the problems of violent husbands and violent wives should be
analyzed within the framework of family violence and dysfunctional

families. In Chapter 7 I pointed out the serious consequences of these recent attempts to merge these issues, as well as the equally serious consequences of the failure to differentiate between issues such as who initiates the violence, the difference in physical strength and fighting capacity between husband and wife, the degree of willingness to use this strength, and whether or not the violence is in self-defense.

If, for example, the issue of violence in self-defense were to be ignored in violent situations between non-intimates, it would mean that a victim of murder or attempted murder who puts up an enormous struggle for her life, and is able to wound her attacker with his own weapon in the process, would be rated as an extremely violent person. This method of analysis is no less ridiculous when it is a spouse who is the victim.

There *are* some battered husbands. In the 175 marriages of our study in which either wife rape or wife beating occurred, two clearcut, serious cases of battered husbands emerged. Both are quoted below. There were other instances where the women responded to the husbands' violence with some violence of their own, but in none of these cases did the violence appear to be dangerous. In only two additional cases was it explicitly mentioned that the wives actually initiated the violence. In both these instances the violence only happened once, and was far from lethal. For example, Mrs. Clarke reported: "We were having an argument. I was real frustrated because he wouldn't talk. I was pounding on his shoulder, and he smacked me on the face with his hand." And Mrs. Eriksen said: "I struck him in anger and he whacked me back across the face with his open hand."

A brief reminder about the limitations of our data is in order here. First, respondents were not asked who took the initiative. Nevertheless, a careful reading of the narrative accounts enabled us to conclude that in 97 percent of the cases the husband initiated the violence. In 1 percent the wife did so, and in 1 percent it could not be ascertained who did. However, since the original question was biased toward finding out about the violence of the husband rather than the wife (*Was your husband or ex-husband ever physically violent with you?*), cases where the wife was violent and the husband was not might simply not have been mentioned. Therefore these data cannot tell us how many wives are physically violent toward nonviolent husbands, but any case where a husband was violent, including in response to the wife's violence, should have been mentioned. Since males seem so much more prone to be violent than females, a fact to be documented later in this chapter, my guess is that the percentage of husbands who have never been physically violent in response to a violent wife is very low. Hence, although it is important to remember the limitations of our data, these do not seem to be too serious in this instance.

Here now are the only two cases in which the man qualifies as a battered husband. Neither wife was a victim of wife rape.

Mrs. Randle was a thirty-two-year-old woman at the time of the interview. She had a fourteen-year-old child and had remarried. She was working part-time as a sales representative.

Mrs. Randle said that violence occurred from 2–5 times over a period of 2 years. Mrs. Randle started out by describing the most upsetting time.

It was when I almost killed him.
    We fought all the time. When he'd get home he would get angry with me. We would end up fighting. When we started to argue, he hit me. He felt he should talk and I should shut up. He didn't just beat me, we fought. That's why we separated; I almost killed him. *What led up to this?* He promised to take me someplace. I got dressed and waited. He didn't come. I went to visit my friend and went out with her. I saw him out with another woman, so I tapped him on the shoulder and said, "Make sure you get home before I do!" When I got home I said nothing. He tried to explain. For a month I kept house and wouldn't talk. I haunted him with silence. He got really angry and hit me in my eye to make me speak. I fell to the floor, then I picked up a knife and stabbed him. Blood was flying and I screamed. I was really scared. When he returned from the hospital we separated. I was too young and afraid I'd kill him. *Age?* Sixteen.
    Our sex life was a beautiful thing, and it continued after we separated. We got along better not living together. Adjusting to home life is hard for men to do. He was older than me. He was twenty-three, so I felt he should adjust better than I. Even though he went out with other women and came home at three or four in the morning, he still wanted sex with me. I didn't want him to touch me at those times. He didn't drink or gamble, so what else was he doing till three in the morning? Men use sex to make you feel important. He would make me feel he still wanted me. Most men can only express real feelings in bed.

Mrs. Clarke and Mrs. Eriksen initiated violence rather mildly by "pounding" or striking once; Mrs. Randle's husband initiated violence more forcefully. Yet Mrs. Randle appears to have wanted to separate from her husband because she was afraid of her own violence toward him. She was clearly very alarmed when she saw how seriously she had hurt him, and apparently could not trust herself not to do this again. No cases of husbands leaving their wives in similar circumstances emerged in our survey.

Mrs. Owen was a thirty-year-old woman at the time of the study. She was still married and living with her husband and two small children. She was working full-time doing wiring for an electronics firm.

Mrs. Owen said that violence occurred only once in her marriage.

We were in a bar drinking with another couple and my husband flirted with a couple of younger girls at another table. I wasn't going to let him get away with that. "If I'm not enough for you," I said, "I'm leaving." I made a scene, knocked down a few chairs, slammed the door, and left the bar. I was on the street planning to catch a bus home. He came out after me and was very mad at me for embarrassing him. "Don't you ever do that in front of anybody again," he said, and he grabbed me by the coat and pushed me up against the car and started to choke me very hard. I was so angry, I wanted to kill him. I kicked him and he rolled down the sidewalk downhill. I was going to kick him and beat him and I would have killed him if one of his friends hadn't come out on the street and held me back. That's how mad I was.

He has never hit me since. I told him many times: "If you ever hit me again, don't ever sleep, because I'm going to kill you." My father used to beat my mother up all the time when he was drunk and I won't have any of that. I put the fear of God into him.

Mrs. Owen is exceptional both in believing that she would have killed her husband but for the intervention of a friend, and in remaining righteous about her actions and intentions. Because of her background Mrs. Owen felt the violent behavior on the part of her husband was totally intolerable. Since her background was one in which her mother was beaten up all the time by her father, she offers a striking exception to the cycle theory that maintains that daughters will behave like their mothers. One exception does not disprove the theory that such violence is often cyclical, but it should serve to caution against an overly ready application of the theory. Mrs. Owen's assertiveness and her threat appear to have been an effective strategy to forestall her husband's violence, both during the incident she described and perhaps in the prevention of any later incidents.

Any attempt to equate the problems of battered husbands and battered wives, or to merge the two, requires serious distortion of the data and misrepresentation of the problem. It also requires ignoring some crucial distinctions, for example, between self-defensive violence and assaultive violence.

Few people are willing to face the fact that statistics on crimes of violence make absolutely clear that violence is overwhelmingly a male problem in this society—and that both women and men suffer the consequences. Sixty-two percent of homicides involve men murdering other men; only four percent involve women murdering other women.[1] In 1979, 99 percent of the arrests for forcible rape, 88 percent of the arrests for aggravated assault, and 86 percent of the arrests for homicide were of males.[2] When crimes of murder, rape, aggravated assault, and robbery with violence or threat of violence are added together, we see that 90 percent of those arrested for these crimes were men and only 10 percent were women.

No explanation is ever offered for the 0.8 percent of females arrested for rape. Since it is exceedingly rare for women to be convicted as actual rapists, the majority of these cases are those in which women have cooperated with, or assisted men in the raping of, another woman. Judging from the few cases of this kind that get reported in the newspapers, these women are rarely the instigators of the rape; frequently they are taking orders from the man or men, or at least in a powerless position in relation to him. A shocking example of this phenomenon that involved murder as well as rape is provided by Susanne Perrin, who helped her husband—who repeatedly raped and strangled her—to hunt down other potential victims for him. This case is described in some detail in Chapter 20.

If rape is omitted from the count of people arrested for committing crimes of violence because it is overwhelmingly a male-on-female crime (only in some states does the law recognize male-on-male or female-on-female rapes), the percentages of men and women arrested hardly changes; in 1979, 89 percent of those arrested for violent crimes were men and 11 percent were women.

Two findings at first appear to be inconsistent with the many statistics showing that violent crimes are primarily perpetrated by men. The National Commission on the Causes and Prevention of Violence reported that 18 percent of homicides involve men killing women and 16 percent involve women killing men.[3] Similarly, the most recently published *Uniform Crime Reports* indicates that husbands are victims of wives in 4.1 percent of homicides while 4.9 percent of wives are victims of husbands. The fact that these rates are so close could appear to support the notion that women are as violent as men. But when seen in the context of a 62 percent male-on-male homicide rate, and only 4 percent female-on-female, it suggests quite the opposite. Since women are usually at a substantial disadvantage in a violent altercation with a man, it is difficult for them to win, particularly if their assailant is an intimate—like a husband—unless they totally and permanently incapacitate the man. If he is not permanently incapacitated he might have all the more motivation to get back at her violently on another occasion. Hence, the fact that women kill four times more men than women is probably explained by their having to resort to extreme means in order to avoid being brutalized or killed themselves. This is another way of saying that women who kill men are more likely to be motivated by self-defense than men who kill women.

Another reason why women kill more men than women might be because they are more intimately involved with men. But by the same argument men would kill more women than men because they too are more intimately involved with women. But men, on the contrary, kill from 3–4 times more men than they do women.

In his classic study of murder, Marvin Wolfgang reported that beating

was the usual method used by men to kill women.[4] In general, his con-
trasting of male and female homicide patterns supports our observation
that despite the fact that almost as many women kill men as men kill
women, men are by far the more violent sex. Wolfgang writes that:

When women kill men it is commonly done by stabbing or shooting—methods
that do not require as much repetition of action to kill as does beating. To beat
someone to the point of death almost of necessity requires severity of the method
as well as considerable repetition of the action. Differential physical strength possessed by the sexes means that it is virtually impossible for a female to beat a male
to death (except in cases where the male victim is an infant or a child).[5]

Wolfgang goes on to say that "even a female life is not easily snuffed out
by one or two blows struck by a male fist, and, since most female victims
are beaten to death by males, it follows that more females are killed violently than are males."[6] When focusing in on husbands and wives rather
than males and females in general, Wolfgang noted that in his study, of
the 53 husbands who killed their wives, 44 (83 percent) did so violently,
as compared with 18 (38 percent) of the 47 wives who killed their husbands violently."[7]

Not only are males overwhelmingly responsible for most violent
crimes, but they are responsible for more and more of them every year.
To ensure that population increases do not account for the increase in
violent crimes, it is helpful to look at the rate of crimes per one hundred
thousand inhabitants, rather than the total number of crimes. And to ensure that an increase in the rate of reporting violent crimes does not account for the increase, it is best to look at the murder rate, since this crime
is least subject to variations in reporting. The rate of homicides in the
United States almost doubled between 1959 and 1979 from 4.8 to 9.7 per
100,000 inhabitants.[8] When the homicide rate per one hundred thousand
people is compared with other countries, it is evident that it is substantially higher than any other western nation. In 1960, for example, when
the homicide rate in the United States was 4.5, it was 1.8 in West Germany, 1.7 in France, 1.5 in Australia, 1.5 in Greece, 1.4 in Canada, 1.4 in Italy,
1.1 in New Zealand, 0.9 in Portugal, 0.9 in Switzerland, 0.8 in Spain, 0.7 in
Belgium, 0.7 in Sweden, 0.6 in England, 0.5 in Denmark, 0.5 in Norway,
0.3 in the Netherlands, and 0.2 in Ireland.[9] This means that the homicide
rate in 1960 was twenty-three times higher in the United States than in
Ireland.

The desire to deny the fact that violence is primarily a male problem
has had a great impact on research on battered women. Feminist and liberal researchers succeeded in bringing the issue of battered women to
public attention in a way that offered some understanding of the needs
and circumstances of battered women, yet some of these same liberal researchers are now undermining these very hard-won achievements by ex-

aggerating the problem of violence against husbands and by using terms such as "marital violence" and "family violence," terms which equate violence against wives and husbands, and ignore the direction in which most of this violence flows. These researchers, though apparently benign and well-intentioned, may succeed only in confusing the public and in reversing the progress already made in this area.*

Theories to explain the continuing increase in crimes of violence abound, but they invariably ignore the 9:1 ratio of male to female arrests for violent crimes. They refuse to confront the fact that violence is predominantly male-induced. Hence, most attempts to solve the problem are off the mark. Until the dangerous consequences of this culture's idea of masculine behavior are recognized and changed, male violence toward women, as well as toward other males, will not be halted.[10]

The fact that Black men are greatly over-represented amongst those arrested for violent crimes is cited by some to justify their racism, by others to demonstrate the consequences of racism, either because they purportedly reveal discriminatory arrest practices, or because they show that racist oppression causes criminal behavior. What is invariably overlooked is that the factor that is most highly related to violent crimes is not race, nor social class, but sex. Many theories that relate crime to lack of economic well-being and opportunities, as well as other deprivations, overlook the fact that Black women should then be the most over-represented group among criminals. But they are not. If 90 percent of the crimes of violence were perpetrated by a particular minority group or social class, that minority group or social class would be viewed as a distinct problem and treated accordingly. But when 90 percent of the ruling gender is responsible for such crimes, the fact of this collective responsibility is totally ignored. This demonstrates that those in power also have the power to define what and who the problem is. The primary cause of violence in this country is related to notions that connect masculinity and violence, plus the power imbalance between the sexes that allows men to act out this dangerous connection. For it to be considered unmanly to be powerful, dominant, or violent, great changes will have to be made.

*For example, in an article titled "The Battered Data Syndrome," Elizabeth Pleck, Joseph Pleck, Marilyn Grossman, and Pauline Bart quote from a letter to Suzanne Steinmetz, one of the researchers most associated with exaggerating the problem of battered husbands. The letter was writtein in 1977 by an active member of the Chicago Abused Women Coalition who maintained that Steinmetz's data were "now being quoted and used to prove that battering is not a women's problem. I have been told recently by a hospital social service department that requested a speaking engagement, 'Violence is a family problem. We don't want to hear about social or political factors. Dr. Steinmetz showed that we must look at violent women and family cycle pathology, not broader social factors.' " *Victimology*, Vol. 2, No. 3–4, 1977–78, p. 683.

Women who are seriously and repeatedly abused by their husbands find themselves in an impossible and contradictory situation. If they don't defend themselves they are often seen as masochistic, as passively accepting their fates, or as inured to the pain. (Erin Pizzy, the woman who is credited with actually starting the whole movement to support battered women in England, is one of those who has argued that some of these women enjoy the beatings.[11]) If they do defend themselves, then they are seen as violent (by Straus, Gelles, and Steinmetz's evaluation [see Chapter 7]; indeed, they may be seen as equally violent as the men against whom they are defending themselves). And if they kill their husbands in self-defense, they are seen as murderers and usually tried as such—even when there is no legal or penal process that can effectively protect them against a husband who threatens to murder them.

In short, exaggerating the seriousness of the problem of battered husbands and/or subsuming the problems of battered wives and battered husbands under the heading of family violence, denies that violence involving adults is primarily a male problem. It is in women's survival interests to recognize the problem of male violence, but many are unwilling to because they recognize that this antagonizes men, and men are their avenue to money, status, and a "normal" life. In the long run this denial may be fatal for all of us, because the steady increase in violent crimes over the years (an increase that cannot be explained away by population increases or higher report rates), points to a critical problem in the collective male psyche that is proving to be lethal—to women, to men, and to the world as a whole.

9 omit

Characteristics
of Wife Rape

> While the research on victim-offender relationships, on vic-
> tims of rape, and on family violence allows us to speculate
> about marital rape, the research carried out to date allows no
> direct insights into the incidence or nature of the phenom-
> enon.
>
> —Richard Gelles, "Power, Sex, and Violence: The
> Case of Marital Rape," *The Family Coordinator,* 1977

Beyond the prevalence of wife rape, and the extent to which wife rape and wife beating are overlapping problems, there are numerous additional questions about wife rape that could be asked. For example, if a woman is raped by her husband, does this tend to happen once only or many times? How much physical violence accompanies the rape, for example are weapons or physical threats used, or is it mainly physical force? How does the wife rape end, and what happens to marriages in which wife rape occurs? Are wives actually afraid of being killed by their husbands? Do they ever blame themselves? These are a few of the questions that will be answered in this chapter.

TYPES OF RAPE

As we have seen, rape by force, rape by threat of force, and rape because the woman was unable to consent can be distinguished. Physical force was used in 84 percent of the wife rapes in this sample; 9 percent were rape by threat of force; 5 percent were rape when the woman was unable to consent. Two percent of the wife rapes did not fit into any of these three categories. In one case of anal rape the woman was taken by surprise, and in another case a combination of force (being tied up and slapped), threat of force, and being unable to consent (she was drugged), was used.

This breakdown is a little deceptive, because often different types of rape will occur in the course of a marriage. If we discovered that rape by force ever occurred in a marriage, we counted it as such. Similarly, if a woman was never raped by force, but she was raped by threat of force as well as when she was unable to consent, the rape was regarded as rape by threat of force. So it was partly as a consequence of these decisions that forced intercourse predominated to such an extent. In fact, in 11 of the marriages (12 percent) in which wife rape occurred, the woman was unable to consent at least once.*

In the eleven cases where the wife was unable to consent: one was helpless from drugs; three from being extremely drunk; five from being asleep (penetration occurred before they woke up). Two of the women were tied up. One had been tied when asleep, the other was heavily drugged.

As was mentioned earlier, the overwhelming majority of wife rapes involving vaginal penetration were completed (82 percent) as compared with 8 percent that were attempted. Seven percent (7 percent) of the assaults involved forced oral or anal sex, and 2 percent were attempted forced oral or anal sex. There was only one case of forced digital penetration.

There were several reasons why some rapes were attempted and not completed. Sometimes the husband was unable to obtain an erection. Sometimes he used violence to punish his wife for refusing sex rather than using it to pursue the goal of sexual intercourse. Sometimes the woman was able to escape. At other times she was successful in overcoming his attempt.

FREQUENCY OF RAPE IN MARRIAGE

Almost one-third (31 percent) of the wife rapes were isolated cases—i.e., wife rape occurred in the marriage once only; the exact same percentage happened over 20 times; and just over one-third occurred from 2–20 times (14 percent occurred from 2–5 times, 12 percent occurred from 6–10 times, and 11 percent occurred from 11–20 times).

Of those wife rapes that occurred more than once, 16 percent occurred over a period of less than 6 months; 21 percent occurred over a period of more than 6 months and less than 2 years; 18 percent occurred over a period of more than 2 years but less than 5 years; 27 percent occurred over a period of more than 5 years but less than 10 years, and 18 percent occurred over a period of more than 10 years.

---

*In one additional case the husband claimed that he had intercourse with his wife when she was asleep, but she didn't know whether or not this was true; hence, it was not included as an incident of rape.

VERBAL THREATS

In exactly half of the wife rapes (50 percent), no verbal threat was used. However, in just over one-third of the wife rapes (35 percent), husbands were reported to have made verbal threats of physical harm. For example: "He said if I didn't do what he wanted he'd choke me"; "He pulled a knife on me and a gun. He said he was going to shoot my head off"; he threatened that "if I gave him too bad of a time, he'd call in a group of men and have them rape me, and take pictures to prove me unfit"; "He said he was going to beat me"; "He threatened my life several times. He said, 'You do as I say or I'll kill you.' "

And in 15 percent of the wife rapes there were verbal threats that were not physical. For example, "When I say no now and won't submit, he says, 'Ok, I'll go find me a whore' "; "He said, 'You have sex now or I'll get sex elsewhere. I'll leave you. If I wanted a maid, I'd have one' "; "He said he'd arrest me for hooking or vagrancy. He was a cop"; "He threatened that he was going to try to get his son back."

WEAPONS

In the vast majority of cases (83 percent), no weapon was used to accomplish the wife rape. Thirteen percent (13 percent) of the husbands had a gun, and 1 percent a knife. These weapons were sometimes used to threaten and intimidate; they were not actually fired or used to stab. Other weapons were used by 4 percent of the husbands. For example, one woman was beaten with a belt, another was beaten with an oak closet pole, another was whipped, and a fourth was burned with cigarettes.

PHYSICAL FORCE AND INJURIES

In well over half the cases of wife rape (58 percent) the physical force was at the minimal level of pushing and pinning down. In 16 percent of cases, it was at the level of hitting, kicking, or slapping; in 19 percent of cases it was at the most extreme level of beating and slugging. In 7 percent of the cases no force was used; either threats of force were sufficient or the woman was unable to consent because she was drugged, drunk or asleep.

Eleven percent (11 percent) of the victims of wife rape mentioned without being asked that they had received some degree of injury as a result of the attack(s). Had the women been asked specifically about injuries, this percentage might have been higher. The mildest cases involved being bruised. For example, Mrs. Henderson: "I was badly bruised. I was all black and blue. I had bruises every day." Some suffered black eyes. For example, Mrs. Freeman said, "He'd hold me so hard I'd have black and blue marks on my throat. And he gave me black eyes too. . . . One time I was so full of blood, the neighbor called the police." And in the more extreme cases, there were broken bones or concussion, and hospitalization was necessary. For example, Mrs. Sutherland said: "I had concussion. I was in the hospital for three weeks. He almost killed me." And Mrs. Ashmore said: "I had broken fingers, a broken jaw, a concussion, and bruises all over. I ended up in hospital after all the beating and throwing finally concluded." The injury suffered by one woman was unique to wife rape. Mrs. Joyce said she suffered vaginal bleeding every time her husband forced her to have sexual intercourse "because I was built so small and he was built so large."

In reading through each case we tried to make a judgment as to whether the husband had used only the amount of force necessary to accomplish the rape, or whether he used more than was necessary. The consensus of 2 of us was that where it seemed possible to make such a judgment (which was in the majority of cases) and where force was in fact used, 62 percent involved the amount of force necessary, and 29 percent used an excess of force or violence. In 9 percent of these cases the husbands did not in fact accomplish their goal.

For about 1 in 5 (21 percent) of the women who were victims of wife rape, the verbal threat(s) mentioned included the threat to kill the wife. We have no way of knowing how serious the husbands were in making these threats, or how serious the wives perceived them to be. However, without specifically being asked, 7 percent of the victims of wife rape volunteered that they were afraid of being killed. After a careful reading of each case by 2 people, there was consensus that for 12 percent of the victims of wife rape there was a substantial risk that they would be killed by their husbands. In two cases, suicide seemed possible, and was in fact attempted.

LOCATION OF WIFE RAPE

The women were not specifically asked where the wife rapes occurred, but frequently a location was mentioned in the course of their description of the attack(s). It occurred almost always inside their home or hotel room or other private dwelling. In only 9 percent of the cases did a woman mention that an attack occurred in a non-private situation such as outside. However, occurring in a "private" situation does not necessarily mean that others in the home would not be able to hear or know what was going on. Some women specifically mentioned that the attack was in earshot of others or in front of the children. For example, Mrs. Henderson said, "Once after I left his home and was with my mother, he came and raped me when there were other people in the house, . . . my little brothers and sisters were around."

WIFE RAPE DURING AND AFTER THE BREAK UP OF THE MARRIAGE

David Finkelhor and Kersti Yllo suggested that wife rape is particularly likely to occur during and after the break-up of a relationship.[1] There seems to be some support for this observation in our data. In 7 percent of the cases, the first wife rape occurred just prior to the break-up of the marriage, and in 8 percent of the cases the couple were already separated.

Only in approximately one-fifth (21 percent) of the marriages in which wife rape occurred, was the couple still married. Just over three-fifths (63 percent) of the marriages had ended in divorce, and 10 percent in separation. In 6 percent of the marriages the wife had been widowed. Even though we cannot assume that almost three-quarters of the marriages (73 percent) broke up *because* of the wife rape, this high percentage does at least suggest that when wife rape occurs, whether or not it is perceived as rape, the marriage is not likely to last in the majority of cases.

THE END OF WIFE RAPE

Our respondents were asked what brought the rapes to an end only in cases where wives were subjected to more than one rape by their husbands. It is unfortunate that wives who were only raped once were not asked this question, since it would be of great interest to know why it only happened once. Nevertheless, sometimes these women provided an answer to this question in their account of what happened to them.

In over two-fifths (42 percent) of the cases where data were available on how the wife rape was brought to an end, the wife left the marriage; in 3 percent of the cases the husband left; and in 17 percent it was clear that the marriage had ended, but not who was responsible for ending it. In 5 percent of the cases, the husband-rapists died or killed themselves; in 2 percent the ending of the wife rape was attributed to counseling. In just over one-quarter of the cases, some other factor was mentioned. Those that involved some effective strategies on the part of the victims of wife rape will be mentioned in Chapter 23. Examples that do not so qualify because the wives' strategies were not effective follow: Mrs. Fulton tried to commit suicide; she ended up in a "psycho ward." Mrs. Jackson said "I finally took an overdose of pills. I was in a coma for eighteen hours." Mrs.

Mayfield's explanation for how the rapes ended was: "He obtained a girl friend, and stopped making sexual advances"; Mrs. Williams said that it only happened once because "I suppose I learned not to be so stubborn."

WIFE RAPE AND OTHERS

It appears that one or more other persons were aware of the attacks suffered by over one-quarter of the victims of wife rape (27 percent). However, this awareness did not necessarily include the fact that they were raped; quite often it was only the other violence that was known about. Those aware of the attacks included police, relatives, neighbors, priests, and children. Once again, the percentage might have been much higher had a specific question been asked about this.

Sometimes informing another person proved very helpful to the victim of wife rape. Supportive relatives played a key role in a few of these women being able to end the abuse or the marriage. Some of these cases will be cited in Chapter 23. The response of the police is the subject of Chapter 22. In 11 percent of the cases, the fact that one or more of their children knew about or witnessed the attacks was mentioned.

However, there were some who knew about the attacks and who were totally unwilling to help. For example, Mrs. Osborne said, "My parents wouldn't take me back. They said, 'You made your bed so lie in it.' " Mrs. Ashmore reported a similar experience: "I moved home with my parents. They threw me out of the house. . . . That was one of the most terrifying parts of the whole experience. That I actually could get no help from anyone. It was an inter-racial marriage and people would say, 'What do you expect?' "

WIFE BEATING AND SEX

Murray Straus, Richard Gelles, and Suzanne Steinmetz explored the relationship between violence in marriage and conflict over five different issues: money, housekeeping, social activities, sex, and children. They found that conflicts over children were the most likely to lead to violence, with conflicts about money following in second place; conflicts about sex and affection were as likely to lead to violence as conflicts over housekeeping and social activities.[2] However, the more conflict there was about any of these five issues, the more violence was reported.[3]

We tried to ascertain to what extent the violence described in response to the question about the husband's physical violence (not the rape) was related to sex—including sexual jealousy on the part of the husband—and to what extent it was related to other factors. This analysis only applies to the victims of wife rape. Where it was ascertainable, it seemed that the violence was totally related to sex in 33 percent of the cases; primarily related to sex in 12 percent of the cases; equally related to sex and other factors in 8 percent of the cases; and not at all related to sex in 39 percent of the cases.

That sex played some role in 53 percent of the wives' experiences of wife beating seems very high, and is probably partially due to the prior questions about sexual abuse in marriage, as well as the focus of the entire interview.

WIFE RAPE AND SELF-BLAME

Victims of wife rape were not specifically asked who they blamed for the rape, or whether they experienced any self-blame. In only 10 percent of the cases of wife rape did these women say something which was indicative of self-blame. This surprisingly low percentage is similar to findings on self-blame reported by Irene Frieze. In her study, 6 percent of wives who were raped once blamed themselves, 8 percent of the wives who were raped twice, and 20 percent of the wives who were raped "often."[4] Indeed, Frieze found that the women generally blamed their husbands more for their own experiences of wife rape than they had blamed the husband in a hypothetical rape situation.* In contrast, battered women blamed themselves more for their own battering experiences than for those of another hypothetical woman.[5]

Frieze also reported that only 20 percent of women who had themselves been raped by a husband blamed a hypothetical victim of wife rape as compared with 40 percent of wives who had not been subjected to wife rape. The experience of wife rape evidently results in a greater understanding of the problem.

Of course there are many other questions of interest about wife rape that have not been addressed here, for example, how upset and traumatized are wives by being raped by their husbands? Are they as upset as women who are raped by strangers or acquaintances? Are the women who are most upset the ones to leave their marriages? And why do some husbands rape their wives in the first place? These and many other questions will be addressed in the chapters to follow.

---

*An example of a hypothetical rape situation used by Frieze is the following: "A close friend of yours named Ruth tells you that her husband has physically forced her to have sex with him several times in their five years of marriage" ("Causes and Consequences of Marital Rape," p. 10).

PART FOUR

THE HUSBANDS

10

Husbands Who Rape
Their Wives

"I have never raped a woman, or wanted to. In this I guess I
am somewhat odd. Many of my friends talk about rape a lot
and fantasize about it. The whole idea leaves me cold."

—Male respondent, *The Hite Report on Male Sexuality*,
Shere Hite, 1981

"The way I see it, Cathy and I were having problems in our
marriage for the last two years. She could have claimed 'rape'
any time during that time. Half of the married men in the
country are guilty of the same thing if that's rape."

—Hughlen Watkin, the first husband to be convicted
of raping his wife in California while still living
with her, *San Francisco Chronicle*, September 3, 1980

Many people would be relieved if they could believe that men who
rape their wives are insane, because only the health of a few men—not
the health of the whole institution of marriage—would then be subject to
question. However, it appears from the women's descriptions of husband-rapists that only a small minority might be regarded as clinically insane. But even if all husband-rapists were insane, it would be necessary
to face the fact that insane men get married and married men go insane,
that some insane people are dangerous, and that wives, trapped in a
shared living situation with them, can be raped and otherwise sexually
terrorized by them. The absence of legislation outlawing rape in marriage
in most states reminds us that insane people may not be able to vote, but
that insane men (as well as those not so designated) can rape their wives
with impunity.

Some of the characteristics of husband-rapists have been enumerated
by two scholars: Irene Frieze and Nicholas Groth. Groth's data are based
on rapists convicted for assaulting unrelated victims, some of whom had
also raped their wives; these men are not representative of men who rape
their wives in the population at large. Nevertheless, this fact does not appear to have deterred Groth from attempting to delineate the common
characteristics of "marital rapists."

Marital rapists have been described by Groth as men whose sexuality has become invested with many other psychological meanings aside from sexual gratification *per se.* According to him, their sexual experiences tend to be impersonal rather than interpersonal, and their sexual feelings are often split off from their needs for affection. In general, they are uncomfortable with emotional intimacy, and their relationships with their wives are not characterized by "equality, reciprocity, mutuality, and sharing." Instead, "wives are regarded as possessions or even opponents to be used, controlled, or dominated." Being the boss, setting the rules, and giving the orders are all very important to these men. Sex is seen as the solution to all marital problems, as well as the source of validation for their masculine identities.[1]

Groth himself recognizes that these characteristics are not limited to men who sexually abuse their wives.[2] Some of them are common to many men, for example, the separation of sexual feelings from needs for affection (which helps us to understand the wide appeal of pornography to men, including magazines like *Playboy, Penthouse,* and *Hustler* with circulations of 5.7 million, 4.7 million, and 1.6 million, respectively*). Further, many men see sex as a solution to all problems in their marriage, as well as a means to validate their masculine identity. Many men also find it difficult to express and experience emotional intimacy in nonsexual ways. And finally, many men prefer unequal marriage relationships. In short, although Groth does not appear to be making the point that wife rape itself is the norm, many of the characteristics enumerated by Groth are common to men in general.[3]

Groth attempted to explain why sex becomes the mode of expression of wife abuse for these men. He maintained that a high incidence of sexual victimization had occurred to these men when they were growing up and he hypothesized, that "such trauma serves to distort the experience of sexuality into a way of punishing or controlling others. Much as a battered child may become a battering parent, a sexually victimized child may become a sexual victimizer."[4] By this theory, many women would rape their husbands if they were physically able to do so. But this seems most unlikely, since few women, for example, sexually abuse children, though they are not only physically able to do so, but also have a great deal of access and opportunity.

While clearly inapplicable to women, future research will help us understand whether or not this element of Groth's theory is valid for men.

---

*81 *Ayer Directory of Publications,* 1981. It is customary to estimate the total readership of these periodicals by multiplying by three; hence the readership for *Playboy, Penthouse,* and *Hustler* is approximately 17 million, 14 million, and 5 million respectively.

Irene Frieze's research does not help answer this particular question, since her data on men who rape their wives were obtained from the wives only. However, she does report a number of differences between the men who did and did not engage in wife rape.

Because of Frieze's sampling procedures,* her data on husband-rapists are biased toward husbands who are also batterers. For example, she found that 34 percent of the sample of 137 battered women (solicited from shelters for battered women, lists of women who had filed a legal action against a physically abusive husband, and other volunteer self-described battered women) reported being raped by their husbands (i.e., 47 women). This compared with only 3 percent of the 137 women in the matched control group (i.e., 4 women). Hence 92 percent of Frieze's sample of victims of wife rape were self-selected battered women; it is not possible to generalize from this group of wife rape victims. Nevertheless, Frieze's research has yielded some extremely interesting findings.

One of the major differences between the men who raped their wives and those who did not was in their use of violence toward their wives.[5] The more violent the husbands were in general, the more likely they were to rape their wives.[6] The violence of husband-rapists toward their wives tended to start earlier in the relationship, and "was more severe and more frequent than the violence of men who did not rape their wives."[7] These men were more likely to be drinking when they were violent, and to beat their wives when they were pregnant.[8]

Frieze also reported that "The men who had raped their wives were significantly more likely to want to have sex after being violent and to associate sex and physical force in other ways." For example, the husband-rapists were more likely than the other violent husbands to have sado-masochistic sexual relations with their wives. Further, husband-rapists got into more fights with people outside the home as well as in it.[9]

Frieze also found that husband-rapists were especially dominant in their marital relationships. For example, "They decided where the couple would go when they went out together and they were more likely to visit his friends than hers."[10] The husbands often went out alone, and their wives were not likely to know where they were when they were away.[11] The wives, on the other hand, "spent more time at home than the other women, and they were more likely to tell us that they felt they could not go places that they wanted to because their husbands wouldn't let them go. The raped wives reported generally doing what their husbands wanted them to do. Their husbands wanted to be seen as experts, although they also acted as though they were helpless at times to get what they

*The methodology of her study was described in Chapter 5, p. 61.

wanted from their wives. Other ways the men tried to get their way included more use than other men of emotional withdrawal, restricting their wives' freedoms, threatening to leave them and using physical force against their wives and their children. . . . When they had arguments, the husbands who raped their wives were more likely to get angry and fight verbally or physically. They also were more likely to get their way than the other men."[12]

Husband-rapists were also found to have a greater likelihood of drinking problems than other husbands:[13] They drank more, and they drank every day on the average.[14] They were also more often drunk when violent than the violent husbands who did not rape their wives.[15] They had fewer close friends, and the friends they did have were more often drinking companions.[16] In addition, they were more jealous of their wives, even though their wives were somewhat less likely to be engaging in an extramarital affair than the wives who were battered but not raped.[17]

Differences in the family backgrounds of the husband-rapists and other men in the samples also emerged. The parents of the rapists were "less affectionate to them when they were children, and they were less affectionate to each other" than was the case for the non-rapists in the samples.[18] The parents of the rapists were also more violent to one another, but this violence did not necessarily extend to the children. In general, the rapists appeared to have a "more distant and violent family upbringing."[19] Frieze says little about other social characteristics except that the husband-rapists tended to earn less money than the other men, and that they were less religious.[20]

The portrait of the husband-rapist that emerges from Frieze's research is of a tyrannical, violent man, who uses violence as well as other techniques to get what he wants, both with his wife and with others. Since he associates sex and violence, this means he also rapes his wife. This, surely, is the portrait also of a patriarch—of a man who sees himself as the master in his own home, and who does indeed have a great deal of power over his wife. How different from the depiction of husband-rapists by Groth in *Men Who Rape* for whom "sexual domination is their *desperate attempt* to establish control *in the face of overwhelming powerlessness.*"[21]

Can this totally different picture of husband-rapists presented by Frieze and Groth be explained by the fact that Frieze has interviewed only the wives, and Groth, the husbands? This is probably part of the explanation. But also, Groth's incarcerated rapists are likely to be very different from those whose abusive behavior can continue undisturbed and unchecked. Groth's depiction implies a degree of psychological sickness which, while applicable to some husband-rapists, is likely not the norm.

Since our study did not attempt to ascertain the psychological charac-teristics of the husbands who rape their wives, we can't really develop de-tailed psychological profiles of the men, but we can nevertheless see some of their attitudes in action. In Chapter 1, I argued that wife rape is largely a consequence of the abuse of the power husbands have over their wives in the patriarchal family. If this is so, we can anticipate that husband-rap-ists would often subscribe to patriarchal attitudes which are a logical ex-tension of patriarchal power, both reflecting a position of power, and helping to maintain it. Patriarchs see themselves as superior to their wives because they are men; they believe their wives are their property and that it is the duty of their wives to accommodate them sexually whenever they want; they believe they should be the boss in the marriage, and that wives who behave in an insubordinate fashion deserve punishment; they see the cooking, housework, and childcare as their wives' responsibility; they believe it is not right for women to work outside their homes or, if they do, they should not earn more than their husbands; they subscribe to a sexual double standard in which it is acceptable for husbands to have other sexual attractions or affairs, but it is totally unacceptable for their wives to do the same; they believe it is the duty of wives to obey them not only in bed, but out of it as well (note, all wives who go through the traditional Christian marriage ceremony promise to obey their husbands).

These attitudes emerge in many of our cases. Let us hear from Mrs. Kearney, Mrs. Eriksen, and Mrs. Henderson about three husbands who appear to have been particularly extreme in their patriarchal behavior or attitudes.

Mrs. Kearney was a forty-eight-year-old divorced woman at the time of the interview. She had raised two children but was living alone and working part-time as a waitress when interviewed. Her husband had been a student at the time he first raped her when she was twenty years old. She reported that her husband had raped her more than twenty times over a period of fourteen years.

It was a very brutal marriage. He was so patriarchal. He felt he owned me and the children—that I was his property. In the first three weeks of our marriage, he told me to regard him as God and his word as gospel. If I didn't want sex and he did, my wishes didn't matter. Our third child was a result of out-and-out rape.

One time we went out with two cronies of his. I got tired and went to sleep in the car. He drove us home and then he insisted on intercourse. I didn't want it so we really fought. He was furiously angry that I would deny him. I was protesting and pleading and he was angry because he said I was his wife and had no right to refuse him. We were in bed and he was able to force himself physically on me. He's bigger than I am and he just held me down and raped me.

Other unwanted sex with husband? Continually. I was miserable. We had no personal relationship. He was mean. He twisted what I said and used it against me. And he always used physical force. *Describe force?* It was never anything besides his using his strength.

What brought it to an end? I didn't realize there was a way out. After fourteen years, I cracked up and he got a divorce.

Weapons? Guns. But we lived in the desert and both shot.

How upset? Extremely upset. *How much effect on your life?* A great effect. It got me to the point of non-existence where "me" had to react in order to survive. I realized I was in bad shape, but not how withdrawn I was. So I've had to rebuild myself from the beginning.

He was so awful that he didn't seem real. He was a psychotic brute. After I left him, I fell in love right off with a gay man and never went to bed with anyone for twelve years. I have had super lovers since then, but I'm terrified of remarrying— of being in a position where I can't leave.

Other physical violence? He put his fist through the bedroom wall once after he missed hitting me. He couldn't tolerate opposition of any sort. He'd get furious. He kicked me another time. And on another occasion he knocked me down and kicked me repeatedly in the head and chest with heavy combat boots.

Mrs. Kearney said that in addition to the rape incidents her husband had been physically violent toward her 2–5 times during the 14 years of their marriage.

Mrs. Eriksen is a sixty-year-old divorced woman who was living alone at the time of the interview. She was working part-time as the manager of a travel agency. She had raised two children. Referring to her ex-husband, an MD, she said, "I can't tell you more. He'd be recognizable."

Mrs. Eriksen was first raped by her husband when she was twenty-four. She said she was raped by him more than twenty times and that these attacks occurred over their twenty-six-year marriage. The interviewer commented that Mrs. Eriksen was initially adamant about having no experiences to report. She was constantly surprised and then increasingly upset when she came to recall these experiences during the interview.

Which experience upset you the most? One that occurred a year after we married. It involved physical forced sexual . . . *Intercourse?* Yes. He was very angry. *Did he hit you?* No, he only struck me one time in the whole marriage, and I had struck him first. *Physical weight used?* Yes, he was a big man. That's how it was accomplished. *What else happened?* He would frequently insist that I have fellatio with him, yet he would never do cunnilingus. That was dirty to him. He felt fellatio was a means by which a woman was made subservient to a man. He enjoyed the gesture; that I was bowing my head to his penis. It was the subservient posture that he wanted as much as the physical pleasure he derived from it.

Was the fellatio forced? He insisted on it. He would use force, but not physically as much as verbally. If I neglected my "wifely duties" he wouldn't speak to me, or he wouldn't bother to come home, or he would pick quarrels for weeks on end.

His vocabulary was frightening. He grew more and more adept at word imagery that was very dreadful. He felt equally incensed by our daughter. He was a sick man. He would insist she was headed toward whoredom.

It's very painful. It was a horrible marriage. I only put up with it because I had nowhere else to go. [Mrs. Eriksen started crying profusely at this point, so I stopped the interview.]

How long did forced intercourse go on? Twenty-six years—the length of our marriage. There was never any tenderness or understanding of my needs as a person or as a woman. I tried to talk to him, but he always said it was my fault and insisted I seek psychiatric help. It was all much more involved than I'm saying—I'm just glossing over it. I'm afraid to say more. I'm sorry. [Mrs. Eriksen was crying hard throughout this section of the interview, so I did not probe further.]

Verbal threats? He had an aura of violence about him. He was very verbally abusive. His dreadful word or idea images could have every bit as much effect on a woman's sexual responses as a razor.

Weapon? We all had guns. We lived in the country, and that was the custom, I guess.

What brought it to an end? Divorce.

How upset? Extremely upset. I was devastated. *How much effect on your life?* A tremendous effect. I very much doubt that I could ever remarry. I would *never* put myself at the mercy of a man again. I don't think I could manage a relationship. I don't have the confidence, though I have a lot to offer and would like to have a man.

It probably made me very interested in what motivates people to act the way they do. I had to find some reason for not hating him. I knew that hate was destructive to me, that if I hated, I would go down the drain. I got a kidney stone, and have constant kidney trouble from the anxiety I experienced in my marriage.

Other physical violence? I struck him in anger and he whacked me back across my face with his open hand. That was it. It happened only once.

The interviewer said that there were long periods where Mrs. Eriksen was unable to speak. She "really put herself out to answer questions. It was *very* difficult for her." At the end of the interview the interviewer commented as follows:

Mrs. Eriksen was literally terrified that her husband might someday read a report of the study and recognize her verbatim comments and identify her, so she wouldn't give details and talked a lot off the record, which I feel honor-bound not to betray. Her ex-husband is prominent professionally and socially.

Mrs. Eriksen's eldest son has totally rejected her as a result of her divorcing her husband and is violent verbally toward her and aggressively hostile. She is terrified of him as well as her ex-husband. Mrs. Eriksen lives extremely privately as a consequence. Her marriage greatly affected her entire life in many suggested but not always explicit ways.

Mrs. Eriksen is a good example of why the problem of wife rape cannot be seen as merely one more abuse suffered by battered wives. The one instance of physical violence was relatively trivial, as well as being initiated by Mrs. Eriksen herself.

Mrs. Eriksen is very clear that she sees her ex-husband's assaults on her as rape. She is one of the few victims of wife rape who actually mentioned her husband in answer to the question: *At any time in your life, have you ever been the victim of a rape or attempted rape?* Although Mrs. Eriksen left her husband eight or nine years before the interview, her extreme distress during it was very obvious. Her explanation for why she stayed with him for twenty-six years was that "I had nowhere else to go," which shows that women who are not physically beaten can feel as trapped in their marriages as battered women. She finally felt able to leave when her children were in their twenties.

Mrs. Henderson's husband is a third example of an extreme patriarch. Drawing on the Pacific culture that they shared, he viewed his wife as his property, and was righteously angry when she refused his sexual advances.

At the time of the interview Mrs. Henderson was thirty-nine and married to her third husband. Her first husband was the only one to rape and beat her, which began to take place when she was only thirteen and he twenty-three years old. Mrs. Henderson had raised two children; when employed she worked as a maid or waitress, but at the time of the interview she described herself as "keeping house."

Mrs. Henderson said her ex-husband raped her over twenty times in the two and one-half years of their marriage. These experiences occurred on one of the Pacific Islands where she and her husband were born.

I was married when I was thirteen. I had never met my husband before. The marriage was arranged by our families. The first time I saw him was when we went to have the papers for the marriage filled out twenty-one days before. It takes twenty-one days for the marriage to be legal. Our custom is to go to the in-law's house on the first night after the marriage. So I traveled 150 miles to my in-laws after the marriage. In the Islands, people live with their parents or in-laws. It's hard when you go to a strange place and you don't know anyone—when you have never even *met* his family or anybody else.

I arrived in the night. He just took me in the room and closed the door. As soon as we went to bed he started raping me. He started stripping me like a horse, very fast. I didn't like him doing that, so he gave me a couple of black eyes, kicked me, and hit me like a man, on my face and stomach. He left me all black and blue. I think they call it legal rape. Because I didn't want him he thought I had a boyfriend or someone else. He didn't know I was a virgin. He didn't understand. He was a city boy from a big town who knew too much. *Hit, then what?* He tried to rape me. But we didn't have any intercourse that night. I was badly bruised. His parents came in and they took me out of the room. I spent the night with his mother.

The next morning my brother came and took me back to my mother. I stayed with my family for one year. Then I claimed maintenance through the court because I was his legal wife. It was settled in court, and he and his parents took me back to their home. I lived with him for one year; he raped me every night of that year. I had bruises every day. He was always accusing me of having a different lover because I didn't want him. It was crazy.

At last I could leave, and I never came back. That was the end of it. I left when I was seven months pregnant. Even when I was pregnant he raped me all the time. I went to my mother's house and she saw my body covered with bruises. [Mrs. Henderson showed me places on her body where she still has scars from cigarette burns where her husband burned her.] Once after I left him and was with my mother, he came and raped me when there were other people in the house. I was eight months pregnant at the time.

By law on the Island, if both parties don't agree, you can't get a divorce. He is mean. He did not give me a divorce for seven years. He now lives here, and if I see him, I turn my face.

Verbal threats? He said: "I'll never let you go while I live. I'll kill you if I catch you with someone else." When he'd see me on the road, he'd give me a beating right on the street.

What was the result of the police report? The police told him to go back to his town. For five months, by court order, he couldn't come to my town.

What brought it to an end? I left the house and stopped living with him. He raped me once after I left when my little brothers and sisters were around. He didn't respect me.

How upset were you? Extremely upset. *How much effect on your life?* A great effect. I don't trust anybody in the world; not my mother, my brothers, my sisters, nor my own husband. I feel very alone at times. I feel I get no help and that I was treated badly. Whatever a husband says, people believe him. They don't question it, but judge you badly.

It hurt me very much that my husband called me cheap, saying that I had other men before my marriage. It still hurts me. I can't sit and talk to people because of what he said about me. Of all the things he said, not one thing was true. But I feel small because people know what he said and think it's the truth. I never even *dreamed* of men when I married him; I was an ignorant kid.

I'm upset whenever I look at my daughter. She wants to see her father sometimes, and it hurts me because he's not a part of our lives. He even said she is not his kid. It still hurts me *very* much. It hurts me to think what an animal I was married to. That's how I look at all men. They are nothing but animals.

When I look at him now, I feel pity. I feel pity for all people like that. They are human beings, but they act like animals.

Everything that's happened to me is because of him. I wouldn't be here today if it wasn't for him. If he had been a good husband to me, I wouldn't have to find another man, to have the children of another man. When my second husband died, I had to marry again to protect my children from other people so they wouldn't think I was cheap.

When a young kid gets married and this kind of thing happens, you lose hope in living, and especially in your sexual life. All those beatings affect you always. The most beautiful time of your life is ruined.

Mr. Henderson's behavior—particularly his brutality toward his wife on their wedding night—provides an extreme example of a husband seeing his wife as his sexual property. Moreover, the whole culture seems to have reinforced this view. Both families appear to have been fully aware of the extent of the abuse, but they and the court forced her to return to it.

Mrs. Henderson is also one of the minority of wives who perceive their husbands as having raped them. Even though she was married for only two and one-half years, and even though twenty-three years had passed since she left her first husband, the trauma was still intense and eloquently described.

If we assume a continuum with extreme patriarchs at one end, and non-patriarchs at the other, most men would likely be closer to the midpoint than to either extreme. Many husbands use the so-called conjugal rights argument to get their wives to submit to them, or to justify their forcing wives who will not submit. These attitudes and actions show us that wife rape can be a logical consequence of patriarchal attitudes toward women; it does not, however, explain why some men with patriarchal attitudes rape their wives while others do not. Future research will have to clarify this question.

SOCIAL CHARACTERISTICS OF HUSBAND-RAPISTS

Data showing that violent crimes are generally more prevalent in the lower class, and consequently among Black people, while well documented by official statistics,[22] are nevertheless a sensitive subject for some people. Whatever one believes about this, it would be wrong to presume that these statistics can be applied to violence and sexual abuse within the family, since such acts are even less likely to be reported than violence and sexual abuse outside of the family. We'll examine this controversial question as it relates to wife rape.

Education

There has never been consensus among sociologists as to what is the best measure of social class: some believe occupation is the most valid, some education, some income, and some a combination of two or more of these factors. We have looked at each of these indicators of social position.

With regard to the education of the husband-rapists who were twenty-five years and older in our survey,* 20 percent were reported by their wives to have had some high school or less, 24 percent were high school

*Information about education and occupation was only sought for men who were twenty-five years and older. Many persons under this age are still in the process of being educated and/or training for an occupation.

graduates, 22 percent had had some college education, 20 percent were college graduates, and 14 percent had at least some postgraduate education. On the face of it, it seems then that there may be little relationship between wife rape and a man's education. However, because we do not know the education of all the men our 930 respondents were ever married to, we cannot be sure that some educational groups are not over-represented and others under-represented among husband-rapists.

Occupation

Our findings on the occupations of husband-rapists are quite contrary to the findings reported in studies of wife beaters.* Almost one-third of husband-rapists (32 percent) had lower-class occupations (operatives, laborers, and service and transportation workers), as compared with the exact same percentage who had middle-class occupations (sales, clerical, crafts), and just over one-third (36 percent) who had upper-middle-class occupations (professional, technical, managerial).

As with education, on the face of it wife rape appears not to be associated with social class. But again, to be sure of the validity of this finding, it would be helpful to know the occupations of all the husbands these 930 women were ever married to. It could be, for example, that there were many more in one social class than another. Unfortunately this information was not obtained.

Income

Raped wives were asked what their total household income was at the time their husband first raped them. We used standard procedures to adjust these incomes to make them comparable with the dollar value for 1978, the year of our survey. Taking into account the number of people that were dependent on this income, 20 percent of husband-rapists and their wives were living below the poverty line at the time. This is a much lower percentage than would be anticipated on the basis of available data on the victims of extramarital rape. For example, the National Commission on Causes and Prevention of Violence found that females with a family income of under $6,000 in 1967 (the equivalent of $10,890 in 1978) reported being raped 3–5 times more frequently than those with family incomes over $6,000.[23] In our survey the family income of approximately 41 percent of wife rape victims was below $10,890 while 59 percent had family incomes above this figure.

*Murray Straus, Richard Gelles, and Suzanne Steinmetz have reported that "the rate of violence between husbands and wives was twice as high in the families of blue collar workers (men and women) than for white collar workers" (*Behind Closed Doors*, p. 149). Other studies, not based on random samples, have reported the same finding (*Ibid.*, p. 123).

Race or Ethnic Identification

Murray Straus, Richard Gelles, and Suzanne Steinmetz have reported that wife abuse is nearly 400 percent more common among Blacks than among whites.[24] However, they offer no other information on other race or ethnic groups with regard to wife abuse.

In our study, while husband-rapists are found in all racial or ethnic groups, the frequency between the groups varies considerably. While 68 percent of the respondents were white women, 73 percent of the husband-rapists were white. The percentage of Latino husband-rapists (10 percent) was also slightly larger than the percentage of respondents who were Latinas (7 percent). On the other hand, 10 percent of the husband-rapists were Black, exactly the same percentage as Black women respondents. The biggest discrepancy of all was in the Asian group; while they constituted 12 percent of the wives interviewed, only 4 percent of the husband-rapists were Asian.

These differences are intriguing, particularly the fact that, in contrast to the finding of Straus *et al.* about wife abuse, white husband-rapists are slightly over-represented, whereas Black husband-rapists are not. Nevertheless, the differences are small. We also do not know whether the differences (or the similarities) noted reflect true differences (or similarities), rather than discrepancies in willingness to disclose.

Age

Many different studies report that the extramarital rapist is primarily a young man between the ages of fifteen and twenty-four.[25] In our study, just over one-third (37 percent) of the husband-rapists were twenty-five years or younger; only 9 percent were twenty years or younger whereas 57 percent were between twenty-one and thirty years of age, 25 percent between thirty-one and forty, and only 9 percent were forty-one years and older. It seems then that husband-rapists are an older group of men than what Susan Brownmiller refers to as "the police blotter rapist"—that is, rapists who are recorded in the police statistics. Since the age of the husband-rapists was gauged by their age the first time they raped their wives, the difference between marital and extramarital rapists is even greater than indicated by these figures. The reason may be simply that a large proportion of fifteen- to twenty-four-year-old men are not married.

In general, then, while our survey is not definitive on these matters, it seems that husband-rapists are almost equally likely to come from the upper middle, middle, and lower social classes. In addition, husband-rapists are disproportionately white and Latin (to a very slight degree), while

Asian men are very under-represented. The percentage of Black men who are husband-rapists is exactly the same as the percentage of Black women who were raped wives. This in itself tends to confirm the lack of relationship between social class and wife rape; because of racism, Black people are disproportionately situated in the lower class. Our data on household income, while suggesting that wife rape more commonly occurs in lower income groups, also show that it occurs frequently in higher income groups. It appears, then, that the social characteristics of husband-rapists may differ greatly from men who rape women other than their wives.

11

Why Men Rape
Their Wives

The man who is not master of his wife is not worthy of being
a man.

 —French saying of the 18th century[1]

"[A] psychiatrist once told me that there was no excuse for
my not having raped my wife since she was depriving me
needlessly."

 —Male respondent, *The Hite Report on Male Sexuality*,
 Shere Hite, 1981

But, if you can't rape your wife, who can you rape?

 —California State Senator Bob Wilson[2]

Given the fact that wife rape has been traditionally sanctioned by law
in most countries in the world, including in this country until the past
decade, instead of the question "Why do men rape their wives?," one
might ask "Why do men *not* rape their wives?"

Obviously, some men don't rape their wives because they care about
their wives' feelings and/or because they abhor the idea of rape. Others
who don't rape their wives don't need to; their wives acquiesce to their
husbands' wishes regardless of their own feelings (see Chapter 6). These
wives are obeying what is still current law in most states, which, by saying rape is impossible in marriage, implies that wives should be sexually
available to their husbands at all times. A man can only rape an uncoop-
erative woman. Men whose wives always submit to them have to look
elsewhere if they want non-consenting sex. And of course many married
rapists do just that: they rape women other than their wives. Others create a non-consenting situation in their marriages by beating up their
wives and then having sex with them.

Another reason why it seems appropriate to ask the question "Why
do men *not* rape their wives" is that recent research indicates that a considerable percentage of men would *like* to rape a woman (some of this research was presented in Chapter 1). For example, in several recent studies

approximately a third (35 percent) of male college students said that there was some likelihood that they would rape a woman, if they could get away with it.[3] The particular rape story that was used at the University of California, Los Angeles, in the original research of this series of studies, involved rape at knife point of a woman who was a total stranger in response to a mild rebuff (see page 8).[4] In this initial study, an even higher percentage of the male students (51 percent) said they might emulate the rapist's behavior if they could avoid any punishment. The results of these experiments raise the question: How many more men would be willing to rape their wives if their sexual advances were rejected for two weeks or two months?

From these facts, and from careful reading of the descriptions of wife rape by the women in our survey, and from the literature on rapists, rape in general, and contemporary research on male sexuality, the following typology of husbands has emerged. It differentiates husbands according to their varying attitudes and behavior with regard to wife rape.

TYPOLOGY OF HUSBANDS IN RELATION TO WIFE RAPE

(1) Husbands who prefer raping their wives to consensual sex with them;

(2) Husbands who are able to enjoy both rape and consensual sex with their wives or who are indifferent to which it is;

(3) Husbands who would prefer consensual sex with their wives, but who are willing to rape (or to try to rape) them when their sexual advances are refused;

(4) Husbands who might like to rape their wives, but who do not act out these desires;

(5) Husbands who have no desire to rape their wives.

Since this typology was not developed until after the survey was completed, we did not ask the raped wives about their husbands' preferences in these terms. However, we can look to other sources as well as our survey data for cases exemplifying these five types of husbands.

Husbands Who Prefer Rape

Nicholas Groth describes one of the husband-rapists in his study, Sam, as "a wife beater" who, as part of the battering, also sexually assaulted his wife. (In fact, it is not clear from this description why Groth regards the wife beating as primary to the wife rape.)

When Sam was eighteen years old he married his girl friend, Carol, who had become pregnant as a result of having been raped by him. One day, while they were walking along the seashore, Sam suddenly knocked Carol to the ground, held her down, tore off her underpants, and raped her. Carol continued to be a target of Sam's physical and sexual violence for the two years that their marriage lasted. He would take offense at such things as the baby's crying or his food not being prepared to his liking and react by attacking his wife. He would kick and beat Carol and sexually abuse her. On one occasion, he forced his fist into her vagina; on another occasion, he strangled her until she passed out and then sodomized her. Any refusal of sexual relations by Carol was certain to bring violent reprisals from Sam, not only against her but also against their infant daughter.[5]

From this brief description of Sam's behavior it appears clear that his knocking his wife down and raping her when they were walking along the seashore was not a response to her rejection of his advances. This, as well as his forcing his fist into her vagina, and raping her anally after she became unconscious through being strangled by him, suggests that he is a sadist who prefers forcing sex on his wife to consenting sex with her.

Jed, another of Groth's husband-rapists, was apprehended for raping a fifty-year-old woman who was a stranger to him. The following excerpt focuses on his rape of his wife.

Jed found himself increasingly preoccupied with fantasies of sodomy and bondage of women. He began reading pornographic novels with titles such as *The Dominant Male, Punishment and Discipline of the Female,* and *Whipping and Spanking,* and prior to his sexual offense, he attempted to live out his fantasies with his wife.

Kathy noted that "Jed seemed possessed with sex. He demanded relations at least once a day and frequently more often, and he spent most of his spare time around the house reading dirty books on sex! He kept this material in a bureau drawer, and in another drawer, he collected all kinds of ropes—some were even jump ropes that he said he used in practicing to keep fit. Since he was athletically inclined, I believed him."

Kathy described Jed as having a bad temper and resenting ever being questioned or criticized. On more than one occasion, when in a bad mood, he had struck both her and the children.

When Jed demanded that Kathy submit to sodomy, she refused and became quite angry with him and accused him of raping her before their marriage. Jed then took some rope and bound her hands behind her back. Although Kathy fought and struggled, he succeeded in inserting his penis into her rectum. Kathy told him it hurt and cried because it was so painful, but Jed paid no attention to her cries and continued performing the act. He tried to justify this assault by telling Kathy she had "brought it on herself." Jed claimed that he did not have any interest in inflicting physical pain on his wife but wanted, instead, to dominate and degrade her.[6]

The picture that emerges from Groth's brief sketch is of a man whose preoccupation with sex finally became overtly sadistic. Though he rationalized his raping his wife anally as being her fault, and though he claimed not to enjoy inflicting physical pain on her, these claims are not very convincing in light of his preoccupation with sadistic literature and paraphernalia, as well as the description of the rape itself.

The following case was described in an article on a treatment program for rapists. The unnamed man was charged with rape (though not of any of his wives) four times beginning at age thirty. According to Gene Abel, Edward Blanchard, and Judith Becker, the article's authors, each of the rapes involved increasingly more severe sadistic beatings of the victims.[7] This man's apparent inability to relate to his wives without raping them makes him an extreme example of husbands who prefer rape to other forms of sex.

The patient was a thirty-five-year-old male, referred for treatment after his fourth arrest for rape. . . . At age nine he began having fantasies of injuring women, and by age twelve was masturbating to sadistic or rape fantasies twenty times per month. His rape and sadistic fantasies continued. He married at age twenty-two, and shortly thereafter, he began physically beating his wife as a routine part of intercourse. He also began having extramarital affairs during which he frequently raped the woman.

When his first marriage ended after eighteen months, he married his second wife. He would sadistically rape her twice per week, reporting, "I couldn't put my hands on her without hurting her." This marriage ended after nine months, because of the rapes and his continued extramarital affairs. His third and fourth marriages lasted five and three years, respectively, and were both associated with progressively more serious sadistic attacks on the wives. His usual sexual activity with his wife would include his beating her breasts and vagina with his fists, sticking pins into her external genitalia, beating her with a coat hanger, and pulling out her pubic hair.[8]

Husbands Who Enjoy Both Rape and Consensual Sex

Mr. Goodner, the husband of one of our survey respondents, appears to have believed that his wife had a duty to satisfy his desire for oral or anal sex; if she would not do so voluntarily, he forced her to do as he wished.

Mrs. Goodner was in her late twenties at the time of the interview and separated from the husband who forced anal and oral sex on her. She was living with an unrelated man and raising her young child. The first rape by her ex-husband, which, she said, occurred more than twenty times over a period of two years, happened when she was twenty-one.

There were certain positions I didn't want to do. I'd tell him so and he'd get defensive. He would fuck me real fast and get it over with. I didn't like oral sex at all. I thought it was degrading and that he should respect my feelings. He'd force me to do it. He'd push my head down on top of him and hold it there. He made me do it because I was his wife. "It's your duty," he said.

He'd be drunk and not affectionate. When I didn't want to have sex, he'd do it anyway. Once he wanted to have anal intercourse. I didn't want to so he held me down and did it. He didn't care that it hurt. When I was in pain—when sex was painful—he didn't care.

What brought it to an end? I left him.

How upset? Extremely upset. *How much effect on your life?* A great effect. I don't ever want to get married again. I was very untrusting of men for a long time, and very afraid of physical violence. For a long time I didn't want to have any sex with anyone. I went through a long period of celibacy after I left him. I feel like I want to be in control of my sexual experiences. I've become real self-centered about my sexuality, real protective of my sexual space, refusing to let myself be somebody else's sexual object!

Other physical violence? Yes, right before I left him. We had just come from seeing a marriage counselor whom I'd been seeing alone. He'd been making excuses for not going, but he finally went with me. I was bewildered at his anger, as I was the one who was angry. When we got home, he grabbed me and pushed me out of the car. We were on the sidewalk and he was sitting on my chest, punching me and beating my head on the sidewalk with my hair. I was screaming. Then he left and ran off. We had many steps to the house and he finally came back to help me up them. He was sorry and gentle by then.

Mrs. Goodner said the physical violence occurred from 2–5 times over a two-and-one-half year period. After the one violent episode that Mrs. Goodner described, her husband was very apologetic about his behavior; he was clearly not, however, after the rapes. It appears that he felt he was simply taking what he was owed when it came to sex, and that he was indifferent as to whether his satisfaction required force or not. At that time the law in California would have been in agreement with him.

Husbands Who Prefer Consensual Sex but Who Are Willing to Rape (or to Try to Rape) Their Wives

Many of the men who raped their wives in our survey probably belong in this category.

Mrs. Harvey was thirty-one, and still married to the man who raped her once about two years ago. She had one six-year-old child and was working full time in a clerical position. Her husband was also a clerical worker.

He wanted to make love with me, and I didn't want to. He got mad and tried to force me to take off my panties. He actually did it himself, so I fought back. I pushed him away, but he was stronger than me, so he forced me down, spread my legs, and forced penetration.

Penetration? Forced intercourse.

How upset? Very upset. *How much effect on your life?* No effect.

The interviewer commented that Mrs. Harvey felt uncomfortable talking about her experience with her husband, and that she had never talked about it with anyone before.

Mrs. Valentine was thirty-one and divorced at the time of the interview. She had no children and was living alone. She worked full-time as a secretary/administrative assistant in a research firm. Her husband had worked as an economist.

Mrs. Valentine was twenty-three years old when her husband first raped her. She reported that this happened more than twenty times over a period of two years.

It happened in the last two years that we were married. I was bored and not interested in having sex at that time. I would be asleep in bed when he would force me to have intercourse with him. He realized that I was not interested in sex so he would wait until I was asleep. Then he would start to caress me and when I woke up, he would be on top of me. I would make a mild protest, but he insisted on doing it. I felt that was the way it was, so I went along. *Kind of physical force?* It was sheer physical force. He is much bigger than me. He lay on top of me and forced me to have intercourse with him.

What brought it to an end? We had a divorce.

How upset? Somewhat upset. *How much effect on your life?* Some effect. These experiences made me realize that I had lost control over my body and myself in my relationship with my husband. I lost interest even more in him and sex. I was more determined to have a divorce as a result, and I am glad that I did.

Sometimes, husbands who fall into this category have been willing to rape their wives, but only one time. One man answered the question in Shere Hite's questionnaire regarding whether he had ever raped a woman as follows:

I have only raped a woman once and that was my ex-wife. I did not like it. It was recommended by a psychiatrist and I think that it was a lousy recommendation.[9]

It is not clear from the answer of a second man how many times he tried to rape his wife.

I tried to rape my wife when I felt frustrated and angry with her because we weren't having a good sexual relationship. At the time I felt men had the "right" to do this with their women and can recall innumerable men talking about that being "what women really wanted" or that "women like being treated roughly or forcefully." This was about six years ago and I feel awful about it now.[10]

Husbands Who Would Like to Rape Their Wives, but Who Do Not Act Out These Desires

Mrs. Altman, one of our respondents, was thirty-three years old and, at the time of the interview, still married to the husband who had raped her. She was childless, and was working part-time as a lecturer at a university. Her husband was the president of an insurance company.

The unwanted sexual experiences started when Mrs. Altman was in her early twenties, and occurred more than twenty times over nine years, "as long as we've been lovers." The vaginal intercourse described appears to have been unwanted but not forced. Mrs. Altman's husband appears to be a sadist, but something (perhaps his conscience) makes him reluctant to act out his desire to hurt his wife consistently. Mrs. Altman uses the word rape to describe the unwanted sexual experiences with her husband.

It was the way husbands rape their wives; you don't want to do it but they talk you into it. Sometimes he respects my wishes when I don't want it, but sometimes he doesn't. *What happens then?* He usually puts his penis in me. *Does he use force?* He gets no encouragement—let's put it that way. He has to do all the work. He inserts his penis and I remain passive. About 50 percent of the time I end up participating. *But is it forced?* It's hard to tell—it's like game playing. He's rubbing up against me, fondling me, trying to turn me on. I'm not participating, but I'm not leaving the bed either.

He says he's done it when I'm asleep but I don't remember that, so I don't know if it's true. I used to have a couple of martinis and aspirin before bed and sleep soundly the first couple of hours, so maybe he does do it. I think it turns him on to think of it.

Verbal threats? He would guilt-trip me. He'd say: "Oh come on—it feels so good for me."

How upset? Somewhat upset. *How much effect on your life?* A little effect.

Information about Mrs. Altman's unwanted experiences of anal intercourse emerged in response to a question on pornography: *Have you ever been upset by anyone trying to get you to do what they'd seen in pornographic pictures, movies, or books?* Mrs. Altman said yes. She was then asked to describe the most upsetting time. She did not reveal that she'd been describing her husband until specifically asked afterward.

It was S and M stuff; being asked if I would participate in being beaten up. It was a proposition. It never happened. I turned it off. I didn't like the idea of it.

Also there was anal intercourse. I have been asked to do it but I don't enjoy it at all. I have had to do it—very occasionally. As soon as the man penetrated me, I realized it hurt and I'd say no, but it was too late, and the person did it anyway. It happened twice.

How did it get to that point? I really didn't want to do it, but I said yes, I'd be willing to give it a try. But when it would start to happen, I'd change my mind and say no, and I *meant* no, but he'd say I really did like it. He'd grab my thighs and I couldn't crawl anywhere—he was in control—and it would take one and a half minutes longer. I'd say "Stop, it really hurts," but that turns some people on, and he'd keep going until he ejaculated. He kept saying, "It will get better. It will get better." And, "Tell me if I'm *really* hurting you." *Physical force?* He grabbed my thighs and grabbed me under my stomach and around my waist and hips so he could control my motions. After he ejaculated, it was fine.

In answer to the question, *What finally brought it to an end?*, the interviewer wrote that the anal intercourse was no longer forced because Mrs. Altman uses a drug to dull the pain.

Other physical violence? He only really lost control of it once. The rest of the time it is gaming. *Gaming?* A couple of slaps in lovemaking. A little hurt doesn't hurt. But that one time he slapped me as hard as he could across my face. We were arguing about my responsibilities and his responsibilities around the house. He made more money than I did, and so he thought I should do more than he did. I guess I felt I did the shit work. So we had a huge argument. I said something and he flew off the handle. He hit me across the face—the cheekbone—with the flat of his hand and knocked me into the glass door. He was flushed and breathing rapidly. His fists were clenched and he was rigid. I ran out and decided I was leaving. I walked around the park and only came home two hours later. He was hysterical trying to find me. He thought something had happened to me. It scared him. That was it. It never happened again.*

One problem with placing Mr. Altman in the category of husbands who would like to rape their wives, but who do not act out these desires, is that the anal sex does appear to have been forced on his wife on two occasions. However, it seems apparent that for the most part he wants his wife's consent to his sadistic desires. Hence, I consider him to be a sadist with a conscience; since Mrs. Altman won't give her consent to his more extreme sadomasochistic proposals, such as his beating her up, he more often stays with the milder ones, such as slapping her.

Shere Hite's questionnaire survey on male sexuality also yielded several cases that illustrate this fourth category of husbands very well.

My wife's sexual ardor cooled off beginning with the honeymoon. Except for when she is "horny," she will have sex with me only because she feels an obligation or because she doesn't want me to have an excuse to seek sex elsewhere. She is uninterested most of the time. I am sure that the problems I have had with my professional life have resulted from the intense and constant frustration I have felt resulting from such deprivation. I can't get along with the people I work with, but it is only because she rejects me. I finally grew to hate my wife so much so that once, just after I had lost my last job, I decided to rape her. Had I not been given a powerful faith to hold on to by my extraordinary parents, I would have done it.[11]

The next man appears to see himself as exceptional for not believing rape in marriage to be appropriate even though he acknowledges having wanted to rape his wife.

I don't think I have ever wanted to rape a woman except maybe my wife and I am not sure why I would want to rape her at this point. I certainly would not mind going to bed with her again, though. There were many weeks during the course of my marriage when my wife did not feel like sex with me. But I don't even believe in rape in marriage. If a woman does not want me, I certainly do not want her.[12]

---

*Mrs. Altman's experience of physical violence by her husband is a good example of a one-time-being-the-last-time story. It is not clear whether he was scared because of her decision to leave, or because he was alarmed at feeling so out of control, or both. But the case breaks the stereotype of once beaten, later battered.

The contrast between Mrs. Altman's assertive rejection of her husband's violence and her passive acquiescence to unwanted vaginal intercourse and her use of drugs to dull the pain of unwanted anal intercourse, is very noticeable. However, it is quite common; there are many more cases of wives refusing to accept beatings but accepting rape, than there are cases of wives refusing rape and accepting beatings.

The last two examples involve men who started to rape their wives but stopped before completing the act. Hence they are borderline cases between this category of husbands who would like to rape their wives, but who do not act out these desires, and those who do act them out.

I tried to rape my wife once, after we were married. We had an argument. I tore off her panties and tried to mount her. After we had a short fight, which was exciting to me, she gave in. She just lay there, spread her legs, and shut her eyes. I looked at her, my erection left, and I laid my head on her chest and cried. If she didn't want me, I didn't want her. I felt sorry for the way I had treated her. I couldn't perform.[13]

I have never raped a woman. I did something near it once and I felt like hitting myself or burning my hand off. One time she [his wife] was not in the mood, so I picked her up and put her in the bed and got on top of her. I started to kiss her and move my body on her, then she started to cry softly, and all the wanting just went out of me. I think I'd have killed myself if I had a gun. My erection disappeared and I was not in the mood for sex. She cried for a while and I held her after a while, but I did not touch her again for the whole night. I only touched her after three days after she made the first move. She told me why she cried and I understood.[14]

Husbands Who Have No Desire to Rape Their Wives

We cannot be sure that husbands whose wives always submit to their sexual desires belong in this category because they have not been put to the test. Given sexual rejection, some of them could belong in the third or fourth categories, that is, husbands who would prefer consensual sex with their wives but who are willing to rape, or husbands who would like to rape their wives, but who do not act out these desires. Due to the nature of this study, husbands belonging strictly in this fifth group were rarely noted. However, the case of Mrs. Raymond illustrates that though a husband may have no desire to rape his wife, there still may be sexual abuse.

Mrs. Raymond was fifty-three, divorced, and living alone at the time of the interview. She had reared two children, and was working full-time as a painter and art teacher. She had been raped once by her second husband; this experience is described in Chapter 23. Mrs. Raymond was twenty-one when the unwanted sex with her first husband began. The following description clearly reveals the difficulty the interviewer had in determining whether the husband's pressure constituted physical force or not.

Whenever he wanted to have sex I had to do it. He said he had to have sex because we were married. Usually I enjoyed it. He only woke me up for sex once, but after that experience I really felt that if he wanted it I had to do it. The time he woke me up, he just kept telling me he wanted to have sex. He kept after me until I did it. I didn't want to; I was tired and wanted to sleep. *Feel forced?* Yes. *Was he violent?* No. He just wouldn't take no for an answer. He said, "I'm married and I need it." I used to sleep soundly and it was difficult for me to wake up but he wouldn't let me sleep. He just kept talking to me until I was awake. Finally when I was awake I did have sex with him. *Did he use physical force?* Not in terms of violence, but he wouldn't take no for an answer, so I had no say about what I wanted to do. The only way I could have changed that pattern would have been to leave him—in no way would he change his behavior. *When you say force, how do you mean?* It was insistence more than physical. *Any physical?* Yes, but violence was not in his nature. *What kind of physical?* Waking me up, talking to me, kissing me, getting me aroused. *Did he hold you, grab you, pin you, restrain you?* He just kept waking me up, kissing me and talking to me; I felt forced. It was an old pattern of sex as women's duty. I think that's what it comes down to.

What brought it to an end? I got pregnant. After the baby was born we separated.

How upset? Somewhat upset. *How much effect on your life?* A great effect. I think it turned me off sexually. I really feel like it affected my entire adult sexual life. I became so turned off to him that I never was really spontaneous sexually after that.

Several of the men who completed Hite's questionnaires appear to fall into this fifth category of husbands who have no desire to rape any woman. For example:

I have never raped a woman. I have never wanted to rape a woman. I like sex and enjoy sex and the most enjoyment that I get out of sex is to see my partner enjoy herself to the point of ecstasy. Knowing and feeling that I am causing this sensation for my sex partner is thrilling and exciting and it gives me a sense of power because *I know she wants me.* I don't believe these feelings would be possible for either partner in case of rape. A person who would rape a woman must be extremely emotionally unstable, a sick mind, irresponsible, one who has no consideration for the rights and feelings of another human being. I consider such a person a scum and reprobate.[15]

Rape is a perversion. It's not a crime of passion. I can understand someone who gets angry and shoots someone else. I have a temper too. But rape isn't like that. A rapist is a sick s.o.b. By raping a woman, he's degrading her. He doesn't really *like* women. I like women and not just in bed. I don't want to hurt anyone. I like women too much. Rape is a calculated degradation of another human being.[16]

The sexual act can be so beautiful and so delicate and tender, that it seems particularly cruel to have it contaminated with violence, pain, and humiliation. I have to say that I find rape a particularly unpleasant crime. I don't want to hurt women. Rape would take the fun out of sex. I might as well punch her in the mouth.[17]

I cannot see anything which could be attained by rape which doesn't depend on a degenerate view of other people, women especially. I do my best to exorcise everything to do with "masculinity," which includes a view of women which can include rape, even the socially acceptable forms of persuasion through status, etc. Even when I detect that my partner is "performing for my sake," when she's not really into it, I get turned off instantaneously. Rape is one of the few things pertaining to sex which really is obscene.[18]

Sometimes a husband's motivation not to rape his wife is not particularly complimentary.

I have never raped a woman. I never had any intention of raping a woman and never will. If any woman, whores included, does not make me feel as though they want me as bad as I want them—*they are not worth having.* I wouldn't even rape my wife—many is the time I thought about doing it, but even a whore was a better piece of ass.[19]

Though I believe this typology is useful in conveying the range of husbands' attitudes and behavior *vis-a-vis* wife rape, like all typologies, it has limitations. One is common to all typologies: the borderline cases that don't quite belong in *any* category. For example, the following man admits to having raped his wife "a few times" but claims he couldn't maintain an erection in an extramarital rape situation. In addition he seems no longer to be willing to rape his wife.

I would never think of taking it by force—except from my wife. I don't think I could get it up in a rape situation. It so appalls me that I couldn't do it. I have forced myself on my wife when she has repeatedly refused me and has led me to believe I could have some and then closed up. This has only happened a few times and I feel bad afterward. I would rather get a divorce than do it again.[20]

This man seems to have belonged in our third category of husbands who prefer consensual sex but who have been willing to rape their wives when rejected. However, he appears to have moved from this category to the fourth one, since he no longer would act out this desire. Typologies are static but people are not.

Implicit in my typology, particularly the third category of husbands who prefer consensual sex with their wives but who have raped them when their sexual advances are refused, is the notion that rape in marriage can be sexually motivated. Most of the theories of rape that have developed have focused on stranger rape, not rape in intimate relationships. In this context feminist analysis of rape has tended to emphasize that rape is *not* sexually motivated, but motivated rather by hatred of women, or the desire to dominate and humiliate them. However, when examining wife rape I believe it is necessary to recognize that it is sometimes motivated by sexual needs, such as when the wife is not a willing partner, for whatever the reason, or when she rejects a particular form of sex that her husband desires. Some husbands have sex whenever and however they wish, regardless of whether or not their wives are willing, since, they, like the law, see this as their right. They are *exercising* power when they do this, but they are not necessarily *motivated* by the desire for power. The experience of Mrs. Sanders seems to be a case of rape for sex.

Mrs. Sanders was a seventy-two-year-old widow who was childless and living alone at the time of the interview. She was retired but had worked as a salesperson in a department store. She was twenty-eight years old when her husband first forced her to have oral sex with him. She said this had happened 11–20 times over a period of years.

He got excited by looking at pictures of the faces of movie stars. After he looked at them, he'd be very sexually excited and want to do strange things to me. He especially wanted me to do oral sex. I didn't want to do it. He made it unpleasant for me. I was naive, and it was a bad experience.

To my mind, he was obsessed with sex. He wanted sex so very often. He used me as a sex object. He didn't really want regular intercourse. I guess when people love each other it's ok, but I married him hardly knowing him. I knew nothing about sex then; my mother told me nothing. She hadn't even told me about menstruation when I was young. *Did he force you?* Yes. To do oral sex. *Forced verbally or physically?* Physically. *Did he succeed?* Yes, he did. *Was he ever violent?* Not violent. But sexually he was off his rocker. That was my first marriage. My second husband was fine.

How brought it to an end? I ended the marriage.

How upset? Extremely upset. *How much effect on your life?* I realized my marriage was a mistake. I should have known him better before I married him. When I married my second husband, I knew him better.

My suggestion that sexual motivation can be primary in wife rape does not mean that I think it usually is. From our survey data, it seems that rape as an assertion of power is most common, but there also appear to be cases of rape from anger, and sadistic rape. These are the three types of motivation to rape that Nicholas Groth has suggested.

NICHOLAS GROTH'S THEORY

In terms of the frequency with which power, anger, and sadistic rapes occur, Groth surmised: "The sadistic rapist, who may maim and murder, is extremely rare. . . . The anger rapist, who brutalizes his victim, leaving her with injuries, torn clothing or other obvious signs of attack, is more common, and the power rapist, who asserts his masculinity by coercing and subduing his victim, is by far the most typical. The relative frequency of these motives is the same in marital rape as in the rape of strangers."[21]

Of course, not all men who are angry with women (or their wives), who want to assert power over them, or who act sadistically toward them, rape them. Nevertheless, Groth's categories seem to be useful for understanding husband-rapists.

Groth speculates that "Probably, the majority of men who rape their wives do not rape other persons."[22] Though evidence to support this view is not yet available, I agree with Groth's surmise. Wives are the most legitimate of all victims. But I disagree with his notion that in all cases where husband-rapists do not rape anyone but their wives, the rape is "a product of family dysfunction."[23] This conclusion places equal responsibility for wife rape on both offender and victim, and denies the significance of the culturally existing power imbalance between husband and wife. Most husbands not only have physical power over their wives; their power is imbedded in the structure of the family and reinforced by cultural notions. Groth's *Men Who Rape* is commonly seen as the most authoritative source on the subject available today. Unfortunately such statements as the preceding one seriously undermine his data analysis, much of which is accurate and helpful.

FINKELHOR AND YLLO'S THEORY

Groth's theories about husband-rapists are based on his work with incarcerated rapists, Frieze's (to which we have referred) on her research with battered women, and Finkelhor and Yllo's on interviews with women who have experienced rape by a husband or lover with whom they were living. As sociologists, Finkelhor and Yllo attempt to place the problem of wife rape in a general social context, rather than to explain why one man rather than another becomes a husband-rapist.

Finkelhor and Yllo point out that physical force is commonly used in marriages as a way of "resolving" conflicts, citing the estimate of Straus, Gelles, and Steinmetz that at least one episode of violence occurs in about 56 percent of marriages in the United States. Sexual conflict is also common in marriage.[24] Putting these two facts together, Finkelhor and Yllo observe that "since the use of force is relatively widespread in resolving marital conflicts, it is a virtual certainty that such force is common in the resolution of conflicts over sex."[25] They cite confirming data from the national survey on violence in American families undertaken by Straus, Gelles, and Steinmetz who reported that husbands in their sample were nearly four times more likely to be violent toward their wives if the couple reported that they "never" agreed on sexual matters, and twice as likely to be violent if they reported agreeing only "sometimes." Hence Finkelhor and Yllo conclude that "it is reasonable to guess that much of this additional violence was triggered by these couples' specifically sexual conflicts, and was sometimes used to coerce sexual activities."[26] It does indeed seem a reasonable conclusion to draw.

In their preliminary analysis of interviews with fifty women whose husbands or cohabiting partners had forced or threatened force to obtain sex with them, Finkelhor and Yllo report that three different types of rape emerged.[27] Although the authors focus on the women in their description of these types, the descriptions are also revealing of the men and the marriages.

(1) *Battering Rapes.* The majority of women they interviewed were "typical battered women" who were subjected to a great deal of physical and verbal abuse, most of it unrelated to sex, by men who often had alcohol and other drug problems. The sexual violence was simply another aspect of the general abuse.[28]

(2) *Non-Battering Rapes.* Little physical violence was reported in marriages of this type. The violence that occurs results from sexual conflicts. At some point, the conflict "spills over into violence. The man decides he is being denied and frustrated and that he is going to get what he wants by force."[29]

(3) *Obsessive Rapes.* A few women among the fifty interviewed described husbands who were obsessed with sex. These men "tended to be heavily involved in pornography and were extremely demanding of sex from the start. These wives reported having sex several times a day to keep their husbands satisfied. As the marriages progressed, the husbands' sexual demands became more and more sadistic and unusual.[30]

More interviews will likely reveal to Finkelhor and Yllo that there are more than three types of wife rape. Certainly there are many examples obtained from our survey that could not be placed in any of their three categories. For example, their typology implies that either the husbands are the classic type of batterers or they are virtually non-violent. What about all the moderately violent husbands who rape their wives? And what about the men who are only somewhat violent outside of sexual situations, but who rape their wives when they are asleep or drunk—without violence? What about men who rape their wives only once just before a divorce or after they have separated, to "make a point," to act in revenge, or to try to "repossess" their wives? What about husbands who are very violent but where the violence is always or primarily sex-related? Despite these questions about their typology, the context within which Finkelhor and Yllo place the problem of wife rape seems extremely helpful: taking it out of the realm of pathology, and showing the connections between wife rape, the use of force in marriage, and the common occurrence of sexual conflicts between partners.

In general, it seems that the less extreme forms of wife rape are being neglected, and, more seriously, theories are sometimes being developed as if these forms of wife rape did not exist. I believe psychologist Irene Frieze in particular is in error in concluding that wife battering and wife rape are always very closely linked.[31] They are closely linked in the sense that many battered wives are also raped, but there are probably many more wives who are raped by their husbands but not battered (the word "battered" here refers to extreme violence that is repeated, not the milder forms of violence, or one-time occurrences).

We did not specifically ask the women interviewed in our survey why they thought their husbands raped them. Nevertheless, various reasons did emerge from many of the women's descriptions. I shall attempt to fit these cases into Groth's typology of sadistic, anger, and power motives for wife rape.

SADISTIC RAPE

Some might argue that a man who can rape a woman must be sadistic to some degree, since he is able to become sexually excited when hurting another human being. Others use the word more sparingly to describe husbands who enjoy hurting their wives in the course of raping them. The experiences of Mrs. Basinger, Mrs. Jones, and Mrs. Upton provide three examples of sadistic rape.

Mrs. Basinger was twenty-six years old at the time of the interview. While she said she was still married to the man who first raped her when she was twenty years old, he and their two young children were out of the country at that time, and he was employed as an economist in that country. Mrs. Basinger was working full-time in a managerial capacity.

Mrs. Basinger said that the sexual abuse had occurred more than twenty times during the six years of their marriage.

I had a hangup about sex when I got married. He introduced sex to me but I didn't want to do it. The days I would let it happen, I was scared. At times he would force me. After the first week of marriage I had to go to the hospital. The doctor said I should have no sexual intercourse for two weeks because my vagina was swollen and needed a rest. I didn't feel like it; it was painful for me. So he would pin me down and force me because he said I was obliged to him.

One time when he wanted to have sex and I didn't, I woke up in the morning and found I was tied up in bed. This was possible because I'm a very heavy sleeper. He tied my hands and feet to the bed posts so I could hardly move. To make a long story short, he assaulted me. Then he said, "You're never supposed to refuse your husband." *What did he do?* It was almost like rape. He hurt me. When I would jerk to get him off, he would keep on. I still have scars. [Mrs. Basinger showed me.] He's very rough. It's like getting branded. He bites me on my arms often. *Vaginal assault?* Yes. And he kept coming back for more until I was totally exhausted. I feel he actually enjoyed seeing me in that condition—fighting. *How many times did he assault you?* Seven times. *How long did it go on?* From 8:00 A.M. through noon. He bruised my whole body up to my nipples; he punched my legs, and bit me all over my neck and body.

After that, I tried not to say no to him any more. I didn't want to end up like that again. There were other similar incidents, but I never allowed myself to get tied again. He makes love in a very rough manner.

What brought it to an end? It's not at an end.

How upset? Very upset. *How much effect on your life?* A great effect. I didn't know a husband could force a wife, or that I am obligated to give in to my husband. Being treated roughly like that—I didn't know it could happen. I didn't know it was even termed assault. *How affected?* I love my husband, so I went out of my way to learn things about sex. I had a call-girl friend teach me. I asked my brother to go to the baths and tell me what they do there. I never said no to my husband after that. I made an effort to make him happy in sex, in the long run to please myself too.

Other physical violence from your husband? He has a bad temper. He knocked me down when I was nine months pregnant, and I almost lost the baby. I should have known better because when he argues, he doesn't want to lose. All my married life I thought only of him. But he lost his mind, went after me, grabbed my head and banged it on the headboard. He said, "I'm going to kill you." He slapped me all over my face. I had bruises. My four-year-old son came in and started to cry. Everyone could hear, but they were afraid to interfere. He continued to slap me, then he left the house.

He went to the hospital and was in the intensive care unit. He told the doctor, who was his best friend, that he had had a heart attack. I think he was embarrassed to come home. *Else?* No, that was the only time he ever laid a hand on me.

When Mrs. Basinger discounts the violent sexual experiences with her husband (by saying that he only laid a hand on her once), she exhibits a surprising though common attitude. When force or violence is connected with sex, the fact that force or violence has been used is often ignored. It is seen as sex, not violence nor sexual violence. The violence in much contemporary pornography is discounted in a similar fashion.

Mrs. Basinger's description of her experience is a little confusing. On the one hand, she said that she learned not to deny her husband's sexual demands; on the other hand she said she experienced his sexual abuse over twenty times. It seems that regardless of her willingness to accommodate him, he is continually very rough with her. While she was shocked to find out that her husband could be so cruel, and that she had no right to say no to him, she learned this lesson so well that she proceeded to try to tolerate his wishes, even when this meant continuing pain to her.

The interviewer paraphrased Mrs. Basinger's discussion of some of the cultural norms prevailing in her home country (the Philippines): "When you're married, you're married. Even if you don't see your husband for years, you wait. Women are trained to be martyrs. They wait until their husbands come back to them after they are through with sleeping around. They are looked down on if they don't. There is a strict double standard." This may throw some light on why Mrs. Basinger is still married to her husband—a topic to be dealt with more fully in another chapter.

While Mrs. Basinger's husband has been classified as a sadist, power and anger also appear to play a significant part in his behavior toward his wife. The episode in which he tied her up and repeatedly and brutally raped her seems to be an expression of his anger at her refusing him, as well as of his need for power (he wanted to teach her that "you're never supposed to refuse your husband").

Mrs. Jones was thirty-one at the time of the interview. She had two children both of whom lived with other relatives. Mrs. Jones was separated from her fourth husband. She had been raped and beaten by her third husband, and beaten but not raped by one of the others. Although Mrs. Jones was generally unwilling to talk about the rape and beating she received from her third husband, the interviewer recorded the following information:

Mrs. Jones explained that she had married her third husband without knowing him well. He had kept her locked in the apartment for five weeks, raping her repeatedly. She also referred to being tied up by him and to the use of whips. It had obviously been extremely painful to her and when we got to this part of the interview all she would say was: "It happened day and night for five weeks. I don't want to talk about it any more."

While Mrs. Jones experienced violence in two out of four marriages, she got out of this one at the end of the five weeks, and the other after eight months. The fact that many abused wives leave their husbands in a fairly short time is often forgotten.

Mrs. Upton was forty and divorced at the time of the interview. She had six children, three of whom were still living with her. She was keeping house, but had previously worked as a clerical worker.

Mrs. Upton was sexually abused by two husbands, though only the first of these experiences met our definition of rape. Both these husbands were physically violent toward her as well. She had been in two other marriages in which she reported no sexual or other violent abuse.

Mrs. Upton started by saying which of the more than twenty times she was sexually abused over a period of seven years had upset her the most.

We'd separate and get back together. This event was after I hadn't seen him for almost two years. He found me and he insisted on calling someone who had advertised in the *Berkeley Barb* that he wanted to be a spectator to various sadomasochistic exploitations, like being tied down to a bed. It's vague because I was on heavy drugs at the time. He slapped me a few times. He had vaginal intercourse with me while I was tied up. I was tightly tied but it was just my arms and legs. The guy paid, then just sat in the corner and watched. It was so sick it was unbelievable. Once the man in the corner got his nut [climaxed] the show was over.

Other unwanted sex with him? Yes. Group sex, and sometimes he'd want me to whip him. And there were two years of sex clubs and sex orgies. After two years I dropped out of that whole thing.

What brought it to an end? I had him put in a therapeutic community. Later he left and beat me half to death. He's now serving time in jail for that and other things.

Verbal threats? He said that he'd kill me if he ever got the chance. He's getting out of jail in a few weeks and still says he's going to do it. *Why?* We just hate one another.

Weapon? He had guns and a knife. He used them in fighting me; not in anything sexual.

Result of police report? Nothing much. In fact, nothing ever happened until he put me in the hospital for six months.

How upset? Extremely upset. *How much effect on your life?* A great effect. It has changed my whole outlook. I gained one hundred pounds and I learned how to hate. I'm pretty down on men.

Other physical violence? After he left the therapeutic community he kicked me, beat me, anything he could. All my ribs were broken, my skull fractured. I had concussion, a lot of cuts and bruises. He gave me a few hairline fractures and he beat me unconscious. I spent six months in the hospital.

At other times, he attacked me with knives, broken bottles or anything he could get his hands on. He would cut me up—very severely sometimes, very deep. I still have scars.

The rape Mrs. Upton described at the beginning of her account appears to involve a mixture of force, threat of force and helplessness due to being drugged. What comes through more strongly than her husband's raping her *per se,* is a more general desire to use and control her body in whatever way he wished, as if she were a total object. In addition his hatred of her and violence toward her are very apparent.

ANGER RAPE

Although many husbands appear to be angry when they rape their wives, judging from the wife's description, there did not seem to be many cases where anger was the primary motivation. Mrs. North's experience appears to qualify as one such case.

Mrs. North was thirty-nine years old at the time of the interview. She was separated from the husband who raped her, and living with one of her two children. She was working full-time as a social worker. Her ex-husband was a physician.

Mrs. North said that her husband had forced himself on her twice over a period of one year. The first time occurred when she was thirty-two.

He forced me to have sexual intercourse and physically threatened me. It was done in anger. He hit me with a belt, slapped me, and forced himself on me. It happened when he lost his temper. He was very angry. Usually when he lost his temper, he walked away, so I was shocked both times that this happened. I cowered in the corner and he beat me up.

Verbal threats? "I'll kill you."

What brought it to an end? I've no idea.

How upset? Extremely upset. *How much effect on your life?* A great effect. I'm still angry. That's it. That's enough. It keeps me unobjective about men and authority figures.

Mrs. Dean was twenty-eight years old at the time of the interview. She was living alone with her seven-year-old child and working full-time as the coordinator of a community project. The common-law husband who raped her was a counselor.

Mrs. Dean said the forced sex occurred from 2–5 times, but that she was able to prevent it on many other occasions. The attacks occurred over 3–4 months, starting when she was twenty-five years old. However, judging from her own description, 2–5 times seems to be an .underestimate of her husband's sexual assaults.

When we lived together we'd always argue and quarrel and fight. After arguments he'd want sex, like arguing got his adrenaline up or something. It didn't matter where we were—it could be in the basement and he'd want it! One time he was in the bedroom on the bed when I came in from work. We were supposed to go out, but he'd changed his mind. We argued and he twisted my arm back. I threw the phone at him and ran out of the house.

He had a son, Duncan who was ten last year. I had serious problems with how he treated the boy. One day Duncan was having trouble with his school work. My husband asked him if he was stupid and hit him, and we argued as a result of this. I went to the bedroom, turned on the TV, and lay down on my stomach across the bed. He jumped on me, pinned my arms back and said, "You've got to learn to behave." We rolled around, fell on the floor, and started fighting. I turned to try to hit him. I grabbed his genitals, squeezed, and hit up. Then I ran out of the house to my mother's house.

I returned later and went to bed. He wasn't there at the time, but when he came home he wanted to have sex. I didn't want it. *Did you have it?* Yes. I wasn't able to lubricate and when that happened, he'd just force himself in. *How force you?* Sometimes he would wake me up and sometimes he wouldn't bother. I'd just feel the penetration. He said: "It doesn't matter if you move or not. I'll get what I want anyway."

Our relationship had deteriorated to the point where the sex act was not desired or wanted by me. Whenever he had the urge, he'd do it, especially during the last months. We argued more and more about his son, and he'd always be out of work. I was supporting a family of four.

What brought it to an end? I kicked him out of the house.

How upset? Extremely upset. *How much effect on your life?* A great effect. It made me very bitter. I had a lot of sleepless nights. I kept expecting him to come back at any minute. I was not open to any relationships with men for about a year. I was very adamant that I wouldn't go out with anyone. It's only been recently that I've started dating again. *Other effects?* I believe all men are no good. Men in general, regardless of their age, are basically evil creatures, composed of mass insecurities. They want educated, intelligent women but they want them to be barefoot in the kitchen. I'm not as open now and I'm more skeptical. Hopefully I'm also more careful in the relationships that I form.

Mrs. Dean's experiences were classified as anger rape because of her husband's pattern of wanting sex after arguments, "like arguing got his adrenaline up or something." This seems to be a very common male pattern, mentioned by many of these women. However, other elements in her description suggest power rape; for example, her husband's unsuccessful attack on her which was accompanied by the statement, "You've got to learn to behave," and his attitude toward having intercourse with her while she was asleep: "It doesn't matter if you move or not, I'll get what I want."

Mrs. Dean's resistance tactics were aggressive, though they were always defensive behaviors: grabbing his genitals, throwing the telephone at him. And unlike many other wives whose husbands would not let them go, she was able to end her husband's abuse by ousting him from the house.

Anger, although it appears to be part of the descriptions of many wife rapes, usually seems to be secondary to the husband's attempt to dominate or control his wife. As Groth found with stranger rapists, power rape seems to be the most common form of rape in marriage as well.

POWER RAPE

According to Morton Hunt, one of the first people to write about wife rape:

The typical marital rapist is a man who still believes that husbands are supposed to "rule" their wives. This extends, he feels, to sexual matters: when he wants her, she should be glad, or at least willing; if she isn't, he has the right to force her. But in forcing her he gains far more than a few minutes of sexual pleasure. He humbles her and reasserts, in the most emotionally powerful way possible, that he is the ruler and she the subject.[32]

This analysis overlooks the fact that it is not just husband-rapists who believe that husbands are supposed to rule their wives. This is the *prevailing* belief, rejected by many liberals and radicals in *theory,* though often not in their own lives. Truly egalitarian marriages are still extremely rare. Nevertheless, Hunt's notion that the typical husband-rapist seeks power over his wife rather than sexual gratification fits with Groth's and our findings.

The following cases illustrate different reasons for power rape by husbands.

Power Rape—To Show Who Is Boss

Mrs. Metcalf was a forty-eight-year-old woman living with her son at the time of the interview. He was the youngest of the five children she had reared. Mrs. Metcalf had worked as a housekeeper in private homes, but she was on welfare when interviewed. She was separated from the husband who had first raped her when she was in her early or mid-thirties. Mrs. Metcalf said that her husband had forced sex on her from 2–5 times over a period of 3 years, and had been physically violent toward her 6–10 times over a period of 19 years.

It was more like a wrestling match. "No, I don't want to." "Yes, you are going to do it." I ended up with bruises. "I'm your husband, you have to," he said. The most upsetting time was when he bruised my legs and tore off my nightgown. It scared me. I was sleeping when it started. When I woke up I tried to get away from him. As I was leaving, he grabbed my nightgown, caught my legs, and was squeezing them. I broke away and went to the children's room. He didn't follow me there.

Verbal threats? He threatened my life several times. He said, "You do as I say or I'll kill you." It was plain and simple. I'd usually manage to get where people were.

What brought it to an end? I'd usually get away, but if I saw I couldn't, I wouldn't resist. For a long time I thought you couldn't reproach your husband. *What brought it to an end?* We separated.

How upset? Extremely upset. *How much effect on your life?* A great effect. I don't trust men very much. It takes me a long time to have any faith. *Was there other physical violence?* We were arguing and when I turned around he flung me across the room. I tumbled over several pieces of furniture. The impact of the fall blew the wind out of me. Then he stomped me with his foot and punctured my lung.*

Both Mrs. Metcalf and her husband articulated complementary patriarchal ideas. He said, "I'm your husband, you have to"; she said, "For a long time I thought you couldn't reproach your husband."

Power Rape—To Force Wife Not to Be Upset

Mrs. Foster was twenty-five years old at the time of the interview. She was separated from the husband who raped her, and working full-time as a recruiter for a market research firm. She was childless and living with an unrelated woman. Her husband had worked as a geologist.

Mrs. Foster was first raped by her husband when she was twenty-two and was raped again from 6–10 times over a period of 3 years. She reported no other experience of physical violence from her husband.

---

*When completing the brief self-administered questionnaire at the end of the interview, Mrs. Metcalf admitted that she had not felt comfortable enough to answer one or two of the questions accurately. The interviewer specifically mentioned that Mrs. Metcalf had told her she didn't go into the full details about the time her husband grabbed her nightgown. When asked why not, she replied, "I'd just rather not. I want to put it behind me. I don't have to deal with him any more."

We had had an argument and I was very upset and his solution was usually at times like this to force me to have intercourse. Then everything was supposed to be ok. Each time was the same: he forced himself on me. *Did you feel physically threatened?* Yes. I was helpless. I couldn't do anything. I couldn't have refused. *Did he know you did not want intercourse?* Yes. Whenever he felt threatened he would want to force me to have intercourse. There were other times when I felt that it made things easier to give in.

Verbal threats? He'd say things like, "I'll go out and get it somewhere else," or that I was inadequate in fulfilling his needs.

How upset? Very upset. *How much effect did it have on your life?* Some effect. I saw he wasn't as gentle with me as I had earlier thought. I felt disadvantaged and put down. I still feel somewhat intimidated by him. He makes a lot of money and has a lot of power that I don't have. I'm afraid of what power he still has, legally and financially.

Frequently an argument precedes wife rape, and husbands commonly want to have sex after the argument, while their wives do not. The use of force to try to make things better is neither humane nor logical, but it is common among husbands with very patriarchal attitudes.

Power Rape—To Repossess a Wife After a Confrontation

Mrs. Stanley was a thirty-four-year-old divorced woman at the time of the interview. She had no children, was living alone and was working full-time as a receptionist-typist. Her husband was a taxi driver.

She was twenty-one years old when her husband first raped her. She said this had happened more than twenty times over a period of one year.

We had a fight and I went to some friends' house. I returned and was taking a shower. I was still upset, when he came into the shower. He started touching my body. *Breasts?* Yes. *Genitals?* Yes. He was trying to patch things up. I said, "I don't want anything to do with you right now!" He grabbed my face and forced me to go down on him. I tried to fight him off but he grabbed my neck and forced me. Then he turned off the water, grabbed my arm, and forced me out of the shower. I begged him to leave me alone, but he wouldn't. He then threw me on the bed and forced intercourse on me unwillingly. *Force?* He had me pinned down with his elbows on top of me while he had intercourse.

Other times when I wouldn't cooperate, he would hit me across the face or put a pillow over my head. I felt like he was going to choke me. I think I felt most helpless in the shower. I was really scared.

He was having an affair with a girl from Latin America. A friend of his told me about it. When my husband came home one night I asked him, "How can you mislead a girl and not tell her that you're married?" He asked me how I found out, and I told him. Then when I got into bed he tried to force me to make love to him. I told him to fuck off; I thought what he had told her was really lousy. He was stronger than I, and he sat up on my torso and forced his penis into my mouth. I bit it, so he got off of me immediately, saying that if I expected to keep the marriage together I would have to cooperate sexually.

He was also having affairs with other women in the building.

Kinds of verbal threats used? He said if I didn't do what he wanted, he'd choke me.

What brought it to an end? I couldn't take it any more. I just left. I'd left him before, but come back. This time I took some money and left the state.

How upset? Extremely upset. *How much effect on your life?* A great effect. I was very bitter—up until a few months ago. The men in my life have changed completely. I hated him [husband] so much. When I found out he was married again it made me feel better.

Other physical violence? He choked me. He also gave me a black eye a couple of times. One time was just before I left him. We had had a fight and he got angry and hit my eye. He also came to my job and pulled a gun on me because I wouldn't go back with him. They put him in the funny farm jail hospital.

Mrs. Stanley's husband's reaction to her biting his penis after he had forced it into her mouth might earn a prize for patriarchal arrogance (he said that "if I expected to keep the marriage together I would have to co-operate sexually."). His behavior is particularly outrageous since it was preceded by her confronting him about his dishonest exploitation of an-other woman.

One highly unusual aspect of this case is that Mrs. Stanley's husband was sent to the "funny farm jail hospital." Yet besides his pulling a gun on her once, Mr. Stanley was not nearly as violent as many of the other husbands.

I've focused this analysis of why men rape their wives on what ap-pears from their wives' accounts to be their psychological motivation to do so; I have omitted various social and cultural factors, such as their be-ing encouraged to do so by laws that deny that wives can be raped, and by values that equate wife rape with proper masculine behavior. But as I argued in Chapter 1, because the structure of marriage gives so much more power to husbands than to wives, it is highly conducive to wife rape. The wife rape described in Galsworthy's *The Forsyte Saga,* which Su-san Brownmiller has described as "the most famous marital rape in litera-ture,"[33] shows us both psychological and social motivations. In what Brownmiller describes as "the logic of Everyhusband," Galsworthy's sex-ually rejected husband "at last asserted his rights and acted like a man. In his morning-after solitude while he hears Irene still crying in the bed-room, Soames muses, 'the incident was really of no great moment; women made a fuss about it in books; but in the cool judgment of right-thinking men, of men of the world, such as he recollected often received praise in the Divorce Court, he had but done his best to sustain the sanctity of marriage, to prevent her from abandoning her duty. . . . No, he did not re-gret it.' "[34]

The notion of "manhood" in patriarchal culture is built on the suc-cessful domination of women, particularly wives. But why some men pursue this ideal by actually raping their wives while others do not, cannot be adequately explained by a sociological analysis. Nor does the psychological analysis pursued in this chapter explain it: we have no definitive answer to the question as yet.

12 *omit*

Abusive Husbands, Alcohol and Other Drugs

> We have consistently found that 50 percent of rapists were DATCO [drinking at the time of the commission of the offence], the great majority of whom were drinking heavily. . . .
>
> —Richard Rada, *Clinical Aspects of the Rapist,* 1978

> Abuse of all types is frequently connected with the abuse of alcohol. The statistics are remarkably consistent, showing over half of abuse incidents, either physical or sexual, as being related to alcohol.
>
> —David Finkelhor, "Common Features of Family Abuse," Unpublished paper, 1981

When reading accounts of wife rape and beating, one is immediately struck by the frequent mention of alcohol, and the frequency with which the women associate the occurrence of rape and other violence with alcohol. This is true of other studies as well as ours; for example, 29 percent of the wives who were raped by their husbands in West Germany considered the fact that "he was drunk/under the influence of alcohol" as *the* reason, or one of the reasons that their husbands raped them.

In between one-fifth and one-quarter of the wife rapes in our sample, the husband was drinking at the time of the rape (in cases of multiple attacks, this was so in at least one of the rapes). Almost one-quarter (24 percent) of the husbands who raped their wives were described in such a way as to suggest that they were habitual drinkers. Since our respondents were not specifically asked about the consumption of alcohol or other drugs, our data can be assumed to greatly underestimate the consumption of alcohol and other drugs.[1]

The relationship between the consumption of alcohol and wife abuse is a controversial one. Although the victims of wife abuse, along with the general public, believe there is a causal relationship between the consumption of alcohol and violent behavior by husbands, researchers do not necessarily agree.[2] Researchers have acknowledged the strong association between battering and high levels of alcohol consumption; however, in her study of battered women, Irene Frieze pointed out that:

Several researchers suggest that alcohol is used as an excuse for battering (e.g., Bard and Zacker, 1974; Gelles, 1972). Others appear to see the relationship as ambiguous (e.g., Walker, 1979). Relatively few actually propose a direct causal relationship between alcohol and marital violence. The main supporters of this view are the battered women themselves and public opinion.[3]

Since no studies have used a control sample, it is impossible to determine whether heavy drinking is peculiar to violent men or whether many men who are not violent are equally heavy drinkers.[4] Frieze's methodology (described in Chapter 5) does not suffer from this limitation, though, since she had a control sample for her battered women.

Her findings were consistent with other research on battered women in that "there was a high rate of alcohol problems among the battering husbands, especially among the men married to battered women who had specifically identified themselves as battered."[5] Sixty-three percent (63 percent) of these women reported that their husbands were sometimes, usually or always drinking when they were violent, a much higher percentage than battering men married to women in the control group (31 percent).[6] In general, Frieze interpreted her results to suggest that "men who do drink heavily are usually violent to their wives as are heavy drug takers. However, . . . the most violent men were not necessarily the heaviest drinkers."[7] And in spite of this high correlation, as Frieze points out, correlation does not prove causation.

Frieze has suggested five ways in which alcohol and drugs may be related to violence in marriage.

(1) Some of the husbands have problems with impulse control and their violence is attributable to their disturbed personalities rather than to their drinking. In fact, the drinking is a symptom of this poor impulse control. Hence, treatment for alcohol abuse would probably have little effect.

(2) With some husbands, the alcohol problems seemed to be more pervasive than the violence. Frieze argued that treatment for alcoholism would likely help greatly in preventing the violent behavior of these men.

(3) Some husbands and their wives argued a great deal when drinking but were not especially heavy drinkers and were not violent.

(4) The fourth pattern of male violence was related to drug taking. Frieze did not make this relationship clear; she only noted that it has been little discussed in the literature and deserves further study.

(5) Finally, Frieze mentioned that "we found some cases of women

who were violent when drinking or when taking drugs but whose husbands were not violent except in self-defense." However, she went on to point out that "little physical damage occurred in these marriages. The severe violence was nearly always associated with male violence."[8]

The results of our study don't allow us to evaluate or even to illustrate patterns (3) and (5) since we did not ask about marriages in which there was no physical violence. Nor did we ask about marriages in which only the wife was violent. Drugs were mentioned very rarely in connection with wife abuse as compared with alcohol in our study. In only two cases did victims of wife rape specifically mention that their husbands were taking drugs other than alcohol at the time of the rape, and in only one case was a husband mentioned as habitually on drugs.*

Frieze's distinction between patterns (1) and (2) is particularly helpful because it separates cases in which alcohol abuse is and is not the main cause of the husband's violence. Though this distinction is difficult to apply to our cases, it is worthwhile to try to look at them in its light.

HUSBAND-RAPISTS UNDER INFLUENCE OF DRUGS

Mrs. Ingram was fifty-six at the time of the interview, separated from her husband and living alone. She had raised three children. She was keeping house at the time but had worked as a sales clerk. The husband from whom she was separated had been unemployed, and she had supported him.

Mrs. Ingram's husband had raped her one time. He had also slapped her once on a different occasion.

I married a man twenty years younger than myself. I was angry because he was staying away so much, so I wasn't going to give in to him. But he threatened to kill me if I didn't give in to him. He said, "You better not try to get away or I will kill you." He was on something. His eyes were glazed. We were sitting on the couch. He had his leg hooked over my leg. I tried to get away, but I couldn't. He got me on the floor. He was babbling. *Intercourse?* Yes, he forced intercourse on me. He held me around the throat and pinned me down with his body. After he got his way he was all right.

How upset? Somewhat upset. *How much effect on your life?* A little effect.

Other physical violence? Once he came home and I asked where he had been, and he slapped me.

Mrs. Bloom was twenty-eight at the time of the interview. She was separated from her husband and living with her three children. She was

---

*In two cases the wives themselves were on drugs at the time. In one of these cases the husband forced drugs on his wife.

In only two cases was it mentioned that a husband was on drugs when he beat his wife. There were no instances mentioned where the wife was on drugs during these incidents.

keeping house but had previously worked as a typist. Her husband had worked as a warehouseman. However, Mrs. Bloom also said that he had been in and out of jobs, and that she had supported him when he was unemployed.

Mrs. Bloom said her husband had forced sex on her more than twenty times over a period of one and a half years. He had been violent toward her from 6–10 times over a period of 3 to 4 months.

He started taking Bennies and then shooting speed. He expected me to have sex for six hours at a time every time he got loaded on uppers. It was the main reason why I left him. *Physical force?* Yes, he'd get out of his mind. He also forced me to take dope—to shoot it. We'd be in the bedroom for six to seven hours. I'd wind up sore. *Sex?* Vaginal intercourse. He'd try to get me to do it orally. *Fellatio?* Yes.

What brought it to an end? He got really doped up and tried to rape my sister. After that, I left him.

How upset? Extremely upset. *How much effect on your life?* Some effect. I stay away from guys who take dope. I never got married again. I keep putting off legal divorce as a way out of a relationship with the father of my second son. I don't want to get tied down again.

Other physical violence? He'd be on uppers or drunk, and we'd get into an argument and he'd slap me a couple of times. *More than once at any given time?* No, because I used to leave.

WIFE ABUSE NOT CAUSED BY ALCOHOL ABUSE

Mrs. Judd was forty-nine and divorced at the time of the interview. She was childless, living alone, and working full-time as a salesperson. The husband who raped her was a butcher.

Mrs. Judd was twenty-two years old when her husband first raped her. She said that he raped her more than twenty times over a period of two years, and gave the same frequency and duration for his other physical violence.

He drank a lot, and he got violent when drunk. He outweighed me by two hundred pounds. He got me to do what he wanted because of his size. *Force?* Yes, that's why we're no longer married. *Most upsetting time?* I can't tell you about the most upsetting time. They were all upsetting. Well, I guess the most upsetting is when he tore out my diaphragm and said, "I'm going to make you stay with me." He was a big man, stronger than I was, and he did what he wanted. He forced himself on me. *Vaginal intercourse?* Yes. Sometimes he slugged me, but when he forced me sexually, it was regular sex. *Did you resist?* No, I never even had the chance to resist, he was so strong. *How did he tear your diaphragm out?* He just reached in and tore it out. He had me down so I couldn't get up.

He said he was jealous that other men would look at me. But I was never a pretty woman, so I couldn't believe that. The very night we married, I knew it was wrong. He was not violent at that time, but just the way he spoke was upsetting. *How?* We invited friends over but he said they were *my* friends. Later he saw to it that I didn't have any friends.

Verbal threats? He reduced my character any time he could. One time he locked me out of the house. The time I told you about he probably threatened to hit me.

Weapon? He was a butcher, so he had a knife. He never meant to kill me, but he threatened me with it.

What brought it to an end? I wouldn't take any more. *Divorce?* Yes.

How upset? Very upset. *How much effect on your life?* A little effect. It kept me from remarrying; it made me look very carefully at other men.

Other physical violence? Yes. *Which time was most upsetting?* The time he tore my diaphragm out. Another time he cut me with a knife. Actually, he *meant* to use it on somebody else, and I stepped in front of him. Had I not stepped in front, he would have done major harm to the other person.

Were you cut? Yes, but it wasn't serious. *Anything else?* He bruised me sometimes when he hit me. *When he hit you?* Oh, that happened very often, whenever he was annoyed with me for thinking other men were looking at me.

Mrs. Judd seems to need to discount the impact of her husband's violent behavior. For one thing, she admits that the wife rape was responsible for her divorcing him ("That's why we're no longer married."). Few women would regard divorce as having little effect on their lives. But we have seen that Mrs. Judd is not alone in her desire to discount the trauma. Most often it seems to be women who are still living with the husbands who raped them who discount the experience. Mrs. Judd, however, is an exception to this.

Mrs. Judd attributed her husband's violence to his drinking. However, it seems that aside from his violence he was an excessively jealous man, who "reduced my character any time he could." He appears to be a classic type of battering husband who is tyrannical and uses coercion to get his way, and to show who is boss. Were he to have given up alcohol, it is quite possible that his violence would have decreased, but it is unlikely that he would have stopped being tyrannical and abusive in other ways.

While alcohol seems to undermine some men's capacity to be effectively violent, with others it has quite the opposite consequence. This difference may well be due merely to the degree of the husband's drunkenness. Whether or not this is the case, alcohol caused Mrs. Upton's husband to become relatively ineffectual.

Although Mrs. Upton's unwanted sexual experiences with her second husband did not meet our definition of rape, they are relevant to the subject at hand—the relationship between alcohol and the abuse of wives. Mrs. Upton described her husband as an alcoholic, but it seems most unlikely that the abuse of alcohol was the cause of his other abusive behavior toward her.

Mrs. Upton said that unwanted sexual experiences with this husband had occurred more than twenty times over a period of six years.

I had sex against my will, when I didn't want to be bothered with him. *Physical force?* Yes. He was into sadomasochistic trips. *The most upsetting time?* It was when he brought a male lover home with him. I was forced. We were all three in the same bed together. This was under the threat that he would be very violent. I was threatened and warned not to leave the bed. Only he and the other person did anything—I faced the other way. Other times he brought people into the house—strangers—both male and female. He always wanted both of us to relate to them but it was really for him. *S and M?* Yeah, as well as bisexual stuff. He also molested his own daughter.

Forced you to do S and M? He tried, but he wasn't strong enough. He was an alcoholic so it was easy to get away. He'd swing and miss. We belonged to clubs that switched partners, etc. He'd try tying me up and I'd end up beating his ass. I just wasn't afraid of him. *Was the club a mutual decision?* Yeah, in the beginning it was a try at making a marriage that wasn't working work. It was suggested by a psychiatrist.

What brought it to an end? I divorced him.

Verbal threats? That he'd hurt me. His brother was a detective in the police force and he threatened to take the kids away.

Physical force? He tried but was unable. He has to be one of the weakest men I've ever met.

How upset? Very upset—somewhat upset—it fluctuated. *How much effect on your life?* A little effect.

Other physical violence? He tried to be violent but his attempts were so feeble. He'd slap me or knock me down if he caught me off guard. He also threatened me with a knife once.

Despite her husband's largely ineffectual attempts at violence, Mrs. Upton said that he had been physically violent toward her from 2–5 times over a period of six years. Several other victims of husband violence related that alcohol rendered their husband's violence harmless or at least less harmful, but Mrs. Upton seems to be a little inconsistent about this. On the one hand, she said that "he tried but was unable" to use physical force; on the other hand, she reports that he slapped her and knocked her down, and threatened her with a knife. In addition, she said that she had participated in unwanted sexual experiences "under the threat that he would be very violent." Perhaps she was intimidated initially and then found his bark to be worse than his bite. Finally, one of the most unusual details in this case is the suggestion of a psychiatrist that Mrs. Upton and her ex-husband join "wife-swapping" clubs in order to try to help their marriage.

Judging from the accounts of Mrs. Judd and Mrs. Upton, it seems unlikely that their husbands' violent and abusive behavior was caused by the alcohol. Alcohol may have played a role in their acting out their impulses, but it does not appear that were they to have stopped drinking, their abusive behavior toward their wives would have ceased.

Alcohol-induced Abuse of Wives

The experiences of the first two women to be described here (Mrs. Phillips and Mrs. Nolan) include abusive sex, but not wife rape. Both husbands were described as alcoholic. It seems apparent, particularly with Mrs. Phillips, that her husband's abusive behavior was highly related to his drinking.

Mrs. Phillips was a sixty-eight-year-old widow who was living alone at the time of the interview. She had raised six children and was retired. She had previously worked as a waitress. Her husband had worked as a bus driver.

Mrs. Phillips said that her second husband had been violent toward her from 2–5 times over a period of 9 years. The unwanted sex described by Mrs. Phillips did not meet our definition of rape, but it occurred from 11–20 times over a period of 9 years.

He was a periodical drunkard. When he was drinking, I didn't want to have anything to do with him. But I did—it was out of a sense of duty. Half the time he'd pass out before he got wound up [finished]. He was a real gentle person except when he was drinking. He was really Dr. Jekyll and Mr. Hyde.

Forced Sex? He didn't really force me, but more or less to keep him happy or quiet around the children—I'd do it rather than have him go somewhere else. Once I got him quiet, he was all right. Half the time he would pass out. *Unwanted?* Yes, it was. Otherwise my husband was a gentle person—and very gentle in his lovemaking.

We were married twelve and a half years. During the last nine years, he drank. He took liquor cures. He joined AA, but with him it was more of a disease. He was horrible when he drank. He was a different person. He'd drink and go blank; it was pitiful. With him it was a disease; he was a good man, a good worker. Finally it killed him.

What brought it to an end? He died from drinking. He got a clot in his brain.

How upset? Very upset. I didn't know how to cope with it. There was no one to turn to to get help.

How much effect on your life? A great effect. I never wanted to get married again. I worked to support my children. I had been married twice and couldn't cope with another one. Men were out. It was up to me to support my family. I became very bitter against liquor or anyone who drank. I had to get myself in hand after my husband died. I was very bitter and emotionally upset. I talked with a doctor and a priest and they helped me out.

One day I slapped a man and went home and cried. That was the breaking point. The man was drunk and it reminded me of my husband staggering up the street and I guess it was a jolt. I'm not patient with drinking people. I come away disgusted from my son-in-law's family. They're drinkers. I have to keep a tight rein on myself. I did one horrible thing after my husband died. My son, sixteen, after three or four beers, came home, out of gas, racing up and down the street. The police came. My son is quiet and meek. I told the police to take him away and put him in the tank with all the drunks. His drinking really floored me. It's my emotional handicap. I'm diabetic and I don't drink. I'm extremely sensitive around people who drink, that's all.

Other physical violence? My husband liked to pick fights when drinking. He pushed me around when drunk but he never touched the children. *Most upsetting time?* They were all upsetting. Once I tried to get his wallet. He gave me a shove and upturned the table. The police came to see what was happening. He said for them to take me! He left and went to San Francisco. He came back ten days later. And he wouldn't remember things; that's what got me. He shoved me down, pushed me around. I don't think he deliberately hit me. One time when he and a guy were fighting and I got between them and they both swung at the same time, they both hit me in the eyes. What a sight! I had two black eyes. Never again! They can kill each other. We were walking down the street, they started arguing and I said, "You're like a couple of kids, shut up," and I went between them.

Sometimes a drunken husband is ineffectual sexually, including an inability to rape his wife, while his capacity for other kinds of violence is unimpaired. Mrs. Nolan provides an example of this. The unwanted sex in her case did not quite meet our definition of attempted rape since her husband did not use force, or threat of force, nor did he try to attack her when she was unable to consent. Rather he badgered and cajoled her.

Mrs. Nolan was a sixty-nine-year-old divorced woman who was living alone at the time of the interview. She had raised two children and was working part-time as a salesperson. Her ex-husband had worked as a truck driver.

Mrs. Nolan said that she had had unwanted sex with her ex-husband more than twenty times over a period of ten years.

He used to drink. The drinking was why I got a divorce. I wouldn't say he raped me, but it was unwanted. *Force?* Yes, I guess you might say that. No, maybe you should change that because I excused it. Most of the time he didn't know what he was doing, and I just gave in. *Physical threat?* Not really, no. *Helpless?* It's an idea that you just accept with being married. It was no big thing. You put up with it. He'd be drinking and he wouldn't be able to do the act, and yet he'd feel it was his right to try. It was routine. He'd have the desire but not the starch! He'd try to consummate the act, that's all I can say to describe it.

We had an active sex life, very active. *Unwanted?* I was married and it was just one of those things. I must have enjoyed it, except when he was drinking. *Intercourse?* Most of the time it didn't result in consummation. After an hour or two I really didn't care much if it was consummated or not. I wished I could go to sleep!

In the final years he'd be out till 3:00 A.M. drinking nearly every day of the week. He said he'd be able to do the job if I'd help, and he accused me of not helping him. He'd keep on until he'd done what he started out to do.

How did this keep happening? Because I was married. It's a wife's duty, I suppose. *What brought it to an end?* Divorce.

How upset? Somewhat upset.

How much effect on your life? A great effect. It led to our divorce after thirty-three years of marriage. I've really had a grand life since. I've traveled. My life had been very narrow. It was work and home at night. I had no female friends. Now my life is much fuller. I have friends. I'm a member of [a large voluntary organization].

It did something to my relationships with men. I don't know how I act with men. I'm self-conscious with them. I usually have a boyfriend, but I'm not at ease with a group of men.

Was husband ever violent? Yes, in the last two years—because liquor got the best of him. He became paranoid. I got a black eye one time right before I got the divorce. I don't even remember why he slapped me now. He'd been drinking. The liquor brought out in him this persecution complex. I don't think he knew what he was doing and he was sorry the next day. He had slapped me on the face with his hand.

Mrs. Nolan said that her ex-husband had been violent toward her "only twice" over a period of two weeks.

Though Mrs. Nolan described the unwanted sex with her ex-husband as only "somewhat upsetting," she mentioned it in answer to a question about which of all the experiences she had had did she find most upsetting. More specifically, she said:

I used to get so tired. I'd have given anything just to be able to go to sleep. I'd sleep at the office just to catch up. He'd wake me by calling me up to tell me where he was, and then he'd call forty-five minutes later and then he'd come home. I'd have given anything for a good night's sleep in those days.

It is very common for the wives to describe, as Mrs. Phillips does, a "Dr. Jekyll and Mr. Hyde" change in personality which their husbands undergo with the consumption of alcohol. For Mrs. Atkins, the change in her husband's behavior with alcohol was less dramatic, but significant none the less.

Mrs. Atkins was a thirty-one-year-old divorced woman who was living alone at the time of the interview. She had no children and was working full-time as an interior designer. Her ex-husband had been a commercial artist.

Mrs. Atkins was first raped by her ex-husband when she was twenty-two years old. She said he had raped her from 6–10 times over a period of four years. However, she did not see herself as having been the victim of physical violence by her ex-husband.

I view it as being raped. He was drunk and obnoxious. He forced me to have sex with him against my wishes.

Which time was most upsetting? We had come back from a party and he had drunk too much. He became obnoxious when drunk. At six feet four inches and two hundred pounds he was quite powerful. We had left the party late and he insisted on driving. I had wanted to drive but he wouldn't let me. He ran off the road once. When we got home I went to bed immediately. He came in, got in bed, and wanted to make love. I wasn't in any mood to do that. He forced himself, by using his strength to pin my arms down. He started kissing me, touching me, aggressively grabbing me, all the time holding my arms down. I would turn my head away, and he would turn my head around to kiss me. I fought him for a long time. I tried to free my arms, but I couldn't. I yelled abuse at him, told him to leave me alone and to stop it. Finally, because it was obvious I wasn't going to get my way, I ended up just lying there. *Intercourse?* Yes, he had intercourse with me.

Experiences like this continued to a lesser degree on other occasions, usually when he had been drinking. He drank more than was necessary, and he ended up dominating conversations with others, which was embarrassing. And he wanted me to be more submissive, to listen to him—that kind of thing. He wasn't an alcoholic, but when he drank he got very aggressive. At other times he was a very nice man.

What brought it to an end? I divorced him.

How upset? Extremely upset.

How much effect on your life? Some effect. It was part of why I got a divorce. There were other reasons, but that was part of it. It made our sex life slightly unpleasant. I wasn't able to be really responsive to him sexually since I felt he had violated me. It has made me more aware of when a similar circumstance is possibly happening again. In a dating situation, if a man is into making love when I'm not, I don't continue the relationship if I feel he could potentially be aggressive. It's made me more aware of my rights as a person and in touch with my rights not to be taken advantage of in any way.

Mrs. Atkins downplays the impact of the rapes on her sexuality. While on the one hand she says that she wasn't able to be really responsive sexually because she felt violated, she also describes this as merely "slightly unpleasant."

Several of the husbands who might appropriately be placed in this category of alcohol-induced abusive behavior were described by their wives as "the nicest person when he didn't drink." Mrs. Freeman provides one such account. She was fifty-nine at the time of the interview, married for the third time and retired. She had previously worked for a large dry cleaning company.

Mrs. Freeman's first husband had forced sex on her from 11–20 times over a period of 2 years. Her second husband had also subjected her to alcohol-related experiences of rape and battery. However, her third and current husband was not physically or sexually abusive toward her.

He was the nicest person when he didn't drink. But there was many a night when he had one too many. He'd come home drunk and I'd be asleep and he'd try and get on top of me. He tried to hold me down. It was easier to lie there and let him do it and get it over with.

One time we were driving back from Tahoe and we stopped at a hotel. I got undressed, showered, and went to bed. He grabbed me and shook me and said, "Have a couple [of drinks] before we do it." He took his clothes off in a big hurry and jerked the bottom of my pajamas off. He held me down by pinning my arms down. Then he stopped, poured himself a drink, and came back and did it [had intercourse] again. He said, "turn over," so I turned over. He wanted to do everything. He hit me, left marks on my wrists, and bruises between my legs.

The last case is one in which the couple were actually separated when the most upsetting experience happened. The wife got back together with her husband after that, and their problem appeared to be solved by his quitting drinking. Mrs. Quinn was twenty-nine at the time of the interview. She was raising two young children, and attending school. She had previously worked as a social worker trainee. Her husband worked as an operator at a spare parts company.

Mrs. Quinn was twenty-six years old when her husband first raped her. It happened from 2–5 times over a period of 3 months.

We had been separated and I was still staying in the same apartment we had lived in. He came over one night real drunk. He can't handle drink at all. He started bamming on the door, and broke it down. He wanted to have sex but I didn't want to. He pushed me, knocked me down, and tore all my clothes off. I was hollering and screaming and wouldn't keep still, so he just slapped me across the face and made me have sex. *Anything else?* One other time he got mad and tried to jump on me. *Intercourse?* No.

Verbal threats? Yeah. He said he was going to kill me if I didn't let him come back.

What brought it to an end? We got back together and I told him he couldn't drink because he can't handle it.

How upset? I was extremely upset at the time. *How much effect on your life?* A great effect. I always remind him about it, but he won't deal with it directly.

The experience of Mrs. Quinn provides a clear-cut case of the problem of violence ending when her husband stopped drinking. However, there is no way of knowing whether her husband's problem was temporarily or permanently solved.

Perhaps wives find it easier to blame alcohol than to blame their husbands; perhaps many husbands would behave in the same way if they did not drink. However, the account by Mrs. Quinn and the others quoted in this segment of the chapter, provide a serious challenge to such an assumption.

Our data are not an adequate test of the usefulness of Frieze's five categories. Nevertheless, it seems that the distinction between men whose drinking and violence are both symptoms of poor impulse control, and whose violence would probably not stop if they ceased drinking, and those men for whom stopping drinking would likely lessen or even end their violent behavior, is particularly useful. It raises the debate from the oversimplistic polarization of views that "alcohol *is* the problem versus alcohol is *not* the problem," to the notion—not as simple as it sounds—that sometimes it is, and sometimes it is not.

PART FIVE

THE WIVES

13

The Victims of
Wife Rape

A woman who's still in a marriage is presumably consenting
to sex. . . . Maybe this is the risk of being married, you know?

—Charles Burt, John Rideout's defense attorney, 1978

"I think basically the reason that our marriage failed was that
I was not prepared for the kind of sex my husband had to offer. . . . I wasn't able to have orgasms when he was in me, and
this just drove him right up the wall. He was determined to
make me have them, but I couldn't. Sometimes he'd force me.
He would hold me down on the bed, and sometimes I was
raw, and it would really hurt, and I'd be screaming my head
off."

—Mrs. Downing, rape victim, *The Politics of Rape,*
Diana E. H. Russell, 1975

"Our marriage really deteriorated after it [being raped by a
stranger]. It was the end of my pedestal days. He approached
me sexually when I was still very injured, and I said, 'No,
please don't. Not now. . . .' His reaction was, 'I have rights,
and you're my wife, and as long as you're my wife, it is my
conjugal right. So don't fight me.' . . . When I saw that he was
determined to go ahead, I really couldn't believe it, and I
started crying. He proceeded, and when he was finished he
left the room and slammed the door."

—Mrs. White, rape victim, *The Politics of Rape,* Diana
E. H. Russell, 1975

Since the study of wife rape has only just begun, no theories have
been developed yet about which kinds of women get raped by their husbands.* However the most current thinking about battered women holds
that they are highly traditional women.[1] For example, battered women

---

*Irene Frieze has compared wives who are raped with those who are not, but as ex-
plained in Chapter 5, all but four of the raped wives were obtained from a sample of battered women. Hence, her comparisons are more revealing of the differences between
battered women who are also raped and those who are not raped, than of wives in general
who are raped by their husbands versus those who are not.

have been described by psychologist Lenore Walker, author of *The Battered Woman*, as "traditionalists" who strongly believe "in family unity and the prescribed feminine sex-role stereotype."[2] Frieze also reported that the severely battered women seemed to be more traditional, finding, for example, that they married at a younger age than wives who were not battered and had more children.[3] They were also more restricted in the places they went to and in the amount of money they had access to.[4] Because many raped wives are also the victims of at least some other violence from their husbands, we decided to see if perhaps they too were more traditional than wives who are not raped.

We devised our own measure to try to find out if the finding that battered women are often very traditional also applied to victims of wife rape. Our index of traditionality for married women was developed on the basis of three factors: whether the woman supported herself in whole or in part, or whether she was supported by her husband; whether she had raised one child, more than one, or no children; and whether she had worked most of the time, about half the time, or less than half the time in her adult life (see Table 13–1).

This measure of traditionality does not indicate the wives' general political beliefs, nor the degree to which they subscribe to traditional beliefs about sex roles, but rather, how traditional or non-traditional the women are by virtue of the degree to which they have conformed to the traditional female sex role. Just over one-third (36 percent) of the raped wives were quite traditional (11 percent scored 0, 8 percent scored 1, and 16 percent scored 2); approximately two-fifths (41 percent) were quite non-traditional (14 percent scored 4, 17 percent scored 5, and 10 percent scored 6);

TABLE 13–1   Traditionality Scale*

	Score
1. *Motherhood*	
Raised no children	2
Raised 1 child	1
Raised 2 or more children	0
2. *Work History*	
Worked most of the time during adult life	2
Worked about half the time during adult life	1
Worked less than half the time during adult life	0
3. *Main Provider*	
Herself	2
Herself plus some other person	1
Other(s) (not including herself)	0.5
Husband	0

*On this 0–6 point scale, 0 indicates the extreme in traditionality, and 6 indicates the extreme in non-traditionality.

and just under one-quarter (23 percent) fell at the mid-point of the scale. Hence it appears that, contrary to expectation, slightly more of the raped wives were non-traditional rather than traditional.

Similarly, when comparing raped wives with those who had been beaten but not raped, and those who had been neither beaten nor raped, there was virtually no difference in their average traditionality scores. Hence women with greater independence from their husbands by virtue of supporting themselves, working most of their adult lives, and having no children, are no less vulnerable to wife rape than women who are more dependent on their husbands. The same is true for wives who were beaten but not raped. That is, according to our survey, *raped wives are no more traditional than non-raped wives, and in addition, wives who are subjected to at least one experience of wife-beating are no more traditional than wives who are never a victim of their husband's violence.*

However, the traditionality of the wives does affect whether they stay or leave abusive husbands; the more traditional women (more traditional by virtue of having fewer resources) are more likely to stay. (The subject of wives who stay will be further explored in Chapter 15.) This finding is very significant, for it suggests the possibility that wife rape (and wife beating) can happen to any married woman, but that how she deals with the experience will be affected by how traditional she is. If this is the case, it would also explain the apparent inconsistency between our finding and those of other researchers. The battered wives described as traditional by Lenore Walker, Irene Frieze, and Mildred Pagelow, for example, were also women who had usually stayed in their marriages for a long time.[5]

A few examples of women who range from the most traditional·(by our measure) to the least traditional, follow. These examples should convey that a great range of types of women are raped in marriage.

Mrs. King was one of the most traditional wives.* She was sixty-two and retired but had worked as a secretary. She was one of the minority of women in our study who was still married to the man who had raped her. She had raised three children. Her husband was a foreman for a manufacturing company.

Mrs. King said she had unwanted sexual experiences with her husband from 11–20 times over a 10 year period, but that the forced (vaginal) intercourse happened only twice. The assault by her husband first occurred when she was in her early thirties.

*On the 0–6 point scale, with 0 representing the most traditional and 6 the least traditional, Mrs. King's score was 0.

It happened two times. One time we had been separated a couple of months. I was staying with my sister. He came to the house, grabbed me and demanded sex. Then he forced intercourse on me. *Describe force?* He was extremely insistent, and he threw me down. I could not resist; he was stronger than I was.

The other time we were out camping with the children. It was midday, and he forced me in front of the children. It was very upsetting to me.

Any other unwanted sex? Probably no more than usually happens between husband and wife. There were other things that bothered me. At the time I thought he tried to force me to do these other things, but I've realized since that those things were really more normal than I had thought. *Meaning of things?* Oral sex and anal intercourse and other things I had never experienced. I definitely felt they were abnormal at the time, and I felt a hate for him because he insisted I do things that were distasteful to me and that I thought were deviant. *Other things?* Putting objects in my vagina which I didn't want. He forced or put whatever he enjoyed into me. He worked with men and they were always talking about sex and he lost track of what love making is.

What brought it to an end? He accepted the fact that it drove us apart rather than causing the sexual liberation of his wife, and he became less sexual. His urges slowed down.

How upset? Extremely upset. *How much effect on your life?* Some effect. It made me read and study and try to understand the difference in our approaches to sex. We had lots of talks and sharing of ideas. Looking from his angle, it was probably a necessary thing because I had a prudish sort of approach because of my earlier experience [of sexual assault]. I suppose I was not as good a sexual partner because of that. But he tried to "educate" me in such a way that it only brought back the earlier roughness I had experienced.

Mrs. King herself relates her lack of interest in sex with her husband to an earlier experience of sexual assault. She seems to discount the effects of her husband's sexual abuse on her although he had raped her in broad daylight in front of their children, had forced objects into her vagina, and pressured her to have oral and anal sex against her wishes. However, she says all this was "probably no more than usually happens between husband and wife," and that these incidents only had "some effect" on her life, even though they continued over a period of ten years. A major reason for her discounting the effects may be that she largely blames her "prudishness," and identifies with his position: "looking from his angle. . . ."

Mrs. King's notion of norms appears to have undermined her own feelings ("I was always upset . . . until I learned this is not as deviant as I used to think."). One wonders how her ideas about these norms came to change. In general, then, Mrs. King reveals a great willingness to discount the trauma, as well as to tolerate her husband's preferences at the expense of her own. However, she was not the only one to adapt. She reported that her husband did finally listen to her argument that his sexual behavior was driving them apart.

As measured by our scale, Mrs. Williams is a moderately traditional woman (with a score of 3). She was fifty-nine years old at the time of the interview and still married to the man who raped her. She was working full-time as a nurse; her husband was a hospital security guard. She had raised three children. She had been raped by her husband once only, when she was twenty-three years old.

This happened within the first year of our marriage. Ordinarily I was very agreeable to my husband's ideas, but that day I had decided we were going out to dinner. When my husband came home he said he was not going to go out. He lifted me onto the bed and I said, "No," but he took off my clothes and proceeded to have his way with me, as they say in Victorian novels. He was much bigger than I, and I suppose I stopped resisting after it was inevitable. *Did you have intercourse?* Yes. *Did you feel physically helpless?* Yes. But this was my husband and I blamed myself for not being in the mood. I didn't feel I could resist because he was so strong. I was being forced to do something I wasn't in the mood for, but I didn't feel threatened.

It never happened again. I suppose I learned not to be so stubborn.

How upset? Not very upset. *How much effect on your life?* A little effect. It made me learn what was necessary to live together; I learnt not to provoke him. I wanted to push my own way sometimes, and I learned to be more understanding.

Other physical violence? My husband was overseas for three years as an infantryman in World War II. He ended up in a psychological ward with fatigue for a year, and even now he can't tolerate stress. The physical violence happened when I was pregnant with our first youngster. We had an argument about one of those little things, and he hit me on the head. It was an open hand slap. He knocked me to the floor and I screamed. It was unexpected. Women can be bitchy when pregnant, but I did not think he was that provoked. Eventually we discussed this incident and he apologized. I learned not to provoke him when he was upset.

This case makes it clear that the objective measures of traditionality used in our scale (such as, whether or not the respondent was a mother, whether she had worked most of her adult life or not, whether she or her husband provided for her), do not necessarily coincide with attitudinal measures (such as acceptance of sex roles, the double standard, a husband's right to have sex when he wants it, etc.). Mrs. Williams would be classified as much more traditional by such attitudinal measures than she is by our scale.

Mrs. Williams illustrates how women in patriarchal society are supposed to act and think. Instead of expressing anger at the rape by her husband, she learns the lesson that she should never say no. Similarly, she learns from his other physical violence to treat him with kid gloves when he is upset, and she sees herself as "provoking" him if she does not do so. Rape and violence serve to keep women like this in their traditional position of giving up power.

Both cases cited so far in this section involve wives responding to being raped by their husbands by trying to be more accommodating to them; these responses seem to be the exceptions rather than the rule. Mrs. Olson exemplifies a very different response.

Mrs. Olson was a childless twenty-seven-year-old woman, who was separated from the husband who raped her. She worked part-time as a waitress at the time of the interview, and qualifies as a non-traditional woman (with a score of 5). Mrs. Olson said she had been raped from 11–20 times during the last 4 months of her 6-month marriage. She was twenty-three years old at the time.

After a few months of marriage, we began to disagree. If I don't like someone morally, it affects me sexually. It got so that I didn't want him to touch me. Whenever he wanted to have sex with me, he forced me. I couldn't tolerate it; so I left him. *Most upsetting time?* I worked as a secretary in Iran. I came home from work very tired. He was waiting for me in bed like a lover. He came and hugged and kissed me. I didn't want this; I was tired. He started to undress me. He said I didn't want sex because I wanted someone else, but I said this wasn't true. The problem was that I had no feeling for him.

He took my dress off. His eyes were different; he was smiling, but acting pushy. He moved me onto the bed and held my hands by the wrists above my head. [Mrs. Olson demonstrated how her wrists were held together with one hand, with her hands clasped above her head.] I asked him what he planned to do and told him to stop what he was doing. I was struggling. *Intercourse?* Yes.

Did he try to get you to do anything to him? No, he did everything. I didn't even hug him. The problem was that two hours later he wanted to do it again, even though he couldn't [get an erection].

For a while I hated men. It was a bad experience for me. He would be waiting for me in bed. That's terrible! When I fall in love, it [sex] is nice. But the night before, we had argued. Then you feel it's forced.

He had trouble with his self-confidence. He didn't believe in himself. He had small genitals. I didn't realize that, but he accused me, saying: "You started arguing with me because I am small." He wanted sex with me to prove to me that he was strong.

What brought it to an end? I left him.

How upset? Very upset. I became crazy. *How much effect on your life?* Some effect. Marriage was my hope for the future. My hopes were gone. I saw it as a big loss. It changed me a lot; in some good ways and some bad. It made me depressed. Nothing was important anymore. I felt that men were nothing. I hate to look at men. I don't trust them that much. I was very dependent and now I am independent. I think of myself, no one else.

I married a second time. I tried to improve my spirit, to change my attitude. My second husband was nice, but of a different culture. I couldn't get that close to him.

Mrs. Olson was raped by force by her husband but without violence; yet the considerable trauma she experienced is quite vividly described. Her second marriage did not last very long, but she reported no rape or beating in it.

So, we have seen that traditionalism (as we measured it) does not predict which wives will be raped. The question then is, what does differentiate them from other wives? One obvious answer is that raped wives are the ones who say no to their husbands. Obviously, this is not to say that all wives who say no are raped. But some are. Perhaps many. We have no way of knowing the frequency at this time. First, we shall hear from a few of the women who wanted *no* sexual contact with their husbands.

WOMEN WHO REFUSE ALL SEXUAL CONTACT WITH THEIR HUSBANDS

Many women accept the notion that they have no right to refuse their husbands' sexual advances. The impact of the women's liberation movement may encourage a growing number of wives to say no: some of these women enjoy sex with their husbands when they are in the mood, but feel able to reject them when they are not. There are other women who never want to have sex with their husbands. These are the women for whom many people will probably have least sympathy; after all, what's a man to do if his wife never wants sex? Many people are likely to think that even if such wives do not "ask for it," they certainly deserve it.

Few would argue that in a marriage in which one partner wants no sexual contact, the other partner should accommodate by accepting celibacy, or by seeking sexual pleasure elsewhere right from the beginning of the marriage. Clearly this is an example of incompatible needs, and raises the question of why the marriage occurred in the first place. Sometimes the woman has had no choice; her parents may have decided for her. But regardless of who chose or chooses her husband, in most cultures in the world, particularly pre-industrial societies, there simply is no place for the woman who does not marry and have children.

While there is more tolerance of women who have never married and borne children in this and other industrial nations, women who do not marry are still often looked upon with pity or contempt or seen as sick or unfeminine. A great deal of pressure is still placed on women and men to marry in this and all other cultures. This state of affairs has been referred to as compulsory heterosexuality.[6] As a result, people marry who never should; others marry before they are ready. Some keep trying to maintain heterosexual relations when this may not be their true preference.

Mrs. Ashmore was forced into marriage by her father. She describes the brutal consequences that can result from a very sheltered and overprotected upbringing.

Mrs. Ashmore was thirty-four and divorced at the time of the interview. She had no children and was living alone. She was working as a self-employed artist. Mrs. Ashmore said that her first husband had raped her over 20 times during the 3 months they were together, and that his other physical violence had occurred from 6–10 times.

I was sixteen when I married. I was forced into the marriage by my father. Whatever sex we had was forced. I never wanted any of it. I didn't realize that sex went along with marriage. That may sound naive, but I was young! And when he first tried to do it, I was almost in shock.

We'd been married four days before he wanted to have sex. I said no because, as I said, I really wasn't aware that sex and marriage went together. He got me extremely drunk, but instead of becoming interested in sex I got deathly ill. He made overtures to me; he was feeling me, but I got sick to my stomach, and stayed in the bathroom throwing up for four days. He was banging on the door getting angrier and angrier. Finally when I was out in the kitchen he grabbed me, pushed me into the bedroom, pulled off all my clothes, hopped on top, and proceeded to have sex. I fought him, but I was too weak to fight him real hard. That was that. He didn't really beat me up, but he literally forced me. There was no way out of it for me. I really did not want it.

Anything else? He'd try to get me to touch him, that kind of stuff. The whole marriage, whenever there was sex, maybe once a week, it would always border on threatening. *Always unwanted?* Yeah. I didn't want to have sex with anyone. I didn't think it was for fun—only for babies, and I didn't want any babies.

Verbal threats? He would use verbal abuse, he'd say "you cunt," all that sort of stuff.

What brought it to and end? My father. I told my father that my husband was hitting me and he came and took me away from him.

How upset? Extremely upset. *How much effect on your life?* A great effect. It caused me to be paranoid. I haven't been able to flow and enjoy a lot of things. It made me very uptight and frigid for a long time during my younger years. During my later teens and most of my twenties I was sexually a fiasco! It wasn't until recently that I got out of this traumatic sexual existence.

Other physical violence? There were a couple of times we had fights and he'd knock me around. He'd tear my clothes. He punched me and knocked me down on the ground. That, and his being verbally abusive. In those days nothing could have been more shocking to me because I'd been so sheltered from that kind of thing.

Other physical violence? He threw things at me. He hit me with a radio once which cut my leg.

Despite the fact that force rather than violence was used to achieve the rape, the trauma of these experiences is quite evident. This is one of the many cases where rape seems to be a far greater problem than the other physical violence. However, it was the hitting rather than the rape that Mrs. Ashmore told her father about, and that led to her rescue. Difficult as many women find it to talk about being beaten, to talk about rape is often felt to be impossible. There is no way of knowing if her father would have been as supportive had she reported the rape incidents instead.

Mrs. Ashmore is one of only two women out of eighty-seven who was raped by more than one husband. Her first marriage involved rape and beating; her second marriage, neither; her third marriage, both.

Mrs. Goodwin's experience provides another example of a fifteen-year-old girl who was not ready for sex when she married. Mrs. Goodwin's sister legitimized her dislike of sex with her husband by saying that it wasn't normal for him to want it so often; only then was she willing to refuse him, and this in turn is "when the fights started."

Mrs. Goodwin was a sixty-three-year-old widow who was living with relatives at the time of the interview. She had raised two children and when employed, had worked as a chambermaid. Mrs. Goodwin said that her husband had forced intercourse on her more than twenty times over a period of five years.

Almost always it was against my will. I was young—fifteen years old—and I'd get scared. He'd get insane. He'd get angry and even want to hit me. *Forced sex?* Yes. *Most upsetting time?* He'd always bother me about the same. I'd cry a lot and get very upset. *What would he do?* We had normal relations. *Normal?* Vaginal intercourse. I was a normal young lady. There was none of that other depravity.

Verbal threats? Yes, he would threaten to take me back home to my parents. And he said he would break my mouth once.

What brought it to an end? We got divorced.

How upset? Extremely upset. Later, I wasn't that upset but at the time I sure was. *How much effect on your life?* It had no effect. I didn't know anything at first. But later I asked my older sister and she told me it wasn't normal for him to want to be on top of me morning, noon and night. When she told me it wasn't normal, I began refusing him and that's when the fights started. *How did it affect your life?* Well, I learned not to let someone do something if I didn't want it.

Mrs. Goodwin conveys a sense of superiority because she was only subjected to forced vaginal intercourse, not other kinds of "depravity." Her reaction reveals the additional humiliation that many women feel from "deviant" sex acts, even though the law has long viewed vaginal intercourse as the most significant and serious form of sexual assault.

Before Mrs. Goodwin's sister had provided her with a rationale for refusing to have sex with her husband, she consented presumably out of a sense of duty. This case illustrates how when sex-out-of-duty ceases, some women will be raped.

One might expect that only some of the women who say "no" to their husbands are raped by them, and assume that those who believe they must acquiesce to their husbands' sexual desires are never raped. But

there are times when some wives are in no position to consent, for example, if they are asleep, drugged or unconscious. And in some cases, rape is
part of a battering attack, where consent to sex is meaningless. In addition, the notion that men only rape when they are denied sex implies that
rape is primarily motivated by sexual need, whereas it seems clear from
the women's accounts that many of the men want to rape their wives as
an expression of anger or sadism or out of a desire to feel powerful. Some
reports show that husbands deliberately make advances to their wives
when they *know* she will be turned off: for example, right after a wife has
confronted her husband with her knowledge of an affair he is having, or
the couple are in the midst of a fight, or a husband has just humiliated his
wife.

WOMEN WHO ARE SEXUALLY TRAUMATIZED

One of the very significant findings from our study is that victims of
wife rape were much more likely to have been sexually abused in childhood as well as in their adult years—by people other than their husbands.*

Frieze also reported that victims of wife rape in her study more often
reported that they had been sexually molested as children. The majority
of the molesters in her study were close relatives, and "the most common
reported effect of this molestation was a negative impact upon the woman's adult sex life or guilt feelings."[7] However, Irene Frieze emphasized
that although these findings are statistically significant, over two-thirds
of the victims of wife rape did not report an experience of childhood sexual abuse.[8] Frieze also reported that many more victims of repeated wife
rape (nearly a third) had been raped by other men as well, in contrast to
only 8 percent of the women who did not report wife rape.[9]

Wife rape victims in our study, as a group, reported more experiences
of unwanted sexual intercourse in childhood; unwanted sexual experiences with a relative, an authority figure, or a female at some time in their
lives; and experiences that they perceive as rape or attempted rape, than
did wives who were beaten but not raped, or wives who reported no such
abuse by a husband (as we can see in Table 13–2). Wives who were beat-

---

*For example, the mean number of sexual abuse experiences with different people re-
ported by the victims of wife rape (excluding the experience of wife rape) is 3.01, almost
twice as high as women who were beaten by a husband but not raped by him (the mean for
these women is 1.69 incidents), and just over three times as high as the mean for all other
women who have ever been married. This association is significant at < .001 level. This
means that the probability is less than one in a hundred that the relationship between childhood sexual abuse and wife rape could have occurred by chance.

TABLE 13–2   Wife Abuse and Other Sexual Abuse

OTHER SEXUAL ABUSE*	RAPED WIVES (Sample size: 87)		WIVES BEATEN BUT NOT RAPED (Sample size: 75)		OTHER WIVES (Sample size: 482)		SIGNIFICANCE LEVEL
	Percent	Number	Percent	Number	Percent	Number	
Unwanted intercourse before age fourteen	24	21	8	6	6	29	< .001
Unwanted sexual experience with a female	16	14	8	6	7	35	< .05
Victim of rape or attempted rape (i.e., respondent perceives one or more experiences as rape)	46	40	28	21	14	68	< .001
Victim of forced intercourse or attempts at forced intercourse (not previously mentioned)	37	32	17	13	19	90	< .001
Victim of unwanted sexual experience with authority figures (excluding relatives)	52	45	32	24	26	126	< .001
Sexual contact with blood relatives	35	30	20	15	10	49	< .001
Sexual contact with non-blood relatives	25	22	15	11	8	37	< .001

*The relationships between wife abuse and these other forms of sexual abuse are all significant at < .05 level, which means that there is less than a 5 percent probability that these associations could have occurred by chance.

en but not raped also reported more of some of these forms of sexual abuse than wives who reported no beatings.

It is possible, as Frieze has suggested, that the association between wife rape and other sexual abuse may be partially because "men might rape their wives in response to their being raped by someone else."[10] However, while it appeared in Frieze's study that the men who raped their wives used rape by another man as an excuse to abuse her, this abuse often took forms other than rape. Frieze has tentatively concluded that some women learn to accept rape, and she cites as an example a woman who reported "being sexually abused by her father and grandfather both as a child and as an adult and being raped by her brother-in-law as well as her husband. For her, "rape is seen as one of the ways in which men treat women."[11] But it is unclear why the view that "rape is one way men treat women" indicates an acceptance of rape by these women, and further, why an acceptance of rape would cause a person to be raped. It may be that such a woman does not resist as strenuously, or does not try as energetically to outwit her attacker.

An alternative explanation may be that the long term impact of sexual abuse results in some women disliking sex. Frieze reported just such a response,[12] and she also reported that the raped wives were more likely to refuse their husbands' sexual advances than the non-raped wives.[13] It seems quite plausible that wives who dislike or refuse sex with their husbands are more likely to be raped by them than wives who like sex and/or do not refuse their husbands' advances. This is all the more likely if Frieze's finding that victims of wife rape use refusal of sex to try to get what they want from their husbands, is applicable to victims of wife rape in general. Women who use sex in a power struggle with their husbands, as this tactic implies, may be particularly subject to power rape.

The experience of Mrs. Tomkins provides an example of a wife whose traumatic experiences of sexual abuse prior to her marriage engendered extremely negative feelings about sex in general, including with her husband. He responded to her refusals by raping her.

Mrs. Tomkins was forty-three years old at the time of the interview. She was separated, living alone and had raised four children. She was working full-time as a clerk typist. She said that her husband had forced himself on her from 11–20 times over a period of 13 years.

It was just like rape. He forced himself on me. He hit me, then pinned me down and had sex with me. Sometimes he would come home after drinking and he would wake me up and force himself on me. He would hold me down and take it. One time he came home after he had been out drinking and he wanted to go to bed with me and we had a fight about it. He started hitting on me and finally I stopped fighting. He had sex with me and then went to sleep.

The experiences that resulted in Mrs. Tomkins wanting no sexual contact with her husband started when she was thirteen years old when she was raped by her brother-in-law. She described her response during this assault: "I was screaming so loud that I began to have seizures. He cried after he found out I was a virgin. I had to eventually go to the doctor. He had damaged the entrance to my vagina." In describing the effect of this experience on her subsequent life, Mrs. Tomkins said:

I'm sure I drove my husband to drinking because my view of sex is that it's dirty, obscene. I can't stand to see people kissing. After my baby, it got worse. I couldn't have sex at all. If the experiences hadn't been so close to home it wouldn't have been so bad. Men only have one thing in mind and that's to mutilate the body. I've been to several psychiatrists but it doesn't seem to go away.

After being sexually assaulted by a policeman when she was eighteen years old, Mrs. Tomkins said: "I was under a doctor's care for quite a while. When my husband tried to touch me I would jump out of the bed and start screaming. I will never get over it."

Then at the age of twenty-three the husband of a very good friend tried to rape her. In describing the effect, Mrs. Tomkins said:

I stopped having sex with my husband. I just couldn't get ready. I think that's why my husband started to drink more and more. I didn't want anything to do with men. I cared about my husband but I couldn't go to bed with him. He would come home and get in bed and I would hop out.

It is not difficult to understand Mrs. Tomkins' abhorrence of sex when one learns of her history.

An additional explanation for the higher rates of sexual abuse reported by victims of wife rape that emerged from our survey is that these women are more willing to disclose abusive experiences. Given common cultural attitudes toward sexual victimization (for example, that the victim must have asked for it or deserved it), many women are reluctant to admit such experiences to others, even today. Being a victim of wife rape or a childhood experience of sexual abuse by a relative is even more taboo than being raped by a stranger. We have seen many examples (in Chapter 3) of women who admitted that abuse by their husbands was the most difficult of all forms of sexual abuse for them to talk about. If a woman is willing to admit wife rape, she would probably also be more willing to admit to other less or equally taboo experiences if she has had them. Similarly, if a woman is unwilling to admit one taboo experience, she is likely to be unwilling to admit another. Our data support this notion.

In response to our survey, 44 percent of the victims of wife rape strongly agreed with the opinion that "It is usually helpful to talk about painful experiences," compared with 27 percent of women who had been beaten but not raped by a husband, and 26 percent of women who had been married but reported no rape or other violence by a husband. Similarly, 58 percent of the victims of wife rape strongly disagreed with the opinion that "sex is not a subject to be discussed," compared with 40 percent of the women who had been beaten but not raped by a husband, and 36 percent of women who had been married, but reported no rape or other violence by a husband.[14]

Finally, only 29 percent of the victims of wife rape agreed that "unpleasant experiences of *any* kind are best forgotten," compared with 31 percent of the women who had been beaten but not raped by a husband, and 41 percent of women who had been married, but reported no rape or other violence by a husband.[15]

It seems reasonable to infer that women who have been sexually abused and who feel comfortable about talking about it, even to a stranger, are more likely to find the topic of the survey interesting, and to cooperate with the interviewer during the interview, than women who have been sexually abused but who feel uncomfortable admitting or talking about it. Our interviewers rated the initial attitude toward being interviewed of almost half (48 percent) of the victims of wife rape as "very interested or enthusiastic," as compared with 31 percent of the women who reported being beaten but not raped by a husband, and 33 percent of the other women who had been married at least once but never assaulted; given the above point, this is significant. Too, almost three-quarters (74 percent) of the victims of wife rape were described by the interviewers as being "friendly and eager" during the interview, as compared with 64 percent of the women who reported being beaten but not raped by a husband, and 63 percent of the other ever-married women. Victims of wife rape know more victims of rape or sexual assault compared with victims of wife beating but not rape. These women in turn know more victims than other women who have been married but not beaten or raped by their husbands, according to our survey.[16] To personally know rape victims suggests that rape is an issue that the woman has been able to discuss with someone (or someone has been able to discuss with her). The topic is clearly not unmentionable, and the victim would not feel as isolated in having been victimized. This might result in less self-blame, which in turn might make it easier to disclose her experiences to a strange interviewer.

One of our findings contradicts those reported above: 18 percent of the victims of wife rape admitted on the self-administered questionnaire (completed at the end of the interview) that they had not felt comfortable enough to answer all questions accurately, compared with 11 percent of the victims of wife beating but not rape, and only 6 percent of the other women who had ever been married. This finding is ironic because it seems to indicate that the victims of wife rape were the most honest in being able to admit that they hadn't always been quite honest.[17]

WOMEN RAPED BY MORE THAN ONE HUSBAND

Although 42 percent of the eighty-seven victims of wife rape were married more than once, only two were raped by more than one husband, a minute number of repetitions.

Many researchers on battered women have observed that battering husbands and battered wives grew up in violent homes where they witnessed wife battering and were subjected to child abuse.[18] For example, Elaine Hilberman and Kit Munson, in their analysis of "sixty battered women," have written:

Life-long violence was the pattern for many of these women who gave remarkably similar histories. Violence between parents, usually the father assaulting the mother, paternal alcoholism, and the physical and/or sexual abuse of these women as children were described by half of the women. . . . Once married, the women found themselves with alcoholic battering husbands who also kept their wives and daughters at home, thus replicating exactly their lives prior to marriage.[19]

Women in our survey were not asked about parental violence or prior experiences of non-sexual abuse. However, the fact that only two of the eighty-seven victims of wife rape were raped by two separate husbands indicates that it is very rare for victims of this form of abuse to repeat "their mistake." Rather, it seems that almost all the women learned from the experience how to avoid this eventuality, either by not remarrying, or by choosing a very different kind of man. While this finding in no way contradicts those reported by Hilberman and Munson and others doing research on battered women, it does remind us yet again that one cannot generalize to all beaten women findings drawn from highly select samples.

Of 75 wives who were beaten but not raped, only 4 were subjected to physical violence by 2 husbands, and one by 3 (i.e., 7 percent). This is strong evidence that the responsibility of wife rape should not be placed on the women, and disaffirms the notion that wives might enjoy the experience (since almost all of them manage to avoid any future experience of it).

SOCIAL CHARACTERISTICS OF VICTIMS OF WIFE RAPE

The Social Class of the Wives

Just as many people would be more comfortable if they could believe all or most rapists were from a social class, racial or ethnic group, age group, or religion, other than their own, it would be equally reassuring if this applied to all victims.

Husbands and wives are customarily considered to have the same social class, and sociologists (and in fact the general public) have commonly
used the husband's occupation as the measure of social class. We have
seen that husband-rapists appear to be almost equally distributed by social class.

Although we have the wife's occupation at the time of the interview,
unfortunately we do not have that information for the time of the rape.
Forty-six percent (46 percent) of these women were working full-time, 13
percent were working part-time, 12 percent described themselves as
"keeping house," 10 percent were retired, and 20 percent were looking for
work, going to school, on welfare, or disabled. Responses of women who
were not working indicated that all had worked at some time in their
lives; 59 percent of them had worked most of the time, 13 percent about
half the time, and 28 percent less than half the time.

The current or main occupation of one-third (33 percent) of the wom-
en who had been raped by a husband was in clerical work, 26 percent
were service workers, 15 percent professionals, and the remaining 26 percent fell into other categories. In terms of social class, 29 percent had upper middle class occupations (professional, technical, managerial), 42 percent had middle class (sales, clerical, crafts), and 28 percent had lower
class occupations (operatives, laborers, service and transportation workers).[20] There were no differences in social class (as so measured) between
wives who had been raped, those who had been beaten but not raped,
and those who had been subjected to neither of these experiences.

The more traditional measure of social class (the husband's occupation) is a problematic one for us, since only thirty-five of the eighty-sev-
en raped wives were married at the time of the interview (and only nineteen of these wives were married to their rapists). Bearing this limitation
in mind, it appears that by this criterion almost half of the victims of wife
rape (45 percent) who were currently married were in the upper middle
class, as compared with 35 percent in the middle class, and 21 percent in
the lower class. As may be seen in Table 13–3, these figures are almost
identical for women who had been married but never subjected to wife
beating or wife rape. However, the husbands of well over twice as many
wives who had been beaten but not raped had lower class occupations as
compared with victims of wife rape (48 percent as compared with 21 percent), and substantially fewer had upper class (28 percent) or middle class
(24 percent) occupations.[21]

Education, which is less likely than occupation to change during the
adult years, is also often used as a measure of social class. Just over one-
quarter (28 percent) of the wives in our study were college graduates, over
half of them (55 percent) were high school graduates or had some college

TABLE 13–3   Social Class at Time of Interview
(Measured by Husband's Occupation)

	WIFE RAPE VICTIMS*		WIFE BEATING VICTIMS		WIVES NOT VICTIMIZED BY HUSBAND	
	Percent	Number	Percent	Number	Percent	Number
Upper middle class	45		28		41	
Middle class	35		24		36	
Lower class	21		48		22	
TOTAL	101	29	100	25	99	290

*Includes women who were beaten if they were also raped.

education, and only 17 percent had not graduated from high school. There were no differences between the education of these wives and those who had been beaten but not raped, or those who had been subjected to neither form of abuse.

Race/Ethnicity and Country of Birth of Victims of Wife Rape

Just over three-quarters of the victims of wife rape in our study (76 percent) were born in the United States. Of the twenty-one women born in other countries, fifteen were born in Third World or Latin countries, and six were not.[22] Of course race/ethnicity cannot necessarily be inferred from the country of birth. Canada, for example, has a sizeable population of Native Americans.

Researchers generally argue that Black women are far more vulnerable to rape than white women.[23] The National Commission on Causes and Prevention of Violence, whose data were based on surveys in seventeen cities in the United States, observed that 60 percent of the rape victims who reported their victimization to the police were Black, at a time (in 1967) when, at least officially, Black people were only 10 percent of the population (though the percentage of Black people in cities is considerably higher).[24] This enormous over-representation of Black women does not show up in our survey of wife rape victims. Nevertheless, a significant relationship did emerge between the race and ethnicity of the victim and whether or not she was a victim of wife rape or wife beating, or neither. By far the least amount of wife abuse is reported by Asian women, as may be seen in Table 13–4. Only 3 percent of the Asian women reported wife rape, 6 percent wife beating, and 91 percent neither form of abuse. The next lowest amount of wife abuse was reported by Latinas, 13 percent of whom reported wife rape, 9 percent wife beating, and 78 per-

TABLE 13-4 Race/Ethnicity of Victims of Wife Abuse

	WIFE RAPE VICTIMS*		WIFE BEATING VICTIMS		WIVES NOT VICTIMIZED BY HUSBAND	
	Percent	Number	Percent	Number	Percent	Number
Asian	3	2	6	5	91	74
Latina	13	7	9	5	78	42
White	14	61	12	51	74	313
Black	18	11	20	12	62	37
Other	25	6	8	2	67	16
TOTAL		87		75		482

Significant at < .01 level.
*Includes women who were beaten if they were also raped.

cent neither form of abuse. Fourteen percent (14 percent) of white women reported wife rape, 12 percent wife beating, and 74 percent neither. And finally, 18 percent of Black women reported wife rape, 20 percent wife beating, and 62 percent neither. While the rate of wife rape and beating is slightly higher among Black women than among women in other groups, the difference (though statistically significant) is small, particularly in comparison with the findings reported in other studies.

Age of Wives

The average age of the victims of wife rape at the time they were interviewed was forty-three years old. Almost one-fifth of these women (19.5 percent) were twenty-nine years or younger, 31 percent were between thirty and thirty-nine years, 19.5 percent were between forty and forty-nine years, and 30 percent were fifty years and older. What, then, about their ages when they were raped?

Females of all ages have been reported as victims of rape, from five months old to ninety-one years.[25] However, numerous studies show the high-risk ages to be from thirteen to twenty-four.[26] Our survey revealed that these are also the high-risk ages for wives; almost two-thirds of the wives who were raped by their husbands (64 percent) were raped for the first time between the ages of thirteen and twenty-five. Twenty-nine percent (29 percent) were first raped between the ages of twenty-six and forty, and only 6 percent were forty-one and over. The average age of the victims of wife rape at the time of the first rape was 25.5 years.

While 64 percent of the wife rape victims were twenty-five or younger, only 37 percent of the husband-rapists were in this same age group at the time of the first rape. Victims of extramarital rape are also commonly younger than their assailants. For example, sociologist Menachem Amir's

Philadelphia study showed 19.6 years to be the median age for victims compared with 23 years for the offenders.[27] Husbands are commonly older than their wives in marriages where no wife rape occurs as well. This age disparity is one more factor that is intended (not necessarily consciously) to bolster the superiority and domination of the husband over the wife.

Because many of these women were raped many times over many years, it would be wrong to interpret these findings as indicating that wife rape is primarily a young woman's problem. The findings show rather that wife rape most often *starts* when wives are still young.

Religious Upbringing and Current Religious Preference

Almost half of the victims of wife rape (47 percent) were reared as Protestants, as compared with 35 percent who were reared Catholic, 6 percent Jewish, 6 percent with no religion and 7 percent with some other religion. As may be seen in Table 13–5, this distribution of religious upbringing is similar to that of the entire sample, except that Protestants are slightly over-represented among victims of wife rape, and Catholics are slightly under-represented.

With regard to current religious preference, over one-third (35 percent) of the victims of wife rape have no religion. This large number reflects a trend toward secularization in the whole population, since 33 percent of the entire sample also have no religion. Twenty-four percent (24 percent) of the victims of wife rape described their preference as Catholic, 23 percent as Protestant, 5 percent as Jewish and 13 percent preferred some other religion. As may be seen in Table 13–5, this distribution of religious preference is rather similar to that found in the entire sample.

TABLE 13–5 Religious Upbringing and Current
Preference of Victims of Wife Rape

	RELIGIOUS UPBRINGING OF MARITAL RAPE VICTIMS		RELIGIOUS UPBRINGING OF ENTIRE SAMPLE		CURRENT RELIGIOUS PREFERENCE OF MARITAL RAPE VICTIMS		CURRENT RELIGIOUS PREFERENCE OF ENTIRE SAMPLE	
	Percent	*Number*	*Percent*	*Number*	*Percent*	*Number*	*Percent*	*Number*
Protestant	47	40	41	380	23	20	26	241
Catholic	35	30	39	358	24	21	28	257
Jewish	6	5	6	59	5	4	5	44
Other	7	6	7	61	13	11	9	80
None	6	5	7	69	35	30	33	305
TOTAL	101	86	100	927	100	86	101	927

Marital Status at the Time of the Interview

The majority of women (60 percent) who had been raped by a husband were not married at the time of the interview; 38 percent were divorced, 13 percent separated, and 9 percent widowed. Forty percent (40 percent) of the victims of wife rape had been married more than once, as compared with 39 percent of the victims of wife beating, and 22 percent of wives who had not been abused in either of these ways.[28]

The association between wife abuse and the break-up of the marriage is particularly evident when the marital status of the abused wives is compared with those who reported no abuse. As may be seen in Table 13-6, *almost three times as many victims of wife rape were separated or divorced at the time of the interview (51 percent) as compared with married women who had not been raped by their husbands (18 percent).* Victims of wife beating but not rape were equally likely to be divorced. This finding is telling evidence of the trauma of wife rape and wife beating.[29]

Maternal Status

Just over one-quarter (26 percent) of these women had raised no children at the time of the interview. Of the sixty-four women (74 percent) who had raised a child, 28 percent had raised only one, 17 percent two, 15 percent three, and 14 percent had raised from three to eight children.

We can better predict the likelihood of rape from the husband's characteristics than from the wife's; the wife's characteristics appear to be more relevant to how the raped wife handles the rape. For example (according to our survey data), there is no relationship between how traditional or non-traditional a wife is and whether or not she is raped by her

TABLE 13-6   Wife Abuse and Marital Status at the Time of the Interview

	WIFE RAPE VICTIMS*		WIFE BEATING VICTIMS		WIVES NOT VICTIMIZED BY HUSBAND	
	Percent	Number	Percent	Number	Percent	Number
Married	40	35	35	26	63	305
Widowed	9	8	12	9	19	92
Divorced or separated	51	44	53	40	18	85
TOTAL		87		75		482

Significant at < .001 level.
*Includes women who were beaten if they were also raped.

husband; however, the more traditional wife does handle wife rape differently from the less traditional wife, and is more likely to blame herself and stay in the marriage.

The data on the social characteristics of victims of wife rape reveal that wife rape occurs to married women in all social classes, in all racial or ethnic groups represented in our sample, in all religious groups, and in a great range of age groups. Aside from age, none of these social characteristics is very strongly related to the occurrence of wife rape. In these respects, wife rape appears to be very different from rape by non-intimates, as well as victims of other forms of violence. Most researchers agree, for example, that extramarital rape victims are predominantly Black and from the lower socio-economic classes.[30] For example, the National Commission on Causes and Prevention of Violence reported that 60 percent of rape victims are Black women.[31]

A particularly interesting finding in our survey is that wives who reported being beaten but not raped were more likely to be from the lower class, in contrast to wives who were raped. Hence it appears that wife rape, and possibly by implication other forms of rape by intimates as well, may be more evenly distributed in the population than other crimes of violence. If this conjecture is supported by future research, one explanation may be that the viewing of wives, and to some extent other intimates as well, as the sexual property of men, may be equally common in all social classes. For the majority of the population who are accustomed to believing that most of society's ills occur more frequently and severely in the lower classes, confirmation of this tentative finding would constitute a refreshing breakthrough in conventional thinking.

14

The Trauma of
Wife Rape

Rape is a man's fantasy, a woman's nightmare. Rape is all the
hatred, contempt, and oppression of women in this society
concentrated in one act.

—Andrea Medea and Kathleen Thompson, *Against
Rape*, 1974

"There's something worse about being raped than just being
beaten. It's the final humiliation, the final showing you that
you're worthless and that you're there to be used by whoever
wants you. . . . He used to boast about it to his friends!"

—Victim of wife rape, *The Politics of Rape*, Diana E. H.
Russell, 1975

[I]nstances of women who attempted to drown themselves
in order to escape domestic brutality were not exceptional
or uncommon.

—R. Emerson Dobash and Russell Dobash writing
about the late 1800's, *Violence Against Wives*, 1979

It is widely believed that wife rape is much less traumatic than stranger rape. The author of one article maintains that: "Many U.S. jurists agree that when a husband compels his wife to engage in sex relations she suffers relatively little of the psychological trauma incurred in rape by a stranger."[1] This presumption lies behind the more lenient treatment of husband-rapists than other rapists, written into the statutes in a few states that have seen fit to outlaw the marital rape exemption. (See Appendix II for detailed state-by-state information on the laws about rape in marriage.) This belief is also prevalent in other countries. For example, in Denmark and Norway, where rape in marriage is prosecutable, the penalty is milder when the woman has previously had a long-term sexual relationship with the perpetrator.[2]

The experiences of wife rape cited in this book show instances of wife rape that are not particularly traumatic; however, many more cases show wife rape to be extremely traumatic and sometimes life-threatening as well. Many different factors affect the degree of trauma experienced.

We tried to obtain a subjective evaluation of the impact of wife rape by asking two multiple choice questions:

(1) Overall, how upset were you by this experience—extremely upset, somewhat upset, (or) not very upset (or not at all upset)?*

(2) Looking back on it now, how much effect would you say this experience has (these experiences have) had on your life—a *great* effect, *some* effect, a *little* effect, or *no* effect?

Where data were available, the answers of victims of wife rape to the first question were as follows: 56 percent extremely upset, 21 percent very upset, 18 percent somewhat upset, 5 percent not very upset, and 0 percent not at all upset; and the answers to the second were as follows: 49 percent said the experience(s) had had a great effect on their lives, 28 percent said it/they had had some effect, 14 percent said it/they had had a little effect, and 9 percent that it/they had had no effect. It is difficult to interpret these figures in a vacuum. More about the trauma of wife rape is revealed if we compare these findings on upset and long-term effects with data on the impact of rape by strangers, acquaintances, friends, dates, lovers, authority figures and other relatives.

THE TRAUMA OF WIFE RAPE COMPARED WITH RAPE BY OTHER ASSAILANTS†

Wife rape is one of the more upsetting kinds of rape, as we can see from a comparison of the degree of upset reported for different kinds of assailants. Table 14-1 indicates that 65 percent of the women who were raped by a relative other than a husband (usually in their childhood), and 61 percent of women raped by a stranger, report being extremely upset, as compared with 59 percent of women raped by a husband, 42 percent of women raped by an acquaintance, 41 percent of women raped by an authority figure, and 33 percent of women raped by a friend, date, or lover.

---

*The final choice was put in parentheses because it was believed that sometimes this part of the question would be experienced by the respondent as insulting or insensitive. For example, if a woman has already described feeling devastated by an experience of wife rape, to ask her if she was "not at all upset" by the experience could be very alienating. It was therefore left to the discretion of the interviewers to decide when to read that particular segment of the question.

†As before, the term "rape" here includes attempted rape. Since it was only with wife rape that acts of completed or attempted forced oral, anal and digital sex were included, for purposes of making this comparison, these forms of rape will be excluded.

TABLE 14–1 Rape Victim's Upset by Relationship with Assailant

UPSET	HUSBAND/EX-HUSBAND		OTHER RELATIVE		AUTHORITY FIGURE	
	Percent	Number	Percent	Number	Percent	Number
Extremely	59	41	65	20	41	23
Very	19	13	16	5	34	19
Somewhat	16	11	13	4	23	13
Not very	6	4	7	2	2	1
Not at all	0	0	0	0	0	0
TOTAL	100	69	101	31	100	56
UPSET	FRIEND/DATE/LOVER		ACQUAINTANCE		STRANGER	
	Percent	Number	Percent	Number	Percent	Number
Extremely	33	96	42	73	61	70
Very	27	80	26	46	24	28
Somewhat	27	79	23	40	12	14
Not very	11	31	8	13	3	3
Not at all	3	8	1	2	0	0
TOTAL	101	294	100	174	100	115

Missing data: 40
Significant at < .001 level

TABLE 14–2 Long-Term Effects by Relationship with Assailant

LONG-TERM EFFECTS	HUSBAND/EX-HUSBAND		OTHER RELATIVE		AUTHORITY FIGURE	
	Percent	Number	Percent	Number	Percent	Number
Great	52	36	52	16	33	19
Some	29	20	23	7	44	25
Little	10	7	10	3	12	7
None	9	6	16	5	11	6
TOTAL	100	69	101	31	100	57
LONG-TERM EFFECTS	FRIEND/DATE/LOVER		ACQUAINTANCE		STRANGER	
	Percent	Number	Percent	Number	Percent	Number
Great	22	65	25	43	39	45
Some	32	95	32	56	40	46
Little	30	87	29	50	14	16
None	16	46	14	25	6	7
TOTAL	100	293	100	174	99	114

Missing data: 38
Significant at < .001 level

Table 14-2 shows that in terms of long-term effects, 52 percent of women raped by a husband and 52 percent of women raped by a relative other than a husband report that the rape(s) had a great effect on their lives, as compared with 39 percent of women raped by a stranger, 33 percent of women raped by an authority figure, 25 percent by an acquaintance, and 22 percent by a friend, date, or lover.

These data argue strongly against the notion that wife rape is less traumatic than other forms of rape. They also suggest that rape by assailants in intimate extramarital relationships (friendship, dating, lover) is the least upsetting (perhaps because fear of death or injury is less common in these situations), and is on a par with rape by acquaintances as having the least long-term effects. We shall explore further why wife rape is so traumatic later in this chapter.

When victims of wife rape reported that the rape had had some or a great effect on their lives, they were asked to briefly describe what these effects were. The results would have been very different if each woman had been asked specifically if she had experienced any of a list of effects. Data based on spontaneous mention considerably underestimate particular effects. Furthermore, the effects listed are only those mentioned in answer to one question; other effects were often referred to in the description of the rape. Table 14-3 indicates the specific effects mentioned by one or more of the wife rape victims who reported that the rape had some or a great effect on their lives.

TABLE 14-3   Percentage of Negative Long-Term Effects of Rape on Wives*

	Percent
Increased negative feelings/attitudes/beliefs/behavior about (toward) men in general	37
Increased negative feelings/attitudes/beliefs/behavior about husband	32
Resulted in deterioration in marriage, including divorce	27
Increase in wife's negative feelings/attitudes/beliefs/behavior about herself	18
Wife changed behavior specifically associated with the rape (e.g., getting drunk, never getting married again)	19
Increase in wife's general worrying, fear, anxiety, depression, withdrawal, general mistrust	16
Increase in wife's general anger, vengeance, desire to hurt	13
Negative impact on wife's sexual feelings (other than about specific sexual acts) or on her perception of her sexuality	11

*Only wives who said that the rape had had some or great long-term effects were asked to enumerate what the effects were. Hence, these percentages are based only on the wives who answered this question.

TRAUMA AND SUICIDE

Two of the raped wives to whom we spoke attempted suicide. Other potential respondents may not have lived to tell their story because of murder or successful suicide attempts. Still other severely traumatized women may have been excluded from our household sample because institutions of all kinds were omitted from our survey, for example, mental hospitals, prisons, half-way houses, and nursing homes. Mrs. Jackson was one of the two women who mentioned that she attempted suicide.

Mrs. Jackson was forty-five at the time of the interview. She had raised five children, had remarried, and was living with her husband. She was working part-time as a dental assistant.

Mrs. Jackson was eighteen years old the first time her husband raped her. The rapes happened from 11–20 times over a period of 7 years. Other physical violence occurred over twenty times over a period of twenty-two years.

Mrs. Jackson started by describing the attack that had upset her the most.

He was drunk. I was willing [to have sex], but then he got nasty and took an oak closet pole and chased me down the stairs. He was acting like a dirty old man. *What was he after?* I don't know. I think sex. He chased me down the stairs and caught me on the phone. I was calling my neighbor for help. He came down and hit me across the head. He broke my nose, which required eighteen stitches. I got out of the door and ran into the clothes-line pole. I went to my neighbor's house and they sent me to the hospital.

I was chicken and I would not sign a complaint because I was scared that he might lose his job.

Other experiences? In November I went up to my son's graduation in Boston. He [husband] bought me roses and fancy things. He proceeded to get drunk after my son's graduation. We shared a room with twin beds. I was tired; it was in the middle of the night, and I went to sleep. Then he came to my bed and forced me to have intercourse. I was scared after all I'd been through. I gave in. He weighed 175 pounds and I was scared of him. He took my clothes off and touched me.

Other forced sex? Oral sex. I do it to him, not him doing it to me. What happened in Boston happened other times. Any time he got drunk and wanted sex, I went along with it because I did not want to get hit or beaten. *Verbal threats?* He said, "I'm going to kill you," and he used a pillow to suffocate me.

What brought it to an end? I finally took an overdose of pills. I was in a coma for eighteen hours. After I recovered I let him send me to a school to become a nurse. Then we got divorced.

How upset? Extremely upset. *How much effect on your life?* A great effect. I'm not going to trust *any* man.

Mrs. Jackson's experience highlights again how difficult it often is to dissociate wife rape and wife beating. The most upsetting experience of her husband's violence appears to revolve around sex, yet it would not seem reasonable to describe it as an attempted rape since she said she was willing to submit, and since he did not attempt intercourse on that occasion. Also his violence toward her on other occasions made her too scared to resist his unwanted sexual demands, making these experiences rape by intimidation rather than by force.

Despite Mrs. Jackson's final declaration, it appears that she has trusted another man, at least enough to marry him. Mrs. Fulton also attempted suicide. Again it is impossible to separate the destructive effects of her husband's sexual abuse from his other violence. Mrs. Fulton was a forty-six-year-old divorced woman at the time of the interview. She had raised seven children and was living with one of them. She was working full time as a probation officer.

Mrs. Fulton was twenty-one years old at the time her twenty-four-year-old ex-husband first raped her. She said he forced sex on her more than twenty times over a period of eleven years, and she gave identical figures for the frequency and duration of his other violence toward her.

He degraded me and slapped me around. He woke me up when I was asleep and forced me. He pushed me, held me down, and slapped me. That's why I liked being pregnant. He wouldn't hit me then. Otherwise, he would abuse and force me.

He was a jealous man. He always asked me dumb questions like why did I look at him, and what did I think about other men. When I'd say something nice about a man, he would not say anything till we'd go to bed. I'd fall asleep and then he'd wake me and ask me all these questions while holding me down and making me look at him and touch him. He sat on me and forced himself inside me. [Mrs. Fulton became very upset at this point. She started crying and we had to stop the interview.]

Verbal threats? He used them against the kids. He beat me and the kids up all the time. With the kids he would hit them with a stick or use a fork to pin their hands to the table until they bled. He did this especially to the boys.

What brought it to an end? I tried to commit suicide. [Mrs. Fulton again became very upset. She said she ended up in a psycho ward.]

How upset? Extremely upset. *How much effect on your life?* A great effect. I have a lot of bitterness. I can't look him in the face. I had to force him to pay child support. The kids love and respect him dearly and that bothers me more than anything else. He's now remarried and he's become a minister.

Any other physical violence? [Mrs. Fulton was unwilling to answer this question. She was very upset and crying at this point.]

The last attack occurred when Mrs. Fulton was thirty-two years old—fourteen years before the interview. But she still cannot talk about her husband's abuse without repeatedly crying.

WIFE RAPE AND FORCED MOTHERHOOD

The women we interviewed were not asked about whether or not they had had any unwanted pregnancies as a consequence of being raped by their husbands, so we have no idea how frequently the trauma of wife rape was compounded by that of forced motherhood. Mrs. James was one of the few women who specifically mentioned this as happening to her.

Mrs. James was a forty-eight-year-old divorced woman at the time of the interview. She had reared six children, three of whom were still living with her. She was working full-time as the owner-manager of a small business.

Mrs. James was first raped by her ex-husband when she was twenty-three years old. She said he had forced sex on her from 11–20 times over a period of 11 years. Mrs. James' husband beat her up once only, and she reported the incident to the police (see Chapter 22). This violent incident had nothing to do with sex.

I had put my trust in him. Nobody told me I had to put up with someone who fooled around with someone else. I didn't want sex with him because he'd been with someone else, so he forced himself on me. He held my hands down—I'd be kicking him and pushing him away from me but he just forced himself on me. It happened many times. I told him: "If you fool around with someone else you can, but not with me too. I don't want to share you with anyone else. You wouldn't want to share me."

Then for a long time we had nothing to do with each other. Especially while I was pregnant, he never touched me. Every time I was pregnant it was because he forced me. He'd kiss my breasts and try to make me submit; if I wouldn't, he'd hold my hands and take advantage. It was like forceful rape.

Other unwanted sex? He always wanted me to have oral sex with him which I wouldn't do. *Did he force you?* He would have if he could have. Also he was always trying all different kinds of positions. I don't know where he got those funny ideas. He'd try to put his penis close to my face. I told him I'd hurt him if he tried that again.

He made me feel guilty about being pregnant like it was my fault. I felt lonely when I had children. He'd have sex with someone else to punish me. After the second child was born he had to force me every time. He knew when to take advantage of me—when I'd be asleep after I had been drinking—and every time we had a child. I am not ashamed. I just didn't want him.

What brought it to an end? He had an affair with my sister-in-law in my own home. I figured that was it—good-bye!

How upset? Extremely upset. *How much effect on your life?* A great effect. I vowed I'd never ever marry again. I'd never be in a position where men have authority over me. Marriage is license to do anything you want. You're not a whole person because no one respects your rights as a human being.

Despite the fact that this was not one of the more violent marriages, Mrs. James describes an extremely oppressive situation. She was repulsed by her husband's infidelities and did not want sex with him. As a result he raped her, and she became pregnant (five times from repeated rapes). Her husband then punished her for being pregnant by ignoring her and having affairs. His infidelity finally included her own sister-in-law. This last humiliation finally enabled Mrs. James to leave her husband. Mrs. James said that she would never marry again as a result of this experience. At the time of the interview she had been divorced from her husband for fourteen years, and had not remarried.

WIFE RAPE WITHOUT VIOLENCE

We have seen in earlier chapters that the impact of wife rape is not always so dramatic, nor the experiences that led to them as terrible as those just cited. The following two women experienced wife rape involving some force or threat but no violence, yet the impact still appears to have been considerable.

Mrs. Dudley was fifty-two at the time of the interview. She had raised one child and remarried. She was working full-time as an insurance broker.

Mrs. Dudley was twenty-two-years old when her twenty-two-year-old ex-husband first raped her. He raped her from 6–10 times over a period of 3 years.

It was like a rape except I was on the same bed. It doesn't give you much enjoyment. He was more physically strong than I, and I was his wife, so he did it. He had sex with me.

What brought it to an end? I made it so uncomfortable for him to live with us, that he left.

How upset? Very upset. *How much effect on your life?* Some effect, but only in my sex life. Unless I'm terribly anxious, I feel I have to provide for my [second] husband, but I'm not as responsive as I might be if it had never been forced on me. This hurts my husband more than it hurts me, unfortunately.

Other physical violence? The most upsetting time was in front of our daughter. He beat me around the kitchen. He hit me on the face with his hands, and on my back and front.

Mrs. Dudley said her ex-husband was physically violent toward her more than twenty times over a period of three years. Yet at first we can find it difficult to take her experience very seriously. She discounts her husband's abuse, and she even discounts the impairment of her sexual responsiveness that continues thirty years later. Mrs. Dudley also discounts herself by saying that this impairment hurts her current husband more than it does her—"unfortunately." Mrs. Dudley is a traditional woman who feels that "unless I'm terribly anxious, I feel I have to provide for my husband." She downplayed the initial trauma of the wife rape, saying "it doesn't give you much enjoyment." And we also hear her say the familiar "it was just *like* rape"—not that it *was* rape.

Unlike Mrs. Dudley, Mrs. Patterson took the matter very seriously, although her experience of rape by her husband sounds comparatively mild. Mrs. Patterson was a thirty-year-old divorced woman who was living with her two-year-old child at the time of the interview. She was working full-time as a registered nurse. She was twenty-five years old when her husband, who was working as a physician at the time, raped her. It happened once.

We were having a fight and he wanted to make love and I didn't. We were sunbathing in the backyard. I didn't put up any resistance after a certain point. I just lay there. He came over and started getting on top of me. First, I tried to push him off but he was obviously stronger than I was, so I went ahead and had intercourse. *Ways forced?* He used his strength. He pinned me down.

How upset? Extremely upset. *How much effect on your life?* Some effect. I wouldn't let it happen again. If it were now and things had gotten that bad in a relationship, I would have gotten out of it. *Any other violence?* Only once. We were having a fight and he was getting extremely frustrated. He struck me in the face—a slap—and I turned around and walked out of the room. He apologized afterward.

Mrs. Patterson rated her experience of wife rape as more upsetting than when she was the victim of an attempted rape by a stranger. She considers it a symptom of how bad the relationship had become, so bad that it should have been ended prior to this. If all women took such an experience as seriously as Mrs. Patterson did, the problem of wife rape would be recognized much sooner.

Rape in marriage, then, is no less traumatic than rape outside of marriage. Indeed, I believe that wife rape is potentially more traumatic than stranger rape, usually perceived as the most dreadful form of rape. As previously mentioned, wife rape can be as terrifying and life-threatening to the victim as stranger rape. In addition, it often evokes a powerful sense of betrayal, deep disillusionment, and total isolation. Women often receive very poor treatment by friends, relatives, and professional services when they are raped by strangers. This isolation can be even more extreme for victims of wife rape. And just as they are more likely to be blamed, they are more likely to blame themselves.

Much more is at stake for a victim of wife rape than for a woman who is raped by a stranger. When a woman has been raped by her husband she cannot seek comfort and safety at home. She can decide to leave the marriage or to live with what happened. Either choice can be devastating. Leaving involves all the trauma and readjustment of divorce, economically, socially, and psychologically, including feeling responsible for the suffering of the children, if there are any. But staying with someone who has raped you often results in a loss of self-esteem, unless the wife is able to effectively threaten or persuade her husband that it must never happen again. However, staying usually means being raped again, often repeatedly. As mentioned in Chapter 9, wife rape occurred more than once in 69 percent of the marriages, and in 31 percent of them it occurred more than 20 times. Since the victim of wife rape "accepted" it the first time, why not the second, and the third, and so on? We have seen how this happens with wives who are beaten. Being raped or beaten by a husband is likely to progressively lower a wife's sense of self-worth as the abuse continues. And the lower the self-esteem, the more difficult it is to stop the abuse or leave the marriage. A vicious cycle is set in motion that can lead a wife to suicide or madness.

A QUANTITATIVE ANALYSIS OF TRAUMA

In this next section I shall explore what aspects of the experience of wife rape tend to make it more or less upsetting. Though common sense would suggest, for example, that the more frequent and the more violent the experiences of wife rape, the more traumatic they would be, common sense is not always correct. That is why it is helpful to quantify variables of interest where possible, and test what factors are indeed significantly related to trauma. For example, Mildred Pagelow was surprised to find in her sample of battered wives that the more severe the physical injuries inflicted on them by their husbands, the longer they remained with them.[3] (Acknowledging that this finding contradicts common sense, Pagelow suggests that it may actually merely reflect that wife abuse tends to increase in severity and frequency over time.[4])

Trauma and Type of Rape

While there was no statistically significant relationship between the degree of upset and the type of assault, a trend is evident.* Sixty percent (60 percent) of the completed rapes (penile-vaginal penetration) were reported as extremely upsetting, as compared with 50 percent of the attempted rapes, and 33 percent of the other forms of rape (involving oral or anal sex). The relationship between type of assault and long-term effects was statistically significant but here acts that were attempted but not completed proved to have much less effect. Specifically, 57 percent of completed penile-vaginal rapes were reported as having a great effect; as

---

*All associations reported in this chapter are statistically significant at < .05 level unless otherwise stated.

compared with 29 percent of completed forced anal or oral sex; and 0 percent of attempted but not completed sex acts (see Table 14-4).

Although the numbers are too small to place great confidence in the trend that is evident, rape when the wife was unable to consent appears to be the least upsetting type of rape: 33 percent of these wives reported being very upset as compared with 57 percent of wives who were raped by force, and 67 percent who were raped by threat of force. Similarly only 33 percent of these wives reported great long-term effects, as compared with 49 percent and 50 percent who reported great long-term effects for the other types of rape. These findings seem understandable, since rape when one is unable to consent does not involve a battle of wills, nor the sense of being overcome. Rape by threat of force may involve a greater sense of powerlessness than being taken advantage of when one is already powerless.

Trauma and the Frequency and Duration of Wife Rape

The degree of upset reported by wives and the frequency of wife rape, as well as the period of time over which these attacks occurred, were not significantly associated. However, there was a clear trend: 61 percent of wives who had been raped more than once reported being extremely upset as compared with 41 percent of the wives who were raped once. The lack of a significant association may be due to the structure of our study: in cases of multiple rapes, the respondents were asked to focus on the most upsetting experience, but they were not asked to give an overall cumulative assessment. There is a statistically significant relationship between the long-term impact of wife rape and the frequency and duration of the rapes. As may be seen in Table 14-5, only 18 percent of the victims

TABLE 14-4   Long-Term Effects by Type of Wife Rape

Type of Rape	Great Long-Term Effects (Percent)	Some Long-Term Effects (Percent)	Little or No Long-Term Effects (Percent)	Total Percent
Completed penile-vaginal rape	57	25	18	100
Completed forced anal or oral sex, or digital penetration	29	29	42	100
Attempted forced sex acts including penile-vaginal rape	0	50	50	100

Significant at $< .01$ level

TABLE 14-5   Long-Term Effects and Frequency
of Wife Rape

Frequency of Wife Rape	Great Long-Term Effects (Percent)	Some Long-Term Effects (Percent)	Little or No Long-Term Effects (Percent)	Total Percent
One time only	18	32	50	100
2–10 times	57	29	14	100
11 times and more	61	27	12	100

Significant at < .01 level

of wife rape reported great long-term effects from a single experience, as compared with 57 percent of women who experienced wife rape from 1–10 times, and 61 percent of women who experienced it over 11 times.

In addition, 71 percent of the women who were subjected to wife rape over a period of five years or more reported great long-term effects, as compared with 50 percent of the wives who had been raped over a period of less than 5 years, and 18 percent of the wives who had been raped only once (see Table 14-6).

Trauma and Verbal Threats

Seventy percent (70 percent) of the women who were physically threatened while being raped by their husbands reported being extremely upset by the experience compared with 39 percent of women who were not physically threatened. This finding is to be expected. Surprising, however, is the fact that non-physical threats (such as that the husband would find himself another woman, or that he would leave her, or that he would lose his love for her) were the most upsetting. Eighty-three percent (83 percent) of the women receiving such threats reported being extremely upset.

TABLE 14-6   Long-Term Effects and Duration
of Wife Rape

Duration of Wife Rape	Great Long-Term Effects (Percent)	Some Long-Term Effects (Percent)	Little or No Long-Term Effects (Percent)	Total Percent
One time only	18	32	50	100
More than one month to less than 5 years	50	33	17	100
5 years or more	71	21	8	100

Significant at < .01 level

However, this difference between physical and non-physical verbal threats was no longer evident for long-term effects. Sixty-eight percent (68 percent) of the women who had received either physical or other kinds of verbal threats reported great long-term effects as compared with 31 percent who were not threatened.

Weapons and the Trauma of Wife Rape

Seventy-seven percent (77 percent) of the victims of wife rape whose husbands had or used a weapon reported being extremely upset as compared with 52 percent of the victims of wife rape whose husbands never had or used a weapon. Similarly, 69 percent of the victims of wife rape whose husbands had or used a weapon reported great long-term effects compared with 45 percent of the victims of wife rape whose husbands never had or used a weapon. However, these associations do not reach statistical significance at the .05 level.

The lack of a strong association between weapons and trauma is probably caused by uncertainty over what exactly constitutes "using" a weapon. In stranger rape, the would-be rapist's having a gun, knife, or other weapon is often sufficient to intimidate the woman. It is often unnecessary for him to use the weapon or even to threaten the woman with it; the mere presence of a weapon can be extremely intimidating.

However, many wives may not take a husband's possession of a weapon so seriously. Hence there is a less clear-cut relationship between a husband's having a weapon and his wife's being threatened by that fact. Nevertheless some wives are clearly intimidated simply by their husband's possession of a weapon.

Violence and the Trauma of Wife Rape

Seventy-three percent (73 percent) of the wives who were subjected to physical violence during one or more rape attacks (i.e., from hitting and slapping to beating and slugging) reported being extremely upset as compared with 48 percent who were subjected to no force or the minimal level of force (e.g., pushing, pinning; only four wife rapes involving no force were reported).

With regard to long-term effects, 86 percent of the women subjected to the most severe physical force (at the level of beating, choking, slugging) during one or more rape attacks reported great long-term effects, as compared with 75 percent of wives who were hit or slapped, and 31 percent of wives who were pushed or pinned.

"Excessive" Use of Force and the Trauma of Wife Rape

We attempted to determine whether or not husbands used more force or violence than was "necessary" to achieve their goals. Some husbands use force and violence to get what they want, particularly when they see it as their right to have what is being denied them. Other husbands use more force or violence than is needed to obtain sexual intercourse or whatever they are seeking, suggesting that they may be enjoying an excuse to be violent, or they may be obtaining sadistic pleasure from it.

In 74 percent of the wife rapes where it seemed that excessive force was used by the husbands, the wives reported being extremely upset, compared with 56 percent of the wives where it appeared that only the amount of force necessary was used.

Similarly, 84 percent of the wives who were subjected to excessive force reported great long-term effects, as compared to 40 percent of the wives who were not so subjected.

Physical Injuries and the Trauma of Wife Rape

Though women were not specifically asked about whether or not they were injured, some information about injuries was volunteered. Of the nine women who mentioned one or more injuries in connection with wife rape, 78 percent reported being extremely upset, as compared with 54 percent who did not mention any injury. All nine of the women who mentioned any injury reported great long-term effects, as compared with 42 percent of the women who did not mention an injury.

Reporting to the Police and the Trauma of Wife Rape

Only nine women who were raped by their husbands reported to the police. However, since wife rape was not against the law at that time, they reported being beaten rather than being raped. Of these nine women, seven reported that they were extremely upset and two that they were very upset.

Of the nine women who reported to the police, eight (89 percent) reported great long-term effects compared with 43 percent of those that were not reported. To what extent the long-term effects result from the reporting process and what follows it, and to what extent this association indicates that the wives who are most traumatized by the experience are likely to report it, is not clear. Likely it is a combination of both these factors.

Wife Rape, Wife Beating, and Trauma

We have strong evidence that rape in marriage can be extremely traumatic, particularly when accompanied by violence, and that it tends to be much less traumatic when not accompanied by violence.

Forty-two percent (42 percent) of the women who were raped but not beaten by their husbands reported being extremely upset by the experience; compared with 61 percent of the women who were raped and beaten by their husbands *on different occasions;* and 71 percent who were raped and beaten *on the same occasion(s),* once, sometimes, or always.

Eighty-six percent (86 percent) of the women who were raped and beaten on the same occasion(s), once, sometimes, or always, reported great long-term effects, as compared with 48 percent of wives who were raped and beaten on different occasions, and only 17 percent who were raped but not beaten. These findings clearly indicate that violent rape is the form of wife abuse most upsetting to these women.

When differentiating between women who were primarily battered or primarily raped by their husbands, we find the following relationship: 73 percent of the women who were classified as primarily victims of wife rape reported great long-term effects, as compared with 63 percent of those who were mostly beaten (but also raped), 60 percent of those where rape and beating were of approximately equal significance, and only 17 percent of those who were exclusively victims of wife rape (i.e., non-violent rape).

An attempt was made to use all the quantitative and qualitative data available to arrive at an overall assessment of how violent each husband was toward his wife, and to examine the connection between violence and the trauma of wife rape. The results showed that in 82 percent of the cases where the husbands were judged to be extremely violent, wives reported great long-term effects as a result of the rape(s), compared with 63 percent of the cases where the husbands were judged to be very violent, and 24 percent of the cases where they were considered only "fairly" violent. (This relationship was significant at the .001 level.)

THE TRAUMA OF WIFE RAPE

Using all the quantitative and qualitative data available, including but by no means necessarily coinciding with the victims' own subjective assessment of the degree of upset and the seriousness of the long-term effects, two of us working on the survey were able to reach consensus on the following assessments. In just over one-third of the marriages in which wife rape occurred (34 percent), it resulted in extreme trauma, 30 percent resulted in considerable trauma, 19 percent in some trauma, 7 percent in little trauma, 1 percent in no trauma, and in 9 percent of the cases the degree of trauma was not ascertainable.

This quantitative analysis of some of the factors that are associated with wife rape being more rather than less traumatic has yielded no real surprises. More trauma tends to result from completed rather than attempted vaginal rape; from rape by force or threat of force than rape when the wife is unable to consent; from the use of violence during the rape, particularly the use of excessive violence, rather than the use of force or no force; and from the use of verbal threats rather than no threats.

While not particularly surprising, one of the findings that deserves emphasis is that it was almost exclusively wives who were extremely upset and who claimed great long-term effects who reported their husbands' violent behavior to the police. Many men appear to be afraid that outlawing rape in marriage might result in a deluge of reports, including cases that are mild in comparison to other reported rapes. But our finding suggests that this fear is likely to be unwarranted. Instead we can anticipate that wives who report to the police are likely to be among the most traumatized by the experience.

15

Why Some Wives Stay

It has become a truism that our women are like dogs, the more you beat them the more they love you.

—Quoted in R. Emerson Dobash and Russell Dobash, *Violence Against Wives*, 1979

Like other dominated people, we have learned to manipulate and seduce, or to internalize men's will and make it ours, and men have sometimes characterized this as "power" in us; but it is nothing more than the child's or courtesan's "power" to wheedle and the dependent's "power" to disguise her feelings—even from herself—in order to obtain favors, or literally to survive.

—Adrienne Rich, *Of Woman Born*, 1976

"I said no, no, no, I didn't want to do it, so he [her husband] forced me. He took my clothes off. There were about six or seven people there. It was a very gross scene. Everybody was really appalled, but nobody would do anything to stop him."

—Mrs. Michel, victim of wife rape, *The Politics of Rape*, Diana E. H. Russell, 1975

Martin Seligman, an experimental psychologist, administered electrical shocks at random and varied intervals to caged dogs. By this process the dogs learned that no matter what they did, they could not control the shock. The dogs became helpless:

The dogs ceased any further voluntary activity and became compliant, passive, and submissive. When the researchers attempted to change this procedure and teach the dogs that they could escape by crossing to the other side of the cage, the dogs still would not respond. In fact, even when the door was left open and the dogs were shown the way out, they remained passive, refused to leave, and did not avoid the shock. It took repeated dragging of the dogs to the exit to teach them how to respond voluntarily again.[1]

This concept of "learned helplessness" has been offered by psychologist Lenore Walker as one explanation for why battered women don't try to free themselves from battering relationships: "Once the women are operating from a belief of helplessness, the perception becomes reality and they become passive, submissive, 'helpless.' "[2]

While this is a plausible enough theory, in reality many beaten and battered wives *do* leave their relationships, and often with little or no assistance from anyone else.[3] Nevertheless, the theory may be helpful in understanding those abused wives who stay with their husbands for a long time.

Another theory suggested by Lenore Walker to explain how battered women fall into learned helplessness behavior and why they do not try to escape describes the process as dividing into distinct phases: "the tension-building phase, the explosion or acute battering incident, and the calm, loving respite."[4]

This "cycle theory of violence" holds that the woman is most likely to flee after the brutal incident that characterizes phase two, but that it is at this point that the batterer is apt to behave in an "extremely loving, kind, and contrite" fashion. "He knows he has gone too far, and he tries to make it up to her."[5] It is also at this time that the men, who are so resistant to seeking help since they rarely see themselves as having a problem, are most likely to seek help: "*after* the woman has left him and he thinks psychotherapy or other help will enable him to get her back."[6] This unusual behavior on his part may give the wife reinforcement for staying in the relationship. Hence, according to Walker, "she becomes an accomplice to her own battering. The women interviewed consistently admitted, although somewhat shamefacedly, that they loved their men dearly during this phase. The effect of their men's generosity, dependability, helpfulness, and genuine interest cannot be minimized."[7]

The third phase of calm and loving respite after the attack seldom occurs, according to the findings of our study. I do not dispute that when husbands, be they batterers or not, act in winning ways, they are often successful in getting what they want, but I do reject the idea that this phase necessarily occurs in many battering relationships. Many of the husbands in our survey appeared to be without remorse about their violence, except if they risked losing the woman. I believe this phase is far from inevitable, and is most likely to occur if the woman leaves her husband or if he fears she will do so, or if she is able to enlist help that gives her more power in their relationship. At this stage the husband can not use physical coercion and verbal abuse to try to bring her in line because those are the very tactics that have resulted in her determination to leave. These men are in a less powerful situation in relation to their wives for a change, and they try to woo them back. They do not always succeed. When they do, the pattern is frequently repeated, but by no means always.

For women who are too broken to rebel, there is no such cycle, only continual abuse, as can be seen in some of the cases we'll consider in this chapter.

Only 22 percent of the eighty-seven raped wives in our survey were still married at the time of the interview to the husbands who raped them. While some of these women were widowed rather than divorced or separated, and others were not the ones to initiate the end of the relationship, nevertheless the fact that only one in every five of the raped wives was still married to her rapist is evidence that many wives do not in fact stay. Let us begin by examining some of the 22 percent of women in our sample who did stay married to their husbands.

WIVES STILL MARRIED TO THE HUSBANDS WHO RAPED THEM

Mrs. Warren was thirty-three at the time of the interview. She was working full-time as an administrative assistant at a university, and living with her husband and eight-year-old child. Her husband was an aeronautical engineer. Mrs. Warren said that her husband had forced sexual relations on her from 6–10 times, and that these experiences had occurred over a 2-year period early on in their 11 years of marriage. She appeared to connect these assaults with her husband's drinking.

I work full time outside my home, and sometimes I'm not in the mood to do it. Because it's a wife's duty, I submit. It's to please him but there is no enjoyment for me. *Most upsetting time?* One time is not more upsetting than the others. *Force?* Yes, he gets rough, especially when he drinks. He grabs me hard. He's ready to go and I am not. He sees I am not responding. He thinks by being rough he will perk me up. He grabs my shoulders and my breasts. It hurts. He puts his finger [Mrs. Warren motions to her vagina]. *Force?* Yes. But now everything's different. He doesn't use as much physical force any more. He loses his head when he drinks, but now he can't drink because it's bad for his health. In age, he has mellowed.

Other unwanted sex? He tries to get me to kiss and suck his genitals, but I don't like it. *Physical force?* No, when he sees I don't want to, he'll forget it. I have done it when I have not wanted to, to please him, but he won't force me. I say yes every now and then to please him.

Verbal threats? When I say no, I don't want to submit, he says, "OK, I'll go find me a whore."

How upset? Somewhat upset. *How much effect on your life?* Some effect. I never did enjoy it and I still don't enjoy it now. *Other effect?* I don't think so. It doesn't affect me, I guess.

Mrs. Warren said that "I never did enjoy it," which I take to mean sex with her husband. From her rather confusing account it seems that mostly she submits out of "duty" but that a few times when he's been drinking, mainly in the past, he has forced her. Whether her husband forced intercourse or other sexual acts, including manual penetration, is not entirely

clear, but we interpreted what Mrs. Warren described as forced intercourse.

The key distinction for Mrs. Warren is not the same as the differenti-
ation we make in our study between forced or violent sex and unwanted
sex. She feels she has to oblige her husband, including a treat of fellatio
"every now and then to please him," and her words indicate that feeling
compelled to make oneself do certain sexual acts can be as upsetting as
being compelled by someone else. However, Mrs. Warren, while saying
that she had been experiencing unwanted sex for the last nine years of
her life, also claims that "it doesn't affect me, I guess." This tells us how
limited her expectations of life, marriage, and a woman's lot are. It also
tells us a great deal about why she would stay in the marriage.

Mrs. Lind's interview is a study in evasion. Until the end of it, one
would never believe one was hearing from a victim of wife rape. Clearly,
she herself would not use that word.

Mrs. Lind was forty-two at the time of the interview. She had raised
two children and was working part-time as a nurse's aide in a convales-
cent home. Her husband worked in a mortuary.

The first incident of forced sex occurred when she was twenty-three
years old. Mrs. Lind said these experiences occurred more than twenty
times over a period of fifteen years. The first question about whether or
not she had experienced any unwanted sex with her husband yielded a
long pause. The interviewer repeated the question, and she replied as follows:

Not outside of the average. *Explain?* I'm not the most sexual person in the world
and there was some unwanted sex but never to the point where I couldn't say no.
But when I tried to say no, he would make me say yes. Here again I think my
feelings go with my husband's, though I have real feelings about this. It is very
possible for men to take sexual advantage of a woman. Also women take advantage of men.
Because I'm not as sexual a person as he, he has demanded it—as much as I
may also make demands of him. *Explain how sexually forced?* Just the fact that he has
been sexually aroused and goes right ahead even if I'm not in the mood or not
ready. I'm really a very tight person. I don't send out signals about sex. I was not
sexually communicative and my husband wanted the full gamut of sex, like lots
of foreplay. I really felt I didn't want to do this but I gave in to him. I think he
wanted to satisfy me and help me to loosen up more, and also to help his virility.
Did you ever feel physically threatened? Yes, but only in the sense that I was made to
feel inadequate. *It would help if you could be very specific. Was there force?* Yes. When he
would make me do things within our marriage that I couldn't accept. *Explain?* Men
are made to feel that they have to force women to have good sex. *Explain?* [Long
pause.] It is very hard for me to accuse my husband of forcing me, but that is
what really happened. *I know it's hard, but please be specific.* There were times when

my husband took advantage of my being smaller. If he really wanted sex, he would force me to have sex.

What brought it to an end? He's now fifty-eight and he's slowed down.

How upset? Somewhat upset. *How much effect on your life?* Some effect. I went to a psychiatrist for a year. I wanted to learn about it, but it wasn't too helpful.

Of all the experiences that have happened to you, which was the most upsetting? What happened with my husband. You are living together and want to have a satisfying relationship. It is more upsetting [than other experiences] because it's a more lasting relationship.

There is no way of knowing whether Mrs. Lind was reluctant to disclose her husband's forcing her to have sex to the interviewer or whether she was also reluctant to confront it herself. I'm inclined to suspect the latter, which would also help to explain why she stayed in the marriage. Her description of life with her husband contains a great deal of self-blame and denial, and many excuses for her husband's sexual coercion. If a woman is unwilling or unable to face her own anger about being abused, she is much more likely to stay in the situation. And if the psychiatrist she saw for a year had the sexist values of many traditional psychiatrists, this might well have contributed to her blaming herself.[8]

While Mrs. Nelson is able to articulate that she feels overpowered by the forced sex with her husband, like Mrs. Warren and Mrs. Lind, Mrs. Nelson also reports a low level of upset and trauma. This raises the question of whether these women play down the trauma because they are still married, or whether they are still married because they are not that traumatized.

Mrs. Nelson was forty-two and a student at the time of the interview. She was raising six children, aged from seven to fifteen years, and had previously worked as a clerk in a drug store. Her husband had worked at a gas station, but was on Social Security income at the time of the interview.

Mrs. Nelson was first raped by her husband when she was thirty-nine. She said he had forced her to have sex from 6–10 times over the past 4 years of their marriage, and he had been physically violent toward her from 2–5 times over a period of twelve years.

Did the forced sex happen more than once? Yes. *Which time was most upsetting?* They are all alike. I heard about him having an affair and I was upset at the time and I refused to go to bed with him. Then he would grab me and once or twice he tore the neck of my clothing when he grabbed me. He'd force me to go upstairs, and then proceeded to have sex. *Forced intercourse?* Yes.

What brought it to an end? It hasn't ended.

How upset? Somewhat upset. *How much effect on your life?* Some effect. It makes me feel overpowered. I feel I have a right not to do whatever he wants. I don't like to have to do what I'm not prepared to do.

Other physical violence? The worst time was around a week ago. We had had an argument and I refused to stay in the bed as usual, and I told him to go some-where else. He went out and had a drink. Then he came back and went after my throat. He held a knife to my throat and said, "If you don't, I'll kill you." After a while he cooled down. He explained that he was upset after all these years to think of having to start over again. He said that I had messed up his life. He talked and talked until after a while it wore off. He had never held a knife against me before.

Unfortunately the interview itself does not provide much insight into why Mrs. Nelson has stayed in the marriage. Her six children may pro-vide part of the answer. Also, Mrs. Nelson is on welfare and has only some high school education. She is currently increasing her options by being enrolled as a student, but as a Black woman, she has yet another burden of discrimination to deal with.

In the self-administered questionnaire at the end of the interview Mrs. Nelson wrote: "I was a bit uncomfortable to explain what had happened with my husband." Does this suggest some self-blame on her part? Cer-tainly, her husband blames her for his most recent episode of violence toward her. He held a knife to her throat threatening to kill her, but in-stead of apologizing when he cooled down, he told her that she had messed up his life. It is not clear whether or not Mrs. Nelson is able to reject his view.

When asked *Which of the experiences that have happened to you, would you now say was the* most *upsetting?* Mrs. Nelson responded with the incident in which her husband pulled a knife on her. Her answer indicated that she views this incident, unlike the forced sex, as extremely serious. Perhaps this helps to explain why Mrs. Nelson reports only being "somewhat up-set" by the forced sex, and "some effect" as a result of her husband's sex-ual attacks. A life-threatening experience is probably much more devas-tating than a few experiences of unwanted sex, even when forced.

In addition, the fact that she had been through many extremely trau-matic experiences prior to the rape by her husband could contribute to her finding her marriage a relative haven. Mrs. Nelson was raped by two strangers, brothers who attacked her together when she was thirteen years old. Later in the same year of her life a stranger who pretended he was a policeman and who offered to protect her attempted to rape her. She was raped by another stranger when she was twenty. Regarding the latter experience, she described herself as "extremely upset" and that it had a "great effect" on her life. When asked to describe the effect she said: "I had terrible dreams about it afterwards. It's something I wouldn't tell anyone—not the children or nobody else. This is the first time I've told anyone." Her distress about her husband's violence toward her must have been acute; for even with these kinds of experiences in her past she said it was the experience with him that upset her the most.

Mrs. Hill, another wife who appears to have down-played the impact of rape by her husband, was fifty-three at the time of the interview. She had raised three children, and was living with her husband and adult son. She was working full-time as a post office clerk. Her husband was a mechanic.

Mrs. Hill was raped one time only when she was twenty-six years old.

After we'd had an argument, and I wasn't in any mood for lovemaking, he forced me to have intercourse with him. *Force?* He sat me right down on the bed and then he got on top of me. I'm not very big, and he just rolled onto me and that was it. I was very bruised and hurt. It took me quite a while to get over it. Of course, he regretted it right after it happened. It doesn't hurt as much now as it did at that time. *Physical threat?* No, he just said: "You're my wife, and that's what you're supposed to do!"

Verbal threats? "You're my wife, that's part of your function. Is there someone else?"

How upset? Somewhat upset. *How much effect on your life?* A little effect.

Mrs. Hill's claim that she was only "somewhat upset" and that the rape only had "a little effect" on her life doesn't quite mesh with her saying, "I was very bruised and hurt. It took me quite a while to get over it." Even though the rape occurred twenty-seven years ago, Mrs. Hill implies that it is still a source of pain: "It doesn't hurt *as much now* as it did at that time" (emphasis mine). It seems perhaps that some denial of the pain might have made it easier to stay in the situation. The fact that her husband apologized and that it only occurred once are probably even more crucial factors.

Though Mrs. Hill prefaced her statement that "he regretted it right after it happened" with "of course," few women report expressions of regret by their husbands. More typical behavior on the part of her husband includes his "conjugal rights" argument, and his wanting sex after an argument, when his wife did not want it.

Finally in this series of women who reported low levels of trauma, Mrs. Thornton claims that she experienced none. A woman who is not upset by an experience will, of course, not leave a marriage because of it.

Mrs. Thornton was thirty-nine years old at the time of the interview. She was living with her husband and their two children. She described herself as "keeping house" but said that she had worked as a bank teller. Her husband was training as a certified public accountant. He raped her only once, two years before, when she was thirty-seven.

I was fast asleep and I woke up to discover he was on top of me. He was having sexual intercourse with me. He also got me to touch his genitals. *How?* He physically took my hand and put it on his genitals. *Else?* No.

How upset? Not very upset. *How much effect on your life?* No effect.

It appears that when the woman is unable to consent, significantly less trauma is evident than for rape by force or threat of force. In these rapes the woman does not experience being overcome; there is also less likelihood of violence, and even force is unnecessary. In addition, the victim is less likely to blame herself.

Mrs. Heller is still married to her husband, but in contrast to the previous five women she reports a great deal of trauma as a result of the rapes.

Mrs. Heller was forty-five at the time of the interview. She was living with her husband and one of their two children and described herself as "keeping house." She had worked previously as a secretary. Her husband was a butcher.

Mrs. Heller was first raped by her second husband when she was thirty years old. The rape was accomplished by intimidation rather than by force; she was afraid of being beaten up if she refused. This happened from 2–5 times over a period of 14 years. Mrs. Heller gave identical figures for the frequency and duration of her husband's other violence.

He doesn't always force me physically—it's more of a mental type trip. A few weeks ago he fractured my finger in a fit of temper. The main reason he did that to me was that he hadn't had sex for four days. I had to have my wedding ring sawed off. A couple of days later, he had the nerve to insinuate that we were going to have sex, but I was scared to refuse. We were watching TV and he started getting amorous. I pretended he turned me on. It makes you want to vomit. *Did you have sexual intercourse?* Yes, I didn't want him to go through one of his tantrums. He's never actually forced me to do anything. I am strong-minded and I know how to run out the front door. *Why concede?* Just to humor him—to keep him happy.

There are ways he has of walking down the hall, of pushing me against the wall, so I know he's in a bad mood. He has ways of letting me know that I'd better get sexy and get him out of his bad mood. He also threatens me with his pay check: "Be a good girl, or you won't get much of the pay check." *Be a good girl equals sex?* That's about it.

Verbal threats? He threatens to move out. Or he says: "I'll break the furniture," and he picks it up. He threw a chair at me once.

How upset? Extremely upset. *How much effect on your life?* A great effect. It made me very insecure. I'm scared all the time. I wonder what will happen next. It's forced me to drink more in order to take courage.

Other physical violence? One time he was chasing me. We had had an argument over our son. I stick up for him [son] because he [husband] gets violent with him. He pushed me out of the kitchen and went after G. Then he grabbed me and twisted my finger; that's when he fractured it. He said, "I'll take care of you!" He grabbed a chair and swung it at me, but it missed. I got my jacket and snuck out and went around the corner to the bar.

Other times it has occurred when he lost his check gambling, so naturally we argued about that. He goes after me out of a guilty conscience and starts chasing me around. He breaks furniture first as a warm-up. He sits in the front room with a bottle of booze and with the radio blaring, like a mental case, and I have to watch out when he comes out of the room because he'll shove me all over the place. He'll knock me against the wall. Then the next day he'll want to make it up by having sex. *Does he hit you?* No, he pushes, but he's very heavy. When he pushes, the wall bruises me anyway.

It can be extremely difficult to separate sexual abuse from other violence, as we see in this case. Mrs. Heller feels intimidated into cooperating with her husband sexually because of his violence. "Why get beat up?" she rhetorically asks. Because Mrs. Heller submits out of fear of her husband's violence, she is able to comfort, as well as to deceive herself, that "he's never actually forced me to do anything. I am strong-minded and I know how to run out the front door."

Mrs. Heller's description suggests that she has had many unwanted sexual experiences with her husband, of whom she is afraid, yet she said she had only had from 2–5 experiences. Such underestimates are probably quite common, because of a tendency to discount experiences that result from fear of physical harm rather than from the direct application of force.

Why does Mrs. Heller stay in such a marriage? The most significant clue comes from her previous marriage: she says quite explicitly that "if it weren't for my first marriage, I would have left this one." Her experiences in her first marriage do not meet our definition of rape, but her account does shed light on why Mrs. Heller stayed in her second marriage. She was seventeen at the time of her first unwanted sexual experience with her first husband.

Every time we did it, I didn't like him at all. I went to the doctor [for not wanting sex with her husband], but it can't change your feelings.

We were in bed talking about the sexual part of our marriage. He knew I had seen a doctor. Though I would put on an act when we had sex, I told him I didn't enjoy it. While discussing this, he asked me to give him a blow job. I said, no way! We argued. He begged and pleaded and threatened me. He wasn't forcing me down on him, so I gave him a straight one [vaginal intercourse] as a consolation prize—then I left him. *Force?* No. I don't really see how any man who loves you could really force you. But it was unwanted. I was always a pacifist after the flame died. But you don't want them catting around and bringing a little VD home. It's really not that much of an effort to do it.

How upset? Very upset. I thought when I got married it was forever. *How much effect on your life?* A great effect. It was my first marriage. It affected me enough to be staying with this one for twenty years. If it weren't for my first marriage, I would have left this one. You just have to make the best of it. Use your wits and make it alright. Who knows what the next one would be like.

Mrs. Heller sees herself as having no real choice to live outside of the institution of marriage, no matter how miserable she finds it. Many women in our society, one that evidences little respect for women who reject the institution of marriage, feel as compelled to marry as do women in a society where marriages are arranged.

At the end of the interview Mrs. Heller wrote on the self-administered questionnaire: "I felt I was betraying my husband by answering truthfully. But I did anyway."

Mrs. Kent, our final example of a wife who was still married to the man who raped her, was fifty-two at the time of the interview. She was childless and described herself as "keeping house," but she had previously worked in a garment factory. Mrs. Kent's husband had owned a small grocery store, but he was looking for another job.

Mrs. Kent said the forced sex had occurred from 2–5 times over a period of one year; the other violence had happened more than twenty times over more than ten years.

We argue so many times. He gets unreasonable and I hate him at those times, so I don't want anything to do with him then, let alone to have sex, but he'd take it away from me. He wants to have everything done his way, and if I do it any other way, it isn't acceptable. *Take it away?* Yes, he'd take my body away from me. He'd take me to bed and force me. *Most upsetting time?* No, I can't really distinguish times. It's one argument after another all the time. His business went bad, and he lost a lot of money, but he'd never ask my opinion about it or anything else. If I tell him anything he doesn't listen. I can't even explain myself to him. He leaves me with my tongue out. He lost all we had in savings and is now looking for a job.

Ten years ago I was going to get a divorce. He said he wouldn't hit me again, and that he'd be nice, and my mother said to stay together; if I left, what would I do? Now I'm on nerve pills and going through the change [menopause], and I receive no sympathy from him.

Verbal threats used? He'd say he was going to kill me and all that kind of damn stuff. *Else?* "You do as I say, you're here to do as I wish."

Experience ever reported to police? One time I threatened to call the police, but he yanked the phone out of the wall.

What brought it to an end? I threw it in his face. I said, "How could you do that? It makes me hate you and go against you even more when you force yourself upon me. What's the matter? Do you get your jollies that way?" I guess he realized what he was doing and stopped.

How upset? Extremely upset. *How much effect on your life?* A great effect. I used to be a happy person. I used to go out a lot, but now he keeps me in this shell all the time. I never go out any more. *Effect of forced intercourse?* I hated him and never wanted him to put his hands on me again. I believe no one should force anyone to do anything. You can suggest, and that's all.

Other physical violence? Yes. *Most upsetting time?* I've been upset with him all the time. When I ask him a question and he won't answer, if I pressure him to answer, to this day he threatens to bop me one. Like I said, he doesn't discuss anything with me. *Most violent episode?* It was a long time ago. It happened for no reason at all. He made both my eyes black and blood-shot, and he pulled my hair until he had gobs of hair in his hand. We were supposed to have an anniversary party the next night. I told him to call everyone up to tell them not to come because I couldn't see people in that condition, and I didn't want people to know about it. My mother and brother got worried and came over. When they saw the condition I was in, they were shocked and my brother wanted to kill him. He said, "You did this to my sister! I'll kill you!" My brother was ready to get me out of the house. But my husband apologized and told my brother he'd never do it again. You know how it is. You cool down after a while and think it will never happen again. But I've had many slaps and other humiliations since then. He's short-fused and has a bad temper. He doesn't think or take time to collect himself.

Mrs. Kent was successful in getting her husband to stop raping her, but his other violence continues. However, his violence appears to have diminished quite markedly since the time she described as most upsetting. Her brother's supportiveness might have played a key role in this change, because her husband saw that she had help she could call on.

While Mrs. Kent's brother seems to have been instrumental in lessening her husband's violence toward her, her mother seems to have played a role in her staying in the marriage, not only in directly advising her not to leave it, but also in implying that she would not be able to manage outside of the marriage.

Mrs. Kent's husband is an extreme patriarch in his unwillingness to discuss his work with his wife, particularly his work problems, his hitting her if she merely presses for an answer to a question, and in general, his servant-like treatment of her ("You do as I say. You're here to do as I wish."). Her unhappiness at being so treated is also very apparent, along with her regret that she stayed in the marriage.

Women who stayed, as we have seen, often reported fairly low levels of trauma as a result of their husband's attacks, but Mrs. Kent and Mrs. Heller reveal that some women who stay in their marriages can be very much aware of having suffered considerable trauma.

WIVES NO LONGER MARRIED TO THE HUSBANDS WHO RAPED THEM

We can also gain insight into why some women stay with a husband who has raped them, or who continues to, from women who are no longer married to their husbands, but who stayed with them for some years. Mrs. Robertson stayed many years with her husband before she was widowed, and Mrs. Ramsey stayed four years.

Mrs. Robertson was a fifty-six-year-old childless widow who was living alone at the time of the interview. She said she was disabled because of "nerves," but that she had worked as a domestic in private homes. Her husband had worked as a meat packer in a slaughterhouse.

Mrs. Robertson said she was twenty-seven the first time she was raped by her husband. She said that she had been raped only twice by him over a period of one and a half years; but she discounted many subsequent experiences, which qualify as rape by our definition, when she submitted to her husband out of fear of force. There is no way of estimating the frequency with which these latter experiences occurred.

Mrs. Robertson said that her husband had been physically violent toward her more than twenty times over a period of four years.

The last two years of the marriage, he actually raped me. My husband was the only person who raped me. I found that I lost desire with him. One time when I was not in the mood, he forced me to have intercourse with him. He couldn't arouse any feelings, so he forced me. I felt it was brutal and that he got a kick out of it because I wouldn't give in. *How force?* He made me have him. I let him go on because otherwise I knew he would beat me. I didn't want none of it. It really killed my feelings for him. I felt he was a stranger.

The second time he raised a vicious argument as soon as we got in the door. Then he had to have intercourse, so he made me do it. There was a painter outside the window looking in. It made me mad. Those two times were rape. After that, I just submitted. Being Pentecostal, I had to stay with him.

What brought it to an end? I came to California and left him. He never sent me no money to go back. God fixed it. He died in 1974. We never got back together.

How upset? Extremely upset. *How much effect on your life?* A great effect. That's why I haven't married again, so I wouldn't make the same mistake twice. I was suspicious of men. Relationships would break up because I would see something that reminded me of my husband. Because of the way he treated me, I was always looking for signs of what I had seen in him.

Other physical violence? I was not a rough person. I didn't want any violence. He would come in telling me about some other woman, taking his feelings out on me. He always hit me on my face or head, never more than two or three times. One night, he was humiliated by this woman's husband catching them in bed, so he jumped on me. In the morning he started an argument, which gave him an excuse to hit me. He got evil. That's when I found out people could be like that. He closed the window and said, "Woman, I'm going to beat you to death, to make you glad you be leaving." I just laid there and said, "Brother, do whatever you plan to." He changed his mind and stopped.

Mrs. Robertson is very clear about why she stayed in her marriage as long as she did, until God "fixed it." Her religious faith apparently made divorce impossible. But though she felt compelled to stay, she was nevertheless able to perceive at least two of the incidents as rape. Often women who remain in the marriage cannot acknowledge this. We do not know, though, whether she perceived her husband's attacks as rape when they occurred.

It is commonly assumed that if a woman does not resist a rape, she probably does not care a great deal about it. Indeed, resistance often has to be proved in cases that go to court in order for them to be regarded as legitimate rape cases. Mrs. Robertson demonstrates great passivity. When her husband tells her he is going to beat her to death, she responds: "Brother, do whatever you plan to." But she nevertheless reports considerable trauma as a consequence of her husband's attacks. She provides poignant demonstration that passivity does not necessarily mean that a woman does not care intensely about what has happened to her.

Even when wives stay only a few years, it is still important to know why they stayed as long as they did. Mrs. Ramsey, who stayed with her husband for four years, was a fifty-six-year-old divorced woman who was living alone at the time of the interview. She had raised two children, both now adults, who had left home. She was working full-time as a staff assistant in a large paper company. The husband who raped her had repaired television sets.

Mrs. Ramsey was forty-four years old when her husband first raped her. She said that the incidents of forced sex had occurred from 6–10 times over a period of 4 years.

He was very demanding; at times I would say he was *extremely* demanding. There were a few times when he was drinking that he pinned me down. He never physically hurt me, but he did force intercourse.

Which time was most upsetting? It was the time he came home drunk. He forced me to have intercourse, then decided once wasn't enough and did it again. He got extremely rough with the re-run. I'm referring to the way he treated my body the second time. He pinned me down like he was raping me. He twisted my arm behind me. He did this after I asked him not to be an ass. Maybe that was the wrong time to say that.

Verbal threats? He said that he'd break my neck. But I guess he never actually made *real* threats. He just made a lot of noise. When he'd had too much to drink, his actions spoke louder than his words. He had funny expressions like "I'll bust your ass," but I don't consider them threats because I knew him too well.

What brought it to an end? We got divorced.

How upset? Extremely upset. *How much effect on your life?* A great effect. These incidents changed my life. I couldn't live with him any more like that. It seemed like these incidents were becoming more frequent. I'm alone now; that's the big thing.

Who or what helped in dealing with this experience? Nothing and no one. He was the only one I could talk to about it. He made great apologies, and said that it wouldn't happen again. It took four years for me to realize that he wasn't a nice guy. I did speak to a priest about it, and had him drop in, but my husband left when the priest came.

Mrs. Ramsey explains that she stayed four years because it took her that long to realize "that he wasn't a nice guy." Despite his apologies, the incidents of forced sex were becoming more frequent. While finally able to perceive her husband in this new way, she could not quite manage to see what he was doing to her as rape: "He pinned me down *like he was*

raping me" (emphasis mine). However, she was clear that it was these incidents that "changed my life" and made living with him intolerable.

A QUANTITATIVE ANALYSIS OF WHY WIVES STAY

To repeat, only 22 percent of the victims of wife rape were still married to their husbands at the time of the interview. When we compare
these women with those who were no longer with their husbands, we
find that a number of the explanations that came to light from the analysis of the case material are supported. Quantitative analysis revealed the
following factors as significant.*

Low Level of Trauma

A small minority of women reported to us that they were not very upset by their experience of wife rape, and that it had little effect. Fifty percent (50 percent) of those who were still married to the men who raped
them reported being only somewhat or not very upset as compared with
16 percent of those who were no longer married to their rapists. Similarly,
only 38 percent of wives who stayed reported great long-term effects as
compared with 52 percent of those no longer married (this relationship
was not significant). As we saw, some of these women appear to need to
discount the impact of the rape; because, for example, they did not want,
or feel able, to leave the marriage. To continue living with someone
toward whom they would normally feel so much anger or hurt required
repressing those feelings. However, a few women did not appear to be repressing their feelings; they were not much affected because it only happened one time and their husbands were extremely apologetic; or because
the rape involved having intercourse when they were asleep, which did
not bother them particularly; or because their expectations of marriage
were so low that this kind of abuse was seen as part of a woman's lot in
life; or because they blamed themselves. Whatever the reason, it is of
course hardly surprising that women who are not particularly negatively
affected by an experience, or who *believe* they are not, will stay with their
husbands.

Some Husbands Stop Abusing Their Wives

Almost a third (31 percent) of the wife rapes happened "only" once.
As we have seen, one time can be devastating. However, like other painful and upsetting experiences that occur within relationships, sometimes

---

*All relationships to be described in this section are statistically significant at < .05 level
unless otherwise stated.

rape can be integrated in a nondestructive way. Other times, it can be integrated, but in a destructive way, as in the case of Mrs. Williams, who learned never to say no again. (In Chapter 23 we shall explore further how some wives stopped the rape and other violence in their marriages.)

It should be noted here that of the nineteen women who stayed in their marriages, five (26 percent) were raped for the first time in the last twelve months. Since their experience of wife rape is so recent, there is no knowing if they really belong in the category of wives who stay. In general, the first incident of wife rape occurred more recently for those who stayed than those no longer married.

Some Wives Have Few Resources, Particularly Economic Resources

Irene Frieze found in her study that many of the raped wives who did leave their husbands "tended to return and then to leave again."[9] Frieze reported that this pattern of leaving and returning was associated with the wives "having a lower educational level and having pre-school children." Hence Frieze concluded that "these women may have had fewer outside resources to support them while they were away."[10]

The wives who stayed in their marriages, according to our survey, were significantly more traditional than those who were no longer married to their rapists. We should remember that our measure of traditionality was not based on ideology and values but on whether or not the woman had a child or children, whether she had worked outside the home most of her adult life, and whether her husband was the main provider or not. More specifically, 47 percent of the wives who stayed worked less than half their adult lives outside of the home, as compared with 24 percent of the wives who were no longer married. For 90 percent of the women who stayed, their husbands provided the money they lived on at the time of the survey, as compared with 24 percent of the wives who were no longer married to the men who raped them. However, some of the latter women had not remarried, so it is probably more relevant to note that the husbands were the sole providers at the time of the first wife rape for 69 percent of the wives who stayed, whereas only 22 percent of the husbands were the sole providers at the time of the first attack for wives who were no longer married to these men.

Most significant of all is that all nineteen of the wives (100 percent) who were the sole providers of the household income at the time of the first wife rape were no longer married to the men who raped them. This is powerful evidence that economic resources play a key role in why raped wives stay.

We anticipated that the more children a woman had, the more likely she would stay with an abusive husband. However, it turned out that wives who stayed were more likely to have had one or two children, whereas those who were no longer married to these men were more likely to have had three or more children or none at all.

In terms of total income for the year prior to the interview (1977), 53 percent of the wives who stayed reported a total household income of $15,000 or over, as compared with only 22 percent of the wives who were no longer married to the men who raped them. This is striking evidence of the economic sacrifice involved for many wives who leave abusive marriages.

Wives' Fear of Sexual Assault Outside the Home

Considerable evidence suggests that wives who stay are more fearful than wives who leave about being sexually assaulted outside their homes. First, they are more likely to perceive sexual assault as a big problem than the other wives; 90 percent of these wives are very or somewhat afraid that someone will rape or sexually assault them compared to 60 percent of the other wives. Ninety-five percent (95 percent) of the wives who stay change the way they do certain things because of their fear of sexual assault, as compared with 78 percent of the other wives; wives who stay report being more upset by men's sexual comments or advances in the street, and more of them report being upset in their adult years by someone exposing their genitals than the other wives. (Not all these associations reach statistical significance at the $< .05$ level. However, the overall pattern seems clear.) Perhaps wives who stay prefer the known risks and abuse at home than the unknown risks involved in leaving it.

Wives Who Blame Themselves for the Rape

Though we did not specifically ask about self-blame, we noted any evidence of it in their accounts of their experiences of wife rape. In 32 percent of the cases where self-blame was evident, the wives stayed, as compared with only 4 percent of the wives who did not stay.

Cultural Differences

Unfortunately the numbers in each racial or ethnic group are too small to allow us to make meaningful comparisons, though it is evident that white wives are much less inclined to stay with the husbands who rape them than wives from all other groups. When Black, Asian, Latina, and other Third World wives are grouped, we see that 42 percent of them stayed with the husbands who raped them as compared with 13 percent of the white women.

Lack of Support for Leaving

It is clear that support for leaving the marriage—by members of the family, friends, neighbors, doctors, and priests—can be very important. For example, though Mrs. Osborne's life was constantly in jeopardy because of the violence of her husband, her parents wouldn't take her back. They told her: "You made your bed, so lie in it." Similarly, Mrs. Ashmore reported that: "I moved home with my parents. They threw me out of the house. . . . That was one of the most terrifying parts of the whole experience. That I actually could get no help from anyone. It was an interracial marriage and people would say, 'What do you expect?' "

In contrast, Mrs. Phillips received the support she needed: "I yelled for my brother. My husband left because he knew that my family was behind me. My mother told me to go ahead and get a divorce."

Excusing Husbands' Behavior

Blaming the violent and abusive behavior on alcohol was the commonest example of this phenomenon. "He was the nicest person when he didn't drink," said Mrs. Freeman. Mrs. Baker also attributed her husband's violent behavior to alcohol. "Otherwise, he was a good dad. We had a good sex life other than that." So the fact that these men are not abusive all the time, and that when they are, alcohol is seen as responsible, enables some women to excuse their husbands' behavior; they stay in the marriage when they otherwise might not.

Mrs. Osborne said that her exceedingly violent and dangerous husband "was an ideal husband till he had a motorcycle accident which affected his head." Hence, she did not blame him but instead felt sorry for him. She finally left only after he tried to kill her.

They Had No Place to Go

None of the women quoted in this chapter said they stayed with their husbands because they had nowhere else to go, but of course, this is a common reason, and one that was mentioned by a few women in our sample. For example, Mrs. Eriksen said: "I only put up with it because there was nowhere else to go." And Mrs. Scott said: "Now they have shelters; then, there was no place to go."

Although this question was not directly asked, none of the women in our sample specifically said that she had gone to a battered women's refuge.

A method of analysis known as multiple regression makes it possible to ascertain which of the factors that we were able to quantify had the greatest weight in explaining which wives stayed. Wives blaming themselves for the rape emerged as the most important one. Future research will, I hope, illuminate why some wives blame themselves rather than their husbands.

Other factors that are also important (according to this method of analysis) in predicting which wives will stay with husbands who have raped them as opposed to which wives will not, are as follows: that the wife is a Third World woman; that less violence was associated with the rape in terms of the degree of physical force used, the presence or use of a weapon, and the making of verbal threats in connection with the rape; that the husband was the main provider at the time of the (first) rape; that the wife perceives there to be a high likelihood of being raped (outside of marriage) at some time in the future; that the wife reports less upset and long-term effects as a result of the rape; that the wife is foreign-born; and finally that the wife is more traditional.* Presumably foreign-born wives are often more isolated from relatives and friends than those born in this country, and so are more likely to stay in their marriages.

Frequently, wives who stay in abusive marriages have been assumed to be masochistic. This chapter suggests that many social factors play a significant role in who remains in the marriage. Blaming the victim (or the wife or the mother of offenders) has been a common practice among psychologists and psychoanalysts.[11] Hopefully this book will contribute to an ending of this prejudiced and wrongheaded perspective.

*Together these eight variables explain 41 percent of the variance.

PART SIX

WOMEN AS PROPERTY

16

Husbands Who Won't Let Their Wives Go

Rape entered the law through the back door . . . as a property crime of man against man. Woman, of course, was viewed as the property.

—Susan Brownmiller, *Against Our Will,* 1975

[He] put it to the House of Commons that the country should treat its married women no worse than it treated its domestic animals.

—Henry Fitzroy, 1853[1]

Every brutal-minded man, and many a man who in other relations in life is not brutal, entertains more or less vaguely the notion that his wife is his *thing.*

—Frances Power Cobbe, 1878[2]

Men who view their wives as their property believe their wives have no right to decide their own fate as long as they still want them. No matter how much the husbands have abused their wives, their wives belong to them. Husbands can defile their property, let it run down, get rid of it, or take care of it well. However they treat it, the decision is theirs alone. The runaway wife is like the runaway slave in the eyes of these husbands; runaway slaves were beaten or killed, and so are some runaway wives.

When writing about battered women in her book *Women Who Kill,* Ann Jones suggests that "if researchers were not quite so intent upon assigning the pathological behavior to the women, they might see that the more telling question is not 'Why do the women stay?' but 'Why don't the men let them go?' "[3] This provocative and valuable insight allows us to look at the situation in a new light, for as our survey revealed, in many cases women stay because of the fanatical determination of some husbands not to let their wives go. The experiences to be described in this chapter make it apparent that one of the most underestimated factors in

why some wives stay in abusive situations for so long is that their husbands simply will not let them go.

All the women we interviewed were survivors, but many women are
not so fortunate. Articles about wives whose husbands preferred to kill
them than lose them, appear quite frequently in the press. Four examples
from our survey of husbands who did whatever they could to prevent
their wives from leaving them—short of murdering them—will now be
presented.

Mrs. Ashmore, a thirty-four-year-old divorced woman, was childless
and living alone at the time of the interview. She was a self-employed artist, and her husband had been a freelance writer. Mrs. Ashmore reported
that her husband had raped her from 6–10 times over a period of a year,
starting when she was twenty-five. She gave the same figures for the frequency and duration of his other violent behavior. The incident she starts
out by describing occurred after they had already separated.

He came over to my house in a jealous rage. He accused me of seeing other men
and he wanted me to say what I was doing with them. Then he proceeded to beat
me up for a long time. He started at 10:00 P.M. that night. By 6:00 A.M. the next day
it was over. After all the beating, kicking and throwing finally concluded, I ended
up in the hospital with a broken jaw, broken fingers, concussion, and bruises all
over. Then before he left, he made me lie down and have sex with him on threat
of doing me more bodily harm if I didn't.

Another time he drove me out in the country, threw me out of the car, then
raped me in the woods. He forced me to carry all his heavy camera equipment
around the trails for hours. Then he took me fishing! Meanwhile he was threatening me the whole time. I was hysterical. When we got home, he beat me some
more and raped me again! He was a psycho. Things like that just kept happening!

Result of police report? They said there was nothing they could do. There were no
witnesses. They said if I wanted to kill him, fine. This was in another state. He
followed me there after the divorce.

What brought it to an end? I got a gun and decided to kill him and moved away.

How upset? Extremely upset. *What effect on your life?* It affected me a great deal. It
has made me extremely wary of men, to the point where it has affected my relationships with them. He's my last husband. I carried a loaded gun in my purse for
three years. He had kidnapped me on two separate occasions before that [the incident already described] after we'd separated. It was really gross. I'd move into an
apartment and he'd show up, take me back to his apartment and tie me up. *Sexual
assault?* Sometimes, if he felt like it. He really did all he could to prove to me that I
was absolutely helpless, and I think he convinced me for a while!

What helped most in dealing with this experience? Nothing and no one. I was in desperate straits for help. I went to the church which I had been completely away
from and moved home with my parents. They threw me out of the house! I got
pneumonia for six months. One of the more terrifying parts of the whole experience was that I actually could get no help from anyone. It was an inter-racial marriage and people would say, "What do you expect?"

In addition to her husband's abuse, Mrs. Ashmore was driven to desperation by the response of the police, by the reaction of her parents, and by the punitive and racist notion that because Mrs. Ashmore had married someone of another race (Mrs. Ashmore was white and described her husband as Cuban), she should expect the violence she was subjected to.

Mrs. Ashmore's husband's violence occurred only over a one-year period; she decided early that she wanted to get out of the marriage. But her husband would not let her go. When asked what brought the marriage to an end, Mrs. Ashmore replied that she obtained a gun and decided to kill her husband and moved away. Had she really planned to kill him, she would probably not have had to move away; it seems likely that she meant that she planned to kill him if she could not successfully get away from him.

Mrs. Clayton was a thirty-five-year-old childless woman married to another man at the time of the interview. She was working full-time as a college professor. Her ex-husband had worked as a reporter for a large newspaper. Mrs. Clayton was twenty-eight years old when she was raped by her husband. It happened only once, whereas the other violence occurred 11–20 times over the last 6 years of a 9-year marriage.

We were separated. I came to visit to see my dog. It was a Friday night. I said something that made him angry. He came up behind me, picked me up holding my arms behind me, and threw me across the floor, cutting my eye and the side of my face. He then tied me up and held me prisoner until Monday, releasing me only when he felt I would not go to either a doctor or the police. While I was tied up he raped me.

One month later he asked me to come back to cat-sit while he was away. It turned out that he had a complex scheme to murder me, and was only pretending he would be away. I became alarmed about 1:00 A.M. because I realized he wasn't away and something strange was going on. I called the police. They sent somebody out at 3:00 A.M.

The police and I rehashed this and previous mysterious attempts on my life. We both realized it was my husband. The policeman set up an appointment for me to see the D.A. The D.A. explained that in spite of the evidence, they could do nothing until he killed me. He suggested I leave the state fast, since the assaults were getting more serious. So I left.

Verbal threats? He said he'd kill me if I left him.

Other violence? He was a paranoid schizophrenic and an alcoholic. He was raised by his mother and her parents. His mother would get hit by her parents to sober her up. He said he hit me to "bring me to my senses." In fact, he'd simply hit me when I made him mad. One time he threw an iron across the room at me. The worst stuff was a series of dirty tricks that occurred about six months prior to the final assault I described to you. For example: he cut the brake cables of my car so when I drove home that night I had no brakes. Another time he hid a gun in my car, then called the police to say I was carrying a concealed weapon. He planted white powder and syringes in the glove compartment of my car, then called my job anonymously and said I'd stolen illegal drugs and was smuggling them to California.

How upset? Extremely upset, not by the rape, but by the attempted murder. *How much effect on your life?* A great effect. He was my husband. I had tolerated him for nine years because he was afraid that if I left him, he'd die. He was a hindrance to my career and he tried to murder me, even though I stayed with him. I realize now that I was cruel and stupid because I didn't do him a favor to stay with him when I didn't love him. He died a year later anyway when he was thirty-three.

If anybody ever tried to physically assault me now, I would kill them. I am deliberately accruing money so I can have them murdered. That is one of my main motives for making money. Nobody will ever do that to me again.

Mrs. Clayton's decision to save money so that she could hire a murderer should anyone attempt to physically assault her again may seem to be the action of someone who is mentally unstable. But when seen in the context of her experience of a crazy husband who tried to kill her, and of the police who knew and believed her story but claimed to be able to do nothing, her behavior seems more understandable.

Mrs. Clayton reported no physical violence or unwanted sexual experiences in her current marriage. She is one of many women whose subsequent lives refute the notion that women who experience such extreme abuse must seek it out.

Mrs. Freeman is a fifty-nine-year-old childless woman who was married to her third husband at the time of the interview. She was retired but had worked for a large catering company. Her ex-husband had owned and run a nightclub. Mrs. Freeman was twenty-eight years old when her second husband first raped her. In her two-and-one-half-year marriage to him, Mrs. Freeman said she had been subjected to forced sexual intercourse at least three times a week. Regarding her husband's other physical violence she said: "I couldn't even count the times. There'd be just long enough for a black eye to heal and then he'd do it again."

He'd have one too many drinks. Then he'd hold me so hard I'd have black and blue marks on my throat. I would be sore from his holding my neck.

Which time was most upsetting? Each one was upsetting. He'd come in drunk and if I didn't spread my legs he would whack me. He was an ex-boxer. I would try and fight back. If he was too drunk, I'd throw him over the edge of the bed and put a blanket over him.

Two months after we got married, he hit me so hard I fell out of bed. He pulled me up on the bed while undressing himself, then told me to stay lying down. I just spread my legs and let him do it, have his sex. Sometimes if I was lucky he'd pass out and go to sleep.

When he'd have a few drinks something in him would change. He'd come home and knock me in the head, "Here's for what you did today. If you didn't do it today, you'll do it tomorrow!" Afterward he'd beg me not to go to any bar or night club where friends would be, so they couldn't see my black eyes. He'd say, "Honey, please don't let anyone else see you."

I finally left him after two and a half years. I rented a place under my maiden name. A bartender who was good friends with him told him where I was. He came there and kicked the door, and I finally opened it. He said, "You're going to come home." He pushed me into the bedroom. I didn't fight him that time; I saw he was sober enough that I would lose. The manager asked me to move, so I packed my clothes and left.

I served papers on him. If I could have gotten my divorce, that would have been it. But then Dr. L. called me and told me he was seriously ill, and that he thought my husband had cancer. So I went back. We made up for two days. He went in the hospital and was operated on and died. Before that I was trying to get a divorce. I would never have gone back to him permanently. One time I was so full of blood, a neighbor called the police.

Verbal threats? He was going to knock my block off.

Weapon? He had a gun. He threatened to shoot me a number of times.

Result of police report? They took him to jail until he sobered up. Then they let him loose.

How upset? Very upset. *How much effect on your life?* A great effect. I wouldn't trust a white man again. [Mrs. Freeman is Latina and her husband was white.] I didn't get married for a number of years after that. I knew if I did they'd use that piece of paper to beat up on me. It was better if I lived with a man without getting married. My second marriage ruined my feelings for men.

The bartender, the manager of her apartment building, and her husband's doctor, each played a role in supporting Mrs. Freeman's husband's attempts to get her back, regardless of whether her health or life were in danger. Mrs. Freeman's experience shows that a woman may have to be extremely determined to leave her husband over his objections.

Mrs. Goddard was a forty-six-year-old woman who had raised two children and was living alone at the time of the interview. She was working full-time as a salesperson. Her ex-husband had worked as a meat cutter. Mrs. Goddard was raped by her husband for the first time when she was twenty-three. Mrs. Goddard said that these experiences of forced sex had occurred over a period of twenty-two years—the duration of their marriage.

He would try to get me to go to bed; sometimes I ended up going to bed with him because I felt threatened. *Most upsetting time?* I had a couple of most upsetting times. The first one I remember he was drinking. He threw me down on the floor and tried to make me have intercourse, while knowing that I had my period. He succeeded, and I wouldn't talk to him afterward. The other time he tried to put his thing in my face when I was sleeping. I woke up, and said, "What's going on?" He stopped when I woke up. Just the thought that he had it in his head to do something when I was sleeping outraged me. I never lost a thing when I divorced that pig!

Frequency of forced intercourse? I wouldn't say very frequently, but sometimes.

From six to ten times. Afterward he'd drink, then he'd stay away for weeks or even months. He would be chasing around [after other women]. I never knew this till after the divorce. When my son was born I was pretty torn up inside. It finally healed, but I used that as an excuse. I couldn't stand him to touch me.

What brought it to an end? Divorce. Since we divorced, he has gotten a gun. One of the last things he said was, "I'm going to get you. It may take me five or six years, but I'm going to get you!"

How upset? Extremely upset. I ended up with high blood pressure, and taking four tranquilizers a day, starting in 1968. I've been off them now for four years. *How much effect on your life?* A great effect. My house and everything is still back there. It is terrible to have to be living here, and always to live in fear of him. I am working at a low paying job, paying a high rent, just to be away from him. And I miss my family back there so much. The lawyer said my son was better living with me, but my husband went and bribed my son. [Mrs. Goddard told a story about her ex-husband taking her son to a tavern and turning him against her. She started crying at this point.]

Other? I suffer from a nervousness, a fear. Any little thing that happens and I'm right up in the air.

The most upsetting time he was physically violent? Oh, so many of them were upsetting! One Thanksgiving Day, he didn't come home. When he finally arrived, he dumped a plate of food on my head, knocked me up against the sink and said: "Bring more and I'll do it again!" One time he took me by the hair and dragged me all around the kitchen by my hair. I could hardly move for three days one time. I was black and blue from my waist to my shoulders with two black eyes from him beating me. He threw me across the room, then put his knee on my stomach and was hammering on my head with his foot.

After the divorce, he followed me home to my daughter's house. I was lying on my grandchild's bed. He followed me, then got on the bed with me and started socking me in the head. They called the police, and my son-in-law took me to the hospital. I thought I had a concussion. There were big lumps on my head. My ear was as black as could be. [During this part of the interview, Mrs. Goddard got enraged and furious, and I couldn't slow her down. As soon as she'd tell me one incident, she'd remember something else that was worse. Finally she started crying and said she didn't want to remember any more.]

Result of police report? The police told my ex-husband to stay away from me.

Who or what was most helpful in dealing with these experiences? My friends. I found I had a lot more friends after I left him. In fact it was hard to leave them to come here, but I had to. I was scared. He said he was going to get me and I don't dare go back there. But my friends helped.

Advice to others in same situation? Don't ever, ever live a life like I did that long. When you're having troubles, leave! Don't ruin your life for something like that.

Elsewhere in the interview Mrs. Goddard said that she had contributed most of the money to pay for their home and to put the kids through school "because I made more money." She said she was going to marry again soon; she felt that she had learned from all the pain she had gone through, that she knew what she wanted this time, and that she would never have to go through such suffering again.

Mrs. Goddard is the only one of the four women cited so far in this chapter who had children. She also stayed in her marriage longer than the other three (twenty-two years as compared with nine years, two and a half years and one year).

Often women with children stay in bad marriages both for the sake of the children, as they see it, and because the responsibility of having to care for children as a single parent is frequently awesome. So, if these marriages end in divorce, it may often be the husband who initiates it, or, to put it another way, perhaps childless women are more willing to initiate divorce than those with children, and thus it is their husbands who are more likely to try to coerce them to stay.

The experiences of these four women illustrate the extraordinary lengths some women have to go to to get away from abusive husbands, and the enormous sacrifices they sometimes have to make; these are likely major reasons why some women stay with abusive husbands. As Ann Jones pointed out, it is a fact that has rarely been explored. Mrs. Ashmore was kidnapped three times by her husband after they were already separated. He followed her to another state even after their divorce. According to Mrs. Ashmore, the police even said that it was fine if she killed him, since there was nothing they could do to protect her.

Mrs. Clayton's husband tried to murder her several times. She claimed that the police concurred in this conclusion, but said they could not protect her, and advised her to leave the state, which she did. Fortunately for Mrs. Clayton, her husband died a year later.

Mrs. Freeman left her husband, but a bartender, her landlord, her doctor, all cooperated with her husband's efforts to find her again and/or to make it difficult for her to leave him.

Finally, Mrs. Goddard had to leave her home, her family, a good job, her friends, and move to another state because she believed her husband's threat to kill her was serious. She is still living in extreme fear for her life.

Leaving husbands who view their wives as their property can mean risking death, and some who take this risk are killed. These possessive husbands are also sometimes killed by their wives. Mrs. Ashmore said she bought a gun and decided to kill her husband. Mrs. Clayton reported that she was deliberately saving money so that she could kill anyone who tried to physically assault her as her husband had done previously. Other cases have been cited in the literature, and many have been reported in newspapers.[4]

The well-publicized case of Joyce DeVillez is one such case. It shows the extreme solutions to which a woman like Mrs. Clayton could be pushed. For Joyce DeVillez murder appeared to be the only way out of a prison—the prison of life with her husband, which seemed far worse to her than the prison sentence she received.

Joyce DeVillez received a 15–25-year sentence for hiring someone to kill her husband after he had abused her for twenty-three years. Although sexual abuse of Mrs. DeVillez by her husband is not mentioned in the following account, his sexual molestation of their daughter is referred to, but not elaborated upon. My guess is that as usual the hideous descriptions of non-sexual violence are still easier to disclose than experiences of sexual abuse.

It was 1974 when Joyce DeVillez decided not to take it any more. For twenty-three years the Evansville, Ind., housewife had served as her husband Bernard's personal punching bag. He beat her, choked her, denied her medical care, sexually molested their daughter Roxann and beat their sons Kevin and Kirk.

"When I was about four my father slammed my face into the table edge, and my nose and face swelled until my eyes were pulled apart," Kevin recalled.

The family says Bernard terrorized them with knives, guns and belt buckles but mostly with his fists and volcanic temper.

He was a powerful man who stood six feet tall and weighed 220 pounds. Joyce was submissive and fragile, four feet eleven inches tall and weighed ninety-five pounds, soft-spoken and polite.

She sought help over the years, but said police and social agencies were reluctant to interfere in family matters. Besides, she says, whenever she threatened to take the kids and leave, Bernard punched her across the room and vowed to hunt them to the ends of the earth and scatter their parts in the wind.

Joyce believed him. He had fractured Kevin's skull once for making a noise, so she was convinced divorce proceedings would sign her death warrant. Joyce also admits to not being very smart then.

Bernard monitored her every movement. He refused to allow a phone in the house, picked up the mail at the post office so the mailman wouldn't flirt with his wife and wired the door shut when he left.

Finally, Joyce had had enough. She phoned a woman named Charlotte Hendricks, a local underworld character. Hendricks said it would cost $1,500 to have Bernard killed. Joyce said, do it.

Hendricks contacted Terry Walker, seventeen, a regular visitor to the juvenile courts and not very smart himself. He said he would do it.

Walker rented a room at the Jackson House Motel, lured Bernard to the parking lot on June 6, 1974, and shot him three times before a crowd of lunchgoers.

Bernard died three hours later. He was forty-three. . . .

On Sept. 30, 1974 [Detective Sgt.] Overby walked into DeJong's Dress Shop, clamped the handcuffs on employee Joyce DeVillez and charged her with first-degree murder.

DeVillez hired one of Evansville's top criminal lawyers. He advised her to plead guilty and billed her $7,000. He told her no jury would care that Bernard possibly needed killing. She would surely be convicted and spend the rest of her life in prison if she insisted on a jury trial. DeVillez was confused and frightened, so she told the lawyer she would plead guilty.

Judge Morton Newman sentenced her to 15–25 years in prison. The lawyer never told the judge about the beatings. Neither did DeVillez. Her lawyer said it wouldn't matter.

Now DeVillez is near forty-five, five years into her sentence. Pleading guilty was the dumbest thing she ever did, she says. Dumber than staying with Bernard for twenty-three years.

A jury, she believes, would have freed her once the story of Bernard's brutality was told. No one ever doubted it was the truth. Even Bernard's family knew it. "I too have felt fear of my brother. . . . I knew Joyce felt threatened and trapped in her marriage," said Bernard's sister, Bernadette Burgess. . . .

The judge who sentenced her says to let her go. "I wasn't aware of the extent of the beating at the time of sentencing," said Newman. "When I heard about the provocation I wrote to the governor and asked for her release. . . . The provocation to which she was subjected was of such magnitude as to invite retaliatory action."

Bernard's brother, Roscoe DeVillez, even appeared at a clemency hearing to plead for her release. Bernard was a brute, everyone admits, and had it coming. "I don't doubt that he knocked her around," conceded Overby.

Scores of pscyhologists and experts on the subject of battered wives have also argued for DeVillez's freedom. "He created a climate of violence that truly invited retaliation," said Temple University psychologist Claire Wilson. "She had a realistic fear that she and her children might be killed."

The CBS *60 Minutes* program examined the case a year ago and triggered an avalanche of mail demanding DeVillez's freedom. Unswayed is the man who holds the key to the prison—Indiana Gov. Robert Orr. Like his predecessor, Gov. Otis Bowen, Orr says there are no "unique circumstances" to warrant an early release.

Although she dreams of freedom, she insists prison was a reasonable price to pay to escape Bernard's poundings. She is without remorse. "I was relieved when he died. I regret the situation that led him to be killed. I don't regret that he's dead because he was a sick and twisted man," she says. "My life in prison is much better than my life with Bernard and given a choice I would take this in a minute. Jails are hard places—there is nothing soft in them. They are all angles and metal. But at least in jail I can sleep with my eyes closed and not worry about being beaten."[5]

However, Mrs. DeVillez expressed considerable fear that the psychological damage Bernard inflicted on their children might eventually ruin their lives. They remain close to her and visit her regularly. But time has not diminished their hatred for their father.

According to one study, men were more than ten times as likely as women to both define their spouse as "an object of personal property" and to treat them as such.[6] Like Mr. DeVillez, some of these men literally imprison their wives in their own homes. Jones argues that it is these men who are most likely to be killed by their wives; murder is a last resort for women (not always for men), and "it most often occurs when men simply will not quit."[7]

At the beginning of this chapter I made a comparison between the runaway wife and the runaway slave in the eyes of some husbands.

Though obviously there is no comparison between the way wives become members of families and the way men and women were enslaved, it could be argued that, like slavery, the exploitation of women is intrinsic to the structure and functioning of the family: supporting evidence being that wives are treated as property; that they can be raped and beaten by their husbands with little or no censure; that they receive no wages for their work in the home, even if this involves an eighty-hour work week, with no pension or security. Nor do they enjoy freedom of movement; if they are unwilling to live where their husband lives, including if he moves domicile without consulting her, she can be found guilty of desertion, lose custody of the children, and so on. However, the institution of the family was not specifically and consciously set up for the purpose of exploiting women in the way slavery was. Nevertheless, a notable similarity between slavery and the patriarchal family is that both involve relationships within which there is a considerable power disparity. Where there are power disparities there are abuses of power; the greater the disparity, the greater the abuse can (not necessarily will) be. When a husband does not abuse his power, the relationship between husband and wife can be a happy one. But when he *does* abuse his power, and when moreover he is a brutal person, who, because of his power, can get away with acting out his brutality, then there are many similarities between the predicament of wives and slaves.

17

mut

Once a Wife,
Always a Wife—
Rape by Ex-Husbands

"I have only raped a woman once and that was my ex-wife. I
did not like it. It was recommended by a psychiatrist and I
think that it was a lousy recommendation."

—Male respondent, *The Hite Report on Male Sexuality*,
Shere Hite, 1981

Some wives are raped by their husbands for the first time *after* they are
already divorced or separated from them. Strictly speaking, these cases
don't qualify as "rape in marriage," but they do share many of its characteristics. The phenomenon of rape by ex-husbands is another manifestation of the concept of wives as property; even divorce, for some men,
does not alter their right to their property.

Though not specifically asked, ten of the eighty-seven women in our
study mentioned spontaneously that they were raped by their husbands
after they had separated. For six of these women it was the first time their
husbands raped them, and for four of them it was not. Three women were
raped by their ex-husbands after they were divorced; thus 15 percent of
the raped wives in our study volunteered that they were raped after the
marriage was terminated, or about one in every seven victims of wife
rape. It is often assumed that if an abused wife will only decide to leave
her marriage, abuse will end; but these and other cases show that this is
often not so.

Separated husbands who rape their wives are examples of the phenomenon of husbands who won't let their wives go. In many states, divorced wives are officially protected by the law; they can charge their
ex-husbands with rape. Women who are merely separated are rarely offered this protection (see Appendix II for detailed information on which
states permit prosecution of rape after separation). The fact that separated
wives may be raped with impunity by their husbands in many states indicates that the notion of once a wife, always a wife is also sanctioned by
the law.

Mrs. Irving was thirty-eight, divorced, childless, and working full-time as a personnel assistant at a private college at the time of the interview. Her ex-husband had worked as a draftsman. He had attempted to rape Mrs. Irving on one occasion three years prior to the interview when she was thirty-five years old.

He was my ex-husband at the time. He came over to visit and forced himself on me. He thought that since he had prior claims, he could reinstitute them. He pinned me up against the kitchen table and was touching me all over. I was able to ridicule him into stopping. *Was he attempting intercourse?* That's what he had in mind. He had me pinned with his body up against the table and he was touching my breasts and genitals. When I ridiculed him, he stopped.

How upset? Not very upset. *How much effect on your life?* It had no effect.

Mrs. Irving's ex-husband stopped trying to force himself on her when she ridiculed him. This borderline rape, not surprisingly, had no long-term impact on her, although a similar experience might affect some women more; the degree of upset may depend partly on what illusions a woman still has about her ex-husband and what sort of relationship they have at the time. Some women, for example, would have been appalled by the notion that "since he had prior claims, he could reinstitute them," while others find this a totally consistent and unsurprising attitude in their ex-husbands.

Mrs. Langer, another of the three women who was already divorced the first time her ex-husband raped her, was twenty-nine and still divorced at the time of the interview. Like Mrs. Irving, she was childless; she worked full-time as a real estate agent. Her ex-husband raped her when she was twenty-one years old; she was unable to consent because she was severely sedated and asleep at the time.

My sister died and my ex-husband came over to comfort me. I took a strong drug, and went to bed. I was scared, so he came to spend the night at my house. I woke up four hours later and he was pumping away. I tried to push him away. It was very unpleasant. I told him to get off. I just remember falling asleep again with him inside of me. I'm not sure what else happened. I was in a fog.

How upset? Very upset. *How much effect on your life?* A little effect.

Mr. Langer took advantage of his wife in a moment of great vulnerability, but apparently Mrs. Langer, though very upset by it at the time, felt that it had only a little effect on her subsequent life. Some women might be enormously disillusioned by such an experience.

Mrs. Porter was raped by her husband both while they were still married and after the marriage ended. She was thirty-one, divorced, and living alone at the time of the interview. Like Mrs. Irving and Mrs. Langer, she had not raised any children. She was going to school, but had previously worked as a clerk. Mrs. Porter was supporting her husband when he started forcing her to have sex during their marriage; they were both twenty years old at the time. The rapes occurred more than twenty times over a period of nine years. She had been divorced for a year when her ex-husband raped her again.

We had been divorced for a year. One night he came to my house when he was drunk. I had been drinking too, which didn't help. He started slapping me, then pushed me on to the bed and started raping me, and what I would term, physically abusing me.

There were also times in our marriage when he was really forceful. I'm not really fond of fellatio, so he forced me to do it. I remember I threw up all over his crotch. After a while I got used to it. The instances where I was forced happened throughout our nine-year marriage. If I didn't do what I was told it would go from verbal threats to threats of physical violence.

How upset? Very upset. *How much effect on your life?* Some effect, but I consider my marriage in a whole different category from other relationships. We're still very good friends. The physical violence calmed down as our marriage went on. It worked out that he wasn't nearly as physically violent in the later years. *Most upsetting time he was physically violent?* That time when he came to my house and raped me.

Mrs. Porter estimated the number of times her husband had been physically violent toward her as more than twenty, and despite her last statement that he had become less violent, she said that the violence had occurred over a period of nine years. Although Mrs. Porter uses the word rape to describe the attack by her ex-husband, she seems to have a great need to underplay the probable trauma of nine years of rape and other violence. Her previous experiences of sexual abuse shed some light on this.

Mrs. Porter was sexually fondled by one uncle at the age of four years, by an old man when she was seven, by another uncle when she was eleven, and by her pediatrician when she was seventeen. The two experiences that seem to be most significant in terms of her own assessment of their impact on her, occurred with lovers, one at the age of seventeen and the other at eighteen. Though the experience she had when she was seventeen did not meet our definition of rape and is therefore simply categorized as an unwanted sexual experience, Mrs. Porter said that she was extremely upset by the unwanted intercourse with this man, and that it had a great effect on her subsequent life.

It added to my overall feeling toward men, which wasn't good. I became sexually active at sixteen, so I began to think that if you go out with a guy, you have to end up having sex with him.

At eighteen, Mrs. Porter was raped by a lover from 2–5 times over a period of 4 months. She described this also as extremely upsetting and said that it had had a great effect on her life: "I became so disillusioned with men. This was partially responsible for my marriage. My husband was the first nice man that I met. He was respectful and kind. I think it led to my having a very low opinion of men." (Mrs. Porter's experience of rape by this lover is described in Chapter 19.)

Mrs. Porter's responses to these prior experiences of sexual abuse make it clearer why she would downplay the abuse she suffered from her husband: to be disillusioned one has to have illusions.

Divorced men can often get back at their wives through their children. Ex-husbands who do not have this option may be more inclined to strike at the wife directly by raping her. Each of the three women we interviewed who were raped by ex-husbands were childless. Only two of the ten women who were raped after they were separated had no children.

Mrs. Gordon was raped once after she had separated from her husband, but never during her marriage. At the time of the interview she was thirty-two, had remarried and was living with her husband. She had no children, and was working part-time as a masseuse. She was twenty-eight years old when her husband first raped her.

He wanted to get back together after our separation. Because of his attitude I experienced fear. He had a temper and I was terrified of him. He started making sexual advances and I was cold and indifferent. I kept moving around the house. He continued with the sexual advances and it was threatening because he was a lot bigger than me. He wanted to go to bed but we took a hot tub instead. I hoped that would put him off. But he then actually picked me up, carried me into the bedroom, and threw me on the bed. He didn't beat me up though. It wasn't like rape because I did submit. I just didn't want it.

How upset? Somewhat upset. *How much effect on your life?* A little effect.

Other physical violence? When we were about to separate, I went out and stayed out until 2:00 or 3:00 A.M. He started pushing me around, threw me on the bed and slapped me. He broke my beads and ripped my shirt. But I don't think it was really "violence."

Mrs. Gordon said that such incidents had occurred from 2–5 times over a period of 2 weeks. Although she said "it wasn't like rape because I did submit," intercourse was obtained by threat of physical harm since she submitted to him out of fear of force or violence, and so we do consider this rape. Mrs. Gordon specifically mentioned that her husband "had a temper and I was terrified of him," that "he was a lot bigger than me," and that he had picked her up and thrown her on to the bed. Her discounting this experience is consistent with her statement that he had not been violent on another occasion even though at that time he had thrown her on the bed, slapped her, broken her beads, and ripped her shirt. This downplaying of her husband's abusiveness is also expressed in her describing the rape as only "somewhat upsetting" and having only "a little effect."

Mrs. Marks was separated when her husband first raped her. She was forty-five at the time of the interview, and although she described her marital status as married she was not living with her husband, but with two other men and her eight-year-old child. She was working full-time as a custodian.

We were separated and I had a live-in job. He came out there and made a scene, twisting my arm and carrying on so that I went on home with him. He was okay—he just didn't want me in those people's home. But he's kind of rough too. He forced me to go to bed with him when we got home. He twisted my arm until it hurt. *Other than twist your arm?* No, but that was enough. He's a strong man.

Mrs. Marks too seems to need to discount the tyrannical nature of her husband's behavior. He went to her place of work, caused a scene, physically forced her to return home, then forced her to have sexual intercourse with him, yet Mrs. Marks describes this as if no outrage was done. Hence, the interviewer, in error, did not complete the questionnaire. Perhaps Mrs. Marks was not more outraged because she saw her husband's behavior as typical, and believed it was his right as a husband to so behave.

Mrs. Tipton was raped for the first and only time by her ex-lover. She is the only woman included in the sample of eighty-seven women who was not actually married (even by common-law) to the man who raped her. They had been live-in lovers and had parented a child together. The role of the child in this case is quite central; so we include it in our analysis of wife rape.

Mrs. Tipton was twenty-five and living with her child and the husband she had married a short time prior to the interview. She was working full-time as a supervisor in a factory. The father of her child raped her when she was twenty-four.

I lived with him for two years. We split up and a month after we split I found out that I was pregnant, so we got back together again for about three months. Then I had the baby and was living on my own. I hadn't seen him for about a year. One night I got a phone call from him. He was back in town, and he asked if I could see him. I told him I'd see him in a bar with other people around. He picked me up and he started driving down toward the beach. Then he stopped off at a motel. He said, "I want to go in and rent a room so we can talk privately." I said that wasn't our agreement. I was upset and in tears. He parked the car and went in and got a room. I was very indecisive in the car. I didn't know what to do. I had to get legal stuff straightened out like child support for our son, so we went in the room and we talked for a while. Then he told me that he wanted to go to bed with me. I told him that I didn't want to. He started to kiss me, and he started getting rough and saying, "I didn't come all the way back here just to talk to you!" I kept trying to walk away from him, but he'd grab onto my arm, holding me so I couldn't walk away. He was verbally very angry, while I was upset and crying. I told him every-thing was finished between us and I wanted to go home. He threw me on the bed and started taking my clothes off. I kept saying, "I want out! I want out! I want to go home!" Then I gave up; I knew how angry he was, so I just gave in. *Sexual inter-course?* Yes. After that neither one of us said anything. He wasn't violent in his love making after I gave in. *Other unwanted sex with him?* No. In fact, when we were together in a relationship, it was nice.

Verbal threats? He used to threaten me that he'd have L. [their son] taken away from me. He's a police officer and knows a lot of attorneys. *Verbal threats in the motel room?* He was still saying that he was going to try to get his son back; that I had no right to keep him from seeing his son.

How upset? Extremely upset. *How much effect on your life?* Some effect. I'm always in a state of fear, not knowing when he'll show up again. He's an extremely jeal-ous person. I don't know if he'd harm G. [her current husband]. That's my major concern.

The child played a central role in Mrs. Tipton's experience; because of him she was willing to see her child's father and to go into the motel. Her ex-lover used the child to manipulate her, through his threats to have the child taken away, and in his stance that "I had no right to keep him from seeing his son." Probably the last chapter of Mrs. Tipton's experience with her ex-lover had not yet occurred by the time of the interview.

Most of these women were only raped once. Three of the women who were raped when they were separated (Mrs. Gordon, Mrs. Marks, and Mrs. Tipton) were raped once, as were two out of the three divorced women. Of the remaining seven women who were raped when separated, three were raped only once. Why did the men rape their wives at this time, and not before? And if they were willing to rape once, then why not more often?

Mrs. King was raped when separated from her husband for a couple of months, but the couple later resumed their marriage and the rapes contin-ued from 11–20 times over a period of 5–10 years. She was still married to this husband at the time of the interview, but he had stopped raping her when "he accepted the fact that it drove us apart."

Mrs. Quinn, who was raped from 2–5 times over a period of from 1–6 months, also returned to her husband, but this appears to have been be-cause she attributed his violence to alcohol, and he had stopped drinking.

The most upsetting experience for Mrs. Upton occurred after she had been separated from her husband for 2 years, but the rapes had also oc-curred over 20 times over a period of 5–10 years prior to the experience when she was separated. And Mrs. Henderson was raped by her husband every night for a year, but only once after she left him.

When a wife is raped one time only it can indicate that she was successful in discouraging her husband from repeating his behavior. It can also happen once because the husband rapes out of a desire to make a point—a point that only needs to be made once. It is quite common, for example, for estranged husbands to try to get their wives back by raping them. If they do not succeed, then they must realize that it is not an effective strategy. For example, Mrs. Yates' husband raped her once in an effort to effect a reconciliation.

Mrs. Yates was thirty-four and divorced at the time of the interview. She was living with her one child, and working full-time as a sales manager for an insurance company.

We were separated. I had left him. He came to where I was staying and we had a big fight. He wanted me to come back to him. He forced me to have sex with him. Since he had been my husband, I couldn't resist like I could with a stranger. *How force?* He pushed me down on the bed. I resisted, saying, "Don't" and pushing him away, but he's very strong. He took off my clothes, my pants, and at that point I just gave up. It really shocked me. He had never been like that before.

Other physical violence? We used to have really awful verbal fights. The issue was that I didn't want to live with him. He finally became really angry, and he pushed me hard up against a corner. It wasn't like he beat me—but it *was* violent.

The fact that rape is used by some men out of a desire for reconciliation provides us with an astonishing insight into patriarchal thinking. Somehow intercourse, even if forced, is seen as an act of repossession that the victim is expected to honor.

What about the separated wives who were raped more than once? There were four of them. The husbands of Mrs. Gordon (whose case is quoted in this chapter), of Mrs. Clayton and Mrs. Quinn (whose cases are quoted in other chapters) also raped them because they wanted to resume their marriages. Two of the thirteen women who were raped after separation or divorce did actually go back to their husbands: Mrs. Quinn's husband stopped drinking and she appears to have believed that the problem was solved. In Mrs. King's case it is not clear why she went back or whether the rape had anything to do with it. Even though Mrs. King described herself as married, she was in fact not living with her husband at the time of the interview—which is to say, she was actually still as separated as she had been at the time of one of her experiences of wife rape. Rape appears to be a poor tactic to employ if a reconciliation is desired. Some husbands rape their wives prior to separation for the same reason:

their wives want the divorce, the husbands do not, and rape is supposed to get the wives to change their minds. The experiences of Mrs. Ellington and Mrs. Fletcher illustrate this point. Both women were among the few who mentioned the rape by their husbands in answer to the question as to whether they had ever been raped at some time in their lives.

Mrs. Ellington was a thirty-one-year-old divorced woman at the time of the interview. She was living alone with her three children and working full-time as a school teacher. The husband who had raped her seven years before worked as a bank clerk. Mrs. Ellington was twenty-four years old on the one occasion her husband raped her. It was on the eve of their divorce, which she was instrumental in seeking. In spite of the fact that she was already sufficiently alienated from him to want a divorce, the trauma of the experience appears to have been considerable.

I was still living with my husband. We got into an argument about the divorce. He didn't want it and he told me he wanted to get me pregnant so I wouldn't leave him. I told him if that happened I would get an abortion and still leave him. Then he slapped me and threw me around, tore my clothes off and raped me.

Verbal threats? "I'm going to get you pregnant. You are going to submit to me." He used foul language, obscenities.

Physical force? It was slapping, pushing, throwing me down, tearing my clothes off. He never hit me in the face; he was afraid it would show. He hit me on my arms, legs and back. Once on the floor, I went into an embryonic position.

How upset? Extremely upset. *How much effect on your life?* A great effect. It really turned me off men and sex. If my husband could do something like that, anyone could! It made sex dirty. When both people want sex, then it's great, but forced sex is wrong. It made me sad that such a neat thing could be turned into something so bad. If he could do it to me, he could also do it to the kids. So I won't let the kids spend the night with him unless he gets remarried.

Mrs. Fletcher was a forty-one-year-old divorced woman living alone at the time of the interview. She was childless and working full-time as a social worker. Her husband was a counsellor who had raped her once when she was thirty-two.

I had asked him for a divorce. We were still sharing the apartment because I hadn't moved out yet. He made some overtures which I repelled, so he forced me. I was wearing jeans. He tore the zipper and he forced me to have sex. We were struggling. He held my hands down, tore off my clothes and penetrated me, though he didn't hit me. *Anything else?* That was it. I was very nasty after that.

Verbal threats? He said he could force me to do anything he wanted to, and that I was going to do what he wanted whether I wanted to or not.

How upset? Extremely upset. *How much effect on your life?* A great effect. It made me very angry. It made me feel degraded and humiliated. It made me feel really resentful that someone would use my body without my permission. I felt whatever I had to do to keep it from happening again, I'd do it.

Other physical violence? He came to slap me. I moved back so he didn't, fortunately for both of us. I told him if he ever tried again, I'd kill him.

Which of all the experiences that happened to you was the most *upsetting?* The experience with my husband, because of the sense of betrayal.

Mrs. Fletcher also reported three other attempted rape experiences, two with dates and one with an acquaintance, but she said that the wife rape was the most upsetting in spite of the fact that she had already decided she wanted to divorce her husband. Her feeling of betrayal provides some insight into why rape by a husband can be more traumatic than rape by a stranger.

Mrs. Fletcher's assertiveness in dealing with her husband's attempted slap raises the question: if women were absolutely definite about not tolerating violence, and were willing to act on this by threatening their husbands, and leaving them if the threat was ineffective, would the problem of husband violence be greatly diminished? Although many women feel they cannot take such actions because they have dependent children, a significant minority of these women have no children, so this is often not the reason they tolerate their husbands' violent behavior.

Obviously we do not simply want to advocate that rape of separated wives be made illegal in every state, since rape in marriage itself must be outlawed where it is not already. The law aside, we have seen that the rape of ex-wives is simply one more consequence of the view of wives as the property of their husbands.

18 ~~crint~~

Women Who Marry
the Men Who
Rape Them

The consent of a woman to sexual intercourse awards the man a privilege of bodily access, a personal "prize" whose value is enhanced by sole ownership.

—*Yale Law Journal,* 1952–53

After the first fuck she was like a well-broken horse; she obeyed me in everything, blushed, was modest, humbled, indifferent, conquered, submissive.

—Anonymous Victorian gentleman, *My Secret Life,* c. 1890

When men regard women as their property, the consequences can be devastating. When women internalize this view of themselves, the results can be equally so, and often it is expressed in very self-destructive ways.

The fact that there are, even today, a few women who marry their rapists, is often taken as evidence that women enjoy being raped. This myth, vigorously fostered and promoted by many pornographers, is tremendously resilient.

Historically, rape was an accepted way of acquiring wives, a custom embedded in Christian and Judaic culture. Susan Brownmiller in *Against Our Will* and Florence Rush in *The Best Kept Secret: Sexual Abuse of Children* provide us with excellent documentation and analysis of this aspect of our history. For example, Rush writes that:

Judaism ordained that a bride could be legally acquired by contract, money, or sexual intercourse, but since the church eschewed materialism, sexual intercourse emerged as the validating factor. As early as the sixth century, Pope Gregory decreed that "any female taken by a man in copulation belonged to him and his kindred." And since copulation with or without consent established male possession of the female, vaginal penetration superseded all impediments. Gratian, twelfth-century Italian ecclesiastic and founder of common law, set forth that while consent was desirable, conjugal union was rendered indissoluble, regardless of age or mutual consent, by coitus. And twelfth-century Pope Alexander III also advised that consent was desirable, but that copulation established a marriage as forever binding.[1]

The notion that intercourse establishes possession of the female by the male is still common in contemporary thinking. This is presumably why thirteen states have actually extended the marital rape privilege to apply to cohabiting couples, and in one state, Virginia, to any couple who has engaged in prior voluntary sexual relations. Shere Hite actually argues that sexual intercourse is and has been symbolic of men's ownership of women for the last three thousand years.[2] Four men who appear to see intercourse as a means of gaining ownership of a woman answered Hite's questionnaire as follows:

Intercourse means I've gotten the woman. I enjoy a woman's subservience.[3]

When I have intercourse with a woman for the first time, it is a feeling of having wetted her with my sperm, or conquered her, and becoming sure that for later meetings she is now my girl.[4]

On occasion I have been so frustrated in dealing with a woman who had willingly had sex with me before that I entertained thoughts of rape. . . .[5]

Why do I want to rape women? Because I am basically, as a male, a predator and all women look to men like prey. I fantasize about the expression on a woman's face when I "capture" her and she realizes she cannot escape. It's like I won, I own her.[6]

Rape by dates and lovers has always been more suspect than rape by strangers in the eyes of the police and the culture at large because of this view. Even prior acquaintanceship is frequently sufficient to cause police to doubt the authenticity of a rape charge.[7]

In her book *Woman-Battering*, sociologist Mildred Pagelow presented the stories of two of her respondents who had married their rapists, but not voluntarily. The rapist of the first woman, Anne, forged her signature on a certificate of marriage. When she became pregnant as a result of the rape, she gave in and moved in with her "husband."[8] The other woman, Sue, was coerced by threats of violence into marriage by her rapist so that she could not testify against him for the rape.[9] The marriage lasted three weeks and Sue was beaten on a daily basis. In contrast, the few women in our study who married their rapists were not coerced into doing so.

Some women have internalized men's perceptions and made them their own. A few even accept the notion that completed rape means successful conquest, and that marriage to the conqueror is the only way that some virtue can be restored.

The first case to be cited here involves a woman who married twice. Mrs. Edwards' first husband attempted to rape her, and her second husband succeeded in raping her. The attacks by both husbands occurred *prior* to the marriage. (Mrs. Edwards is not included as one of the eighty-seven raped wives since she was never raped by these men while they were married to her, nor after the marriages had ended. But I include her experiences here because they are relevant to the issue of why a few women marry the men who rape them.)

Mrs. Edwards, who said she was fifty at the time of the interview, was separated, disabled, and living alone. She had raised one child, who had died in her late teens. She had been an assistant credit manager in a department store. The attempted rape occurred when Mrs. Edwards was seventeen years old.

On the self-administered questionnaire given at the end of the interview, Mrs. Edwards wrote that she had felt very uncomfortable during the interview but "I did answer truthfully *all* of the questions to the best of my ability with the exception of my age." Presumably that means she was older than fifty.

He was an acquaintance whom I met at a party. He was drunk and followed me home. He asked me to go for a hamburger or something. I got in his car, and after a bit, he pulled off the road at a deserted place. Then he took off my clothes. He did everything but actual fornication. *Did he try to force intercourse?* Yes of course. *How?* He tried to force himself on me. He shoved me down on the seat. I struggled, but he had all his weight on me. I don't remember if he took himself out of his pants or not. I sort of flip-out when something like this happens. I block it out. Maybe he put it between my legs, I don't remember, but nothing went inside, and I don't think I touched him anywhere. *Kind of force?* It wasn't violent in that he wasn't beating me; it was just struggling. He may have pushed my shoulders down on the seat, put his knee between my legs, but I know he didn't penetrate me.

That was the first night I met him. After that I felt he had to marry me. *Other unwanted sex with him?* No.

How upset: Extremely upset. *How much effect on your life?* A great effect. I married somebody I would never have considered marrying otherwise, and I had his baby though I hadn't planned on having children so soon. It tied me down and I had to live a lie, hiding things from my family, like that he was a drunk and a gambler.

Mrs. Edwards' reasoning is very evident: "after that I felt he had to marry me." Otherwise, according to this reasoning, she would have been rendered even more impure, because sex without marriage is a sin. If there is sex, even if it is forced, there must be marriage. She could retain purity only at the price of an unhappy marriage with a man she did not respect or care about. Even at the time of the interview she did not appear to question the rightness of her decision.

The second rape and marriage followed a similar pattern. This husband also did not rape Mrs. Edwards during the marriage, but she said he had been violent toward her more than twenty times over a period of four years.

He grabbed my hand, got my keys, forced me on the bed and raped me. *Then you married him?* I told you, I had to marry him after that. I didn't consider him even a boyfriend at the time, he was just a date. *He put his penis in your vagina?* Yes. *Anything else?* No. *What kind of force did he use?* He manhandled me. He pushed and shoved me and threatened to arrest me for hooking or vagrancy. He was a cop. *Other unwanted sex with him?* No. He was violent, but that's the only time he raped me.

How upset? Extremely upset. *How much effect on your life?* A great effect. I hate and despise all bullies and brutes. He used the police force to cover up his own lousiness.

Other physical violence? It happened all the time. I ran away many times but he would always find me and beat me up. I reported him to the police many times too. I was a nervous wreck.

One time he broke my nose. We were in the car and he had a gun. He said he was going to kill me because he said I'd lied to him. He reached over with his fist and broke my nose. He also broke my fingers, and did things to my vagina.

Not only does Mrs. Edwards specifically use the word rape when describing her second husband's assault on her, but she volunteered this experience to the question regarding whether she had ever been a victim of rape or attempted rape. Once again Mrs. Edwards' belief system is clear: even though she was raped by a date whom she hated, she "had to marry him after that."

Mrs. Creedon, who was forty-six and married to her second husband, was not only raped by her first husband before her marriage, but more than twenty times during the six months that it lasted. She was childless and at the time of the interview was working full-time as a clothes designer. Mrs. Creedon was twenty-one years old when her husband first raped her. First, her account of the premarital rape:

We had coffee together at my house after a date. He twisted my arm around me and threw me down on the floor and raped me. He bit my breasts, as I recall. He was armed. He had a pistol. He didn't actually wave it at me, he just talked about it. He wondered whether he should kill himself, or kill me, or whether we should both go together. It was spooky. He was an unbalanced guy. He forced intercourse on me.

Verbal threats? He was threatening suicide and murder. He described how the blood would splatter over the ceiling and the floor.

How upset? Extremely upset. *How much effect on your life?* A great effect. I probably married him because I felt guilty. That was a real black time. I can't sort it out, and never have been able to. I think I felt half responsible for his mental state. I was young and stupid.

Other unwanted sex with him? Yes, after I married him. The most upsetting time was when he had my arms tied behind me. He had a shotgun that he put in my face. I was awfully scared. He liked to describe gore. *Forced intercourse?* Yes. It couldn't have been anything else. He seemed to prefer that [forced rather than consensual intercourse]. *Anything else that he tried to do?* No, he was pretty straight-arrowed as far as the sex. It was straight intercourse.

Weapons? He had a hand gun, a shotgun, and a knife too.

What brought it to an end? He killed himself.

How upset? Extremely upset. *How much effect on your life?* A great effect. It was a good eight years before I married again. I still don't like the idea of marriage, that piece of paper. I don't know if that has to do with him or not.

Most upsetting incident of physical violence? That time I told you about, when he tied me up. I sure didn't like that at all! He put the shotgun in my face and described how cute it was. He described how it would be with the blood and the brains splattered all over. He was a violent man.

It is interesting that he volunteered as a policeman. He had been in the Marine Corps. He wanted to enlist a third time but they wouldn't let him.

The fact that Mrs. Creedon married a man as violent and dangerous as Mr. Creedon appears to have been, certainly testifies to the danger that can result from feeling responsibility when it is not appropriate. This in turn is something females are reared to do in this culture.

Had Mrs. Creedon obtained some perverse gratification from her husband's violence, she might have married another man like him. But Mrs. Creedon chose a second husband who appears to be neither disturbed nor violent. She did mention experiencing some unwanted sex with her current husband, but she said that these experiences were not forced. This is how she described them: "They usually have to do with his drinking too much, but they really aren't forced. Not physically. I think that if I let him know [that they were unwanted], he would stop."

In her second marriage Mrs. Creedon appears still to have a problem with asserting herself. Feeling guilty or responsible inappropriately is surely one of the most critical factors in keeping women from acting in their own best interests. Mrs. Creedon certainly provides a very extreme example.

Mrs. Garrison's experience of premarital rape differs from that of Mrs. Edwards and of Mrs. Creedon; she was raped by her fiancé. At the time of the interview, Mrs. Garrison was sixty-seven years old, married (but not to the man who raped her), and had raised one child. She was retired, but had been the manager of a daycare center when she worked.

Mrs. Garrison was eighteen years old at the time her fiancé raped her. She said these experiences continued to occur after they were married, and that she had been raped more than twenty times over a period of seven years.

We were engaged and the marriage date was set. He was eleven years older than me. A few days before we were to be married, he was drinking, and then it happened. I stayed overnight at his place. I was young and in love, but when he was tipsy he would push me around. He smelled of alcohol. I cried; it was a very terrible experience. I didn't want it but I went through with it because I felt I had to. It was a very messy marriage; everything was unwanted. I would say, "You've been drinking again," and that would make him mad and he would force me to have intercourse. He demanded his rights as a husband. Other times if I didn't obey, he would leave the house. Sometimes I would give in to get it over as quickly as possible. He's dead now; I don't want to put the fault all on him.

Verbal threats? "I'll kill you."

What brought it to an end? I couldn't stand it anymore. He was going down with his drinking.

How upset? Not at all. *How much effect on your life?* No effect.

Mrs. Garrison wanted to discount the trauma of the experience because her husband was dead. However, while maintaining that the experiences had neither upset her, nor affected her life in any way, Mrs. Garrison also reported that she had cried, that "it was a very terrible experience" and "a very messy marriage," that her husband had threatened to kill her, and that at some point she "couldn't stand it any more" and they got divorced.

Mrs. Garrison mentioned in her interview that she was "in love," and that she was eleven years younger than her fiancé. Because she spontaneously mentioned the latter as if she thought it significant, her husband may have been something of an authority figure to her. In addition to these aspects of their relationship, the fact that the rape occurred on the eve of her becoming her fiancé's "legitimate" possession, as well as a feeling of commitment toward him, probably played a role in her marrying her rapist. Mrs. Garrison also seemed to feel her youthfulness was a relevant factor in her premarital rape.

Mrs. Lucas was even younger than Mrs. Garrison. She was only thirteen the first time the man who was to become her husband raped her. At the time of the interview she was a thirty-year-old divorced woman, living alone with her two children. She was looking for work, but said that she had been a school bus driver.

The man who raped her was sixteen. Mrs. Lucas said the rapes had continued and had occurred more than twenty times over a period of nine years. The first attack is an example of rape when unable to consent; having drunk an excessive amount of alcohol, Mrs. Lucas was unconscious.

I was thirteen. It was the first time. This was my ex-husband. There was no physical force, but there definitely was mental pressure. I played my part because of my insecurity. If I was a different person it might never have happened. He got me drunk with half a bottle of Seagram's 7. Then he took my virginity from me. He was sixteen at the time. I remember being in the kitchen and then waking up in the garage. He had undressed me and had sexual intercourse with me. *Vaginal intercourse?* Yes. *Did he ever use physical force?* One time. He was stronger than me and he just held me down.

Verbal threats? He threatened never to see me again if we didn't have sex. He said that he would leave me and no one would ever want me. He said that if I gave him too bad a time he'd call in a group of men, have them rape me, and take pictures to prove that I was an unfit mother. I never wanted sex with him then, so this went on for nine years until I desired him.

What brought it to an end? I came into my own person. He was someone who was able to manipulate people and I was easily influenced by others. As long as I didn't realize I was being manipulated, it didn't end. After I had Gestalt therapy for four years, I started realizing things.

How upset? Extremely upset. *How much effect on your life?* A great effect. I think it set up tremendous mental blocks in me. It left me with a very worthless attitude toward myself. I was more of an object than a person. It fed into my insecurities.

Other physical violence? He belted me in the mouth once, and I lost a front tooth. But basically he was a nonviolent person. I was with him seventeen years of my life. He did physical damage to me twice. The other time when wrestling with me he twisted my arm pretty badly. He sprained it. *Why did he hit you?* Because I was screaming at the top of my lungs about him and other women.

Mrs. Lucas said her husband was only violent when he was drunk, and that his physical violence had occurred only twice over a period of two years. She described him as a basically nonviolent person, which seems inconsistent with his vicious threat that if she gave him too bad a time, he'd call in a group of men, have them rape her and take pictures to prove that she was an unfit mother.

Mrs. Lucas explained her marriage to a man who raped her as being due to her insecurity, and by implication, her low self-image. She also specifically mentioned that "he took my virginity from me." This fact might have played a part in her marrying him: since she had "lost her virtue," as the culture sees it, marrying the man may have constituted partial redemption. In addition, the fact that she was raped when she was drunk may have caused her to blame herself for getting drunk in the first place.

Finally, her extreme youth—being only thirteen years of age at the time—probably made her far more vulnerable to a manipulative man who was three years her senior than most adult women would have been. A three-year age difference for teenagers is a much greater difference in power and authority than a three-year difference later in life.

Mrs. Field provides perhaps the only clear-cut case of a victim of wife rape who participated in her own victimization. She was forty-one at the time of the interview and still married to the man who raped her. She was raising three children and going to school, but she had previously worked as a stewardess, a model, an office worker, and the manager of a dress boutique. Her husband was an investigator for the District Attorney's Office.

Mrs. Field was twenty-seven years old the first time she was raped by her husband; this and subsequent rapes were achieved not by force but by her husband's taking advantage of her when she was helpless because she was drunk. The rapes occurred over twenty times over a period of ten years.

I would literally black out. It happened before and after we were married—for two years before and eight years afterwards. We had a ritual. We'd drink a lot, I'd get loose and sexual, but I didn't want to have intercourse. He wouldn't take no for an answer. He could drink better than I could. I'd get passive and inert and he'd do whatever he wanted. When we were married I felt I had to.

Much of the intercourse was physically forced. I suffered from vaginismus, which I went into therapy for. I was just a body, and he would fuck me to get his orgasm. *Anything else?* Yes, oral sex. *Did he succeed?* Yeah. Again, through begging or psychological manipulation, and through positioning me and himself. He always proceeded on to intercourse. All my life I was told I had to do it. When drunk, I felt physically helpless. It got to be a destructive pattern. I had to be drunk.

What brought it to an end? Talking it out. My becoming militantly feminist. Therapy. His becoming more aware and calming down.

How upset? Extremely upset. *How much effect on your life?* A great effect. I thought there was something wrong with me; that it was all my fault. I felt my marriage was threatened, and I was into preserving the marriage. I reminded myself that I hadn't had good sexual experiences before. All the literature said I was a frigid woman. It took a long time to sort through. I went into therapy and joined women's groups and talked about it a lot.

Which of the experiences that happened to you upset you most? What happened with my husband. I had to deal with it to survive.

In the self-administered questionnaire at the end of the interview Mrs. Field wrote that it was "rather difficult to talk about the sexual experience with my spouse. Though the problems have been resolved, the memory is still painful."

Given Mrs. Field's cooperation with the "ritual"—as she called it— this is a borderline case of rape due to the victim being unable to consent. Nevertheless it seems important to understand why she participated in it, and why she married a man with whom she spent two years having such an unsatisfactory sexual relationship. The fact that she blamed herself for sexual inadequacy seems crucial.

Mrs. Field described herself as suffering from vaginismus—a condition in which the vagina is so contracted that penetration by a penis is usually painful or impossible. It is usually caused by sexual trauma. Mrs. Field had been subjected to a great deal of prior sexual assault: forced oral sex over a period of eight months with a date when she was twenty-one; forced oral sex with a lover over a period of three years starting when she was twenty-two; attempted rape by an acquaintance when she was twenty-two; attempted rape by a boss when she was twenty-four. Hence, abusive as her experiences with her husband-to-be were, she said that she reminded herself that she hadn't had any good sexual experiences before. On the other hand, in retrospect, she also considered her experiences with her husband the most upsetting of all because "I had to deal with it to survive."

Mrs. Field's experience is tragic and poignant; it shows some of the worst consequences of compulsory heterosexuality. Because she was blamed or blamed herself for her experiences of sexual assault, when someone came along who she felt abused her slightly less than the others, she married him. She felt her very "survival" was at stake, even though she had a college degree and had previously obtained many different kinds of jobs. These facts suggest that it was not her economic survival as much as her survival as a woman that she felt was at stake. She appears to have believed that she could not avoid unwanted sexual relationships with men.

Mrs. Anderson was also very young when she was raped by the man she later married. At the time of the interview she was twenty-eight and had just the day before divorced the husband who raped her. She was living with her grandmother and young child. Mrs. Anderson described herself as "keeping house" but had previously worked as a dental assistant. The husband who had raped her had been a student whom she had supported.

Mrs. Anderson was fifteen or sixteen years old and in the tenth grade when her husband-to-be first started to sexually abuse her. He was sixteen years old himself. When asked how many times he had assaulted her Mrs. Anderson replied that she "couldn't even count"—they had been so numerous. Her husband's sexual abuse occurred over a period of two years, and his other physical violence occurred more than twenty times over a period of seven years.

For about two years we had a problem because he wanted to go all the way, and I felt I should stay a virgin. I was afraid of what others would say. We'd do everything but have intercourse. He used to take pictures of me with my bra on and he'd insist that I pose for him. *Did you feel forced?* Yes, I felt at his mercy. He would come over when I was babysitting and he'd make me do things like walk outside without clothes on, or take his clothes off. Also, he often forced me to have oral sex. *How?* By pushing my head down and holding it there until he was finished. Once he attempted rectal intercourse with me. He just pushed me down and did it. *Did you feel physically threatened?* Yes. He had a bad temper, and I felt that he wouldn't let me resist. I felt that he had to do it his way, and that there was no way I could refuse. His threats were physical and also verbal, and he wouldn't let me go out until he was through.

When we married he continually forced intercourse on me and also physically hurt me. After I had a child I had no sex drive for a while, and my husband would rape me often. I felt forced to have intercourse every night. He'd hold me down, hit me, verbally abuse and bully me, and pull guilt trips on me. He would force me to have oral sex by pushing my head down or shoving it down my throat. He would hold off coming for hours and was obsessed that we had to have sex every night as a torment to me.

Verbal threats? "I can't wait forever." And when we were married, he'd say, "I can't tolerate this. You have sex now or I'll get sex elsewhere. I'll leave you. If I wanted a maid, I'd have one."

Physical force? If I'd say no, he'd throw me against the wall or onto the bed. He'd also push me out of bed when I resisted him. He'd punch me on the arm and body, shaking me hard, throwing me against the wall.

How upset? Extremely upset—it was hell. *How much effect on your life?* A great effect. I'm afraid to get involved in another relationship. I'm trying to become more selfish. I had the strength to get out of this relationship somehow, and now my security is very important to me.

Which experience of physical violence upset you most? I was holding the baby and he threw both of us onto the bed and started hitting me really hard. I thought he was crazy. I thought he at least loved the baby. She was screaming and very frightened for me, but he kept hitting me anyway. *Did he hurt her?* Physically no, but emotionally a great deal. Who knows how much effect that has had on her. *Other physical violence?* He pushed me against the wall once when he was angry. Another time he tried to take the baby away from me and he tried banging me against the wall. He'd squeeze my arms very hard or hit me and slap me hard on my arms or my back. Any time he'd get angry he could get violent like this; usually it involved the same kinds of hurting.

Aside from the fact that Mrs. Anderson was young and thus more vulnerable than most older females, she gives us no clue as to why she married this sadistic young man after he had intimidated her and been so sexually abusive. However, the impact she described of an earlier experience with her first boyfriend who was almost her peer (she was twelve and he was eleven at the time) appears to have played a significant role.

It was my first boyfriend. I was twelve and we were playing hide and seek. One day when we were in his parents' car, he grabbed me on my breasts with his hands, then he pulled me down on top of him. *Did you feel physically forced?* Yes. He laid on top of me and kept his hands on my breasts and I couldn't push him away. I felt I had been made dirty by him and that he got something. *Was this against your wishes?* Yes. Extremely so.

How upset? Very upset. *How much effect on your life?* A great effect. I felt very ashamed and guilty as if it was my fault and he had taken something of my own from me and then left me. I felt easy, cheap, robbed of something. It made me very afraid to *feel* in a relationship because if you give too much they'll tire of you and leave. It made me hung-up sexually. My sister read about it in my diary and she told his mother and my mother, and I was very ashamed and embarrassed. Later when my husband heard about it he went and beat him up.

Often the first sexual abuse experienced by a young girl or adolescent, if it is traumatic, is repeated at a later time. Mrs. Anderson was very upset by the feeling that her first boyfriend had, after abusing her, tired of her and left. This may have contributed to her willingness to marry and stay with her husband after his abuse of her, because at least he didn't abandon her after defiling her like her first boyfriend had. Her husband's act of beating up this boyfriend adds an ironic twist to her story. Abusive husbands are commonly outraged by abusive behavior on the part of other men. It also illustrates that the other side of the protector role can often be abusive behavior. Though the former is commonly revered in patriarchal culture while the latter is not, both are intended to demonstrate power.

Many wives feel unable to leave husbands who are abusing them when they have a young child or children to care for. Hence the fact that Mrs. Anderson had the responsibility of a young daughter at the time she left indicates that she was finally able to muster up considerable determination.

The common theme that seems to connect all six of these cases is the link between sexual relations and a woman's becoming the property of a man. Many women feel they belong to a man once they are married to him. Some women, however, feel they belong to a man they have sex with, even when it was unwanted or forced on them, as was the case with these women.

The young ages of most of these women—one was thirteen, one fifteen or sixteen, one seventeen, one eighteen, one twenty-one, and one twenty-seven—helps us to understand this attitude. Their youthfulness also probably made it difficult for them to cope with unequal power situations. The twenty-seven-year-old was the only woman who was described as participating in her own victimization. The rapists who became the husbands of the two youngest females appear to have been particularly domineering and tyrannical toward them before and after their marriages.

Though many people interpret the fact that a few women marry the men who rape them as evidence that women enjoy being raped, these accounts demonstrate various degrees of trauma and no discernable enjoyment.

19

Lovers and Daughters
Are Property Too

"She is *mine*. I have a right to orgasm through intercourse.
God gave me this right when he made women for men."

"Two previous girl partners (separately) said 'no' and I did it
anyway. I was thrilled out of my mind that I could be such a
beast and it was really satisfying."

"I let her know that if she was going to have a relationship
with me, she was going to fuck when I wanted to. Sometimes
I want to and she don't, if we are in bed I will get on top and
force my way into her."

> —Male respondents, *The Hite Report on Male Sexuality*,
> Shere Hite, 1981

Many of the fathers seemed to consider it their parental prerogative to introduce their daughters to sex.

> —Judith Herman, *Father-Daughter Incest*, 1981

That women are the property of men is an idea that is applied to situations other than marriage. Lovers are also often seen as property, a view
that is also sanctioned by law in many states where the marital rape exemption has been extended to protect men in nonmarital cohabiting relationships. (Even date rape is protected in Virginia: see Appendix II for
further information on these laws.) Too, children are almost universally
seen as the property of their parents, and some fathers assume that this
includes the right of sexual access, particularly to their daughters.

DAUGHTERS AS PROPERTY

Although the eighty-seven raped wives in our survey were not asked
whether their husbands had also abused their children, two of them
spontaneously mentioned that the same husband who had raped them
had also sexually abused their daughters. One victim of wife rape mentioned that another husband who had beaten but not raped her had sex-

257

ually abused a daughter; and a fourth woman who had married a man who raped her, reported that he had tried to rape her daughter.

This means that husbands of 5 percent of the raped wives also sexually abused their daughters, if we include the one woman who married her rapist along with the eighty-seven victims of wife rape. Another way of looking at this figure is to note that out of the 292 women in our sample who had ever been married *and* had a daughter, 1.4 percent spontaneously mentioned that a daughter was abused by her husband. Alternatively, since there were altogether 175 marriages within which wife rape and/or some other violence occurred, 4 cases represents 2.3 percent of these marriages. These percentages are likely gross underestimations of the true prevalence of father-daughter incestuous abuse, since wives were not even asked about this issue. Louise Armstrong, author of *Kiss Daddy Goodnight: A Speakout on Incest,* concludes that: "It seems apparent, both by its incidence and by the noticeable absence of any sincere, widespread dread of retribution, that incest is not truly a taboo. Just a very, very long-lived, well-suppressed secret."[1] In support of this viewpoint, Armstrong maintains that the offending fathers of the incest victims she interviewed for her book who did not get caught showed no signs of guilt.[2] Armstrong also believes that an incestuous father must have "a sense of paternalistic prerogative in order to even begin to rationalize what he's doing. . . . He must have a perception of his children as possessions, as '*objects.*' "[3]

Mrs. Lucas, a thirty-year-old divorced woman whose account of wife rape was cited in Chapter 18, was initially very suspicious of how her address was selected, fearing that one of the agencies she had applied to for help with the problem of incest may have given out information. After investigating the authenticity of the study and its sponsoring agency, she became very interested and involved.

Mrs. Lucas was only thirteen at the time her husband-to-be raped her. He continued to rape her for a period of nine years when they were married "until I desired him." A few years after she started desiring him, he started sexually abusing their daughter.

When asked which of her experiences had been the most upsetting Mrs. Lucas disclosed the incestuous abuse of her daughter.

There was a sexual relationship between my husband and one of my children. It went on for five years. It ended when my daughter told me because she reached an age where she felt that what was going on wasn't right. I got medical help from the local Medical Association of Psychiatry. *Who received services?* My daughter, myself, and her father—for a while. *What happened?* Sexual intercourse. *What was the age of your daughter?* It happened from when she was seven to twelve years old. *How old was your husband then?* He was twenty-five when she was seven.

He'd never been in any trouble as far as crime went. *Did he bother other people?* In retrospect, I started remembering other incidents I hadn't realized at the time might be like that—with other young girls. I found out about my daughter one and a half years ago.

Was this ever reported to the police? Yes. The juvenile child abuse center listed my daughter as being abused by him. But nothing happened to him because of it. He got no record for it.

Psychologists have often attributed the sexual abuse of daughters by fathers to the "fact" that the wives of these men are frigid or otherwise sexually rejecting. But while Mrs. Lucas had sexually rejected her husband for the first nine years of their marriage, she subsequently changed, and he had stopped raping her. Within a couple of years, however, he started sexually abusing their daughter. Perhaps Mr. Lucas preferred an unwilling partner. Perhaps he enjoyed the sense of power that can accompany rape of an adult or the sense of power that can accompany relating sexually to a child to whom one is a supreme authority.

Mrs. Fulton was a forty-six-year-old divorced woman at the time of the interview. She had been married twice and had raised seven children. One husband raped her (this experience was described in Chapter 14). The other was violent toward her more than twenty times over a period of eleven years, and also abused their daughter.

He tried to choke me to death when I saw him with my daughter once. He said it wasn't anything, and to forgive him. He called me ignorant and alcoholic.

I used to beg him to go to bed with me, but all the while he was having something with my daughter. When I approached him about it, that's when he started beating me.

I couldn't approach my daughter about it because she put him on a pedestal. Toward the end when I wouldn't want to come home, he slapped me around in front of the kids.

In this brief description, Mrs. Fulton presents a picture that contradicts two stereotypes about the wife or mother of father-daughter incest victims. First, one stereotype has it that wives often know when their daughters are being sexually abused but refuse to do anything about it and so collude in the crime. Mrs. Fulton, however, confronted her husband as soon as she realized what was going on, as a result of which he tried to choke her to death.

The second stereotype, mentioned earlier, is that these wives sexually reject their husbands. Mrs. Fulton was not sexually rejecting but sexually deprived, and assertive about this ("I used to beg him to go to bed with me").

One feature that commonly occurs in cases of father-daughter incestuous abuse is alluded to by Mrs. Fulton; the distance (often hostility) that this relationship creates between the mother and the daughter. Many daughters end up blaming their mothers for not protecting them, more than they blame the fathers for abusing them.

Like Mrs. Lucas, Mrs. Edwards married her rapist. Her account of this experience was described in Chapter 18. Her husband also abused their daughter.

He tried to rape my daughter. He performed cunnilingus on her. I reported it and he got kicked off the [police] force. She later became a hooker and committed suicide. I could have killed him.

Many prostitutes have one or more experiences of childhood sexual abuse, particularly incestuous abuse.[4] Like Mrs. Lucas and Mrs. Fulton, Mrs. Edwards took action against her husband on behalf of her daughter. She was even successful in getting him dismissed from the police force.

The fact that two of the four cases of father-daughter incestuous abuse spontaneously mentioned by the wives in our survey occurred in marriages in which women had married the men who raped them, may be more than coincidental. We have discussed why women married their rapists, it is also important to consider why rapists would marry their victims. Perhaps men who believe that rape is a way to gain possession of a woman—men who subscribe particularly ardently to the idea of women as property—are also more inclined than most men to see their female children as their sexual property.

Roland Summit and JoAnn Kryso have differentiated what they describe as "imperious incest" from nine other types. This is how they describe the men involved:

These men set themselves up as emperors in their household domain. They play out an incredible caricature of the male chauvinist role, requiring wife and daughter to perform acts of sexual fealty. The man, who initiated three daughters into his service, even constructed a throne for himself.[5]

Another type is described by Summit and Kryso as "misogynous incest." This also involves fathers seeing their daughters as their possessions. These researchers believe that for these types of fathers, possessing their daughters sexually is an assertion of their invulnerability to the control of women, as well as an act of "punitive defiance" toward their wives.[6]

While Shere Hite does not deal with the issue of incestuous abuse in her voluminous book on male sexuality, she cites one case of a father sexually abusing his wife and his daughter.

Often, fellatio was a prelude to "normal" intercourse between my wife and I. Sometimes I used it as a means of demeaning her. Sometimes I told her to, other times I asked her to. I also forced my youngest daughter to perform fellatio on me two or three times. Not because I was sexually attracted to her.[7]

Given that research on wife rape is in its infancy, the connection between wife rape and incestuous abuse has never before been explored. This discussion is but a first step. It seems possible that there is more of a link between these two forms of sexual abuse than has been thought heretofore, and that the status and perception of females as property may be a key factor in the etiology of both.

LOVERS AS PROPERTY

There are both similarities and differences in rape by husbands and rape by lovers. Some lover relationships differ from marriage only in so far as there is no legal sanction of the relationship, and because psychologically, the partners realize they are not legally woman and husband. Other lover relationships have little in common with marriage other than that they involve a sexual relationship. The latter type of relationship turns up quite often in our study since our definition of "lover" was very broad: it included any nonrelative with whom the respondent had had consensual sexual intercourse at least once. However, another thing that many lover relationships have in common with marriage is that once a woman has voluntarily consented to intercourse, many men believe she has given up her right to refuse them on future occasions. Once again, the woman is seen to have become the man's property by virtue of having been penetrated by his penis. Like a wife, she has lost the right to say no.

Mrs. Morgan, whose experience of wife rape was described in Chapter 4, left the husband who had raped her over a period of six months. Subsequently, she was raped by a lover. She saw her relationship with her lover as essentially the same as that with her husband—though in fact, it seems to have been considerably worse.

Mrs. Morgan was twenty-eight and separated at the time of the interview. She was living with her lover and one of her two children, and working full-time as a clerk-typist. Her lover worked as a legal secretary. She said that he had raped her more than twenty times over the last eight months of their four-year relationship.

It's the same [as with her ex-husband] with the boyfriend I'm living with now. Men are all the same. He comes home after he's been with someone else and has sex with me. *Forced intercourse?* Yes. When I know he's been with someone else, I don't have any desire to have sex. *Verbal threats?* The same ones as my husband—

they're all the same. He said he'd get gasoline and pour it on me and set me alight. He even went to a garage to get the gasoline. I never reported it because the police said they wouldn't do anything. I called them just to ask.

How upset? Somewhat upset. *How much effect on your life?* A great effect. I'm beginning to hate men as far as ever sharing a house with them. It's affected my mood. I get depressed—very depressed. I worry a lot. I've developed hypertension.

Other physical violence? Yes. I've lost track of how many times. More than twenty—ever since we've been together, which is four years. He loses his temper and starts fighting me. I never fight back.

That Mrs. Morgan's stayed with her lover is particularly remarkable since she was willing to leave her husband after only six months. She reiterated that "men are all the same," and perhaps she has resigned herself to the notion that living with any man involves being subjected to abuse. Sometimes bad experiences strengthen a woman's resolve not to accept abuse again, and sometimes they undermine her belief that she can successfully avoid abuse. Mrs. Morgan seems to fall into the latter category.

Ms. Holland's relationship with her lover was not like a marriage. Nevertheless her lover refused to recognize her right to say no. Ms. Holland was thirty and had never been married; she was living alone at the time of the interview. She was working full-time as a secretary. At the time of the rape she was twenty-six years old—the same age as her lover, who worked as a clerk in a department store. The rape had occurred once.

I knew him for six years. Then we started dating and being lovers. I had thought of him as a friend, but he started to become offensive and I didn't want to be his lover any more. I was at his apartment and I wanted to go home and he said, "Stay. Why not?" I tried to tell him my feelings had changed. I was trying to be rational with him. I asked him to take me home.

He's about six feet five inches and weighs about two hundred twenty pounds, so it wasn't hard for him to push me back on the couch and for him to get on top of me. His hands were all over me. I could feel his hands against my groin. He pinned me down with his body. He had both of my hands held down with one of his. He told me to stop struggling. Then he said, "Maybe you'd enjoy it if I tied you." I burst into tears and I said "You goddamned bastard." I was so upset that he would even suggest something like that. Also I knew I would never get out of there without having sex, and I didn't want to get hurt. My reaction was tears and frustration. I thought, "Who'd believe me if I screamed? After all we had been lovers." So he had sex with me.

Verbal threats? He threatened to tie me up. He wanted it to be a turn-on but it wasn't.

How upset? Very upset. *How much effect on your life?* A little effect.

The fact that Ms. Holland had known this man for six years before they became lovers was no protection against his raping her, nor against his imagining that she might get sexual stimulation from being tied up.

It is clear from Ms. Holland's rhetorical question: "Who'd believe me if I screamed? After all, we had been lovers" that she recognized the cultural myth that lovers, like wives, cannot be raped. This is one reason why women in this situation are often less able to resist optimally. They are disarmed by the very fact that they are being raped by an intimate.

Mrs. Porter's lover also denied her the right to say no, raping her from 2–5 times over a period of 4 months. Like many women who are raped by their husbands, she did not at the time see the assault as rape.

Mrs. Porter was thirty-one, divorced, and living alone at the time of the interview; she had no children and was going to school. She was eighteen years old when she was first raped by her lover. Her subsequent experience of rape in marriage was described in Chapter 17.

I was having an affair with this man, but I wasn't in love with him. It was the middle of the night. I was home in bed. The kitchen door must have been unlocked. He came in and got in bed with me. I told him to go home because he was drunk. God, that really made him mad. It also really scared the shit out of me. He essentially raped me. He was very big and strong and we had sex which was totally against my wishes.

Another time I was at his house and I wanted to go home. He simply picked me up and carried me into his bedroom and forced me to have sex with him. I was almost smothered—I could hardly breathe. At the time I didn't look at it as rape. My definition of rape has changed now.

What brought it to an end? I was really scared of the dude and just avoided him like crazy.

How upset? Extremely upset. *How much effect on your life?* A great effect. I became so disillusioned with men, which was partially responsible for my marriage. My husband was the first nice man I met. He was respectful and kind. I think it led to my having a very low image of men.

When women like Mrs. Porter do not see themselves as victims of rape, it is more difficult for them to feel outraged by what has happened to them. Their unawareness that the act was rape also makes it more likely that it will happen again.

Like Mrs. Porter, Mrs. Kerr articulated that she had not seen herself as a rape victim at the time "because I'd been sleeping with him a month." Mrs. Kerr was a forty-one-year-old divorced woman who had no children and was working part-time as a pharmacist's assistant. She had previously worked for many years as a physical therapist.

Mrs. Kerr was thirty-eight years old when she was raped by her lover. It happened once. She described him as a professional gambler.

I had picked him up in San Francisco and went out with him. I didn't take him home the first night, but I gave him my phone number. He called the next day and I wanted to see him. We went out. He was a very attractive, well-dressed Italian. The second night we went out, I brought him home and we went to bed and everything was fine. I continued to see him for a week. He was very possessive and I liked that at first. After three weeks, he admitted to me that he was a gambler. I told him I didn't approve of his lifestyle and I wouldn't get along with him. I really provoked this whole thing because I got upset with his lifestyle and asked him *not* to talk about it with me. After four weeks he asked to move in with me. He hadn't asked for money or anything, and it seemed to be all right. The only problem was that he flew to Reno every day to gamble.

He moved in and everything went smoothly for two and a half weeks. One Sunday after he left to go to Reno, I knew when he came back I would get beaten up. I knew something violent would happen because he said he'd taken his last five thousand dollars. So I took precautions. I made sure the doors of the house were open so I could get out quickly, and I asked a neighbor to stand by, though he hadn't been violent before.

He came back and as I opened the door, he beat me up. He threw me on the floor and really pummelled me. I was fighting back really hard and all of a sudden the fighting turned into lovemaking. I tried to push him off and the more I tried to push him off the more violent he became. He started fucking me hard and hurtfully, like he was really trying to hurt me sexually as well as hurt me physically by smacking me in the face. Even after he succeeded in penetrating me he continued to beat on me. The whole time I was fighting back, but he was really strong. Then I said, "Let's go into the bedroom, it'd be more comfortable in bed." We got up and I ran out the back door, screaming and yelling and threatening to call the police. I was out in the backyard for half an hour and he was gone when I went back inside. I got dressed to go to the police. He'd said his brother was a policeman, so I tried to call his brother at the precinct but they said they had no cop by that name. So I decided that I'd provoked it. I didn't think I was raped actually because I'd been sleeping with him for a month.

I went to a friend's house and he came over there but she didn't let him in. I threatened to call the cops and he never showed up after that. He called on the phone every day, but I refused to see him, so he stopped. I felt I'd provoked it mentally by stifling him from speaking about the thing nearest and dearest to him, which was his gambling. I never saw it as a rape. It's rape with a total stranger, not with someone you live with. I don't think this guy was a rapist. He was very macho; maybe too macho.

Verbal threats? He said: "I'm going to fuck you to death," if that's a threat.
How upset? Extremely upset. *How much effect on your life?* A little effect.

Mrs. Kerr knew she was going to get beaten up and she took a number of very sensible precautions because of this, but she was still unable to prevent what happened. She was able, however, to end the relationship quickly. Mrs. Kerr, unlike most raped wives, is able to shut this abusive man out of her life much more rapidly than can women who share property, children, and years of living together with their rapists.

Although Mrs. Kerr articulates very clearly that she didn't think her lover was a rapist and that "I never saw it as rape," she mentioned the experience in answer to the question regarding whether she had ever been raped. On the other hand, at the beginning of the interview the interviewer reported that Mrs. Kerr didn't think she had any experiences to talk about. This reveals how complex the issue of perception can be in experiences like this. Mrs. Kerr's unwillingness to consistently see her lover as a rapist, and her self-blame, may account for her assessment that the rape had only a little effect on her subsequent life.

Some women accept the idea of themselves as the property of their lovers even though they might hate them. They have "commited" themselves to them and feel that they have to accept any abuse, including rape. Ms. Luke is such a woman.

Ms. Luke was forty-two years old at the time of the interview, had never been married and was living alone. She worked full-time as a secretary. Ms. Luke was thirty-two when she was first raped by her lover. She said he had forced sexual intercourse on her more than twenty times over a period of three years.

I lived with him for three years. I did not realize that he was an alcoholic until we started living together. He had sex with other people and there was the risk that he would have VD. He was dirty; he did not clean his body. I did not care for sex with him when he was on his binges. One time he forced me to have oral sex when he was drunk. *Physical force?* Yes. He was a big, strong man and he just overpowered me. Whenever he was on his binges he forced me to have intercourse against my will. And he would beat me up when he was not satisfied enough. When he was on his binges he wanted it even though he did not remember the experiences afterward.

Verbal threats? He'd say: "God damn it. If you won't let me in, I'll break down the door. If you don't fuck, I'll beat you up."

Experience reported to the police? Yes, I called the police to get him out after he beat me up. The police said that since I let him in, it was my fault. He had broken down my door once, and I did not have money to replace the door every time. But they told *me* to get out.

What brought it to an end? I could not stand him around. He would not leave and I put up with him until he found someone else. I had a friend who found another girl friend for him, so he left.

How upset? Extremely upset. *How much effect on your life?* It was in the sixties when all this happened. People were not living together as often as now. I did not let my parents know. I went into it with the idea that it would lead to a marriage. It was my first experience living with a man. I stopped thinking about marriage after he left. *Other effects?* Maybe I scrutinize men too much. Also, I cannot put up with alcoholics any more. I think alcohol brings out the worst in a person. He was out for himself. He had absolutely no respect for women. It affected my seeking male relationships. I am afraid of men and do not want to let myself get into that situation anymore. I enjoy my own independence and freedom.

Like beaten wives, beaten lovers receive little sympathy from the police. Although lovers are not exempt from the charge of rape according to the letter of the law, in fact prior sexual involvement has usually been regarded by police as well as by jurors and members of the public at large as proof that rape could not have occurred.

Some women do not feel that they are their lovers' property. Some also believe that they have as much right as their lovers to relate sexually to other people. However, because of the strength and power disparity between men and women, if the man a woman is involved with doesn't agree with her, her notion of equality won't necessarily provide her with protection. Mrs. Martin's account illustrates this point. She was a thirty-year-old married woman at the time of the interview. She had no children and worked full-time. She was undergoing training for management in accounting. The one time her lover raped her she was twenty-two years old.

I was living with a guy with whom I was tremendously in love. He was fucking around on me. At a party a guy made a pass at me, and I accepted. We went upstairs and screwed. The guy I was living with was aware of it. Later at home he proceeded to throw me on the floor and hold me down by half-sitting on me. He started slapping me, and hitting me on my upper arms and face. He became even angrier because I didn't cry, so he hit me more. I was fighting back, to the best of my ability. I finally broke away and tried to get out of the house. He stopped me by grabbing me; he was six feet tall and weighed two hundred pounds, whereas I was smaller then than I am now. He carried me into the bedroom, tore my clothes off, and raped me. He said he would fuck me any way he damn well chose, and if I didn't like it, he could kill me. He also used an inanimate object, a cucumber, after he used himself. I was very afraid. I felt he could kill me. The violence ended after he raped me. Then he became very solicitous and gentle. I was afraid of losing him because I was in love with him.

How upset? Extremely upset. *How much effect on your life?* A great effect. Basically I resolved never to put myself in a situation like that again, though the emphasis was more on what he did to me emotionally than physically. I went through at least a year of having numerous relationships with men without any deep involvement at all. In fact, I didn't have any deep involvement until I met K. [her current husband]. I didn't trust any of them. I attribute the change also to maturation. I was insecure for a while and, to be honest, after I settled here, I only got involved with married men, so there would be no commitment.

Mrs. Martin's mentioning her feelings of love for her lover is rare in these accounts; the reader may have noticed that few of the victims of wife rape expressed such sentiments.

Where Mrs. Martin's experience is a strikingly clear cut example of rape as punishment—rape motivated by both power and anger at her breach of the traditional double sexual standard—Mrs. Fulton's lover seems to have been motivated more by sadism than by power or anger. In addition, he appeared to believe that his lover had no right to say no to whatever sex acts he desired.

Mrs. Fulton was a forty-six-year-old divorced woman, one of whose daughters was sexually abused by one of her ex-husbands (this experience was described at the beginning of this chapter, and her experience of rape in marriage was presented in Chapter 14). Mrs. Fulton was thirty-two years old when her twenty-eight-year-old lover forced anal intercourse and fellatio on her. This was the same year that her abusive marriage ended (see Chapter 14). She said these incidents occurred from 6–10 times over a period of 3 months.

This was a real rough one for me. I got involved with him seriously. I really wanted him. It turned out to be real ugly in the end. I was trying to learn about sex, to do what he wanted. When he asked me to do things, I'd try, as difficult as they were for me, but there were times I just didn't want to, and I was afraid. He changed; toward the end he was real cruel to me. He tried all kinds of things with me. One New Year's Eve he was drinking and he bashed the hell out of me. He wanted to go up my rectum. I couldn't do it, it was too painful. I got upset. He put his penis in my rectum. I begged him not to. That's when he started hitting me. He beat me up and pulled me down the hall by the hair. I was screaming and asking for help. He turned wild, very wild. He slapped me, socked me all over, and when I fell on the floor he grabbed my hair and kicked me all over. He was very rough, biting me on my breasts. He left me in the hall crying. He went in the bedroom and slammed the door. About an hour later I left and walked home alone.

Another time he tried to force me to go down on him, but I couldn't do it. He'd hold me down on him and I couldn't breathe.

What brought it to an end? I walked away. I didn't want to see him again. Then I met my second husband.

How upset? Extremely upset. *How much effect on your life?* Some effect. I was disappointed. I lacked trust. It turned me into a very bitter woman. I used to condemn a man before he even sat next to me. He'd say something nice, but I wouldn't believe it.

Ex-lovers, like ex-wives, have no right to say no as far as some men are concerned. Ms. Newell provides a good example of this phenomenon. She was a twenty-five-year-old woman who had never been married at the time of the interview. She was working full-time as a carpenter. Ms. Newell was twenty-two years old when she was raped by her ex-lover, who worked as a chef for an expensive restaurant. He raped her once.

After he moved out and he couldn't deal with the separation he got drunk all the time. One time he climbed up the balcony and broke into the house. He slugged me a couple of times and then forced himself upon me, saying violent things like that he'd kill me. I didn't fight him. I was terrified. I just wanted him to go away. *Forced himself?* He was erect and forced my legs open. After he hit me, I did not resist. I was still in bed. I let him go ahead and do whatever he wanted. He was really drunk. He came [to orgasm] and that was it. He had broken in before. Before then it had been mutual and he was not violent. The next time I called the police and reported the break-ins. *Result of report?* Nothing. But later he was arrested for raping another woman. The police were very prejudiced because he was Latino—and he was convicted and put in prison.

Verbal threats? He had written notes before and left a knife and a hammer on the bed. He said "I am going to kill you."

How upset? Extremely upset. *How much effect on your life?* A great effect. It was my first experience with love and I had totally given myself to the situation and made every effort to make it work. Since then I have been very inhibited about giving myself physically, mentally, or with money.

The ex-lover of Ms. Orloff also ended up in jail—but for murder, not rape. Her experience demonstrates even more powerfully than Ms. Newell's that some lovers, like some husbands, refuse to let women leave them.

Ms. Orloff was thirty-two and had never been married at the time of the interview. She was living with a man and raising her eight-year-old child, and described herself as keeping house, but she had previously worked as a legal secretary. She was twenty at the time her ex-lover first raped her. He had raped her from 2–5 times over a period of 6 months. When asked his occupation she replied that "he stole."

I stayed with this man for several weeks. He did something violent and I left him. He followed me here from Southern California and found me. He wanted me to continue to be with him. He came to my apartment and my friends let him in. It was early morning and I was in bed. He came into the bedroom and he wanted me to have sex. I definitely didn't want anything to do with him. I had seen him hit another woman. He threatened to hit me and I said, "That's why I left you," and I told him to leave but he wouldn't go. There were other people in the house and I got out of the room, scantily dressed, and I told him to go away. He continued on and I told my friends to get him out. They were confused because he was a smooth talker, but he finally left.

He came to my house one more time, but I wasn't alone. He was on a big ego trip. He was going to try to have intercourse with me but he didn't even have a hard-on. He was kind of physically roughing me around and he was mad because his body wasn't cooperating. I tried to get out of bed and he threw me back. I was trying to get out of the room and he tried to keep me there. He didn't hit me—he wanted me to be "his woman" more than just having sex with me. But he also wanted to have sex, except he didn't have a hard-on. I was really verbally attacking him.

He found me again in a different place in a different city. I was with my date's father who made it clear to him to get on his way. He's in jail now for life—for murder.

How upset? Extremely upset. *How much effect on your life?* Some effect. It made me know I have to protect myself. I became a legal secretary and I got into martial arts. I am a legal secretary to know what my rights are under the law. Because of who he eventually became [a murderer], I have this fear he'll come after me. I have an unlisted phone number now, I lock my doors, and I'm careful when I get out of my car.

It is clear from these womens' stories that in cases of rape by lovers, the more marriage-like the lover relationship, the more we find the same dynamics that are found in cases of wife rape. When lovers live together, have children in common, and see each other as long-term partners, it becomes more difficult for the woman to resist or to end the relationship and hence she is likely to be subjected to more abuse. Multiple rapes are more likely to occur in these cases. Conversely, the less marriage-like the lover relationship, the greater the likelihood that the woman will be able to end the relationship after one experience of rape, and the more likely she is to perceive it as rape.

Bearing this continuum in mind, rape by lovers is similar to rape by husbands in a number of ways. First, in both situations there is frequently a lack of recognition by both parties that forced intercourse, or intercourse because of threat of force or inability to consent, is rape. Second, the rape often occurs more than once; frequently it occurs many times. Third, the woman is often unwilling to employ all her resources, particularly her capacity to be violent, when trying to fend off the rapist. Fourth, there is often more of a sense of disillusionment and betrayal as a consequence of rape by intimates than when a woman is raped by an acquaintance or stranger. Fifth, the police and public at large are often even more skeptical, unsympathetic, and unhelpful than in cases of rape by non-intimates. Sixth, as with a husband, the woman often has a hard time getting rid of an unwanted male lover when she wants to. The male lover frequently seems to feel his masculine role threatened if it is not he who decides on any major changes in the relationship, particularly the ending of the sexual side of it. Even when the relationship is over, she may have a hard time getting rid of an ex-lover or ex-husband. And seventh, the perception of the woman as an unequal partner with unequal rights, indeed, as the property of the man, is also evident in both types of relationships.

But there are also important differences between rape by husbands and lovers. It is usually easier to end lover relationships than marriage relationships for legal, economic, social and psychological reasons. Hence, abused wives are likely to be subjected to more abuse than lovers before they try to break up the relationship. For this and other reasons, there is often somewhat less trauma in lover relationships. Given the enormous value placed by society on marriage, failed marriages are more likely to result in the internalization of negative feelings toward the self than lover relationships that fail.

PART SEVEN

TORTURE AND FEMICIDE

20

Torture and Marriage

No one shall be subjected to torture or to cruel, inhuman, or degrading treatment or punishment.

—Article 5, Universal Declaration of Human Rights

A man's home may be his castle, but for his wife, it is sometimes a prison. The tactics some abusive husbands use to make their wives comply with them are equivalent to torture, as cruel and destructive of the will as the treatment received by prisoners of war.

Americans were recently outraged by the treatment of the hostages in Iran, even though according to an unnamed senior State Department official who received all the evidence available at that time, they suffered no "systematic"or "sadistic" beatings.[1] Much worse treatment is going on every day and every night in many American homes. But because much of this torture is inflicted on wives by husbands, and because of general public ignorance of the situation, and finally, because most of those in power are husbands with wives, little attention is paid to it.

Amnesty International, an organization whose aim is to protect the rights of political prisoners world-wide, defines torture as follows:

Torture is the systematic and deliberate infliction of acute pain in any form by one person on another, or on a third person, in order to accomplish the purpose of the former against the will of the latter.... It can be safely stated that under all circumstances, regardless of the context in which it is used, torture is outlawed under the common law of mankind. This being so, its use may properly be considered to be a crime against humanity.[2]

Amnesty International distinguishes between physical and mental torture. They maintain: "In general the effect of physical torture such as beating, electro-shock, near-drowning, sleep deprivation and drugs will be the same on any human system."[3] On the other hand, mental or psychological torture "usually depends on the value system of the victim for its effect."[4] Both kinds of torture occur in some marriages, as we will see in the following pages.

There is no organization specifically concerned about the torture of women within the family; one form of torture—rape—is widely regarded as a husband's prerogative and is legal. Other physical violence is widely tolerated. Although murder of wives is illegal and punishable, sexual torture of wives is usually neither. Refuges for battered women are, of course, concerned about abuse of wives, but the word torture is rarely used to refer to this abuse even though it is frequently warranted.

As we have seen in previous chapters, many cases among the eighty-seven victims of wife rape in our study would qualify as torture. But we can draw examples from other sources as well.

The Powell Case

When violence and abuse are seen as related to sex, many people discount the violence. For example, pornography, even when it includes extreme violence, tends to be seen as sexual rather than violent. The case of Bernadette Powell illustrates this point.

Mrs. Powell was a battered and sexually abused wife who finally killed her husband. Her defense counsel contended that her husband, Herman Smith, had repeatedly threatened to shoot her, and that she was defending herself when she shot and killed him.[5] In court there was testimony by Mrs. Powell, her brothers, a friend, and the police who intervened, that her husband had crushed burning cigarettes into her body, kicked her down the stairs, beat her with a metal ring in a closed fist, forced her to have hot and cold water showers (referred to as "tortures" by her attorney), and attempted to assault her with a linoleum knife. Mrs. Powell explicitly stated that this violence, in one form or another, occurred on an average of twice a week.[6]

The District Attorney, Joseph Joch, argued that Smith's "acts of abuse were sex-related" in that they were "sexually motivated."[7] Use of this line of argument was intended to undercut the evidence that his client had a violent and quarrelsome temperament or character. For example, Joch writes in his brief defending his approach: "The cross examination . . . was aimed at emphasizing that Powell's brothers and Powell herself could not point to any fact that Herman was motivated by meanness instead of by sexual drive."[8] Hence, because it was sexually motivated, Joch concluded, Bernadette had no reasonable fear of serious injury or death at his hands, and "claims of mindless violence and vicious cruelty" were unjustified.[9]

Mrs. Powell was found guilty of murder and given a fifteen-year-to-life prison term.

As her defense counsel argued in his appeal brief after the trial was over: "While the sexual motivation may have been present on occasion, it was Herman Smith's motivation and not Bernadette Powell's!"[10] However, here too, Joch had attempted to argue that she was a masochist wh⌐ had enjoyed and encouraged the abuse.[11] Judging from the verdict it appears that the jury found his arguments convincing.

Two other battered wives who were raped by their husbands, but who were also subjected to numerous beatings quite unrelated to sex, received more understanding from the juries who heard their cases. Francine Hughes actually killed her husband; Dolores Churchill shot her husband, but did not kill him.

The Hughes Case

One of the most remarkable case studies of torture in marriage has been documented in the book *The Burning Bed: The True Story of Francine Hughes—A Beaten Wife Who Rebelled.*[12] Mrs. Hughes was also a victim of wife rape, though other forms of violence predominated in the Hughes marriage. Faith McNulty describes the last such incident just prior to Mrs. Hughes' killing her husband Mickey by setting him on fire on March 9, 1977. Before the final rape, he had brutally beaten her, forced her to burn her school books and term paper, forbidden her to return to school—her one escape from him—and humiliated her in other ways. He had also told her in front of the police that he was going to kill her that night. Then:

Mickey yelled for me and I went into the bedroom. He had finished eating. His empty plate was on the floor. He was lying on the bed and he had unzipped his pants. My stomach jumped inside me and I shut my eyes. I thought "Oh no!"

Mickey grinned at me. "How about a little?" he said and began to pull down his pants. He already had an erection. I stood there frozen. I thought I might vomit. I had an impulse to run, but I stopped myself. I thought, "If you resist, this will go on all night. If you give in, it will be over. He'll go to sleep."

I sat down on the edge of the bed. Mickey got up and took off everything: shirt, pants, underwear. God, I hated to look at him sexually aroused. "Come on," he said, "hurry up!" I was wearing slacks. I took them off. "Everything!" Mickey said. "I want everything off!" So I took off my sweater and my bra and underpants and stood there naked. He shoved me down on the bed and began.

I hated it worse than I ever had before. The idea of him inside me, owning even my insides, shoving deep into me, made my flesh crawl. Because he was drunk it took a long time. At one point he wanted me on top. I looked down at him and I had an impulse to put the pillow over his face and smother him, but I knew I wasn't strong enough. I clenched my teeth to keep from screaming. He said nothing; he just went on sawing at me until, after about thirty minutes, he finished. He lay there on his back and I got up and picked up my clothes and went to the bathroom to wash him off me as quick as I could.

I dressed and went into the living room and sat down. There is no way to describe how I felt: a helpless, frozen fury; a volcano blocked just before it erupts.[13]

A short time later Francine Hughes poured gasoline on the floor of the bedroom in which her husband slept and set fire to it. While he burned to death, Mrs. Hughes turned herself into the police. Francine Hughes was acquitted on grounds of temporary insanity.

The Churchill Case

Twenty-nine-year-old Dolores Churchill was tried for shooting her estranged husband, Frank, on a crowded San Francisco street in February 1981. Frank was a policeman. According to Bill Mandel, a newspaper reporter, Mrs. Churchill said "she feared for her life that February day, and finally turned the tables on her tormentor, using his gun. In seven harrowing hours of testimony last week,"[14] Mandel wrote, "Dolores Churchill described the last seven years of her marriage as a private hell of beatings, grotesque sexual abuse, rape, threats with weapons, and harassment administered by her husband. . . .

On the day she shot him, Dolores Churchill testified, Frank had already punched her in the head, raped her and held a gun to her temple. . . .

Even when she moved out on her husband, she testified, he turned up every day, either at work or on the San Jose platform where she caught a train to her San Francisco office. She couldn't shake him, she said. She told the jurors that on several occasions after she'd left, her husband forced her into his car, drove her to their former home and held a gun on her until she submitted to him.

At another point in her testimony, she said Frank Churchill held a revolver to her head and ordered her to go into the street and proposition any passerby for sex while he watched. She said her husband planned to position himself in view of the door so he could shoot her if she tried to call for help. . . .

On another occasion, she told the jury, Frank Churchill fired a pistol at her, putting two bullet holes in the pillow she held to her chest for protection. (Schwartzbach entered a two-holed pillow into evidence.)

Three days later, William Carlsen, another reporter, described what happened as follows:

A San Francisco Jury took less than two hours yesterday to decide that twenty-nine-year-old Dolores Churchill was justified in shooting her policeman husband in the stomach and chest on Market Street one afternoon last February.

The eight-man, four-woman jury accepted her story of seven years of physical and sexual abuse from her husband, Frank, and found her not guilty of attempted murder and assault with a deadly weapon. . . .

One woman juror held the weeping defendant, consoling her and saying over and over again: "It will be all right now, thank God."

But Mrs. Churchill, speaking briefly with reporters, said that she was "still fearful" and worried about retaliation from her husband. . . .

Mrs. Churchill recounted from the witness stand repeated incidents of being beaten by her husband with his fists and a belt and being sexually assaulted by him with a wine bottle, a broom handle, and his gun.

She testified she was so badly beaten that she twice sought medical attention, although she never told anyone how she received the injuries. . . .

She testified that Churchill constantly threatened her with his police revolver.

The defense also offered testimony claiming that Churchill had beaten his wife at a San Jose shopping mall and had to be restrained by security guards.

On four occasions the couple, who had met in high school, took turns initiating separations.

The shooting occurred during the last separation. On February 20, the couple got together to look for their ten-year-old daughter who had not shown up for school.

After they found their daughter, Churchill drove his wife to his house to get a property deed, which Mrs. Churchill testified he forced her to sign by threatening her with his .38 caliber pistol.

Churchill then offered to drive her to work in San Francisco, placing the gun in the glove compartment of the car. Mrs. Churchill testified that when he went into a liquor store to buy some wine she put the gun in her purse because she was afraid he would shoot her.

When they arrived on Market Street, an argument started over the deed and she got out of the car. Mrs. Churchill said she walked quickly to the building where she worked and heard him running after her.

Fearing that she was about to be beaten once again, she grabbed the gun, turned and pulled the trigger three times, she testified.

The first time it did not go off, but the next two bullets hit her husband in the chest and the stomach. She was arrested in her office.

Bernie Horowitz, one of the jurors, said yesterday the jury took only three votes. "The first was 10 to 2 for acquittal. The only problem was whether she was justified in using the kind of force she used," he said.

"But we looked at the law, which stated you have the right under those circumstances. And on the third vote it was 10 to 0 not guilty on both charges."[15]

In other cases the husband's violence appears to be more connected with sex than in the previous cases. Hence, it is more likely that these other cases would be dismissed were they to be brought to trial in states that still permit wife rape, even though the fact that the violence is sex-related makes it no less violent. The next two cases are excerpted from Lenore Walker's *The Battered Woman*.

The Case of Millie

Millie had met her husband at a school dance when she was fourteen and he was sixteen. She had come from a home where there was a lot of violence, as had he. He was the first person who paid attention to her. Millie describes the sexual abuse as follows.

I did not like to be tied up and begged him not to do that. He promised he would not hurt me. The times that he didn't hurt me, it wasn't so bad, but I never knew what to expect. Of course, if you're tied up, you can't do anything about stopping it. Most of the time he would want me to suck his cock. Sometimes I liked doing it, but it got to the point where I had to do that all the time or he couldn't come. He would tie me up and force me to have intercourse with our family dog. The dog was a big German shepherd, and the first time he told me to do this, I thought I'd vomit. He'd get on top of me, holding the dog, and he would like hump the

, while the dog had its penis inside of me. I used to cry sometimes. I didn't
...t to do it. I mean, the dog seemed like another child of mine. It was such a
part of our family. But every time I would protest, I would get beaten and then
tied up and then he'd force me to do it anyhow. I mean what can you do when
your legs are spread apart? So after a while, I just used to close my eyes and make
believe that it wasn't really the dog, that it was really him. After the dog would
finish fucking me, then Jeff would get on top of me and mount me just like the
dog did. . . .

Once he tore me up so badly that I had to go to my gynecologist and have
stitches. I'm not sure what he did. I think he ripped the scar from when I had the
babies. In any event, it was painful. He reopened those stitches by forcing me to
have intercourse again before they were healed, and I had to go back again.[16]

The Case of Lois

According to Walker, Lois looked at least twenty years older than her
age and had innumerable scars, particularly on her face.

He would take out his knife and he would cut marks in my skin with it. He would
tie me whenever we had sex to a bed or a chair or whatever. Sometimes he would
force me to suck him and would stick his penis in my mouth all the time. Sometimes he would tie me around facing the other way and would have anal sex with
me. He ripped my rectum so many times that the doctors in the emergency room
used to laugh when I'd walk in. I think his favorite was when he would masturbate and I had to masturbate him at the same time with various objects. He would
use whatever was around. Sometimes he was very creative. Once he found a can-
taloupe that I was saving for dinner, and he cut a round hole in it just about the
size of his penis, and then he would put his penis in and out of the canteloupe,
and he used to make me watch it. He would make me say things and scream
things at the same time to get him even more excited. The time with the canta-
loupe, after he came all over it, he wanted to cut it up, and then he wanted me to
eat some. I just couldn't do it. I gagged and I vomited, which seemed to turn him
on even more. He had to be weird. He would stick all kinds of things in my vagina, like the crucifix with the picture of Jesus on it. One time he took a whole
bunch of St. Christopher medals to see how many he could get in at one time.
That time he was jerking off at the same time, and then just when he was about to
come, he would stick his penis right by my vagina and get his sperm all over. I
remember one time crying because he took some goldfish I had just bought for the
children. He wanted to see what would happen if he took a goldfish and put it all
the way into my vagina. I'll never forget the sensation of that goldfish flapping
around. Then he took his penis and stuck it in my vagina afterward, and it was
him and the goldfish. I just remember him and goldfish, him and the goldfish,
him and the goldfish. I can't remember all the times he'd stick, push, and stuff all
those objects inside of me. Sometimes I used to get up when he'd untie me, and
I'd go into the bathroom and douche to clean myself out. I'd feel so filthy and so
degraded. Once he caught me doing it and decided that that was a new toy for
him to use, so he would take the douche bag and fill it up with all kinds of liq-
uids, stick them in me, and watch them come out. I got a bad infection from that,
and my doctor told me to throw the bag away, which I did.[17]

The Burnham Case

This is the only case we'll discuss in this chapter where a conviction for wife rape was obtained. Prior to the recent California legislation that made rape in marriage illegal, Victor Burnham could not have been prosecuted for these rapes. He had in fact tortured two previous wives, who had not reported his abuse to the police, but who did testify against him in the first wife rape trial to occur in Merced, California.

In an article entitled "Sex torture charges unveiled in Burnham trial,"[18] reporter Sylvia Wharton cites the prosecutor as describing Rebecca Burnham's marriage as "a bondage similar to that of a prisoner of war."

Episodes of torture with a battery-charged cattle prod and an egg beater, as well as forced intercourse with large dogs, were recounted in Merced County Superior Court Thursday by two of Victor Burnham's former wives.

The thirty-five-year-old Burnham is charged with several counts of spousal rape and is being tried before a seven-woman, five-man jury. The lengthy trial is the first of its kind here.

Burnham's present wife, Rebecca, a petite twenty-year-old ash blonde, testified she managed to escape from her two-and-one-half-year bondage with her husband in January after he repeatedly sent her out into neighborhoods to solicit sex with other men.

Burnham was arrested Jan. 17, [1981] and has been in custody in lieu of $30,000 bail. He is represented at the trial by Clovis attorney Val Dornay.

The present Mrs. Burnham told the jury her husband forced her to submit to sex with dogs as well as his acquaintances. He took photographs which can only be described as pornographic. . . .

A tally sheet done in Burnham's handwriting listing men with whom Mrs. Burnham supposedly had sex along with a calendar with similar notations also are in evidence at the trial.

Burnham's divorced wife of 1976 to 1978 told the jury in carefully worded terms how she was threatened with death at gunpoint, how she was isolated from friends and family, and how she was forced to perform sexual acts beyond description. Women in the jury shed tears during the testimony. Men jurors clenched their chins with their hands.

The former Mrs. Burnham said her reaction to such episodes was that she felt "filthy." She then described her mental and physical preparations as she managed to escape from her husband. She said she abandoned everything she had taken to their Arkansas home, taking the car and driving with only $20 in her pocket to Fort Worth, Texas. There, she said, she obtained help from family and friends and returned to California. This witness said she offered to testify in the case after reading an account of Burnham's arrest in the newspaper.

Mrs. Burnham of 1964 to 1969 testified next. She said Burnham's peculiar sexual preferences became apparent about two years after their marriage when she failed to become pregnant. "His first idea was to have me get pregnant by another man so he wouldn't have to go [in the service]," she said. She said Burnham began beating and choking her, forced her to take other men into the bedroom where her husband would fondle both her and the other men. She said he purchased a large dog and trained it to have sex with her, then he would become excited enough to have intercourse with her.

All three women have told the court they were unwilling participants in the events recounted, but feared for their lives. All three have said they have been choked, beaten, struck with gun butts, held at gunpoint, and continually threatened.

A Merced man testified he went at Burnham's request on several occasions for sex-and-photo sessions with two of the defendant's wives. Thursday's male witness said he believed Burnham would harm his present wife if he, as Burnham's friend, did not do as he was requested to do.

On June 5, 1981, Sylvia Wharton reported that Victor Burnham was found guilty as charged after the jury deliberated a little more than four hours.

The sweeping verdict included four counts of raping his wife, one count of bestiality, and a final count of assault with intent to commit great bodily injury. . . .

The thirty-five-year-old defendant initially was charged with from sixty-five to seventy counts of spousal rape but the bulk were dismissed because the state's new spousal rape law set a thirty-day time limit on reporting.

State law provides a penalty of three, six, or eight years in prison for each count of spousal rape; half of the same penalty for the charge of attempted rape with a foreign object (dog); and two, three, or four years in prison for felony assault. Burham faces yet another trial on child molesting charges in July.

Burnham's attorney, Val Dornay of Clovis, maintained throughout the two-week trial that the defendant was wrongly accused, saying everyone involved consented to his admittedly strange sexual lifestyle. Dornay told the jury during closing arguments that the accused man was "made to look like a Dracula who seduces women and keeps them in his possession to have sex with other men. Pure nonsense," continued Dornay, adding that prosecution allegations were pure "figments of the imagination."

However, it must not have been difficult for the seven-woman, five-man jury to believe Mrs. Burnham's horror story of her two-and-one-half-year marriage when Dornay placed two photo albums in the hands of jurors in open court. The books contained a pictorial record of Burnham's wife's forced sexual activities. He flipped pages pointing out specific photographs, telling the jury during his argument to "see for themselves." Horrified, each juror merely glanced as Dornay pointed out specific poses.

Prosecutor Clifford Johnson argued that people faced with death or the threat of violence could, as Mrs. Burnham had testified, be forced to do unthinkable things, terming the twenty-year-old woman's marriage a bondage similar to that of a prisoner of war.[19]

The Perrin Case

The case of Phillip Hughes and Susanne Perrin is perhaps the most shocking of all those cited in this chapter. In particular, it demonstrates that one of the consequences of brutal oppression can be the condoning and participation in brutality not only toward oneself, but to others. Bruno Bettelheim, a well-known psychoanalyst, has referred to the mechanism that explains such behavior as the "internalization of the aggressor," a concept developed in his attempt to understand how some of the inmates of German concentration camps would imitate the behavior of the SS guards, and would even torture and brutalize fellow inmates in the same manner they had been subjected to.[20] Susanne Perrin did not go that far; but she did condone and assist her husband's murder of other women.

In a transcript released this week (October 1979) of a closed preliminary hearing held last month, Suzanne Perrin told of a seven-and-one-half year marriage and relationship that she said was an unending insanity of forced sex at home followed by periodic homicides outside.

Perrin finally went to the police last July. As a result, her husband, Phillip Joseph Hughes, of Pleasanton, has been charged with murdering three women between 1972 and 1975.

Perrin said her blind commitment to the suspect initially led her to accept his incredible rationale that he had strangled the first victim as a humanitarian act to relieve her of pain from stab wounds.

But Perrin said she knew the two other murders were calculated, cold-blooded affairs, and still she did nothing to stop them. She said she even helped hunt down potential victims and continued living with her husband and the terrible knowledge. . . .

Perrin testified that in 1975 she complied with her husband's request to give him names, addresses, and physical descriptions of four of her co-workers at the French Bank of California in San Francisco.

At first, she said, Hughes—who made his living then by "burglary and bowling"—claimed he was only interested in burglarizing their homes. Later he admitted he was looking for "possible victims—for murder."

Nonetheless, she said, she went so far as to inform him when the husband of the bank's head teller, Letitia Fagot, twenty-five, would be away from their Walnut Creek home.

Fagot was the last of three women Hughes is charged with killing.

Deputy Public Defender Ken Dothee, asked Perrin in the preliminary hearing: "You pretty much knew or thought you knew Phil was going to kill Letitia Fagot, didn't you?"

"Yes," she said. "Why didn't you try to stop him?" "Being afraid of him, being controlled, and wanting to help," she explained.

Perrin said Hughes attributed his urges to kill to furious emotions he harbored against a former girl friend named Cathy.

Often, Perrin said, "He [Hughes] expressed a need to kill Cathy, and being afraid of being caught if he killed her. He expressed to me that he was going to use other people as victims to relieve his desire."

Perrin said that some 230 times over the years she submitted to the following sadistic ritual: Hughes would choke her to a point short of producing unconsciousness, and then, with his hands still forcefully about her throat, have sexual intercourse with her.

"I had to assume the position of being dead," she said. ". . . it wasn't anything I enjoyed, and I was afraid."

She claimed she consented to these attacks "to make him—to relieve the tension of the feeling that he had to kill people."

Perrin said that during the weeks before her husband went out to kill, the strangulations at home tended to become "heavier."

"One time I recall that he had been looking for a victim and to my knowledge wasn't able to find one and he just increased the attacks on me," she said.

She said she lived with Hughes for two years before their December 1973 marriage, and thus had plenty of warning of what she was getting into.

She said there had been thirty premarital chokings. A month before the marriage, on Thanksgiving, he tried to drown her, she said.

Perrin said she called police after the drowning try, but he avoided prosecution as she kept quiet about everything else.

She said that on Nov. 16, 1972, Hughes arrived home late in dirty and bloodied clothes and with this explanation for the naked body of Maureen Fields, nineteen, he had in his car: "He had seen a man chasing a naked woman," Perrin said, and when Hughes ran to her rescue he supposedly found her alone and suffering from several stab wounds.

"She was in a lot of pain," Hughes allegedly told Perrin, ". . . and he figured she was going to die anyway, so he strangled her to kill her and relieve her [of] the pain."

Perrin said she believed him and helped him dispose of the body. . . .

But Perrin acknowledged she was with Hughes when they picked up the girl [another victim] and drove her to their house—where the dutiful wife waited upstairs with "the television on just as a matter of noise" while Hughes allegedly raped and murdered Beery.

How did she abide all this?

"There had to be some sort of control . . . I wouldn't do anything without asking him, not even going out and spending $10 on myself," she claimed.

" . . . I felt that the way he treated me and talked to me that he sort of tried to manipulate my thoughts and actions."

Perrin said Hughes first "gained control" of her about a year after they began living together. She said that this year she began to "feel a little more independent," and urged by a new, extramarital boyfriend she went to police with her story.[21]

The term "brainwashing" became fashionable after the Korean War to explain the submissive and often collaborative behavior of American and other prisoners of war. Responsibility for debunking the myth that the Chinese had used mysterious or magical means to achieve these effects is attributed to A. D. Biderman,[22] who argued along with his colleagues that the effects were achieved by manipulative techniques they referred to as DDD—Dependency, Debility and Dread. Some husbands seem to use the same techniques on their wives—albeit not consciously—and to achieve the same effects.

Debilitation may be effected by depriving a person of food, sleep, or human contact. Subsequently, the victim "becomes paradoxically dependent on his torturer for these things. The only person who can provide these reliefs is the torturer, and in the induced abnormal environment where deprivation and stress are the norm and other social contacts are withdrawn, the victim becomes dependent on him as the sole source of support. Occasional unpredictable brief respites, when among other things the torturer becomes a sympathetic listener, make the victim feel obligated toward him."[23]

Husbands in traditional patriarchal marriages need not actively manipulate their wives in order for a considerable power differential to exist between them. In such marriages, debilitation is not necessary to bring about dependency. Husbands in non-traditional marriages may need to manipulate the dependence, if that is what they want. In the marriages under study, deliberate deprivation of food is rarely involved, although some wives are deprived of sleep as long as they refuse to have sex with their husbands. More commonly the abused wife is isolated from people except for her husband and, if she has them, her children; some husbands manage to keep their wives in virtual seclusion. But many other factors— economic, cultural, and psychological—make the dependency of wives on husbands common in marriage. The superiority in physical strength enjoyed by most husbands also contributes to an unequal power relationship between husbands and wives, particularly when husbands are willing to use their strength to coerce their wives.

According to Amnesty International's *Report on Torture,* which gives considerable credence to Biderman's research, debilitation leads to dependency, and dependency leads to dread.[24] The *Report* concludes that "the combination of these three factors, carefully contrived and nurtured, prepares a resistant prisoner for complete compliance." Such coercive stresses seriously affect a person's customary ways of looking at and dealing with themselves.[25]

Biderman developed a "Chart of Coercion" listing eight general methods of coercion with their effects[26] (see Table 20-1).

Biderman's scheme can be applied very easily to the tactics used by some abusive husbands; examples of the many similarities between the two types of torture follow.

Isolation: Social isolation has frequently been cited as a characteristic of the modern nuclear family; as we have seen, the social isolation of battered women is even more pronounced. Linda Lovelace, the well-known star of the pornographic movie *Deep Throat,* describes in her book *Ordeal* how her husband Chuck Traynor forced her to perform on and off the movie set, and how he successfully imprisoned her wherever they went.[27]

Monopolization of perception: The possessiveness that some husbands display toward their wives not only regarding their relationships with other men, but also with other women, their jobs, school, or any other interest

TABLE 20–1　Biderman's Chart of Coercion*

General Methods	Effects (Purposes)
1. Isolation	Deprives victim of all social support of his ability to resist
	Develops an intense concern with self
	Makes victim dependent upon interrogator
2. Monopolization of perception	Fixes attention upon immediate predicament; fosters introspection
	Eliminates stimuli competing with those controlled by captor
	Frustrates all actions not consistent with compliance
3. Induced debility; Exhaustion	Weakens mental and physical ability to resist
4. Threats	Cultivates anxiety and despair
5. Occasional indulgences	Provides positive motivation for compliance
	Hinders adjustment to deprivation
6. Demonstrating "omnipotence"	Suggests futility of resistance
7. Degradation	Makes cost of resistance appear more damaging to self esteem than capitulation
	Reduces prisoner to "animal level" concerns
8. Enforcing trivial demands	Develops habit of compliance

*The column suggesting variants has been omitted.

they may have, effects a monopolization of perception as well as isolation and dependence.

Induced debility: Physical violence is clearly one common method of inducing debility as well as forced sex or the imposition of unwanted sex. Psychological means such as insulting, derogatory, humiliating, or cruel put-downs can be very effective too. The cases in this book provide examples of all these methods.

Threats: Verbal threats by husbands to hurt or even to kill their wives are fairly common. Many wives are intimidated by their husbands' superior strength even when they are not threatened directly. Non-physical threats can also be devasting.

Occasional indulgence: In many marriages there are good times and bad; the good times can keep the wife in the marriage.

Demonstrating "omnipotence": Coercion clearly serves to convey "omnipotence"; much wife rape and imposition of other unwanted sex appears to serve this purpose.

Degradation: We have seen many examples of women who comply with their husbands because they believe that resistance is more damaging to their self-esteem than capitulation. Thus many wives submit to unwanted sex; others do not fight back when being raped or beaten.

Enforcing trivial demands: It is common for battered women to describe their husbands' violence as being set off by the most trivial things, such as an undusted shelf, a meal they do not care for, or food not being ready when they get home, even though the wife may have no way of knowing when they will be home. Such tyrannical behavior helps to develop the habit of compliance in some wives.

All these methods, effective in obtaining the compliance of POW's, have been effective in obtaining the compliance of wives. POW's are trapped by barbed wire, locks and keys; wives can be trapped initially by all the economic, social and cultural factors that make them dependent. They can subsequently be trapped as a result of the torture itself.

The now-popular term "battered woman syndrome" suggests a complex psychological response that is unique to battered women. But the psychological response we see occurring in some raped and battered wives has much in common with victims of torture in other situations.

21

Femicide: The Murder of Wives

Till death us do part.

—Christian marriage ceremony

In New Delhi [India] alone, more than 200 women were burned to death last year by their husbands and in-laws because they brought an insufficient dowry, women's groups here estimate. . . .

Until last summer, when women's organizations began publicizing bride burning, police generally refused to investigate the cases.

—Stuart Auerbach, "Bride Burning," *San Francisco Chronicle*, April 12, 1980

The issues of wife rape and wife beating overlap with the issue of *wife killing*. There is a word for this phenomenon in English—*uxoricide*—but few would understand it. A more general word for the killing of women *because* they are women is *femicide*. This word cannot be found in dictionaries yet, but it is important because it focuses attention on the fact that when women are killed it is often not at all accidental that they are women. Just as the word genocide was needed to refer to the systematic killing of people because they belong to a particular racial or national group, so too do we need a word to refer to the same phenomenon when females are the victims. This point was made in 1976 in the testimony on Femicide delivered at the International Tribunal on Crimes Against Women:

We must realize that some homicide is in fact femicide. We must recognize the sexual politics of murder. From the burning of witches in the past, to the more recent widespread custom of female infanticide in many societies, to the killing of women for "honor," we realize that femicide has been going on a long time. But since it involves mere females, we have to invent a name for it—femicide.[1]

The testimony goes on to discuss the killing of wives by their husbands as another form of femicide.

We have encountered, in Chapter 16, two wives whose husbands attempted to kill them: Mrs. Ashmore and Mrs. Clayton; throughout this book there are many other examples of husbands who threatened or tried to kill their wives. Of the eighty-seven raped wives, nineteen (22 percent) specifically mentioned that their husbands had threatened to kill them, even though they were not systematically asked about this. A careful reading of the data available on each woman indicates that at least eleven of the women appeared to be in danger of being killed by a husband or ex-husband; and in another sixteen of the cases evidence is not sufficient to draw any conclusion. Obviously the victims of femicide cannot speak for themselves, but the experiences of a few of the women in our survey who came close to being murdered by their husbands can be quoted.

Mrs. Osborne was a seventy-five-year-old divorced woman at the time of the interview. She had raised five children and was retired and living alone. She had previously worked as a special education teacher. Her ex-husband had worked as a cook.

Mrs. Osborne was thirty-four years old when her husband first attempted to rape her. She said that he had forced sex on her more than twenty times over a period of ten years.

When he got drunk, he'd just pin me down. *Force you?* Yeah, only when he was drunk, but he drank quite a bit.

Which was the most upsetting time? They were about the same all the time. He'd get exhausted and then give up. He had a vicious temper, so I'd give in. He always tried to see if he could get sexual satisfaction, but he never did. He'd quit because he'd be too drunk. *He never had sexual intercourse with you even when he tried to force you?* No. He'd try but couldn't do it.

Else? He scared me. He'd go to bed with guns, knives and pipes. I held my rosary praying all the time. *What do exactly?* He had me up against the wall with a pipe. He held it up to my neck, pinned me against the wall, and threatened me. *Threats?* Like, "Tonight I'm going to kill you." He used profanity—language like in the movies. I passed out. Fainted. When I came to there was water all over my face. He would snap out of it when I fainted. Another time he pinned me down with a gun and a butcher knife, all the while I had a rosary and prayed. He did many, many things that were frightening. *Hit you?* No, he never hit me but he would throw things at me. He'd throw knives. Anything! Everything just missed me. I never told anybody this. He also destroyed things that I treasured, like flushing my rings down the toilet. He was a sharp shooter but he never beat me up. I would duck when he threw things at me.

When I quit giving in to him is when he became physically violent. When I did what he said, he wouldn't be. My parents wouldn't take me back. They said, "You made your bed, so lie in it."

He was terribly jealous. He was always accusing me of being with other guys. I would *never* tolerate such behavior now. I would leave him, then he'd beg and beg and I'd go back to him. I'd have another baby. I used to forgive him because he had had a motorcycle accident that affected his head and caused this behavior. Aside from this he was an ideal husband. He was ideal in all ways, sexually and everything else, when he wasn't like this. It wasn't his fault. I was never bitter about him and I still pray for him. At the beginning of our marriage he was good except for a few months of the year. Then he was good for a long time, but he was always like that [violent, etc.] at the end.

Reported to police? The police said I had no business leaving home. And a Catholic priest said I was an unfit mother because I'd leave to spend time with friends. *Arrest?* No. He acted ok when the police came.

What brought it to and end? He tried to kill me. That's when I left him in 1933. I didn't tell him. I just got my kids and left.

How upset? Very upset. *How much effect on your life?* Some effect. I am a religious person. I pray for him. Even to this day I don't have any hatred for him. It's a wonder I didn't crack up. This is the first time I have told someone. My daughter is fifty, but I have never told her. I never remarried. I didn't want to have a step father for my children who might abuse them.

In addition to the appalling reactions of Mrs. Osborne's parents, the police and the priest, religion seems to have played a signficant part in keeping Mrs. Osborne in her dangerous marriage, along with her compassion. In addition to these factors, her own sense of shame ("I never told anybody this") seems to have contributed to her extreme isolation. The trauma of such experiences can only increase when there is no one with whom to share them.

Like Mrs. Osborne, a number of women claim that *now* they would never accept the behavior they were once willing to tolerate. One reason for this conviction may be that once outside of the power relationship in which they were trapped at the time, many women feel more able to act in their own interests. When the woman is no longer in the oppressed role, hindsight shows her own and her husband's actions in a different light.

Mrs. Sutherland was fifty-five years old at the time of the interview. She was a widow who had been married five times. She had raised one child but was living alone. She was on disability but had worked as a credit collection manager.

Mrs. Sutherland's husband attacked her sexually once only, two years prior to the interview. This is the only case of the eighty-nine rapes reported in our survey in which some form of penile penetration was not completed or attempted. The rather unsatisfactory term "digital penetration" was invented for this case.

We were married three months before his death. He got drunk and almost killed me. He beat me up. He was an alcoholic. He threatened me with a knife and put his fist in my vagina. He went berserk. I have no idea why it happened. He had been drinking and taking medication and decided I was someone else. I was in the hospital for three weeks. [Mrs. Sutherland started to cry.] I didn't know what he was doing. It was a horrible experience. He continued to beat me for twelve hours. I had a concussion and two black eyes. He beat me with his fists on my head, and shoved his fist in and out of my vagina. I never told this to anyone in my life. I still can't believe it.

After three weeks in the hospital, I was afraid, but I came home.

Verbal threats? Yes, he said he was going to kill me. I didn't know why. He said he loved me and felt he was going to leave this world, and he wanted to take me with him. He was maniacal and suicidal, but I didn't know it then.

Reported to police? Yes, but I dropped the charges the next morning when my husband agreed to get treatment at a VA hospital. He died three weeks later of heart condition right here in this room. He was the last of five husbands. I thought I finally "had it made."

How upset ? Extremely upset. *How much effect on your life?* [Mrs. Sutherland was very upset at this point.] The man's dead. Why defame him? There is no need. Put "no effect" down. I know if he was alive today it would never happen again.

The interviewer noted that there had been no history of violence or violent sex in Mrs. Sutherland's marriage to this husband. It appears that he did indeed go "berserk." Nevertheless Mrs. Sutherland was lucky to survive the episode.

Like Mrs. Osborne, Mrs. Sutherland also mentions that she had "never told this to anyone in my life." This notion of privacy helps to perpetuate the myth that the family is a haven of peace and security not only for men, but for women.

In the cases of Mrs. Osborne and Mrs. Sutherland, their husbands specifically threatened to kill them, and the information provided suggested that their lives were at risk.

The remaining cases are drawn from the seventy-five women who were beaten but not raped by their husbands. Because less detailed information was obtained on husband violence that did not involve rape, it is not always clear in the following cases how much the respondents' lives were really at risk. However, Mrs. Watson's husband actually shot her.

Mrs. Watson was a sixty-seven-year-old divorced woman who lived alone at the time of the interview. She had raised one child. Her husband's violence had occurred over a three-year period, but Mrs. Watson refused to estimate how many times these attacks had taken place beyond saying "a lot of times."

Which was the most upsetting time? The time he shot me was the worst. He shot half my side off.

One day we went fishing. After we got home, he started drinking. The woman he was going with called him. He and his friend were in the room whispering and then he made some excuse to leave. I also left. When I got back he had returned too and we started to argue. He went in the back room and got his gun, came back and said "I'll shoot you." I threw up my hands and started to turn and he shot me.

He said he was sorry and that he didn't know why he did it. He was crazy; he had been in Napa hospital a couple of times.

How many casualties—in terms of lives and human suffering—are there as a result of the policy of trying to get mentally ill people to be taken care of in the community? How often is this care provided by women? Mrs. Wright's husband had also been hospitalized in a public mental hospital.

Mrs. Wright was a sixty-five-year-old divorced woman who had raised no children and was living alone at the time of the interview. She said her third husband's violence had occurred more than twenty times during their seven year marriage.

He beat me up whenever he got the chance. He was a mental case. He'd get drunk. Then he took a whip after me. He tried everything. I was always half dead. I was in terror most of the time. He tried to kill me too. *How?* I crawled under the bed one time to get away. He crawled under with me and tried to strangle me. I started praying and he stopped. But the next day, he didn't remember anything.

Most of the time I would run to try to get away from him. I became ill and the doctor put me on disability insurance. He kept beating me until I divorced him. We were married for seven years. He was in Napa most of the time. He was crazy. For example, one day we went out to the pound to get a dog because I had started raising dogs. They wouldn't give him the dog because they thought he was too crazy. They'd only give it to me.

Mrs. Wright, who was married three times, was beaten by all three husbands. She described the first two as alcoholic; the third, described above, had a pattern of getting drunk and not remembering his violence toward her. She was the only respondent who was beaten by as many as three husbands, and the only one who experienced alcoholism and violence so repeatedly. The first marriage only lasted a year; the second husband died from liver trouble after three months.

Mrs. Reid, whose life was endangered by her husband's violence whether or not he was actually trying to kill her, was seventy years old at the time of the interview and still married to the husband who had beaten her from 6–10 times over a period of 12 years. She had raised no children.

His violence started since he retired. Before that, it wasn't as serious. One time I made cream soup. He had a fit because he didn't want milk in the soup. He took the chair and tried to hit me with it. Luckily I got out of the way. He's really disagreeable and hard to get along with. I had to call the cops that day. They said to me, "You've got no scratches," and they merely told him to stay out of the kitchen.

During the last episode, he threw things at me in the basement and I had a heart attack on account of it. I was in the hospital two days later. I've had episodes with a sore arm from the heart attack.

Research on battered women suggests that violence starts early on in battering relationships. Statistics on violent crimes support the view that many men mellow with age. But Mr. Reid's violence became a problem only after his retirement. The failure of the police to provide any help is not unusual, but should not be overlooked.

Mrs. Fraser, who believed her husband came close to killing her, was sixty-two years old, divorced, and living alone at the time of the interview. She had raised one child. Her husband was violent toward her three times over a period of one year, but he was not sexually violent ("He never forced me, but I had sex when I didn't really want it").

During the first year we were married, he'd hit me if I crossed him in any way. He'd hit me with his fist in the head or any place he felt like. He had an uncontrollable temper. He would get drunk, and he'd really go wild. I was pregnant when we separated. He came home drunk and had a gun pointed at me for half an hour. If I'd let him know how scared I was, he would have killed me.

I never remarried because of that.

The interviewer had additional comments about this marriage at the end of the interview. "Mrs. Fraser's husband didn't want children, and she was barely pregnant when they separated because of his violence. After their son was born, they reunited for ten months, and then split up again. Mrs. Fraser said that her husband's mother had told her not to deny him anything because of his temper."

Mrs. Fraser left her husband even though she was pregnant. She is one of the many abused wives who are successful in leaving their husbands relatively quickly. Such women have tended to be left out of the literature on battered women, which as a result often gives the impression that part of the "battered woman syndrome" is that the woman is unable to get out of the marriage.

Mrs. Vogel was a forty-eight-year-old disabled woman who was separated and living with her father at the time of the interview. She had raised no children. She reported that her husband was violent toward her over twenty times over a period of six months.

We have no way of knowing how serious Mrs. Vogel's husband was in his threat to kill her if she didn't drop her suit against him. It does seem that she believed him; furthermore, she risked her own life to try to get away from him.

One time he was going to a class where I think he met the girl he later married. By accident I passed by and I saw him, and as I turned, he turned. I didn't say anything, but when I got home he was very angry. It must have been because I had discovered him with the girl. He grabbed a knife and put it to my throat and told me it was a warning not to yell about his girl friend to other wives or tell the family.

When I filed suit against him he found out my address from one of the lawyer's papers. He followed me and grabbed me and got me into his car. I tried to throw myself out of his car. I preferred to die—but he grabbed me and took me to a hill. He said that we would go back to court and I would drop the suit, and if I said anything, he would kill me with the knife in front of the judge, because no one would be able to reach me in time.

He had once tried to take the immigration papers that were for my mother. When I suggested that he had married the other girl for immigration papers, he hit me very hard in the face. He picked up a mallet and raised it as if he was going to hit me with it, then he threw me on the bed and hit me many times.

Mrs. Vogel was assertive; she challenged her husband and filed for divorce. Her husband punished her for this assertiveness. Like Mrs. Fraser, Mrs. Vogel is one of the battered women who left her violent marriage in a relatively short period of time (six months).

In two of the three violent incidents, Mrs. Vogel's husband appears to have felt guilty or defensive (when his wife saw him with his "girl" friend, and when Mrs. Vogel accused him of marrying to obtain immigration papers). Is guilt perhaps a common occasion for males to become violent?

In the case of Mrs. Peters it appears that her husband did not actually try to kill her, but that his callousness was such that she might have died in his presence without his trying to prevent it.

Mrs. Peters was a divorced woman of forty years at the time of the interview. She raised three children, and was living with two of them at that time. She said that her husband had been violent toward her three times over a period of three years.

There were times when I had sex against my will because of psychological force, and when I was filled with anger against him. I did so simply to avoid more verbal or financial abuse. It was a pattern. He was not often into sex, but when he was, there would be the mental abuse and the withholding of money to force me to have it. I can't say there was physical force. I have to give him credit for that. He never hit me or held me against my will for sex.

He broke my nose one time. Another time he dragged me across the floor by my hair. He smashed my head against the wall which broke two of my teeth. When I was seven months pregnant, he found me hemorrhaging. I came to, and he was reading *Variety* magazine. He was angry with me because I was getting the rug dirty. I would have bled to death if I hadn't come to.

I knew I had to leave him then.

When asked about unwanted sex with her husband, Mrs. Peters claimed that "it was not a physically violent marriage, but there was psychological violence." Then when asked about whether or not her husband had ever been physically violent toward her she admitted that she hadn't intended to tell about this, but that she would do so in the interest of this scientific study and because the interviewer had made an oath of confidentiality. However she did not change her statement that she was not a victim of forced sex.

Mrs. Stewart's husband said he was going to kill her, but then decided she wasn't worth the consequences.

Mrs. Stewart was a forty-three-year-old widow who was living alone at the time of the interview. She had raised two children but was retired. She had formerly worked as a bank teller. Mrs. Stewart's husband had been violent toward her over the entire period of their eight-year marriage during "drinking spells."

He drank whisky, which finally killed him. Usually he hit me on the bottom or side with his fist. I was scared of him.

A colored friend of his came over and sat next to me on the bed and tried to hold my hand. After he left, my husband got violently angry and said I had had intercourse with him, which I never had. He said we were reminiscing in front of him about it. *Drinking?* Always. He drank three bottles a day. He hit me on my behind and he grabbed a knife and said he was going to kill me. I told him to go ahead and do it, I didn't care about living anyway. "No," he said, "you're not worth going to the chair for," and put his knife away.

Enormous contempt was displayed by Mr. Peters in ignoring his wife's hemorrhaging and only expressing concern about the carpet getting dirty, and by Mr. Stewart's telling his wife she wasn't worth going to the chair for.

IS MURDER IN MARRIAGE ON THE INCREASE?

Since the rate of homicides in the United States almost doubled between 1959 and 1979 (from 4.8 to 9.7 per 100,000 inhabitants),[2] we would expect that the rate of murder of wives and husbands would also have increased. But the opposite is true. Data on the percentage of total homicides that involved spouses is available for 1963, and then from 1967 to 1979.[3] From these data it is possible to calculate that the spousal murder rate per 100,000 marriages has declined from 3.0 in 1963 to 1.9 in 1979.[4] The explanation for this is probably that the divorce rate has more than doubled in this same time span; it has increased from 9.6 per 1,000 married people over fifteen years of age in 1963 to 21.9 per 1,000 in 1978 (1979 figures are not yet available).

Separate statistics have been reported in the *Uniform Crime Reports* for homicide victims who are wives and husbands of their assailants since

TABLE 21-1 Murders of Husbands and Wives, 1977–1979

	Number of Wives Murdered by Husbands	Wife Victims as a Percent of Total Homicides	Number of Husbands Murdered by Wives	Husband Victims as a Percent of Total Homicides	Number of Spouse Murders	Spouse Victims as a Percent of Total Homicides
1979	1,051	4.9	880	4.1	1,931	9.0
1978	1,095	5.6	841	4.3	1,936	9.9
1977	1,071	5.8	918	4.8	1,989	10.6

Source: *Uniform Crime Reports*

1977. These statistics indicate that the difference between rates for wives and husbands is not great (see Table 21–1). However, approximately 22 percent of the total number of female murder victims were murdered by their husbands in 1979, as compared with only approximately 6 percent of the total number of male murder victims who were murdered by their wives.[5]

While the statistics cited show that the rate of spousal murder is decreasing, it is nevertheless a serious problem. In Chapter 20 the cases of Mrs. Powell, Mrs. Hughes, and Mrs. Churchill illustrated the amount of wife abuse that often precedes the murder of a husband. In this chapter we have heard from wives whose lives appeared to be at risk, all women who were obtained by our random sampling process. Three other cases of wife murder (near-murder in one instance) have appeared in the popular press. The three cases to be described also involved wife rape.

Gerald Stanley, Shasta County, California

A Shasta County trapper, on parole for the 1975 murder of his second wife, is under investigation for the murders of two women and the disappearance of a third.

Gerald Frank Stanley, thirty-five, is being held at the Shasta County Jail in Redding on charges of rape by threat, spousal rape, oral copulation, and felony wife-beating.

The victim of those alleged crimes was his fourth wife, who was slain after she told authorities she feared Stanley intended to kill her.

"His first wife he divorced, his second wife he murdered, his third wife is missing and his fourth wife is deceased as of the eleventh of August and he's being questioned on that," said Officer Ed Neiderberger of the police department in Anderson (Shasta County), Stanley's hometown.

Stanley was arrested at his mother's house in Anderson last week by twenty-six heavily armed law enforcement officials from five Northern California counties. Stanley surrendered without incident. Several high-powered rifles were found in the house.

While Stanley is being held without bail as a parole violator, authorities consider him a suspect in the disappearance of his third wife and the deaths of his fourth wife and a Redding woman.

He was convicted in Contra Costa County in 1975 of firing two bullets into his second wife's head and sentenced to five years in prison for second-degree murder. Stanley—who claimed diminished capacity in his 1975 defense—was paroled from San Quentin last October and took a job cutting wood in Anderson, authorities said.

He married again, but last Valentine's Day his third wife, Diana Lynn Stanley, disappeared in a rural area east of the town of Red Bluff. Investigators are still searching the area with dogs.

Tehama County Sheriff Ron Koenig said Stanley is known to have quarrelled with his wife shortly before she vanished.

Stanley tried marriage a fourth time—to Cynthia Rogers, a twenty-nine-year-old Lake County bookkeeper. "They met in Hayfork on July 4 and were married in Reno on the 7th," said Rogers' father, Frank Spatig. "She'd met him on the rebound."

But on July 29, Stanley was charged by Trinity County sheriff's officials with threatening, raping and beating his new bride. After she got out of the hospital, the latest Mrs. Stanley feared for her life. "She said he was going to hunt her down like he did them animals," Spatig said. Spatig said he notified Lake County sheriff's officials of his daughter's fears, but they couldn't provide protection around the clock and suggested she leave the county.

On the night of August 11, Rogers was gunned down while she was sitting by the pool of her father's Clear Lake resort.

Stanley is suspect in his wife's murder, but no formal charges have been filed, Lake County officials said.[6]

Kevin Green, Santa Ana, California

While Kevin Green's wife survived his attack, it was certainly a very close call.

In April 1980, Kevin Green, twenty-one, was "ordered to stand trial for murder, rape and assault, after allegedly causing the death of his unborn child by beating and raping his pregnant wife."[7]

Prosecutor Cliff Harris alleges that Green is guilty of first-degree murder because the child died during a rape. Municipal Judge John Teal, after a two-hour preliminary hearing Wednesday, bound Green over for Orange County Superior Court arraignment April 18 on charges of murder, attempted murder, rape, and assault.

Green was first arrested in October after he allegedly beat and raped his wife Diana, then twenty, for refusing to have sex with him. After the alleged attack, the woman, who was nine months pregnant at the time, was rushed to the hospital in a coma. When delivered several hours later, the infant was not breathing, and attempts to resuscitate the baby failed.

Because Mrs. Green was in a coma, charges against her husband were dropped and he was released from custody. Harris said the woman came out of the coma about two weeks later, but her speech was impaired and she could not communicate. After three months of intensive speech therapy, investigators said they were able to piece together her story, and Green was rearrested.

Wednesday's preliminary hearing was closed to the public at the request of defense attorney Richard Curran, but an Orange County newspaper, *The Register,* reported Thursday that it had learned the woman testified about forty-five minutes Wednesday and had to use hand signals because her injuries still cause her difficulties in speaking.

The paper said she testified that her husband came to her in their Tustin bedroom and tried to force her to have sex with him even though her baby was two weeks overdue. Mrs. Green said that when she resisted her husband, he picked up a large metal key container and belted her in the forehead. She said she remembers little of what happened after that.

According to the prosecution, the baby died from lack of oxygen because the placenta became detached. Mrs. Green continues to suffer from "aphasia," an ailment in which a person gets confused with word patterns, the prosecutor said. "It's real rewarding to see her progress," Harris said. "She had to work very, very hard to learn to speak again and you could see her frustration on the stand, when she couldn't come up with a word."

Harris said Wednesday was the first time Mrs. Green had been in the same room with her husband since the alleged attack on September 30, 1979. Green has been held in Orange County Jail in lieu of $200,000 bail since his arrest last month.[8]

Kevin Green was sentenced to fifteen-years-to-life in state prison.

Michael Lowe, El Cajon, California

Cecilia Lowe was a battered wife. After she had filed for divorce she was raped and beaten by her ex-husband; then, after the police claimed they could not help her, she was murdered. This nightmare occurred in 1977, before wife rape was illegal in California. Had it been recognized as a crime at that time, Cecilia Lowe might not have been murdered, since there would have been legal grounds for arresting Lowe.[9]

The dawn of Michael Lowe's madness came on a sunny July day as he watched his shaggy white sheepdog chase playfully after a pet chicken in the family's rural Ramona yard. "Come here!" shouted Lowe to the dog. The animal, bought for Lowe's wife as a puppy, pranced over and sat at her master's feet. "I told you not to chase the chickens," Lowe said to the dog. "I told you not to chase the chickens."

Lowe went inside the house and returned with a .357 magnum revolver. Cecilia Lowe knew what was about to happen, having become uncomfortable at that look, that tone of voice. She fell to her knees, pleading with Lowe not to harm the animal. She grabbed her husband around the legs and begged while the couple's 20-month-old son stood by crying.

Lowe casually pumped a shot into the dog. The sheepdog ran under the family's truck, cowering in pain as Lowe went back into the house and returned with a .30-.30 Winchester rifle. He called to the animal and made her sit in front of him as he fired five more shots, killing the family pet. Three months later he did the same to his wife. Then he killed himself.

During the three months between the killing of his dog and the killing of his wife and himself, Michael Lowe wandered his way through madness, largely es-

caping public notice—and help. His wife, swirling in the insanity that was engulf-
ing her, sought aid . . . from her parents . . . her attorney . . . and finally, on the
day before she died, from law enforcement officers. But in the end, it was not
enough.

It was in September when Cecilia had left him for the last time, after he shot
the family's dog. She reinstated the divorce proceedings, which included placing
Lowe under a restraining order and allowing him to see his son only once a week.
And she called the Humane Society to report Lowe's killing of the dog. After an
investigation, a Humane Society investigator ordered the animal exhumed, took
away Lowe's two guns, and filed a complaint against him in El Cajon Municipal
Court. He was to appear on the charge in mid-October.

Profoundly disturbed, Lowe took a shotgun, called the California Highway
Patrol and said he was going to shoot himself or someone else unless the police
could stop him.

It was shortly after 3:00 A.M. Within minutes, two El Cajon police officers
found Lowe sitting on a curb along El Cajon Blvd., a major thoroughfare. He
looked up at the officers and told them he bought the shotgun to kill Cecilia. But
he didn't really want to. "I just want to talk to someone," he said.

The officers took Lowe to the Community Mental Health clinic where they
related Lowe's threat to kill his wife and his actual killing of the family dog. He
was held for forty-eight hours then released. Michael Lowe was released because
he did not fall neatly into that category of persons who may be kept in custody.
"If a person is not gravely disabled or in danger to himself or others—out he goes.
It's a violation of his civil rights to keep him," explained James Boyle, Community
Mental Health spokesman.

Singling out a profoundly disturbed person isn't always an easy task. And it
can be more complicated at a place such as the mental health center where Lowe
was taken. Each month, it handles an average of 600 persons who are evaluated
for psychiatric difficulties. If the psychiatrist evaluating Lowe had determined
that it was necessary to examine him further, the psychiatrist could have autho-
rized an additional fourteen days' treatment. But in this case, he decided otherwise.

Upon his release Lowe learned that he had also been released from his job. It
was not just because of his days of absence, but because he had been generally
"neglecting his work," his former boss said. Frank Karash remembered Lowe's de-
spondency: "He had lost his job, he had no money, he was working here and
there, and the bills were piling up. He was so depressed. He had nothing to live
for." And within one month, Michael and Cecilia Lowe were dead.

The day before the murder-suicide, Lowe called his estranged wife and asked
her to bring Mike to his Ramona house for the weekly visit. Normally Lowe
would come to her house. But his truck had broken down, he lied.

"She really didn't want to go," Mrs. Karash said, "but she did. When she got
into the house he closed all the doors, he put a gun to her stomach, and he told
her to make a promise to him, to cross her heart, that she would honestly come
back to him. "Well she had no choice, she told him yes. . . . " Frank Karash, his
voice a whisper, filled in the more graphic details. "He held her for four hours and
he raped her, he threw her on the bed and raped her. And he said if you say no (to
a reconciliation). . . . I'm going to tie you to the truck, to the wheel, . . . and run
you over the cliff. That way no one will know. And he showed her the ropes."

During those four hours of rape and confinement, Dora Karash worried about her daughter. She called and spoke to Cecilia and would later learn that, during that conversation, Lowe held a gun to his wife. "I noticed in her voice right away that there was something wrong," said Mrs. Karash. "I really didn't know what to do, and now I question myself that maybe I should have called the sheriff and had him checked out. But then he would have killed her right there. . . ."

That afternoon, shortly after she returned home, Cecilia called the sheriff's office. Two deputies came to her house, a man and a woman. They spoke in the front yard, and Cecilia later told her mother that she had reported everything to them. "Mother, can you believe this!" Cecilia exclaimed as she rushed into the house after the deputies left. "They tell me there is nothing they can do because there was no bodily harm done. There is nothing they can do."

Desperate, she called her attorney, George Hurst, who is still pained at the thought that he might have helped more at the time. "She was still distraught and upset," he said. "Obviously she had gone through quite a trauma. She said that she told the deputies that he had threatened her before, that he had raped her and she was really afraid of him, that he had been picked up a month earlier with a shotgun, that he killed the family dog and that he tried to drown her in the bathtub in March. She said that she was really afraid and wanted them to do something to protect her. And they said, 'It's just a civil case and we can't get involved,' " said Hurst, adding that Lowe should at least have been held for assault and battery.

He assailed a system which allows a man to rape a woman, as long as she is his wife. But the law is clear on this. "You can't be arrested for raping your wife," said San Diego County sheriff's spokesman Jim McCain. "They (the deputies) told her they couldn't do it (help her), and it's true," he said. "She told them she had a restraining order against this guy . . . and they told her the restraining order was a civil matter and she was going to have to contact her attorney. . . . And they left."

The matter was so routine to the deputies that they did not make a report on the call when they returned to the station.

The next day, Michael Lowe's madness came to an end.

Twenty-three-month-old Mikie Lowe was standing with his grandmother in her kitchen when suddenly his father came crashing through the glass patio door, yelling, waving a lead pipe.

. . . His grandmother and his mother screaming . . . his mother running to the phone to call the police . . . his father crushing his grandmother's arm with the pipe, hitting her on the head and making her fall . . . his father lunging for his mother while his grandmother ran screaming from the house. . . . Within minutes his father fired the rifle and his mother collapsed in a bloody heap on the floor near the front door. Then his father fired the rifle at himself and he crumpled next to her.[10]

The tendency to downplay women's oppression as having more to do with psychological notions of identity, than economic or physical survival has been widespread. But this has never been accurate, and with violence against women increasing every year (see Chapter 8), as well as the continual rise in the numbers of women living in poverty, it becomes ever more inaccurate. While murder of wives by husbands is one of the few forms of violence that is not increasing, and while murder of spouses is one of the few areas where the numbers of husbands and wives who are victims is fairly close, this does not mean there is not cause for alarm. We have seen that wives who murder their husbands have often been subjected to such horrendous abuse, not only by their husbands but by those they turn to for help as well, that their act of killing their husbands appears a healthy, though often unwise, assertion of their self-respect and determination to end the abuse. Hence, the statistics on the murder of husbands, along with the statistics on the murder of wives, are both indicators of the desperate plight of some wives, not a sign that in this one area, males and females are equally violent.

PART EIGHT

WIVES' STRATEGIES

22

Wives Who Report to the Police

In dealing with family disputes the power of arrest should be exercised as a last resort. The officer should never create a police problem when there is only a family problem existing.

—Training Manual issued by the International Association of Police Chiefs, 1967[1]

(L)aws are invoked almost automatically when one person beats up another—provided the two are not bound together by a marriage contract.

—Del Martin, *Battered Wives*, 1976

It is generally acknowledged that forcible (extramarital) rape is the most under-reported of the four types of violent crime—murder, aggravated assault, rape, and robbery.[2] The results of our survey show that only 9.5 percent of all the extramarital rapes disclosed to an interviewer by the 930 women interviewed were ever reported to the police; slightly less than one in ten rape or rape attempts. It is also generally believed that the majority of beaten wives do not report, even though the wife beater often commits one or more of the following crimes when he abuses his wife: assault and/or battery, aggravated assault, intent to assault or intent to commit murder.[3] Frequently when wives do report their husbands, they regret it. Murray Straus, Richard Gelles, and Suzanne Steinmetz sum up the situation regarding the police response to wives who report violence by their husbands as follows:

Because family violence is dangerous for police and because its rewards are few, police, for the most part, are reluctant actually to get involved in its prevention. In some jurisdictions the police use a "stitch rule." They arrest an abusing husband only if his wife has been injured badly enough to require a specific number of surgical sutures. At best, police officers offer to take the husband out of the house and walk him around the block until he calms down. At worst, they offer to remove the woman from "his" house, or do nothing, or even sympathize with the abusing man.[4]

Since rape in marriage was not against the law in California, the location of our survey, in the summer of 1978, it was not surprising that very few of the victims of wife rape with whom we talked reported to the police. The nine exceptions appear to have reported their husbands' violence without mentioning rape. Of these nine cases, three husbands were arrested and there was one conviction. However, since the police response was in no way affected by the fact that these women had been raped, our analysis will include wives who were beaten but never raped along with the raped wives. But first, we should add a note about the limitations of our survey data on this issue.

The victims of wife rape we interviewed were systematically asked if they reported their husband's behavior to the police, but wives who were beaten but not raped by their husbands were not. Hence the analysis of the police response presented in Table 22–1 is limited, in the cases where there was no rape, to information that was spontaneously offered to the interviewer. This means that our data probably underestimate the number of wives who called the police. Nevertheless, as may be seen in Table 22–1, in almost one-fifth of the 150 marriages (19 percent) in which women were subjected to physical violence by their husbands, the wives mentioned having reported this behavior to the police at least once. This rate can be seen as surprisingly high when we recall that 20 percent of the wives included were subjected to violence only once, our definition of violence included relatively mild forms (arm twisting, a slap) as well as extreme forms, and the women who were beaten but not raped were not specifically asked if they had ever reported their husband's violence to the police.

TABLE 22–1 Outcome of Wives' Reports of Their Husband's Violence to the Police

	WOMEN SUBJECTED TO VIOLENCE WHO REPORTED*		
	Percent		*Number*
Reported, but police would/could not help	7	19%	10
Reported, but wife would not file a complaint or press charges	3		5
Reported, arrest made / husband detained or convicted	5		8
Reported, some other outcome† or no information on outcome	4		6
Not reported or no information about whether or not reported	81		121
TOTAL	100		150

*The twenty-five incidents of wife rape not accompanied by violence are not included here because such behavior was not against California law until 1980.

†For example, getting a restraining order from the D.A. and filing for divorce; the police came to see what was happening, and the respondent's husband told them to take her instead of him; neighbors called the police but there was no information on the outcome.

As with all our data, the fact that they were obtained from a random sample of women makes them particularly valuable. In this instance, for example, we can use them to evaluate whether or not the generally bad reputation of the police on this issue is fair. When there is selective reporting, a question is raised as to whether it is only the most disgruntled and most badly treated women whose stories are being told. In contrast, we obtained information from all women who reported, regardless of whether their experience was positive or negative. Some of these cases will now be quoted, starting with those in which the police either would not or could not help.

HUSBAND VIOLENCE REPORTED, BUT POLICE WOULD/COULD NOT HELP

Mrs. James was forty-eight and divorced at the time of the interview. She had raised six children, two of whom were still living with her. She was working full time managing her own small business. Mrs. James was raped by her ex-husband 11–20 times over a period of 11 years, but she was beaten only once. That one time she reported to the police.

He beat me up once. I had been in bed for two weeks after an operation. I wanted to use the car to visit friends. He had a date with my sister-in-law. He said, "I don't want you to go." I said, "Then *you* can't go." I ripped the wires out of the car. He tried to shove me down the stairs, but he couldn't. I held on, and our daughter screamed at him. He tried to hit me with my own hands, then with his own. I called the police. He tried to tear the phone out of the wall, and hit me on the face. It was all black and blue. The police said it was a family affair. They told my husband to leave the house. And they told me it was my fault and to shut up. That's all. The police are not interested in women's point of view.

Mrs. James' behavior does not fit the stereotype of the "typical" battered wife. The first attack, though very violent, was also the last one. Even though the police were so unhelpful, it is possible that Mrs. James' willingness to call them might have deterred her husband from being violent again.

Mrs. Campbell was thirty-one, married, and raising a four-year-old child at the time of the interview. She was working full-time as a clerical assistant. Mrs. Campbell was not a victim of wife rape, but experienced other violence from her husband 2–5 times over a period of one year.

When we used to go out and drink, he would slap me. And he threatened to beat me up. One time, he came home with a couple of guys. He came into the bedroom and next thing I knew he put a switchblade knife at my neck, and he accused me of going with other men and having boyfriends. Then he left to join his men friends in the other room. After that I left. I wouldn't be around him when he was drinking again.

I reported the last incident to the police but they didn't do anything. They said they couldn't do anything because we were legally married. So I knew that if he threatened me again and I called the police, it would be pointless. So I stayed away from him when he was drinking or partying around. But I felt very upset that I couldn't trust him [husband].

Mrs. Orr was forty-six, divorced, and living on her own at the time of the interview. She had no children and was working full-time as a real estate agent. Mrs. Orr was not a victim of wife rape, but she had experienced other violence once in both her marriages; each time she dealt with it very assertively. She reported the violence of her second husband to the police.

We had recently moved to a new location. I knew no one except two friends. We had invited them over for dinner, but my husband didn't come home till 2:00 A.M. Then he plopped into bed and I said, "Not in my bed." We had an argument and he became violent. He pressed so hard on both sides of my head with his hands that my face was bruised. Then he banged my head against the wall. I went to the police station, but they didn't take it seriously. They offered to take me home and said: "You can't stay here, lady."

Mrs. Orr's experience, though mild in comparison with many of the other wives, highlights the need for places for abused women to go so that they can escape their violent husbands.

Like Mrs. James, Mrs. Campbell, and Mrs. Orr, the following women also complained of lack of help from the police. Their cases are all fully cited in other chapters, so the accounts here are limited to brief descriptions of the violence and information on the response of the police.

Mrs. Ashmore was beaten and raped from 6–10 times by her ex-husband over a period of one year. Once, after she was already separated from him, he beat her from 10:00 P.M. one night to 6:00 A.M. the next morning. At the end of the attack he raped her. She ended up in the hospital with a broken finger, a broken jaw, and a concussion. Mr. Ashmore's verbal threats included the threat of murder, and he followed her to another state after they were divorced.

Mrs. Ashmore reported her husband's violent threats and attacks to the police, who told her that there was nothing they could do since there were no witnesses. "They said if I wanted to kill him, fine." (See Chapter 16 for more complete information on Mrs. Ashmore's experiences.)

Mrs. Clayton said her ex-husband had beaten her from 11–20 times over a period of 6 years. He had raped her once. She said that he had a complex scheme to murder her, and because of this she called the police. The policeman who arrived at 3:00 A.M. apparently agreed with Mrs. Clayton that her ex-husband was trying to kill her, so he arranged for her to see a D.A. However the D.A. explained that in spite of the evidence "they could do nothing until he killed me. He suggested I leave the state fast since the assaults were getting more serious. So I left." (Mrs. Clayton's experience is more fully described in Chapter 16.)

Mrs. Osborne said her ex-husband had raped and beaten her more than twenty times over a period of ten years. He had also tried to kill her. Prior to that he had terrorized her with weapons and threats more than with actual violence. Mrs. Osborne finally reported his behavior to the police. "He acted okay when they came," she explained, and as a result they would not arrest him. In fact, they told her that she had no business leaving home. (See Chapter 21 for more complete information.)

Mrs. Reid said her husband had never raped her but he had been violent toward her from 6–10 times over a period of 12 years after his retirement. She described an incident in which her husband "had a fit because he didn't want milk in the soup," so he tried to hit her with a chair. She called the police but they only remarked that she had no scratches so all they did was to tell her husband to "stay out of the kitchen." Mrs. Reid subsequently had a heart attack as a result of one of her husband's attacks.

Other varieties of police ineffectiveness were reported by Mrs. Goddard and Mrs. Henderson. Mrs. Goddard was beaten more than twenty times by her ex-husband over a period of fifteen years. She was also raped by him from 6–10 times. Not only was her husband's violence toward her extreme, but she was still living under the threat that he would kill her, even though they were divorced. When Mrs. Goddard reported her husband's violence to the police after the divorce, they merely instructed him to stay away from her. (See Chapter 16 for more information.)

Mrs. Henderson reported that she was raped every night for a year, and seriously beaten many times by her husband with whom she had an arranged marriage. In the Pacific Island where they lived under British rule at the time, she maintained that "If both parties don't agree, you can't get a divorce." Mrs. Henderson's husband refused to divorce her. When she reported his violence to the police, they told him to return to the town he came from. By court order he could not come to her town for five months, but this restriction does not appear to have been very effective. She said that "when he would see me on the road, he'd give me a beating right on the street." (See Chapter 10.)

The fact that Mrs. Rhodes, whose experience will be fully described in the next chapter, was willing to report her husband's violence to the police, successfully intimidated him. No credit for the effectiveness of her strategy can be given to the police, however, for they merely wrote a report when her ex-husband broke down the door in an effort to gain entry into her house. However, she found that her husband was deterred by her calling the police on subsequent occasions.

HUSBAND VIOLENCE REPORTED, BUT WIFE WOULD NOT PRESS CHARGES

There were five cases in our survey of wives who found the police wiiling to help but who for various reasons were unwilling to press charges.

Mrs. Bowman was thirty-seven, divorced, and childless. A freelance photographer, she was looking for work at the time of the interview.

Mrs. Bowman was not a victim of wife rape, but her husband was violent toward her twice over a period of three weeks. Her parents reported his violence to the police on the second occasion, but Mrs. Bowman maintained that she herself would have had him locked up had he been violent again. He never was.

He was drunk. He knocked me down and started punching me. He was beating the shit out of me. I started pleading with him and screaming and yelling. He stopped. I didn't fight back. I couldn't. All I could do was plead.

I called my parents and told them. He heard me and pulled out the cord. My parents called the cops. He dragged me out of the house and packed my suitcase and threw me into the car. He was opening the car door when the cop cars came up. Their coming freaked the shit out of him. One cop tried to make me on the way to the station. Men are fuckers. *Was he arrested?* No, I didn't file a complaint because he pleaded with me. The police got the keys from him so he couldn't come after me. But it never happened again. If it had, I'd have had the fucker locked up.

Mrs. Raymond was a victim of wife rape whose experience is fully described in Chapter 11. Her husband hit her twice over a period of two weeks. On the second occasion she called the police. Mrs. Raymond said she would have had him arrested but for the fact that "my daughter got really upset. I mostly wanted to teach him a lesson—that I wasn't going to sit around and let him punch me. I wanted to nip that pattern of behavior in the bud by calling the police. And I accomplished that purpose."

Although Mrs. Bowman and Mrs. Raymond did not press charges, they were not fearful, downtrodden, non-assertive women. They intimidated their husbands through the police, thereby exerting some control over future outbursts of violence.

Mrs. Jackson is very different from Mrs. Raymond or Mrs. Bowman. In addition to raping her, Mrs. Jackson's husband had been violent toward her over twenty times over a period of twenty-two years. She described the most upsetting time as one in which he hit her across the head with an oak closet pole, breaking her nose. She went to a neighbor's house and they sent her to the hospital. This attack, which required eighteen stitches, was reported to the police, although probably by the neighbors rather than by Mrs. Jackson. Mrs. Jackson said that nothing came of the report because "I was chicken and I would not sign a complaint because I was scared that he might lose his job" (see Chapter 14).

Mrs. Joyce's husband had beaten and raped her more than twenty times over a period of twenty years. Though she reported his violent behavior to the police, and he was arrested and put in jail, she said that she was too scared to convict him. She believed it would have been worse for her at home if she had pressed charges (see Chapter 7).

Mrs. Sutherland's fourth husband was violent toward her one time only. He went berserk and violently attacked her, including forcing his fist into her vagina, for twelve hours; as a result, she was in the hospital for three weeks. "He almost killed me," Mrs. Sutherland said. After reporting the attack to the police, Mrs. Sutherland dropped charges the next morning when her husband agreed to treatment at a VA hospital. He died three weeks later.

Mrs. Sutherland decided not to press charges because she realized her husband's behavior had been psychotic and she wanted him to get treatment, not out of lack of courage or extreme fear (see Chapter 21).

People tend to assume that if abused wives are unwilling to press charges they are, like Mrs. Joyce, fearful of consequences such as that their husbands may lose their jobs, or that they will be even more badly beaten as punishment. However, we have seen that some wives do not press charges for more positive reasons. For example, Mrs. Bowman and Mrs. Raymond decided against doing so because they believed their husbands would be sufficiently intimidated by their merely having called the police. They were right, though of course not all husbands are as easily restrained. Mrs. Sutherland decided pressing charges was unnecessary as long as her husband would obtain treatment.

HUSBAND DETAINED, ARRESTED, OR CONVICTED AS A RESULT OF HIS VIOLENCE

Mrs. Armstrong was one of two women in the sample whose husbands were sentenced to jail for violence toward their wives. Mrs. Armstrong reported that though her husband had not raped her, he had beaten her more than 20 times over 2–3 years, "until I got rid of him." She reported that she accomplished this by calling her father, who "came running" to her assistance. As a result, her husband spent two years in jail. She said she hadn't seen him for five years and that he was "long forgotten."

Such a smooth and happy outcome is very rare; the case of Mrs. Upton (discussed in Chapter 11) is more typical. She reported that she was raped by her husband more than twenty times over a period of seven years. She had him placed in what she called a "therapeutic community," but after two years he left and beat her "half to death." As a result she was hospitalized for six months with a concussion, broken ribs, and other broken bones. When asked about the outcome of her report of his violence to the police, Mrs. Upton said that he was serving time in jail "for this and other things." She mentioned that prior to this episode nothing had ever come of her reports to the police. She also said that he was getting out of jail in a few weeks' time, and that he had threatened to kill her if he ever got the chance. Mrs. Upton felt her life was still in danger, in spite (or because) of the fact that she was one of the few battered women who had succeeded in getting her husband to receive treatment and to be convicted and sent to jail for his violence toward her.

Women are quite frequently successful in having violent husbands detained when they are drunk, but for only as long as it takes to get them sober. This can no doubt be helpful temporarily, but it does not alter the wife's predicament.

Mrs. Logan was seventy-four, divorced, and living alone at the time of the interview. She had raised two children, was retired, and had been employed as a drapery worker.

Mrs. Logan's husband had not raped her, but he had been violent toward her "almost every other week" over a period of eight years.

My first husband came home drunk and would get violent. He used to strike me. He used to have a gun or a knife. I told him if he kept it up I would leave him, because it was unhealthy for me. He'd stop for a week and start again. One time he came home with a gun. He pointed it at me to scare me. I called the police. He dropped the gun in an alley, but they caught him and locked him up overnight. That sobered him, and then they let him out. *Where strike you?* Right here. [Mrs. Logan indicates her head and eye brow.] I almost lost my eye. I had to go to the hospital. *Else hit?* My back. It was only when he drank that he beat me up. He was violent almost every week. That's why I left him. I was afraid of him.

Mrs. Taylor said she had been beaten more than twenty times during a period of seven years as well as raped by her husband. Mrs. Taylor said that she had once had him put in jail overnight. She had called a policeman who lived downstairs from her. He had come when she called and had taken him down to headquarters. However, her husband was released when he was sober the next day (see Chapter 4).

Mrs. Freeman had a similar experience. She said that her second husband had beaten and raped her more than twenty times over the two-and-one-half years they were married. "One time," she said, "I was so full of blood the neighbor called the police." When asked about the result of this report to the police, Mrs. Freeman said that "they took him to jail until he sobered up and then let him loose" (see Chapter 16).

Mrs. Stanley was one of the few women who was actually able to get long-term protection from the legal and penal systems. Mrs. Stanley reported being beaten and raped more than twenty times over a period of one year by her ex-husband. The last incident involved his going to her place of work and pulling a gun on her because she would not go back with him. As a consequence, he was placed in what she called "the funny farm jail," where he remains (see Chapter 11).

Mrs. Sutherland, whose experience with her fourth husband has already been cited in this chapter, is our final example. She had another husband arrested twice in the same night. He beat her up on one occasion.

I had him arrested for assault and battery. He came home drunk and got me against the wall, and gave me a black eye. He was hitting me all over. I had the police there twice in one night. His daughter bailed him out right away the first time, and he came back right away. He broke down the door. I hid in the boiler room. He found me there but I was able to run to the gas station where I called the police again. *Weapon?* No, just his fists, and he weighed 250 pounds. *Threats?* That he was going to kill me. He imagined I had been with another man. *Other?* No, there was no way there would be anything else. [Mrs. Sutherland was shaking and upset.]

While Mrs. Sutherland was able to use the police to obtain protection, having to get her husband arrested twice in one night can hardly be regarded as an acceptable police response.

Of the twenty-nine women who reported to the police, very few reported a response that they found helpful. In most cases, even extremely severe ones involving serious threats to the women's lives, the police were reported to claim there was nothing they could do. It is very clear that both the legal and law enforcement systems fall woefully short in their handling of abused wives. This fact has been documented by many others.[5] But this is the first time that the inadequate and sometimes scandalous treatment of battered wives has been documented on the basis of a random sample, allows us to be sure that we are not hearing only the negative stories about police handling of these problems because of selective reporting. There seem to be very few positive stories to tell. Why is this?

I believe the primary reason is that most police are men. Many are husbands and some might themselves beat and/or rape their wives. Whether or not they do so, many are likely to assume that the woman probably provoked or deserved the treatment she received. Susan Brownmiller has emphasized the importance of having a more integrated police force (in terms of female participation) in order for rape cases to be more justly handled.[6] Her point has been substantiated by a recent, rigorously conducted study in Philadelphia in which it was found that "where a policewoman is present, even if only in the capacity of a secretary, cases disappear or receive nonoffense labels less often, and are marked as founded more often."[7] This is to say that women's reports of rape experiences are believed and followed up more often if another woman is involved in the case, even if only at the level of a clerical worker. This finding is probably applicable to beaten wives, and perhaps even more applicable to victims of wife rape.

The implications of this analysis for social policy are obvious: we need more women police officers, and we need the mandatory involvement of women police officers in all cases of wife rape, extramarital rape, and wife beating. All police need to be properly educated on these issues, which means for the men, being confronted with their sexist attitudes and assumptions, and learning not to automatically identify with husbands and other male offenders.

23

How Some Wives
Stop the Violence

Relationships that have been maintained by the man having
power over the woman are stubbornly resistant to an equal
power-sharing arrangement. Thus, even with the best help
available, these relationships do not become battering
free.... The best hope for such couples is to terminate the
relationship.

—Lenore Walker, *The Battered Woman,* 1979

Women who are raped in intimate relationships appear to resist less
forcefully than women who are raped by strangers. One reason for this,
as noted by sociologists Finkelhor and Yllo, is that "many of the women
felt that they could not deter their partner's aggression no matter how
hard they tried."[1] These women frequently perceived their partners as
very strong, and Finkelhor and Yllo observed that there was often a considerable size disparity between these women and their partners, leading
them to speculate that women who are much smaller than their partners
may be particularly vulnerable to rape.[2] Whether or not this speculation
is correct, many of the women interviewed by these researchers were
afraid that if they resisted they would be hurt even more seriously. The
women whose partners had a history of violence were especially likely to
be afraid to resist. Another reason, according to Finkelhor and Yllo, is that
"many of the women believed they were somehow in the wrong.[3]

In discussing styles of resistance, Finkelhor and Yllo observe that
"certain kinds of ultimate resistance tactics appeared to be out of the
question for these women."[4] Few, for example, ran out of the house, or
threatened to leave; nor did they resist in the ways some women raped by
strangers resist, by gouging eyes and aiming kicks to the groin. "Moreover, unless they were prepared to leave they knew they had to face their
partner later on, in the morning, or the next day. Since most were not prepared to end the relationship at that point, an overarching goal was 'keeping the peace.' They were not willing to bring out ultimate weapons, because they had to coexist with this person. And they wanted to make

things more tolerable for themselves. So appeasement rather than massive resistance appeared to be the preferable solution, from their immediate point of view."[5]

Despite these valuable insights into why many raped wives do not offer optimal resistance, the fact remains that most wives do utilize some strategy or another, and many do so effectively. Raped wives more often sought help from others for their marital problems than did battered but not raped wives, and were more likely to have called the police for protection from their husbands' violence, according to Irene Frieze's study.[6] In addition, the victims of wife rape were more likely than other battered women "to want to leave their husbands, to go ahead and try leaving and to leave and then return to him." They also filed more legal charges against their husbands, and more of the raped wives were separated or divorced from the husbands who abused them. However, Frieze points out that the fact of rape alone may not account for the differences, since the raped wives in her sample suffered more severe violence than other battered wives.[7]

Frieze analyzed which of the reactions noted above were most related to wife rape, and found that the factor most related to the rapes was "the wife trying to leave her husband." On the other hand she also reported that the husbands' violence, not the rapes, was the strongest predictor of the wives wanting to leave them.[8]

In summary, while Finkelhor and Yllo point to why raped wives and other partners feel particularly helpless, Frieze maintains that these women are more apt to try to get out of their situations than other battered wives. Although these viewpoints are not mutually exclusive, they certainly represent very different emphases. However, as we shall see from our survey data, it seems that both views are in fact valid.

As shown in the chapter on the characteristics of wife rape, 10 percent of the raped wives in our study (including victims of forced oral and anal sex) were successful in avoiding being raped by their husbands. That is, these women were victims of attempted, not completed, rape. In addition, in almost one-third (31 percent) of the cases, rape occurred only once. Do one-third of the wives develop effective strategies for dealing with their husbands' aggression, or do they never again refuse their husbands' sexual advances?

We have seen in previous chapters a few examples of women who, after being raped once, never again refuse their husbands. Other women have developed strategies for deflecting their husbands' attacks. We can draw examples from the experiences of wives who were raped as well as of those who were beaten but not raped; I include examples of the latter group because there is a paucity of information about such wives in the literature on battered women in contrast to the great attention given to those who respond more passively.

LEAVING THE MARRIAGE PERMANENTLY

In 42 percent of the cases where we could determine what brought the wife rape(s) to an end or what prevented a recurrence, the wife left her husband; in most cases she divorced him.

Mrs. Wheeler was sixty-nine, divorced, and living alone at the time of the interview. She had raised two children. She was retired but had previously been employed as a hairdresser. Her husband attempted to rape her once.

We were fighting, and I didn't want to have sex. He was almost on the verge of being a wife beater when I left him. He was trying to force me to stay. *Force intercourse?* Yeah. He tried to force intercourse. He choked me, and tried to throw me downstairs. *More than once?* No. *Succeeded in intercourse?* No. We were living with my mother then, and she kicked him out.

Any other physical violence? No, it was just that one time.

Although her husband had never previously been violent, Mrs. Wheeler defined his behavior in clear terms; he was "on the verge of being a wife beater." She was aided in her refusal to tolerate rape or other violence from her husband by her mother's refusal to accept his behavior.

Mrs. Blake was forty-six, divorced, and living with her only child at the time of the interview. Mrs. Blake usually worked as a legal secretary, and was looking for work. She was not a victim of wife rape, but she had been the victim of other violence from her husband 2–5 times over a period of 3 years.

When we argued or if he was drinking, he would hit me. He had a drinking problem. Once he was drinking a lot and I was washing the baby and I locked the bathroom door. He got mad and took a hammer and started hammering the door, breaking it down. It scared the heck out of me. Then he said, "I'm going to hit you," and I said, "Oh, no." After he said that he left and stayed away, then later he came back. *Did he hurt you physically?* No, not that time, but other times I would get black eyes. He would beat me up. It was all because of his drinking problem. He didn't know what he was doing. It was when my son was five or six years old. I finally decided to get a divorce, and the divorce stopped everything.

He has stopped drinking now, so I see him and he supports me and my son.

Had Mr. Blake been able or willing to stop drinking when he was married, perhaps his violence would also have stopped.

Mrs. Farrell was twenty at the time of the interview. She had remarried and was living with her husband and one-year-old child. She described herself as "keeping house" but had worked as a waitress. Her ex-husband, who had been on social security because he had "bad legs," had done odd jobs occasionally.

Mrs. Farrell was eighteen years old the one time her ex-husband attempted to rape her.

He was jealous because he believed what someone else told him—that I had gone to bed with this other guy. So he told me to suck his peter or he'd beat me up, and I wouldn't do it so he beat me up. He pulled a knife and a gun on me and said he was going to shoot my head off. I walked out and left him. He had no other chance. *More than once?* Only once. *Ever violent before?* No.

Verbal threats? He said he would beat me up, and that he was going to shoot my head off.

How upset? Very upset. *How much effect on your life?* A little effect.

Mrs. Farrell not only remained defiant but did so successfully in spite of being beaten and threatened with weapons. Not all wives would be so fortunate in the face of threats to their lives. Nor can Mrs. Farrell's assertiveness be easily explained in terms of her background, for she had less than a ninth-grade education and, according to the interviewer, was unable to read. Thus she would seem to have had relatively few options open to her aside from her marriage.

LEAVING THE MARRIAGE TEMPORARILY

Mrs. Smith was fifty-three at the time of the interview. She said she was married but living alone; she had raised no children. She worked part-time as a receptionist. Her husband had been violent toward her 2–5 times in the first year or two of marriage. Although Mrs. Smith was not a victim of wife rape, she reported that "I had sex when I didn't want to."

He slapped me a few times. It was nothing dangerous. He was very jealous and had a very bad temper. He would fly into a jealous fit and slap me. It happened very seldom, and I was never really afraid of him as far as anything dangerous happening to me. But I left him a couple of times because of it so he gradually quit it.

The strategy of leaving a marriage temporarily is often unsuccessful; but it can be effective.

Mrs. Brooks was twenty-four years old at the time of the interview. She had one child and was working part-time as an insurance clerk. She was still married to the man who had been violent toward her one time.

He'd been home from being overseas for about six months and he didn't want to return there and be away from me and our daughter. He got upset about our daughter crying and he spanked her and sent her to her room. We had company over and it was late and she was tired and hungry and he spanked her. I understood what was bothering her and went up to comfort her. He got mad that I didn't agree with what he'd done and kicked me right in the rear. I started crying and went upstairs. He came up and started crying too. I left and stayed at my parents' house until he phoned and apologized.

Mrs. Brooks took what many people would see as a relatively small amount of violence very seriously. Possibly this played a part in her husband's not repeating that behavior.

FIGHTING VIOLENCE WITH VIOLENCE

Some women respond violently to attempts at violence directed at them. The five women to be cited in this section were all able to use violence effectively to stop their husbands' abuse.

Mrs. Phillips was a sixty-eight-year-old widow who was living alone at the time of the interview. She was retired, but had previously worked as a waitress. She had reared five children. The husband who attempted to rape her one time had worked as a drugstore clerk.

We'd been quarreling for a long time. We were separated. He came over and said we should get back together and try married life again. I said no. He shoved me, held my shoulder and tried to push me onto the bed. We wrestled back and forth, then he tried to attack me again. He pushed and shoved me, called me names, and was very rude. Again he tried to force me onto the bed, so I got a vase, hit him, and stunned him. Then I yelled for my brother. My husband left because he knew that my family was behind me. My mother told me to go ahead and get a divorce.
Verbal threats? He said I was his wife and he was going to see I lived up to it.
How upset? Extremely upset. *How much effect on your life?* Some effect. It made me cautious and leery of him, over-protective about my daughter, and strict with my son.
Other physical violence? Sometimes he'd slap me for no damned reason. He was very handy with his hands. If there was dust on the leg of the chair he'd slap me. He was abusive to my oldest child too.

Mrs. Phillips asserted herself both by hitting her husband and by yelling for her brother. The supportiveness of Mrs. Phillips' brother and mother played an important role in making Mrs. Phillips' strategy effective.

Mrs. Emery was fifty-one at the time of the interview, separated, and living with the youngest of her three children. She worked full-time as the coordinator of print materials for a newspaper. She was seventeen years old the one time her ex-husband tried to force her to perform fellatio.

We were both very young when we married. I didn't care for sex or married life. We had an argument. He wanted oral sex and it went against my feelings and so it ended up in a fight; I didn't do it but there was a terrible scene! *Force?* Yes. We were in bed beginning to make love. My not liking sex may have had something to do with it. All of a sudden he was forcing my head under the covers and that's when I rebelled. I fought and got away from the situation. I jumped out of bed and went to the bathroom and locked the door and cried, "I want to go home." He wasn't bad; he never tried it again.

How upset? Very upset. *How much effect on your life?* No effect.

Other physical violence? Yes, but I was also physically violent with him. I wasn't a little flower myself. We were like two overgrown kids. So on second thought, I'd say no.

Mrs. Emery's answer to the last question was highly unusual in the context of this study, because her words convey a rare sense of mutuality, as well as of equality in physical strength and willingness to use it.

Mrs. Emery's experience also highlights the fact that the success of the wife's strategy depends on the husband's response. Some husbands in Mr. Emery's situation would have persisted with the sexual assault. This point is brought home even more strongly by the experience of Mrs. Jefferson.

Mrs. Jefferson was a fifty-seven-year-old divorced woman who lived alone at the time of the interview. She had reared one child and was working full-time as a medical file clerk. Her ex-husband had worked as an electrical engineer.

Mrs. Jefferson was twenty-three years old the one time her husband tried to rape her.

We were getting ready to divorce. We were staying in a hotel, and I told him I didn't love him any more and he got very upset. He started to rip my nightgown off. I was very angry; I pushed him away and kept fighting him off. *Attempted intercourse?* That's what he wanted, but once he saw how angry I was, he stopped. I left the next day.

How upset? Not very upset. *How much effect on your life?* A little effect.

Mrs. Jefferson had not been subjected to any extramarital experiences of sexual abuse, which may have helped her to be outraged and assertive with her husband. Repeated experiences of abuse, as we have seen, can break a woman's spirit so that she is not able to be righteously angry. An inability to respond with anger is one way in which multiple experiences of sexual abuse destroy women.

Mrs. Allen was another woman for whom violent retaliation appears to have been effective. She was a thirty-two-year-old divorced woman living alone at the time of the interview. She had no children and was working full-time as a legal secretary. She had never been raped by her ex-husband, but had experienced physical violence from him once.

He got angry because I didn't want to go somewhere with him after dinner. He hit me in the chops [meaning face]. I was cooking so I hit him with a frying pan, and he left. I found out later he had a tendency to react violently. He was very immature and did not have a strong sense of self. He was never violent again after that.

Mrs. Murray was twenty-seven and living with her husband and two children at the time of the interview. She had previously worked as a security guard but was looking for work. She had never been a victim of wife rape, but her husband had been physically violent toward her twice.

Mrs. Murray's description of the most upsetting incident follows:

I had stayed out too late and wrecked his car. When I came in he punched me in the side and it really hurt. I've never been hit like that before and I picked up a lamp and hit him with it. He saw that I wasn't going to stand there and be punched like that and he left me alone and went on upstairs.

There are wives who would have felt they "deserved" to be punished—even physically—under such circumstances. But in spite of having wrecked her husband's car, Mrs. Murray was outraged by her husband's violence and responded with violence of her own.

The last case to be cited as an example of effective use of physical force by a wife is a little more ambiguous than the others. Mrs. Bennett's husband was violent toward her from 11–20 times over a period of 10 years; thus she was a rather seriously abused wife. Although she was only raped once, her strategy of dealing with that episode was far from successful.

Mrs. Bennett was a thirty-nine-year-old divorced woman at the time of the interview. She had raised six children, and was living with three of them. She worked full-time as a receptionist.

After going out he would come home and want to lay on me. This particular night I decided to let him know I didn't want to be bothered. We were in the bed and he pinned me down. We wrestled for a while. I didn't want to wake up the kids. If the children had heard us fighting, they would have come to see about me, and I didn't want them in there when we were naked. But we fell on the floor and did wake them up. When they came to the door I told them I was all right. After that I struggled some more with him, but to keep the kids from becoming too upset, I went on and submitted because I knew he wouldn't stop struggling with me. So he just took it. *Meaning?* He had intercourse with me.

Verbal threats? He said he would beat me to death.

How upset? Extremely upset. *How much effect on your life?* A great effect. It goes to show that men have no respect for what you want when they want something. I couldn't trust again. You must believe what you see and little of what you hear.

Any other violence? Yes. *What was the most upsetting time?* We had gone to a party my instructor gave at his home. After we left and got home, he was drunk. He accused me of having some kind of relationship with the instructor. He beat me so badly in my face that I became senseless and I guess I started fighting back. He had me pinned in a chair and he sat on me and kept hitting me in the face. He really messed my face up. I started to fight back for the first time since we'd been married. He hit me so hard that he reinjured his hand that he had previously injured in a car accident.

When he saw I would fight back he never hit me too much after that.

Fighting back was effective against the violence she describes at the end, but Mrs. Bennett was not able to be as assertive in dealing with the rape. Her concern to protect her children inhibited her inclination to fight her husband.

EFFECTIVE THREAT OF VIOLENCE

Mrs. Evans was seventy-two and retired at the time of the interview and was still married to the man who had been violent toward her from 2–5 times. She had raised one child and had been a waitress. Mrs. Evans was not a victim of wife rape.

He kicked me once a long time ago. I don't remember what brought it on. I threatened that I'd call the police or break a chair over his head. *More than once?* He's hit me a couple of times—but not seriously. He'd be considered a gentleman I think. The guy's still alive. He wouldn't have been if he'd kept it up. I could hold my own pretty well, I guess.

Though Mrs. Evans' statement is less forceful than Mrs. Emery's, her last comment indicates a similar sense of strength and equality. Of course, many women are unable to feel this way because of past experiences with their husbands and/or because it simply is not realistic. Finkelhor and Yllo's finding that there is often a considerable size disparity between wives who are raped by their husbands was mentioned at the beginning of this chapter. Obviously, making idle or unrealistic threats of violence could be dangerous.

EFFECTIVE THREAT TO LEAVE MARRIAGE

Mrs. Clarke, a thirty-year-old divorced woman at the time of the interview, was working full-time as a bookkeeper and office manager and raising her twelve-year-old child. Although her husband had tried to pressure her to have sex when she didn't want it during the last year of their marriage, he had never used force. He had been violent toward her once, but Mrs. Clarke herself had initiated the violence.

We were having an argument. I was real frustrated when he wouldn't talk, so I was pounding on his shoulder. He then smacked me on the face with his hand. It freaked me out. He'd never hit me before, and it was the only time it happened. It made me realize how frustrated he was. I told him never to hit me again or that would be it.

Mrs. Rice was raped in her sleep by her husband. Although she was very angry about this, she threatened to leave him because of his violence. Her account of what happened follows:

One time he was really mad. We had been together six months. A gossipy woman told him that I was going out with another man. We began to argue. I told him that he was stupid if he thought that being with him, I would go out with another man. He got angry. He gave me a hard blow with his hand and my nose bled but later he repented. After that happened I said, "I'll leave you forever if you're like that. I didn't imagine you were like that. You're an animal." I wanted to hit *him*. I threw the pillows at him. "I'd better leave. I don't want to argue any more," he said. He came back three hours later, very calm and said, "Let's not get like this. I promise you I won't do that to you again. If that woman writes to me again, I won't believe her."

Other violence? Sometimes he hits the furniture but nothing's happened to me again. We calm each other down so as not to argue too much. If we can argue calmly we do. If not, the other one starts singing or watching TV or something like that.

It seems to me that if wives were in a position to threaten to leave the marriages in which husbands were violent toward them, and if they really meant it and were able to convey this to their husbands, we would be at least half way toward a solution to the problem of violence against wives. Some men, because of their prior socialization and experiences, are undoubtedly unable to control their violence no matter what the consequences. But other men only appear to have no control—because they think they can get away with it. No woman should have to live with a man who falls into the first category of those who cannot control their violence. If the threat does not work, it would seem the woman and her children are well out of the situation.

EFFECTIVE USE OF THE POLICE

We have seen many examples of wives who were willing to call the police, but who received little or no help from them. The two wives whose accounts are cited here were able to use the police effectively, not because the police were particularly helpful, but because their husbands felt intimidated by this strategy.

Mrs. Rhodes was a twenty-four-year-old divorced woman living with her three young children at the time of the interview. She was going to college but had worked as a nurse. Her ex-husband had been violent toward her 2–5 times over a period of 3 years, but he had never forced sex on her.

It was after we were separated that he became violent toward me. Nothing had happened before then. He came to the house and broke the door down. I lived with my sister-in-law and she called the police. The police just took the report. I didn't say anything because I was afraid he'd slap me again. He'd say, "You want violence, right?"

He's been locked up for assaulting one of his friends. *Most violent incident with you?* Slapping me in my face. This only happened once. The other times he tried to push me to the floor. *Did he succeed?* No, but he tried a couple of times.

Right now he's not violent. At first I kept quiet and he thought he could do what he wanted with me. Being in jail cooled him off a bit. Anything that happened after that I'd call the police. Because I call, he's not violent any more.

Mrs. Rhodes took her husband's violence very seriously. Her rejection of what some people would regard as mild forms of violence, along with her tactic of calling the police, enabled her to keep a man who had been jailed for assaulting one of his friends from continuing to be violent toward her.

Mrs. Raymond was a fifty-three-year-old divorced woman who was living alone at the time of the interview. She had reared two children, and was working full-time as a painter and art teacher. Her ex-husband had worked as an insurance underwriter.

Mrs. Raymond was twenty-six years old when she had her first unwanted sexual experience with her second husband (her experience of unwanted sex with her first husband is described in some detail in Chapter 11). Though she *felt* forced on this occasion, her description of her husband's behavior suggests pressure more than force. The second incident which, unlike the first incident, meets our definition of rape, occurred nine years later. The rape and other violence were totally unrelated; as is typical of these cases, it was the other violence that was reported to the police.

I had sex with him one time when I really didn't want to. We had sex in the car in front of a girl friend's house. I kept mentioning where we were, but he went ahead and did it anyway. I was pretty uncomfortable about that. *Intercourse?* Yes. *Feel forced?* Yeah.

Another time after the baby was born he showed no responsibility about birth control. He was very careless about it. *Forced?* Yes. I would say that he physically forced me. I don't think he would have let me out of the car if I didn't give in to him. He was physically forcing me by using his strength. He didn't let me up. He just held me down with his body. I told him I didn't want to do it and didn't particularly enjoy it.

How upset? Extremely upset. *How much effect on your life?* A great effect. After the first experience I decided that I would never do that again. I wasn't going to make love in the car after that. I always was very responsible about birth control after I thought I was pregnant and found out I wasn't. I would never take those risks again. I was upset that my husband didn't care about birth control.

Other physical violence? I came home from school at noon one day and he was supposed to be watching the baby but he was asleep. I was afraid that something had happened to the baby, being alone all that time. The baby was ok; he was just playing in the crib, but when I picked him up I started yelling at my husband because I was mad at him. He then punched me in the face. I saw it coming but I couldn't get away fast enough because I had the baby in my arms.

What happened the second time? He started to hit me. I was able to get out of his way, and I called the police. *Arrest?* No, I would have but my daughter got really upset. I mostly wanted to teach him a lesson that I wasn't going to sit around and let him punch me. I wanted to nip that pattern of behavior in the bud by calling the police, and I accomplished that purpose.

Even though a fairly low level of force accompanied the rape, Mrs. Raymond was very traumatized by it and was unable to oppose her husband's sexual demands. She responded more assertively to her husband's other violence. Her outrage that her husband might think hitting her was acceptable is evident in her immediate call to the police. Women like Mrs. Raymond might be helped greatly if rape in marriage were made illegal throughout the United States, assuming they were aware of such a law, because Mrs. Raymond was willing to use the police to put an early end to her husband's other violence. In the case of the rape, no law gave her the option to use the police to convince her husband never to repeat this behavior.

WILLINGNESS TO TURN TO SUPPORTIVE RELATIVES

A supportive family as well as neighbors and friends can be a very effective deterrent to husbands' violence toward their wives.

Mrs. Armstrong was twenty-two years old at the time of the interview, raising a young child, and working part-time as a nurse. She had remarried and was living with her second husband. Her first husband had been violent toward her more than 20 times over a period of 2–3 years "till I got rid of him." Mrs. Armstrong said that he had not forced sex on her.

The most upsetting time was when he threw me down the stairs when I was seven months pregnant. He also used to slap me on the face practically every day. And once he threatened to run me over. *Did you lose the baby?* No, but it was one month late. I called my dad who came running. So I was able to get rid of him [husband]. He went to jail for two years. I haven't seen him for five years.

Mrs. Ashmore, who was raped and beaten by her first and second husbands, also told her father about the beating by her first husband, and as a result "my father came and took me away from him." The supportive role of Mrs. Wheeler's and Mrs. Phillips' families were cited earlier in this chapter. Mrs. Phillips yelled for her brother and "my husband left because he knew that my family was behind me." Mrs. Phillips' mother encouraged her to get a divorce. Mrs. Wheeler's mother, with whom she and her husband were living at the time, "kicked him out" after he tried to rape and beat her.

When Mrs. Kent had to cancel her anniversary party because she was so badly beaten up, her mother and brother became worried and came to visit (see Chapter 15 for the full account). "When they saw I was in that condition they were shocked and my brother wanted to kill him." Her brother also wanted to get her out of the house. Mrs. Kent's husband promised her brother that he would never beat her up again. Though he did not keep this promise, future beatings were not nearly as severe.

Some times the respondent's children were helpful or supportive. Mrs. Nash asked her daughter to call the police; Mrs. James said her daughter screamed at her husband when he hit her. Mrs. Gray said her daughter ran for help. Mrs. Polk said her thirteen-year-old son "intervened," which resulted in his getting beaten up too. When Mrs. Austin's son grew to be six feet, two inches tall at age fifteen, she said her husband was too scared to try beating her up again because her son would have defended her.

INSISTENCE THAT HUSBAND STOP DRINKING

Mrs. Holmes was sixty-three at the time of the interview. She had raised three children, and was living with her husband and son. She described herself as keeping house though she had previously worked as a commercial artist. Mrs. Holmes' husband had been violent toward her at least twice over a period of 5–7 years, but he had never forced sex on her.

When he was drinking he'd come home and start fussing at the top of his lungs. He'd scream and yell and if that didn't work he'd throw things around. Once or twice he struck me and I told him it was either me or the bottle. He gave up the bottle. I had a father who drank and I didn't want to live that life again. That was it.

Two other wives mentioned that their husbands' violence had stopped after they quit drinking. Mrs. Blake's husband gave up drinking only after his wife divorced him, at which time they resumed a relationship (but not their marriage).

While Mrs. Quinn and her husband were separated, he got drunk and raped her. He wanted to get back together with her, and in spite of the rape she agreed. She attributed his violence to his drinking problem, and made him quit drinking as a condition of their getting back together; there were no further incidences of rape.

The following examples of successful strategies were all used by victims of wife rape, whose accounts are fully quoted in other chapters. Some of these women were only partially successful in that they were raped many times before they could get their husbands to stop. In addition, considerable sacrifice was involved for a few. For example Mrs. Clayton was advised by the D.A. to leave the state, and she did so. With regard to her second husband, Mrs. Ashmore said, "I got a gun and decided to kill him and moved away."

When asked what brought the rape to an end, Mrs. Dudley said that she made it "so uncomfortable for him to live with us that he left." Mrs. Irving was able to ridicule her ex-husband to make him stop forcing himself on her. "I made him feel ridiculous," she said.

Mrs. Lucas said that the therapy she had obtained had brought the rapes in her marriage to an end. "I came into my own person. He was a person who was able to manipulate people and I was easily influenced by others. Until I realized I was being manipulated, it didn't end. After I took Gestalt for four years I started realizing things."

Mrs. Field said that "talking it out" had brought the rapes to an end in her marriage, plus "my becoming militantly feminist. Therapy. His becoming more aware and calming down." When asked what brought the rapes in her marriage to an end, Mrs. Kent replied: "I threw it in his face. I asked: 'How could you do that? It makes me hate you and go against you even more when you force yourself upon me. What's the matter with you! Do you get your jollies that way?' I guess he realized what he was doing and he stopped."

ASSERTIVENESS BY WIFE LIMITED TO HUSBAND'S NON-SEXUAL VIOLENCE

Some women are able to be very assertive against wife beating but not against their husbands' unwanted sexual advances nor against acts of rape.

Mrs. Baker was thirty-six at the time of the interview. She had remarried, and was working full-time as a hairdresser and raising three children. At the time of the first wife rape, Mrs. Baker was twenty-one years old. She said the rapes had occurred from 6–10 times over a period of 10 years, and that her husband's other physical violence had occurred the same number of times over a period of 12–13 years.

I was in bed and he was drunk. He wanted to make love and he was insistent and forced me to. I fought it a little bit which is what made it so hard. We struggled. He pinned me down and wouldn't let me out of bed. I didn't fight him too much because he was drunk and would have hit me. So he forcibly took me. I had no choice in the matter. *Other physical force?* He didn't punch me but I always had a few black and blue marks. He completed the act and then went off into a stupor.

How many unwanted sexual experiences with him? We were married sixteen years. A lot of times I just gave in. If I didn't, it was harder on me. Forced entry hurts. I usually tried to talk him out of it. Most of the time he didn't know what happened. He'd say I exaggerated—a sign of an alcoholic. I never let him touch the kids when he was drunk. Otherwise, he was a good dad. We had a good sex life other than that.

What brought it to an end? I divorced him because of his drinking, which caused everything.

Verbal threats? He said: "I'll kill you!" Other threats meant the same thing. When I left him he said, "You're afraid I'd come after you with a gun." I said that I was.

Ever have a weapon? His fist. He split his hand open one time. I didn't want weapons in the house. The last five years, he had hunting weapons, but kept them stored.

How upset? Extremely upset. *How much effect on your life?* A great effect. I divorced him and I think that that was the best thing in the world I could have done. I'm not bitter over it. When you are young you think it's going to get better, but when you lose your respect for someone, there's no sense in going on. Divorce was the best thing that ever happened to me, and I initiated the whole thing. I am a much happier and more relaxed person although I gave up a bit of security. That doesn't mean a thing if you are not happy.

Other physical violence? Yes. *Which time was most upsetting?* He came home drunk and he wanted to make love. He proceeded to pin me down on the bed. I don't like that. I am claustrophobic. I let loose hollering. It was the first time I rebelled when I was being treated like that. He slugged me and bit me on the arm. He pulled my hair and hit me in the face. I was very sore. It went on for hours. He finally let me get up. I was sobbing. I made a cup of tea, but he felt I was taking too long. I said, "I'm letting the tea cool down," and then he put his fist through the cup at ninety miles an hour. It immediately started bleeding all over the place. So someone took him to the hospital. This was the only thing that stopped the incident.

I told him that if he ever hit me again I'd leave him. There were minor incidents after that, but he knew I meant it.

Even though Mrs. Baker's husband punished her severely when she finally rebelled against his sexual coercion, she was nevertheless able to stand up to him and give him an ultimatum after his most extreme act of violence. Many women would have been intimidated into submission. A refusal to accept the violence is often the first step toward stopping it.

Women who are willing to put their marriages on the line to stop their husbands' non-sexual violence are often not willing to take the same risk over sexual abuse. The same woman who righteously rejects a husband's attempt to beat her may not reject his attempt to rape her because she feels that sex is his right and that she is wrong to refuse him. She knows that even the law condones his behavior.

WIVES RESPONSIBLE FOR ENDING THE WIFE RAPE:
A QUANTITATIVE ANALYSIS

In our study, only wives who were raped more than once by their husbands were specifically asked what ended the wife rapes if indeed they had ended, although some wives who were only raped once volunteered an explanation for why the rape did not occur again. In some cases the wives' answers did not reveal whether they or their husbands were responsible for bringing the rapes to an end. For example, a few replied that "we divorced" without indicating who initiated the termination of the relationship. Nevertheless, we studied each case to try to determine whether or not the wife was responsible for ending the rapes. All eighty-seven of the raped wives were then placed in one of two categories: (1) those where the wife's actions ended the rape(s); and (2) those where her actions did not end the wife rape(s), or where we could not ascertain who was responsible, or where the rapes were ongoing.

As may be seen in Table 23–1, we found that raped wives were more likely to be responsible for ending the rapes in the following circumstances: (1) if they reported being extremely upset by the rape(s), and suffering from more serious long-term effects as a result of them; (2) if their husband had also threatened to kill them; (3) if the first rape occurred just prior to the break-up of the marriage. The first two of these findings require no explanation. If the first rape occurs just prior to the termination of the marriage, this generally means the decision had already been made to end the marriage. It may also indicate that the wife initiated the break up.

Wives who reported less fear of sexual assault, who were less upset by men's sexual comments in the street, and who were less upset by witnessing a man exposing himself in their adult years, were also more likely to act to end the rapes. Whether or not being upset by, and fearful of, sexual assault intimidates some wives into inaction, or whether their inaction is a symptom of their fearfulness, is impossible to know. Wives who acted to end the rapes were also less likely to have an unwanted sexual experience with an authority figure at some time in their lives. Whether the unwanted experience with the authority figure contributed to the raped wives' inability to act to end the rape is an interesting possibility, but our results don't allow us to speculate fruitfully about causation.

Some economic and social class factors are also significantly associated with wives successfully ending rape in their marriages. Wives who were the primary breadwinner at the time their husbands first raped them were more likely to take effective action. In addition, the husbands of the women who were effective in ending the rape were more likely to be ser-

TABLE 23–1   Factors Associated with Raped Wives
Successfully Ending the Rapes

	Wife Ended Rape(s) (Percent) (Sample size: 39)	Not Ended Rapes/Other Ended Rapes/No Information (Percent) (Sample size: 50)
Factors Relating to the Rape		
Wife reported being extremely upset by rape(s)	76	38
Wife reported rape(s) having great long-term effects*	61	38
Husband threatened to kill the respondent	33	12
The first rape occurred just prior to the marriage breaking up	16	0
Factors Relating to Upset/Fears/Experiences of Other Sexual Assault		
Wife reports no fear at all of sexual assault at the time of the interview	24	4
Wife reports not upset by men's sexual comments on the street	37	16
Wife reports not upset by man exposing himself in adult years	68	42
Socio-Economic Factors		
Wife more likely to be the primary breadwinner at the time of the first rape	24	5
Husband-rapists more likely to be (1) service workers, and less likely to be (2) upper middle class	(1) 41 (2) 18	11 39
Wives' occupations more likely to be upper middle class or lower class, less likely to be middle class. (These percentages refer to middle class occupations.)	26	55
Wives' fathers' occupations more likely to be lower class	31	12

*While this is the only factor listed in this table that does not reach statistical significance at < .05 level, when the means of these two groups are compared for the effects variable, wives who end the rapes report significantly greater effects (at < .05 level).

vice workers (the occupations with the lowest status). These findings suggest that economic factors are important in whether or not raped wives act to end the rape.

However, when we examine the occupations of the wives who ended the rapes, the picture looks slightly more complicated. These wives were more likely to be either upper middle class or lower class; they were less likely to be middle class. In addition, their fathers were more likely to have had lower-class occupations. They were either the most privileged or least privileged in terms of their own occupations, and the least privileged in terms of their fathers' occupations. However, privilege is relative; in terms of an ability to take action against wife rape, perhaps the more significant fact is that the wife is the primary breadwinner, not how much she earns.

Battered wives are generally depicted as losers not only by society in general but also in existing studies.[9] The wives are shown as passive, and as Lee Bowker and Kristine MacCallum have noted: "this way of portraying beaten wives does them a disservice by underemphasizing their active coping strategies and by specifically excluding women who have successfully beaten wife-beating in their own homes from being research subjects."[10] I strongly agree with Bowker and MacCallum's critique. The cases in this chapter show that most (perhaps all) wives employ some strategy to cope with wife rape, and that a significant number are successful.

Economic factors emerge from our study as extremely important in terms of why abused wives remain with their abusers. This is not evident from the women's accounts of what happened and what they did about it. Frequently people are not aware when social factors such as age, religion, race, education, and economics affect their behavior, and for this reason it is important not to rely only on people's subjective accounts. Our quantitative analysis has shown that wives who were primary breadwinners at the time their husbands first raped them, were more likely to take effective action. Similarly, in Chapter 15 ("Why Some Wives Stay"), I reported that all nineteen of the wives (i.e., 100 percent) who were the sole providers of the household income at the time of the first rape were no longer married to the men who raped them. These findings are consistent with other research on battered wives. For example, based on three hundred and fifty interviews and many case studies, Mildred Pagelow found that "wives with the most resources were the first to leave physically abusive husbands."[11] The solution to this major contributor to the problem—economic equality between men and women inside and outside the home—is obvious, if not easily achieved.

PART NINE

AN INTERNATIONAL
PERSPECTIVE

24 *print*

Wife Rape in
Other Countries

> With regard to rape in marriage, the law in Portugal states
> that marital relations have to be maintained. The expression,
> "He used me" is the usual way rape in marriage is expressed
> in Portugal. . . . The husband seems to be able to use his
> wife's body in any way he wishes—to force her to have an
> abortion she does not want, to have her sterilized, to lock her
> up, or to beat her.
>
> —Portuguese witness, *Crimes Against Women,* Diana E.
> H. Russell and Nicole Van de Ven, eds., 1976

I have long believed in the importance of taking an international perspective, particularly for feminists. It was demonstrated repeatedly at the
International Tribunal on Crimes Against Women held in Brussels, Belgium, in 1976, that in spite of great differences in the cultures and econo-
mies of the countries represented, there were striking similarities between
some of the problems women faced.[1] For example, the testimony at the
Tribunal revealed that a victim of extramarital rape or wife beating is
viewed and treated pretty much the same in Japan, France, England, Portugal, Holland, Norway, Denmark, and the United States. In all these
countries it is usually the rape victim who appears to be on trial. Both
raped and beaten women tend to be blamed for the abuse they suffer, and
outside of feminist-initiated institutions, such as rape crisis centers or
battered women's shelters, neither kind of victim has anywhere to turn
for help. The battered woman in particular is trapped in her abusive situation, whatever the country in which she lives.[2]

Little is known about the prevalence of wife rape in pre-industrial societies. Anthropologists have largely ignored the topic of extramarital as
well as marital rape.[3] However, given the connection we have seen in our
study between patriarchal family relationships and wife rape, and given
the fact that the majority of world cultures are patriarchal in nature, my
guess is that wife rape occurs in every country in the world today. Understanding wife rape in other countries should give us additional perspec-
tives on the problem in this country.

To investigate the subject, I solicited personal accounts from women who had experienced rape in marriage. In a flyer mailed to all members of the International Feminist Network,[4] as well as to many other women in other countries whom I know, I mentioned my interest in obtaining such personal accounts. I noted in addition that I would like to learn how widespread wife rape is in their country, whether or not rape in marriage was permitted by law, and how other people reacted to a woman who was raped by her husband. In Australia, the Australian Broadcasting Commission aired a radio program on wife rape, made in the U.S., including a request that women contribute their experiences to this book.[5] By far the largest response to my request has, as a result, come from Australia. Before citing some of these letters, in whole or in part, we should have a brief overview of countries where wife rape is against the law.

LAWS AGAINST WIFE RAPE IN OTHER COUNTRIES

The U.S.S.R. and other countries in the Communist bloc, such as Czechoslovakia and Poland, do not exempt husbands from the charge of rape.[6] Czechoslovakia's law predates Communism, having originated in 1932.[7] However, most Communist countries are unwilling to divulge statistics on crime and other social problems, so it is impossible to find out how these laws work in practice, including how often the charge of rape is brought against husbands by wives, if ever. Tatyana Mamonova, one of the first public feminists to emerge in the Soviet Union, from where she was deported, reported that rape in marriage is "prevalent" there; indeed Mamonova maintained that it was "not covered by the law," which I interpret to mean that in her opinion, wife rape was legal.[8] She also said that husbands' terrorizing their wives is a widespread and serious problem in the Soviet Union, and that both wife rape and wife beating "are furthered by widespread male alcoholism."[9]

Sweden, Denmark, and Norway allow husbands to be prosecuted for wife rape, though, as it was noted in Chapter 14, husbands who rape their wives in Denmark and Norway are subject to milder penalties, as are all men who rape women with whom they are having a sexual relationship "of a more lasting kind."[10]

Some European countries, including Switzerland and Yugoslavia, "equate economic threats, such as the threatened loss of a job, with threats of physical force in cases of rape."[11] This reveals an advanced understanding of the predicament of wives in traditional patriarchal marriages since clearly economic threats can often be as effective as physical threats in obtaining sex against a woman's wishes. The recent recognition in this country of the widespread problem of sexual harassment on the job also reflects this understanding; however, this recognition has not yet been incorporated into legal definitions of rape.

The situation with regard to wife rape is unclear in Italy and the Spanish-speaking countries.[12] For example, after examining Mexican law on the issue, one writer affirmed the principle that wives can be raped by their husbands. However, the majority of writers on Spanish and Italian law have concluded otherwise.[13]

South Australia, the most progressive state in Australia, outlawed rape in marriage in 1976, followed by New South Wales in 1980.

At the beginning of this chapter I noted that rape victims and battered women tend to be treated in very similar fashion even in countries which seem to be different in many ways. Male resistance to progressive change vis-a-vis women is often similarly universal. For example, Australian author and feminist Anne Summers wrote of the "spirited attack" on what came to be known as the "rape-in-marriage" bill in South Australia: "Their objections were that the law would be impossible to enforce, and 'an unenforceable law is a bad law,' that it would destroy the institution of marriage by bringing the law into the bedroom, and that it would place a powerful weapon in the hands of 'a vindictive wife.' "[14] One conservative parliamentarian complained that the bill was "minority legislation designed to protect the few, yet putting at risk an institution revered and respected by the majority of Australians." "It was not clear," concluded Summers, "whether he was referring to rape or marriage."[15]

Five years after this law was passed in South Australia, no husband has yet been convicted for wife rape unassociated with general physical violence. This extraordinary fact has been explained by Aileen F. Connon of the South Australian Health Commission:

Rape in marriage ... is still rarely reported. ... The general public, while they may be aware of this complaint, have been slow to implement the opportunity as there has been a great deal of difficulty with such matters as protection, intimidation, emotional distress to the children, custody, etc.[16]

However, Connon added that:

a number of women who have reported sexual assault resulting from [their] husband or ex-husband have taken their case to court. As it happens there has been a significant associated component of general violence and this tended to be the charge which finally is carried into court. ...[17]

In Israel, a precedent-setting verdict was reached on January 29, 1980. Moshe Cohen was found guilty by the Jerusalem District Court of raping his wife, and of committing an assault on her, causing bodily harm, and of attempting to induce his wife to withdraw her charges against him by threatening to kill her. The District Court sentenced him to three years imprisonment. Cohen appealed against the rape conviction and against the severity of the sentence.[18]

On September 24, 1980, the Supreme Court of Israel dismissed an appeal against this judgment. Though most law in Israel is based on English law, which grants husbands the right to rape their wives, Justice Bechor commented, "Happily for us, we in Israel are not obliged to follow the English law unless it has been expressed by (Israeli) legislation." Instead, he argued, the marital rights and duties of Jewish men and women are subject to rabbinical law. Citing the Talmud, Justice Bechor noted that:

it speaks of a man's obligation to have sexual relations with his wife, but not of a corresponding obligation on her part. The Talmud prohibits forced sexual intercourse between a man and his wife. Even if the wife's refusal to comply is unjustified, she may be declared a "rebellious" wife and denied certain privileges, but under no circumstances is she to be forced to have intercourse with him....[19]

However, the Supreme Court saw fit to reduce Cohen's sentence to eighteen months actual imprisonment plus a suspended sentence of eighteen months:

in view of the fact that the appellant's wife had, shortly before the assault on her had taken place, gone abroad with another man; of the fact that her desire for a divorce (which she had subsequently obtained) had been one of the reasons for the assault; of the fact that the wife, herself, had testified that their small son was very attached to his father and needed him; and of the fact that this was the first time that a Jewish husband had been found guilty of raping his wife....[20]

This interpretation of the law does not mean all wife rape in Israel is against the law. Civil marriages which are celebrated outside of Israel, whether between Jews or mixed couples or adherents of other religions, are recognized in Israel because of private international law. Hence, it may be possible "that not all husbands who have sexual intercourse with their wives against their will and by force would be regarded as equally guilty under the secular law."[21]

The fact that there has not been a single conviction for wife rape in South Australia in the five years since the law was passed there in 1976, points up the fact that a change in law does not put an end to the problem. Seeing that the law is implemented is clearly also crucial, and this means changing attitudes.

WIFE RAPE IN OTHER COUNTRIES

Information about wife rape in eleven countries, obtained from personal letters and other sources, will be presented by country in alphabetical order: Australia, Belgium, The Dominican Republic, France, Germany,

India, Israel, Norway, Peru, Sweden, and The United Kingdom. The fact that materials from countries other than these are not included only means that my attempts to get information from them were incomplete or unsuccessful. The reports that follow clearly demonstrate that wife rape is not merely a problem for women in the United States.

Australia

The experiences of wife rape reported by Australian women range over all its forms, from extreme violence to the use of no force at all because the woman was unable to consent. To convey this range, the letters will be presented in order of violence, from the least to the greatest amount.

Mrs. Farnham:*

My husband does not ask me to have sex. He just pushes me over or onto my back and pushes his penis in, no matter how dry my vagina is. This can be painful. There is no word of thanks, no expression of any love. If asleep, I am poked and prodded until woken. Sometimes intercourse takes place and I am scarcely aware of it. My husband drinks every day and his alcoholic breath and smoke is everpresent. Over a certain quantity of drink his breath becomes putrid, the smell of a dead sheep almost pleasant in comparison. When my husband has too much to drink, his penis is too limp to do anything, but I am still manhandled until sleep gets the better of him.

Prior to having the children he insisted on having intercourse "dog fashion" until I went to the hospital, and he expected to have sex as soon as I was home.

Some women say they have a headache but no consideration is ever shown to me. My husband is not brutal but very selfish and inconsiderate. Today there was a woman saying on TV that love means closeness and sex, and that it should be wonderful. I have had very few experiences of pleasure. I can remember once my husband and the fellow up the road had a bet to see who could screw the most in twenty-four hours. From talking to my doctor, many other women are in the same position—afraid to leave because of what the family will say, and reluctant to leave the home and garden they have taken years to try and build and find some sort of security in when alone.

Outwardly I guess our marriage is regarded as solid but my opinion is that I know what "hell" is all about.

Although it is abundantly evident that Mrs. Farnham was subjected to a great number of unwanted sexual experiences in her marriage, it is not clear that they meet our definition of rape (i.e., sexual intercourse obtained by the use of force, the threat of force, or because the person is unable to consent). Mrs. Farnham does say that "sometimes intercourse

---

*To preserve the anonymity of the woman who wrote this letter, her name, like those of the other victims of wife rape who wrote to me, is a pseudonym.

takes place and I am scarcely aware of it," but this does not quite meet our definition of being unable to consent, since she was not totally unaware. However, her case serves to illustrate one form of abuse on the continuum of abusive sex in marriage; many experiences that do not qualify as rape, clearly qualify as abuse.

Mrs. Brown introduces the notion of "blackmailing rape" which she says is widespread in Australia. Even her horrendous experiences with this form of abuse does not meet our narrow definition of rape, for it lacks physical coercion. However, she was also raped when asleep.

I will tell you the story of my first marriage.

His rape would take this form: having been drinking and God only knows what else until midnight at the earliest, he would stagger home and climb into bed. I would be asleep, having long given up the pointless practice of waiting up for him. He would shake me to wake me up. He would then caress (ugh!) me, saying repeatedly, "Come on V., how about it? How about it? Come on, come on." I would indignantly say no, and roll away. He would roll after me, saying again, "Come on, come on." This he would do for half an hour, an hour, and sometimes two hours, going on and on until he was nearly dementing me, for just as I could feel sleep returning to me, he would shake me from it and continue his nagging. It was only after I cried in desperation, "All bloody right," and he would hop on for his two minutes of delight, that I was allowed to sleep. For the last eighteen months of this dismal marriage, I had to buy my sleep by opening my legs to him.

On other occasions, I would stir in the morning from sleep and find that he had stuck his penis into me and was going for his life (from behind, for I always averted myself from him) quite without my being conscious of it. I didn't even have to be awake for it; he raped a sleeping body. This has left me with a profound aversion to being touched while I'm asleep, and my new (and excellent) husband has had to learn not to casually stroke me in the mornings until he knows I am completely awake.

The worst raping occasion was the morning I awoke in labour with my first child. The hospital I was booked into was a thirty-minute drive away, and this being the first time I had undergone childbirth, I had no idea of how close I was to giving birth, or what was to happen to me next. I laboured at home for a few hours until perhaps 11:00 A.M., and then said to my ex-husband that I thought we'd better go to the hospital. The pains were acute and I was panicking that I would not be able to bear them. He looked at me, and said, "Oh, all right. But we'd better have a screw first, because it'll be a week before you're home again." I couldn't believe it, even of him. "Please, W., take me to the hospital," I begged as another contraction stormed across my body. "Not until we have a screw," he insisted. I wept, I cried, I pleaded, but he wouldn't budge. The pleading went on until midday, by which time I was frantic to get nursing help. He stood adamant with his arms crossed, a smirk on his face, and jiggling the car keys as a bribe. In the end I submitted. It took two minutes, then we dressed and drove to the hospital. The baby was born five hours later.

I might add that after we separated, I had no taste for a man for nearly a year, and when I did first venture it, I was terrified that it would make me sick. I must have spent an adequate time in chastity to live out my distaste, because I found this initial man enjoyable, and have had little trouble since, except, as I said, I cannot bear even a gentle arm on my shoulder while I'm asleep.

I believe that this blackmailing rape is an epidemic here in Australia. Many friends have shared their secret pains with me, and the stories are alike: "Screw me, or I'll go to the pub." "Screw me, or I'll screw someone else." "Screw me, or we won't go to that film you want to see," etc., etc., *ad nauseam*.

Mrs. Burdick believes her experience of wife rape (which does meet our definition) was not only related to her ex-husband's drinking but also to his adaptation to the Australian way of life.

It's a daunting task to write of these things, and even more difficult to chronicle them correctly since the emotional trauma remains for much longer than the act itself.

My experience is peculiar (aren't they all?) in that I'm an Australian who was married to an American. We lived the first five years of our uneventful marriage in the U.S. and sexual relations seemed quite "normal." The last eight years we lived in Australia, and that's when the drink-related rapes began to occur. I think my ex-husband couldn't cope with life in Australia, just as I found it difficult to cope with life in the U.S. His answer was to throw himself into the Australian way of life, which is basically going to the pub every night after work with the "mates" and getting very drunk, coming home to me and trying (and succeeding) to fuck me. For the first year I accepted this behaviour as a transitional period, but then life became a nightmare.

Although violence was not involved, other than the fact that even while in a drunken stupor, he was still strong enough to physically overcome me, I'll never forget the fear I lived through each day wondering what would happen that night. This was in fact an irrational fear because for eight years life was quite predictable. It was my illusory hope that "tonight might be different" which brought on my fear and anxiety about not being able to predict my future. Of course most of the problem was that I could not control my own body or my future; both lay in the hands of some drunken idiot. (Great for the self-esteem!)

My husband developed a pattern of drinking and raping me four nights out of the week (he was very tired on the other three in-between nights). Nothing I could do or think of, could prevent these rapes.

Another problem with rape in marriage is the trouble-free facade we put forward to the outside world. We were in fact a beautiful family, well dressed, well housed, doing all the right things, taking the kids to sporting events, picnics, nights out at restaurants (where my husband became increasingly amourous). People commented on how much my husband "adored" me. If rape in marriage is adoration, they can keep it!

During the marriage I sympathized with my husband's shortcomings, and the fact that he'd given up so much in the U.S. to live in Australia. As a feminist I can now see that like most women I saw the world through its effects on others, not putting my own needs first, or giving them equal status. I hurt emotionally during those years, with no one to talk to, protecting the children from the knowledge (as much as one can), with no money to call my own, and nowhere to run to.

The physical experience of rape no doubt has many sordid variations. Mine would certainly pale into insignificance compared to many—but it is still my tragedy, my experience. It is an experience men don't have to suffer when they decide to marry. I am slightly built; my husband was stocky and no stronger than the average male. The feeling of powerlessness and lack of control of my actions, lack of any choice in the matter, tended to kill any sexual feelings I may have had for him. I became repulsed by the sight of him. I could only feel contempt for him (as no doubt he did for me, his victim). In fact, his drunken stupor coupled with his non-adult behaviour (or should I say criminal behaviour?) slowly led me to believe in myself as an intelligent and worthwhile person, finding consolation and validation in my role as a competent housewife, a loving and caring mother, and a worker in the outside world. So I grew, and I fled—terrified that he could come back into my life again at will, the same way he could have sex with me at will.

I wished I could say that I left these experiences behind me when I left the marriage. Although I certainly haven't let them traumatize me to the extent that I can't live a relatively happy life, these experiences will never be erased from my memory. I could not look at a man for two years afterward, and I had to work through much hate and anger during that period. In the subsequent two years I've settled down to a standoffish acceptance of men who exist in my life and work. I had my first sexual experience with another man last month, and was pleasantly surprised to find my responses satisfying. I felt totally divorced from my past sexual experiences with my ex-husband, as if a new life had begun. Even so, it was a casual encounter which will not be repeated.

I cannot honestly write that the rapes in my marriage have affected my ability to form relationships with men because I found it nearly impossible before marriage, and the same after. Basically, men are not worthwhile as friends.

Force was not involved in most of the experiences described by Mrs. Hammer, though it was very clear to both her and her husband that the sexual intercourse was unwanted. The one time she refused, he was very violent. That particular attack would qualify as an attempted rape by our definition.

I had no say as to whether we had sex or not. It went on without fail, regardless of me, Tuesday night, Thursday, Saturday, and Sunday. When I asked him to change the nights around, all he did was to throw back his head and laugh. If we were going out on say a Sunday afternoon, and he saw me getting dressed, or in stockings, slip, and bra, that was the signal for it to happen. But when I had a period, oh how he changed his tune. All he could say then was that I stank.

After years of the four nights a week sex routine, which bored me out of my mind, one night I decided I was going to have my way just for once, and I dared to say "no." Well, it was on in no uncertain fashion—him trying to force himself on me, and me fighting him off. In the end he picked me up bodily from the bed and threw me out onto the floor. I landed on the top of my head, I must have jarred my neck or the top of my spine because I had a stiff neck for a week. Thank God there was a thick carpet on the floor and a rug on top of that, or I might have really been in trouble.

One time when I was in hospital for three weeks in a private room, he used to come to the hospital early, before anyone else got there, and all he did was to nag me for sex. He used to say things like, "Oh, there's nothing wrong with you!" I hadn't had an operation; I'd cracked up from working all my life and running the house as well for twenty-five years. He tried to fight with me to get into the hospital bed, and tried to drag me out of the bed. This was all his coming to see me consisted of. I think that hoping for some sex was the only reason he came to the hospital at all.

Eventually he found another woman to have as a sex partner. We are still living together in the same house and he goes off every weekend to his other woman. It's not a very happy life for me, of course, but at least I have peace. He took himself off to another bedroom about fourteen years ago, which I was glad of, but up until about four years ago, he still used to come into my room of a morning before I got up to get him off to work. But I gradually turned him off. I refused to move or lift a finger, so at last he must have taken the hint.

Another incident shows how he thought I was his property or that my body was his. One night I was reading when he got into bed. This night, according to him, was going to be the night. I refused to put down my book, but as usual he started to go into the sex act from behind. I said I was reading before he came into the bed, and I would continue to read. But he would not be put off. So it ended with me reading (or making out I was reading) and him having sex. He always said that a woman's place was in the kitchen and the bedroom. He used to laugh when he said it, but I'm sure he meant it.

Another thing he liked to do, was to pull and bite my nipples. One day at work I discovered my nipples were very sore, so I went off and had a look at them and that creature the night before had apparently pulled so hard he had broken all the skin away from around the base of them. It never mattered what I said to him; when I told him that he was hurting me, he used to say I was moaning and to shut up.

So that was my experience of sex in marriage for about twenty-five or twenty-six years; the last few years I have had peace from his constant sexual wants, thank God, because he has this other woman.

I stay in the marriage as I can't afford to do anything else. I was sacked [fired] from my job about twelve years ago, so I am now dependent on his money, such as he gives me, to run the house. Anyway, I've had enough of working after twenty-seven years, so I'll put up with not much money. Also at fifty-five, I probably couldn't get a job now. And the house is in both our names; I am going to live in my home, just the same as he is, no matter what.

Mrs. Peel describes what would also be an attempted rape, one that involved considerable violence.

Four years ago I married a very nice man—the "pick of the bunch." After two years he met an old flame and got hold of some kind of drugs which upset his behaviour. He was a clumsy lover, but I had previously talked him into being considerate. Then one morning, it happened. I was dressing and he was about to tear my clothes off. He was standing naked and "extended." I knew in a split second that if he did approach me in that manner I would surely be physically injured. Also I knew that if he did, I would never *love* him again; I had loved him dearly. He then knocked me down, pinned me on the bed, clenched his right fist, and gave me its full force on my left ear. I screamed and got three more punches on the side of my head. That was supposed to knock me unconscious, I believe. His intention was obvious, but I got away. I grabbed some clothes and fled.

He packed up and left while I was out of the house, but I live behind locked doors. I am now half blind through his cruelty. I can write as you see, but I cannot see to read anything even with glasses.

Mrs. Rathburn was a battered wife who was terrorized by her husband into submission. Most of the rapes she was subjected to were achieved through threat of force.

Although I feel uncomfortable about writing, I feel that I owe it to someone to do so. My story is not all that dramatic. I have not told very many people about it. I found that when I did, and then only to women, I was regarded as some kind of idiot. How could a married woman be raped by her husband, which is a legal impossibility? Or they would say that I was exaggerating the situation. So I have not talked about it for some time.

At the time these events took place, I felt very angry at my humiliation. Over the years that reaction has changed to pity for my former husband. Fortunately for me, the man that I subsequently married—having vowed never to remarry after the previous horrific experience—is the antithesis of my ex-husband. I now know that it is possible for a man to be healthy and masculine without feeling the need to prove his sexual prowess at all times.

I do not want to refer to my former husband by name, but shall simply call him A. To give a little of A.'s background: his father was in the military, a homosexual, who A. claimed had sexually assaulted him when he was age ten. Our marriage was his third, my second. Physical abuse was not infrequent in our relationship, but A. always managed to persuade me that I had provoked the attacks. I went to a social worker after the last attack and was convinced by her that I had to leave him, having been told by him that if I did so he would kill me. At that time I was living in the United States with very few friends, only my colleagues at the university for which I worked.

This seems a long, perhaps unnecessary preamble, but I feel that it is necessary to fit the actual marital rape into a context. I suspect that if my former husband had not come from a specific social background (upper-middle class, English, with a violent father etc.) he might not have had to prove himself sexually.

When I first went to bed with him I found him sexually exciting. He was a charming, social creature, considerably older than I, and I was flattered by his attentions. He taught in a university and I was a student of his. I knew that he was given to fits of rage that he would take out on me, but I always felt that I could understand why he had been provoked. Perhaps I loved him or wanted to explain away an undesirable trait. I was also absolutely terrified of him and am to this day. As a child I had been beaten by both parents, but had no conception of how vicious a spouse could be. No one I knew talked about it, and my father certainly did not beat up my mother.

When I did finally get up the courage to leave, vowing that I would not allow myself to be beaten up again, I did so in the full knowledge that he would try to kill me. As for specifically sexual events, these were as follows: I would be expected to "perform" every night, so that it became a grind, literally. I found it messy to have sexual intercourse during my period, but that was no excuse. After having been beaten up, I felt very unhappy about having my breasts fondled during love making (I vaguely remember being punched in the breast on one occasion), but my self-protectiveness in this regard was thought of as peculiar. A.

thought that I was being absurd not to want to make love after a fight. Perhaps he found it arousing—I found it more of a turn-off. He also expected me to wear a raincoat during our love making which was intolerable because it was one of those plastic ones that are very hot to wear. At first this seemed a bit kinky, but not impossible because I did not have to wear the coat every night, but latterly if I did not wear it he would not have an erection.

Whenever I protested about going to bed with him, he would say that if we waited until I was in the mood we would never make love. And he was right. I stayed with him out of fear and used to lie awake fantisizing how I would kill him.

When I talk about marital rape I am talking about being forced to make love, i.e., lie there and be used. The alternative was to fight against it, be beaten up and then have to submit anyway. It was less painful physically to submit without the violence.

After I left him that last time (I had done so before but I'd always been persuaded to come back: he would kill himself or me or both of us if I did not) I continued to work at my job, but lived in hiding. One Saturday afternoon I sat out in the sun by the side of the house eating strawberries. I was not visible from anywhere, and I was enjoying my solitude when he came to stand over me. I was terrified because I knew that there was no one around to protect me, that I was totally on my own. I thought that if I cried out, he would beat me up. The best course of action was to go quietly into my room on the ground floor, lie back and let it happen. I shall never forget lying on my bed, tears of humiliation and anger and terror streaming down my face. He probably thought it was joy, so out of touch was he with my feelings.

After he left I took a shower and douched myself. I felt really degraded. I was always afraid he would come back, but I later heard that he had gone overseas. Those events finished happening over ten years ago, but I still feel afraid of him.

Fortunately for me, I do not think that I have let the fears and horror of the past interfere with my relationship with M. He is very loving and understands my feelings. I thank God. . . .

I hope this helps. It is difficult to write about after years because the details that were so devastating at the time, fade with time. Also I have actively tried to forget about the details because I do not want them to intrude on my life or on that of my family.

Mrs. Selby was also a battered wife, battered by her husband physically, and battered psychologically by many besides her husband. She conveys well the prison in which many battered women live, and the fact that sometimes other people have access to the prison keys even if many of them don't use it.

For many years I had the experience of being little more than an unpaid hooker to a drunken, violent husband who used to bash me and force his attentions on me. I complained to the police, who would not take action in "domestic arguments." I was told by the police woman that I was "selfish" because I did not want my drunken husband to have intercourse with me. This was my "duty," said this unmarried, middle-aged police woman!

My husband, a devout Catholic, used to get drunk Saturday nights and then go to mass on Sundays. Nobody believed me because he was a pillar of the Church. A priest told me that I ought to pray to St. Jude, St. Monica, and the Blessed Virgin Mary and other saints for a happy home life, because the greatest saints had to suffer, and God sent suffering to those he loved most. I attempted suicide twice, but nobody believed me when I talked about my ill treatment. A lawyer whom I went to see said he had known my husband and his family, he'd gone to school with them, and he would not believe that a devout Catholic behaved in such a manner. Instead he recommended a psychiatrist for me.

My husband is afraid of my sons who are now grown up because my sons said they would never stand for him hitting me again. We are now "separated" though we live in the same house, and he goes his own way. I can't leave the house because it's in our joint names. My husband and I no longer have sex (thank God), and at last I have a doctor who *believes* me.

I also want to tell you about my girl friend, Kathy, who was constantly raped and bashed during pregnancy. Most of the funding for Women's Refuge Shelters had been cut, and many of the shelters have had to close.

Kathy had nowhere to go and she could no longer stand being bashed and raped by her husband and not having anybody believe her, so she was forced to leave her home without her children. Since then, her husband has "shacked up" with another woman, and Kathy has lost custody of her children as an "unfit mother." She was the most devoted, loving mother anyone ever saw, but she couldn't stand being bashed and raped by her drunken husband anymore. She was on the verge of suicide when she left. She visits her children, but her husband and his defacto [common-law wife] make her visits as uncomfortable as possible. The law is stacked against women in Australia.

Mrs. Selby's description of her role as being "little more than an unpaid hooker to a drunken, violent husband" highlights an interesting contradiction. In most societies prostitutes are looked down upon for their ability or willingness to have sex with men they may find revolting, obnoxious, or immoral; other women, especially wives, are admonished if they *cannot* or *will not* perform sexually for husbands whom they find revolting or immoral.

Belgium

According to a Belgian lawyer, wife rape in Belgium is "an everyday thing," and as such, the commonest form of rape to occur. However, there has only been one trial of a husband for wife rape in Belgium to date.[22]

Bruno De Ridder, a twenty-five-year-old grocery store clerk, forced his wife, Lisette, to have sexual intercourse with him repeatedly between March 1976 and December 1977. According to testimony, "De Ridder beat his wife and tied her to a bed when she refused his advances." Mrs. De Ridder said she "tolerated the beatings and forced intercourse for almost two years before complaining to police in December 1977." She further testified that "she had stayed with her husband for the sake of their two children."[23]

A local Brussels court cleared De Ridder of the charge of rape, but convicted him of assault. They agreed with a defense argument that "by not submitting to intercourse with her husband, the wife was neglecting her marital responsibilities." However, an appeals court overturned this decision. The three-judge panel ruled that "rape is an act of violence no matter whether the two persons involved are married." They argued that "by marrying a man, a woman 'agrees to have intimate relations'—but the husband does not have the right to force her into intercourse through use of 'his greater physical strength.' "[24] This decision apparently provoked a great deal of controversy and protest in Belgium.[25]

Dominican Republic

A feminist organization called Centro de Investigacion Para la Acción Femenina published a request for contributions to this book about wife rape in a weekly national newspaper. There was no response to this request. Magaly Pineda, the coordinator of this group, wrote in explanation that this lack of response was caused by a lack of consciousness regarding women's rights. She added that a few women had told her that it was not possible to have rape in marriage because it is a wife's duty to always be at the disposal of her husband.[26]

France

Wife rape is not against the law in France. However, for the first time in France an all-male jury in Grenoble found a husband, Didier Pongi, guilty of raping his wife.

Twenty-five-year-old Didier Pongi was convicted by the court in Grenoble to serve an eight-year sentence and his accomplice Jean Chevallier-Chambet was convicted to serve five years. A lawyer said that this conviction will "become part of the history of the regulation of marital rights and duties. The husband cannot any longer do with his wife what he wants to, as if he had gained absolute ownership of her with marriage." Pongi had beaten his wife shortly after the marriage. That was the reason she filed for divorce after a few months. After a day in court on November 30, 1978, Pongi lay in wait for his wife together with his friend, attacked her, tore her clothes off, and raped her. His friend had to hold her down during the rape. The prosecutor demanded ten years. The usual laws which do not acknowledge marital rape were not applied because in this case it was not possible any longer to talk about there being an intimate or marital relationship.

Since this is the first time a man has been found guilty of raping his wife in France, in spite of there being no law against it, the verdict is likely to be very significant and possibly precedent-setting.[27]

Germany (West)

Imogen Seger-Coulborn writes in the introduction to an unpublished report on wife rape in West Germany prepared by Institut für Demoskopie Allensbach:

Eighteen out of one hundred wives felt that they had been raped by their husbands—rarely or repeatedly, in the past or on a continual basis—and said so in their interviews. . . .

This 18 percent represents roughly two and a half million married women in West Germany and West Berlin. Two and a half million women is no small number. But they have been silent up to now. They did not know whom to talk to. They did not know whether they might be abnormal or might be "bad wives."

Now the issues of rape and of rape in marriage have come to public attention. This changes many things.

Now it is possible for women who till this time have brooded alone over their problems in sorrow, anger or bitterness, to read what other women are saying. . . . Only the fact that the problem has been publicly defined as a problem makes it easier for the individuals involved to talk about it, and that is almost always the basis for the beginning of change.[28]

Even though the results were published in the popular magazine *Stern,* this report did not appear to change anything. West Germany has not been in the vanguard of legal reform on this issue even though it is the only country in which a national poll on wife rape has been conducted. The women's movement has not mobilized around the issue, and many German feminists seem both unaware of and unconcerned about the problem.

I believe two reasons may account for this lack of concern. First, movements don't just happen; they are based on social conditions, and develop out of what has happened before. The time simply does not appear to have been "ripe" in 1976 for women in West Germany to become incensed by the injustice of wife rape. Nor were the women's movements in any other countries working on this issue at that time. Further, the Institut für Demoskopie Allensbach seems to have placed the issue of wife rape in the context of male-female marriage problems. For example, the introduction states: "Perhaps ultimately, they [wife rape victims] will be able to talk with their husbands, making it clear that something in the marriage isn't working."[29] This implies that the problem can be solved by more and better communication, and that husbands are unaware that the wives find being raped a problem. Undoubtedly there are some cases like this, but judging from our data, this is not what most wife rape is about.

Roswitha Burgard, a German feminist who has worked at a center for battered women in West Berlin for some years, was commissioned to write about wife rape for *Stern* magazine, but they then refused to publish what she wrote, an excerpt of which was as follows:

Almost daily, women who have fled to our battered women's shelter tell me:

"He told me not to make a fuss, that, ultimately, I'm his wife, and he can do what he wants with me." "When I didn't have sex with him twice a day, he'd threaten to go find another woman, and then I'd be left with my three children." "I've only been able to stand it by drinking. . . ."

If a woman was ever able *before* marriage to express her sexual needs, she finds her ability terminates in the motto: "A wife must serve her husband's wishes and demands." According to this rule, it makes no difference whether she doesn't feel in the mood—physically or emotionally; whether she's pregnant or has just given birth; whether the children are sleeping in the same bedroom or even sleeping in the same bed; whether he's showing off for friends or colleagues; or whether the wife is being forced, in order to increase his excitement. . . .

Wives submit to all these, otherwise risking "not only" rape, but also battery by the husband. Repeatedly, women in our shelter say that they have been beaten bloody and almost unconscious, and have been raped by their husbands immediately afterward.

The husbands described are neither sick nor criminal by nature, as is often claimed. Men who rape their wives and still consider it their "legal right" are not so much the gas station attendant on the corner, according to district social workers, as they are judges who should be "administering justice" over rapes in dark alleys. The assaulted women who have experienced marital rape are less frequently economically dependent women, such as women working in the home, and more often highly skilled women, such as nurses.

Women have always been forced into marital intercourse. What is new is that women are beginning to talk about it and to defend themselves against it.[30]

In *Vergewaltigung in der Ehe (Rape in Marriage)* published in 1979, Dierk Helmken argued for the need for a change in the law in Germany so as to make rape in marriage illegal, and traced the history of discussions about this issue, particularly in the late 1960s.[31] It appears that these discussions came out of the sexual criminal law reform movement and had nothing to do with the women's movement.[32] However, more recently, a women's group in Germany has finally taken the initiative to try to change the law.[33]

India

Mrs. Chowdhury wrote to me that in Indian culture, there is a total failure to acknowledge the issue of rape in marriage, but that she was inspired by the title of this book to start collecting information about it. Mrs. Chowdhury, a member of the Brahmin caste who observed Purdah (the covering of the face) though she did not believe in the custom, was doing her Ph.D. thesis on the Meena Tribe of Rajasthan in India. Before talking about her own experience of rape in marriage, Mrs. Chowdhury wrote about what she had learned on this subject from the Meena Tribeswomen.

It seems that the dominant husbands enjoy rape more than normal intercourse, and that the drunken husband has no consideration for the consent of the wife. Most of the wives are very cold and the partner has no alternative. Because of the Purdah system [the covering of the face and relations of avoidance] as well as all sorts of other constraints due to poverty, lack of privacy, and social fear or shyness, most of the husbands do not get a chance to have intercourse in a smooth manner, except when they find their wives due to the grace of God. Nothing but rape is the solution for the sexually frustrated men when their wives are at their disposal just by chance. (Daily bed-sharing is not arranged by elder members of the family.) One of the informants said that she is the mother of seven children and till now she had been raped seven times by her husband which resulted in conception every time, no misfire!

I suppose the position in the rest of Indian society is the same, with a few differences here and there. After I started enquiring about this subject, I learned a striking fact: that there is no concept of rape in marriage in our culture. We only think that intercourse outside marriage is illegal, and if it is by consent of the partner, it can be termed adultery; if it is without consent, then it is rape. But inside marriage everything is sacred and worthy to be taken for granted.

Not only do we not consider rape as something criminal in marriage, but rather it is thought to add to the status of the husband. If such treatment is known about it proves that the wife is a total virgin and she is praised for being raped, because it shows her innocence. But in my case, which may be like many other Indian females, I was shy enough to cry and make a noise, but like all the newly married women, I had to yield.

There is no bedroom for spouses in most joint families, and the male and female family members are supposed to sleep in separate apartments. I belong to a joint family of about eighty members where I was brought up, and till my marriage took place, because of the arrangements in my parents' house, I had no idea of sharing a bed with my husband. My married sisters and sisters-in-law used to talk secretively, but whenever the unmarried girls came near them, they used to change the topic. It was all a mystery. Sex, being considered obscene, could not be talked about in the presence of elders and youngers, nor openly in any company. So when I entered into the institution of marriage, like a total confused girl, I took my husband as a real scoundrel. Later I came to know from my married sisters and sisters-in-law that they also took it the same way.

You will be surprised to know that this condition is the same even today in most of the semi-urban areas where the joint family is still prevailing. I suppose that the situation will improve fast as parents like me are aware of the difficulties we had.

There is one more thing I would like to inform you about. I gathered the information on this subject from the Meena Tribe, but I am unwilling to include this part in my thesis because at the time of my viva-voce [oral examinations], my examiners will question me regarding this. I don't want to be embarrassed, and I feel that most of my sisters might feel the same way.

It was only you being a lady that I dare confide in you. I would not have responded if the author was a male. We do not converse on such topics even with our husbands.

I am really happy that by writing of my past experiences to you, I could get relief from the repressed desire to share with someone. There is a real need to liberate women from such kinds of atrocities, which are never thought of as such.[34]

Norway

The first time a man was convicted of wife rape in Norway was in 1974.[35] Through their contact with women, Krisesentret, a shelter for battered women in Oslo, and an organization called Free Legal Aid for Women, "discovered that rape in marriage occurs quite frequently." The Norwegian correspondents answered the question "Why is rape in marriage so seldom reported?" as follows:

We believe that there are two reasons: (a) Men do not think of it as rape—they believe it is a right following from being married; (b) Nor do women define sexual violence in marriage as rape. They believe that the husband actually has the right he thinks he has. This is to some extent due to myths, and to some extent due to the idea that what happens within the home (between spouses) is part of people's "privacy."...

Rape in marriage may be looked upon as an even greater strain—a greater defeat—than "ordinary rape." She—the wife—must either have rejected the myth, or the rape must be of such an extreme character, that it "undoubtedly" is rape!... Judging from legal practice, only the very severe cases of rape in marriage come to light, such as in the Supreme Court decision of 1974.[36]

In order for wife rape to be punishable, it must be proved to have been committed "with intent," i.e., the man must be conscious of what he is doing. However many rapists neither see their acts as rape nor perceive that the victim does not want forceful sex. The fact that the perception of the husband-rapist is given priority over the reality for the rape victim makes it evident that the law in Norway is intended to protect husbands rather than wives.

Peru

The response to my request for information on wife rape in Peru was virtually identical to the response from the Dominican Republic. When my flyer requesting information on wife rape in other countries arrived in Peru, an organization called Accion para la Liberación de la Mujer Peruana (ALIMUPER) decided to do a poll on the subject. A questionnaire on wife rape was included in their quarterly bulletin *Accion*. However, there were no responses. "Perhaps we should have expected it," wrote Ana Maria Portugal. Her letter continued as follows:

It seems this subject is still very much taboo around here where Machismo is so deep and so strong; women are certainly not ready to share their experiences about rape in marriage with anybody—maybe they don't even acknowledge it to themselves. We don't really know. What this experience has given ALIMUPER proof of is that rape in marriage can not be measured; it can not even be estimated in our country because it is such a serious problem that women are just too embarrassed to even consider talking about it.[37]

Sweden

Swedish researcher Ulf Linderholm undertook a study of rapes reported to the police during 1970 in Stockholm. Wife rape had been made illegal in 1965. Nevertheless, wife rapes constituted a relatively small proportion of the total number of rapes. "There were four instances involving a wedded couple, and two in which the pair was engaged—a status in Sweden that very nearly approximates marriage."[38]

According to Geis,

These cases seemed somewhat more brutal than the usual rape incident coming to police attention, and more often involved a revenge motive. In one instance, for example, a young woman who had left her fiancé was attacked in her apartment by him and a friend. They forced her to engage in repeated acts of intercourse, shot at her feet with a pistol, and struck her with various objects. In another case, the offender forced the victim to undress and thereafter, before intercourse, took photographs of her in different positions.[39]

Geis' own review of Stockholm police files for 1976

found only two cases resembling rape-in-marriage; in neither was the couple legally married. The first involved two former mental hospital patients, who had met at the institution and then upon their release set up housekeeping together. The offender was returned to the hospital after his roommate's rape report, and she withdrew her complaint. In the second episode, the engaged couple had separated, then reunited. The fiancé's rape charge was prosecuted as assault, and the man received a forty-five day sentence.[40]

A brief article titled "Matrimonial rape" reported a five-year prison sentence and a five thousand dollar fine in Sweden for a man who raped and assaulted the woman he lived with. According to this article, "the number of unreported cases (of wife rape) has been estimated to be as high as 60,000 a year."[41] No basis for this estimate was offered.

United Kingdom

In March 1976 a Labour member of the British parliament proposed an amendment to the Sexual Offenses Act which would have eliminated the marital rape exemption. The amendment was defeated by opponents whose position Geis summarizes as follows:

We have to keep our feet well on the ground and bring to bear a little earthy common sense. There are some women who are so unscrupulous that if they were given the encouragement of a statutory provision such as (the rape-in-marriage) amendment they might be prepared to commit perjury and bring their husbands into a criminal court for the sole purpose of breaking up the marriage.[42]

The similarity in the arguments made by the legislators opposing the elimination of the marital rape exemption is as strikingly similar across national boundaries as is the treatment of raped and battered women. Most of all, men's fears of vindictive or unscrupulous women is exploited to the hilt. The privacy of the bedroom is another favorite, as if crimes cannot be committed in that sanctuary, or if they are, they should not be prosecuted out of concern for the larger issue of man's-home-is-his-castle.

More recently, in November 1980 the Criminal Law Revision Committee, a British government-appointed committee of judges and lawyers, recommended among other changes in the law that "a husband who forces his wife to have intercourse should be guilty of rape."[43] The majority of the Committee criticized the present law "as archaic and based on the subjection of a wife to her husband, which is 'totally out of accord with present-day attitudes. . . . It is difficult to explain why wives should be outside the protection of the law on rape when unmarried cohabitants are not.' "[44] At the time these recommendations were made, a husband in England could be charged with rape only if a divorce was pending, if the couple was legally separated, or if a court had issued a non-molestation order.

WALES Mrs. Christie:

My husband was a very violent man and he used sex as another means of hurting and degrading me. He would order me to do things and if I refused or gave any sign of being unwilling, he would hit me until I obeyed, and then hit me for getting it wrong or being too slow. Subsequently he would just walk in, order me to strip, and then rape me.

I was too afraid and humiliated to do much about this for years, except for pretending to be ill. He said he'd cut me up if I tried to leave. He would go at me until I bled, and humiliate me verbally at the same time. He would finish by ejaculating or even urinating over me, preferably in my face if I couldn't avoid it.

When he thought I'd told my doctor what was happening, he punished me with sodomy. That damaged me, and the fear of that overrode my fear of leaving him, and I ran off with the children. I'm still running, and he's still trying to find me.

I don't think the law here is interested in rape in marriage, but it is quite common, especially when the man is violent anyway. But women don't like admitting that it's happening. It's not easy to admit that the man you once loved and trusted could do that to you. It's the worst sort of violence—but the bruises don't show.

ENGLAND Mrs. Reese is a thirty-eight-year-old woman who was married for fourteen years. Her testimony came in the form of two letters which have been combined.

In 1976 I found I couldn't climax and it eventually annoyed my husband who believed I was having an affair. After a few months we argued every time I let him make love to me. I begged him to help me to climax, but he refused.

By 1977 I was getting extremely sexually frustrated as my husband kept working me up into a frenzy but leaving me once he had climaxed. I begged him not to over and over again but he wouldn't listen, so I began refusing him sex. After a month he began holding me down and climbing on top of me, although I asked him not to. I hated him touching me and hurting me. At one point he held me down and masturbated into my eye sockets. Then another time while my two children were downstairs and I was looking after a neighbour's children who were downstairs also, I was ordered upstairs and made to strip naked so he could hold me down and make love to me. One day in November 1977 I was being held down by him and started crying. I cried so much I feared he would hit me. He told me to stop crying but I couldn't, so he got up off me and threw me off the bed. I never let my husband near me after that—though I lived and slept in his bed for another two years before we divorced.

I was told I could not divorce him for rape, as rape in marriage did not exist, but *he* could divorce *me* for refusing him sex. Yet at my eventual divorce in 1980 the only consolation my solicitor gave me, was that if we had lived together unmarried, my husband would have been in prison. As it was, I was only able to divorce him on grounds of unreasonable behavior, and what he actually did to me was *never* disclosed to the courts.

Since my divorce, I have lost my two children and was made homeless and penniless. When I've told people of both sexes about my experiences, they have gossiped afterward saying, "Oh well, she must be a prude." They think it's unnatural for a woman to refuse her husband sex unless she's odd, and men keep me at a distance saying I am frigid. It's a problem that has very long *AND* lasting consequences, and a problem that has unjustly labeled me as "odd."

As far as I am concerned, I was "raped" by my husband—no matter what the law says. Rape by one's own husband is as horrendous as any other form of rape. With me, it is the long term effects that worry me—for believe me, after all the years since my husband last touched me in Nov. 1977, I am still nervous of men, yet I love them.

I never told anyone of all the things my husband did to me as they would never have believed me. Now you are printing my letter, and I feel that the truth is finally coming out.

I wish to add one final comment. My husband at no point ever believed he was doing wrong—and therefore he was totally blind to my pain. As far as he is concerned, I enjoyed myself.

Maybe if I had lived in the States I would not have been made homeless and penniless the way I was in England. Where rape in marriage is concerned, in Britain there is very little sympathy for the woman. As a result of the lack of emotional support, it has made me very bitter and resentful, and this in turn makes it more difficult for me to help myself. When I go to my General Practitioner for help, he just tells me to pull myself together and stop being silly. Yours is the only support I've had that has not condemned me.

SCOTLAND   Mrs. Burns:

I am a forty-seven-year-old grandmother, still living with my husband, and I have experienced a great deal of male violence in all its forms in the past twenty-seven years.

I could simply tell you my "sad tale of woe," but that leaves me in an almost "blind" state of rage at the end, which takes me about a week to work off.

One thing I can state however, is that there is no such thing in Scotland as "rape" in marriage. The general attitude is that a woman has a duty to her husband, and if a husband has to resort to force to obtain his conjugal rights then there is something deficient about the woman, i.e., she is not carrying out her "wifely duties" and attending to his physical *NEEDS*.

As regards other people's reactions, I can't speak on behalf of younger women today who are still going through this experience, but for my age group, it was extremely difficult. One just did *NOT* talk about these things. On the few occasions I plucked up courage to try to talk to "a close friend" I was very sympathetically, but embarassedly "put off." I was told that this really is a very private thing, and one shouldn't discuss it other than with one's marriage partner. Or the response was: "Isn't it awful what we women have to put up with? But, that's the way men are—isn't it?" So I continued to seeth and rage inside about the fact that this bastard seemingly had the right to use me and my body in whichever way he pleased.

On thinking back I realize now, that even the couple of women I tried to discuss it with were defining rape as "man's *gentle* force." I doubt very much now, had I mentioned the extreme violence I was experiencing, if I would have been believed. It's also very clear to me now that they too were undergoing the coercive type of rape, but that they didn't see it as rape.

Years later, by which time my rage had exploded, I openly made a very angry statement about my experiences in front of my husband and one of these women and her husband. I was told later by my husband that they had told him they thought it disgusting I would say such things (they obviously were not disgusted by the fact that my husband did them); this from my "closest" friend.

After a rapid loss of weight (4 stone [56 lbs.] in 3 months) due to the continual mental abuse and physical violence from my husband, I was told by my G.P.: "for God's sake, go home and have a dozen kids, and then you won't have so much time to think about yourself." When I eventually objected vocally and very angrily to his attitude, he threatened to have me committed if I did not "behave" myself.

In 1974 when I was traveling in Italy, I asked feminists about the problem of rape in their country. At that time they told me that is was not a problem. I had been told the same in France, Sweden, Norway, Holland—wherever I traveled in Western Europe. In Denmark I was even told, not by a feminist, but by a woman probation officer: "In Denmark we are sexually liberated, so we don't get upset about rape—if it happens, we lie back and enjoy it." This woman was not describing her own feelings, but instead, she was articulating what she believed to be the ideology in Denmark at that time.

I was skeptical about the constant denial of this problem, and by the time I arrived in Italy, I followed up my questions about rape by asking about forced sex in marriage: how common was that? "Oh, that happens *all the time*," I was told. Similarly, in the letters I received from India, the fact that wife rape happens frequently was conveyed, along with the idea that this was a shocking and taboo subject that no one talked about. In the letter from Peru cited in this chapter, the woman who wrote me understood the silence of the married women polled on this topic in her country to indicate not that it is no problem, but on the contrary; this silence showed how big a problem there is.

We are only just starting to deal with the issue of wife rape in the United States. Most other countries are not willing to deal with it yet. The more advanced the women's movement is, the more likely there will be a willingness to confront the issue of wife rape. This is not to say that the women's movements in all countries have to evolve at the same slow pace; the process of reaching a new awareness about particular issues can be hastened. For example, England was the first country where women dealt with the issue of battered women. The United States was the first country to deal with rape. Scandinavian feminists were the first to deal with pornography. Many countries have learned a great deal from England about the problems of battered women, and from the U.S. about the problems of rape victims (though for some reason, not much seems to have been learned from the Scandinavian feminists' actions against pornography—possibly because they have been too feeble). I hope very much that women in many countries will be able and willing to learn from the attack on rape in marriage in this country, as well as that there will soon be much to learn from what happens here.

25

Conclusions and Solutions

[T]oo many men do not realize that the slogan "An End to Rape" does not so much refer to grand rapes committed on the crime-ridden streets of the cities as to the brutalization of contact between brother and sister, father and daughter, teacher and pupil, doctor and patient, employer and employee, dater and datee, fiance and fiancee, husband and wife, adulterer and adulteress, the billions of petty liberties extracted from passive and wondering women.

—Germaine Greer, "Seduction Is a Four Letter Word," *Playboy*, 1973

In order that we stop being victims we ourselves must take up the struggle against rape. Individually and collectively we can break the silence and make it no longer a taboo subject, or something shameful which weighs us down

—French witness, *Crimes Against Women*, Diana E. H. Russell and Nicole Van de Ven, eds., 1976

Almost all the knowledge about rape accumulated to date relates to rape by strangers; to a lesser extent, rape by acquaintances; and to an even lesser extent, rape by dates. Rape by lovers and close or long-term friends, as well as wife rape, have rarely been studied. Though there are similarities in experiences of rape no matter what the type of relationship within which it occurs, there are significant differences too. Wife rape is the most extreme form of rape by intimates, and probably differs most from rape by strangers, except that both are often extremely traumatic. The sense of betrayal combined with the many obstacles to leaving the situation when rape occurs in marriage, often causes an even stronger negative impact on the woman's other (and future) intimate relationships than when the rape is perpetrated by a stranger.

Like any other act, wife rape does not occur in a vacuum. It is one of the consequences of the unequal power relationship between husband and wife, and if we are to understand the problem, it is important to see it in this broader context. An unequal power relationship is fundamental to, indeed enshrined in the traditional family, where the husband is the primary breadwinner, and the wife is the primary homemaker and rearer of children. The role of breadwinner gives the husband the economic power while the wife's role makes her his dependent. This structural arrangement does not mean wife rape is inevitable, but it does encourage it. The more powerful person is apt to get what he wants, or take it if necessary. As John Stuart Mill said over a century ago, "It is perfectly obvious that the abuse of power cannot be very much checked while the power remains."[1] As long as the division of labor in the family entrenches the power of the husband, wife rape will continue to occur.

The view that wives belong in one of two categories—those who are raped in marriage or those who are not—can be misleading and counterproductive. Many women have experiences that are not rape, but are very *like* rape; it is important to bear in mind the notion of a continuum of abuse, with mutually wanted sex, free of sex-role playing, at one end, and rape at the other. Our study suggests that a considerable amount of marital sex is probably closer to the rape end of the continuum. Many men believe their wives do not have the right to refuse their sexual advances, and though many of these men may be unwilling to rape their wives, they are nevertheless willing to have intercourse with them even when they know it is totally unwanted. And we have seen that many women feel obliged to accommodate their husbands' sexual wishes no matter how repelled they are by them.

In addition, as we have seen, some women even marry men with whom they have no desire to have sex, and some have no desire for sex with anyone. Some are very young and not yet interested in sex, some are sexually traumatized, some may be lesbians, either conscious of their preference or unaware of it. Whatever the reason that some women do not want sex with their husbands, it seems clear that wife rape is likely to occur as long as women feel forced or pressured to marry. It is a sad cultural fact that women who are not involved in an intimate relationship with a man do not receive as much respect as those who are involved. As long as this is true, we can be sure that a situation of forced heterosexuality will prevail. And it seems clear that this in turn means that wife rape will continue to occur.

With regard to husband-rapists, it is helpful to see them in the context of other husbands. According to the typology proposed in Chapter 11, some husbands prefer raping their wives to consensual sex, others enjoy both, yet others prefer consensual sex but are willing to rape their wives when their wives reject their advances. Yet other husbands would like to rape their wives but do not act out this desire, and others have no inclination whatsoever to rape their wives (though many of these husbands in the last group may never have been denied sex by their wives).

As rape exists at one end of the continuum of sexual behavior, another such continuum exists in marriage and other intimate relationships: one of violence, with the most violent rape/murder of wives or lovers at one extreme, and, at the other, the non-violent marriage in which there is no forced sex or beating. The continuum of violence and the continuum of sex merge in the act of wife rape. Wife rape then should be considered in discussions of both the issue of violence in marriage and the issue of sexual relations. To date, it has been ignored in both contexts.

Wife rape is but one of the consequences of two very serious primarily male problems: one is violence; the other is predatory sexuality. It is a fact that 90 percent of the arrests made in this country for crimes of violence are of men and only 10 percent are of women.[2] In cases of murder, women who murder men quite frequently do so in self-defense or after years of abuse. But in spite of the overwhelming evidence, there appears to be a strong desire by most people to deny that violence is primarily a male problem, even though recognition of this fact is a prerequisite to solving or diminishing it.

Wife rape is equally a manifestation of a male sexuality which is oriented to conquest and domination, and to proving masculinity; masculinity unfortunately is defined in terms of power, superiority, competitiveness, control, and aggression.[3] A "real man" is supposed to get what he wants, when he wants, particularly with his wife, and even more particularly, in his sexual relations with her.

These two male tendencies are greatly aggravated and have become the problems they are today, because men have had the power, inside and outside of the family, to act them out. Indeed, these tendencies may be a manifestation of the corruption of their power. The notion that power corrupts is an old one, and it is also often true.

SOLUTIONS

Wife rape is a much more serious problem than most people have realized. The fact that it remains legal in most states and most countries not only perpetuates the problem but probably helps cause it, because it allows men and women alike to believe that wife rape is somehow acceptable. The first step toward reversing the destructive attitudes that lead to this destructive act is to make wife rape illegal; it must also be stripped of the stereotypes and myths that attach to it and be understood for what it is.

Both the phenomenon of wife rape and the legal protection of husband-rapists by exempting them from prosecution are consequences of the age-old conception of wives-as-men's-property, particularly their sexual property. Hence the solution to this problem requires that wives no longer be so regarded, neither by the law, nor by men and women. Outlawing rape in marriage is the first and easiest step in this process.

There are several other important reasons for deleting husbands' rape privilege from the law, where it still exists, including in states that have implemented reforms but which still do not regard wife rape as seriously as extramarital rape. The National Center on Women and Family Law has argued that when the law makes it permissible for married women to be raped by their husbands, it is a breach of wives' constitutional right to the equal protection of the criminal law.[4] The "equal protection" could refer to equality as between married and unmarried women, or as between husbands and wives.

Married women have an "equal right" by law to rape their husbands, but clearly this fact does not make sexual relations between husbands and wives equal. Few women have the physical strength to rape a man and few women appear to have such inclinations. If more women did enjoy imposing their sexual desires on others, much higher rates of sexual abuse of children by females would occur than is reported by researchers on child sexual abuse.[5] Strength aside, it is difficult to force intercourse on men because their cooperation is required, at least to the extent of obtaining and sustaining an erection.

Without this equal protection, as the laws now stand in most states, men are taught that they can rape their wives, and women are taught that they have no right to say "no." The possibility of charging a husband with the rape of his wife offers an important symbolic endorsement of the principle that all women have the right to decide if, when, how and with whom they will relate sexually (subject, of course, to the consent of the other person[s]).[6]

Current laws concerning rape in marriage, as we have seen earlier, stem from Matthew Hale's argument that by virtue of "their mutual matrimonial consent and contract, the wife hath given up herself in this kind unto her husband. . . ." But as suggested by Susan Barry, such an agreement would not survive the classical tests for an express or implied contract. "[I]n order to make a contract there must be an objective manifestation of intent to agree. A new bride would be surprised indeed to find that she has agreed to give up her right to bodily privacy and to submit to any force, brutal or otherwise, her new spouse might use against her."[7] Barry also points out that: "the proper remedy for breach of contract, moreover, is damages, not forced performance. In accordance with this analysis, a husband should seek legal redress for breach of an implied contract. Violent enforcement clearly violates the spirit of the law."[8] Simply spoken, proper redress for breach of contract is not forced compliance.

In a similar vein, it must be recognized that the identity of the perpetrator is irrelevant to the judgment that a crime has been committed. Murder is murder, no matter who is the perpetrator of the crime. Robbery is robbery, no matter who is the perpetrator, and rape is rape no matter who is the perpetrator.[9] It is illogical, inconsistent, absurd, and unjust that rape outside of marriage be recognized as a very serious crime, deserving of penalties of years of incarceration to death (depending on the state), while inside of marriage it is seen as acceptable male behavior against which a wife has no recourse. This truly is a state of legalized sexual slavery.

One argument used in attempts to justify this state of affairs has to do with the erroneous notion that wife rape is less traumatic than stranger rape. Abundant evidence has been presented in this book that the consequences of wife rape are often very severe, and that wife rape is not infrequently accompanied by life-threatening violence. In fact, wife rape appears to be the most traumatic form of rape by intimates, and many factors cause wife rape often to be more traumatic than rape by strangers and other non-intimates; for example, the sense of betrayal, the disillusionment, the fact that it frequently contaminates the entire marriage, and the additional fact that wife rape is often repeated, sometimes for years on end. As Gilbert Geis argued, rape law should focus on the consequences of the crime, not on the intimacy of the relationship between the parties, except as they affect the consequences.[10]

The marital rape exemption is not merely an archaic and outdated law. On the contrary, it serves to protect a significant percentage of men from the charge of rape and from the perception of themselves as rapists. Many of their wives, on the other hand, learn from this exemption that they have no legal or socially acceptable right to refuse their husband's sexual advances. Hence, the issue of wife rape is not simply the concern of those wives who are willing to acknowledge that their husbands forced them to have sexual intercourse at least once (14 percent of women who had ever been married in our survey); it directly affects many more women, and indirectly affects all women.

Also looking at the potential of the law to have a deterrent effect, it is possible that some or even many husbands would be deterred by the threat of prosecution, particularly if more victims of wife rape were to start pressing rape charges. For it is clear that toleration of violence helps perpetuate violence, and that the reverse is also true. Del Martin, author of *Battered Wives*, has pointed out that one way to contribute to the culture of violence in this country is to overlook certain crimes of violence such as rape in marriage. As long as any violence is tolerated by the legal system, its perpetuation as a cultural norm is sanctioned.[11]

Similarly, accepting wife rape contributes to "criminal rape." Peter Volk of Frieburg University's Institute for Forensic Medicine in West Germany, who has been conducting research on rape for some years, expressed the opinion that "as long as rape within a marriage remains permissible, criminal rape must be viewed as the mere tip of an iceberg which will only disappear once the idea of the constant sexual availability of the woman has been made baseless."[12] This is a very important point. It makes no sense to treat rape by strangers as a heinous offense, then to shut one's eyes to date and lover rape, and to make wife rape legal. Yet this is exactly what the situation has been in this and most other countries for years.

Finally, mounting a campaign to change a law is often a very effective means of obtaining access to the media, and in general, getting an opportunity to raise awareness about an issue. Were the laws in all the remaining thirty-four states* of this country that still have total or partial marital rape exemptions to be changed overnight, much work would still be needed to inform married women about their newly recognized right, and to encourage them to charge guilty husbands. A greater impact is often achieved if the struggle to change the law can be accompanied by an educational campaign about the meaning and significance of the change. Recall that in South Australia, though there has been a law against wife rape since 1976, not a single conviction has been obtained. In states where laws against wife rape do already exist, women need to be made more aware of their rights in this regard. Whether or not wife rape is against the law in their state, women must be informed about what they can do in the event that they are raped by their husbands. Even though there are woefully few refuges for battered women, nevertheless these are of invaluable assistance for wives who want to get away from their abusive husbands and who have nowhere else to go. These refuges as well as their older sister institutions, rape crisis centers, can also offer advice and counseling to victims of wife rape.

Clearly, though legal reform is a crucial step in dealing with wife rape, it is not enough. Our survey data have shown that many women who are economically dependent on their husbands do not feel able to leave the husbands who rape them. Hence, the struggle against wife rape and other wife abuse is connected with the struggle for women to obtain greater economic independence, in their marriages and outside of them. Ultimately it is not possible to eradicate wife rape as long as women are subordinate to men in the family and in society. Hence, the struggle for equal power, which means more for women and less for men, is part of the struggle against wife rape.

*This figure has been changed to reflect the situation in 1989.

Nevertheless, refusal to tolerate rape and other violence in marriage is surely something for which women should strive. Every woman has her breaking point; that is, some behavior that she simply will not tolerate from her husband. Often this breaking point is reached when he hurts the children; many women are much less compassionate toward themselves. Of course, it is a symptom of women's oppression that we have had to take so much abuse from men for so long. But men will not change unless they have to. If no woman would stay in an intimate relationship with a violent man, this might provide quite effective shock therapy. Violent treatment by men must become something women refuse to live with. And the concept of "conjugal rights" must be reinterpreted to include women's right to say "no" to their husbands. To continue to see rape in marriage as a husband's privilege is not only an insult, but a danger to all women. We must strive to stop wife rape, including working to eliminate the conditions that have given rise to it.

APPENDIX I

Husbands Accused of
Wife Rape in the United States:
Selected Cases

I have cited throughout the book several cases of wife rape that were reported to police. Most of these were later tried in court: for example, the Rideout case in Oregon (Chapter 2); the De Villez case in Indiana (Chapter 16); the Churchills, the Burnhams, Phillip Hughes in California, and Mickey Hughes in Michigan (Chapter 20); and the Stanleys and Lowes, also in California (Chapter 21).

A selection of other cases will be presented here, as they were reported in the press at the time. None of these cases has received nearly as much attention as the Rideout case; indeed, most of them have only appeared in the local presses. These cases make it clear that at least some women in this country have been willing to charge their husbands with marital rape when the law permits them to do so.

An attempt was made to select a sample of cases from the newspaper clippings available in the files of the National Clearinghouse on Marital Rape in Berkeley, California, that would convey a sense of the great variety of cases that have gone to court, or that have come close to doing so, in the country as a whole. California cases are over-represented because this is one of the few states that has outlawed rape in marriage, and because more cases have been prosecuted in this state. There has also been a phenomenal rate of conviction for wife rape in California.[1] The National Clearinghouse uses a national clipping service; thus the over-representation of cases in California is not on account of its location in this state.

Six of the first seven cases to be presented went to trial with varying results, including a mistrial due to a hung jury (Beglin), two men who received three years probation (Romagno and Chiarpotti), a one-year jail sentence (Waddingham), a three- to five-year prison sentence (Chretien), and a sixteen-year sentence (Martinez). These indicate the great range of outcomes possible in these cases. The first case to be cited never went to trial, partly because there was no law against wife rape at that time in Florida.

Based on these and the remaining cases, it is clear that the charge of

362

wife rape is made most often when the couple is already separated. Some states are only willing to prosecute such cases, but even where separation is not a precondition for charging wife rape, these cases tend to have a better chance of resulting in a conviction.

Unnamed man, Lakeland, Florida

The incident occurred on the evening of Nov. 8, 1979. The wife told police her husband entered the home he had left about two weeks earlier, using the pretext of wanting to retrieve his television set.

She said she asked him to leave after he made sexual advances toward her in the kitchen. She pulled away and walked toward the front door, but he grabbed her, forced her into the bedroom and sexually assaulted her, police said.

The woman told officers her doctor had ordered her not to have sexual intercourse because she had a hysterectomy three weeks earlier. She said her husband had ruptured her by kicking her in the vagina.

Uncertain what to charge the man with, the Lakeland Police Department turned the investigation over to the state attorney's office. On Feb. 18, Brock charged the twenty-two-year-old man with aggravated battery.

After weeks reviewing the law, Brock said, "I finally concluded that what I believed all along was correct—that a husband cannot rape his wife in Florida."

Lakeland Police Capt. Gene Nipper said that in twenty years he has never before worked on such a case.

When he saw the twenty-three-year-old woman, at Lakeland General Hospital after the incident, she was able to walk, but bleeding and obviously in pain.

"My initial opinion was that it was a sexual battery. I had reservations about it being prosecuted as such, because of the husband-wife stigma. But in her medical condition there is no way that she would have consented. It would have been too painful," Nipper said.

Examinations confirmed the presence of sperm and the recent surgery. One doctor reported that any act of intercourse would have caused extreme pain, Nipper said.

Brock also said he has never been confronted with a husband-wife rape case.

If Brock had charged the man with sexual battery, his attorney could have claimed that he did not violate any law, because "we're talking about the absence of state law."[2]

While Assistant State Attorney Glen Brock said he couldn't think of "an issue that is more ripe for a judge to take it by the horns," he also felt that "these were not the circumstances under which the court would have felt enough sympathy for her."[3] Why? Because the couple had recently pleaded no contest to dealing in marijuana and each was sentenced to five years on probation.[4]

John Beglin, Santa Ana, California

Pauline Beglin told the jury that her husband of two years had tied her to a bed, took nude photographs of her, and then raped her.

Beglin, however, told the jury that his wife screamed rape only after he announced he intended to seek alimony payments from her if she followed through on her plans to divorce him. Testimony placed her income at $41,000 last year as a sales manager.

Beglin said that he had been watching the Miss America beauty pageant with his wife when they engaged in sex by consent that she later claimed as rape.

His wife, however, testified that she watched the beauty pageant alone upstairs while Beglin watched an X-rated movie downstairs. She said that after the pageant was over, her husband came upstairs and sexually attacked her.

The jury was "hopelessly deadlocked" and a mistrial was therefore declared. The District Attorney said he believes he can get a conviction in a second trial.[5]

Joseph Romagno, Bakersfield, California

Joseph Romagno, twenty-seven, was arrested on a charge of "spousal rape" on July 15, 1980. He is reported to have told officers, "I won't lie to you. I forced my wife into sex."[6]

According to Bakersfield Police Department reports on file in support of the felony criminal complaint, the twenty-seven-year-old Romagno is separated from his wife but still is legally married to her. They have different homes.

The reports allege he invited her to his 4812 Summertree Lane apartment to discuss financial matters.

But once there, the complaint alleges, he raped and hit her.

He is charged with spousal rape and "inflicting corporal injury on a spouse."

Romagno's wife sued him for divorce a year ago; he countersued her; the matter was dropped, and she sued him again in May.

At the time of the alleged attack on his wife he was free on $1,500 bail after she told police he kicked in the door of her apartment, ripped up furniture and spray painted obscenities about her on the walls.[7]

On August 1, 1980, Romagno was given three years' probation and ordered to obtain psychiatric counseling. If he violates probation during that period, he will spend one year in the county jail.[8]

John Chiarpotti, Livermore, California

Lisa, the estranged twenty-two-year-old wife of John Chiarpotti, twenty-three, told sheriff's deputies that:

She had been living with her parents in Dublin for several weeks when Chiarpotti phoned her one night. He reportedly said he had "something important" to tell her, according to the sheriff's department report.

The sheriff's report said the wife got into Chiarpotti's van to talk with him when he drove to a secluded area of the Delta near Stockton where the alleged rape occurred. . . .

He [Chiarpotti] was arrested April 28, 1980, while at work at a Livermore grocery store after his wife reported to sheriff's deputies that she had been raped. . . .

Chiarpotti pleaded "no contest" to the misdemeanor. He was placed on formal probation for three years and ordered to complete twenty-five days of community volunteer work. The felony rape and kidnapping charges were dropped in the plea bargain.

Judge John A. Lewis noted that the defendant does not have a prior criminal record and that he has been undergoing counseling.

"I am confident both parties feel the disposition is a fair one and that the public's interest is adequately safeguarded," Lewis said.

"It would appear under the circumstances that a jail sentence would not be constructive in this case," the judge added.

Lewis cautioned Chiarpotti that he could be sentenced up to a year in the county jail should he violate conditions imposed by his probation officer.

He further warned the defendant "not to molest, annoy or attempt to approach in any way" his wife, from whom he is separated.[9]

David William Waddingham, San Mateo, California

Victoria Waddingham told police that on October 28, 1979, her estranged twenty-eight-year-old husband "took her against her will to the Santa Cruz mountains and sexually assaulted her."[10]

She and Waddingham had been separated for about two months. A court order had been issued that restricted him from getting closer than 300 feet to his wife's residence.

The woman told police that on the morning of Oct. 28, she received a telephone call from a distraught friend, who said David Waddingham was at her home and drinking whisky.

When she arrived at her friend's house, the report said, she talked with her estranged husband for more than an hour before agreeing that he could visit the couple's child—which he had insisted on. Then they got into her car and left.

The probation report said that David Waddingham drove erratically as he told his wife he wanted to make love to her.

He then drove to a remote area in the Santa Cruz mountains and sexually assaulted the woman, the report said. He threatened to beat her with his belt and said he had a gun in the glove compartment of the car.

She told officers she tried several times to get out of the car, but that the man tore her clothes off and prevented her from leaving. She managed to get out once but was overtaken.

He again forced her into sexual activity, the report said, and this time she was scratched and bruised.

The report said the two left the area before dark and on the way home David Waddingham said he intended to kill her and himself. Then he stopped the car and again sexually assaulted her, the report said.

David Waddingham eventually drove the woman home, and she called police.

He told police he didn't remember what happened but said he made love with his estranged wife by mutual consent.[11]

David Waddingham was sentenced to one year in jail for sexually assaulting his wife. The two were divorced at the time of the sentencing.

James Chretien, Salem, Massachusetts

One year after John Rideout was acquitted for marital rape in Oregon, James Chretien became the first husband in the United States to be convicted of raping his wife. He received a sentence of from three to five years in prison.

An unemployed bartender was convicted yesterday of raping his wife, apparently the first such conviction in U.S. history. James Chretien, thirty-three, faces life imprisonment.

An Essex County Superior Court jury of four women and eight men deliberated for more than five hours before reaching the verdict.

Chretien had been living apart from his wife Carmelina, but they were not legally separated or divorced. The prosecution contended that Chretien broke into his wife's Haverhill apartment February 8 and raped her.

The trial was all the more unusual because of the testimony of the couple's nine-year-old son, James Jr.

Before allowing the boy to testify, the judge asked him if he understood the difference between a lie and the truth.

"Yes, a lie is when somebody is not telling the truth," the youngster answered.

The boy testified for about fifteen minutes as his parents watched and wept.

"I woke up and heard my mother screaming downstairs, and I ran downstairs. My father was pulling my mother by her arm," James said. "My father told me to go upstairs, and I obeyed."

"I didn't hear them arguing when they were in the bedroom," said young James, a fourth grader. "My father dragged my mother into the bedroom."

"I never saw my father hit or choke my mother, but I think my mother didn't want to come upstairs," the boy said.

He said he went back to bed, but couldn't sleep, and he heard his father again around 5:00 A.M.

"That time my parents were in my mother's bedroom. I heard words but can't remember what. There was no screaming that time," James said.

Chretien also was found guilty in the case of one count of breaking and entering, which carries a minimum sentence of ten years. . . .

The defendant, a former Vietnam veteran, showed no emotion when the verdict was announced, and he held out his hands as the court officers approached him with handcuffs to take him away.[12]

Frank Martinez, Pomona, California

Frank Martinez, twenty-one, was the first man in California to be charged under the new spousal rape law. He was arrested on January 8, 1980, just eight days after the law took effect.

Along with the four counts of spousal rape, Martinez was held to answer five counts of rape and one count of oral copulation with the other woman, plus two counts of kidnapping and one count of grand theft.

Martinez was arrested on Jan. 8 by Riverside County sheriff's deputies as he was driving near Blythe in a van allegedly stolen from the California Coach dealership in El Monte two days earlier.

Deputies had been alerted to watch for the stolen van by a state worker at a rest area where Martinez had stopped along the way.

Martinez' wife, Rena, eighteen, told police investigators she passed a note to a woman while they were in the restroom saying she had been kidnapped by her husband, raped and needed help. The woman gave the note to the state worker.

According to El Monte police detectives, Martinez had picked his wife up at work in South El Monte on the morning of Jan. 7, telling her he had some Christmas presents in a van outside for her and her mother.

Martinez and his wife had separated in September after being married for six weeks. Prior to their marriage, they had dated for about five years, part of which they had lived together. No legal action has as yet been taken toward a divorce.

Responding to her husband's request, Mrs. Martinez walked to the van parked outside her office and her husband allegedly forced her inside and drove off.

A day earlier, Martinez allegedly kidnapped a female employee of California Coach during a test drive of the van, and until about 3:00 A.M. on Jan. 7, drove her around and forced her into oral copulation once.

The nineteen-year-old victim was freed near the Pomona Freeway and Interstate 5 where the van ran out of gas, police investigators said.

The California Coach employee and Mrs. Martinez were the only witnesses to testify during the preliminary hearing, during which a judge must determine only if there is probable cause to believe the defendant might be guilty of the crimes charged.

While waiting in the hallway outside the locked courtroom, Martinez' halfbrother, Louie Guillen, also of El Monte, said Martinez had been suffering from emotional problems lately, which he blamed on the young man's recent use of the drug PCP.[13]

Martinez was found guilty of thirteen felony counts that included the kidnapping and rape of his estranged wife. He was sentenced to sixteen years in state prison.

One factor that likely contributed to this heavy sentence is that another woman besides Mrs. Martinez was kidnapped and raped; the similarity of their experiences probably also enhanced the credibility of both their testimonies.[14]

Aside from estrangement, another factor that seems to be present in many of the cases of wife rape that reach the courts is that the wife is also a victim of battering. The next two cases to be presented here are classic examples of battered wives. Catherine Watkins even sought out a refuge for battered women. The Ramos case provides another example. The cases that follow these two include progressively bizarre behavior on the part of the husbands. Such cases are also more likely to be reported to the police.

Hughlen Watkins, Redding, California

Hughlen Watkins, twenty-four, was the first husband to be convicted of raping his wife in California while they were still living together. He was sentenced to eight months in jail as part of a three-year probation term.[15]

Watkins was arrested after his wife called police from a women's refuge center, and he was booked for investigation of spousal rape, penetration with a foreign object, and sodomy.[16] Mrs. Watkins was treated at Memorial Hospital. She filed for divorce on the day of the attack.

Catherine Watkins lay awake in bed last March after her husband had choked her and forced her to have sex. The last thing he told her before dropping off to sleep was to "call the cops if you want."

That's exactly what she did.

Last month, Hughlen "Cliff" Watkins pleaded guilty in Shasta County's first case of spousal rape. He'll be sentenced Aug. 25 in Superior Court.

Ms. Watkins, a petite, soft-spoken woman, talked of the ordeal last week as she sat beneath a poster in a small room at the Shasta County Women's Refuge in Redding. The poster read "There can be no free men until there are free women."

The twenty-three-year-old woman has a similar message for women who are victims of abuse by their husbands or men with whom they live.

"There is an alternative," Ms. Watkins said. "If I can get that point across to even one woman who is as scared and miserable as I was, then I have to try. I want her to understand she doesn't have to remain a prisoner at the hands of a man."

It took Ms. Watkins six and one half years to understand. They were years filled with loneliness and pain—pain, she said, that was caused by mental, as well as physical, "beatings."

She was married to Watkins for three and one half years, and lived with him before the marriage.

Watkins, twenty-four, has a much different view of the relationship.

"I pleaded guilty because I didn't want the whole thing to be made public—I didn't want my kids to have to go through it," Watkins said. "And after thinking it over, I decided it could be called 'rape,' if it's possible to rape your own wife."

Watkins, who faces a maximum of eight years in prison for what he terms a "marital problem," said he has met several men who are as puzzled as he is about the wife-rape law that became effective Jan. 1.

"The way I see it, Cathy and I were having problems in our marriage for the last two years. She could have claimed 'rape' any time during that time. Half of the married men in the country are guilty of the same thing, if that's rape."

Watkins said he advises married couples who are going through a similar situation to separate temporarily instead of "forcing the issue."

And because he said he recently "found Jesus again," he advises men to obey all the laws of the land—even if they are "terrible" laws.

"This law is wrong. I don't doubt that for a minute," Watkins said.

Ms. Watkins said she would have left her husband sooner, but she believed she had no place to go. And she also had three small children to consider.

"I filed for divorce the same day I called the police to report my husband had raped me," Ms. Watkins said. "I would have done it sooner, but Cliff convinced me that I had no choice but to stay with him. He kept telling me no other man would want a woman who has three kids, and he kept pounding in the point that there is nothing I can do to get a job.

"I believed he was right for a long time, but I finally had enough. When I left him, I found there was another choice."

With help from women—and men—at the refuge center, Ms. Watkins found she had the strength to face a court trial and the widespread publicity surrounding her case. The case never went to trial because of Watkins' guilty plea, something Ms. Watkins feels is a mixed blessing.

"I'm glad it didn't go to trial, because I wasn't looking forward to what I knew would be some adverse feelings from the public," she said. "But I did want to tell my story, in case it might help another woman who is going through something similar."

Ms. Watkins, who does volunteer work at the refuge center, said she immediately heard from two other women who "were going through the same thing" when her case was made public.

Steve Cilenti, the Redding police investigator who handled the Watkins case, agrees there are more cases of "wife rape" than most people would imagine.

"The entire marriage system, including nuptial rites, makes it difficult for a woman to protect herself from abuse from her husband," Cilenti said. "American society hides sex, making it something shameful that isn't supposed to be discussed. Until attitudes change, women and men will remain in the same roles— and that means sexual abuse inside marriage will continue."

Cilenti said although the Watkins case never was considered by a jury, the case will make it easier to prosecute future spousal rape trials.

"There was an almost audible sigh of relief from law enforcement officers when we heard about the outcome of this [Watkins] case, and I think if there is another wife-rape trial, it won't hit the community quite as hard," the investigator said. "I've never handled anything like it before, and now that I've gone through it, it will make it easier to face the next one. It's given me more confidence."

"Confidence" also seems to be the best word to describe Ms. Watkins. She smiled as she told of her plans to go to school and learn a skill that will help her maintain the independence she never enjoyed until last March.[17]

John Ramos, East Chicago, Indiana

An East Chicago man, accused of raping his wife, is expected to testify today in the first such case in Indiana.

John Ramos, Jr., twenty-five, is accused of raping his estranged wife, Priscilla, twenty-two, on June 4, 1980, after the woman had filed for divorce and obtained a restraining order prohibiting him from living with her or physically abusing her.

Mrs. Ramos testified Monday Ramos also choked her and hit her as she tried to fight off his sexual attack in the bathroom of her East Chicago apartment.

Photographs, showing bruises on her arms, and medical records of her treatment at St. Catherine Hospital the day of the alleged rape were introduced into evidence by Deputy Prosecutor Karen Coulis.

Under questioning by Coulis, Mrs. Ramos sometimes cried as she testified for the third day in the courtroom of Judge Richard Maroc. Mrs. Ramos, talking about another treatment at the hospital, said her husband threw her from the bed and jumped on her stomach with his feet.

She said that treatment consisted of medication for pain and wearing a brace on her stomach for several weeks.

Evidence was also introduced concerning the divorce of the couple, granted July 14, 1980 by Lake Superior Court Judge Morton B. Kanz. Maroc read several orders entered by Kanz after the divorce, including a contempt finding of Ramos for failure to pay child support and later entries showing Ramos had paid some support and was attempting to sell musical equipment to make more payments ordered by the court.

Defense lawyers Thomas Bullard and Kenneth Anderson are attempting to prove Mrs. Ramos had sex with her husband willingly and that she filed the rape charge for revenge.

"You hate John Ramos, don't you?" Anderson asked Mrs. Ramos Monday.

"Yes," the petite woman answered. She denied she has hated him for a long time but did admit her marriage had not been a happy one.[18]

Larry Roberson, Burlington County, New Jersey

A Browns Mills man jailed this week for the alleged rape of his wife will be the first county resident tried under the new criminal code that acknowledges rape by a spouse as a punishable crime.

Larry Roberson, thirty-two, of Cactus Street was in Burlington County Jail last night on charges of aggravated sexual assault against his thirty-two-year-old wife on Monday morning in their home. Bail was set Friday at $2,500.

Police said the couple had been separated for a week at the time of the alleged assault and were living in the same house but sleeping in separate rooms. The separation was by verbal agreement, said police.

Police said Roberson allegedly entered his wife's bedroom at 10:30 A.M. Monday, removed her clothes and tied her wrists and legs to the bedpost. He allegedly sprayed her with whipped cream, photographed her, and raped her.

The couple's four children were at school at the time, said police.

Roberson was still in the house when his wife released herself after twenty minutes, said police. She attempted to telephone police but Roberson had apparently cut the telephone wires. He also reportedly disabled the car. Police said she reported the incident at 6:00 P.M. that evening and Roberson was arrested Monday night.[19]

Manuel Gonzalez, Los Angeles, California

In an article written on January 7, 1980, Elaine Warren reported that:

Authorities said the thirty-three-year-old wife of Manuel Gonzalez went to sheriff's deputies Saturday and told authorities she has been living in fear for her life the past five years, during which time her husband has repeatedly forced her to engage in sexual activities with him and with strangers, and beat her when she resisted.

According to Sgt. Douglas Lapenna of the East Los Angeles sheriff's station, the woman said Gonzalez would drive around with her in his car, pick up a third person and bring him to the Gonzalez home, where the trio then would engage in sexual activity.

Lapenna said deputies were told by Mrs. Gonzalez that on Saturday she refused to engage in the activity and decided to flee to authorities.

Sheriff's spokesman Mike Santander said Gonzalez apparently left his home after the incident and has not been seen since. If found, he may be charged with felony rape and battery against his wife, Santander said.[20]

Mrs. Gonzalez decided not to press charges, despite the urgings of the District Attorney that she do so. The reasons are unknown, but fear of being killed or brutally punished is a common factor in such situations.

Daniel Morrison, Medford Lakes, New Jersey

Daniel Morrison was the first man in New Jersey to be convicted of marital rape. He and his wife, Rosita, were legally separated at the time of the attack.

Morrison was found guilty on May 25, 1978, of abducting his ex-wife at gunpoint from a railroad station, taking her to his home, roping her to a bed and raping her three times during a day-long attack.

Morrison also took pictures of his ex-wife and showed her a snapshot of a freshly dug grave he said was for her.

Psychiatrists testified during the trial that Morrison had been a paranoid-schizophrenic for years. Judge Paul Kramer said: "I don't think there is any question that all of this was done in an effort to keep his wife . . . it was a perverted demonstration of his love."

The conviction was later overturned by a three-judge panel on the grounds that the defendant was still legally married to his victim on the date of the rape.[21]

Morrison was released from jail in February 1980. However, he was "jailed once again in March when the county prosecutor appealed to the State Supreme Court to reinstate the conviction."[22]

Unnamed Man, Largo, Florida

The young Largo woman sat in her home for three hours agonizing about whether she should report the brutal sexual attack. She feared no one would take her seriously.

The twenty-six-year-old mother of two was about to accuse her estranged husband of being a rapist.

Later, the woman said she was surprised to learn, while talking to law enforcement officers, that she was not the only wife who has made such an allegation.

However, she is among a tiny number of women around the country who have pursued rape charges against their husbands.

Other women have been thwarted by state laws that exclude prosecuting a man for raping his wife as well as by social and economic pressures that often keep the woman at home performing her "wifely duties."

"I had to do it. I feel by going to trial, I will be helping other women," the Largo woman told The Tribune.

National and local authorities knowledgeable on the subject of marital rape say the Pinellas case, set for trial today, could be the first test of Florida's law.

According to the woman's own account, her husband, a hospital technician, had been living with a nurse during the couple's six-week separation prior to the attack.

"I wonder how many nights he sat outside watching to see who I came home with," she said.

It was about 12:30 A.M. last Jan. 20, when she did come home with another man.

The charges filed contend the enraged husband pulled her into the house and during the next three to four hours forced her to have sex. He also sexually assaulted her with a bottle and a pen and struck her with a baseball.

When questioned by detectives, the twenty-nine-year-old man allegedly admitted to the sexual activity, telling them the encounter was "rough, a bit. . . ."

The woman said she believes her husband has "a sex problem" and is assured he will get psychological treatment if he is convicted. He could get life imprisonment, although the woman says she does not favor such a harsh sentence.

Besides the criminal prosecution, the woman is seeking to end the couple's nearly eight years of marriage, claiming she has been the victim of physical abuse. The divorce petition was filed eight days after the alleged rape.[23]

Pinellas Circuit Judge David Patterson told the twenty-nine-year-old man he would be a candidate for probation if his wife agrees and if an investigation of his background record is favorable.

The man's twenty-six-year-old wife has said her main interest in pursuing the case was to see that her husband gets psychological help for his "sex problem."

Defense attorney Charles Morachnick said counseling probably would be a condition of his sentence if he is granted probation. . . .

Pinellas prosecutor Larry Hart also revealed a bizarre plot by the husband to use the incident as a weapon to gain custody of the couple's seven-year-old and five-year-old sons.

Hart said the man hoped to "manufacture evidence" by taking nude photographs of his twenty-six-year-old wife, photographs that were supposed to portray her infidelity.

The photos, however, also revealed that the woman "appears distressed and in pain," Hart said.

The camera and film were recovered at a woman's home where the man had been living since leaving his wife about six weeks prior to the rape.

After their separation in December, the wife began steps toward getting a divorce, but the actual divorce petition was not filed until eight days after the sexual assault. The divorce decree is not yet final.

According to Hart, the three-hour sexual assault occurred after the man barged into his wife's Largo home and found her in bed with another man.

The woman claims that it was the first time she had brought a man to her home since the couple's separation.

Following a scuffle between the woman's date and her husband, the woman tried to leave the house with her date but was stopped and forced back into the house.

The date, however, left.

Hart quoted the husband as telling his wife that "because she had hurt him, he would hurt her."[24]

John Ludwig, Montgomery County, Pennsylvania

A Montgomery County woman accused her estranged husband yesterday of assaulting and raping her, then dangling her nude over a bridge early last Sunday as he professed his love for her.

John Ludwig, twenty-seven, of Tennis Ave. in Ardsley, was arraigned before District Justice M. William Peterson in Abington Township yesterday on a variety of charges lodged by his wife, Rita, twenty-three.

Mrs. Ludwig, who lives in Roslyn with her mother and two-year-old child, said her estranged husband drove her to a secluded spot in Abington Township after volunteering to take her home from a party they had attended Saturday. He allegedly held her captive from 2:00 A.M. to 6:00 A.M., disrobed her, then raped and choked her, and finally dangled her nude over a bridge in Abington, all the time professing his love for her.

Ludwig allegedly ran red lights so his wife would not have a chance to escape by jumping out of his van. Then Ludwig drove her to a spot where Old Huntingdon Pike deadends, in Huntingdon Valley, Abington, according to Abington Detective John Thompson. After raping her, Mrs. Ludwig said he took her clothes to a bridge which spans Pennypack Creek, twenty-five feet away from the parked van. When she ran, unclad, to retrieve her clothes at the bridge, he grabbed her ankles, dangled her head-first from the bridge and threatened to drop her, vowing that he loved her.

"I'd drop you if I didn't love you," Mrs. Ludwig said he told her.[25]

William Schacklett, San Jose, California

A San Jose concert promoter has been charged with beating his wife and sexually assaulting her with a tire iron and a crowbar. William Schacklett, thirty-one, was charged yesterday in Municipal Court with assault with a deadly weapon and two counts of rape with a foreign object. He was freed on $13,000 bail pending a Jan. 19 arraignment. Schacklett's twenty-eight-year-old wife was hospitalized with vaginal bleeding and internal injuries after Tuesday's attack, which also left one side of her face puffy and one eye bruised. Officer Mike Mendez said Schacklett, a private promoter of rock concerts and other events, had been drinking after his wife went to bed and later assaulted her when she refused his advances. He struck her in the face, raped her with the tire iron and crowbar, tore her breasts with the crowbar, struck her in the abdomen with a belt and poured brandy on her, police said. She received numerous stitches for the breast wounds, police said. Mrs. Schacklett escaped to a neighbor's home when her husband freed her to feed their three-month-old son. When police arrived, Schacklett was holding the baby in his arms.[26]

Finally, two cases in which the tortured wives killed their husbands will be cited. One of them was found not guilty (Curnutt), and one received a ten-year sentence (Davenport).

James Curnutt, Kansas

Deborah Davis, a twenty-two-year-old white woman from Lyndon, Kansas, was found innocent in the shooting death of her husband, James Curnutt, thirty-eight. They had been married six months, but he had already sexually abused her for five years by torturing her with rubber balls, pins, and an electric cattle prod. He had also imprisoned her in an underground tank.

James owned books on torture, brainwashing, and hypnotism. According to Diane Wiley, . . . James made Deborah's suffering bearable by giving her "reasons" for it. For instance, he'd say, "I'm going to stick pins in your breast because you don't cry enough, and crying is good for you." Of course, she would cry, and that would bring some relief.

But her torture became unendurable when James announced his plans to keep her wrapped in tape, like a mummy, in a coffin beneath the bed. Deborah discovered he was serious when she found a catheter and air pump for keeping her alive.

She testified that she was afraid for her life, so she shot James in the back of the head while he was sleeping on Christmas, 1979. The jury in her June 1980 trial sympathized with her ordeal and cleared her of murder.[27]

Roland Davenport, Oregon

Juanita Davenport, a white forty-eight-year-old mother from Cave Junction, Oregon, pleaded no contest to the manslaughter of her husband who had sexually abused her during their thirty-year marriage. Her husband, Roland, fifty-nine, was described in court testimony by their twenty-eight-year-old daughter, who had also been sexually abused by Roland, as "somewhat of a cross between Charles Manson and Hitler."

According to a call to District Attorney Bob Burrows, Roland had been impotent so he "engaged in vicarious sex" by making her have sex with others while Roland looked on. Burrows also indicated that Roland even attempted to mate her with a dog once.

The press reported that Burrows, who prosecuted her, said she killed her husband under extreme stress and provocation because of Roland's sexual perversions and domination of her. She shot Roland in March 1980. She then dismembered his body; boiled the hands, feet, and head in a pressure cooker; and cremated his remains in their barbecue pit. She testified that her husband told her that when he died he wanted to be cremated. Other witnesses said that she did anything to please him, including abnormal sex acts. . . .

Juanita's adult son found his father's remains in the barbecue pit and buried them in the garden. Five months later, the son showed the authorities where the grave was located.

Juanita pleaded no contest to first degree manslaughter after a murder charge against her was dismissed. Judge Larry Cushing sentenced her on January 12, 1981, to up to ten years at the Oregon Women's Correctional Center in Salem.[28]

APPENDIX II

State-by-State Information on Marital Rape Exemption Laws

Original 1981 Research by
Joanne Schulman, Staff Attorney
National Center on Women and Family Law, Inc.

Updated by
Laurie Woods, Executive Director
National Center on Women and Family Law, Inc.

and
Laura X, Director
National Clearinghouse on Marital and Date Rape

Edited by
Diana E. H. Russell

A husband's rape of his wife is not recognized as a crime equivalent to non-marital rape in most states. This legal right of wife rape is known as a "marital rape exemption," and is included in most states' rape statutes.

There are many types of marital rape exemptions. This state-by-state summary divides the exemptions into the following catgories.

CATEGORY	
1	*Absolute Exemption.* A husband can never be prosecuted for rape of his wife as long as the parties are married. The exemption still applies even if the parties are separated by court order. The exemption only ends when the parties are divorced. No state belongs in this category at this time, but there were 10 states with absolute exemptions as recently as 1981.
2	*Partial Exemption.* A husband can be prosecuted for rape of his wife in some circumstances. Some states allow prosecution if the rape occurred after one spouse filed papers in court to end the marriage, or when the parties were not living together. The event or

circumstance that ends the exemption differs from state to state. Many states in the 1980s have changed their statutes to grant wives the right to consent to sexual intercourse in marriage by permitting the prosecution of their husbands for raping them, even when the rape occurred while they were living together. Perversely and cruelly however, if a wife was in a situation so vulnerable as to automatically constitute rape were her husband to commit the same act on any other woman, some of these statutes grant her no such protection. Specifically, if this woman is legally unable to consent because of her temporary or permanent mental or physical condition, her husband is exempt from prosecution for rape.

3   *Cohabitant Exemption.* A man who is living with a woman to whom he is not legally married cannot be prosecuted for raping her. Often this exemption is stated as a "defense" rather than as a bar to prosecution. For example, the district attorney may institute rape charges against such a man, but he cannot be convicted of rape if he can prove he was living with the victim.

4   *Voluntary Social Companion Exemption.* This exemption may apply to husbands, cohabitants, and social companions (i.e., dates). There is no requirement that the rapist live or have lived with the victim.

5   *Silent Statute.* Sometimes the law does not mention whether or not husbands can be prosecuted for raping their wives. It was assumed, until recently, that husbands could not be prosecuted for such behavior in states with silent statutes. This assumption was based on the widespread acceptance of England's Chief Justice Hale's posthumously published treatise in the eighteenth century in which he maintained that marriage gave husbands the right to sexual intercourse with their wives whenever they so wished. However, recent court decisions in four states with silent statutes—New Jersey, Massachusetts, Florida, and Georgia—have held that no such common law exemption exists. Hence, it is not yet clear if husbands can be prosecuted for marital rape in other states with silent statutes. Whether or not marital rape is considered a crime in these states will depend on future judicial decisions or legislative interpretation of their statutes.

6   *No Exemption.* The marital rape exemption has been abolished so husbands can be charged with rape of their wives in all cases.

Rape Degrees   In some states, the law recognizes different types of rape, murder, assault, etc. In most states, the criminal laws punish rape more or less severely depending on the circumstances of the rape (e.g., whether or not a weapon was used, the age of the victim and perpetrator, mental and/or physical condition of the victim, whether or not the assault involved illegal sexual penetration, conduct, contact, or use of a foreign object). These differences in the law are called "degrees." It is not possible to give a uniform definition for each "degree," as each state bases its rape degrees on different factors.

The fact that the marital rape exemption may apply in some rape degrees and not others has political and practical significance. The lawmakers are saying that they will tolerate certain violence by husbands against their wives that they will not tolerate between strangers. Practically, the different application of the exemption, based on the degree of rape charged, may determine whether marital rape cases will ever be prosecuted, or what penalty will be imposed, if any. This is especially true if it is only a crime in the first degree. In this case, plea bargaining is blocked and most prosecutors will not bother to pursue justice. This is also the case when the crime of spousal rape is separated from non-marital rape.

Gender-Neutral Statutes Traditionally, the law defined rape as a crime only men could commit. Thus, only husbands were granted the "immunity" or protection of the marital rape exemption. Today, many states have rewritten their laws in gender-neutral terms. Under these new rape laws, women can also be prosecuted for rape, and the immunity granted under the marital rape exemption is extended to both spouses. The following chart does not incorporate these gender-neutral changes since it is intended to reflect reality rather than pure "legalese."

Age of Consent This is the age (which varies by state) under which males or females are considered too young to decide to have sexual intercourse. Such acts are chargeable as statutory rape.

States may fall into more than one of the categories described above. Since considerable legislation and litigation have been occurring over the last eight years, the following chart reflects the law as of January 1, 1990.

STATE AND CATEGORY	STATUS OF MARITAL RAPE LAW	CITATIONS
Alabama 6	Husbands can be charged for rape of wife.	500 So2d. 1301 (1988) and Merton v. State 500 So2d. 1301 (1986)
Alaska 6	Husbands can be charged for rape of wife.	Stat. § 11.41.443
Arizona 2	Husbands can only be charged with the crime of "sexual assault of a spouse" if they use force or threat. However, a judge can lower the sentence for the first offense to the highest degree misdemeanor if counseling is mandated. Husbands cannot be charged with any other sexual assault crimes against wives.	Chapter 301, S.B. 1458. July 7, 1988 R.S. § 13-1404-06
Arkansas 5	The statute only exempts husbands who rape wives under the age of consent. Whether marital rape is a crime will depend on judicial decision or legislative interpretation of alleged "common law" exemption.	Stat. § 41-1803, *et seq.*
California 2	Husbands can only be charged with felony or misdemeanor crime of "spousal rape" if they use force or threat and if rape is reported within 90 days. They cannot be	Pen. C. § 262

STATE AND CATEGORY	STATUS OF MARITAL RAPE LAW	CITATIONS
	charged if they use violence without force or threat; or if the wife is incapable of giving consent because of a mental disorder or a developmental or physical disability about which they are/should be cognizant; or if the wife is prevented from resisting due to intoxicating, anesthetic or controlled substances administered by them or with their knowledge; or if the wife is unconscious of the nature of the act at the time it occurred, and this is known to them; or if intercourse if forced on the wife by threat of deportation or incarceration. For further information, see footnote 1 on p. 22.	
Colorado 6	Husbands can be charged for rape of wife.	H.B. 1089, March 16, 1988
Connecticut 2, 3	Spouse/cohabitors can only be charged with first degree rape; marital and cohabitor exemption for all other sexual assaults.	Pen. Code § 53a-67(b), § 53a-70
Delaware *no exemption for first and second degree* 2, 4	Husbands can only be charged for rape of wife in first and second degree. "Voluntary social companion" of victim cannot be charged with first degree rape.	D.C.A. § 763, 764, 772 (b)
District of Columbia 5	U.S. Attorney's Office has stated that its policy is that husbands can be charged for rape of wife.	R.S.D.C. § 22-2801
Florida 6	Husbands can be charged for rape of wife.	S.A. § 794.011 State v. Larry Smith 80-878 (1981). State v. William Rider 83-821 (1984)
Georgia 6	Husbands can be charged for rape of wife.	C.A. § 16-6-1(a), Warren v. State 336 S.E. 2d 221 (1985)
Hawaii 2	Husbands can only be charged for rape of wife in first through third degrees, not fourth and fifth.	R.S. § 707-730 to 732
Idaho 2	Husbands can only be charged for rape of wife if they use force, violence, threat of immediate and great bodily harm, intoxicating substance, narcotic, or anesthetic. They cannot be charged if she is temporarily or permanently/ incapable of giving her legal consent because of "lunacy or other unsoundness of mind."	C. § 18-6107

STATE AND CATEGORY	STATUS OF MARITAL RAPE LAW	CITATIONS
Illinois 2	Husbands can only be charged for rape of wife if force is used and rape reported within 30 days. They cannot be charged with lesser offense of sexual abuse even if they knew that she "was unable to understand the nature of the act or was unable to give knowing consent."	A.S. Ch. 38 § 11-1
Indiana 6	Husbands can be charged for rape of wife.	S.A. § 35-42-4-1(b)
Iowa 2	Husbands can be charged for rape of wife in first and second degree. Husbands and cohabitors can be charged with third degree sexual abuse of mate (with lesser penalty) except when she has "mental defect or incapacity which precludes giving consent."	C.A. § 709.2 to 709.4
Kansas 2	Husbands can only be charged for rape of wife, but not with sexual battery.	S.A. § 21-3501-3
Kentucky 2, 3	Husbands and cohabitors cannot be charged for rape of wife unless parties living apart and one has filed a petition for divorce or separation.	R.S. § 510.010 (3)
Louisiana 2	Husbands and cohabitors cannot be charged for rape of wife unles there is a court order of separation or a court order prohibiting physical or sexual abuse.	R.S.A. § 14.41-43
Maine 6	Husbands can be charged for rape of wife.	R.S.A. 17A § 251, 252
Maryland 2	Husbands can only be charged for rape of wife if force used and if parties living together or separated less than six months. If separated more than six months or if written separation agreement obtained, they can be charged if used force or threat of force, except if wife is "mentally deficient, mentally incapacitated or physically helpless." Husbands can also be charged with lesser crimes of first and second degree sexual offenses.	A.C. § 27-464D
Massachusetts 6	Husbands can be charged for rape of wife.	A.L. Ch. 265 § 22 277 § 39 Commonwealth v. Chretien 383 Mass. 123, 417 N.E 2d 1203 (1981)
Michigan 2	Husbands can be charged for rape of wife except when she "is under the age of 16,	Act No. 138, 1988

STATE AND CATEGORY	STATUS OF MARITAL RAPE LAW	CITATIONS
	mentally incapable, or mentally incapacitated."	
Minnesota 2	Husbands can be charged for rape of wife except when wife is "mentally or physically disabled."	S.A. § 609.349
Mississippi 2, 5	Husbands cannot be charged for "sexual battery" of wife unless parties living apart. Although rape statute does not exempt husbands from being charged for rape of wife, whether or not marital rape is considered a crime awaits the interpretation of the court.	M.C.A. § 97-3-95 to 103 (Suppl. 1980)
Missouri 2	Husbands cannot be charged for rape of wife unless there is a court order of separation.	A.S. § 566.010:2
Montana 2, 3	Husbands/cohabitants can be charged for rape of mate but not the lesser offense of sexual assault, unless parties living apart.	R.C. § 45-5-506
Nebraska 6	Husbands can be charged for rape of wife.	R.S. § 28-319, 320 State of Nebraska v. Charles Willis 233 Neb. 844
Nevada 2	Husbands can only be charged for "sexual assault of a spouse by a spouse" if they use force or threat. They cannot be charged if they know or should know their wife is "physically or mentally incapable of resisting or understanding the nature of his conduct."	R.S. § 200.373
New Hampshire 2	Husbands can be charged for rape of wife except when she is "mentally defective" or under the age of consent.	RSA 632-A2, A3, A5
New Jersey 6	Husbands can be charged for rape of wife.	S.A. § 2C:14-5(b) State v. Albert Smith 85 N.J. 193, 201, 426 A. 2d 38.42 (1981), State v. Daniel Morrison N.J. 426 A. 2d 47 (1981)
New Mexico 2, 3	Husbands/cohabitants cannot be charged for rape of their mates unless parties living apart or legal action started for divorce or separation (petition filed).	Stat. § 30-9-10, 11
New York 6	Husbands can be charged for rape of wife.	People v. Liberta, 64 N.Y., 2d 152 (1984)
North Carolina 2	Husbands cannot be charged for rape of wife unless parties living apart.	G.S. § 14-27.8

STATE AND CATEGORY	STATUS OF MARITAL RAPE LAW	CITATIONS
North Dakota 6	Husbands can be charged for rape of wife.	C.A. § 12.1-20-01, 02, 03
Ohio 2	Husbands can only be charged for rape of wife if they use force or threat of force. They cannot be charged if they substantially impair wife's judgment or control by administering a drug or intoxicant, surreptitiously or by force, threat of force, or deception, to prevent her resistance.	ORC § 2907.01, 02, 12
Oklahoma 2	Husbands can only be charged for rape of wife if parties living apart or one party has initiated legal proceedings, and if husbands have used force or threat.	S.A. Title 21 § 1111
Oregon 6	Husbands can be charged for rape of wife.	R.S. § 163.305
Pennsylvania 2, 3	Husbands/cohabitants can only be charged with lesser crime of "spousal sexual assault" if victim reports within 90 days. Husbands cannot be charged if wife is "mentally deranged, or deficient," including intoxicated.*	S.A. Title 18 § 3103
Rhode Island 2	Husbands can be charged for rape of wife except for first degree rape or if she is "mentally incapacitated, mentally disabled, or physically helpless."	G.L. § 11-37-1-6
South Carolina 2	Husbands cannot be charged for rape of wife unless there is a court order of separation.	C. § 16-3-658
South Dakota 2	Husbands cannot be charged for rape of wife unless parties separated under court order or living apart and the victim filed a complaint within 90 days of the rape.	C.L.A. § 22-22-1
Tennessee 2	Husbands can only be charged with "spousal rape" when rapes result in "serious bodily injury" or if they use a weapon—or what the victim believes is a weapon—to commit "unlawful sexual penetration." They can also be charged with "spousal sexual battery" if the same two conditions apply. Husbands cannot be charged if only force or coercion is used, or if they know	C.A. § 39-2-610

*The word "intoxicated" is not in the statute, but according to the attorney general's office, the concepts "mentally deranged or deficient" include being intoxicated. Personal communication, Jane Ellen Rosenberger, 29 November 1984.

STATE AND CATEGORY	STATUS OF MARITAL RAPE LAW	CITATIONS
	or have reason to know "that the victim is mentally defective, mentally incapacitated, or physically helpless," or if sexual penetration is accomplished by fraud. The penalties for nonmarital rape are vastly more severe than for spousal rape and spousal sexual battery.	
Texas 2	Husbands can only be charged with "aggravated sexual assault" for rape of wife.	§ 21-02(a), 21-12
Utah 2	Husbands cannot be charged for rape of wife unless there is a court order of separation.	Crim. C.A. § 76-5-402, 407
Vermont 6	Husbands can be charged for rape of wife.	S.A. Title 13 § 3252
Virginia 2	Husbands can only be charged with the lesser crime of "marital sexual assault" if there is serious physical injury and the assault is reported within 10 days. They can accept counseling instead of going to prison if the court and victim agree.	Code 18.2-61, *et seq.*
Washington 2	Husbands can only be charged for rape of wife in first and second degrees.	R.C.A. Ch. 9A.44.010, *et seq.* (Supp., 1979)
West Virginia 2	Husbands can only be charged with lesser offense of "sexual assault of a spouse" if they commit first degree rape or the forcible compulsion part of second degree rape. Conviction carries a lesser penalty than for non-marital rape. They cannot be charged if she is "physically helpless, mentally defective, or mentally incapacitated."	Code § 61-8B-1
Wisconsin 6	Husbands can be charged for rape of wife.	S.A. § 940.225 (6)
Wyoming 2	Husbands can only be charged for rape of wife in first and second degrees, but not third and fourth degrees; i.e., if they know or have reason to know she "has a mental illness or deficiency or developmental disability," they cannot be charged.	S.A. § 6-4-032-305
Federal Land	Husbands can be charged for rape of wife when it occurs on federal land (e.g., national parks, wildernesses, Native American reservations, and U.S. Territories).	Sexual Abuse Act 1986 S 2241-2245 chapter 109A

SOURCE NOTES

Introduction to New Edition

I would like to thank Marny Hall and Sandy Butler for their feedback on drafts of this introduction, and Candida Ellis for her excellent editorial assistance on both the introduction and the second revised half of chapter 2. Most of all I am indebted to Laura X (Laura adopted her last name in 1969 to protest the legal ownership of wives by their husbands). She contributed her considerable expertise on wife rape to both new sections of this book. She read several drafts of these and was particularly helpful in providing me with the most up-to-date information on the complicated and constantly changing legal aspect of wife rape, as well as by giving me many useful suggestions for the non-legal sections of these chapters. In addition, she brought to my attention many new bibliographic sources on wife rape and took a great deal of time and effort to ensure that Appendix II, "State-by-State Information on Marital Rape Exemption Laws," is as accurate and current as possible.

[1] Laura X reported reading this quote in connection with the *Liberta* case in New York, personal communication, August 5, 1989.

[2] See pages 367–69 of this book.

[3] May 1983, p. 105.

[4] Ibid., p. 104.

[5] Ibid., p. 104.

[6] Laura X, personal communication, August 6, 1989.

[7] Moira K. Griffin, "In 44 States, It's Legal to Rape Your Wife," *Student Lawyer*, Vol. 9, No. 1 (1980), p. 21.

[8] Ibid.

[9] Margaret Mitchell, *Gone with the Wind* (New York: Macmillan, 1936).

[10] Ibid.

[11] "Rape Within Marriage," *The Boston Globe*, December 29, 1984, p. 8.

[12] I was equally careful to include a similar range of experiences in my book on incest, *The Secret Trauma: Incest in the Lives of Girls and Women* (New York: Basic Books, 1986).

[13] Sylvia Wharton, *Sun-Star*, Merced, California, June 5, 1981.

[14] Sylvia Wharton, "Sex Torture Charges Unveiled in Burnham Trial," *Sun-Star*, Merced, California, May 29, 1981.

[15] Ibid.

[16] *Sun-Star*, June 5, 1981.

[17] For example, see Robin R. Linden, Darlene R. Pagano, Diana E. H. Russell, and Susan L. Star, *Against Sadomasochism: A Radical Feminist Analysis* (San Francisco: Frog in the Well, 1982).

[18] New York: Berkeley Books, 1981.

[19] Even those in the legal profession are aware that male bias is still a serious problem. In an article titled "It's Still Tougher to Be a Woman," the results of a two-year study by the Washington Task Force on Gender and Justice in the Courts found that "more than 70 percent of the lawyers and 60 percent of the judges responding to the statewide survey believed that gender bias is a problem" (*The Seattle Times*, August 25, 1989). In particular, the Task Force described "a lack of understanding about the needs of women in sexual-assault, domestic-violence, and divorce cases" as a "far-reaching problem" in the legal profession (ibid.).

[20] Joyce Faidley, "Judge Mirrors Spousal-Abuse Myths," *Los Angeles Times*, July 9, 1989.

[21] Ibid.

[22] Ibid.

[23] Ibid.

[24] Ibid.

[25] "A Spousal Tragedy," *Los Angeles Times*, July 16, 1989.

[26] Ibid.

[27] April 25, 1989.

[28] J. C. Barden, "Confronting the Moral and Legal Issue of Marital Rape," *New York Times*, June 1, 1981.

[29] Ibid.

[30] Natalie Phillips, "Marital-rape Bill Clears House: Tebedo Votes 'No,'" *Colorado Springs Gazette Telegraph*, January 27, 1988. Ironically, at the same time as Representative Tebedo was expressing these male-identified attitudes, she was sponsoring a bill to make it a criminal offense for psychotherapists to have sexual relations with their clients.

[31] Howard Pankratz, "Marital Rape Law Little Used in 1st Year," *Denver Post*, July 2, 1989.

[32] See "*Warren v. State:* One Attempt to Modernize the Marital Rape Exemption," *American Journal of Trial Advocacy*, Vol. 10 (Summer 1986). Martha Warren's first victory was the Supreme Court decision allowing her husband to be prosecuted. The second was the conviction of her husband in the lower court. Laura X is the source of the information about Martha Warren's firing, personal communication, August 5, 1989.

[33] Ibid.

[34] Ibid.

[35] The survey was conducted by the Gateway Shelter for battered women. Ibid.

[36] "Domestic Violence and Marital Rape," unpublished paper presented at the Third Annual Conference titled "Domestic Violence in the 80s," Columbus, Ohio, May 12, 1989.

[37] Ibid.

[38] Ibid.

[39] Laura X, personal communication, August 2, 1989.

[40] Laura X, personal communication, July 25, 1989.

[41] For an extensive discussion of the literature on the prevalence of wife rape, see chapter 5 of this book; for the prevalence of rape by strangers, acquaintances, friends, authority figures, boyfriends, dates, lovers and ex-lovers, as well as the prevalence of child sexual abuse and sexual harassment on the job, see Russell, *Sexual Exploitation: Rape, Child Sexual Abuse, and Workplace Harassment* (Beverly Hills, California: Sage Publications, 1984); and for the prevalence of incestuous abuse, see Russell, *The Secret Trauma*.

[42] The figure usually cited by the rape crisis centers is that one in three women will be raped in their lifetimes. (I wonder if anyone knows the source of this oft-cited statistic.) I have never heard the center representatives in the Bay Area report any figure for rape in marriage.

[43] See my article, "Pornography and Rape: A Causal Model," *Political Psychology*, Vol. 9, No. 1 (1988), on the causative role of pornography in the occurrence of rape.

[44] Lynn Thompson-Haas, "Marital Rape: Methods of Helping and Healing," unpublished paper, School of Social Work, University of Texas, 1987. Thompson-Haas is planning to publish this paper. (See bibliography for information on obtaining a copy of this paper.)

[45] Ibid.

[46] Ibid.

[47] Ibid.

[48] Lynn Thompson-Haas, personal communication, August 11, 1989.

[49] Thompson-Haas, "Marital Rape."

[50] See footnote 42.

[51] Ibid.

[52] Ibid.

[53] Ibid.

[54] Ibid.

[55] Ibid.

[56] Ibid.

[57] Lee Bowker, *Beating Wife-beating* (Lexington, Massachusetts: Lexington Books, 1983); David Finkelhor and Kersti Yllo, *License to Rape* (New York: Holt, Rinehart and Winston, 1985); Irene Frieze, "Investigating the Causes and Consequences of Marital Rape," *Signs: Journal of Women in Culture and Society*, Vol. 8, No. 3 (1983); Mildred Pagelow, *Family Violence* (New York: Praeger, 1984); Diana E. H. Russell, *Rape in Marriage*; Nancy Shields and Christine Hanneke, "Battered Wives' Reactions to Marital Rape," in Richard Gelles, Gerald Hotaling, Murray Straus, and David Finkelhor (eds.), *The Dark Side of Families* (Beverly Hills, California: Sage Publications, 1983); Lenore Walker, *The Battered Woman Syndrome* (New York: Springer, 1985).

[58] "Women's Responses to Sexual Abuse in Intimate Relationships," *Health Care for Women International*, Vol. 8 (1989), p. 340.

[59] Ibid.

[60] Frieze, "Investigating the Causes and Consequences of Marital Rape"; and Shields and Hanneke, "Battered Wives' Reactions to Marital Rape."

[61] Ibid.

[62] "Women's Responses to Sexual Abuse," p. 344.

[63] Ibid., p. 341.

[64] Ibid., p. 341.

[65] Nancy Shields and Christine Hanneke, "Comparing the Psychological Impact of Marital and Stranger Rape," paper presented at the National Conference for Family Violence Researchers, Durham, New Hampshire, 1987.

[66] "The Dark Consequences of Marital Rape," *American Journal of Nursing*, Vol. 89 (1989).

[67] "Women's Responses to Sexual Abuse," p. 344.

[68] "Misogyny and Homicide of Women," *Advances in Nursing Science*, Vol. 3, No. 2 (1981).

[69] British feminist criminologist Jill Radford and I are currently completing an anthology which includes several articles on wife murder: *Femicide: The Politics of Woman Killing*, to be published by Twayne Publishers, Boston, in 1990.

[70] *Against Our Will: Men, Women, and Rape* (New York: Simon and Schuster, 1975), p. 381.

Preface

[1] *San Francisco Chronicle*, June 22, 1979

[2] Ibid., August 22, 1979.

[3] Ibid.

[4] Press Release Re: AB 546—Chapter 994 Statutes of 1979, September 25, 1979.

1 Introduction: The Crime in the Closet

[1] A short monograph titled *Vergewaltigung in der Ehe* (*Rape in Marriage*) by Dierk Helmken was published by Kriminalistik Verlag in Germany in 1979.

[2] The validity of so generalizing will be discussed in Chapter 5.

[3] *Against Our Will: Men, Women and Rape* (New York: Simon and Schuster, 1975), p. 380.

[4] *Webster's Dictionary*.

[5] See Paul Hollander, *Soviet and American Society: A Comparison* (New York: Oxford University Press, 1973) and Gail Lapidus, *Women in Soviet Society: Equality, Development, and Social Change* (Berkeley: University of California Press, 1978).

[6] For example, the Nayar of India, described by E. Kathleen Gough, "The Nayars and the Definition of Marriage," *Journal of the Royal Anthropological Institute of Great Britain and Ireland*, Vol. 89, Part 1 (1959); and the Kibbutzim of Israel, Mel Spiro's "Is the Family

Universal?—The Israeli Case" in Norman Bell and Ezra Vogel (eds.), *A Modern Introduction to the Family* (New York: The Free Press, 1960).

[7] "Rape Doesn't End With a Kiss," *Viva*, June 1975, p. 40.

[8] *The Family Coordinator*, Vol. 26, October 1977. This discussion of the social scientific literature of wife rape is limited to published works. Research on rape in marriage is being pursued by Irene Frieze (a social psychologist at the University of Pittsburgh), David Finkelhor (a sociologist at the University of New Hampshire), and Julie Doron (a sociologist at Barnard College). Their unpublished work is referred to and cited where appropriate throughout this book.

[9] Ibid., p. 339.

[10] Ibid., p. 344.

[11] Ibid., p. 346.

[12] "Rape of One's Wife," *Medical Aspects of Human Sexuality*, Vol. 12, No. 2 (February 1978), p. 153.

[13] "Marital Rape," *Medical Aspects of Human Sexuality*, Vol. 15, No. 3 (March 1981).

[14] Ibid., p. 127.

[15] *Men Who Rape: The Psychology of the Offender* (New York: Plenum Press, 1979), p. xiii.

[16] For a recent summary of some of these studies, see Mary P. Koss, Kenneth E. Leonard, Dana A. Beezley, and Cheryl J. Oros, "An Empirical Investigation of the Social Control and Psychopathological Models of Rape" (Paper delivered at the Annual American Psychological Association Meetings, August 1981).

[17] *Men Who Rape*, p. 106.

[18] Ibid., p. 107.

[19] Ibid., p. 109.

[20] *Rape Culture* is the title of one of the best-known documentary films about rape. The notion that the United States has a rape-supportive culture has also been argued and substantiated by Martha R. Burt, "Cultural Myths and Supports for Rape," *Journal of Personality and Social Psychology*, Vol. 38 (1980); and "Attitudes Supportive of Rape in American Culture," House Committee on Science and Technology, Subcommittee on Domestic and International Scientific Planning, Analysis and Cooperation, *Research into Violent Behavior: Sexual Assaults*. Hearing, 95th Congress, 2nd Session, January 10–12, 1978 (Washington, D.C.: U.S. Government Printing Office, 1978), pp. 277–322.

[21] Burt, "Attitudes Supportive of Rape" (Hearings).

[22] Ibid., p. 5.

[23] James V. P. Check and Neil M. Malamuth, "Feminism and Rape in the 1980's: Recent Research Findings" (Unpublished paper, portions of which were presented at the Section on Women and Psychology, Canadian Psychological Association Meetings, Toronto, Canada, June 1981).

[24] "Testing Hypotheses Regarding Rape: Exposure to Sexual Violence, Sex Differences, and the 'Normality' of Rapists," *Journal of Research in Personality*, Vol. 14, No. 1, 1980, p. 124.

[25] Ibid., p. 130.

[26] Ibid.

[27] Neil M. Malamuth, "Rape Proclivity Among Males," *Journal of Social Issues*, Vol. 37, No. 4 (December 1981).

[28] John Briere, Neil Malamuth, and Joe Ceniti, "Self-Assessed Rape Proclivity: Attitudinal and Sexual Correlates" (Paper presented at the American Psychological Association Meetings, Los Angeles, August 1981).

[29] Ibid., p. 2.

[30] According to police statistics, those arrested for rape are disproportionately Black (*Uniform Crime Reports* [annual]) and lower class; see also the results of a seventeen-city survey undertaken by the Government Commission on Violence: Donald Mulvihill, Melvin Tumin, and Lynn Curtis, *Crimes of Violence: A Staff Report*, submitted to the National Commission on the Causes and Prevention of Violence, Government Printing Office, Washington, D.C. (1969), Vol. 11; and Susan Brownmiller, *Against Our Will*, 1975.

[31] "Adolescents' Cues and Signals: Sex and Assault" (Paper presented at the Annual Meeting of the Western Psychological Association, San Diego, California, April 1979).

[32] *The Future of Marriage* (New York: Bantam edition, 1972).

2 Wife Rape and the Law

[1] Hubert S. Feild and Leigh B. Bienen, *Jurors and Rape: A Study in Psychology and Law* (Lexington, Mass.: D.C. Heath and Company, 1980), p. 163.

[2] Ibid.

[3] Gilbert Geis speculates that Hale was in fact probably reflecting even earlier standards. "Rape-in-Marriage: Law and Law Reform in England, the United States, and Sweden," *Adelaide Law Review*, Vol. 6, No. 2 (June 1978), p. 285. For two excellent in-depth discussions of the validity or lack thereof of the Hale doctrine, see "The Marital Rape Exemption," *New York University Law Review*, Vol. 52 (May 1977), and Dennis Drucker, "The Common Law Does Not Support a Marital Exemption for Forcible Rape," *Women's Rights Law Reporter*, Vol. 5 (1979).

[4] Geis, "Rape-in-Marriage," p. 286.

[5] Feild and Bienen, *Jurors and Rape*, p. 153.

[6] Ibid., p. 153.

[7] Ibid.

[8] Geis, "Rape-in-Marriage," p. 294.

[9] Joanne Schulman, "The Marital Rape Exemption in the Criminal Law," *Clearinghouse Review*, Vol. 14, No. 6 (October 1980).

[10] The first portion of the account is excerpted from an article by Michelle Celarier, "I Kept Thinking Maybe I Could Help Him," *In These Times* (January 10–16, 1979).

[11] The remainder of this account of the Rideout case is excerpted from an article by Moira K. Griffin, "In 44 States, It's Legal to Rape Your Wife," *Student Lawyer*, Vol. 9, No. 1 (September 1980).

[12] National Clearinghouse on Marital and Date Rape, State Law Chart. Unpublished sheet, updated January 1, 1990.

[13] Ibid.

[14] Diana E. H. Russell, *Sexual Exploitation: Rape, Child Sexual Abuse, and Workplace Harassment* (Beverly Hills, California: Sage Publications, 1984).

[15] Sarah Wunsch of the Center for Constitutional Rights has summarized the significance of the 1984 New York State Court of Appeals' case called *People of the State of New York v. Mario Liberta* in a pamphlet first published in July 1986. The Court of Appeals demolished "the excuses for not having laws to protect women against marital rape" by offering the following arguments:

Marriage does not give a husband a right to forced sex; rape is not part of the marriage contract. While it is understood that sex is a part of marriage, a woman has no 'duty' to provide sex on demand whenever and in whatever way the husband desires it; and often, rape has nothing to do with sex.

Accusing angry wives of making up charges of rape is just another example of discrimination against women. In states where marital rape is treated as rape, there is no evidence that wives are making up charges. In fact, rape is one of the most underreported of all crimes.

Just because a crime may be hard to prove in some cases doesn't mean that prosecutors should be unable to ever present such a case. Actually, there is a high conviction rate in marital rape cases that have gone to trial.

Marital privacy is meant to protect the privacy of husbands and wives to engage in activities they both agree to; it is not a shield for violent, brutal acts.

Making marital rape a crime does not make it harder to keep a marriage going. By making rape in marriage a crime, some rapes can be prevented and the institution of marriage may be strengthened by the respect for women it conveys. (*Stop-*

ping Sexual Assault in Marriage: A Guide for Women, Counselors and Advocates, 1986, pp. 8–9).

3   The Rape Study

[1] For example, see M. Joan McDermott, *Rape Victimization in 26 American Cities* (Washington, D.C.: U.S. Department of Justice, Law Enforcement Assistance Administration, 1979). Some studies of attitudes about rape and rape victimization have been based on random samples, for example, Martha Burt, "Cultural Myths and Supports for Rape," *Journal of Personality and Social Psychology*, Vol. 38 (1980); Shirley Feldman-Summers and Clarke D. Ashworth, "Factors Related to Intentions to Report a Rape," *Journal of Social Issues* (In press); M. T. Gordon, S. Riger, R. K. LeBailly, and L. Heath, "Crime, Women and the Quality of Urban Life," *Signs: Journal of Women in Culture and Society*, Vol. 5, No. 3 (Chicago: University of Chicago Press, Spring 1980).

[2] See, for example, Burt's "Cultural Myths and Supports for Rape."

[3] Ibid.

[4] Philip H. Ennis, *Criminal Victimization in the United States: A Report of a National Survey.* National Opinion Research Center (N.O.R.C.), University of Chicago (Washington, D.C.: U.S. Government Printing Office, May 1967).

[5] E. J. Kanin, "Male Aggression in Dating-Courtship Relations," *The American Journal of Sociology*, Vol. 63 (1957); E. J. Kanin and C. Kirkpatrick, "Male Sex Aggression on a University Campus," *American Sociological Review*, Vol. 22 (1957); Ann Wolpert Burgess and Lynda L. Holmstrom, *Rape: Victims of Crisis* (Bowie, Massachusetts: Robert J. Brady Co., 1974); Diana E. H. Russell, *The Politics of Rape: The Victim's Perspective* (New York: Stein & Day, 1975).

[6] California Volume 1: Characteristics of the Population, Table 81, p. 435.

[7] Alfred Kinsey, Wardell Pomeroy, and Clyde Martin, *Sexual Behavior in the Human Male* (Philadelphia: W. B. Saunders, 1948), p. 120.

[8] Ibid., p. 149.

[9] Ibid., p. 148.

[10] Ibid., pp. 149–50.

4   What Is Wife Rape?

[1] Sedelle Katz and Mary Ann Mazur, *Understanding the Rape Victim: A Synthesis of Research Findings* (New York: John Wiley & Sons, 1979), p. 11.

[2] This point is made by David Finkelhor and Kersti Yllo, "Forced Sex in Marriage: A Preliminary Report" (Paper presented at the American Sociological Association Meetings, New York, August 1980), p. 8.

[3] Irene Frieze, "Causes and Consequences of Marital Rape" (Paper presented at the American Psychological Association Meetings, Montreal, Canada, September 1980), p. 3.

[4] Ibid.; Finkelhor and Yllo, "Forced Sex in Marriage"; Richard J. Gelles, "Power, Sex and Violence: The Case of Marital Rape," *The Family Coordinator*, Vol. 26 (October 1977); and Mildred Daley Pagelow, "Does the Law Help Battered Women? Some Research Notes" (Paper presented at the 1980 Annual Meeting of the Law and Society Association and the ISA Research Committee on the Sociology of Law, Madison, Wisconsin, June 5–8, 1980).

[5] *The Hite Report on Male Sexuality* (New York: Alfred Knopf, 1981), p. 729.

[6] Ibid.

5   The Prevalence of Wife Rape

[1] David Finkelhor and Kersti Yllo, "Forced Sex in Marriage: A Preliminary Report" (Paper presented at the American Sociological Association Meetings, New York, August 1980).

[2] The 1979 edition of the *Uniform Crime Reports* reports that 5.6 percent of all murders in 1978 involved wives as victims of their husbands. The figure of 1,095 wife victims was calculated from the total number of homicides (19,555) in that year.

[3] Irene Frieze, "Causes and Consequences of Marital Rape" (Paper presented at the American Psychological Association Meetings, Montreal, Canada, September 1980); and Mildred Daley Pagelow, "Does the Law Help Battered Women? Some Research Notes" (Paper presented at the 1980 Annual Meeting of the Law and Society Association and the ISA Research Committee on the Sociology of Law, Madison, Wisconsin, June 5–8, 1980).

[4] Richard J. Gelles, "Power, Sex and Violence: The Case of Marital Rape," *The Family Coordinator*, Vol. 26 (October 1977), p. 342.

[5] Morton Hunt, "Legal Rape," *Family Circle*, January 9, 1979, p. 34.

[6] More recently Gelles still cites the figure of two million women as "victims of severe physical violence each year," *Family Violence*, 1979, p. 92. In *Behind Closed Doors* by Murray Straus, Richard Gelles, and Suzanne Steinmetz, the figure of 1.8 million was projected from the same data (New York: Anchor Books), p. 40.

[7] Hunt, "Legal Rape," p. 24.

[8] Ibid.

[9] Ibid., p. 24.

[10] For example, see Barbara Star, "Q & A: Why Husbands Resort to Raping Their Wives," *U.S. Magazine*, Vol. 2 (March 6, 1979), p. 23; Susan Barry, "Spousal Rape, the Uncommon Law," *American Bar Association Journal*, September 1980; and Nicholas Groth and Thomas Gary, "Marital Rape," *Medical Aspects of Human Sexuality*, Vol. 15, No. 3 (March 1981).

[11] Pagelow, p. 5.

[12] Ibid.

[13] Personal communication, June 10, 1981.

[14] Frieze, Table 9.

[15] Ibid., p. 9.

[16] Ibid., pp. 9–10.

[17] Ibid., Table 9.

[18] Ibid.

[19] Ibid., pp. 15–16.

[20] Ibid., p. 16.

[21] Ibid.

[22] Julie Blackman Doron, "Conflict and Violence in Intimate Relationships: Focus on Marital Rape" (Paper presented at the American Sociological Association Meetings, New York, August 1980).

[23] Ibid., data tabulation, p. 1.

[24] Finkelhor and Yllo, p. 13.

[25] Ibid.

[26] Ibid.

[27] Lenore E. Walker, *The Battered Woman* (New York: Harper & Row, 1979), p. 108.

[28] Ibid., p. 126.

[29] Diana E. H. Russell, *The Politics of Rape: The Victim's Perspective* (New York: Stein & Day, 1975); Gelles, "Power, Sex, and Violence"; Nicholas Groth, *Men Who Rape: The Psychology of the Offender* (New York: Plenum Press, 1979); Finkelhor and Yllo, "Forced Sex in Marriage"; Frieze, "Causes and Consequences of Marital Rape"; Pagelow, "Does the Law Help Battered Women?"

[30] Gelles, "Power, Sex, and Violence"; Hunt, "Legal Rape"; Groth, *Men Who Rape* and "Marital Rape"; Frieze, "Causes and Consequences of Marital Rape"; Barry, "Spousal Rape, the Uncommon Law."

[31] Gelles, p. 345.

[32] Hunt, p. 24. Hunt's emphasis.

[33] A. F. Schiff, for example, reports in an article published in 1971 that while the rate per

100,000 was 35 in the United States, it was only 1.9 in France, 1.2 in Holland, and 0.8 in Belgium (A. F. Schiff, "Rape in Other Countries," *Medicine, Science, and the Law*, Vol. 11, No. 3 [1971], p. 25). John MacDonald agrees that "available statistics, despite their deficiencies, suggest that the United States has an unusually high rape rate. . . ." He contrasts his figure of 30 per 100,000 females in the United States (year unspecified) with less than one per 100,000 in Norway, 3 in England, and 7 in Poland (J. MacDonald, *Rape: Offenders and Their Victims* [Springfield, Illinois: Charles C. Thomas, 1971], pp. 25–26).

[34] Imogen Seger-Coulborn, "Vergewaltigung in der Ehe" (Rape in Marriage), Unpublished report (West Germany: Institut für Demoskopie Allensbach, 1976).

[35] Ibid.

[36] Ibid.

[37] Ibid.

[38] Ibid., Table 3, p. 5.

[39] Ibid., Table 5a, p. 10.

[40] This was also reported by Finkelhor and Yllo in their preliminary study of wife rape, "Forced Sex in Marriage."

[41] February 13, 1980.

[42] Barbara Wertheim, personal communication, May 1981.

[43] *The Australian Women's Weekly*, February 13, 1980, p. 27.

[44] Ibid., July 23, 1980, p. 30.

[45] Ibid.

[46] Ibid.

[47] Barbara Wertheim, personal communication, May 1981.

6   A Continuum of Sexual Relations

[1] Diana E. H. Russell, *The Politics of Rape: The Victim's Perspective* (New York: Stein & Day, 1975), p. 261.

[2] "Seduction Is a Four Letter Word," *Playboy*, January 1973, p. 178.

[3] *The Sensuous Woman* (New York: Dell, 1971), p. 179.

[4] Imogen Seger-Coulborn, "Vergewaltigung in der Ehe" (Rape in Marriage), Unpublished Report (West Germany: Institut für Demoskopie Allensbach, 1976), Table 6, p. 11.

[5] *Webster's Dictionary*.

[6] Seger-Coulborn, Table 1.

[7] Ibid., p. 3.

[8] Ibid.

[9] For example, Jessie Bernard, *The Future of Marriage* (New York: Bantam Books, 1972); Mirra Komarovsky, *Blue Collar Marriage* (New York: Random House, 1962); Lee Rainwater, *And the Poor Get Children* (Chicago: Quadrangle Books, 1960); Lillian Rubin, *Worlds of Pain* (New York: Basic Books, 1976).

[10] For example, Seymour Feshbach and Neil Malamuth demonstrate that even "one exposure to violence in pornography can significantly influence erotic reactions to the portrayal of rape." "Sex and Aggression: Proving the Link," *Psychology Today*, Vol. XII, No. 6 (November 1978), p. 116. For three critical reviews of the recent scientific research on the relationship between pornography and violence against women see Irene Diamond, "Pornography and Repression: A Reconsideration of 'Who' and 'What'; Pauline Bart and Margaret Jozsa, "Dirty Books, Dirty Films, and Dirty Data"; and Diana E. H. Russell, "Pornography and Violence: What Does the New Research Say?" in Laura Lederer (ed.), *Take Back the Night: Women on Pornography* (New York: William Morrow, 1980).

[11] Alfred C. Kinsey, Wardell B. Pomeroy, Clyde E. Martin, and Paul Gebhard, *Sexual Behavior in the Human Female* (Philadelphia: W. B. Saunders Co., 1953), Chapter 9, pp. 346–408.

[12] Shere Hite, *The Hite Report: A Nationwide Study of Female Sexuality* (New York: Dell Publishing, 1976), and *The Hite Report on Male Sexuality* (New York: Alfred Knopf, 1981).

[13] Morton Hunt, *Sexual Behavior in the 1970's* (New York: Dell Publishing Co., 1974), Chapter 4.

[14] Ibid., pp. 15–16.

[15] Ibid., p. 178.

[16] Ibid., p. 179.

[17] Ibid., p. 230.

[18] Ibid., Table 36, p. 231.

[19] Ibid., p. 230.

[20] Ibid., p. 232.

7   Wife Rape and Wife Beating

[1] *Behind Closed Doors* (Garden City, New York: Anchor Press/Doubleday, 1980), p. 12.

[2] *Violence Against Wives* (New York: The Free Press, 1979), Table 7, p. 248.

[3] Ibid.

[4] Aside from the works of Mildred Pagelow and Lenore Walker already cited in Chapter 5, Elaine Hilberman and Kit Munson mention that among the sixty battered women they studied, "sexual assaults were common, women describing being beaten and raped in front of the children." ("Sixty Battered Women," *Victimology*, Vol. 2, No. 3/4 [1977–1978], p. 462.)

[5] Irene Frieze, "Causes and Consequences of Marital Rape" (Paper presented at the American Psychological Association Meetings, Montreal, Canada, September 1980), p. 6.

[6] Moira K. Griffin, "In 44 States, It's Legal to Rape Your Wife," *Student Lawyer*, Vol. 9, No. 1 (September 1980), p. 58.

[7] *Behind Closed Doors*, p. 26.

[8] Ibid., p. 37.

[9] Ibid.

[10] Ibid., p. 4.

[11] Ibid., p. 32.

[12] Ibid., p. 36, emphasis theirs.

[13] Ibid., p. 35.

[14] Ibid., p. 36.

[15] Ibid., p. 37.

[16] Del Martin, *Battered Wives* (San Francisco: Glide Publications, 1976); Mildred Daley Pagelow, "Does the Law Help Battered Women? Some Research Notes" (Paper presented at the 1980 Annual Meeting of the Law and Society Association and the ISA Research Committee on the Sociology of Law, Madison, Wisconsin, June 5–8, 1980); and Russell Dobash and R. Emerson Dobash, *Violence Against Wives: A Case Against the Patriarchy* (New York: The Free Press, 1979).

[17] *Behind Closed Doors*, p. 40.

[18] Ibid., p. 40 for 3.8 percent figure, and p. 41 for 4.6 percent figure.

[19] Ibid., p. 41.

[20] Ibid., p. 43. They also make statements like the following: "Traditionally men have been considered more aggressive and violent than women. Like other stereotypes, there is no doubt a kernel of truth to this." (Ibid., p. 36).

[21] Irene Frieze, "Causes and Consequences of Marital Rape," p. 15.

[22] Ibid., p. 8.

[23] Ibid., p. 10.

[24] Ibid.

8   Husband Battering, Wife Battering, and Murder

[1] Donald Mulvihill and Melvin Tumin, *Crimes of Violence: A Staff Report Submitted to the National Commission on the Causes and Prevention of Violence* (Washington, D.C.: Government Printing Office, 1969), Vol. 11, p. 210.

[2] *Uniform Crime Reports,* 1980.

[3] Mulvihill and Tumin, p. 210.

[4] Marvin E. Wolfgang, *Patterns in Criminal Homicide* (Philadelphia: University of Pennsylvania Press, 1958), p. 162.

[5] Ibid., p. 163.

[6] Ibid.

[7] Ibid., p. 214.

[8] *Uniform Crime Reports,* 1960–1980.

[9] Marvin Wolfgang and Franco Ferracuti, *The Subculture of Violence* (London: Tavistock Publications, 1967), p. 275.

[10] Some of these ideas were first expressed by me in "Fay Stender and the Politics of Murder," *Chrysalis,* No. 6 (October 1979).

[11] Bill Bowder, "The Wives Who Ask for It," *Community Care,* March 1979. For an excellent rebuttal of this thesis see Russell P. Dobash and R. Emerson Dobash, "The Myth of the Wives Who Ask for It: A Response to Pizzey, Gayford and McKeith," *Community Care,* April 1979.

9   Characteristics of Wife Rape

[1] David Finkelhor and Kersti Yllo, "Forced Sex in Marriage: A Preliminary Report" (Paper presented at American Sociological Association Meetings, New York, August 1980), p. 32.

[2] Murray Straus, Richard Gelles, and Suzanne Steinmetz, *Behind Closed Doors* (Garden City, New York: Anchor Press/Doubleday, 1980), pp. 171–73.

[3] Ibid.

[4] Irene Frieze, "Causes and Consequences of Marital Rape" (Paper presented at the American Psychological Association Meetings, Montreal, Canada, September 1980), Table 26.

[5] Ibid., p. 30.

10   Husbands Who Rape Their Wives

[1] A. Nicholas Groth and Thomas S. Gary, "Marital Rape," *Medical Aspects of Human Sexuality,* Vol. 15, No. 3 (March 1981), p. 131.

[2] Ibid.

[3] See for example, Shere Hite, *The Hite Report on Male Sexuality* (New York: Alfred Knopf, 1981), as well as any number of books and articles on men's roles, for example, Warren Farrell, *The Liberated Man* (New York: Bantam Books, 1975).

[4] Groth and Gary, "Marital Rape," p. 131.

[5] Irene Frieze, "Causes and Consequences of Marital Rape" (Paper presented at the American Psychological Association Meetings, Montreal, Canada, September 1980), p. 27.

[6] Ibid. The overall correlation between the worst episode of the husband's violence and his raping his wife was 0.34.

[7] Frieze, "Causes and Consequences of Marital Rape," p. 22.

[8] Ibid.

[9] Ibid., p. 28.

[10] Ibid., p. 21.

[11] Ibid., p. 22.

[12] Ibid., pp. 21–22.

[13] Ibid., p. 28.

[14] Ibid., p. 21.

[15] Ibid., p. 28.

[16] Ibid., p. 20.

[17] Ibid., p. 28.

[18] Ibid., p. 21.

[19] Ibid.

[20] Ibid., p. 20.

[21] *Men Who Rape: The Psychology of the Offender* (New York: Plenum Press, 1979), p. 178. Emphasis mine.

[22] *Uniform Crime Reports* (annual); Donald Mulvihill and Melvin Tumin, *Crimes of Violence: A Staff Report Submitted to the National Commission on the Causes and Prevention of Violence* (Washington, D.C.: Government Printing Office, 1969), Vol. 11.

[23] Milton S. Eisenhower, *To Establish Justice, To Insure Domestic Tranquility.* Final Report of the National Commission on Causes and Prevention of Violence (Washington, D.C.: U.S. Government Printing Office, December 1969).

[24] *Behind Closed Doors* (Garden City, New York: Anchor Press/Doubleday), p. 134.

[25] Sedelle Katz and Mary Ann Mazur, *Understanding the Rape Victim* (New York: John Wiley, 1979), p. 101.

11   Why Men Rape Their Wives

[1] R. Emerson Dobash and Russell Dobash, *Violence Against Wives* (New York: The Free Press, 1979), p. 56.

[2] Flyer published by the National Clearinghouse on Marital Rape, P.O. Box 9245, Berkeley, California 94709.

[3] Neil Malamuth, "Rape Proclivity Among Males," *Journal of Social Issues*, Vol. 37, No. 4 (December 1981).

[4] "Testing Hypotheses Regarding Rape: Exposure to Sexual Violence, Sex Differences and the 'Normality' of Rapists," *Journal of Research in Personality*, Vol. 14, p. 124.

[5] A. Nicholas Groth, *Men Who Rape: The Psychology of the Offender* (New York: Plenum Press, 1979), p. 177.

[6] Ibid., pp. 176–77.

[7] "An Integrated Treatment Program for Rapists," in R. T. Rada (ed.), *Clinical Aspects of the Rapist* (New York: Grune & Stratton, 1978), p. 195.

[8] Ibid., pp. 195–96.

[9] Shere Hite, *The Hite Report on Male Sexuality* (New York: Alfred Knopf, 1981), p. 731.

[10] Ibid., p. 730.

[11] Ibid., p. 720.

[12] Ibid., p. 730.

[13] Ibid.

[14] Ibid.

[15] Ibid., pp. 731–32.

[16] Ibid., p. 733.

[17] Ibid.

[18] Ibid., p. 734.

[19] Ibid., p. 732.

[20] Ibid., p. 730.

[21] "Study Shows Men Rape Wives and Strangers for Same Reasons: Anger, Power and Sadism," *New Women's Times*, Vol. 6, No. 6 (1980). In *Men Who Rape*, Groth does not use these three categories in his brief analysis of wife rape. Instead he differentiates five motives: when sex is equated with power; or with love and affection; or with virility; or with debasement; or when it is seen as a panacea, as when it is seen as the solution to any marital problem (pp. 178–79).

[22] *Men Who Rape*, p. 180.

[23] Ibid.

[24] David Finkelhor and Kersti Yllo, "Forced Sex in Marriage: A Preliminary Report" (Paper presented at American Sociological Association Meetings, New York, August 1980).

[25] Ibid., p. 3.

[26] Ibid., pp. 3–4.

[27] Kersti Yllo, "Types of Marital Rape: Three Case Studies" (Paper presented at the Na-

tional Conference for Family Violence Researchers, University of New Hampshire, July 21–24, 1981).

[28] Finkelhor and Yllo, "Forced Sex in Marriage," pp. 25–26.

[29] Ibid.

[30] Yllo, "Types of Marital Rape."

[31] Irene Frieze, "Causes and Consequences of Marital Rape" (Paper presented at the American Psychological Association Meetings, Montreal, Canada, September 1980).

[32] Morton Hunt, "Legal Rape," *Family Circle*, January 9, 1979, p. 38.

[33] *Against Our Will* (New York: Simon and Schuster, 1975), p. 38.

[34] Ibid.

12   Abusive Husbands, Alcohol and Other Drugs

[1] Wives spontaneously mentioned that their husbands were drinking at the time (or at least at one of the times) in almost one-third (32 percent) of the cases of *wife beating* (as distinguished from wife rape). In only 6 percent of the wife rapes did the respondents mention that they themselves were drinking at the time, and in 3 per cent of these cases it appears that their husbands deliberately gave them alcohol in order to facilitate the rape.

[2] Irene Frieze, "The Effects of Alcohol on Marital Violence" (Paper presented at the American Psychological Association Meetings, Montreal, Canada, September 1980).

[3] Ibid.

[4] Ibid., p. 6.

[5] Ibid., p. 20.

[6] Ibid., p. 20 and Table 8.

[7] Ibid., p. 19.

[8] Ibid., p. 21.

13   The Victims of Wife Rape

[1] Irene Frieze, Jaime Knoble, Gretchen Zomnir, and Carol Washburn, "Types of Battered Women" (Paper presented at Association for Women in Psychology Meetings, Santa Monica, California, March 1980), p. 4.

[2] Lenore E. Walker, *The Battered Woman* (New York: Harper & Row, 1979), p. 31.

[3] Irene Frieze, "Causes and Consequences of Marital Rape" (Paper presented at the American Psychological Association Meetings, Montreal, Canada, September 1980), p. 3.

[4] Ibid.

[5] Ibid.; Mildred D. Pagelow, *Woman-Battering: Victims and Their Experiences* (Beverly Hills: Sage Publications, 1981), p. 156; Walker, *The Battered Woman*.

[6] Diana E. H. Russell and Nicole Van de Ven (eds.), *Crimes Against Women* (Millbrae, Ca.: Les Femmes, 1976), p. 40; and Adrienne Rich, "Compulsory Heterosexuality and Lesbian Existence," *Signs: Journal of Women in Culture and Society*, Vol. 5, No. 4 (Summer 1980), p. 631.

[7] Frieze, "Causes and Consequences of Marital Rape," p. 23.

[8] Ibid.

[9] Ibid., p. 25.

[10] Ibid., p. 26.

[11] Ibid., p. 27.

[12] Ibid., p. 23.

[13] Ibid., p. 18.

[14] The findings reported in this paragraph are statistically significant at the .01 level.

[15] This association is statistically significant at $<.05$ level.

[16] The mean number of victims known are 1.64, 1.04, and 0.85 respectively. This association is statistically significant at $<.001$ level.

[17] This association is statistically significant at the .001 level.

[18] For example, see Erin Pizzey, *Scream Quietly or the Neighbors Will Hear* (Baltimore: Pen-

guin Books, 1974); Elaine Hilberman and Kit Munson, "Sixty Battered Women," *Victimology*, Vol. 2, No. 3/4 (1977–1978); and Murray Straus, Richard Gelles, and Suzanne Steinmetz, *Behind Closed Doors* (Garden City, New York: Anchor Press/Doubleday, 1980).

[19] Hilberman and Munson, "Sixty Battered Women," p. 461.

[20] These data on occupation are of particular interest given that researchers Sedelle Katz and Mary Ann Mazur found only one study that reported statistical frequencies on the occupations of victims, and that was a totally unrepresentative study based on victims who responded to an underground questionnaire (*Understanding the Rape Victim* [New York: John Wiley, 1979], p. 43).

[21] This relationship did not quite reach statistical significance at <.05 level.

[22] The Third World and Latin countries are: Aruba—part of the Netherlands' West Indies (1), El Salvador (1), Fiji (1), Iran (2), Jamaica (1), Mexico (2), Nassau (1), Nicaragua (2), Philippines (2), Samoa (1), Sri Lanka (1); and the six non-Third World or Latin countries are: Canada (2), Greece (1), Scotland (1), USSR (2).

[23] Katz and Mazur, *Understanding the Rape Victim*, p. 39.

[24] Donald Mulvihill and Melvin Tumin, *Crimes of Violence: A Staff Report Submitted to the National Commission on the Causes and Prevention of Violence* (Washington, D.C.: Government Printing Office, 1969), Vol. 11, p. 212.

[25] Katz and Mazur, *Understanding the Rape Victim*, p. 38.

[26] Ibid.

[27] Menachem Amir, *Patterns in Forcible Rape* (Chicago: The University of Chicago Press, 1971), p. 101.

[28] This relationship is statistically significant at <.001 level.

[29] This relationship is statistically significant at <.001 level.

[30] Katz and Mazur, *Understanding the Rape Victim*, p. 41.

[31] Mulvihill and Tumin, *Crimes of Violence*, Vol. 11, p. 212.

14   The Trauma of Wife Rape

[1] *Parade*, April 22, 1979, p. 5, cited by Irene Frieze, "Causes and Consequences of Marital Rape" (Paper presented at the American Psychological Association Meetings, Montreal, Canada, September 1980), p. 1.

[2] Gilbert Geis, "Rape-in-Marriage: Law and Law Reform in England, the United States, and Sweden," *Adelaide Law Review*, Vol. 6, No. 2 (June 1978), p. 297. Geis appears to be in agreement with the belief that wife rape is less harmful than rape by non-intimates. For example, he refers to wife rape as involving "acts of a less egregious kind"—less egregious presumably than stranger and acquaintance rape (p. 303). This view seems to be based on Geis' belief that wife rape is less life-threatening. For example, he argues that "there would probably be more general willingness to eliminate affinity clauses if the rape statutes differentiated sharply between more harmful and less harmful acts. . . . [F]eminist rhetoricians tend to concentrate on the sexual ugliness of rape and its chauvinistic hostility to women as a group, whereas rape victims themselves focus overwhelmingly on their fear of death or serious injury" (p. 303). Geis goes on to commend the law reform relating to marital rape in South Australia as pointing "roughly in the right direction of rape reform generally. Given a redefined, more restricted rape offense *tailored to the lesser harm it threatens*" (emphasis mine, p. 303).

[3] Mildred D. Pagelow, *Woman-Battering: Victims and Their Experiences* (Beverly Hills: Sage Publications, 1981), p. 162.

[4] Ibid.

15   Why Some Wives Stay

[1] Lenore E. Walker, *The Battered Woman* (New York: Harper & Row, 1979), p. 46.

[2] Ibid., p. 47.

[3] According to Walker's definition, those women who leave after the first beating, no

matter how severe it was, would not even qualify as battered women. Walker's definition is as follows:

A battered woman is a woman who is repeatedly subjected to any forceful physical or psychological behavior by a man in order to coerce her to do something he wants her to do without any concern for her rights. . . . Furthermore, in order to be classified as a battered woman, the couple must go through the battering cycle at least twice. Any woman may find herself in an abusive relationship with a man once. If it occurs a second time, and she remains in the situation, she is defined as a battered woman (Ibid., p. xv).

This is not only a very cumbersome definition, it is highly problematic because when women don't follow the pattern predicted by her theory, they are, by definition, not regarded as battered women.

[4] Ibid., p. 55.
[5] Ibid., p. 65.
[6] Ibid., p. 67.
[7] Ibid., p. 69.
[8] Research by Inge Broverman *et al.* reveals that clinicians believe a healthy woman has the same characteristics as an unhealthy adult. "Sex-Role Stereotypes and Clinical Judgments of Mental Health," *Journal of Counseling and Clinical Psychology*, Vol. 34 (February 1970).
[9] Irene Frieze, "Causes and Consequences of Marital Rape" (Paper presented at the American Psychological Association Meetings, Montreal, Canada, September 1980), p. 33.
[10] Ibid. Mildred Pagelow and Richard Gelles also both emphasize lack of resources as a major reason for battered wives to stay with their husbands. Pagelow, *Woman-Battering: Victims and Their Experiences* (Beverly Hills: Sage Publications, 1981), p. 133; Gelles, *Family Violence* (Beverly Hills: Sage Publications, 1979), p. 109.
[11] Rochelle Albin argues that "psychiatric theory that places blame for rape on victims, mothers, and wives of the sex offenders" is one of the most striking legacies of the Freudian view of women. Albin refers to these as women precipitation theories. "Psychological Studies of Rape," *Signs: Journal of Women in Culture and Society*, Vol. 3, No. 2 (1977), p. 427.

16   Husbands Who Won't Let Their Wives Go

[1] R. Emerson Dobash and Russell Dobash, *Violence Against Wives* (New York: The Free Press, 1979), p. 68.
[2] Ibid., p. 73.
[3] *Women Who Kill* (New York: Holt, Rinehart and Winston, 1980), p. 299.
[4] For example, Stuart Palmer, "Family Members as Murder Victims," in *Violence in the Family*, edited by Suzanne Steinmetz and Murray Straus (New York: Dodd, Mead & Co., 1974); Teresa Priem, "Marital Rape: What Happens When Women Fight Back," in *New Women's Times*, Vol. 7, No. 5 (1981). Also see Faith McNulty, *The Burning Bed* (New York: Harcourt Brace Jovanovich, 1980).
[5] Bill Shaw, *San Francisco Sunday Examiner*, May 3, 1981.
[6] Jones, *Women Who Kill*. Jones cites as her source an unpublished study by G. Marie Wilt and James Bannon, p. 298.
[7] Ibid., p. 298.

18   Women Who Marry the Men Who Rape Them

[1] Florence Rush, *The Best Kept Secret: Sexual Abuse of Children* (Englewood Cliffs, New Jersey: Prentice-Hall, 1980), p. 32.
[2] Shere Hite, *The Hite Report on Male Sexuality* (New York: Alfred Knopf, 1981), p. 477.
[3] Ibid., p. 334.
[4] Ibid., p. 335.
[5] Ibid., p. 712.

[6] Ibid., p. 718.

[7] See, for example, Menachem Amir, *Patterns in Forcible Rape* (Chicago: The University of Chicago Press, 1971); Diana E. H. Russell, *The Politics of Rape: The Victim's Perspective* (New York: Stein & Day, 1975); Thomas W. McCahill, Linda C. Meyer, and Arthur M. Fischman, *The Aftermath of Rape* (Lexington, Mass.: D. C. Heath and Company, 1979).

[8] Mildred D. Pagelow, *Woman-Battering: Victims and Their Experiences* (Beverly Hills: Sage Publications, 1981), p. 182.

[9] Ibid., p. 194.

19 Lovers and Daughters Are Property Too

[1] *Kiss Daddy Goodnight* (New York: Hawthorn Books, 1978), p. 238.

[2] Ibid., p. 239.

[3] Ibid., pp. 234–35.

[4] For example, see Jennifer James and Jane Meyerding, "Early Sexual Experience as a Factor in Prostitution," *Archives of Sexual Behavior*, Vol. 7, No. 1 (1977).

[5] "Sexual Abuse of Children: A Clinical Spectrum," *American Journal of Orthopsychiatry*, Vol. 48, No. 2 (April 1978), p. 245.

[6] Ibid.

[7] *The Hite Report on Male Sexuality* (New York: Alfred Knopf, 1981), p. 727.

20 Torture and Marriage

[1] *San Francisco Chronicle*, February 2, 1981, p. 20.

[2] *Report on Torture* (London: Gerald Duckworth, 1973), p. 31 and p. 34.

[3] Ibid., p. 32.

[4] Ibid.

[5] *Ithaca Times*, June 11, 1981.

[6] Marty Stoler, Unpublished Reply Brief appealing the conviction of Bernadette Powell, p. 4. On file at marital rape collection, Women's Studies Library, University of Illinois, Urbana, Il. 61807.

[7] Marty Stoler, Unpublished Main Brief appealing the conviction of Bernadette Powell, pp. 29 and 28.

[8] Ibid., p. 30.

[9] Ibid., p. 27.

[10] Stoler, Reply Brief, p. 5.

[11] Stoler, Main Brief, p. 29.

[12] Faith McNulty, *The Burning Bed* (New York: Harcourt Brace and Jovanovich, 1980).

[13] Ibid., p. 174.

[14] Bill Mandel, "His Gun Was Her Escape from a Private Kind of Hell," *San Francisco Chronicle*, June 7, 1981.

[15] William Carlsen, "'Battered Wife' Cleared in Shooting of Husband," *San Francisco Chronicle*, June 10, 1981.

[16] Lenore E. Walker, *The Battered Woman* (New York: Harper & Row, 1979), pp. 120–21.

[17] Ibid., pp. 121–22.

[18] *Sun-Star*, Merced, California, May 29, 1981.

[19] *Sun-Star*, Merced, California, June 5, 1981.

[20] Bruno Bettelheim, "Individual and Mass Behavior in Extreme Situations," in T. M. Newcomb and E. L. Hartley (eds.), *Readings in Social Psychology* (New York: Holt, Rinehart, and Winston, 1947).

[21] George Williamson, "Wife's Grisly Story," *San Francisco Chronicle*, October 11, 1979.

[22] *Report on Torture*, p. 45.

[23] Ibid., p. 46.

[24] Ibid.

[25] Ibid., and p. 25.

[26] Ibid., p. 49.

[27] *Ordeal* (Secaucus, New Jersey: Citadel Press, 1980).

21   Femicide: The Murder of Wives

[1] Diana E. H. Russell and Nicole Van de Ven (eds.), *Crimes Against Women* (Millbrae, Ca.: Les Femmes, 1976), p. 144.

[2] *Uniform Crime Reports,* 1959–1979.

[3] Ibid.

[4] Statistics on the total number of married people for each year were obtained from *Statistical Abstracts.*

[5] *Uniform Crime Reports,* 1980, p. 10. For some unknown reason, the total number of murder victims when broken down by sex (20,591) is slightly different from the total number when not broken down by sex (21,456) (Ibid, pp. 10 and 6 respectively). However, this discrepancy would have little impact on the percentages reported in the text.

[6] "Man's Wives Have A Tragic History," *San Francisco Chronicle,* August 21, 1980.

[7] "Marine to Be Tried for Wife's Rape," *Tri-Valley Herald,* Livermore, California, April 11, 1980.

[8] Ibid.

[9] "Man's Madness: Could 2 Lives Have Been Saved?" *Los Angeles Times,* December 18, 1977.

[10] Ibid. Italics mine.

22   Wives Who Report to the Police

[1] R. Emerson Dobash and Russell Dobash, *Violence Against Wives* (New York: The Free Press, 1979), p. 210.

[2] See for example, Allan G. Johnson, "On the Prevalence of Rape in the United States," *Signs: Journal of Women in Culture and Society,* Autumn 1980.

[3] Del Martin, *Battered Wives* (San Francisco: Glide Publications, 1976), p. 87.

[4] *Behind Closed Doors* (Garden City, New York: Anchor Press/Doubleday, 1980), pp. 232–33.

[5] Martin, *Battered Wives;* Mildred D. Pagelow, *Woman-Battering: Victims and Their Experiences* (Beverly Hills: Sage Publications, 1981); Maria Roy (ed.), *Battered Women: A Psychosociological Study of Domestic Violence* (New York: Van Nostrand Reinhold Company, 1977); Straus *et al., Behind Closed Doors;* Dobash, *Violence Against Wives.*

[6] Susan Brownmiller, *Against Our Will: Men, Women and Rape* (New York: Simon and Schuster, 1975).

[7] Thomas W. McCahill, Linda C. Meyer, and Arthur M. Fischman, *The Aftermath of Rape* (Lexington, Mass.: D. C. Heath and Company, 1979), p. 121.

23   How Some Wives Stop the Violence

[1] David Finkelhor and Kersti Yllo, "Forced Sex in Marriage: A Preliminary Report" (Paper presented at American Sociological Association Meetings, New York, August 1980), p. 29.

[2] Ibid.

[3] Ibid.

[4] Ibid., p. 30.

[5] Ibid.

[6] Irene Frieze, "Causes and Consequences of Marital Rape" (Paper presented at the American Psychological Association Meetings, Montreal, Canada, September 1980), p. 21.

[7] Ibid., pp. 29–31.

[8] Ibid., p. 32.

[9] Lee Bowker and Kristine MacCallum, "Women Who Have Beaten Wife-Beating: A

New Perspective on Victims as Victors" (Paper presented at the American Society of Criminology Meetings, November 6–8, 1980), p. 1.

[10] Ibid.

[11] Mildred D. Pagelow, *Woman-Battering: Victims and Their Experiences* (Beverly Hills: Sage Publications, 1981), Chapter 5.

24 Wife Rape in Other Countries

[1] Diana E. H. Russell and Nicole Van de Ven (eds.), *Crimes Against Women* (Millbrae, Ca.: Les Femmes, 1976).

[2] Ibid., pp. 110–39.

[3] R. A. LeVine's article on the rape of Gusii Women is a notable exception; "Gusii Sex Offenses: A Study in Social Control," *American Anthropologist*, Vol. 61 (December 1959).

[4] An International Feminist Network was initiated during the International Tribunal on Crimes Against Women. It serves as an effective means of mobilizing international feminist support for particular campaigns, struggles, or trials occurring in different countries. Further information about this important organization can be obtained from IFN, c/o Isis Suisse, C.P. 50 (Cornavin) 1211 Geneva 2, Switzerland.

[5] The program was produced by Karla Tonella in the U.S.A., and commissioned by Liz Fell, head of women's programming at the Australian Broadcasting Commission in Australia.

[6] Susan Brownmiller, *Against Our Will: Men, Women and Rape* (New York: Simon and Schuster, 1975), p. 382; Gilbert Geis, "Rape-in-Marriage: Law and Law Reform in England, the United States and Sweden," *Adelaide Law Review*, Vol. 6, No. 2 (June 1978), p. 296.

[7] Geis, "Rape-in-Marriage," Ibid.

[8] Robin Morgan, "The First Feminist Exiles from the U.S.S.R." *Ms. Magazine*, November 1980, p. 108, and personal communication with Tatyana Mamonova.

[9] Ibid.

[10] Geis, "Rape-in-Marriage," p. 297.

[11] Brownmiller, *Against Our Will*, p. 382.

[12] Geis, "Rape-in-Marriage," p. 296.

[13] Ibid.

[14] Anne Summers, "In South Australia Wives Can Charge Husbands with Rape," *Seven Days*, February 28, 1977, p. 37.

[15] Ibid.

[16] Personal communication from Aileen F. Connon, Health Services Co-ordinator, South Australian Health Commission, March 11, 1981.

[17] Ibid.

[18] Doris Lankin, "Sexual Rights in the Marriage Bed," *Jerusalem Post*, October 20, 1980.

[19] "Husband Who Rapes Wife Guilty of Criminal Offence," *Jerusalem Post*, September 26, 1980.

[20] Lankin, "Sexual Rights."

[21] Ibid.

[22] Personal communication, January 31, 1981.

[23] *San Francisco Chronicle*, June 22, 1979.

[24] Ibid.

[25] Personal communication from Dominique Misson.

[26] Personal communication from Magaly Pineda, September 23, 1981.

[27] *Observer*, February 15, 1981, and *Tageszeitung*, February 16, 1981. This article was translated from German into English by Margrit Brückner.

[28] Imogen Seger-Coulborn, "Vergewaltigung in der Ehe" (Rape in Marriage), Unpublished Report (West Germany: Institut für Demoskopie Allensbach, 1976), pp. 1–2. Translated from German into English by Julia Randal.

[29] Ibid.

[30] Unpublished article written for an issue of *Stern*, 1976.

[31] Heidelberg: Kriminalistik Verlag, 1979.

[32] This information is based on a translation of the text by Margrit Brückner.

[33] *Tageszeitung*, March 17, 1981.

[34] Personal communication, 1981.

[35] Information on Norway was sent by Reidun Lauvstad, Turid Steen, and Ellen Anfeldt, members of an organization called Free Legal Aid for Women.

[36] Ibid.

[37] Personal communication, June 25, 1981.

[38] Geis, "Rape-in-Marriage," p. 299.

[39] Ibid.

[40] Ibid.

[41] *New York Post*, July 7, 1981.

[42] Geis, "Rape-in-Marriage," p. 292.

[43] *San Francisco Chronicle*, November 8, 1980.

[44] Ibid.

25   Conclusions and Solutions

[1] *The Subjection of Women* (1869) in *Essays on Sex Equality: John Stuart Mill and Harriet Taylor Mill*, edited by Alice S. Rossi (Chicago: The University of Chicago Press, 1970).

[2] These statistics are discussed in detail in Chapter 8.

[3] Diana E. H. Russell, *The Politics of Rape: The Victim's Perspective* (New York: Stein & Day, 1975). The Chapter on "Rape and the Masculine Mystique" focuses on this issue and offers an explanation for why masculinity is defined in this way.

[4] Amicus brief prepared by Regina Little and Phyllis Gelman, National Center on Women and Family Law, for the State of New Jersey v. Albert Smith, Supreme Court of New Jersey, 1980, p. 1.

[5] For example, see Vincent DeFrancis, *Protecting the Child Victim of Sex Crimes Committed by Adults* (Denver, Colorado: The American Humane Association, Children's Division, 1969); David Finkelhor, *Sexually Victimized Children* (New York: The Free Press, 1979); Florence Rush, *The Best Kept Secret: Sexual Abuse of Children* (Englewood Cliffs, New Jersey: Prentice-Hall, 1980).

[6] Gilbert Geis, "Rape-in-Marriage: Law and Law Reform in England, the United States and Sweden," *Adelaide Law Review*, Vol. 6, No. 2 (June 1978), p. 303.

[7] Susan Barry, "Spousal Rape, the Uncommon Law," *American Bar Association Journal*, September 1980, p. 1088.

[8] Ibid.

[9] Del Martin, Testimony to Assembly Criminal Justice Committee Hearing on AB 546, April 23, 1979, p. 1.

[10] Geis, "Rape-in-Marriage," p. 303.

[11] Del Martin, Unpublished testimony on AB 546, pp. 1–2.

[12] *German Tribune*, October 28, 1979.

Appendix 1

[1] Personal Communication, Laura X, Executive Director of the Clearinghouse.

[2] Cheryl Nordby, "Attorney Wants Husband-Wife Rape Law—But Says He Won't Get It With This Case," *Lakeland Ledger*, Lakeland, March 4, 1980.

[3] Ibid.

[4] Ibid.

[5] Larry Welborn, "Retrial Seen in OC's First 'Wife-Rape' Case," *The Register*, February 18, 1981.

[6] Michael Trihey, "Kern Man Faces Trial Under New Law for Raping Wife," *Californian*, Bakersfield, Ca., July 18, 1980.

[7] Ibid.

[8] Ibid.

[9] "Rape Case Ends in Probation," *Tri-Valley Herald*, Livermore, Ca., June 11, 1980.

[10] Ellen Norman, "Husband Is Jailed for Assaulting His Wife," *Peninsula Times Tribune*, Palo Alto, Ca., May 5, 1980.

[11] Ibid.

[12] *San Francisco Chronicle*, September 22, 1979.

[13] Kay Cooperman, "Husband Ordered to Trial Under New Law," *San Gabriel Valley Tribune*, Covina, Ca., January 25, 1980.

[14] Ibid.

[15] *San Francisco Chronicle*, September 3, 1980.

[16] Ibid., March 19, 1980.

[17] Pat Lakey, "Spousal Rape: A Story of Human Suffering," *Record Searchlight*, Redding, Ca., August 6, 1980.

[18] "Accused Rapist to Testify," *Times*, Hammond, Indiana, February 3, 1981.

[19] "Man Facing Trial in Rape of Wife," *Burlington Times*, Burlington, New Jersey, April 19, 1980.

[20] Elaine Warren, "Man May Face State's First Wife-Rape Charges," *Los Angeles Herald Examiner*, January 7, 1980.

[21] *Trenton Times*, Trenton, New Jersey, February 2, 1980.

[22] *Burlington Times*, Burlington, New Jersey, April 19, 1980.

[23] Karen Wolfson, "Pinellas Marital Rape Case May Test State's Law," *The Tampa Tribune*, April 22, 1980.

[24] Karen Wolfson, "Largo Man Pleads Guilty to Wife's Charges," *The Tampa Tribune*, April 23, 1980.

[25] Ruth O'Bryan, "Wife Accuses Mate of Rape, Dangling Her from Span," *Daily News*, Philadelphia, February 28, 1980.

[26] *San Francisco Examiner*, January 3, 1981.

[27] Teresa Priem, "Marital Rape: What Happens When Women Fight Back?," *New Women's Times*, Vol. VII, No. 5, 1981.

[28] Ibid., p. 20.

SELECTED BIBLIOGRAPHY
ON WIFE RAPE†
(EXPANDED)

Only those works that focus on wife rape, or that include some discussion or experience of it, are cited here. Numerous bibliographies are now available on the more general topics of non-marital rape and wife beating.

"Abrogation of a Common Law Sanctuary for Husband Rapists: *Warren v. State.*" *Detroit Criminal Law Review* (Summer 1986).

Adamo, Sonya. "The Injustice of the Marital Rape Exemption: A Survey of Common Law Countries." *The American University Journal of International Law and Policy,* vol. 4, no. 3 (1989).

"All Marital Rape Outlawed by State Court of Appeals." *New York Law Journal,* vol. 192 (December 1984).

Amdur, Richard. "Conjugal Rape." *Cosmopolitan* (February 1981).

Anderson, Cerisse. "Marital Exemption Denied in Sex Case." *New York Law Journal,* vol. 201 (March 1989).

"Annual Review of Family Law." *Clearinghouse Review,* vol. 20 (January 1987).

Barden, J. C. "Confronting the Moral and Legal Issue of Marital Rape." *New York Times* (June 1, 1981), p. B5.

———. "Marital Rape: Drive for Tougher Laws Is Pressed." *New York Times* (May 13, 1987).

Barry, Susan. "Spousal Rape, the Uncommon Law." *American Bar Association Journal,* vol. 66 (September 1980).

Barshis, Victoria R. G. "The Question of Marital Rape." *Women's Studies International Forum,* vol. 6, no. 4 (1983).

Bart, Pauline B. "Rape Doesn't End With a Kiss." *Viva* (June 1975).

Bayer, Edward. *Rape Within Marriage: A Moral Analysis Delayed.* Lanham, Maryland: University Press of America, 1985.

Bearrows, Thomas. "Abolishing the Marital Exemption for Rape: A Statutory Proposal." *University of Illinois Law Review,* vol. 1983 (1983).

Benedict, Helen. *Recovery: How to Survive Sexual Assault for Women, Men, Teenagers, Their Friends, and Families.* Garden City, New York: Doubleday, 1985.

Bidwell, Lee, and Priscilla White. "The Family Context of Marital Rape." *Journal of Family Violence,* vol. 1, no. 3 (1986).

Bienen, Leigh. "Mistakes." *Philosophy and Public Affairs,* vol. 7, no. 3 (1978).

†I would like to thank the following people for their assistance in compiling this selected bibliography: Jacquelyn Campbell, Roberta Harmes, Meg Gallucci, Dan Guggenheim, Sarah Troutt, and most especially, Laura X. I am also indebted to others whose bibliographies I found useful, for example, Bobbie Ogletree, Nancy Phares, and Kelley Williams.

————. "Rape III: National Developments in Rape Reform Legislation." *Women's Rights Law Reporter*, vol. 6, no. 3 (1980).

————. "Rape IV: Rape Laws of the 50 States." Special Supplement to *Women's Rights Law Reporter*, vol. 6, no. 3 (1980).

————. "Rape Reform Legislation in the US: A Look at Some Practical Effects." *Victimology*, vol. 8, no. 1–2 (1983).

Blay-Cohen, Sue, and Dina L. Coster. "Marital Rape in California: For Better or Worse." *San Fernando Valley Review*, vol. 8, annual edition (1980).

Bogdanovitch, Peter. *The Killing of the Unicorn: Dorothy Stratton (1960–1980)*. New York: William Morrow, 1984.

Bowker, Lee H. *Beating Wife-Beating*. Lexington, Massachusetts: Lexington Books, 1983a.

————. "Marital Rape: A Distinct Syndrome?" *Social Casework: The Journal of Contemporary Social Work*, vol. 64 (1983b).

Braverman, Mara. *Marital Rape*. Cincinnati: Pamphlet Publications, 1979.

————. "Prosecution May Be Difficult Under New Marital Rape Law." *The Western Law Journal* (January–Feburary 1980).

Browne, Angela. *When Battered Women Kill*. New York: Free Press, 1987.

Brownmiller, Susan. *Against Our Will: Men, Women and Rape*. New York: Simon and Schuster, 1975.

Burt, Charles D. "The Crime of Marital Rape." *Family Advocate*, vol. 7, no. 4 (1985).

Calderon, Elaine. "The National Clearinghouse on Marital Rape: Acquiring Material on Something that Does Not Legally Exist in Most States." *Library Acquisitions: Practice and Theory*, vol. 5 (1981).

Campbell, Jacquelyn C. "Nursing Research Helps Change Law." Submitted for publication, June 1988.*

————. "Women's Responses to Sexual Abuse in Intimate Relationships." *Health Care for Women International*, vol. 8 (1989).

Campbell, Jacquelyn C., and Peggy Alford. "The Dark Consequences of Marital Rape." *American Journal of Nursing*, vol. 89 (1989).

Caringella-MacDonald, Susan. "Parallels and Pitfalls: The Aftermath of Legal Reform for Sexual Assault, Marital Rape, and Domestic Violence Victims." *Journal of Interpersonal Violence*, vol. 3, no. 2 (1988).

Carmichael, Vicki L. "Constitutional Law: The Marital Exemption in the Rape and Sodomy Statutes of the New York Penal Law and the Gender Exemption in the Rape Statute Are Unconstitutional as Violations of the Equal Protection Clause of the Fourteenth Amendment." *Journal of Family Law*, vol. 24 (October 1985).

Celarier, Michelle. "I Kept Thinking Maybe I Could Help Him." *In These Times* (January 10–16, 1979).

Chappell, Duncan, and Peter Sallman. "Rape in Marriage Legislation in South Australia: Anatomy of a Reform." *Australian Journal of Forensic Science*, vol. 14 (1982).

*All asterisked items in this bibliography are available from the Women's Studies Library at the University of Illinois at Urbana Champaign, 415 Library, 1408 West Gregory Drive, Urbana, Ill. 61807. The telephone number specifically for this collection of materials on wife rape is (217) 244-1024.

Chase, Sherri. "Outlawing Marital Rape: How We Did It and Why." *Aegis*, vol. 35 (Summer 1982).*

Christensen, Mark. "The Honeymooners: Do Wife-Rape Laws Rape Husbands, Too?" *Oui Magazine* (September 1, 1979).

Clancy, Thomas K. "Equal Protection Considerations of the Spousal Sexual Assault Exclusion." *New England Law Review*, vol. 16, no. 1 (1980–81).

Coady, Carol. Testimony on rape in marriage presented before the House of Representatives Congressional Hearings on HR 4876, September 12, 1984.*

Coen, Geri. "The Marital Rape Exemption: Time for Legal Reform." *Tulsa Law Journal*, vol. 21 (Winter 1985).

Cole, Catherine A. "Husband and Wife—Where the Wife Unilaterally Revoked Her Implied Consent to Marital Sex by Clearly Manifesting an Intent to Terminate the Marital Relationship by Living Separate and Apart from Her Husband, the Husband Can Be Found Guilty of Spousal Rape." *Journal of Family Law*, vol. 23 (April 1985).

Comment† "Rape and Battery Between Husband and Wife." *Stanford Law Review*, vol. 6 (1954).

Comment. "Rape by a Husband on Wife." *Criminal Law Journal*, vol. 10, no. 4 (1986).

"Conjugal Violence: Nursing Intervention for the Wives." *Nursing Quebec*, Supplement (July–August 1987).

Corns, Christopher T. "Liability of Husbands for Rape-in-Marriage—The Victorian Position." *Criminal Law Journal*, vol. 7, no. 2 (1983).

Cowley, David. "Indecent Assault—The Scope of Marital Consent." *Journal of Criminal Law*, vol. 53 (February 1989).

Creyke, R. M. "Indecent Assault: Sexual Intercourse with Wife Without Her Consent—Parties Separated—Whether Husband Can Rape Wife—Criminal Code Act." *Criminal Law Journal*, vol. 7 (October 1983).

"Criminal Law—Rape—Husband Cannot Be Guilty of Raping His Wife." *Dickinson Law Review*, vol. 82 (1978).

Cunliffe, Ian. "Consent and Sexual Offences Law Reform in New South Wales." *Criminal Law Journal*, vol. 8 (October 1984).

Daane, Diane M. "Are Rape Laws Changing." Paper presented at the Academy of Criminal Justice Sciences, San Francisco, April 1988.*

Dabney, Michael. "Spousal Law Held Constitutional." *Pennsylvania Law Journal-Reporter*, vol. 9 (December 8, 1986).

D'Amour, Denise M. "Criminal Law—New York Court Abrogates Marital Rape Exemption as a Violation of Equal Protection." *Suffolk University Law Review*, vol. 19 (Summer 1985).

Davis, Sherri. "Marital Rape: The Legislative Battle." *The Colonial Lawyer*, vol. 15, no. 1 (1986).

de Cardenas, Susana C. "La Violacion en el Matrimonio." *Revista Juridica de la Universidad de Puerto Rico*, vol. 53 (Fall 1983).

De Mott, Benjamin. "Criminal Intimacies." *Psychology Today* (August 1982).

DiCarlo, Melinda S. "The Marital Rape Exemption in Pennsylvania: With This Ring. . . ." *Dickinson Law Review*, vol. 86 (1978).

---

†Student authors of "notes" or "comments" in law journals are still not permitted to have their names published in this male dominated profession.

Doron, Julie Blackman. "Conflict and Violence in Intimate Relationships: Focus on Marital Rape." Paper presented at the American Sociological Association Meetings, New York, August 1980.*

Drucker, Dennis. "The Common Law Does Not Support a Marital Exemption for Forcible Rape." *Women's Rights Law Reporter* (Rutgers), vol. 5, no. 2–3 (1979).

Duffy, Regan J. "Abrogation of a Common Law Sanctuary for Husband Rapists." *Detroit College of Law Review* (Summer 1986).

Elias, Susan. *Rape in Intimate Relationships: Guidelines for Helping the Victim.* Womansource, 1989. [P.O. Box 3432, Dayton, Ohio 45401]

English, Peter. "The Husband Who Rapes His Wife." *New Law Journal,* vol. 126 (1976).

"Expansion of the Marital Rape Exemption." *Woman's Advocate: National Center on Women and Family Law Newsletter,* vol. 1, no. 2 (July 1980).

Faulk, M. "Sexual Factors in Marital Violence." *Medical Aspects of Human Sexuality,* vol. 11 (October 1977).

Field, Hubert, and Leigh Bienen. *Jurors and Rape: A Study of Psychology and the Law.* Lexington, Massachusetts: Lexington Books, 1980.

Finkelhor, David. "Marital Rape: The Misunderstood Crime." In *National Conference on Domestic Violence: Proceedings,* vol. 1, ed. Suzanne E. Hatty. Canberra: Australian Institute of Criminology, 1986.

Finkelhor, David, and Kersti Yllo. "Forced Sex in Marriage: A Preliminary Research Report." *Crime and Delinquency,* vol. 34 (1982).

———. "Rape in Marriage: A Sociological View." In *The Dark Side of Families,* ed. David Finkelhor, Richard Gelles, Gerald Hotaling, and Murray Straus. Beverly Hills, California: Sage Publications, 1983.

———. *License to Rape: Sexual Abuse of Wives.* New York: Free Press, 1985.

———. "The Shocking Story of Marital Rape." *Woman's Day,* July 23, 1985.

Foat, Ginny. *Never Guilty, Never Free.* New York: Ballantine Books, 1985.

"For Better or for Worse: Marital Rape." *Northern Kentucky Law Review,* vol. 15 (1988).

Forte, A. D. M. "Marital Rape: A Cautionary Note." *Law Quarterly Review,* vol. 99 (October 1983).

Freeman, Michael D. A. "'But If You Can't Rape Your Wife, Who[m] Can You Rape?': The Marital Rape Exemption Reexamined." *Family Law Quarterly,* vol. 15, no. 1 (1981).

———. "Doing His Best to Sustain the Sanctity of Marriage." *Sociological Review Monograph,* vol. 31 (1985).

Frieze, Irene. "Investigating the Causes and Consequences of Marital Rape." *Signs: Journal of Women in Culture and Society,* vol. 8, no. 3 (Spring 1983).

Geis, Gilbert. "Lord Hale: Witches and Rape." *British Journal of Law and Society,* vol. 5 (1978).

———. "Rape-in-Marriage: Law and Law Reform in England, the United States, and Sweden." *Adelaide Law Review,* vol. 6, no. 2 (1978).

———. "Rape and Marriage: Historical and Cross-Cultural Considerations." Paper presented at the annual meetings of the American Sociological Association, New York, August 1980.*

Gelles, Richard J. "Power, Sex, and Violence: The Case of Marital Rape." *The Family Coordinator,* vol. 26, no. 4 (October 1977).

———. *Family Violence.* Beverly Hills, California: Sage Publications, 1979.

Glasgow, Jan M. "The Marital Rape Exemption: Legal Sanction of Spouse Abuse." *Journal of Family Law,* vol. 18 (1980).

Gonving, Michael J. "Spousal Exemption to Rape." *Marquette Law Review,* vol. 65 (1981).

Goodman, Ellen. "When Husbands Assault Wives." *Boston Globe,* January 3, 1979.

Griffin, Moira K. "In 44 States, It's Legal to Rape Your Wife." *Student Lawyer,* vol. 9, no. 1 (1980).

Grosfeld, Sharon. "Rape Within Marriage: A Sociological and Historical Analysis." Paper presented at the meetings of the Society for the Study of Social Problems, August 1980.*

Groth, A. Nicholas, and Thomas S. Gary. "Marital Rape." *Medical Aspects of Human Sexuality,* vol. 15, no. 3 (1981).

Hall, Ruth, Selma James, and Judith Kertesz. *The Rapist Who Pays the Rent* (pamphlet). Bristol, England: Falling Wall Press, 2nd edition, 1984.

Hall, Ruth. *Ask Any Woman.* Bristol, England: Falling Wall Press, 1985.

Hanneke, Christine R., and Nancy M. Shields. "Marital Rape: Implications for the Helping Professions." *Social Casework: Journal of Contemporary Social Work,* vol. 66 (1985).

Hanneke, Christine R., Nancy M. Shields, and G. J. McCall. "Assessing the Prevalence of Marital Rape." *Journal of Interpersonal Violence,* vol. 1, no. 3 (1986).

Harman, John D. "Consent, Harm, and Marital Rape." *Journal of Family Law,* vol. 22 (April 1984).

Helmken, Dierk. *Vergewaltigung in der Ehe.* Heidelberg, West Germany: Kriminalistik Verlag, 1979.

Hermann, Dianne. "Rape and Marriage: Public Policy Implications of the Spousal Exemption in the Rape Laws." Paper presented at the meeting of the Northeastern Political Science Association, Mount Pocono, Pennsylvania, Nov. 10–12, 1977.

Hilberman, Elaine, and Kit Munson. "Sixty Battered Women." *Victimology,* vol. 2, no. 3/4 (1977–78).

Hilf, Michael. "Marital Privacy and Spousal Rape." *New England Law Review,* vol. 16 (1981).

Hite, Shere. *The Hite Report on Male Sexuality.* New York: Alfred Knopf, 1981.

Holtzman, Elizabeth. "The Right to Rape." *Glamour* (September 1986).

———. Testimony addressing "Women, Violence, and the Law" before the House of Representatives Select Committee on Children, Youth, and Families, September 16, 1987.*

Hunt, Morton. "Legal Rape." *Family Circle* (January 9, 1979).

"Husband Cannot Be Guilty of Raping His Wife." *Dickinson Law Review,* vol. 82 (1978).

"Husband Convicted of Raping Wife." *Response to Family Violence and Sexual Assault,* vol. 3, no. 3 (1979).

Hutchings, Nancy, ed. *Violent Family: Victimization of Women and Children and Elders.* New York: Human Sciences Press, 1988.

Jeffords, Charles R., and R. Thomas Dull. "Demographic Variations in Attitudes towards Marital Rape Immunity." *Journal of Marriage and the Family,* vol. 44, no. 3 (1982).

Jeffords, Charles R. "Prosecutorial Discretion in Cases of Marital Rape." *Victimology*, vol. 9 (1984).

Jonas, George. "Rape and Marriage Are Not Like Horse and Carriage." *Canadian Lawyer*, vol. 3, no. 2 (1979).

Jones, Ann. *Everyday Death: The Case of Bernadette Powell*. New York: Holt, Rinehart and Winston, 1985.

Kaganas, Felicity. "Rape in Marriage: Developments in South African Law." *International and Comparative Law Quarterly*, vol. 35 (April 1986).

Keeler, James W. "Rape by Husbands More Common than Thought." *Bench & Bar of Minnesota*, vol. 37 (July–August 1980).

Kelly, D., and R. S. Shiels. "Marital Rape in Scots Law." *Journal of the Forensic Science Society*, vol. 28 (July–August 1988).

Kelly, Liz. *Surviving Sexual Violence*. Cambridge, England: Polity Press, 1988.

Kilpatrick, D. G., C. L. Best, B. E. Saunders, and L. J. Veronen. "Rape in Marriage and Dating Relationship: How Bad Is It for Mental Health?" *Annals of the New York Academy of Sciences*, vol. 528 (1988).

Kivett, Lisa. "Sexual Assault: The Case for Removing the Spousal Exemption from Texas Law." *Baylor Law Review*, vol. 38 (Fall 1986).

Klatt, Michael R. "Rape in Marriage: The Law in Texas and the Need for Reform." *Baylor Law Review*, vol. 32 (1980).

Knapman, Lynne, and J. C. Smith. "Rape of Wife by Husband—Separation—Termination of Implicit Consent of Wife—Non-molestation Injunction Ended." *Criminal Law Review* (March 1986).

———. "Indecent Assault Upon Wife—Extent of Consent Implied by Marriage." *Criminal Law Review* (February 1988).

Lanham, David. "Hale: Misogyny and Rape." *Criminal Law Journal*, vol. 7, no. 3 (1983).

Lazansky, Elyse. "1986 Update on Marital Rape Exemption Law." *The Women's Advocate: Newsletter of the National Center on Women and Family Law*," vol. 7, no. 5 (1986).

Lee, Rana. Testimony addressing "Women, Violence, and the Law" before the House of Representatives Select Committee on Children, Youth, and Families, September 16, 1987.*

LeGrand, Camille. "Rape and Rape Laws: Sexism in Society and Law." *California Law Review*, vol. 61 (1973).

Lewis, Bonnie. "Wife Abuse and Marital Rape in a Clinical Population." Paper presented at the Second Family Violence Research Conference, University of New Hampshire, August 7–10, 1984.

Lipsman, Julie A. "Criminal Law: Domestic Violence." *1985 Annual Survey of American Law* (October 1986).

Livneh, Ernst. "On Rape and the Sanctity of Matrimony." *Israel Law Review*, vol. 2, no. 3 (1967).

Lovelace, Linda. *Ordeal*. Secaucus, New Jersey: Citadel Press, 1980.

———. *Out of Bondage*. Secaucus, New Jersey: Lyle Stuart, 1986.

Maidment, Susan. "Rape Between Spouses: A Case for Reform." *Family Law*, vol. 8 (1978).

"Marital Rape and Related Offenses." *University of Richmond Law Review*, vol. 20 (1986).

"Marital Rape Exemption: People v. Liberta." *New York University Law Journal*, vol. 52 (December 27, 1984).

"The Marital Rape Exemption: Time for Legal Reform." *Tulsa Law Journal*. vol. 21 (1985).

"The Marital Rape Exemption, Article 52." *SIECUS Report* (*Sex Information and Educational Council of the United States*), vol. 1, no. 6 (July 1978).

"The Marital Rape Exemption in Pennsylvania: With this Ring. . . ." *Dickinson Law Review*, vol. 86 (Fall 1981).

Martin, Sheila S. Testimony addressing "Women, Violence, and the Law" before the House of Representatives Select Committee on Children, Youth, and Families, September 16, 1987.*

Matthews, Paul. "Marital Rape." *Family Law*, vol. 10 (1980).

McFadyen, Joanna L. "Inter-Spousal Rape: The Need for Law Reform." In *Family Violence: An International and Interdisciplinary Study*, ed. John M. Eekelaar and Sanford N. Katz. Toronto, Canada: Butterworth, 1978.

McLaughlin, Kenneth. "Criminal Law—Sexual Battery—No Interspousal Exemption from Prosecution under Florida Sexual Battery Statute." *Florida State University Law Review*, vol. 10 (1982).

McNulty, Faith. *The Burning Bed: The True Story of Francine Hughes—A Beaten Wife who Rebelled*. New York: Harcourt Brace and Jovanovich, 1979.

Mettger, Zak. "A Case of Rape: Forced Sex in Marriage." *Response*, vol. 5, no. 2 (March–April 1982).

Mitra, Charlotte L. ". . . For She Has No Right or Power to Refuse Her Consent." *Criminal Law Review* (September 1979).

Morris, Jeannie. "The Marital Rape Exemption." *Loyola Law Review*, vol. 27, no. 2 (Spring 1981).

Nadler, Rae. "She [Greta Rideout] Called It Rape." *Hartford Courant* (February 27, 1979).

National Clearinghouse on Marital and Date Rape. State Law Chart. Unpublished sheet, Berkeley, California (updated January 1, 1990).* [P.O. Box 9245, Berkeley, CA 94709. Cost: $2.00.]

O'Donnell, William J. "Consensual Marital Sodomy and Marital Rape—The Role of the Law and the Role of the Victim." Paper presented at the Annual Meeting of the Academy of Criminal Justice Sciences, 1980.*

Okun, Lewis. *Woman Abuse*. New York: State University of New York Press, 1986.

Ominsky, Harria. "TV, Wives, Cows All Breathe Easier." *Pennsylvania Law Journal-Reporter*, vol. 8 (January 7, 1985).

Orchard, Gerald. "Sexual Violation: The Rape Law Reform Legislation." *New Zealand Universities Law Review*, vol. 12 (June 1986).

Paetow, Barbara. *Vergewaltigung in der Ehe: Eine Strafrechtsvergleichende Untersuchung unter Besonderer Berucksichtigung des Rechts der Vereinigten Staaten von Amerika*. Freiburg, West Germany: Max-Planck-Institut für Auslandisches und Internationales Strafrecht, 1987.

Page, Barbara. "Marital Rape Banned: Sex Crimes Reforms in South Australia." *Ms. Magazine* (August 1977).

Pagelow, Mildred D. *Woman-Battering: Victims and Their Experiences*. Beverly Hills, California: Sage Publications, 1981.

———. *Family Violence*. New York: Praeger, 1984.

———. "Marital Rape." In *Handbook of Family Violence*, ed. V. van Hasselt, Morrison, et al., New York: Plenum, 1988.

Pennsylvania Commission on the Status of Women. "Marital Rape Fact Sheet." Unpublished sheet (May 1987).*

Priem, Teresa. "Marital Rape: What Happens When Women Fight Back?" *New Women's Times*, vol. 7, no. 5 (1981).*

"Rape and Battery Between Husband and Wife." *Stanford Law Review*, vol. 6 (July 1954).

"Rape by Husband on Wife." *Criminal Law Journal*, vol. 10, no. 4 (1986).

Reskin, Lauren Rubenstein. "New York Abolishes the Marital Rape Exemption." *American Bar Association Journal*, vol. 71 (April 1985).

———. "No Marital Rape Exemption in Georgia." *American Bar Association Journal*, vol. 72 (March 1, 1986).

Rickenberg, Monica, and Joanne Schulman. "Florida, New York, and Virginia Courts Declare Marital Rape a Crime." *Clearinghouse Review*, vol. 18 (November 1984).

"The Rideout Trial: A Selected Summary." Unpublished paper. Berkeley, California: Women's History Research Center (August 1980).*

Riley, John. "Women's Rights Advocates Praise Marital Rape Ruling." *The National Law Journal*, vol. 7 (January 1985).

Roca, Santiago M. "Breves Comentarios en Torno a la Inmunidad Concedida al Marido para Violar a la Esposa, en el Articulo 99 del Codigo Penal de Puerto Rico." *Revista de Derecho Puertorriqueno*, vol. 21 (January–June 1982).

Ruby, Susan. "Problems of Convicting a Husband for the Rape of His Wife." *Nova Law Journal*, vol. 9 (Winter 1985).

Russell, Diana E. H. *The Politics of Rape: The Victim's Perspective*. New York: Stein & Day, 1975.

Sagarin, Edward. "Rape of One's Wife." *Medical Aspects of Human Sexuality*, vol. 12, no. 2 (1978).

Salveson, Michael N. "Sexism and the Common Law: Spousal Rape in Virginia." *George Mason University Law Review*, vol. 8, no. 2 (Spring 1986).

Sasko, Helen, and Deborah Sesek. "Rape Reform Legislation." *Cleveland State Law Review*, vol. 24 (1975).

Schiff, Arthur F. "*State of Oregon* v. *Rideout*—Can Husband Rape Wife?" *Annual Medical Trial Technique Quarterly*, vol. 26 (1980).

———. "Husband versus Wife: Rape." *Journal of Forensic Science Society*, vol. 27 (May–June 1987).

Schorsch, E. "Vergenwaltigung in der Ehe." *Journal Beitrage zur Sexual Forschung*, vol. 62 (1987).

Schulman, Joanne. "The Marital Rape Exemption in the Criminal Law." *Clearinghouse Review*, vol. 14, no. 6 (1980).

———. "Battered Women Score Major Victories in New Jersey and Massachusetts Marital Rape Cases." *Clearinghouse Review*, vol. 15 (1981).

Schultz, Sandra L. "Marital Exemption to Rape: Past, Present and Future." *Detroit College Law Review*, vol. 11 (Summer 1978).

Schwartz, Martin. "The Spousal Exemption for Criminal Rape Prosecution." *Vermont Law Review*, vol. 7 (Spring 1982).

———. "Domestic Violence and Marital Rape." Paper presented at the Third Annual Conference on Domestic Violence in the 80s. Columbus, Ohio, May 12, 1989.*

Schwartz, Martin, and Gerald T. Slatin. "The Law on Marital Rape: How Do Marxists Explain Its Persistence." *ALSA Forum*, vol. 8 (Spring 1984).

Scutt, Jocelynne A. "Consent in Rape: The Problem of the Marriage Contract." *Monash University Law Review*, vol. 3, no. 4 (1977).

——. "To Love, Honour and Rape with Impunity: Wife as Victim of Rape and the Criminal Law." In Hans J. Schneider, ed., *The Victim in International Perspective*. New York: Walter de Gruyter, 1982.

——. "Marital Rape." In *Even in the Best of Homes: Violence in the Family*, ed. Jocelynne A. Scutt. Melbourne, Australia: Penguin, 1983.

——. "United or Divided?: Women Inside and Women Outside Against Male Lawmakers in Australia." *Women's Studies International Forum*, vol. 8, no. 1 (1985).

Seger-Coulborn, Imogen. "Vergewaltigung in der Ehe." [Rape in Marriage] Unpublished report. West Germany: Institut für Demoskopie Allensbach, 1976.

Seine, Charles. "Criminal Law—Rape—Husband Cannot be Guilty of Raping His Wife. *State* v. *Smith* (1977)." *Dickinson Law Review*, vol. 82 (1978).

"Sexual Assault: The Case for Removing the Spousal Exemption from Texas Law." *Baylor Law Review*, vol. 38 (1986).

Shields, Nancy M., and Christine R. Hanneke. "Battered Wives' Reactions to Marital Rape." In *The Dark Side of Families*, ed. Richard Gelles, Gerald Hotaling, Murray Straus, and David Finkelhor. Beverly Hills, California: Sage Publications, 1983.

——. "Comparing the Psychological Impact of Marital and Stranger Rape." Paper presented at the National Conference for Family Violence Researchers, Durham, New Hampshire, 1987.*

Siller, Sidney. "'Wife Rape'—Who Really Gets Screwed." *Penthouse* (April 1983).

Slovenko, Ralph. "The Marital Rape Exemption." *Victimology*, vol. 4 (1979).

Sprey, Jetse. "Editorial Comments." *Journal of Marriage and the Family*, vol. 47, no. 4 (1985).

Star, Barbara. "Q & A: Why Husbands Resort to Raping Their Wives." *U.S. Magazine*, vol. 2, no. 23 (March 6, 1979).

Stecich, Marianne. "The Marital Rape Exemption." *New York University Law Review*, vol. 52 (May 1977).

"Study Shows Men Rape Wives and Strangers for Same Reasons: Anger, Power and Sadism." *New Women's Times*, vol. 6, no. 6 (1980).*

Thompson, Tracy. "Immunity Limited on Spousal Rape: New Ruling in Georgia." *The National Law Journal*, vol. 8 (November 1985).

Thompson-Haas, Lynn. "Marital Rape: Methods of Helping and Healing." Unpublished paper, School of Social Work, University of Texas, 1987. [Available from Austin Rape Crisis Center, 4326 James Casey, Austin, Texas 78745.]

Ticknor, Joan. "Marital Rape." *Off Our Backs* (November–December 1979).*

Tierney, Abigail Andrews. "Spousal Sexual Assault: Pennsylvania's Place on the Sliding Scale of Protection from Marital Rape." *Dickinson Law Review*, vol. 90 (Summer 1986).

"To Have and to Hold: the Marital Rape Exemption and the Fourteenth Amendment." *Harvard Law Review*, vol. 99 (April 1986).

"Twenty-three States Now Recognize Marital Rape as a Crime." *Criminal Justice Newsletter*, vol. 16 (January 16, 1985).

von Malottke, Caroline S. A. "One Attempt to Modernize the Marital Rape Exemption." *American Journal of Trial Advocacy*, vol. 10 (Summer 1986).

Walker, Lenore E. *The Battered Woman*. New York: Harper and Row, 1979.

——. *The Battered Woman Syndrome*. New York: Springer, 1984.

Waterman, Sallee F. "For Better or Worse: Marital Rape." *Northern Kentucky Law Review*, vol. 15, no. 3 (1988).

Weingourt, Rita. "Wife Rape: Barriers to Identification and Treatment." *American Journal of Psychotherapy*, vol. 39, no. 2 (1985).

"When a Wife Says No . . . Beyond the Rideout Case." *Ms. Magazine* (April 23, 1982).

"Wife Rape: The First Conviction." *Time Magazine* (October 8, 1979).

Williams, John. "Marital Rape: Time to Reform." *New Law Journal*, vol. 134 (January 1984).

———. "Marital Rape." *Family Law*, vol. 15 (April 1985).

Williams, Kelly. "Marital Rape: Annotated Bibliography." Unpublished (December 9, 1988).*

Wise, Daniel. "Women's Groups Join in Test of Rape Law in New York." *New York Law Journal*, vol. 192 (November 1984).

Withers, Nancy A. "Marital Rape." Unpublished paper available from Sociological Abstracts Reproduction Service, 1988.

Witkin-Lanoil, Georgia. "Too Close to Home." *Health Magazine*, vol. 19 (January 1987).

Women's Law Caucus, University of Montana [Holly Frantz, Mary Gallagher, Ann Hefenieder, Karen S. McRae, K. Amy Pfeifer, Tammy K. Plubell, Marylinn E. Smith]. "Montana's New Domestic Abuse Statutes: A New Response to an Old Problem." *Montana Law Review*, vol. 47 (Summer 1986).

Wunsch, Sarah. *Stopping Sexual Assault in Marriage: A Guide for Women Counselors and Advocates* (pamphlet). New York: Center for Constitutional Rights, 1986. 1989 edition in Spanish and English, in press.

X, Laura. "Rape Bill Supporters Get Lesson in Politics." *New Directions for Women* (March–April 1981).

———. Testimony addressing "Women, Violence, and the Law" before the House of Representatives Select Committee on Children, Youth, and Families, September 29, 1987.*

Yegidis, Bonnie L. "Wife Abuse and Marital Rape Among Women Who Seek Help." *Affilia*, vol. 3, no. 1 (1988).

Yllo, Kersti. "A Response to Jetse Sprey's 'Editorial Comments.'" *Journal of Marriage and the Family*, vol. 48, no. 4 (1986).

Young, Marlene. "'Second Injury' Results in Death." *NOVA [National Organization for Victim Assistance] Newsletter*, no. 3 (1989).

INDEX

Diana E. H. Russell is Professor of Sociology at Mills College, Oakland, California. She is author of many books on sexual assault aside from *Rape in Marriage*, including *The Politics of Rape: The Victim's Perspective, Sexual Exploitation: Rape, Child Sexual Abuse, and Workplace Harassment,* and the C. Wright Mills Award-winning *The Secret Trauma: Incest in the Lives of Girls and Women.*